Troubled Children: Their Families, Schools, and Treatments
by Leonore R. Love and Jaques W. Kaswan

Research Strategies in Psychotherapy
by Edward S. Bordin

The Volunteer Subject
by Robert Rosenthal and Ralph L. Rosnow

Innovations in Client-Centered Therapy
by David A. Wexler and Laura North Rice

The Rorschach: A Comprehensive System, Volumes 1 and 2
by John E. Exner

Theory and Practice in Behavior Therapy
by Aubrey J. Yates

Principles of Psychotherapy
by Irving B. Weiner

Psychoactive Drugs and Social Judgment: Theory and Research
edited by Kenneth Hammond and C. R. B. Joyce

Clinical Methods in Psychology
edited by Irving B. Weiner

Human Resources for Troubled Children
by Werner I. Halpern and Stanley Kissel

Hyperactivity
by Dorothea M. Ross and Sheila A. Ross

Heroin Addiction: Theory, Research, and Treatment
by Jerome J. Platt and Christina Labate

Children's Rights and the Mental Health Profession
edited by Gerald P. Koocher

The Role of the Father in Child Development
edited by Michael E. Lamb

Handbook of Behavioral Assessment
edited by Anthony R. Ciminero, Karen S. Calhoun, and Henry E. Adams

Counseling and Psychotherapy: A Behavioral Approach
by E. Lakin Phillips

Dimensions of Personality
edited by Harvey London and John E. Exner, Jr.

The Mental Health Industry: A Cultural Phenomenon
by Peter A. Magaro, Robert Gripp, David McDowell,
and Ivan W. Miller III

Nonverbal Communication: The State of the Art
by Robert G. Harper, Arthur N. Wiens, and Joseph D. Matarazzo

Alcoholism and Treatment
by David J. Armor, J. Michael Polich, and Harriet B. Stambul

A Biodevelopmental Approach to Clinical Child Psychology:
Cognitive Controls and Cognitive Control Therapy
by Sebastiano Santostefano

THE RORSCHACH: A COMPREHENSIVE SYSTEM

VOLUME 2

THE RORSCHACH
A COMPREHENSIVE SYSTEM

VOLUME 2
Current Research and Advanced Interpretation

JOHN E. EXNER, Jr., Ph.D.

A WILEY-INTERSCIENCE PUBLICATION

JOHN WILEY & SONS, New York • Chichester • Brisbane • Toronto

Library of Congress Cataloging in Publication Data

Exner, John E
  The Rorschach.

  (Wiley series on personality processes)
  Vol. 1: A Wiley-Interscience publication—v. 2:
A Ronald Press publication.
  Vol. 2 has also special title: Current research and
advanced interpretation.
  Includes bibliographies.
  1. Rorschach test. I. Title. [DNLM:
1. Rorschach test. WM145 E96ra]
BF698.8.R5E87   155.2'842   74-8888
ISBN 0-471-24964-5 (v. 1)
ISBN 0-471-04166-1 (v. 2)

Printed in the United States of America

10 9

To Doris—

When we were very young and new
I pledged my deepest love to you,
And as we've grown along the way
that love grows deeper every day

—JEE

Series Preface

This series of books is addressed to behavioral scientists interested in the nature of human personality. Its scope should prove pertinent to personality theorists and researchers as well as to clinicians concerned with applying an understanding of personality processes to the amelioration of emotional difficulties in living. To this end, the series provides a scholarly integration of theoretical formulations, empirical data, and practical recommendations.

Six major aspects of studying and learning about human personality can be designated: personality theory, personality structure and dynamics, personality development, personality assessment, personality change, and personality adjustment. In exploring these aspects of personality, the books in the series discuss a number of distinct but related subject areas: the nature and implications of various theories of personality; personality characteristics that account for consistencies and variations in human behavior; the emergence of personality processes in children and adolescents; the use of interviewing and testing procedures to evaluate individual differences in personality; efforts to modify personality styles through psychotherapy, counseling, behavior therapy, and other methods of influence; and patterns of abnormal personality functioning that impair individual competence.

IRVING B. WEINER

Case Western Reserve University
Cleveland, Ohio

Preface

This work reflects a continuation of *The Comprehensive System*. It has involved, literally, a small army of highly enthusiastic and very dedicated people plus the generous cooperation of the nearly 4000 subjects, young and old, who have participated in the more than 200 studies initiated since 1973, when the original manuscript for the System was completed. Not all of those studies have been included here, for some went awry as subjects disappeared, design problems evolved, or data analyses proved disappointing.

Essentially, all of this work has funneled through *Rorschach Workshops,* a sometimes strangely organized unit originally established to test the merits of the several Rorschach systems that were developed between 1935 and 1957; and ultimately a logical extension of that work was the integration of the positive findings into a unified Rorschach approach. The original goals of that integration now appear to have been realized; to create a system that is easily taught, manifests high interclinician reliability, and that will stand up under various tests of its validity.

As the early research progressed, a continuing education "arm" was added to Rorschach Workshops, through which the System has often been presented, sometimes tested, and has also provided important feedback from the field of action. Workshop alumni have also aided considerably in expanding the data pool.

The basic objective, after the development of the System, has been the expansion of knowledge concerning its applicability. To this end, a research advisory council, formed in 1972, has been responsible for the rank ordering of research targets, and most members of the council have served as project team leaders and/or Workshop assistants. Their enthusiasm and commitment are predominantly responsible for major gains in our knowledge about the test, its capabilities, and its limitations. The System in its present form represents the product of their collective efforts, and I have experienced considerable pride in working with them.

In addition to the team leaders, nearly 200 examiners have been involved in the many projects completed to date. Many have been graduate students, but many others, coming from a variety of backgrounds, have ranged from a professional musician to an extremely talented high school senior. Our examiners have included physicians, nurses, social workers, educators, housewives, a retired businessman, and some adept secretaries who discovered that the administration of the Rorschach can sometimes be as boring as typing letters. Their ability to collect Rorschach data in a standardized format has been among the very reassuring aspects of the *Comprehensive System*.

Although the System may now be complete in its formal aspects, the test itself continues to pose many mysteries, and there is no end in sight to the continuing research needs. Some of its features are highly reliable, while others are more questionable. It is valid for some, but clearly not for all, things, and if it is to be "finished," it will require the continued eager commitment of many people like those who have functioned so marvelously in our projects during the past several years. Some of those whose efforts went far beyond what might have been expected should be identified.

Antonnia Victoria Leura was largely responsible for subject recruitment and has directed the extensive standardization project with younger clients; she is a unique jack-of-all-trades without whom we would have faltered badly. Joyce Ruth Wylie functioned as one of my "right arms" and played a major role in almost every project we undertook; her tireless efforts can never be repaid. Elaine Louise Bryant invested herself into most of our laboratory studies, and gave consistently creative input to all of our efforts; she has contributed enormously to our conceptual understanding of new data. George Lee Armbruster played the "devil's advocate" in every project, and awed all of us with his persistent creativity; more important, he has been a friend to all of us. John Roger Kline taught us about computers, practically dismantling one in the process; none of our work could have succeeded without him.

Our senior examiners include Doris Alinsky, Peter Brent, Edward Caraway, William Cooper, Fred Ehrlich, Roy Fishman, Jane Foreman, Christy George, Doris Havermann, Milton Hussman, Mary Lou King, Arnold Lightman, Louis Markowitz, Andrew Miller, Doris Price, Virginia Reynolds, Jane Sherman, Vicki Thompson, Edward Walker, Leslie Winter, and Nancy Zapolski.

Our workshop assistants, many of whom also served as senior examiners, include Francesca Cannavo-Antonini, Miriam Ben Haim, L. Philip Erdberg, Nancy Goodman, Laura Gordon, Beth Kuhn, Donna Levy, Beatrice L. Mittman, Lyn Monahan, Naomi P. Sadowsky, Felix Salomon, Joseph Schumacher, Whitford Schuyler, Donald Viglione, Jane Wasley, and Tracey Zalis.

Working with these people has sustained my excitement for the Rorschach which was inspired years ago by my association with the Rorschach giants. During that period I was often awed by Samuel Beck's preciseness, Bruno Klopfer's charisma, Zygmunt Piotrowski's endless energy, and Marguerite Hertz's warmth, openness, and encouragement. I owe more to them than can ever be repaid. I also owe much to Irving Weiner, who has been a friend, colleague, consultant, and critic over many years; his sharing in our many Workshop ventures has lightened the burden and enhanced the enjoyment.

Finally, I must acknowledge one more unpayable debt to my wife, who has not only managed our continuing education programs, but who has also been deeply involved in every phase of our work. Her tolerance and support of me as I struggled through this manuscript went far beyond any call of duty.

JOHN E. EXNER, JR.

Bayville, New York
April 1978

Contents

PART I   FOUNDATIONS OF INTERPRETATION

1. NEW DEVELOPMENTS IN THE COMPREHENSIVE SYSTEM,   3

   Normative Data for Adults,   3
   Normative Data for Younger Clients,   6
   Matters of Procedure,   6
   Issues of Scoring,   14
   Special Scorings,   21
       Category I: Deviant Verbalizations,   21
       Category II: Autistic Logic,   22
       Category III: Inappropriate Combinations, Perseveration,   22
   Interpretation of Special Scores,   25
   The Structural Summary Blank,   30
   A System Workbook,   30

2. THE RESPONSE PROCESS,   37

   Range of Perceived Responses,   41
   Rating of Reported Responses,   45
   Social Desirability and the Response Process,   46
   Perceptual Accuracy and the Response Process,   51
   Articulation and the Response Process,   53
   Summary,   58

3. THE ISSUE OF RELIABILITY: TEMPORAL CONSISTENCY OF THE
   STRUCTURAL DATA,   63

   Temporal Consistency and Interpretation,   65
   The Research Plan,   66
   The Focal Study,   67
   Temporal Consistency for Brief Intervals,   71
   Summary,   79

4. BASIC PERSONALITY STRUCTURE: THE FOUR SQUARE,   81

   The *EA:ep* Relationship,   82
   The Outpatient (OP) Study,   86
   The *EA:ep* as a Concept,   93

The *Erlebnistypus (EB)*,   94
A Study in Problem Solving *(PS)*,   97
The Experience Base *(eb)*,   104
Case Illustrations,   116
    Case 1: Male, Age 27,   116
    Case 2: Female, Age 28,   117
    Case 3: Female, Age 31,   117
    Case 4: Male, Age 26,   118
    Case 5: Female, Age 13,   119
    Case 6: Female, Age 24,   119

5.   BASIC PERSONALITY STRUCTURE: OTHER STYLE INDICES,   122

The Affective Ratio *(Afr)*,   124
The Role of *Lambda*,   128
The Egocentricity Index *(3r+(2)/R)*,   130
The Active-Passive Ratios *(a:p, M^a: M^p)*,   134
Organizational Activity *(Zf, Zd)*,   138
Case Illustrations,   142
    Case 1: Male, Age 27,   142
    Case 2: Female, Age 28,   144
    Case 3: Female, Age 31,   146
    Case 4: Male, Age 26,   148
    Case 5: Female, Age 13,   150
    Case 6: Female, Age 24,   152

6.   THE FINISHED INTERPRETATION,   156

Some Nonpatient Protocols,   157
    Case 1: A 27-Year-Old Male,   157
    Case 6: A 24-Year-Old Female,   166
    Case 7: A 34-Year-Old Male,   176
    Case 8: A 10-Year-Old Female,   187
Summary,   198

PART II   SPECIAL ISSUES OF DIAGNOSIS AND DESCRIPTION

7.   THE SUICIDE POTENTIAL,   201

A Constellation of Critical Variables,   202
Suicidal Potential in Younger Clients,   209
Case Illustrations,   210
    Case 2: A 28-Year-Old Female—Chronic Isolation,   211
    Case 9: A 37-Year-Old Male—Rapid Disorganization,   221
    Case 10: A 24-Year-Old Female—An Incompatible Hysteroid,   231
Summary,   242

8. DIFFERENTIATION OF SCHIZOPHRENIA,   245

    Rorschach Manifestations of Schizophrenia,   247
    The Schizophrenia Reference Sample,   247
    Borderline Conditions,   250
    Case Illustrations,   252
        Case 11: A 24-Year-Old Female—The Flighty Butterflower,   252
        Case 12: An 11-Year-Old Male—The Whalechild,   265
        Case 4: A 26-Year-Old Male—A Lonely Island,   276
        Case 13: A 20-Year-Old Male—An Incipient Snowman,   287
    Summary,   298

9. SOME FORENSIC ISSUES,   302

    Malingering and Simulation,   303
        Case 14: A 42-Year-Old Male—A Frightened Fake,   304
    Competency Issues,   313
        Case 15: A 27-Year-Old Male—A Growling Mugger,   314
    Custody and Placement,   323
        Case 16: A 12-Year-Old Female—The Unopened Flower,   324
    Summary,   335

PART III   TREATMENT PLANNING AND EVALUATION

10. TREATMENT PLANNING,   339

    The Rorschach as a Starting Point,   340
        Case 3: A 31-Year-Old Female—The Reflective Hysteroid,   342
        Cases 17 and 18: Two 25-Year-Olds—Marital Disarray,   355
    Summary,   377

11. YOUNGER CLIENTS,   379

    Case 5: A 13-Year-Old Female—The Funny Statue,   380
    Case 19: A 15-Year-Old Female—The Hidden Angel,   391
    Case 20: A 9-Year-Old Male—The Mixed Up Guitar,   403

12. TREATMENT EVALUATION,   417

    Cases 21 and 21A: A 24-Year-Old Male—The Little Bird,   418
    Summary,   439

13. AN OVERVIEW,   440

AUTHOR INDEX,   441

SUBJECT INDEX,   447

Tables

1 Group Means for Location, Determinant, and Some Content Scores, and Various Summary Scores for Nonpatients plus Four Psychiatric Groups, 4

2 Group Means for Location, Determinant, and Some Content Scores, Plus Various Summary Scores for Nonpatients and Two Psychiatric Groups, for Ages 5 Through 16, 7

3 Results of an Active-Passive Word Study for Two Groups for 300 Items, Showing the Majority Score for Each Item for Each Group Plus the Number of Subjects Represented by That Majority, with * Indicating Group Disagreements, 18

4 Frequencies and Means for Four Special Scores for Each of Three Groups at the 12 and 16 Year Age Levels, Also Showing the Number of Protocols in Which the Scores Appear, 28

5 Mean Response Frequencies for 60 Seconds, and for Each 30 Second Interval, plus the range of Responses for Each of Five Groups, 43

6 Mean Number of Responses per Card for Each of Five Groups, 43

7 The Frequency of Popular Answers plus Mean Form Quality, Three Location Areas, and Two Contents for Five Groups Shown by First and Second 30 Second Response Intervals, 44

8 A Comparison of Major Structural Features for Two Groups of Outpatients, Half of Whom Were Tested By Their Own Therapists, 47

9 Frequencies of Collapsed Rankings for Two Groups of 30 Subjects Each, for Five responses per Blot, 49

10 Frequencies for Five Responses and Articulation of the Color, for Two Groups, One Administered Standard Cards and the Second Administered Chromatically Altered Cards, 56

11 Correlation Coefficients and Coefficients of Determination for Two Testings, the Second Taken Between 35 and 38 Months after the First, for 100 Nonpatient Adults, 69

12 Test-Retest Frequencies for Five Ratios, with Z Values Concerning Change in Directionality, for 100 Nonpatients, 70

13 Correlation Coefficients and Coefficients of Determination for Two Testings, The Second Taken 7 Days after the First, for 25 Nonpatient Adults, 72

14 Correlation Coefficients and Coefficients of Determination for Two Testings, the Second Taken 60 Days after the First, for 25 Nonpatient Adults, 73

15 Correlation Coefficients and Coefficients of Determination for Two Testings, the Second Taken after 30 Days, for 25 Wait Listed Patients, 74

16 Correlation Coefficients and Coefficients of Determination for Two Testings, the Second Taken after 10 Days, for 20 Inpatient Schizophrenics, 75

17 Correlation Coefficients and Coefficients of Determination for Two Groups, One of 35 Patients in Brief Treatment, with the Second Record Collected after Approxi-

mately 90 Days, and the Second of 30 Long Term Treatment Cases, with the Second Record Taken after Approximately 180 Days, 77

18 Means for Three Reference Groups, Ages 5 Through 16, for Four Variables Comprising the EA and ep Ratios, 84

19 Frequencies for Directionality of the $EA{:}ep$ Relation and the EB for Seven Treatment Groups and One Control Group Across Four Testings During 28 Months, 89

20 Correlation Coefficients for 100 Nonpatients Retested after 35 to 38 Months, for 19 Variables Across Three Groups, Defined by the *Erlebnistypus*, 95

21 Means and Standard Deviations for Six Variables in Four Logical Analysis Device Problems for Three Groups, 100

22 Means and Standard Deviations for Five Adult Reference Samples Concerning the T Determinant, Showing the Total Group and Group Sample for Which T Occurs, 110

23 Frequencies of High, Low, and Normal Egocentricity Indices in Two Broad Groupings of Outpatients Rated after 28 Months as Improved or Unimproved by Ratings of Significant Others, 133

24 Characteristics of Six TAT Story Endings Provided by Two Groups of 12 Subjects Each, Differentiated on the Basis of the $M^a{:}M^p$ Ratio, 137

25 Frequencies of Protocols Identified by Number of Variables, in an 11 Variable Constellation, for Two Suicide Groups Subdivided by Classification of Method Selected, and for Three Control Groups, 205

26 Frequencies of Protocols, Identified by Number of Variables Appearing in an 11 Variable Constellation, for Combined Effected Suicide and Pretested Suicide Attempt Groups, Posttested Attempters, Combined Psychiatric Controls, and Nonpatient Controls, 206

Figures

1 Structural Summary Blank, 31

2 Percent EA Greater Than ep For Three Groups At Twelve Year Levels, 83

3 Subject Display Panel for the Logical Analysis Device, 98

4 Mean Egocentricity Index For Three Younger Client and Five Adult Groups, 130

PART ONE

Foundations
of Interpretation

CHAPTER 1

New Developments in
the Comprehensive System

The manuscript for the first volume of this work, published in 1974 as *The Rorschach: A Comprehensive System,* was completed in late 1973. It included a considerable accumulation of research initiated between 1967 and 1972, plus an extensive evaluation of all earlier Rorschach research that might be relevant to decisions about the format and basic components of an approach to the Rorschach. These decisions, it was hoped, would incorporate the "best" of previously developed approaches to the test. The goal had been, and continues to be, the use of scientifically justifiable methods to test out the host of procedures and propositions that have been applied to the 10 Swiss inkblots with which Hermann Rorschach experimented ingeniously over a half century ago.

As is often the case with research, the results usually raise more questions than they answer. Consequently, what seemed a straightforward investigation of procedures and propositions constantly developed hydra-like research heads. By early 1973, more than 150 studies, many of which were simple "pebble picking" investigations, had been completed—but nearly as many had been initiated. In ending his 1967 revision of *Rorschach's Test, Volume II,* Samuel Beck had written:

> Those younger persons who will be using the test will confirm what is sound. They will discard what they cannot confirm. They will go on from there. It is the way of all scientific flesh (p. 409).

What Beck did not say is how difficult the confirmation or discarding process would be, and in reality, how it may well be that, what Rorschach initiated may never be finished in the sense of being truly complete, because the very process of the Rorschach is so extremely complex. The Comprehensive System, which was conceived as a natural extension of an earlier comparative analysis of the major approaches to the test (Exner, 1969), does provide a basic structure from which continued research may proceed, but there is no end in sight to the research needed. Nonetheless, many gains have been made since the manuscript for the basic system was completed in 1973; and it seems appropriate to begin this volume with a review of how the system has been extended by findings derived since 1973, plus some clarification of material from the earlier work.

NORMATIVE DATA FOR ADULTS

The 1974 text contained a table of group means (p. 217) for each of four samples: nonpatients, outpatients, inpatient nonschizophrenics, and inpatient schizophrenics. Standard deviations were not provided for these data because the sample

3

Table 1. Group Means for Location, Determinant, and Some Content Scores, and Various Summary Scores for Nonpatients plus Four Psychiatric Groups

Category	Nonpatient (N = 325) M	SD	Outpatient Nonpsychotic (N = 185) M	SD	Inpatient Character Problems (N = 90) M	SD	Inpatient Depressive (N = 155) M	SD	Inpatient Schizophrenic (N = 210) M	SD
R	21.75	5.1	25.20	6.3	22.35	4.8	16.50	4.3	24.20	7.2
LOCATION FEATURES										
W	7.04	2.8	6.47	3.1	8.23	3.7	5.29	2.4	7.38	3.2
D	13.50	4.7	15.92	5.6	13.22	5.2	9.42	3.2	11.49	4.1
Dd	1.21	1.1	2.81	1.1	0.91	0.6	1.79	0.8	5.33	2.7
S	1.05	0.7	2.64	1.3	3.48	1.3	1.26	0.9	1.74	1.2
DETERMINANTS										
M	3.48	1.8	3.77	2.2	1.85	0.9	2.13	1.1	3.92	1.9
FM	2.36	1.4	4.12	1.6	3.95	1.2	2.07	1.3	2.96	1.2
m	0.73	0.6	1.21	0.8	1.23	1.1	1.35	0.9	1.18	0.8
FM + m	3.09	1.5	5.33	1.9	5.18	2.2	3.42	1.6	4.14	1.9
FC	3.56	1.2	1.72	1.3	1.41	1.2	0.87	1.1	1.87	1.3
CF	1.23	0.9	2.81	1.4	3.22	1.8	1.93	1.2	3.31	1.6
C + Cn	0.48	0.6	1.13	1.1	1.50	1.3	0.56	0.8	1.56	0.9
Sum C	5.27	2.3	5.66	2.7	6.13	4.3	3.36	1.4	6.74	2.9
Sum weighted C	3.73	1.8	5.37	3.1	6.18	3.9	3.21	1.8	6.58	3.7
FC' + C'F + C'	0.63	0.8	1.41	0.9	0.94	0.7	1.91	1.1	1.18	1.2
FT + TF + T	1.18	0.9	2.57	1.3	1.05	0.8	1.78	1.0	2.36	1.4
FY + YF + Y	1.11	0.6	2.34	1.2	0.82	0.9	2.16	1.1	0.94	0.8
FV + VF + V	0.36	0.3	1.13	0.9	0.21	0.4	1.89	0.8	0.64	0.9
Sum grey black R	3.28	1.8	7.45	3.9	3.02	1.4	7.74	2.9	5.12	2.6
FD	0.92	0.7	1.87	1.2	0.36	0.9	2.61	1.1	0.47	0.9
Fr + rF	0.14	0.7	0.68	1.2	1.41	0.8	0.21	0.6	1.24	0.8
(2)	7.61	2.7	9.84	3.6	10.44	3.9	5.38	1.6	10.74	4.1
F	9.83	3.2	7.87	3.6	7.13	2.8	5.61	2.4	7.29	3.8
RATIOS AND DERIVATIONS										
P	6.45	2.7	7.41	3.1	6.83	3.1	4.94	2.3	2.48	1.8
Lambda	0.82	0.3	0.45	0.4	0.47	0.4	0.52	0.3	0.43	0.2
X + %	0.81	0.12	0.78	0.13	0.75	0.14	0.73	0.09	0.57	0.14
F + %	0.89	0.08	0.83	0.13	0.85	0.11	0.77	0.10	0.62	0.08
Zf	9.41	2.3	9.12	3.1	8.74	3.4	7.71	2.7	9.63	2.8
A%	0.39	0.08	0.42	0.07	0.51	0.08	0.46	0.07	0.31	0.10
Afr	0.69	0.06	0.82	0.09	0.96	0.13	0.61	0.08	0.95	0.12
3r + (2)/R	0.37	0.06	0.47	0.13	0.66	0.18	0.35	0.14	0.59	0.16

4

Table 1 (Continued)

Category	Nonpatient (N = 325)		Outpatient Nonpsychotic (N = 185)		Inpatient Character Problems (N = 90)		Inpatient Depressive (N = 155)		Inpatient Schizophrenic (N = 210)	
	M	SD	M	SD	M	SD	M	SD	M	SD
EA > ep										
(frequency)	229	—	87	—	19	—	68	—	72	—
H + Hd	4.74	1.4	3.93	1.6	3.77	1.4	2.96	0.92	3.14	1.1
Blends	4.90	1.8	5.87	2.3	3.67	1.2	5.84	1.6	4.38	2.7
DV	0.18	0.1	0.41	0.3	0.43	0.2	0.47	0.2	1.01	0.9
ALOG	0.13	0.1	0.22	0.2	0.76	0.4	0.39	0.2	1.75	0.8
INCOM	0.28	0.2	0.51	0.3	0.97	0.6	0.65	0.4	1.18	0.7
FABCOM	0.12	0.1	0.31	0.2	0.58	0.3	0.53	0.3	0.99	0.7
CONTAM	0	—	0.016	0.01	0.02	0.01	0.012	0.01	0.14	0.08
Sum special scores	0.71	0.3	1.48	0.7	2.74	1.3	2.07	0.9	5.08	2.2
PSV (within)	0.05	0.2	0.11	0.2	0.14	0.3	0.18	0.2	0.20	0.2
PSV (across)	0.04	0.1	0.13	0.2	0.18	0.2	0.07	0.05	0.18	0.1

sizes were generally small, and because one or more of the samples might have consisted of an overly heterogeneous grouping. The data were intended to serve as a "reference" rather than a norm. Subsequently, the research pool of protocols has been expanded considerably, making possible a more precise grouping of "homogeneous" subjects, and permitting a more statistically thorough comparison of different groups.

For example, the 1974 reference table contained data for a small number (N = 70) of inpatient nonschizophrenics, a group that contained both depressed and nondepressed subjects. In extending and revising the reference table, those subgroups have been separated. Moreover, the expanded samples have been closely monitored to insure that various socioeconomic strata are proportionally represented, roughly in accordance with the 1970 Census figures. As the sample sizes were enlarged, significance testing was carried out to compare the variety of socioeconomic levels in a group, such as nonpatients, with each other. The results of these analyses are essentially negative. In other words, all manner of protocols will be forthcoming from any single demographic grouping of subjects. This is true *only* for the *structural* data, not the responses themselves, since various groups, such as inner city, rural, and Southern, do often use vocabularies that are subculturally unique. Consequently, if verbal material alone is compared, some differences across demographic groups will be found.

Table 1 provides the revised and expanded reference data for five samples of subjects: nonpatients, outpatient nonpsychotic, inpatient character problems, inpatient depressives, and inpatient schizophrenics. Although the sex distribution for each group is not exactly equal, neither sex is disproportionately represented in any of the groups. For example, the inpatient depressives (N = 155) include 84 females and 71 males, while the schizophrenic group (N = 210) consist of 112 males and 98 females.

NORMATIVE DATA FOR YOUNGER CLIENTS

In late 1972, one of the more ambitious projects of Rorschach Workshops was initiated. The target has been to accumulate protocols from three categories of subjects from ages five through 16: nonpatients, behavioral problems, and withdrawn or socially isolated. Although the optimal goal of obtaining 100 subjects for each cell for each year has not been achieved, 2545 records have been collected, and many of the cells are at or near the 100 mark. More than 200 examiners have been involved in collecting these data, which, like the adult samples, represent various socioeconomic levels. Significance testing comparing the variety of socioeconomic groups has yielded essentially negative findings among the structural data. Table 2 provides the means and standard deviations for each category of subjects by year levels. Caution should be exercised in the application of these data, especially where the sample sizes are small (usually among the withdrawn groups), since the variance is often substantial among small samples. All the records in both the adult and younger client reference samples have been taken and scored according to the procedures and rules of the Comprehensive System. Some of these rules and procedures warrant clarification here.

MATTERS OF PROCEDURE

Encouragement. Most subjects will offer enough answers to make the structural summary data useful. Some are less cooperative, however, and a rule is included in the system for encouragement. It is applied *only* during the first card, and *only* if the subject gives but one answer. The standard encouragement is, "Most people see more than one thing." Unfortunately, some subjects do not respond readily to this form of encouragement, especially children. In that context, Meyer (1977) has suggested a second statement, to be used *in addition to,* or *as a substitute* for the "Most people . . ." statement: *"I think if you look at it a bit longer, you will find something else there, too."* This additive or substitute form of encouragement has been employed quite successfully in the ongoing project designed to collect protocols from large samples of younger clients, and also appears to be a very effective technique with the resistive adult. Unfortunately, there will always be subjects who will not respond to these forms of encouragement. However, no additional form of encouragement should be provided *except* in instances of a potential rejection.

Potential Rejections. Even though this happens infrequently, some subjects will carefully examine a blot and report that there is nothing discernible there. When this occurs on the *first* or *second* card, the examiner should *consider* terminating the test, for usually a rejection or attempted rejection *early in the test* is a sign that the subject is not properly prepared for the examination. It is also a sign that, if the test continues, the yield will be relatively low in terms of R. Quite often, the time that would be devoted to struggling through the remainder of the test can be allocated more profitably in other ways: interviewing, using other tests, or simply making a greater effort to make the subject feel more at ease in the situation. When the potential rejection occurs *after* Card II, and most of these will occur with Card

Table 2. Group Means for Location, Determinant, and Some Content Scores, plus Various Summary Scores for Nonpatients and Two Psychiatric Groups, for Ages 5 through 16

| | 5 Year Olds | | | | | | 6 Year Olds | | | | | |
| | Non-patients N = 70 | | Behavior Problems N = 45 | | With-drawn N = 30 | | Non-patients N = 80 | | Behavior Problems N = 55 | | With-drawn N = 40 | |
Category	M	SD	M	SD	M	SD	M	SD	M	SD	M	SD
R	15.6	4.1	13.7	3.5	13.9	3.4	16.7	4.4	14.8	3.9	15.9	4.6
LOCATION												
W	9.4	3.6	8.6	2.8	7.4	2.6	8.8	3.2	8.2	3.6	7.2	2.9
D	5.8	2.1	4.9	1.8	5.3	1.9	6.3	2.4	5.7	2.5	6.4	3.1
Dd	0.4	0.3	0.2	0.4	2.2	1.3	1.6	1.0	0.9	0.6	2.3	1.8
S	1.1	0.7	1.9	0.6	0.7	0.6	1.3	0.6	1.8	0.7	1.5	0.8
DETERMINANTS												
M	0.9	0.6	0.5	0.4	1.4	0.8	1.2	0.7	0.8	0.6	1.5	0.7
FM + m	2.7	1.3	2.6	1.4	2.2	1.3	3.0	1.3	3.3	1.4	2.1	0.9
FC	0.4	0.6	0.3	0.3	1.4	0.8	0.7	0.5	0.4	0.4	1.3	0.8
CF + C + Cn	1.9	1.2	2.7	1.4	1.8	1.1	2.3	1.2	2.9	1.2	2.0	0.7
Weighted Sum C	3.1	1.6	4.2	1.9	2.7	1.5	3.7	1.8	4.2	1.7	2.9	1.4
Sum C'	0.2	0.3	0.8	0.5	1.0	0.7	0.3	0.2	0.7	0.4	1.2	0.8
Sum T	0.8	0.4	1.2	0.8	1.3	0.6	0.9	0.4	1.1	0.6	1.1	0.5
Sum Y	0.5	0.4	0.7	0.4	0.6	0.4	0.7	0.4	0.3	0.2	1.0	0.6
Sum V	0	—	0	—	0	—	0	—	0.2	0.2	0.7	0.5
Sum all Shading	1.5	0.7	2.7	1.1	2.9	1.2	1.9	1.1	2.3	1.1	4.0	2.3
FD	0.1	0.1	0	—	0	—	0.3	0.2	0	—	0.4	0.2
Fr + rF	0.6	0.4	1.3	0.8	0	—	0.7	0.4	0.7	0.5	0	—
(2)	7.1	3.3	6.7	2.7	6.7	2.9	8.1	3.1	8.2	3.6	7.3	2.8
F	7.7	2.6	5.6	2.3	5.8	2.6	7.9	2.8	5.4	3.1	5.9	2.7
RATIOS AND DERIVATIONS												
P	3.1	2.2	3.5	1.9	3.7	2.1	3.8	1.7	3.4	1.8	4.2	2.4
Lambda	.97	.38	.69	.26	.72	.29	.90	.31	.57	.27	.59	.24
X + %	.79	.11	.72	.19	.74	.13	.85	.13	.74	.09	.77	.12
F + %	.82	.10	.76	.17	.78	.08	.88	.07	.73	.11	.79	.09
A%	.54	.14	.63	.21	.58	.13	.55	.08	.61	.13	.51	.10
Afr	1.06	.27	1.36	.34	0.91	.21	0.98	.29	1.04	.19	0.86	.13
3r + (2)/R	.57	.13	.77	.23	.48	.16	.62	.22	.70	.18	.46	.16
H + Hd	2.7	1.2	1.6	1.0	1.4	.08	3.6	1.4	3.8	1.8	2.9	1.1
Zf	10.3	3.9	9.4	2.6	9.6	2.7	10.7	3.8	9.9	3.1	10.3	2.8
Blends	1.6	0.7	2.3	0.9	2.9	1.4	2.2	1.3	2.9	1.3	3.4	1.2
RATIO DIRECTIONALITY (FREQUENCIES)												
EA > ep	9 (13%)		1 (2%)		5 (16%)		14 (17%)		5 (9%)		9 (23%)	
M > Sum C	4 (5%)		0		7 (23%)		13 (16%)		1 (2%)		10 (25%)	

7

Table 2 (Continued)

| | 7 Year Olds | | | | | | 8 Year Olds | | | | | |
| | Non-patients N = 95 | | Behavior Problems N = 60 | | With-drawn N = 35 | | Non-patients N = 100 | | Behavior Problems N = 85 | | With-drawn N = 45 | |
Category	M	SD	M	SD	M	SD	M	SD	M	SD	M	SD
R	18.7	4.6	17.1	3.7	16.7	3.8	20.3	4.4	18.1	3.8	17.2	3.6
LOCATION												
W	9.1	2.9	9.8	3.0	8.2	2.6	9.5	2.8	9.4	3.1	8.7	2.7
D	8.2	1.8	6.4	2.5	6.1	1.7	9.1	3.2	7.6	2.8	7.3	2.1
Dd	1.4	0.8	0.9	0.7	2.4	1.1	1.7	0.6	1.1	0.6	1.2	0.7
S	2.3	0.9	2.4	1.1	0.9	0.6	1.6	0.8	2.2	1.2	0.9	0.5
DETERMINANTS												
M	1.5	0.8	1.1	0.6	2.3	0.8	1.9	0.9	1.3	0.7	2.8	1.4
FM + m	3.1	1.2	3.4	1.6	2.5	1.1	2.8	0.7	3.6	1.3	2.3	1.1
FC	1.2	0.6	0.4	0.3	1.6	0.8	1.1	0.7	0.6	0.4	1.2	0.8
CF + C + Cn	2.7	1.1	2.9	1.1	2.0	0.9	2.6	0.9	3.1	1.4	1.6	0.7
Weighted Sum C	3.8	1.4	4.9	1.8	2.8	1.2	3.1	1.2	4.2	1.7	2.4	0.9
Sum C'	0.5	0.3	0.4	0.3	1.2	0.6	0.3	0.2	0.6	0.4	1.2	0.7
Sum T	0.8	0.5	1.2	0.8	1.4	0.9	0.9	0.6	1.3	0.7	1.9	1.1
Sum Y	0.4	0.3	0.6	0.2	1.0	0.6	0.2	0.2	0.5	0.3	0.9	0.4
Sum V	0	—	0	—	0.3	0.2	0.2	0.2	0	—	0.6	0.3
Sum all Shading	1.7	0.9	2.2	0.8	3.9	1.4	1.6	0.7	2.4	1.1	3.6	1.5
FD	0.2	0.2	0	—	0.4	0.2	0.5	0.3	0	—	0.4	0.2
Fr + rF	0.8	0.4	1.1	0.7	0.4	0.1	1.0	0.6	1.1	0.8	0.5	0.2
(2)	9.3	3.1	9.6	3.0	5.9	1.8	9.1	3.4	9.9	3.2	6.8	2.4
F	8.3	2.6	6.4	2.1	5.1	1.9	8.5	2.6	7.2	2.8	4.9	1.8
RATIOS AND DERIVATIONS												
P	4.1	1.3	3.7	1.8	5.2	1.9	4.4	1.8	3.5	1.3	5.1	2.1
Lambda	.81	.24	.60	.16	.44	.21	.72	.19	.66	.14	.40	.26
X + %	.85	.11	.73	.15	.79	.13	.87	.13	.71	.16	.74	.13
F + %	.82	.10	.76	.12	.80	.09	.79	.12	.74	.08	.81	.11
A%	.52	.12	.58	.15	.62	.14	.51	.09	.56	.12	.59	.10
Afr	0.89	.19	0.96	.16	0.72	.13	0.82	.13	0.92	.14	0.74	.14
3r + (2)/R	.63	.13	.75	.18	.43	.12	.60	.14	.73	.16	.48	.09
H + Hd	3.9	1.1	3.1	1.3	3.0	1.2	4.3	1.6	3.7	1.4	3.2	1.1
Zf	10.4	2.6	10.7	2.9	9.8	2.1	11.2	3.1	10.7	3.3	10.3	3.1
Blends	2.7	1.2	3.1	1.7	3.3	1.0	3.1	1.2	3.9	1.7	4.1	1.8
RATIO DIRECTIONALITY (FREQUENCIES)												
EA > ep	18 (19%)		8 (13%)		10 (28%)		24 (24%)		14 (16%)		13 (29%)	
M > Sum C	21 (22%)		5 (8%)		14 (40%)		26 (26%)		11 (13%)		16 (36%)	

Table 2   (Continued)

Category	9 Year Olds						10 Year Olds					
	Non-patients N = 100		Behavior Problems N = 90		Withdrawn N = 35		Non-patients N = 100		Behavior Problems N = 100		Withdrawn N = 40	
	M	SD	M	SD	M	SD	M	SD	M	SD	M	SD
R	20.6	4.7	18.2	4.3	17.1	3.8	20.1	4.5	18.9	4.1	16.9	4.1
LOCATION												
W	9.9	3.1	7.8	2.9	7.4	3.0	9.4	2.8	7.0	2.7	7.3	2.9
D	9.2	2.6	9.7	2.6	7.3	2.5	9.1	2.6	10.4	3.1	7.8	2.3
Dd	1.5	0.6	0.7	0.4	2.4	1.1	1.6	0.8	1.5	0.6	1.8	1.2
S	1.2	0.5	2.7	1.1	2.3	0.9	1.4	0.6	2.5	0.8	2.6	0.9
DETERMINANTS												
M	1.8	0.8	1.1	0.7	2.8	1.1	1.9	0.9	1.3	0.7	2.6	0.8
FM + m	3.2	1.2	3.6	1.1	2.7	0.9	3.1	0.7	3.0	1.8	2.8	1.1
FC	1.2	0.7	0.7	0.4	2.1	0.8	1.4	0.8	0.6	0.3	2.3	0.9
CF + C + Cn	2.1	0.8	2.6	1.1	1.9	0.9	2.0	0.7	2.8	1.2	1.8	0.7
Weighted Sum C	2.9	1.1	3.9	1.4	3.1	1.4	2.8	0.9	4.3	1.3	2.7	0.9
Sum C"	0.5	0.2	0.3	0.1	0.9	0.5	0.4	0.3	0.2	0.2	0.8	0.4
Sum T	0.9	0.6	1.1	0.7	1.4	0.6	0.8	0.4	0.9	0.5	1.1	0.6
Sum Y	0.3	0.1	0.2	0.2	0.7	0.4	0.4	0.2	0.3	0.2	0.7	0.5
Sum V	0	—	0	—	0.4	0.2	0.2	0.1	0.5	0.3	0.4	0.2
Sum all Shading	1.7	0.8	1.6	1.0	3.4	1.3	1.8	0.8	1.9	0.7	3.0	1.1
FD	0.6	0.3	0	—	0.4	0.2	0.8	0.3	0.3	0.1	0.5	0.2
Fr + rF	0.3	0.1	0.8	0.5	0	—	0.4	0.2	0.8	0.4	0.2	0.1
(2)	9.7	2.6	10.2	2.9	7.1	1.9	9.5	1.8	10.9	2.6	6.8	1.7
F	8.9	3.2	9.1	3.1	6.1	2.2	9.1	2.4	9.8	2.5	5.8	1.6
RATIOS AND DERIVATIONS												
P	4.8	1.3	4.1	1.6	6.4	2.1	5.7	1.4	4.8	1.4	6.7	2.1
Lambda	.76	.13	1.00	.23	.57	.16	.82	.14	1.07	.27	.52	.16
X + %	.86	.09	.74	.08	.78	.10	.84	.08	.75	.11	.72	.13
F + %	.89	.11	.76	.09	.71	.08	.82	.08	.73	.14	.72	.09
A%	.47	.09	.57	.13	.58	.11	.48	.09	.55	.08	.61	.11
Afr	0.88	.14	1.04	.19	0.69	.12	0.91	.12	1.16	.17	0.71	.16
3r + (2)/R	.51	.09	.69	.11	.41	.08	.53	.08	.70	.14	.43	.07
H + Hd	3.8	1.2	2.9	0.8	3.3	1.1	4.1	1.3	2.7	0.9	3.9	1.1
Zf	10.8	2.6	9.1	2.4	10.6	3.2	10.4	2.3	8.9	2.6	11.2	2.7
Blends	3.8	1.1	3.8	1.6	5.3	1.8	3.7	1.4	3.4	1.1	5.1	1.4
RATIO DIRECTIONALITY (FREQUENCIES)												
EA > ep	29 (29%)		17 (19%)		10 (29%)		33 (33%)		26 (26%)		16 (40%)	
M > Sum C	26 (26%)		16 (18%)		19 (54%)		27 (27%)		18 (18%)		17 (43%)	

9

Table 2   (Continued)

| | 11 Year Olds | | | | | | 12 Year Olds | | | | | |
| | Non-patients N = 100 | | Behavior Problems N = 75 | | With-drawn N = 50 | | Non-patients N = 100 | | Behavior Problems N = 85 | | With-drawn N = 45 | |
Category	M	SD	M	SD	M	SD	M	SD	M	SD	M	SD
R	19.7	4.2	19.6	4.8	17.7	3.8	20.4	4.6	19.8	3.9	18.1	3.9
LOCATION												
W	8.4	3.1	7.0	1.9	7.4	2.6	7.9	3.7	7.3	3.6	6.8	3.1
D	11.0	3.3	10.4	3.1	9.2	1.4	12.3	2.7	11.4	3.2	8.8	2.9
Dd	1.3	0.7	2.2	0.9	1.1	0.4	1.1	0.7	1.1	0.8	2.5	1.1
S	1.4	0.4	2.6	1.1	2.4	0.9	1.2	0.6	2.2	0.7	2.6	0.9
DETERMINANTS												
M	2.5	1.2	1.9	0.8	2.3	0.8	2.7	1.0	1.7	0.8	3.1	1.2
FM + m	3.1	0.9	3.7	1.5	2.4	1.3	3.3	1.2	3.8	1.1	2.8	1.1
FC	2.0	0.8	1.8	0.9	2.2	1.0	2.7	1.3	2.1	0.8	2.1	1.1
CF + C + Cn	2.2	1.0	2.9	1.4	1.7	.07	2.1	0.9	3.1	1.1	2.0	0.7
Weighted Sum C	3.3	1.2	4.6	1.2	3.1	.09	3.4	1.2	4.9	1.6	3.1	0.8
Sum C'	0.3	0.1	0.4	0.1	0.9	0.7	0.5	0.3	0.2	0.2	1.1	0.6
Sum T	0.7	0.4	0.5	0.3	1.1	0.4	1.0	0.4	0.1	0.1	0.9	0.4
Sum Y	0.2	0.1	0.1	0.1	0.7	0.4	0.5	0.3	0.2	0.1	0.6	0.3
Sum V	0	—	0.2	0.1	0.4	0.3	0.2	0.1	0.4	0.2	0.6	0.4
Sum all Shading	1.2	0.6	1.2	0.9	3.1	1.2	2.2	0.8	0.9	0.5	3.2	1.3
FD	0.7	0.5	0	—	0.6	0.4	0.5	0.3	0	—	0.8	0.5
Fr + rF	0.3	0.1	0.8	0.4	0.1	0.1	0.4	0.2	0.9	0.6	0.1	0.1
(2)	8.7	2.8	10.9	2.9	7.8	2.6	9.3	2.9	10.6	2.7	7.0	2.1
F	9.3	3.2	9.6	3.2	5.9	2.1	8.9	2.7	10.1	3.6	6.4	1.9
RATIOS AND DERIVATIONS												
P	6.1	2.1	4.7	1.5	6.8	2.2	6.3	2.1	4.9	1.8	6.2	2.3
Lambda	.89	.17	.96	.13	.50	.14	.77	.12	1.04	.23	.55	.10
X + %	.83	.09	.72	.11	.75	.14	.81	.10	.70	.09	.77	.08
F + %	.81	.11	.74	.13	.72	.08	.86	.09	.76	.07	.78	.10
A%	.48	.08	.55	.09	.53	.11	.49	.11	.56	.09	.59	.09
Afr	0.81	.11	0.96	.12	0.69	.16	0.83	.09	0.97	.13	0.64	.14
3r +(2)/R	.49	.08	.68	.13	.46	.08	.53	.14	.67	.09	.40	.07
H + Hd	4.2	1.2	3.1	1.4	3.7	1.2	4.4	1.3	2.9	1.1	3.9	1.8
Zf	10.1	2.8	8.9	2.6	11.3	3.1	10.7	2.7	8.9	1.4	9.9	2.3
Blends	3.0	1.2	2.8	1.8	3.9	1.6	3.2	1.1	5.1	1.4	5.3	1.9
RATIO DIRECTIONALITY (FREQUENCIES)												
EA > ep	49 (49%)		26 (35%)		17 (38%)		52 (52%)		27 (32%)		20 (44%)	
M > Sum C	31 (31%)		20 (24%)		26 (52%)		34 (34%)		19 (22%)		22 (49%)	

Table 2 **(Continued)**

| Category | 13 Year Olds | | | | | | 14 Year Olds | | | | | |
| | Non-patients N = 80 | | Behavior Problems N = 65 | | With-drawn N = 35 | | Non-patients N = 100 | | Behavior Problems N = 75 | | With-drawn N = 40 | |
	M	SD	M	SD	M	SD	M	SD	M	SD	M	SD
R	20.7	4.9	19.4	5.1	17.6	4.6	21.8	5.3	19.6	4.5	17.2	4.8
LOCATION												
W	7.4	2.1	6.8	2.4	5.7	2.5	7.9	2.4	7.3	2.2	5.9	2.1
D	11.8	3.6	11.4	2.9	9.8	2.1	12.1	3.3	11.2	2.7	9.1	2.3
Dd	1.5	0.7	1.2	0.9	2.1	0.9	1.8	1.1	1.1	0.6	2.2	1.2
S	0.7	0.4	2.4	1.2	1.6	0.7	0.8	0.5	2.6	1.3	1.9	0.8
DETERMINANTS												
M	2.7	1.1	1.4	0.8	3.6	1.4	2.8	1.2	1.6	0.9	3.3	1.2
FM + m	3.4	1.6	3.6	1.5	3.9	1.8	3.1	1.1	3.8	1.4	3.5	1.7
FC	1.8	0.8	0.9	0.7	2.7	1.2	2.0	1.3	1.1	0.8	2.9	1.2
CF + C + Cn	2.1	0.9	2.7	1.3	1.6	0.9	2.4	1.1	2.5	1.3	1.4	0.7
Weighted Sum C	3.8	1.6	4.4	1.8	3.1	1.2	3.6	1.4	4.3	1.5	3.3	1.3
Sum C'	0.3	0.2	1.3	0.8	0.9	0.7	0.2	0.2	1.1	0.8	1.1	0.6
Sum T	0.7	0.5	1.6	0.9	1.2	0.6	0.6	0.4	1.3	0.7	1.0	0.4
Sum Y	0.4	0.2	0.6	0.3	0.9	0.6	0.3	0.2	0.5	0.3	0.8	0.5
Sum V	0.3	0.2	0.2	0.2	0.8	0.5	0.2	0.1	0.3	0.2	0.7	0.4
Sum all Shading	1.7	0.8	3.7	1.4	3.8	1.2	1.3	0.7	3.2	1.6	3.6	1.4
FD	0.7	0.5	0.3	0.2	0.7	0.4	0.9	0.6	0.3	0.2	0.8	0.5
Fr + rF	0.4	0.2	0.9	0.5	0.2	0.1	0.3	0.2	0.8	0.3	0	—
(2)	8.1	2.6	10.3	2.9	6.1	2.3	8.5	2.8	10.6	3.1	5.9	1.8
F	8.9	2.7	9.3	3.1	5.4	1.6	9.3	2.6	10.3	3.9	6.1	1.9
RATIOS AND DERIVATIONS												
P	6.4	2.1	5.4	1.8	6.7	2.3	6.1	2.3	5.5	2.4	6.8	2.2
Lambda	.75	.13	.92	.23	.44	.18	.74	.16	1.10	.26	.55	.17
X + %	.82	.09	.74	.11	.78	.13	.84	.10	.72	.09	.79	.11
F + %	.80	.08	.76	.12	.81	.09	.79	.08	.74	.11	.83	.09
A%	.44	.08	.57	.10	.38	.12	.46	.07	.54	.09	.36	.12
Afr	0.72	.14	0.89	.15	0.63	.16	0.74	.11	0.91	.14	0.61	.19
3r + (2)/R	.45	.07	.67	.16	.38	.12	.43	.08	.66	.14	.34	.09
H + Hd	4.2	1.3	3.7	1.6	3.3	1.1	4.6	1.8	3.6	1.2	3.9	1.7
Zf	9.4	1.6	8.3	1.2	8.1	2.3	9.2	2.2	8.5	2.1	9.0	2.4
Blends	3.4	1.2	4.8	2.3	5.7	2.6	3.2	1.2	4.1	1.8	5.1	2.4
RATIO DIRECTIONALITY (FREQUENCIES)												
EA > ep	36 (45%)		22 (34%)		23 (66%)		54 (54%)		29 (39%)		22 (55%)	
M > Sum C	23 (29%)		9 (14%)		24 (69%)		31 (31%)		11 (15%)		26 (65%)	

Table 2 (Continued)

| Category | 15 Year Olds | | | | | | 16 Year Olds | | | | | |
| | Non-patients N = 100 | | Behavior Problems N = 80 | | Withdrawn N = 45 | | Non-patients N = 100 | | Behavior Problems N = 100 | | Withdrawn N = 65 | |
	M	SD	M	SD	M	SD	M	SD	M	SD	M	SD
R	21.4	5.2	19.9	4.8	17.9	4.6	22.7	5.1	19.4	4.5	18.1	4.7
LOCATION												
W	8.4	3.1	7.6	2.8	6.2	2.1	9.4	3.2	7.3	2.8	6.6	2.9
D	11.7	3.2	11.8	3.6	9.5	1.4	12.1	2.9	11.3	3.1	9.4	2.6
Dd	1.3	0.8	0.5	0.3	2.7	1.1	1.2	0.6	0.8	0.6	2.1	0.8
S	0.5	0.3	2.3	0.9	1.7	1.1	0.6	0.4	2.7	1.2	1.9	0.8
DETERMINANTS												
M	2.6	1.1	2.0	0.8	3.6	1.3	2.8	0.9	1.9	1.1	3.4	1.2
FM + m	3.3	1.3	4.3	1.2	3.1	1.2	3.0	1.2	3.8	1.4	2.8	1.4
FC	2.1	0.8	1.3	0.7	3.2	1.1	1.9	0.9	1.6	0.8	3.1	1.3
CF + C + Cn	2.0	0.9	3.2	1.1	1.6	0.7	2.1	1.1	3.4	1.3	1.8	0.9
Weighted Sum C	3.1	1.2	4.7	1.5	3.0	1.4	3.3	0.9	4.9	1.7	3.3	1.1
Sum C'	0.4	0.2	1.1	0.7	1.4	0.9	0.5	0.3	0.9	0.6	1.2	0.8
Sum T	0.9	0.5	1.3	0.8	1.7	0.8	0.8	0.4	1.0	0.4	1.4	0.9
Sum Y	0.2	0.1	0.6	0.4	1.1	0.7	0.3	0.2	0.4	0.3	0.9	0.6
Sum V	0.4	0.2	0.2	0.2	0.8	0.3	0.3	0.1	0.2	0.1	0.7	0.4
Sum all Shading	1.9	0.8	3.2	1.4	5.0	1.6	1.9	1.1	2.5	1.2	4.2	1.3
FD	1.1	0.6	0.4	0.2	0.8	0.5	0.9	0.4	0.5	0.3	0.7	0.4
Fr + rF	0.4	0.2	0.9	0.3	0.2	0.1	0.5	0.3	0.8	0.4	0.1	0.1
(2)	8.2	2.1	10.1	2.3	5.8	1.1	8.6	1.8	10.3	2.6	5.9	1.4
F	9.7	2.6	9.1	2.4	5.4	1.3	9.9	2.8	9.5	2.8	6.2	1.4
RATIOS AND DERIVATIVES												
P	6.7	1.1	5.5	1.2	6.8	1.6	6.4	1.5	5.2	1.8	6.2	1.3
Lambda	.83	.08	.84	.16	.44	.13	.77	.11	.96	.18	.52	.14
X + %	.80	.08	.73	.13	.78	.09	.84	.08	.71	.09	.81	.10
F + %	.83	.11	.77	.08	.79	.12	.85	.10	.78	.08	.76	.09
A%	.43	.08	.53	.11	.42	.09	.46	.13	.51	.09	.39	.12
Afr	0.79	.17	0.89	.15	0.61	.19	0.73	.10	0.85	.11	0.58	.17
3r + (2)/R	.44	.08	.64	.11	.36	.09	.44	.09	.65	.09	.34	.09
H + Hd	4.6	1.3	3.6	1.2	4.0	1.2	4.8	1.4	3.2	1.6	4.2	1.2
Zf	11.1	2.6	9.1	2.8	9.3	2.6	12.4	2.9	9.8	2.7	10.8	2.2
Blends	3.7	1.2	4.7	1.6	6.2	2.1	3.9	1.1	4.9	1.7	6.6	2.4
RATIO DIRECTIONALITY (FREQUENCIES)												
EA > ep	64 (64%)		29 (36%)		22 (49%)		63 (63%)		31 (31%)		30 (46%)	
M > Sum C	39 (39%)		14 (18%)		31 (68%)		37 (37%)		22 (22%)		44 (68%)	

IX, the examiner should *probably* be unwilling to accept the rejection. Although this is a technique that will create some stress for the subject, at least one answer is almost always forthcoming if the examiner states, *"Take your time. We are in no hurry. Everyone can find something in each of these."* Each examiner must make his or her own decision whether or not to invoke this "ploy," but it does tend to reduce the number of actual rejections to near zero for essentially all populations.

The Inquiry. The objective of the inquiry is to insure accurate scoring of the response given during the Free Association. It is not a new test; nor is this a time when new information is developed. It is simply a time when old information is clarified. The inquiry should *always* be prefaced by a clear statement from the examiner that explains the inquiry procedure: namely, that the examiner wants to see what the subject saw. It follows that if the examiner can actually see what the subject has seen, scoring can be done easily. Thus, it is crucial that the subject understand what is required of him in the inquiry. *Never* begin the inquiry before this goal has been accomplished. A relatively standard introduction is:

Now I want to go back through the cards again. I won't take very long. I'll read what you said, and then I want you to help me to see it as you did. I want you to show me where you saw it, and what there is there that makes it look like, so that I can see it just as you did. Understand?

At this point some subjects ask questions, and they should be answered, with the answers always focusing on the purpose of the inquiry and reemphasizing the fact that the examiner does truly want to see the things reported by the subject, as the subject has seen them. If the subject understands the task, the number of questions necessary for the inquiry will be minimal. A reasonably cooperative subject will "catch on" quickly to the task and will usually provide more than enough information. Questions posed during the inquiry should be logical and to the point, and within the framework that insures nondirectiveness, and as a *general* rule of thumb, no more than one or two questions should be addressed to any single response. Most questioning should work within a broad context, such as, "I'm not sure I see it as you do," or, "I'm not sure what there is about it that makes it look like that," or, "I don't think I see it where you do, put your finger on the. . . ."

There is another category of questions based on specific key words used by the subject during the Free Association *or offered spontaneously* early in the inquiry. Words like "beautiful," "pretty," "ugly," "rough," "soft," "behind," "night," and the like should be pursued if they are not clarified by the subject, for any of them may include a color or shading determinant. However, care should be exercised, inasmuch as some key words do not appear until the inquiry, and the decision to pursue them must evolve with caution. A rule of thumb is to ask only about those key words that occur very early in the inquiry and that appear to have been provided spontaneously.

Inquiry with Younger Clients. It is often extremely difficult for the very young child to attend to any single task for an extended time. Ames (1973) has suggested that, because of this, it may be appropriate to complete the inquiry for children after each card rather than wait for the completion of the Free Association to all 10 cards. This technique has some obvious advantages for the inattentive youngster, but it also has some drawbacks. Part of the system research initiated in 1972 and still continuing has involved the collection of protocols from more than 2000 young clients. The experience of examiners working in that project indicates that, in about 90% of the cases, the standard procedure of conducting the inquiry after the entire Free Association has been completed is effective. On the other hand, there have been a significant number of youngsters, mainly at the five, six, and seven year age levels who "obviously" would have difficulty tolerating the 35 to 45 minutes required. These youngsters are usually identified easily by their pretest behavior, which is marked by overactivity or a distinct resistance. In some of these cases it may be prudent not to perform the test. In cases where the data are seemingly essential, however, it is probably best to modify the method of administration and use a procedure similar to that of Ames. In this case, the introduction to the test must also be altered. Instead of simply saying, "What might this be?" the examiner should say, *I want you to look at this and tell me what it might be, and I want you to show it to me so that I can see it too.* Under this procedure, inquiry questions are sharply limited. Ordinarily, either of the prompting remarks ("I'm not sure I see it as you do" or "I'm not sure why it looks like that") constitutes the limit of questioning, and key words provoked *after* prompting are not pursued.

ISSUES OF SCORING

Certain scoring features of the Comprehensive System have been confusing to some scorers, largely because the criteria provided in the earlier work were unclear or incomplete. To be sure, the scoring format is not absolutely perfect. There will always be some disagreements among scorers about the more subtle scoring issues. Is a response to be scored *FT* or *TF,* or is a movement answer active or passive? Although such disagreements do exist among experienced scorers, they are generally few in number, and in two new scorer reliability studies, one completed in 1975 and involving 10 scorers and 25 records, and second completed in 1976, using 15 scorers and 20 protocols, the .85 level of reliability was achieved or surpassed for all scores. Concurrent with those studies, a survey was made of 20 Rorschach instructors, focusing on the scoring issues that they reported were most difficult for their students. The results of this survey disclose three basic problem areas, all of which seem to be related to incomplete or ambiguous criteria for assigning scores.

Developmental Quality Scoring *(DQ)*

Some scorers, usually those just beginning to use the system, tend to confuse the *DQ* scoring with the Form Quality scoring because the symbols are similar, or possibly because there is a relationship between the Form Quality minus (−) and the *DQ* scoring. These two sets of scores are not the same nor do they relate to the same process, even though there is some overlap. *DQ* scores provide an index of the "cognitive sophistication" of the subject, whereas the Form Quality scores yield information about the perceptual accuracy of the subject.

The assignment of the *DQ* score is best accomplished through a simple process of elimination. The first step in this procedure is to determine whether the answer qualifies for a *DQ* scoring of *vague (v)*. This score is assigned to *any* answer in which the object reported has essentially *no specific form requirement*. In other words, it is used for any object that can take markedly varied shapes, such as blood, water, clouds, islands, smoke, abstracts, rocks, explosions, and the like. Objects that have a specific form requirement—objects like people, birds, fish, chairs, and so on—*cannot* be scored *v*. The second step involves the evaluation of the form quality to determine whether a *minus* (−) *Form Quality* score should be assigned. These are answers in which a gross distortion of the form features of the blot are involved, or answers in which arbitrarily created lines contributed significantly to the perception of the object. *If* the Form Quality score is minus, the *DQ* score can *only* be − or *v*, depending on whether the object has a specific form requirement. If an answer is not a − or *v*, the final step in assigning the *DQ* score is the determination of whether a *synthesis* (+) has occurred. The + score is assigned when the subject has "broken up" a single area of the blot into two or more discrete but related objects, or has combined two or more separate blot areas in a meaningful way. If the *DQ* score is not vague *(v)*, or minus (−), or synthesis (+), then it must be ordinary *(o)*; and that is the precise order of descending priority used in assigning *DQ* scores. Any vague response is automatically scored *v*, even though the *FQ* might be minus. Any minus response *which is not scored vague must* be scored −, even if it involves a synthesis.

Form Quality Differentiation

A second common issue raised by the responses from Rorschach instructors concerns the differentiation of Form Quality. Obviously, the starting point in this process is the Form Quality Table. This table differentiates about 4000 answers, by location, into the categories of "Good" or "Poor" Form Quality on the basis of the frequencies of these answers in a large number of records. The next step is that of differentiation: the scorer must decide whether a Good form quality answer is *superior* (+) or *ordinary (o)*; or whether the Poor Form Quality answer is *weak (w)* or *minus* (−). The task is not as ominous as it may seem. A Good form quality answer can be differentiated easily to a + or *o* score if the scorer focuses on the extent to which the *form features* have been articulated. The *superior* form quality response (+) is one enriched by the subject's precision and care in identifying specific *form* elements. It is *not* necessarily a healthier response; it is merely one in which the subject has taken pains to identify the form elements more extensively than is usually the case. Obviously, all Good form quality responses that are not scored + are scored *o*.

The differentiation of the Poor Form Quality answer into *w* or − follows the same guidelines. The weak *(w)* scoring is assigned to any answer that is *seen easily*. It does not involve any gross distortions of contour, nor does it entail the creation of any arbitrary lines that do not in fact exist in the blot. An *FQ* score of *w* means simply that the subject has identified the blot area in an unusual way; it does not, however, reflect the kind of perceptual distortion found in the *minus* response. Minus (−) answers are marked by a much greater arbitrariness in the use of form features. These responses are much more difficult, and sometimes even impossible, to see. *The reported form is not really there,* even though the majority of minus answers do contain one or two elements that, taken alone might be considered appropriate form use.

Naturally, the distinction between Good and Poor Form Quality need not rely on a "literal" interpretation of the Form Quality Table. Reasonable extrapolation should always be attempted, but within reasonable boundaries that do not violate the main principle of beginning the evaluation of Form Quality with an examination of frequency data. Beyond that level, the scorer should be realistic and straightforward in the scoring decision, knowing full well that decisions to score + will not necessarily be advantageous to the subject, nor will decisions to score weak rather than minus. Poor Form Quality answers are expected, and they often occur, even at the minus level, in the protocols of the well adjusted. Just as a + Form Quality answer signifies a tendency or willingness to give special care to the definition of an answer, so too, in a different way, do the Poor Form Quality answers signify something of the uniqueness of the subject: in most instances a willingness to "see things differently," and in some instances an inability to see things as others do. *No single score* or even a dyad of scores will become overwhelmingly influential to any interpretation, and in that context, it is vitally important that each scorer maintain a sense of objectivity in the assignment of scores. Again, those who teach the Rorschach agree that novices are often overly concerned with the notion that the assignment of a minus Form Quality answer will somehow devastate the interpretation. This assumption is simply not true, and in the matter of form Quality differentiation, the weak or minus score should not be a cause for concern.

Active-Passive Movement Differentiation (a : p)

The third general area in which Rorschach teachers note problems is the distinction between active (a) and passive (p) scoring for movement responses. It is quite true that the 1974 volume contains no defined criteria for these scorings. The reason for the omission is very simple: namely, the distinction is impossible to define precisely. Nevertheless, most people do seem to be able to agree on the meaning of those words when applied to movement answers. At issue here is the fact that every definition applied to movement answers will have exceptions. One need only study the variety of definitions in any dictionary to gain an appreciation of the problem. In the pre-1973 research, when the system was still in a formative stage, scorings of active and passive were almost abandoned because of this "common criterion" problem. As reliability tests were completed, however, a surprising consensus was noted. For example, when 10 postdoctoral fellows were asked to differentiate active and passive M's, FM's and m's, they agreed at a .91 level. Even more surprising was the fact that 10 high school graduates, with no special training in psychology, agreed on the same 150 answers at a slightly higher level than did the postdoctoral fellows. Under those circumstances, it was decided to retain the differentiation in the system—a decision which has since proved very important, as will be noted in a later chapter. Nonetheless, the differentiation of a and p scoring is often one on which even experienced scorers disagree, and one for which no specific definitions exist to help in resolving such issues.

Two more recent studies reaffirm a high level of agreement between scorers when they are asked to make these differentiations. In the first (Wylie and Exner, 1976), 20 nonpatient adults from a variety of socioeconomic levels, none trained in psychology, were asked to "score" each of 300 items, most of them verbs, as either active or passive. They were told that the study involved the extent to which people would agree or disagree on whether certain verbs and adjectives implied an "active sense" or a "passive sense." They were given a few examples, such as "leaping," "brawling," "effusive," and "zooming," to signify the concept "active," and "gliding," "thinking," and "languishing" to illustrate the concept "passive." The subjects were provided with as much time as was necessary to score the 300 items, but were encouraged to work quickly and generally to let their first impressions guide them. In the second study (Exner and Viglione, 1977), 20 second year graduate students completing a one year course in assessment that had focused largely on the Rorschach were used as subjects. They were given the same instructions and same items as the lay group. Table 3 shows the 300 items used in this study, and includes the score for each agreed to by the majority of subjects, plus the actual number of subjects in each group constituting that majority.

Although the simple scoring of verbs and adjectives is not truly commensurate with the Rorschach scoring process, these studies do yield some interesting data. First, the majority of subjects from *both groups* agreed on the scoring of 275 of the 300 items; that is, the group majorities disagreed on only 25 items. Almost half the items involving disagreement included the qualifying verb "looks," as in "looks mean." In all those cases, the lay group majority scored the verbs active, while the student group, following the 1974 text examples, scored those items passive. The other differences between the groups also appear to be a function of the students' experience with the test. Verbs like "hallucinating," "inspecting," "imagining," "sniffing," "watching," and the like were all unanimously scored passive by the students, while varying majorities of the lay group classified the same words as active. The student group agreed unanimously on 213 of the 300 items, while the lay group showed 100% agreement on only 112 of the 300 words. It is much more important, however, to note the high percentage of agreement *within* each group on the scorings· .947% for the student group and .862% for the lay group. In other words, even when verbs implying movement are scored without the context of a full response, there is considerable agreement among those trained in the system; yet even without that training, the level of agreement is very substantial. Although this level of agreement does not suffice for more precisely defined criteria of active and passive, it does indicate the probability of an adequate "functional" level of scoring.

Scoring for Color Projection

Another scoring issue not covered in the 1974 text concerns the appropriate scoring of responses to achromatic blots or blot areas in which the subject identifies the presence of *chromatic coloring*. For example, a subject responding to Card V might say, "It is a pretty butterfly with a pleasant purple coloring." These are rare responses that have been identified by Piotrowski (1957) as "color projections." Usually, when the answer is pursued in the inquiry, the subject gives information implying that the different shades of the blot area aid in creating the "colored"

Table 3. Results of an Active-Passive Word Study for Two Groups for 300 Items, Showing the Majority Score for Each Item for Each Group Plus the Number of Subjects Represented by That Majority, With * Indicating Group Disagreements

Item	Lay Group N = 20		Students N = 20		Item	Lay Group N = 20		Students N = 20	
	Score	N	Score	N		Score	N	Score	N
Abandoned	p	19	p	18	Challenging	a	18	a	20
Accelerating	a	20	a	20	Charging	a	20	a	20
Accusing	a	20	a	19	Chasing	a	20	a	20
Acting	a	17	a	18	Chewing	a	18	a	20
Admonishing	a	19	a	20	Clapping	a	19	a	20
Aggravated (looks)	a	18	a	16	Climbing	a	20	a	20
Aggressive	a	20	a	20	Clinging (helplessly)	p	20	p	20
Agitated	a	18	a	19	Clutching	a	18	a	20
Ailing	p	16	p	19	Composed (looks)	p	16	p	18
Aimless (feeling)	p	20	p	20	Confused (looks)	p	17	p	20
Alarmed	a	18	a	20	Creeping (animal)	a	18	a	20
Amazed (looks)	p	14	p	15	Crouched (animal)	p	16	p	20
Amused (looks)	p	15	p	18	Crying	p	17	p	20
Anchored	p	20	p	20	Cuddled	p	18	p	20
Angry (looks)	a	20	a	20	Dancing	a	20	a	20
Anguished (looks)	p	16	p	14	Dealing (cards)	a	18	a	20
Animated	a	15	a	18	Deciding	a	14	a	17
Annoyed (looks)	p	14	p	16	Defensive (looks)	p	15	p	19
Anxious	a	17	a	15	Defeated (looks)	p	19	p	20
Apologizing	p	16	p	14	Demanding	a	20	a	20
Arguing	a	20	a	20	Demoralized	p	18	p	20
Ascending (smoke)	p	19	p	20	Depressed	p	20	p	20
Aware (looks)	p	14	p	13	Deprived (looks)	p	17	p	20
Bad (looks)	a	11 *	p	12	Deteriorating	p	20	p	20
Baffled	p	16	p	17	Determined (looks)	a	17	a	19
Baking	p	18	p	16	Determined (feels)	a	19	a	20
Balancing (a top)	a	17	a	20	Disappointed (feels)	p	18	p	20
Basking (in the sun)	p	19	p	20	Discussing	a	17	a	20
Bathing	a	14	a	16	Disturbed (upset)	a	14 *	p	13
Battering	a	20	a	20	Dreaming	p	16	p	20
Battling	a	20	a	20	Dripping (water)	p	20	p	20
Beaming (the sun)	p	16	p	20	Drowning	a	13 *	p	18
Bending (in wind)	p	19	p	20	Dropping (leaf)	p	20	p	20
Bewildered (looks)	p	18	p	20	Dying	p	20	p	20
Bleeding	p	20	p	20	Ejecting	a	16	a	18
Blissful (looks)	p	17	p	20	Embarrassed	p	13	p	17
Blowing (hair)	p	18	p	20	Erect (penis)	a	19	a	20
Boasting	a	20	a	20	Euphoric (looks)	a	14	a	15
Bouncing (ball)	a	20	a	17	Excited	a	20	a	20
Breaking	a	18	a	16	Exhausted	p	20	p	20
Bumping (balls)	p	14	p	15	Exploding	a	20	a	20
Burning (fire)	p	13	p	17	Facing	p	14	p	20
Calmly	p	19	p	20	Falling	p	20	p	20
Calling	a	20	a	20	Feeling (physical)	a	16	a	14
Carrying	a	20	a	20	Feeling (mental)	p	18	p	16
Carving	a	18	a	20	Ferocious	a	20	a	20
Casual (looks)	p	17	p	20	Fighting	a	20	a	20
Catching	a	20	a	20	Filling (a pool)	p	14	p	19
Celebrating	a	20	a	20	Firm (muscle)	a	15	a	18

Table 3   (Continued)

Item	Lay Group N = 20 Score	N	Students N = 20 Score	N	Item	Lay Group N = 20 Score	N	Students N = 20 Score	N
Fixing	a	20	a	20	Leading	a	17	a	20
Flapping (in wind)	p	20	p	20	Leering (a wolf)	a	15	a	20
Flapping (bird)	a	18	a	20	Leaning (against)	p	17	p	20
Fleeing	a	20	a	20	Lifting	a	20	a	20
Floating	p	20	p	20	Limping	a	14	a	13
Flowing (river)	p	19	p	20	Loading (cargo)	a	20	a	20
Flying	a	20	a	20	Longing (looks)	p	14	p	18
Frightened (looks)	p	18	p	20	Loosely (held)	p	11	p	16
Gambling	a	16	a	20	Loving (2 people)	a	18	a	20
Gasping (for breath)	a	17	a	12	Lustful (looks)	a	15	a	20
Gazing	p	18	p	20	Lying (down)	p	20	p	20
Glaring (at someone)	a	17	a	20	Mad (looks)	a	17	a	20
Graciously (standing)	a	14 *	p	16	Magical	a	14 *	p	13
					Making (a cake)	a	20	a	20
Grinding	a	17	a	19	Mashing	a	20	a	20
Growing (plant)	a	15 *	p	14	Mean (looks)	a	16 *	p	15
Hallucinating	a	13 *	p	17	Meditating	p	14	p	20
Hammering	a	20	a	20	Menstruating	p	16	p	20
Hanging (man)	p	18	p	20	Miserable (looks)	p	20	p	20
Happy (looks)	a	17	a	19	Mixing	a	20	a	20
Harassed (looks)	p	14	p	17	Modeling (standing)	p	14	p	20
Helping	a	20	a	20	Modeling (clay)	a	11	a	18
Hesitant	p	15	p	19	Mounting	a	20	a	20
Holding	a	17	a	20	Moving	a	20	a	20
Hostile (looks)	a	20	a	17	Mugging	a	20	a	20
Hunting	a	20	a	20	Murdering	a	20	a	20
Hurting	a	20	a	20	Musing (alone)	p	15	p	20
Idle	p	19	p	20	Nervous (feels)	a	13 *	p	18
Imagining	a	13 *	p	18	Nervous (looks)	p	12	p	20
Impatient (looks)	a	14 *	p	14	Nodding (to sleep)	p	20	p	20
Impulsive	a	18	a	20	Noticing (someone)	a	17 *	p	20
Inclining	p	13	p	20	Numb (feels)	p	18	p	20
Inert	p	20	p	20	Objecting	a	20	a	20
Injured	p	20	p	20	Oblivious	p	20	p	20
Inspecting	a	16 *	p	14	Observing	p	16	p	20
Intercourse	a	20	a	20	Offensive (looks)	a	13 *	p	14
Interested	a	13	a	17	Oozing	p	20	p	20
Isolated (feels)	p	18	p	20	Opening (a door)	a	16	a	20
Jeering	a	20	a	20	Opposing	a	18	a	20
Jerking	a	19	a	20	Outraged	a	20	a	20
Jogging	a	20	a	20	Pacing	a	20	a	20
Joining (2 people)	a	18	a	20	Painful (feels)	p	14	p	20
Jovial (looks)	a	17	a	18	Panting (a dog)	p	13 *	a	16
Jumping	a	20	a	20	Passing	a	20	a	20
Kidding (2 people)	a	20	a	19	Peaceful (looks)	p	20	p	20
Killing	a	20	a	20	Perplexed (looks)	p	15	p	20
Knowingly (looks at)	p	14 *	a	17	Picking up	a	20	a	20
Laboring	a	20	a	20	Playing	a	20	a	20
Landing (plane)	a	18	a	16	Pleased (feels)	p	13	p	17
Laughing	a	15	a	13	Pleased (looks)	p	15	p	20
Laying	p	20	p	20	Pondering	p	12	p	20

19

Table 3 (Continued)

Item	Lay Group N = 20 Score	N	Students N = 20 Score	N	Item	Lay Group N = 20 Score	N	Students N = 20 Score	N
Preaching	a	20	a	20	Smoking (fire)	p	17	p	20
Pretending (sleep)	p	11	p	16	Smoking (person)	a	18	a	20
Prowling	a	20	a	20	Sniffing	a	11 *	p	19
Puffed (balloon)	p	14	p	20	Speaking	a	16	a	14
Pulling	a	20	a	20	Spilling (water)	p	14	p	20
Pushing	a	20	a	20	Springing	a	16	a	20
Putting (golf)	a	20	a	20	Squall (rain)	a	14	a	18
Queer (looks)	p	16	p	20	Stabbing	a	20	a	20
Querulous (looks)	p	15	p	20	Standing	p	13	p	20
Quiet	p	20	p	20	Steaming water	p	18	p	20
Quivering	a	13 *	p	14	Stormy	a	13	a	20
Racing	a	20	a	20	Stroking	a	11	a	16
Raging (river)	a	20	a	20	Struggling	a	20	a	20
Raising (a log)	a	20	a	20	Stuck (in mud)	p	20	p	20
Ramming (2 cars)	a	20	a	20	Subdued (looks)	p	16	p	20
Rapturous	a	16 *	p	18	Suffering	a	13 *	p	17
Reaching	a	20	a	20	Suspicious (looks)	p	12	p	20
Ready (to run)	a	20	a	20	Swimming	a	20	a	20
Reckless (looks)	a	12 *	p	20	Taking	a	18	a	20
Refreshed	p	13	p	11	Talking	a	13 *	p	18
Remorseful	p	15	p	17	Tapping	a	20	a	20
Reposing	p	20	p	20	Tearful	p	17	p	20
Resigned	p	16	p	20	Telling	a	14 *	p	18
Resolute (looks)	a	13	a	15	Terrorized (feels)	p	16	p	20
Reticent (looks)	p	11	p	17	Thrilled	a	14	a	13
Revolving	a	17	a	20	Throwing	a	20	a	20
Riding (a horse)	a	20	a	20	Thumping	a	20	a	20
Ringing (bell)	a	14	a	18	Tilted	p	14	p	20
Ripping fabric	a	20	a	20	Toasting (people)	a	17	a	20
Roaring (lion)	a	20	a	20	Tormented (feels)	p	15	p	20
Roaring (water)	a	13 *	p	18	Touching (2 people)	a	14	a	17
Rolling (ball)	p	17	p	20	Tranquil (looks)	p	20	p	20
Rowing	a	20	a	20	Troubled (looks)	p	13	p	20
Running	a	20	a	20	Turning (around)	a	20	a	16
Sad (looks)	p	18	p	20	Unconscious	p	20	p	20
Sad (feels)	p	20	p	20	Unsteady	p	14	p	20
Sagging	p	16	p	20	Upset (feels)	p	13	p	20
Sailing (boat)	p	14	p	20	Vaulting (animal)	a	18	a	20
Satisfied (feel)	p	13	p	19	Vibrating	a	20	a	20
Screaming	a	20	a	20	Vigorous	a	20	a	20
Seated	p	17	p	20	Violent	a	20	a	20
Seeing	p	15	p	20	Waiting	p	16	p	20
Seething	a	16	a	20	Walking	a	20	a	20
Shaking	a	16	a	18	Wanting	p	11	p	16
Shocked	p	13	p	20	Watching	a	13 *	p	20
Singing	a	20	a	20	Weary (feels)	p	15	p	20
Sinister (look)	a	13	a	16	Whirling	a	20	a	20
Skimming	a	17	a	14	Wounded	p	17	p	20
Sleeping	p	20	p	20	Writing	a	20	a	20
Slipping	p	15	p	20	Yielding	p	18	p	20
Smelling	a	12 *	p	17					

effect; and in that context, most would be scored as a variation of Y in the Comprehensive System. Interpretively, color projections probably reflect a form of "ingenuine emotion"; that is, the subject feels somewhat helpless in the test situation and attempts to contend with that feeling by "denying" its existence and substituting a rather transparent and unrealistic positive emotional tone.

SPECIAL SCORINGS

The 1974 text contains less than two full pages on "special scorings." These scorings, developed in some Rorschach systems, or in specific research endeavors, included the scoring for "originality," the Fisher-Cleveland (1958) body-image boundary scoring, and scoring for unusual verbalizations. None were included in the system for one of two reasons: low interscorer reliability or lack of convincing validity. Unusual verbalizations, however, are an important element in the study of cognitive processing; thus the task of creating a format for scoring these kinds of answers was broached in 1975. The authors of such formats (Rapaport, 1946; Schafer, 1954; Weiner, 1966) had not agreed on criteria; moreover, scorers using any of these criteria could not demonstrate a satisfactory level of interscorer agreement.

A major area of variance among the previously established formats for unique verbalization scoring has been the concept of fabulization, usually scored *Fab*. Rapaport (1946) used this category to denote instances in which the verbal material illustrates an "increased loss of distance" from the response. Thus, for Rapaport, the *Fab* score is assigned to most answers in which emotionally charged adjectives are used, *or* in many instances where movement is present. Phillips and Smith (1953) extended this concept to include any response in which elaborative words or phrases are used that are "unique" in nature, such as "fearful man," "person yelling," and so on. Schafer (1954), using the term fabulation, defined the concept as applicable whenever "feelings, motives, qualities, or events are alluded to with marginal support in the blot." Weiner (1966) defined the fabulized answer as one involving greater affective elaboration, or a greater specificity of the response than is realistically justified by the blot features. Each of these definitions is quite subjective, and applied to Rorschach answers, especially those involving movement, yields considerable disagreement among scorers. Consequently, it was dropped from the scoring format.

The variety of other special scorings for unique verbal material were much more amenable to integration into precisely defined categories that could be used with a high level of agreement by multiple scorers (Exner, Weiner, and Schuyler, 1976). Ultimately, five special scores, reflecting three broad categories of unique verbal material, were selected. The three basic categories are: (1) Deviant Verbalizations, (2) Inappropriate Combinations, and (3) Autistic Logic.

CATEGORY I: DEVIANT VERBALIZATIONS (*DV*)

The *DV* score is assigned to those answers characterized by distorted language use or by idiosyncratic modes of expression that impede the subject's ability to communicate clearly. This phenomenon may take any of four forms, all of which create an impression of oddity in the answer.

One form is illustrated by a commentary in the response which is inappropriate to the answer itself. For example, "It's a bat *but I was wishing to see a dog.*" Here the peculiarity is created by the highly personalized "afterthought."

A second form of *DV* is exemplified in answers where the subject appears to lose an appropriate set in describing the object perceived, as in, "A monster *that no one has ever seen.*" Here, the somewhat magical denial phenomenon imparts a distinct peculiarity to the response.

In a third form, the *DV* response is characterized by an *odd* use of language that cannot be justified in terms of subcultural idioms or limited vocabulary skills. In these instances, the responses are typically stilted or redundant, as in, "A matched *brace* of stomachs," or "An x-ray of *somebody's* self," or "A *female* vagina."

The *DV* is most obvious in its fourth form, for here it involves the use of an incorrect word, or a neologism, in place of a correct word that falls well within the subject's verbal capacity. Examples include: "Some things in a *biography* lab," or "Two dogs with their *snoods* together," or "A crocodile with a *slithery* eye."

CATEGORY II: AUTISTIC LOGIC *(ALOG)*

The *ALOG* scoring is used whenever the subject, *without prompting,* uses strained reasoning to justify his answer. The logic involved is clearly not conventional, representing, rather, a form of loose or circumstantial thinking. Usually the *ALOG* response is easily identified because the subject calls attention to size features or spatial elements of the blot. For example, "This is a very small lion *because it is only a part of the picture,*" or "This green must be lettuce *because it's next to the rabbit,*" or "It must be a man and a woman *because they're together,*" or "Its the North Pole *because its at the top.*" In each of these statements, the reasoning becomes attached to, and dependent upon, the size, positioning, or number of objects included in the response.

It is important to reemphasize that *ALOG* is scored *only* when the impaired logic is offered *spontaneously.* There are instances when a subject may offer a complex answer, and in his attempt to use the entire card, or as much as possible, includes features in a more "qualified" vary, as in the statement ". . . and I suppose this could be a . . . if you stretch your imagination." These kinds of qualifications are *not* scored *ALOG.* Similarly, it is not uncommon for some "strained" logic to be manifest in the inquiry *after* the examiner has asked for clarification of a percept. *ALOG* would not be scored in these instances, inasmuch as the element of spontaneity has been removed by the examiner's questioning.

CATEGORY III: INAPPROPRIATE COMBINATIONS *(INCOM, FABCOM, CONTAM)*

These combinative responses involve the inappropriate condensation of impressions and/or ideas into percepts that violate realistic considerations. They are responses in which unreal relationships are inferred between images, blot qualities, objects, or activities attributed to objects. Three separate scorings are included in this category to differentiate the kind of inappropriate combination that has occurred.

1. The *Incongruous Combination (INCOM)* is scored when the condensation of blot details or images are merged inappropriately into a single object. For example, "A person with the *head of a bat*," or "A *four* legged chicken," or "Tree branches with *hands* on them," or "A frog with a *mustache*." Sometimes, the incongruity will be manifest by the inappropriate combination of color with form, as in, "*Red* bears," or "*Black* snow," or "*Blue* people." The *INCOM* will *only* be scored when a single object is involved.

2. *The Fabulized Combination (FABCOM)* is scored when an *implausible* relationship is posited between two or more objects perceived in the blot. This kind of answer *always* involves two or more discrete blot details, such as, "Two chickens holding *basketballs*," or "A woman giving birth to a *cow*," or "A monster chasing *butterflies*," or "A woman attacking an *aircraft carrier*," or "Two ants fighting over a *baseball bat*." Each of these answers presents an inplausible situation and involves two or more distinct blot segments, identified as different objects.

3. The *contamination* response *(CONTAM)* is scored for the most bizarre kinds of inappropriate combinations. The *CONTAM* represents two or more impressions that have been "fused" into a single blot area in a manner that clearly violates reality; in this process of fusion the adequacy of either impression is impaired, in contrast to the situation in which they would be reported separately. Whereas *INCOM* answers fuse impressions of discrete blot areas into a single implausible percept, *CONTAM* responses involve the use of a single blot area to arrive at one percept, but a percept in which impressions that are ordinarily kept distinct from each other are merged into a response of bizarre quality. Contaminations are often marked by the use of neologisms or other peculiar verbalizations to describe the object perceived. A classic illustration of a neologistic *CONTAM* is the condensation of the front view of a bug and the front view of an ox into "*The front of a bug-ox*." A peculiarly verbalized *CONTAM* apparently involving two percepts was given by a young schizophrenic woman to Card IV. She examined the card quite carefully in the upright position, and then examined the card quite carefully in the inverted position, and ultimately said, "It is, no doubt, a *butterflower*." It would seem that she had "fused" an impression of the D3 area as flower with the inverted whole as a butterfly.

In other instances, the *CONTAM* is less obvious but still as crude and apparently pathological. Since it is exhibited in a manner that would stretch the most liberal imagination. For instance, a subject responding to the upper red area of Card II said, "This part looks like blood, and it also looks like an island, so it must be a *bloody island*." In another case, the subject said, "This looks like a flower and the petals look soft and velvety, so it must be one of those *velvet flowers*."

All *CONTAM* responses are automatically afforded a form quality of minus (−), whereas *INCOM* and *FABCOM* responses may be in accordance with Good form fit.

The interscorer reliability for these scores was established through two studies.

The first entailed the use of 40 protocols, 20 nonpatient and 20 schizophrenic, each scored independently by 10 scorers. Here, the reliabilities were .81 for *DV* answers, .87 for the *ALOG* responses, .84 for *INCOM*, .91 for *FABCOM*, and .82 for *CONTAM*. In the second reliability study, 75 responses were selected from 250 protocols. The 75 selected responses appeared to contain at least one feature warranting a special score. These answers were then scored by 18 scorers who had no knowledge that the responses had been selected for their special features. The interscorer reliability was .86 for *DV*; .82 for *ALOG*; .88 for *INCOM*; .82 for *FABCOM*; and .81 for the *CONTAM* answers.

PERSEVERATION *(PSV)*

In the process of researching a format for scoring unusual verbal material, attention was also focused on the issue of perseverated contents. A study of more than 1000 records collected from various patient samples revealed that there are clear instances where an almost identical response is given within a blot, and that there are other cases where a response is alluded to again, later in the record. These kinds of answers appear to represent some sort of cognitive rigidity, or cognitive preoccupation. Logically, it seems important to identify these forms of response, since their presence may provide useful information for the overall understanding of the thinking operations of the subject. Up to this point, all perseveration responses are given the same scoring *(PSV)*, even though it is very apparent that at least three types of perseverative answers do occur.

Within Card Perseveration

The within card *PSV* responses are those that use *exactly* the *same* location, the *same* determinant(s), the *same* content score, the *same DQ* and *FQ* scores, and the *same Z* and *P* scoring if either has been involved, *as the preceding response*. The content may change slightly, but it will remain in the same general content category. The most common examples of this form of *PSV* response occur in Cards I and V, when the subject gives two Popular answers in *consecutive* order. For instance:

   1. "This could be a bat." (described by form and to the *W* and scored, *Wo Fo A P* 1.0)

followed by:

   2. "It could be a butterfly, too." (described by the form to the *W* and scored, *Wo Fo A P* 1.0 *PSV*)

It is quite important to establish the fact that the subject *does* mean to give two responses and not simply an alternative, as is often the case. Usually, when the alternative type of answer is intended, it will be revealed easily in the inquiry by the selection of one of the two answers as being most appropriate, as in "Well the more I look at it it seems like a butterfly rather than a bat." In other instances, a subject may give an alternative type response, "Well it might be a bat, or it could be a butterfly too," but then will clearly differentiate the two in the inquiry. For example, "Well it really could be a bat because it's all black too," scored, *Wo FC'o A P* 1.0; and "Of course it would be a good butterfly if you ignore the coloring," scored, *Wo Fo A P* 1.0.

The real issue in scoring a within card form of *PSV* is that the subject does deliver essentially the same answer *in the context* of the scoring, with *no intervening answers*.

Content Perseveration

Whereas within card *PSV* is scored only for consecutive answers within a card, Content Perseveration, also scored *PSV,* characterizes responses that are not necessarily within the same card or to consecutive cards; but the content is *identified as the same seen earlier*. The scoring of the new response may be quite different than for the answer in which the object was initially perceived, but the subject makes it quite clear that it is the same object(s). For instance, a subject may identify, "Two people in a fight" on Card II, and to Card III report, "Oh, there are those *same* two people but the fight is over now and they're bowing to each other." It is not uncommon for some subjects, especially children, to see a bat on one card, usually Card I or V, and then report, "Oh there's *that bat again*" to a subsequent card.

Mechanical Perseveration

A third type of perseverative response is seen more frequently among subjects who are intellectually handicapped and organically impaired. For the most part, this kind of perseveration is noted in very brief records, and it is easily identified because the subject gives essentially the same answer over and over, in an almost mechanical way. For example, a subject with severe organic impairment gave the answer "A bat" to each of the first seven cards, with no other responses intervening. When Card VIII was presented, he said, "Oh, this bat is colored," and finally on Card IX said, "Where did it go; it's not there anymore." These subjects will often inadvertently emphasize their perceptual rigidity by saying, "Oh, another . . . ," or "This one looks like a . . . too," or "My, they all look like . . . to me." Typically, subjects who manifest this form of perseveration are not good candidates for the Rorschach, and because they are so mechanistic, they are usually distinguished easily from the very resistive subject who is more clearly uncooperative and attempting to conceal through comments such as, "Man, they just don't look like nothing. They all look the same, all bats or something."

INTERPRETATION OF SPECIAL SCORES

Scores for Unique Verbalizations

The presence of a special score for unique verbal material should not be surprising, for they reflect some form of cognitive disruption or inefficiency; and the Rorschach presents the kind of situation that tends to promote occasional disruption. Most nonpatients, both adults and younger clients, usually give at least one or two Form Quality weak or minus responses, which represent a variation or disruption in perceptual accuracy. Similarly, nonpatient adults average about one special score for unique verbal material in every four records; for youngsters, this frequency is considerably greater. Consider, for a moment, the Rorschach situation. Responses are generated in a reasonably short period of time, during which the subject is required *continuously to disregard reality*. The subject must "pretend" that the inkblot figure is not an inkblot figure. If a subject says, "It looks like an inkblot," the examiner cautions the subject with a comment such as, "Yes, that is correct, this is the inkblot test, but your task is to tell me what it looks like, what it might be." The clear implication is that to say "It looks like an inkblot" is wrong, or at least unacceptable. Thus, the subject is not permitted to cling to the reality of the stimulus, but instead must make some transformation of the inkblot into another object; and in doing so the potential for cognitive slippage is considerable. This is especially true if the subject is not especially efficient in his or her cognitive operations. The stress of transforming the inkblot into something that it is not is compounded by another stress, the open ended time element of the test. The instructions contain no reference to time, and the competent examiner *does not* imply this directly by displaying a stopwatch or by carefully scrutinizing a clock or wristwatch. Nonetheless, the test situation itself conveys a temporal element, and most subjects will function during any testing with the hope of "quick" completion. Silence during the Rorschach is embarrassing, and when a subject sits in silence for an extended period after the query, "What might this be?" the situation often becomes discomforting for both the subject and the examiner. Most subjects are prone to deliver a response in a relatively short period of time. Some respond very quickly, in a matter of two or three seconds, while others take longer. It is unusual, however, for a subject to take more than five or 10 seconds before giving the first answer, and, as will be shown in the next chapter, much psychological action occurs during that brief period. It can be a very difficult brief period for those whose cognitive operations are not fully organized or consistently efficient. How often has a contestant on a TV quiz program, operating under a brief time limit, blurted out a completely inappropriate response to a question, only to be punished moments later by the agonized groans of an audience, all certain that they, in the same position, could have functioned "better?" These seemingly stupid responses to questions or tasks do not usually stem from lack of intellectual talent (although TV sometimes seems to convey that impression through the process of selecting subjects). More commonly the inappropriate responses occur because the pressure of the situation has created some form of cognitive disruption. So can it be with the Rorschach.

The Rorschach task is complex and somewhat threatening, and is deliberately made more so by the very procedure of administration in which the subject is *not* told about "right or wrong" answers, and is "kept in the dark" about how the data are used. This does not mean that the presence of special scores for unusual verbal material should be taken lightly in the interpretive framework; but they should be used in perspective. For example, it is not at all uncommon for a child to produce a deviant verbalization in the course of everyday activity, especially if the child is at the preschool level. Children are still at a stage in which they are struggling to sort out the complexities of vocabulary, and they can easily mislabel an object or event in a moment when memory traces are not fully functional. This is a legitimate *DV* response, signifying that the cognitive operations were inefficient or inappropriate or both. Thus the *DV, INCOM,* or *FABCOM* of the child, taken in perspective and not appearing in excess, is both expected and acceptable. Conversely, when the *DV, INCOM,* or *FABCOM* type of answer occurs in an adult, reactions from observers are typically marked by alarm and "raised eyebrows." It is expected that the older subject will have achieved a level of cognitive organization at which those "erroneous" events are not commonplace or acceptable, particularly when they occur with any substantial frequency. It is within this framework that the interpretive propositions concerning scores for unusual verbal material have developed.

An important datum concerning the special scores for unique verbal material is derived from the records of younger clients. In this context, Weiner (1977) has drawn 325 nonpatient protocols and 495 patient records of adolescents, ages 12 through 16, from the Rorschach Workshops pool for comparative purposes. Weiner notes, in his study, that there is an abundant research literature confirming the thesis that unique verbalizations are commonly found among patients who manifest thinking disorders (Watkins and Stauffacher, 1952; Friedman, 1953; Powers and Hamlin, 1955; Pope and Jensen, 1957; Bohm, 1958; Quirk, Quarrington, Neiger, and Sleman, 1962; Blatt and Ritzler, 1974; Quinlan and Harrow, 1974). The 495 patients whose protocols were studied by Weiner included 345 adolescents who had been evaluated in connection with "behavior problems," usually some form of acting out, while the remaining 150 records were taken from subjects characterized as "withdrawn" or socially isolated. Weiner found that *DV, INCOM, FABCOM,* and *ALOG* responses do appear among the protocols of all three groups (nonpatients, behavior problems, and withdrawn) at each of the five age levels; however, three of the response categories, *DV, FABCOM,* and *ALOG,* occur in a significantly smaller proportion of records from the nonpatient group at each of the five age levels. For example, approximately one third of the nonpatient 12 year olds give at least one *DV* and one *ALOG,* whereas about three of every four records of the other two groups contain at least one of these answers. Similarly, the 12 year old nonpatient records reveal a FABCOM in one of each four cases, while FABCOM responses occur in about three of every four 12 year old behavior problems, and in almost all of the 12 year old withdrawn group protocols.

The Weiner data also reveal that, beginning with the 14 year old sample, the *INCOM* response occurs in significantly fewer nonpatient records, than in those of the other two groups, a pattern that continues through the 16 year level. Overall, the data show that, for *DV, INCOM, FABCOM,* and *ALOG,* there is a gradual decrease in both the frequency of these types of answers, and the proportion of records in which they appear, *among the nonpatient samples.* Conversely, the mean frequencies of these answers remain about the same in the two patient groups, across the five age levels, as does the high proportion of records in which they occur. This is possibly best illustrated by the data in Table 4, which shows the three groups of 12 and 16 year olds.

The frequency for the *CONTAM* responses was *zero* in all five nonpatient samples *and* in each of the behavior problem samples. Such responses did appear once among 12, 14, and 15 year old withdrawn subjects, and in two records of the 16 year old withdrawn group. This very low frequency should not be surprising, since the *CONTAM* answer reflects the most marked form of cognitive disarray

Table 4. Frequencies and Means for Four Special Scores for Each of Three Groups at the 12 and 16 Year Age Levels, Also Showing the Number of Protocols in Which the Scores Appear

| | Groups | | | | | |
| | 12 Year Olds | | | 16 Year Olds | | |
Scores	Nonpatients $N = 70$	Behavior Problems $N = 70$	Withdrawn $N = 50$	Nonpatients $N = 65$	Behavior Problems $N = 55$	Withdrawn $N = 30$
DV						
Responses	35	77	33	13	71	27
Mean	0.50	1.13	0.66	0.20*	1.29	0.90
Number of protocols	28*	52	29	12*	39	24
INCOM						
Responses	67	107	70	34	103	51
Mean	0.95	1.53	1.40	0.52*	1.87	1.70
Number of protocols	63	61	44	28*	52	26
FABCOM						
Responses	20	64	55	23	88	36
Mean	0.29*	0.91	1.10	0.35*	1.60	1.22
Number of protocols	18*	49	48	21*	47	23
ALOG						
Responses	28	92	60	24	67	21
Mean	0.40*	1.32	1.20	0.37*	1.21	0.70
Number of protocols	24*	59	43	21	44	17

*Significantly less than the two patient groups at .05 or better.

and is usually found only among schizophrenic or severely impaired organic patients. An examination of Table 1 reveals a frequency of zero *CONTAM* among the nonpatient adult reference sample, and an occurrence of approximately one of each 100 cases in the three nonschizophrenic psychiatric groups. Conversely, the mean *CONTAM* in the schizophrenic reference sample is 0.14, indicating a significantly high frequency.

If the scorings for unique verbal material are conceptualized as illustrating "degrees" of cognitive slippage or disarray, the *INCOM* answer appears to reflect the mildest form of disruption. These responses appear about twice as often in the records of nonpatients as do the other special scorings. They are answers based essentially on the direct use of the blot contours of a single area. In other words, they involve less cognitive manipulation than do the other sorts of responses. In fact, it is not uncommon, especially among nonpatients, both adults and children, to modify the *INCOM* by noting, "It looks like that, but I've never heard of such a thing." All of the other special scores represent a more complex form of processing, in which relationships are mentally established that violate logic and/or reality. The *ALOG* response is clearly the most concrete of these special scores. It represents difficulty with flexibility and probably relates to problems with higher center operations. *ALOG* answers appear with the highest frequency among the records of schizophrenics, which is not surprising, *and* inpatient character problems. The latter are notorious for their poor judgment, and extrapolation suggests that *ALOG* answers do reflect a limitation in the form of logic that constitutes the basis for adequate judgment.

The *FABCOM* response involves considerably more ideational input than either the *INCOM* or *ALOG*. It is a synthesized action in which some element of the processing "goes awry," thereby permitting the integration of elements in a ridiculous and unrealistic manner. *FABCOM* responses occur about four times more often in nonschizophrenic patient records than they do in the protocols of nonpatients, *and* schizophrenics give about twice as many *FABCOM* answers as any other psychiatric group.

Whereas the *FABCOM* involves a form of perceptual synthesis, the *DV* responses manifest an unusual verbal synthesis that seems to be related to difficulties in sorting and/or delay. The *DV* category represents degrees of this form of disarray, with the neologistic *DV* answers illustrating the more severe breakdown in the sorting process, which is the basis of articulation. Whether the neologistic *DV* is a product of the person overwhelmed by needs, or more simply, a product of a major cognitive dysfunction, is not clear. It is clear that it appears most commonly in the records of the severely disturbed, *or* the very young, whereas the more simple forms of "queer" articulation appear among almost all kinds of subjects, although with a significantly lower frequency in nonpatient records.

Some interesting data concerning special scores are reported in a series of treatment effects studies that required following a group of schizophrenics for nearly four years (Murillo and Exner, 1973; Exner and Murillo, 1973; Exner and Murillo, 1977). Seventy patients, tested initially at admission, were retested at discharge or transfer. Of the 70, fifty-three were discharged as "improved" and were retested after one year's postdischarge, then after three year's postdischarge. The mean number of special scores at admission was 7.3. After treatment, the discharged group averaged 5.1 special scores with zero *CONTAM*, and the transferred group averaged 7.4 special scores, with *CONTAM* appearing in approximately one of every two protocols. A variety of behavioral data were collected to determine posthospitalization adjustment. Three years after discharge, 44 ex-patients manifesting *very good* adjustment gave about four unique verbalizations per record. In other words, the presence of the special score does not equal incapacitation; but it does probably represent occasional cognitive slippage or malfunction which can, of course, create difficulties in particular situations, or a more massive disruption if the frequency of these events is substantial.

Perseveration

Much less is known about the *PSV* answers than about the scores for unusual verbal material. When the *PSV* is *mechanistic,* the gross cognitive inflexibility is obvious, and issues of organic involvement must be pursued. The *within* card form of perseveration also seems to involve inflexibility, but it may be *defensive.* In other words, once a subject has decided on an answer, there is some degree of psychological efficiency in "perserverating" variations on that answer rather than undergoing a complete "set" change. While this reaction is inefficient in the context of test performance, it is much safer and easier for the subject. Within card perseveration should not always be interpreted as representing "defensiveness," for there are clear instances in which a subject does have difficulty shifting his perceptual-cognitive perspective, and this can easily promote forms of within card perseveration.

Perseveration *across* cards does appear to represent some form of preoccupation. It may also illustrate instances in which the subject is aware of, and dissatisfied with, his or her own lack of flexibility. Perseveration across cards is not uncommon among very young children, usually in the five to eight year range, and it also appears among very intellectually oriented adults. The frequencies of these answers are low in all groups. In the Weiner study (1977) of adolescent protocols, both within and across card perseveration occurred significantly more often among the 12 and 13 year olds than among the 15 and 16 year olds. However, neither of these types of answer occurred with any greater frequency among the psychiatric subjects when compared to the nonpatients at any year level. In the adult reference sample, a *PSV* occurs about once in every 12 protocols, with across and within *PSV*'s appearing at about the same frequencies. The psychiatric groups all display a higher frequency of *PSV* when compared to nonpatients. Interestingly, the depressed subjects show a relatively high frequency of *within PSV* but a low frequency of across *PSV,* a possible clue to the relationship between within card *PSV* and cognitive inflexibility, a feature very commonly noted among depressives.

THE STRUCTURAL SUMMARY BLANK

Soon after the 1974 text was completed, it became apparent that a form on which to record data from the protocols would be extremely useful, both to the practitioner and researcher. Such a form, the *Structural Summary Blank* (Exner, 1976), was created and modified during the next two years, culminating in a four page blank that includes one page for basic demographic data, a second page for the recording of scores, a third page containing the structural summary itself, and the fourth page which contains the location figures as they are used during the administration of the test.[1] The pages of the Structural Summary Blank are shown in Figure 1.

A SYSTEM WORKBOOK

The previously mentioned canvas of Rorschach instructors using the Comprehensive System revealed that many of the basic scoring features pose difficulties for the beginning student, mainly because their identification and description are often embedded in much historical material in the 1974 text. It soon became obvious that a workbook, which would present these features more concisely, and with some clarification, could be useful to the Rorschach novice. Such a workbook was released during 1976 (Exner, Weiner, and Schuyler, 1976).

---

[1] The Rorschach location figures have been reproduced in the Structural Summary Blank by special agreement with Hans Huber Verlag, Bern Switzerland.

STRUCTURAL SUMMARY BLANK

Developed by John E. Exner, Jr. for use with

THE RORSCHACH: A COMPREHENSIVE SYSTEM

Date: ....

I. SUBJECT DATA

1. Name: .... 2. Age: .... 3. Sex: .... 4. Race:...........

5. Date of Birth: ....   6. Place of Birth: ....

7. Marital Status: 7a. **If** married, divorced or widowed:

    Single ....   Age of Spouse ....

    Engaged ......   Sex & ages of Children ....

    Married ...... Yrs ....

    Divorced ...... Yrs ....

    Widowed ...... Yrs ....

8. Father: Mother: Siblings:

    Living ....   Living ....   Sex .... Age ....

    Deceased ....   Deceased ....   Sex .... Age ....

    Age ....   Age ....   Sex .... Age ....

    Occupation ....   Occupation ....   Sex .... Age ....

9. Current Employment: ....   11. Education Completed:

    How Long? ....   0 - 8 Yrs .... 13 - 15 Yrs ....

10. Prior Employments: ....   9 - 12 Yrs .... B.A. Degree ....

    ....   H.S. Grad .... Grad Degree ....

II. REFERRAL DATA

1. Purpose: 1a. **If** Psychiatric: 1b. **If** Psychiatric:

    Psychiatric ....   Admission ....   In patient ....

    Forensic ....   Progress ....   Out patient ....

    Educational ....   Discharge ....   Day Care ....

    Other ....   After Care ....

2. What is the referral question? ....

3. What is the presenting problem? ....

....

III. TESTING SITUATION

1. Seating: 2. Cooperation: 3. Other Tests Administered:

    Side by side ....   Excellent ....

    Face to face ....   Adequate ....

    Other ....   Reluctant ....

                       Resistant ....

© John E. Exner, Jr., 1976

Figure 1. Structural Summary Blank.

SEQUENCE OF SCORES

CARD	RT	NO.	LOCATION	DETERMINANTS (S)	CONTENT (S)	POP	Z SCORE	SPECIAL

Figure 1 (*Continued*)

STRUCTURAL SUMMARY

R =   Zf =   ZSum =   P =   (2) =

Location Features		Determinants (Blends First)	Contents	Contents (Idiographic)
W =	DQ		H =	=
D =	+ =		(H) =	....
Dd =	o =		Hd =	
S =	v =		(Hd) =	....
DW =	— =	M =	A =	=
		FM =	(A) =	....
		m =	Ad =	=
		C =	(Ad) =	....
Form Quality		CF =	Ab =	=
		FC =	Al =	....
FQx	FQf	FC =	An =	=
		C' =	Art =	....
+ =	+ =	C'F =	Ay =	=
o =	o =	FC' =	Bl =	....
w =	w =	T =	Bt =	=
— =	— =	TF =	Cg =	....
		FT =	Cl	
M Quality		V =	Ex =	**Special Scorings**
		VF =	Fi =	
	=		FV =	Fd =	
			FY =	Ge =	PSV =
o =		Y =	Hh =	
			YF =	Ls =	DV =
w =		FY =	Na	
			rF =	Sx =	INCOM =
— =		Fr =	Xy =	
		FD =		FABCOM =
		F =		CONTAM =
				ALOG =
				=

RATIOS, PERCENTAGES, AND DERIVATIONS

ZSum-Zest =		FC:CF+C =		Afr =	
Zd =		W:M =		3r+(2)/R =	
EB =	FA =	W:D =		Cont:R	
eb =	ep =	L =		H+Hd:A+Ad =	
				(H)+(Hd):(A)+(Ad) =	
Blends:R =		F+% =		H+A:Hd+Ad =	
a:p =		X+% =		XRT Achrom =	
Ma:Mp =		A% =		XRT Chrom =	

Figure 1 (*Continued*)

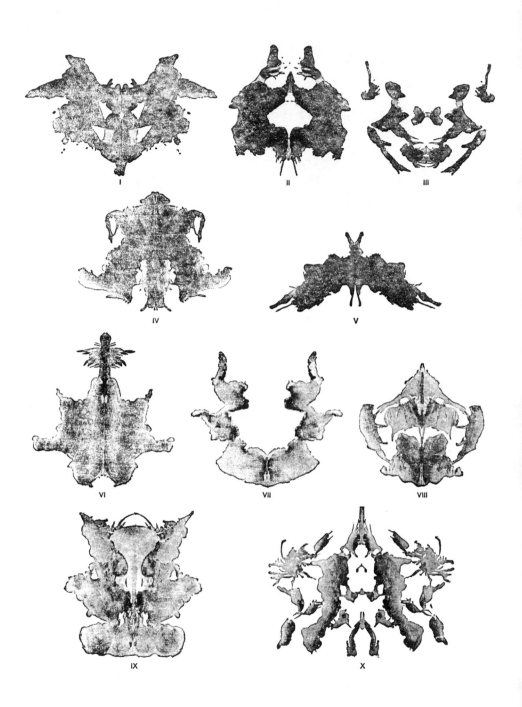

34

SUMMARY

So stands the Comprehensive System today. It has proved sturdy in research and useful in clinical practice. What follows in this volume is a review of the research findings concerning the system since its inception. Data have accumulated from more than 100 studies completed since 1973. Some have been conducted in the laboratory, while others have involved information generated "in the field." The composite of this material appears to make for a better understanding of the test and a more sophisticated description of the subject who has taken the test.

REFERENCES

Ames, L. B., Metraux, R. W., Rodell, J. L., and Walker, R. N. *Child Rorschach Responses*. (rev. ed.) New York: Brunner/Mazel, 1974.

Beck, S. J. and Molish, H. B. *Rorschach's Test. II: A Variety of Personality Pictures*. (rev. ed.) New York: Grune and Stratton, 1967.

Blatt, S. J., and Ritzler, B. A. Thought disorder and boundary disturbances in psychosis. *Journal of Consulting and Clinical Psychology*, 1974, **42**, 370–381.

Bohm, E. *Rorschach test diagnosis*. New York: Grune and Stratton, 1958.

Exner, J. E. *The Rorschach Systems*. New York: Grune and Stratton, 1969.

Exner, J. E. *The Rorschach: A Comprehensive System*. New York: John Wiley and Sons, 1974.

Exner, J. E. *Structural Summary Blank*. Bayville, N.Y.: Rorschach Workshops, 1976.

Exner, J. E., and Murillo, L. G. Effectiveness of regressive ECT with process schizophrenia. *Diseases of the Nervous System*, 1973, **34**, 44–48.

Exner, J. E., and Murillo, L. G. A long term follow-up of schizophrenics treated with regressive ECT. *Diseases of the Nervous System*, 1977, **38**, 162–168.

Exner, J. E. and Viglione, D. Agreement concerning the active-passive definition among graduate students trained in Rorschach scoring. Workshops Study No. 244 (unpublished), Rorschach Workshops, 1977.

Exner, J. E., Weiner, I. B., and Schuyler, W. *A Rorschach Workbook for the Comprehensive System*. Bayville, N.Y.: Rorschach Workshops, 1976.

Fisher, S., and Cleveland, S. E. *Body Image and Personality*. New York: Van Nostrand Reinhold, 1958.

Friedman, H. Perceptual regression in schizophrenia. *Journal of Projective Techniques*, 1953, **17**, 171–185.

Meyer, M. Personal communication, January 1977.

Murillo, L. G., and Exner, J. E. The effects of regressive ECT with process schizophrenics. *American Journal of Psychiatry*, 1973, **130**, 269–273.

Phillips, L., and Smith, J. G. *Rorschach Interpretation. Advanced Technique*. New York: Grune and Stratton, 1953.

Piotrowski, Z. *Perceptanalysis*. New York: Macmillan, 1957.

Pope, B., and Jensen, A. R. The Rorschach as an index of pathological thinking. *Journal of Projective Techniques*, 1957, **21**, 54–62.

Powers, W. T., and Hamlin, R. M. Relationship between diagnostic category and deviant verbalization on the Rorschach. *Journal of Consulting Psychology*, 1955, **19**, 120–125.

Quinlan, D. M., and Harrow, M. Boundary disturbances in schizophrenia. *Journal of Abnormal Psychology,* 1974, **83,** 533–541.

Quirk, D. A., Quarrington, M., Neiger, S., and Sleman, A. G. The performance of acute psychotic patients on the index of pathological thinking and selected signs of idiosyncracy on the Rorschach. *Journal of Projective Techniques,* 1962, **26,** 431–444.

Rapaport, D., Gill, M., and Schafer, R. *Diagnostic Psychological Testing.* Volume II. Chicago: Yearbook Publishers, 1946.

Schafer, R. *Psychoanalytic Interpretation in Rorschach Testing.* New York: Grune and Stratton, 1954.

Watkins, J. G., and Stauffacher, J. C. An index of pathological thinking in the Rorschach. *Journal of Projective Techniques,* 1952, **16,** 276–286.

Weiner, I. B. *Psychodiagnosis in Schizophrenia.* New York: John Wiley and Sons, 1966.

Weiner, I. B. Rorschach indices of disordered thinking in patient and nonpatient adolescents. Ninth International Rorschach Congress, Fribourg, Switzerland, September 1977.

Wylie, J. R. and Exner, J. E. Lay group agreement concerning the active-passive definition. Workshops Study No. 236 (unpublished), Rorschach Workshops, 1976.

CHAPTER 2

The Response Process

It seems impossible to believe that anyone using the Rorschach extensively will not ultimately come to question the manner in which a response is formulated and delivered. It is not a new question, but rather one which has lingered since the inception of the test. Any close reading of Rorschach's *Psychodiagnostics* (1921) reveals that he was very intrigued with the response process. He conceptualized the response as involving basic perceptual elements: sensation, memory, and association. Rorschach postulated that the response is formed through an associative integration of engrams with the complex sensations precipitated by the components of the stimulus. Drawing from his work with severely impaired organics, retardeds, and severely debilitated schizophrenics, many of whom tended to name the blots rather than associate to them, Rorschach concluded that under those conditions, the associational element of perceptual activity failed, either by disruption or decay. This deduction led Rorschach to argue, quite persuasively, that a response can occur only when there is an intrapsychic realization that the sensations created by the blot stimuli are not identical to the engrams. In other words, interpretation evolves from a willingness to identify the blot, or a blot area, as being something that it is not, but to which it has some similarity. He also suggested that differences in ability to *assimilate,* or in thresholds for assimilation, form the basis for the great diversification of responses to the blots. It was, in fact, on these grounds that Rorschach rejected the notion of projection, or unconscious elements, as being influential in the formation of the response. Instead, he preferred to view the response process as one of perception or apperception.

Although it seems likely that Rorschach might have ultimately agreed with Frank's *projective hypothesis* (1939) as relevant to the response process, it is very doubtful that he would have embraced that notion as a major element in the formulation of the response. Whatever might have been had Rorschach lived longer, the question of how a Rorschach answer is formed and delivered remains one of the fundamental mysteries of the test. It is an area of research that has been sorely neglected in the Rorschach literature; and this neglect may well have contributed considerably to the broad divergence that occurred among those attempting to extend Rorschach's work and "complete" the test (Exner, 1969).

One of the earliest efforts to understand the response process was that of Stein (1949). He presented the blots tachistoscopically to two groups of subjects. The first, identified as the "ascending group," was shown the blots for intervals of 0.01 second, 0.10 second, and 3.0 seconds, with a fourth exposure of unlimited time. All 10 cards were shown in their regular order for each of the four trials. The second group, identified as the "descending group," also received four trials, but with the temporal order of exposure reversed, so that they began with an unlimited exposure time. Unfortunately, Stein's project was probably confounded by the rapid test-retest procedure. However, some important clues concerning the response process may be gleaned from the data for Stein's ascending group. In their first trial, when the blots were exposed for only .01 second, the subjects averaged nearly 10 responses, with a range of 5 to 14 answers. Interestingly, when the blots were exposed for a full 3.0 seconds on the third trial, the average number of responses had increased only slightly, to about 12, with a range of 8 to 17. Stein also noted that as the exposure time increased during the first three trials, so too did the frequency of answers invoving form, and a significantly greater number of Popular answers occurred during the third trial. These data suggest that responses can be, and probably are, created very quickly after the initial exposure to the blot stimulus, and that subjects do tend to rely on the contour dimensions of the blots when that is practical.

In a related study, Horiuchi (1961) presented the Card III and VI blots tachistocopically to groups of 80 nonpatients, 80 "neurotics," and 80 schizophrenics. Each group received four exposures, for intervals of .10 second, .30 second, 1.0 second, and unlimited time. Horiuchi found that approximately 60 of the 80 nonpatients, and nearly half of the neurotics and schizophrenics, gave a response when the blots were exposed for only .10 seconds. When the exposure time was increased to .30 second, all nonpatients offered at least one answer, many of which included determinants other than form. However, with the schizophrenic and neurotic groups, neither the frequency nor the complexity of answers increased at the .30 exposure level, and a few subjects from these groups continued to have difficulty presenting a differentiated response even with the blots exposed for one full second. These findings appear to support the Stein data concerning the speed with which a subject can form an answer, and also seem to indicate that this mediational activity is often inhibited in conditions of psychopathology.

Two other works have approached the response process by studying the extent to which perception is differentiated. Friedman (1952) compared the protocols of 30 nonpatient adults, 30 nonpatient children, and 30 schizophrenics. He demonstrated that the schizophrenics' operations were quite similar to those of the children in some ways. Both were marked by a tendency toward global analysis of the figures, but both were also rigid and relatively undifferentiated. Friedman also noted, however, that the schizophrenic orientation is in other respects quite *unlike* that of children, reflecting a more specific discreteness and plasticity, characteristics more commonly found among nonpatient adult percepts. Friedman interpreted his findings as evidence of a perceptual regression in the schizophrenic and argued that this type of decay is a common factor among schizophrenics. Meili-Dworetzki (1956) has reported the results of a very ambitious study in which she studied the levels of perceptual organization and development, using 11 groups of subjects ranging in age from two and a half years to adulthood. She neatly demonstrated a natural progression in perceptual development which coincides with that postulated early by Claparède (1908). In the earliest stage of development, the percepts are marked by a global but primitive analysis. In the second stage, a more sophisticated analysis occurs, but synthesis does not generally follow. In the third stage, analysis and synthesis "interlock," and this forms the highest perceptual level.

The composite of these four studies does render some limited information about the response operation. The Stein and Horiuchi findings suggest clearly that responses are usually formed very quickly once the blot is exposed; at least some responses will be formed in a brief time interval. The Friedman and Meili-Dworetzki findings suggest that the nature of the response will be related to the level of sophistication at which the perceptual process is operating.

Interestingly, while the process of response formulation and delivery have been given little attention, the research that has been produced is often glossed over lightly in the literature on interpretation. Yet most assumptions concerning interpretation are based on assumptions about this very process. For example, if the $X + \%$ is inordinately low in a record that contains a high frequency of minus form quality answers, it is assumed that the perceptual accuracy (or reality testing) of the subject is limited. Similarly, content that is richly unique is generally interpreted on the assumption that elements of identification and/or projection have provoked direct or indirect manifestations of self concept, need states, intrapersonal or interpersonal conflicts, and the like. In fact, there are very few interpretive assumptions or hypotheses that are not based, in some way, on other assumptions about what occurs as the response is formed and delivered. Although most interpretive assumptions are derived from a reasonably sturdy body of research, most are *inferential*—that is, deduced from a comparison of the composite Rorschach data for several populations with a body of valid non-Rorschach data. For example, one source from which the conclusion that a low $X+\%$ equates with poor reality testing is the study of schizophrenia. It has been well established that schizophrenics tend to misinterpret reality quite frequently, and it has also been well established that schizophrenics tend to misinterpret the form features of the blots more than any other group (Weiner, 1966). This leads to the logical deduction that form accuracy in the Rorschach is a valid index of reality testing, a premise supported by numerous replications.

Fortunately, Rorschach interpretation can proceed from propositions that are deduced from solid empirical data, but the more intriguing question lingers: How does the response develop? Why do some subjects appear to struggle to find a single object within a blot, while others will render a seemingly endless array of answers? Or, why do some subjects yield very conventional or easily perceived answers, while others, responding to the same blot areas, deliver responses that are highly unique and even bizarre?

There is a considerable Rorschach literature demonstrating that some features of the Rorschach can be altered under given conditions. For instance, different instructional sets, such as asking subjects to see more details, or more things in motion, will usually produce more of the kind of responses for which the set is established (Coffin, 1941; Hutt, Gibby, Milton, and Potthurst, 1950; Abramson, 1951; Gibby, 1951). Similarly, it has been demonstrated that differences among the basic instructions used by various Rorschach "systematizers" will produce significant differences in the average length of a record (Goetcheus, 1967; Exner, 1974). Several studies also demonstrate that both verbal and nonverbal reinforcement procedures can alter the frequencies of some kinds of responses (Wickes, 1956; Gross, 1959; Dinoff, 1960; Magnussen, 1960; Hersen and Greaves, 1971). The work of Lord (1950) suggested that the "affective atmosphere" in which the test is given may vary the characteristics of the record to some extent; more important, her findings revealed considerable differences across examiners regardless of the atmosphere element. Examiner differences have also been reported by

Baughman (1951), and Gibby, Miller, and Walker (1953); in fact, these accumulated findings, added to those derived from the *deliberate* reinforcement studies mentioned above, plus the finding of Masling (1965) that examiner expectancies can alter some content, led to basic decisions about procedure for the *Comprehensive System* (Exner, 1974). In other words, seating the subject and examiner side by side, thereby reducing the potential for nonverbal reinforcement, and minimizing the complexity of the instructions, thus reducing the potential for a direct ''set,'' tend to reduce the variance in the number of responses and limit the potential for examiner influence.

The literature also reveals that more subtle sets, either toward the subject or toward the examiner, tend to have far less effect on the response yield. For instance, Fossberg (1938) found no major differences in a test-retest design that asked subjects to give their best and worst impressions. Carp and Shavzin (1950) followed essentially the same design with similar results. Similarly, the basic features of protocols do not appear to be affected significantly by ego involving sets (Cox and Sarason, 1954); by requests that the subject respond as quickly as possible (Williams, 1954); when the test is introduced as one of imagination (Peterson, 1957); or when the subject is led to believe that there are right or wrong answers (Phares, Stewart, and Foster, 1960). Although Masling (1965) has demonstrated that examiners, operating under a set to expect either more Animal or more Human content, may inadvertently alter content in line with their expectancies, this same kind of set does not appear to affect basic determinants. Two well designed and executed studies (Strauss, 1968; Strauss and Marwit, 1970) ''set'' examiners to expect either high *M* or high *C* records, and also created an expectancy for long or short records. The results indicate that the direction of the *Erlebnistypus (EB)* was not influenced by the examiner expectations, nor was the length of the protocol.

Although the preceding literature does provide some insights into the kinds of Rorschach features that might be altered under various conditions, and the features that are probably not altered easily, none deal very directly with the response process itself. In other words, does the subject actually report what he sees? Or, viewed from a different perspective, is the subject fully aware of what he is seeing in the blot? Actually, these are two interrelated questions. The first—does the subject report what is seen?—is raised almost every time a brief record is taken, and especially in those cases when, after studying a blot for a long time, the subject says, ''It doesn't look like anything to me.'' This question focuses on the willingness of the subject to share percepts with the examiner. The second question—is the subject fully aware of what is being seen?—focuses more on a mediational aspect of Rorschach behavior. Every experienced Rorschacher has ''suspected'' the presence of a determinant, as for example in those somewhat frustrating ''skin'' responses to Cards IV or VI in which the subject, even with careful but nondirective inquiry questioning, fails to denote textual features. Either of these issues may involve a failure to assimilate or mediate stimulus material; or either may involve a failure to articulate what has been assimilated; or other factors may be at work, contributing to the formation and delivery of the response. A composite of data available from several studies may help unravel some of the threads of this knotty problem.

RANGE OF PERCEIVED RESPONSES

In a pilot study (Exner and Armbruster, 1974) two groups of 10 subjects each were paid to participate in a "standardization" project concerning the Rorschach. They were instructed to give as many responses as they could, with a time limit of 60 seconds for each card. The free association segment of the test was audiotape recorded, with the examiner writing only the basic content of the response, rather than trying to record the answer verbatim. The inquiry was confined to location features. One of the two groups, consisting of 10 nonpatient adult males, gave an average of 104 answers to the 10 cards. Their records ranged in length from 68 to 147 responses, with no fewer than six responses to any single card. The second group consisted of 10 male nonpsychotic outpatients, all having completed at least 20 individual psychotherapy sessions. They produced an average of 113 responses, ranging from 71 to 164, with no fewer than six answers to any one card. Although the very large number of answers given by each group was surprising, an even more unexpected finding was that the form quality of the responses did not appear to deteriorate as a function of the inflated R. The mean $X+\%$ for all responses given by the nonpatient group is 79%, and 75% for the outpatient sample, as contrasted with mean $X+\%$'s of 81 and 78, respectively, for similar subjects tested under standard conditions (Exner, Weiner, and Schuyler, 1976).

The findings of the pilot study suggest that people do see many things that are not ordinarily reported; however, the small sample sizes, plus the fact that the subjects had been paid, raised some question about the reliability of the findings. In addition, it was very difficult to determine in which segments of the 60 second interval most answers were given, since the audio equipment used was a cassette variety and it was discovered that the rewinding of some tapes could alter the digital display as much as 10 units, or the equivalent of between seven and nine seconds. Thus, it was possible that some subjects might have experienced difficulty in seeing, or assimilating, objects in the blots soon after the card was presented, but when working under the instructional set were ultimately able to find objects that they might not have perceived had they been functioning under standard conditions. Consequently, a more sophisticated study was completed (Exner, Armbruster and Mittman, 1978).

Four groups of subjects were used in this study: (1) 40 adult nonpatients, ranging in age from 20 to 41 years; (2) 20 inpatient schizophrenics, ranging in age from 24 to 42 years; (3) 20 inpatient depressives, aged 29 to 51 years; and (4) 20 nonpatient children, age 11 to 13. Each group contained 50% males and 50% females, and none had taken the Rorschach previously. Twelve experienced Rorschach examiners were randomly assigned to subjects, so that each examiner tested some subjects from each group, but no examiner tested more than four subjects from any single group or more than 10 subjects in all. All subjects volunteered and were not paid.

The procedure used in taking the protocol followed the standard method of the Comprehensive system, except that prior to the onset of the free association each subject was told to look at the card for the full 60 seconds that would be allotted and, during that period, report as many things as he or she could find. Instead of introducing the first card by saying, "What might this be?", the examiner began by saying, "Now look at this one and find as many things as you can. You'll hear a beep signal when the 60 seconds are up." The responses were audio recorded on a very sophisticated tape system (Hewlett Packard 3960A) which was actuated by a footswitch that the examiner used with the introduction of each card. The recorder was interlocked with a timer so that it stopped automatically at the end of each 60 second interval and concurrently sounded the beep signal. An inquiry, focusing mainly on location, was conducted after the free association to all 10 cards. The adult nonpatient group was also administered the Form R of the MMPI after the experimental Rorschach was taken.

The data were summarized by a count of the number of answers given by each subject, for each card, and for each of the two 30 second intervals during which the subject was responding to the card. Responses were scored for location, form quality, content, and Popularity.[1] On the basis of the MMPI data, the adult nonpatient group was subdivided into two groups of 20 each; a median split of the K Scale raw scores served as the basis for the classification. This subdivision of the nonpatient adults was made in order to determine if a *social desirability* set, as measured by the K Scale (Dahlstrom, Welsch, and Dahlstrom, 1975), might influence the number of answers given under these varied Rorschach instructions. In other words, would a tendency to respond in a favorable light, as indicated by the higher K Scale scores, tend to facilitate or inhibit the number of Rorschach responses given? An analysis of variance applied to the data yielded a highly significant difference between groups F ratio ($F = 11.63$; $p < .01$).

The average total number of responses given to all 10 cards by each group is shown in Table 5, which also includes the average number of answers given during each of the 30 second intervals, plus the range of responses for the subjects in each group. These data indicate that all groups gave considerably more responses than would be expected had standard instruction been applied. It also seems quite apparent that the majority of answers were formulated and delivered during the first 30 second interval. Even the depressed group, which gave the lowest average number of responses, gave nearly two thirds of all of their answers during that first 30 second interval, while the nonpatient groups tended to give nearly three quarters of all their answers during that same period. When the tapes were studied by 15 second intervals, it was shown that about the same number of answers were delivered during the first and second 15 second periods, and the fewest average number of answers occurred during the fourth 15 second segment. This held true for all groups except the depressives. Depressives delivered their largest average number of answers during the second 15 seconds, and the average number of responses given during the third 15 second interval was only slightly less than that given during the first 15 seconds.

When the average number of responses per card are studied per group, there is considerable variance across cards but a relatively consistent performance across groups when the ratio of responses to each card is considered in the context of the total responses. These data are provided in Table 6. They indicate that the low K nonpatient adults yielded a significantly greater average number of answers on two

---

[1] An attempt to score also for movement, color, and shading determinants was abandoned because most of the responses were very brief, and the inquiry was rarely sufficient to clarify instances in which the probability of a determinant other than F was equivocal.

Table 5.   Mean Response Frequencies for 60 Seconds, and for Each 30 Second Interval, plus the Range of Responses for Each of Five Groups

Group	Total R M	SD	1st 30 Seconds M	SD	2nd 30 Seconds M	SD	Range
Nonpatients, upper half MMPI K Scale, $N = 20$	83.3**	9.2	61.6	8.1	21.7	4.1	56—113
Nonpatients, lower half MMPI K Scale, $N = 20$	100.6	10.4	70.2	9.6	30.4	7.8	73—134
Nonpatient children, ages 11—13, $N = 20$	94.1	9.8	69.6	10.4	24.5	8.3	68—129
Inpatient schizophrenics, $N = 20$	63.2*	9.4	40.8*	7.4	22.4	6.7	37—97
Inpatient depressives, $N = 20$	51.2*	7.8	31.9*	8.6	19.3	7.8	34—82

*Significantly fewer than all three nonpatient groups at .05 level.
**Significantly fewer than nonpatient adult group scoring in the lower half on the MMPI K Scale at .05 level.

of the cards, III and VI, while the depressives gave significantly fewer answers to three of the cards, I, IV, and VIII. Interestingly, it was the schizophrenic group, rather than the depressives, who gave the lowest average number of answers to Cards V and IX. Possibly of greater interest is the fact that the average frequency of responses to each of the cards was substantially greater than that ordinarily obtained in the regular Rorschach routine. Again, even the depressives averaged three or more answers to every card, and gave an average of seven answers to two of the cards.

Table 6.   Mean Number of Responses per Card for Each of Five Groups

	Groups								
Cards	Nonpatients, Upper Half MMPI K Scale $N = 20$ M	SD	Nonpatients, Lower Half MMPI K Scale $N = 20$ M	SD	Nonpatient Children, Ages 11—13 $N = 20$ M	SD	Inpatient Schizophrenics $N = 20$ M	SD	Inpatient Depressives $N = 20$ M	SD
I	7.2	1.6	9.2	1.9	8.6	2.4	6.9	1.4	3.1*	1.1
II	8.4	2.1	9.7	2.4	10.1	3.2	7.2	2.3	4.1	1.3
III	9.3	2.7	11.3**	3.2	9.3	2.1	6.8	1.4	5.7	1.6
IV	5.7	1.3	7.1	1.8	8.1	2.6	4.9	1.1	3.6*	0.9
V	6.1	1.4	7.3	1.7	7.3	2.2	4.2	0.8	5.7	1.3
VI	6.8	1.9	8.6**	2.3	6.9	1.7	5.8	1.1	4.9	1.7
VII	8.2	1.6	10.4	3.2	9.6	3.3	4.2	0.9	4.0	0.8
VIII	11.5	3.1	13.5	3.6	12.8	4.2	9.7	2.9	7.2*	1.7
IX	6.1	1.2	7.2	2.1	6.3	1.7	3.9	0.7	5.1	1.8
X	14.5	3.7	16.3	4.1	15.1	4.7	9.6	2.8	7.8	2.3
Total	83.3	9.2	100.6	10.4	94.1	9.8	63.2	9.4	51.2	9.8

*Significantly fewer responses than all other groups at .05.
**Significantly more responses than all other groups at .05.

Table 7.   Frequency of Popular Answers plus Mean Form Quality, Three Location Areas, and Two Contents for Five Groups Shown by First and Second 30 Second Response Intervals

| | \multicolumn{10}{c}{Groups} | | | | | | | | | |
| Item | \multicolumn{2}{c}{Nonpatients, Upper Half MMPI K Scale $N = 20$} | | \multicolumn{2}{c}{Nonpatients, Lower Half MMPI K Scale $N = 20$} | | \multicolumn{2}{c}{Nonpatient Children, Ages 11–13 $N = 20$} | | \multicolumn{2}{c}{Inpatient Schizophrenics $N = 20$} | | \multicolumn{2}{c}{Inpatient Depressives $N = 20$} | |
	M	SD	M	SD	M	SD	M	SD	M	SD
POPULAR RESPONSES										
1st 30 sec	7.6	1.7	7.4	2.2	7.7	2.0	4.1*	2.1	9.3	3.6
2nd 30 sec	3.2	1.1	1.9	0.9	2.0	1.1	4.3*	1.7	0.9	0.7
$X + \%$										
1st 30 sec	84.7	8.4	81.3	8.2	82.7	8.1	59.1*	10.3	74.8	7.2
2nd 30 sec	89.3	9.6	78.1	8.7	84.1	7.8	49.3*	11.4	68.7	8.3
$W\%$										
1st 30 sec	24.2	8.7	22.1	9.6	40.9*	11.4	29.3	9.1	32.3	11.2
2nd 30 sec	9.3	2.7	8.9	3.3	17.3*	6.7	4.2	2.7	10.6	7.4
$D\%$										
1st 30 sec	67.1	14.2	66.5	11.9	58.6	10.3	49.6	13.2	56.8	9.9
2nd 30 sec	74.4	12.6	76.7	14.2	69.5	11.4	59.6	10.8	60.0	10.2
$Dd\%$										
1st 30 sec	8.7	1.3	11.4	2.9	5.1	0.8	21.1*	5.2	10.9	2.4
2nd 30 sec	16.3	3.8	14.7	4.4	13.2	4.1	36.2	10.7	29.4	11.6
$H\%$										
1st 30 sec	28.4	6.3	26.3	6.7	21.7	6.1	14.7	4.9	17.3	5.9
2nd 30 sec	13.7	3.2	17.8	4.6	17.3	4.3	7.2*	2.3	4.1*	1.1
$A\%$										
1st 30 sec	41.3	11.2	40.6	9.7	58.4	12.1	28.1*	8.1	45.2	8.8
2nd 30 sec	58.7	12.2	47.3	10.6	54.1	11.7	36.4	9.4	29.8	7.9

*Significantly different from all other groups at .05.

The average frequencies of responses given per card by each group are also of interest in light of previous work on card difficulty. Meer (1955) has offered rather convincing data to suggest that Cards VI, IX, and X are the most difficult. The data in Table 6 suggest this is not always the case if number of responses is used as a criterion. All groups, except depressives, yielded the lowest mean frequencies for Card IX, which does coincide with Meer's findings. Conversely, all but the depressives gave fewer average answers to Card VI than to Card IV, and Card X had the highest frequency of responses for four of the five groups, and the second highest frequency for the fifth group. One of the striking bits of data is found in the comparison of the High K and Low K nonpatients. The data in Table 5 reveal that the High K group gave a significantly lower average number of answers to the entire test. This difference is dramatized much more in Table 6, where it will be noted that the High K group averaged fewer responses than the Low K group *on every card*. The element of social desirability does appear to have a very significant influence on what is actually delivered by a subject.

The data in Table 7 show the frequency data for Popular answers and offer information on the form quality of the responses, location choices, and the use of Human and Animal content. It is interesting to note that the High K group, while not differing statistically from three of the other groups, did yield the highest form quality averages, and gave the largest mean number of Populars in *both* 30 second segments. All groups, except the schizophrenics, had significantly more Populars during the first 30 seconds, whereas the schizophrenics gave about as many Populars in each of the two segments. The form quality level remains essentially the same for each of the groups when the first and second 30 second intervals are compared. The children tended to use more W throughout the entire testing, which is not surprising, while the schizophrenics gave more Dd answers during the first half minute. Interestingly, the schizophrenics gave significantly less Animal content during the first interval than any of the other groups.

The fact that the data in Table 7 reveal no deterioration in form quality supports the contention that all, or almost all, subjects were actually responding to objects perceived in the blots, as contrasted with the possibility of simply "creating" responses under these unusual instructions. It is also important to note that the schizophrenic group gave a consistently high frequency of poor form quality answers throughout the test. This was not necessarily unexpected in that schizophrenics tested under standard conditions yield a mean $X+\%$ of 57%; but what was unexpected here was that the schizophrenics averaged more than *eight* Popular answers under this experimental condition. Under standard testing conditions, they usually average no more than three Populars. When content other than Human and Animal was studied, it was found that schizophrenics gave significantly more Blood and Fire responses than any of the other groups, while depressives scored significantly higher for Anatomy and X-ray answers, and the children gave significantly greater numbers of Botany and Landscape answers.

RATING OF REPORTED RESPONSES

It had been expected that the schizophrenic group would deliver a substantial frequency of poor form quality answers, and in that context, the 80 adult subjects used in the preceding study were asked to review their responses immediately after the inquiry had been taken. The tape recording of the free association was replayed while the subjects viewed the cards and had the location sheet available. These subjects were asked to select the "best two" answers that they had given to each card. Thus, each subject selected 20 answers—two per card—that he or she considered to be the best.

Eighteen of the 20 High K group consistently selected two good form answers for all 10 cards. The remaining two selected one good and one weak form response for each of three cards. All 20 subjects from that group selected at least one Popular answer to each card as being "best." Similarly, 17 of the 20 Low K group subjects selected two good form quality responses per card, with the remaining three selecting one good form and one weak form answer for three or four cards. None of the nonpatients selected a minus response as among the best. Although only 10 of the Low K group selected one Popular per card, all 20 subjects in that group selected at least seven Populars. Fourteen of the depressives consistently selected two good form answers as being best, while the remaining six used at least one good form answer for each card. Only one of the depressives considered a minus answer as among the best given, and 18 of the subjects in that group used at least nine Populars among their best 20 responses. The ratings of the schizophrenics are probably most interesting. Only four of the schizophrenics selected more than four Populars among their 20 best answers, and nine of that group failed to include any Populars. Seven selected more minus form quality responses than good form quality answers. Thirteen of the 20 picked at least two minus responses among the 20 best, and all 20 included at least three weak answers in their selections. These findings seem to offer considerable support for the notion that the schizophrenic either does not "see" conventionally, or that he is so overwhelmed by his pathological cognition that he misinterprets conventional objects.

SOCIAL DESIRABILITY AND THE RESPONSE PROCESS

The data from the preceding study illustrate that the High K subjects gave a lower average number of answers, both in the aggregate and to each card, when compared with the Low K group. This finding offers a clue to the "expectancy" factor that may be involved in the response process. Two additional studies add support to the postulate that "expectancy" does play an important role in determining what the subject actually delivers during the test.

In the first (Exner, Armbruster, and Mittman, 1978), 10 therapists agreed to recruit two each of their own patients for testing. All subjects had completed between 20 and 40 individual psychotherapy sessions in a treatment condition that was essentially "insight" oriented. All subjects were judged "well motivated" by their own therapists. Ten of the 20 subjects were used as the "experimental group" and were tested by their own therapists. The remaining 10 were used as "controls" and were tested by one of the other therapists. Assignment to testing was done by randomization, and none of the therapists or subjects was aware of the purpose of the study, all having been informed merely that it involved a standardization project concerning patients in insight oriented psychotherapy. Before the testing, all therapists took part in a review session to insure that the standard procedures of the Comprehensive System would be followed. All testing was also audio recorded to insure that no unusual dialogue occurred during the administration. The protocols were scored by one of three skilled technicians, none of whom was aware of the purpose of the study. Data were analyzed using a series of F tests for frequencies, or Chi Square analyses when proportions were involved. Some of the more important differences between the two groups are shown in Table 8. These data indicate that records taken by therapists from their own patients differed significantly in several respects from the protocols of "control" subjects who were tested by a therapist other than their own. Patients tested by their own therapist tended to give longer records, a significantly higher frequency of M answers, more chromatic color responses, more blend responses, a higher frequency of W and Dd locations, and a somewhat lower $X+\%$. This group also gave *fewer* Populars, fewer shading answers other than those involving texture, and significantly more sex content.

It is most interesting to note that patients tested by a therapist other than their own gave records that were very similar to those given by most outpatients. On the other hand, when the patient's own therapist took the protocol, a longer and more complex record was obtained with fewer conventional answers and more sex content. These findings seem to support the contention that, under the "safer" condition of being tested by their own therapists, the subjects displayed more involvement related to the therapeutic situation. For instance, giving more responses probably indicates a greater willingness to share percepts. Similarly, the substantially higher sex content suggests less caution in reporting what is actually seen, but often not reported, by most subjects. These subjects were willing to "extend" themselves and reveal more; in other words, they were probably less influenced by the element of social desirability than is ordinarily the case. Both Schachtel (1945) and Schafer (1954) have cautioned that the relationship between the examiner and subject can have an important input to the final productivity of the subject, depending on whether the subject feels defensive and threatened in the testing situation, or whether the subject develops a moderate form of "transference" in the context of the situation. In either event, and in light of these data, it seems likely that a subject will tend to reveal, or tend to inhibit, answers as a function of the extent to which he or she is "aware" of the social

Table 8.   A Comparison of Major Structural Features for Two Groups of Outpatients, Half of Whom Were Tested By Their Own Therapists

Item	Tested by Own Therapist $N = 10$		Tested by Other Therapist $N = 10$	
	M	SD	M	SD
Number of responses	34.7*	6.7	24.2	5.6
M responses	7.2*	2.6	4.1	1.8
Color responses	6.9*	2.1	3.8	1.7
Texture responses (shading)	3.7	0.9	3.1	1.1
Shading responses (excluding texture)	1.4	0.7	3.6*	1.2
Blend responses	7.3*	2.4	4.4	1.8
Popular responses	5.1	1.8	7.3*	1.6
$3r + (2)$ index	.43	.14	.41	.11
W responses	9.6*	3.1	6.4	1.7
Dd responses	4.3*	1.9	2.6	0.9
Human responses	5.9	1.3	4.6	1.2
Sex responses	4.3*	1.7	0.8	0.5

*Significantly larger frequency or proportion at .05.

desirability element, and is influenced by the need to react in concert with that awareness. This notion is given added support by the results of a second study completed during the course of this work (Exner and Leura, 1976).

Sixty nonpatient adults, aged 20 to 33, were randomized into two groups of 30 each. None had had previous exposure to the Rorschach. All had volunteered to participate in a "broad" standardization project involving the Rorschach and its interpretation. Both groups were presented the test through the use of slides of the blots. Before the first blot was exposed, each subject was given a list of five responses per blot plus a location sheet on which the 50 answers had been outlined and numbered. The numbering sequence for the responses within each blot had been randomized into five orders, so that no response was numbered first or last for more than six subjects in each group. The five responses listed for each blot included the Popular answer to the card (in the case where more than one Popular has been established for a card, the one with the highest known frequency was included), plus two answers that occur very frequently but are not Popular, plus two answers that occur very infrequently. At least one, and sometimes two, of the five answers had content implying violence, injury, or sexuality. For example, the $D4$ area of Card I was identified as a "naked woman," the $D2$ of Card II as "blood smears," the W of Card V as "rams butting heads," the $D2$ of Card VI as "penis," and the $D11$ of Card X as "insects fighting."

Each slide was presented so that the blot was seen first in the upright position for 30 seconds, and then in each of the three alternative positions for 15 seconds each. Then the blot was returned to the upright position for a 90 second interval during which time the rankings were completed. Subjects in Group I, consisting of 17 females and 13 males, were told that the five responses listed for each blot represented those most frequently reported by *severely disturbed psychiatric subjects,* and that while these objects might be difficult to see at times, the purpose of the study was to determine that very level of difficulty, and consequently, to gain a better understanding of the perceptual process of psychiatric patients. The subjects were instructed to check each of the five responses against the blot and then evaluate the "ease" with which each percept could be recognized as compared with the remaining four answers for the blot, using a rank for 1 for "easiest to see," 2 for the next easiest to see, and 5 for the most difficult to see. Subjects in Group II, consisting of 14 females and 16 males, were given identical instructions—*except* that they were told that the five responses for each blot were those *given most frequently by normal subjects.*

The results, which reflect a form of paired-comparison rankings, were analyzed with the use of a 2 × 2 contingency table chi-square for each response, collapsing the ranks of 1 and 2 into a single category for "easy to see," and, similarly, collapsing the ranks of 4 and 5 into a single category of "difficult to see." Table 9 shows the frequencies for these collapsed rankings for each group and the instances in which the p value for the differences between the groups is at .05 or less. Examination of the data in Table 9 shows that the differences in set—that is, psychiatric versus "normal"—responses, provoked substantial differences in the group rankings for a large number of the responses. A significant difference at .05 or less, occurred between the group rankings for 22 of the 50 responses; although some of these may be attributed to a chance factor, several appear to be clearly related to the "set" phenomenon. For instance, the subjects in Group II, operat-

Table 9. Frequencies of Collapsed Rankings for Two Groups of 30 Subjects Each, for Five Responses per Blot

Card	Response	Area	Ranked 1 or 2—Easiest			Ranked 4 or 5—Difficult		
			Grp I Psychiatric Set	Grp II Normal Set		Grp I Psychiatric Set	Grp II Normal Set	
			N	N	p	N	N	p
I	Animal	>D2	8	9	—	17	20	—
	Bat	W	25	17	.05	1	8	.05
	Bell	Dd24	8	4	—	19	15	—
	Mask	WS	15	11	—	6	15	.05
	Naked woman	D4	4	19	.001	17	2	.001
II	Blood smears	D2	0	13	.001	27	11	.001
	Butterfly	D3	16	8	—	5	18	.01
	Rocket taking off	DS5+ D3	4	14	.02	21	11	.05
	2 animals	D1	26	13	.01	1	8	.01
	2 people	W	14	12	—	6	12	—
III	Blood running down	vD2	3	14	.01	16	10	—
	Bulging eyes	D4	0	2	—	30	19	.001
	Butterfly	D3	21	10	.01	1	9	.02
	Fish	<D5	7	7	—	13	21	—
	2 people	D1	29	27	—	0	1	—
IV	Animal skin	W	24	25	—	2	1	—
	Butterfly	vW	5	6	—	9	12	—
	Flower	D3	7	6	—	20	20	—
	Monster	W	23	17	—	1	8	.05
	Snakes	D4	1	6	—	28	19	.02
V	Alligator head	D1	1	9	.05	29	17	.001
	Butterfly	W	28	26	—	1	1	—
	Human profile	D11	8	5	—	18	17	—
	Rabbit	D7	12	8	—	7	17	.05
	Rams butting heads	W	11	12	—	5	8	—
VI	Animal skin	D1	23	21	—	1	5	—
	Dog	>D9	8	0	.01	12	22	.05
	Human profile	D4	6	1	—	16	19	—
	Penis	D2	1	23	.001	28	3	.001
	Totem pole	D3	22	15	—	3	11	.05
VII	Dog	>D2	18	15	—	0	5	—
	Fried shrimp	W	8	9	—	16	16	—
	Heads of women	D2	29	25	—	0	3	—
	Lampshade	DS7	5	7	—	18	12	—
	Vagina	D6	0	4	—	29	24	—
VIII	Bat	D5	4	3	—	16	22	—
	Flower	W	11	9	—	11	16	—
	Internal organs	W	8	13	—	18	6	.01
	Rib cage	DS3	12	7	—	14	16	—
	2 animals	D1	25	28	—	1	0	—

Table 9   (Continued)

| Card | Response | Area | Ranked 1 or 2—Easiest | | | Ranked 4 or 5—Difficult | | |
| | | | Grp I Psychiatric Set | Grp II Normal Set | | Grp I Psychiatric Set | Grp II Normal Set | |
			N	N	p	N	N	p
IX	Buttocks	D6	0	5	—	23	23	—
	Explosion	W	11	4	—	10	17	.05
	Man's head	D4	23	21	—	4	2	—
	Vase	D8	12	5	—	13	15	—
	Witches	D3	14	26	.001	10	0	.001
X	Bloodstains	D9	4	12	.05	21	14	—
	Fighting insects	D11	12	11	—	14	9	—
	Man's face	Centr DdS	3	7	—	21	19	—
	Rosebud	D15	19	15	—	3	10	—
	Spider	D1	22	15	—	1	8	.05

ing under the set that the responses were commonly given by *normal* subjects, ranked at least six responses as being "easy to see" which in Group I subjects, operating under the assumption that the answers were from *psychiatric* patients, ranked "difficult to see." Interestingly, at least five of these six (naked woman, blood smears, alligator, penis, and witches) were among those included because of their sexual, violent, or aggressive content, and the sixth (rocket taking off) requires a unique figure-ground integration. Similarly, the Group II subjects also ranked the other two blood answers (blood running down and bloodstain) as significantly easier to see than did the Group I subjects. Conversely, the Group I subjects generally ranked as "easiest to see" those responses which usually occur with the highest frequencies among normative data for nonpatients (Card I, bat and mask; Card II, animals and butterfly; Card III, people and butterfly; Card IV, skin and monster; Card V, butterfly; Card VI, skin and totem; Card VII, women and dog; Card VIII, animals; Card IX, head; Card X, spider and rosebud).

The results of this study, although collected from relatively small samples, add credibility to the postulate that, under normal testing conditions, subjects tend to reject, inhibit, or "process out" those responses which do not appear to be *acceptable* in the context of the social desirability issue and/or the set under which the test is occurring. For example, many Group II subjects, who assumed that all the answers were common for normals, found each of the three Blood responses (Cards II, III, and X) easy to see, and ranked them accordingly. More than half the subjects in that group ranked each of those three answers 1, 2, or 3. Conversely, more than half of the Group I subjects, operating under the psychiatric set, ranked those responses as very difficult to see. Possibly, a more striking example occurs in the case of the item "penis" for Card VI. Twenty-seven of the Group II subjects ranked that response 1, 2, or 3, while only two of the 30 subjects in Group I ranked the same answer as 1, 2, or 3. In the same striking context, 28 of the Group II subjects ranked the Popular female figure in the *D*4 area of Card I as 1, 2, or 3 when listed as "naked woman." On the other hand, 17 of the 30 Group I subjects ranked that same response as 4, or 5, and only four of the 30 gave that response a rank of 1 or 2.

It is also important to note that the two groups tended to agree much more when the object has less precise form or color, or involved smaller or less commonly used blot areas. For instance, both groups ranked 13 answers as the most difficult to see (Card I, bell, animal; Card III, fish, bulging eyes; Card IV, flower, snakes; Card V, profile; Card VI, profile; Card VII, shrimp, vagina; Card VIII, bat; Card IX, buttocks; Card X, man's face). This seems to suggest that while the response set can be very influential, such influence is probably restricted to some broad parameters that are contingent on the stimulus features of the blots. These findings coincide with the data in the Exner, Armbruster, and Mittman study (1978), which indicates that subjects tend to maintain the same form quality in their answers, even when they are induced to give many more answers than are ordinarily expected. In other words, most sets concerning the test, including the set involving social desirability, will probably *not* cause a subject to deviate significantly from his *own level of perceptual accuracy.* None of the three Poor form quality answers in the 50 that were listed (bulging eyes, buttocks, man's face) was ranked as "easy to see" by many subjects in either group, and all three were ranked as the most difficult to see by the overwhelming majority of subjects in both groups. This finding is particularly important for its bearing on the interpretation of Poor form quality responses. That is, there is little reason to believe that a poor form quality answer may be provoked somehow by the test situation or by a set concerning the test. Consequently, when a subject delivers a Poor form quality answer, especially a minus response, it is probably because he or she does *see* that object easily, and mentally ranks that potential answer as being "better" than other objects that are also seen. This fact becomes especially critical in differentiating the "malingered" protocol from that given by the true schizophrenic.

PERCEPTUAL ACCURACY AND THE RESPONSE PROCESS

People who try to "fudge" psychosis on the Rorschach are usually confronted with the problem of their own perceptual accuracy. Psychotics, and particularly schizophrenics, tend to see the world through some kind of distorted psychological prism which nonpsychotic people do not share and have difficulty understanding. The true schizophrenic, propelled through a private psychological space by his disturbance, seems to have difficulty seeing, no less comprehending, things that less disturbed people see. This strange distortion or injury to the perceptual process of the schizophrenic makes it very difficult for the nonschizophrenic to simulate the kind of mediational activity that seems to be involved in the formulation of a "minus" answer. Usually, the person trying to feign schizophrenia will use bizarre and/or dramatic wording in his answers, and quite frequently will give unusual answers; but when the form quality scoring is examined closely, the sham has failed. In other words, in spite of the unusual verbiage and the unusual responses, there is little basic distortion in *perceptual accuracy,* so that the $F+$ and

$X+$ percents are typically within normal limits; and even when the $F+$ and/or $X+$ percents are substantially lower than normal, those proportions are created by a higher frequency of *weak* form quality answers with relatively few true *minus* responses appearing. The schizophrenic simply has great difficulty seeing things in the same way that nonschizophrenics see them. This difficulty is demonstrated by the consistently low form quality answers given by schizophrenics in the Exner, Armbruster, and Mittman (1978) study, and even more by the fact that when asked to rate their answers, the schizophrenics tended to select poor form quality responses as representing their "best" answers. Conversely, nonschizophrenics have trouble trying to "see the world" through "schizophrenic-like" eyes.

The sturdiness of this difference in perceptual process is illustrated by two small sample studies completed for this work. In the first (Exner and Wylie, 1975), 12 second year graduate students, completing their first Rorschach course, were asked to "create" a schizophrenic protocol within a two hour time limit. All had reviewed schizophrenic records in the course of their study, and most had actually tested one or more schizophrenics. Nonetheless, only one student was able to create a record that was later judged as "schizophrenic" when reviewed in the blind by three judges having no awareness of the purpose of the study. Six others did produce protocols with $X+$ percents lower than 70%, but in each of those instances the frequency of "weak" answers exceeded the frequency of "minus" responses. In a second study (Exner and Sherman, 1977), 10 schizophrenic patients who were given the Rorschach in the routine course of diagnostic testing, were asked on the same day to repeat that test. They were told that the results of the testing had been reviewed and that the staff agreed that he or she could probably "improve" their performance. The same judges used in the Exner and Wylie study with graduate students evaluated these protocols in the blind. All 10 records were judged a schizophrenic, but, more important: while most of the protocols did differ, when contrasted with the first, in content, location selection, and length, the $F+$ and $X+$ percents remained essentially unchanged, and the frequency of minus responses was almost identical.

A large proportion of subjects, both psychiatric and nonpatient, will yield a minus response in the course of taking the test. It is difficult to speculate what this means. Extrapolating from data concerning schizophrenics, it seems probable that the occurrence of the minus response represents some form of cognitive slippage, provoked by any number of elements. For instance, children who are *not* patients tend to give proportionally fewer minus answers than do nonpatient adults. It also seems clear that children tend to be less cooperative and more defensive when taking the test. It may be logical to infer that the minus is more likely to occur in circumstances when the defensiveness of the subject is less stringent or effective. Another postulate concerning the minus response concerns the element of defense effectiveness, which may be reduced by an intense need state or preoccupation. Under these conditions the appropriateness of the form quality may be considerably less important than the *need* to see an object. For example, several studies have been reported demonstrating a higher frequency of Anatomy and X-ray responses among psychosomatics, depressives, "neurasthenics," and women suffering psychiatric complications related to pregnancy (Zolliker, 1943; Rapaport, 1946; Shatin, 1952; Draguns, Haley, and Phillips, 1967; Exner, 1974). In these instances, it seems logical to assume that the preoccupation has become quite influential in the *selection process* of the answer that, among all those perceived, will actually be delivered. These studies are important here in that many Anatomy or X-ray answers tend to be of Poor form quality, and often minus.

It seems less likely that the social desirability element will provoke minus answers. There is no doubt that more "individualistic" subjects do tend to have reduced $X+$ and $F+$ percents. However, the vast majority of these cases reflect a higher frequency of *weak* form quality answers, and relatively insignificant numbers of minus responses. For example, in a continuing study designed to collect large samples of normative data from younger clients, some of which has already been published (Exner, Weiner, and Schuyler, 1976), it is noted that children and adolescents referred for intervention because of "behavioral problems"—that is, acting out behaviors in school and/or at home—give $X+$ percents averaging about 10 percentage points lower than those of nonpatient children. Examination of this pool of records shows that the proportions of minus responses are no greater than for the nonpatient group; however, the frequency of weak form quality responses is significantly greater.

The weak form quality response is a unique answer that usually does not have the quality of form fit to the blot area, as does the Good form quality response. It is because of this uniqueness that it is seen (or reported) infrequently and thus falls into the general category of Poor form quality. It does not, however, reflect the gross perceptual distortion involved in the minus answer. Rather, it is usually easy to see once the area is identified, and it does not contain the arbitrary use of contours that often occurs in the minus response. Thus, the weak response appears to represent less concern with conformity, preciseness, and social desirability, where the minus response represents a distinct perceptual difficulty.

Whatever the cause, it remains that a *minus is a minus,* and does reflect some kind of perceptual disarray. Whether the disarray is well fixed or merely transitory will be illustrated by the frequency with which minus answers appear in a protocol. This is especially important for interpretation, since almost all responses that are "delivered" in the course of taking the test will be formulated on the basis of the *form features* of the blots. This pattern has been demonstrated quite well in Baughman's (1959) work, which involved the manipulation of several of the nonform features of the blots. In other words, when a minus response appears, it is apparently the result of a malfunction. Similarly, when a weak form quality answer occurs, it is probably a result of some need or preoccupation that does not interfere *significantly* with the operations underlying perceptual accuracy. In this context, the more idiographic responses do illustrate situations in which the more simple, efficient, straightforward delivery of a neatly defined pure form answer has been circumvented by some personal element; and the more idiographic the answer, the more intense the circumventing element. This is a principle of efficiency versus inefficiency, and apparently there are many cases in which the seemingly inefficient "route" is judged more useful by the subject. This principle appears to hold not only for form quality issues, but for a broad variety of articulated determinants.

ARTICULATION AND THE RESPONSE PROCESS

A major issue for Rorschach interpretation concerns the distinction between what is "perceived" and what is articulated. Earlier in this chapter, data were presented indicating that people do see many "potential" answers when they examine each of the blots. Some blots presumably evoke more potential responses than others, but all seem to suggest several possible answers shortly after they are presented. It also appears reasonably certain that the selection, among these several potential responses, of the one that will actually be "delivered" during the test can be influenced to some degree by sets relating to the test or the test situation. Moreover, the element of perceptual accuracy plays an important role. That is, with the exception of subjects with severe perceptual dysfunction, most potential answers will be formulated within boundaries of reasonable perceptual accuracy, usually based on form features, but in some less common cases on color or shading features, as in a "blood" response to an all red area. Ultimately, in many, or even the majority, of responses, it is some form dominated composite of stimulus features that leads to the identification of the potential answer, and then to the decision to deliver a particular response. But this does *not* mean that a subject will necessarily articulate *all* the stimulus features that have contributed to the response formulation. On the contrary, it is very common that some of these features will not be articulated, *yet it is the substance of what has been articulated that forms the basis for interpretation.* This factor poses one of the most difficult problems for the student of the Rorschach, and has probably contributed to confusion about the test and how it should be used. How often has the experienced Rorschacher encountered the subject who responds to a chromatically colored blot or blot area with a response such as "a flower" but then fails to articulate the color as being relevant to the answer? Many such examiners, comfortable in their naiveté, will try to evoke a mention of the color features through semidirect inquiry questions, such as "I'm still not sure why it looks like a flower"; "Is there anything else that makes it look that way?"; or even worse, "If it were a different color, would it look more like a flower, less like a flower, or as much like a flower?" The skilled Rorschacher knows better than to do this, and appreciates the fact that the response process in itself consists of the perceptual mediation factor, the decision to deliver or not to deliver what has been perceived, *plus* the manner of delivery. Articulation, as such, is as vital to the overall interpretation of a record as is the response itself.

It is also established that some blot features very critical to the formation of a response are *rarely* articulated. In fact, when they are articulated, it takes on special interpretive significance. For instance, Baughman (1954, 1959) and Exner (1959) have demonstrated that the achromatic features of Card I are essential to the formation of the Popular "bat" response. If the achromatic features of the blot are modified to reduce their impact, as in the Baughman work, or changed completely as in the Exner work, the frequency of that response can be diminished or even eliminated. Exner presented the cards in various colors, keeping the form and shading features constant. When the blot was presented as a light blue, taken from the $D1$ area of Card X, the frequency of "bat" was reduced to zero among 100 nonpatient subjects. When the blot was presented as green, brown, or magenta, the frequency for "bat" was considerably greater than zero, but in all instances less than the frequency required for designation as Popular. This fact would seem unremarkable but for the fact that the black-grey features of Card I are articulated as relevant to the percept "bat" by slightly less than one in every 12 nonpatients, and by slightly more than one in every seven patients giving that response. Obviously, the grey-black coloring of the blot is very important to the formation of the bat response. Nevertheless, very few subjects do articulate it. Presumably, the coloring element is part of a complex cue system inherent in the stimulus, which is cognitively mediated by the subjects who do see the bat; however, the intensity of that stimulus is apparently more subtle than the form element and the response therefore, is rarely articulated. Conversely, the same stimulus element appears to become more intense for a small number of subjects who do actually articulate the color characteristic. It is this element of awareness that makes the articulation factor very important; or, stated more simply, the strength and accuracy of the interpretation *proceeds from what the subject says about the blot rather than what is inferred* about his percept.

Articulation is not only important to accurate scoring, but in many instances becomes important to the interpretation of the content. For instance, one subject may say, "a bat," a second may say, "a horrible bat," a third may say, "a wicked bat," and so on. Although each of these answers may be scored identically, there are clearly compelling hints of important interpretive information in these answers employing adjectives. Similarly, the manner of articulation will often provide important information about the cognitive operations of the subject. For example, a subject will occasionally respond to Card VIII by saying, "pink bears." When this occurs, it is scored as an Incongruous Combination *(INCOM)* and offers evidence of cognitive rigidity. Other subjects, responding to the same area, will report, "They look like bears, pink ones, but I've never seen pink ones." This is also a form of cognitive rigidity, but the subject is able to recover, at least partially, by dissociating the unreality of the color from the reality of the form. Most subjects never mention the pink, but it does seem highly likely that most process that stimulus feature.

Unfortunately, current knowledge about the entire perceptual process leaves many important questions unanswered, but it does seem certain that different people will process the same stimulus cues differently; and the matter of articulation becomes one of the fundamental avenues through which some understanding of the processing may evolve. Another study, completed for this work (Exner and Wylie, 1976), adds more information concerning this complicated phenomenon. The chromatic coloring for five major blot areas, four of which ordinarily provoke Popular answers, were altered with the use of a monochrome dye-coupling method that holds form and shading constant. The Card III red *D*3 area, in which a butterfly is commonly perceived, was altered to yellow; the Card VIII pink *D*1 area, usually perceived as an animal, was changed to dark brown; the Card IX orange *D*3 area, sometimes seen as a witch, was changed to grey; the Card IX *D*4 area, commonly seen as a human head, was altered to a light tan; and the Card X *D*1 area, usually seen as a spider or crab, was changed to dark brown. The purpose of the study was twofold: The first was to determine whether coloring certain areas in accord with the "natural" colors of objects most frequently reported for those areas would significantly increase the number of common responses above those occuring when the cards are presented in their standard colors. The second and more important aim was to determine whether those common responses, when given, would include more references to color when the blot coloring was more appropriate to the objects. Fifty nonpatient adults, who had volunteered for a Rorschach "standardization" project were randomized into two groups of 25 subjects each. None had prior exposure to the Rorschach. Subjects were tested individually by one of seven experienced examiners, none of whom was familiar with the purpose of the study. Examiners were randomized across subjects so that no examiner tested more than eight subjects or more than five subjects from either group. Subjects were shown *only* the four cards involved in the study, with the same instructions and procedures as if the entire test were being administered. One group was given the four standard Rorschach blots, while the second group was given the four experimentally altered cards.

The data were analyzed, using the chi-square method, only for the five critical responses: butterfly, animal, human head, witch, and spider or crab. The frequencies, by group, are shown in Table 10, which also includes the frequencies with which the color features were also articulated. These data indicate that the color change did provoke higher frequencies for four of the five critical responses, the differences for two of which reach a statistically significant level. Interestingly, the frequency of the spider or crab answer to Card X was lower when the color was altered from blue to brown. It should also be noted that the color feature was articulated with a significantly greater proportional frequency by subjects responding to the altered cards. At first glance, these data are not very consistent. Only in the instance of the butterfly response did both response frequency and color articulation increase significantly as a function of the color change. No significant increase in frequency could have been achieved for the animal response, since the control subjects also gave that answer with a high frequency; but the color change in that area appears to have produced a stronger stimulus effect, provoking a higher frequency of articulation. The change of color from orange to grey in Card IX did provoke more witch responses, but with no proportional increase in color articulation. This may be a case in which the stimulus feature contributes to the formulation of the answer, but is not of sufficient intensity to be articulated. The data concerning the Card X spider or crab response appeared to be the most confusing because the frequency for the answer was actually lower than when the area is colored blue; yet a significant proportion of those responding to the altered card with that answer did articulate the color. Subsequently, all subjects in this study were retrieved and asked to complete a brief questionnaire about their habits and interests. A question on their favorite color was included, the re-

Table 10.   Frequencies for Five Responses and Articulation of the Color, for Two Groups, One Administered Standard Cards and the Second Administered Chromatically Altered Cards

Card, Area, and Response	Standard Set $N = 25$		Altered Set $N = 25$		Chi-Square for	
	R	Color	R	Color	R	Color
III, D3, butterfly	12	6	20	18	5.04*	4.44*
VIII, D1, animal	22	0	25	17	0.07	20.58**
IX, D4, human head	9	2	16	9	2.88	1.50
IX, D3, witch	8	2	17	6	5.12*	0.03
X, D1, spider or crab	16	0	11	4	2.03	4.25*

*p < .05.
**p < .01.

sponses to which revealed that 20 of the 25 Standard Set group subjects, and 18 of the 25 Altered Set subjects, prefer blue to all other colors, a preference that may have contributed to the results. An examination of the other responses given by both groups to Card X did uncover the fact that four of the Altered Set subjects who did not respond to the $D1$ area of the card did, in fact, give a response to the $D6$ area of the blot, which is also colored blue. None of the subjects from the Standard Set group who responded to the $D1$ area also responded to the $D6$ area of the card.

These data offer little in the way of clarifying the complex stimulus features of the blots, but they do illustrate the need for extreme caution in making assumptions about what is seen and *especially about the intensity of the stimulus impact.* In that context, they also illustrate the importance of the articulation element, and, of course, the necessity for recording all material *verbatim.*

One of the best examples illustrating the importance of articulation in the response process is derived from data about Cards IV and VI. It is with these cards that the texture *(T)* determinant is most frequently articulated, ordinarily in the framework of a "skin" response to either card, or in conjunction with an Animal or "monster" response to Card IV. Data concerning the texture determinant lend considerable support to the interpretive postulate that it relates to affective need (Exner, 1974), and most protocols do contain one or two texture determinants. When a record displays a large number of texture answers, the subject is usually one who has a strong need for affective interpersonal contact. In a study completed in the course of this work (Exner and Bryant, 1974), 30 subjects who had recently been divorced or separated and had no "substitute" partner were tested by one of six examiners who had no information about the subjects or the purpose of the study. A second group of 30 married subjects who judged their marriages as being at least average in stability and happiness were controls. When the protocols of the two groups were compared, several statistically significant differences were noted, among them a substantial difference in the frequency of texture determinants. All 30 of the divorced or separated subjects gave texture responses, the average for the group being 3.57 with a *SD* of 1.21. The 30 control protocols included 28 containing at least one texture answer. The mean for that group was 1.31, with a *SD* of 0.96. An *F* test revealed the groups to differ significantly on this variable, at a level beyond .05.

Just as a higher frequency of texture responses becomes quite meaningful, so too does the absence of the texture determinant. Exner (1974) noted that more psychiatric subjects have this "*T* failure" than do nonpatients, and he speculated that the absence of texture may reflect a serious form of interpersonal impoverishment in which the subject no longer strives for meaningful relationships with others. Inasmuch as this state of emotional isolation is often associated with the "burnt child" phenomenon, Leura and Exner (1976) collected protocols from 32 children, ages 7 to 11, who had lived in foster homes since the age of two or less, with no placement lasting longer than 14 months. A control population of 32 children in the same age range who had lived with their true parents since birth was also tested. Both groups were also administered the Wechsler Intelligence Scale for Children (WISC), the results of which showed that the groups did not differ for the I.Q. variable. Twenty of the 32 foster home children failed to articulate texture in their protocols, although 14 of those 20 did give skin, animal, or monster responses to either or both Cards IV and VI. Overall, the mean number of texture responses for the group was 0.457. The control subjects gave very different protocols. Twenty-nine of the 32 controls gave at least one texture answer, and 31 of the group gave the skin, animal, or monster answer to either or both Cards IV and VI. The average number of T responses for that group is 1.47, reflecting a statistically significant difference between the groups on this element, well beyond the .01 level.

These differences, and those reported by Exner and Bryant about subjects who give higher T frequencies, are underscored by two studies that include data on the stimulus features of Cards IV and VI. In the Baughman (1959) study, six variations of the blots were used in addition to the standard blots. With one experimental set all shading features were removed while color and form were retained. Although Baughman does not report the incidence of the shading features, it does seem clear that the frequency of "critical" texture provoking skin, animal, and monster responses to Cards IV and VI was reduced significantly by this experimental alteration. Working on a different factor Exner (1961) altered the coloring of these two blots, keeping the form and shading constant. The blots were presented in four chromatic colors, brown, magenta, green, and blue, plus the standard achromatic versions, one set of each given to five groups consisting of 40 subjects each. No differences were found between any of the groups for the texture determinant. In other words, it seems quite clear that the shading component is very critical to the formulation of the texture oriented answer for either of these cards.

Baughman (1959) had suggested that Rorschach scoring might best proceed through the use of a paired comparison method of inquiry that he had described earlier (1958). The assumption here, developed quite logically, was that the scoring should reflect what is *actually* seen in the context of stimulus input. Such a method could reveal information about stimulus features that were processed. The problem with the method, however, is that it depends on information gathered well after the "free association" occurs, and is also contingent upon a new stimulus input. Although the Baughman recommendation was based on an empirically developed technique, it is probably inappropriate to the Rorschach because it tends to circumvent the important element of articulation. And although the issue of articulation will, no doubt, remain a knotty problem for Rorschach researchers, it does seem to be a vital factor to the overall interpretive process. What a subject says when examining a blot *remains what that subject has said,* and in some mysterious way, those words represent the composite of what has been seen, processed, evaluated, and delivered. It is the combination of these steps that constitutes the response process, and ultimately the data from which scoring and interpretation are derived.

SUMMARY

Rorschach's fascination with the response process was certainly justified, for this is a complicated phenomenon about which much more research is required. On the basis of data developed up to this point, it seems practical to hypothesize that at least four interrelated components are involved in the delivery of the response.

The first is the reception and mediation of the stimulus input, the mental acknowledgment at the moment that the task at hand is to see something other than an inkblot, and the categorization of the many objects which the inkblot or its parts may resemble. This seems to be a rapid process, and most subjects probably generate a host of "possibilities" in the course of a few seconds. The second step in the process involves some form of rank ordering of the possibilities that have been detected. At this stage, several factors merge to determine that rank order. They include needs, internal sets, and sets about the test situation, and it is important to note here that the needs and sets may be integral parts of the personality structure, manifest in the form of basic response styles, or they may be more transitory, created by situational elements. It also seems clear that this stage of the response operation includes concern for perceptual accuracy, if this element has not already become influential.

The third phase of the process appears to involve the element of social desirability. Even if a potential response has "passed muster" in terms of perceptual accuracy, sets, and basic stimulus processing, the subject must feel or believe that the answer will be acceptable. If this feeling or belief is not present, the response will have a low priority for delivery, and for most subjects will not be delivered at all. Finally, there is the manner of articulation, something much more important and complex than simple verbiage. During this stage of the response process, many elements appear to be involved. Some will restrict what is said while others apparently stimulate the idiographic character so frequent in an answer. Some perceptual features are specified and others are not, and somehow, this strange mixture of articulation comes to reflect the manner in which the subject has coped with the stress of the ambiguous stimulus presented to him or her.

It is important to remember that Rorschach answers are, in microcosm, a unique and valuable behavioral sample reflecting the way the individual is most likely to respond in a problem solving situation where there are few rules or principles directing the "psychological traffic." In the Rorschach, the individual is "on his own," forced to used the behaviors with which he is most comfortable, which are easiest for him to display, and which, in his judgment, will lead to acceptable performance. One of the most important features of the Rorschach is that it is "nondirected" and does force the individual to display his "psychological wares" in coping with the situation. When the Comprehensive System was developed, one point became clear above all others: the importance of keeping the task as free as possible from externally induced direction. It is for this reason that the inquiry is severely limited, and that questions in the inquiry must be minimized.

The obvious question that should be posed at this point by the skeptic is whether this response process, purported to reflect basic response styles of the person, will be "stable" over time. It is this issue that forms the subject matter of the following chapter.

REFERENCES

Abramson, L. S. The influence of set for area on the Rorschach Test results. *Journal of Consulting Psychology,* 1951, **15**, 337–342.

Baughman, E. E. Rorschach scores as a function of examiner differences. *Journal of Projective Techniques,* 1951, **15**, 243–249.

Baughman, E. E. A comparative analysis Rorschach forms with altered stimulus characteristics. *Journal of Projective Techniques,* 1954, **18**, 151–164.

Baughman, E. E. A new method of Rorschach inquiry. *Journal of Projective Techniques,* 1958, **22**, 381–389.

Baughman, E. E. An experimental analysis of the relationship between stimulus structure and behavior on the Rorschach. *Journal of Projective Techniques,* 1959, **23**, 134–183.

Carp, A. L. and Shavzin, A. R. The susceptibility to falsification of the Rorschach diagnostic technique. *Journal of Consulting Psychology,* 1950, **14**, 230–233.

Claparède, E. Perception syncretique chez un enfant. *Archives de Psychologie,* 1908, **7**, 195.

Coffin, T. E. Some conditions of suggestion and suggestibility: A study of certain attitudinal and situational factors influencing the process of suggestion. *Psychological Monographs,* 1941, **53**. Whole No. 241.

Cox, F. N. and Sarason, S. B. Test anxiety and Rorschach performance. *Journal of Abnormal and Social Psychology,* 1954, **49**, 371–377.

Dahlstrom, W. G., Welsh, G. S., and Dahlstrom, L. E. *An MMPI Handbook, Volume II: Research Applications.* (rev. ed.) Minneapolis: University of Minnesota Press, 1975.

Dinoff, M. Subject awareness of examiner influence in a testing situation. *Journal of Consulting Psychology,* 1960, **24**, 465.

Draguns, J. G., Haley, E. M., and Phillips, L. Studies of Rorshach content: A review of the literature. Part 1: Traditional content categories. *Journal of Projective Techniques and Personality Assessment,* 1967, **31**, 3–32.

Exner, J. E. The influence of chromatic and achromatic color in the Rorschach. *Journal of Projective Techniques,* 1959, **23**, 418–425.

Exner, J. E. Achromatic color in Cards IV and VI of the Rorschach. *Journal of Projective Techniques,* 1961, **25**, 38–40.

Exner, J. E. *The Rorschach Systems.* New York: Grune & Stratton, 1969.

Exner, J. E. *The Rorschach: A Comprehensive System.* New York: John Wiley and Sons, 1974.

Exner, J. E., Armbruster, G. L. Increasing R by altering instructions and creating a time set. Workshops study No. 209 (unpublished), Rorschach Workshops, 1974.

Exner, J. E., Armbruster, G. L., and Mittman, B. L. The Rorschach response process. *Journal of Personality Assessment,* 1978, **42**, 27–38.

Exner, J. E. and Bryant, E. L. Rorschach responses of subjects recently divorced or separated. Workshops study No. 206 (unpublished), Rorschach Workshops, 1974.

Exner, J. E. and Leura, A. V. Variations in the ranking of Rorschach responses as a function of situational set. Workshops study No. 221 (unpublished), Rorschach Workshops, 1976.

Exner, J. E. and Sherman, J. Rorschach performances of schizophrenics asked to improve their protocols in a second administration. Workshops study No. 243 (unpublished), Rorschach Workshops, 1977.

Exner, J. E. and Wylie, J. R. Attempts at simulation of schizophrenic like Protocols by psychology graduate students. Workshops study No. 211 (unpublished), Rorschach Workshops, 1975.

Exner, J. E. and Wylie, J. R. Alterations in frequency of response and color articulation as related to alterations in the coloring of specific blot areas. Workshops study No. 219 (unpublished), Rorschach Workshops, 1976.

Exner, J. E., Weiner, I. B., and Schuyler, W. *A Rorschach Workbook for the Comprehensive System.* Bayville, N.Y.: Rorschach Workshops, 1976.

Fossberg, I. A. Rorschach reactions under varied instructions. *Rorschach Research Exchange,* 1938, **3,** 12–30.

Frank, L. K. Projective methods for the study of personality. *Journal of Psychology,* 1939, **8,** 389–413.

Friedman, H. Perceptual recognition in schizophrenia: an hypothesis suggested by the use of the Rorschach test. *Journal of Genetic Psychology,* 1952, *81,* 63–98.

Gibby, R. G. The stability of certain Rorschach variables under conditions of experimentally induced sets: I, The intellectual variables. *Journal of Projective Techniques,* 1951, **15,** 3–25.

Gibby, R. G., Miller, D. R., and Walker, E. L. The examiner's influence on the Rorschach protocol. *Journal of Consulting Psychology,* 1953, **17,** 425–428.

Goetcheus, G. The effects of instructions and examiners on the Rorschach. Unpublished M.A. thesis, Bowling Green State University, 1967.

Gross, L. Effects of verbal and nonverbal reinforcement on the Rorschach. *Journal of Consulting Psychology,* 1959, **23,** 66–68.

Hersen, M. and Greaves, S. T. Rorschach productivity as related to verbal reinforcement. *Journal of Personality Assessment,* 1971, **35,** 436–441.

Horiuchi, H. A study of perceptual process of Rorschach cards by tachistoscopic method on movement and shading responses. *Journal of Projective Techniques,* 1961, **25,** 44–53.

Hutt, M., Gibby, R. G., Milton, E. O. and Pottharst, K. The effect of varied experimental "sets" upon Rorschach test performance. *Journal of Projective Techniques,* 1950, **14,** 181–187.

Leura, A. V. and Exner, J. E. Rorschach performances of children with a multiple foster home history. Workshops study No. 220 (unpublished), Rorschach Workshops, 1976.

Lord, E. Experimentally induced variations in Rorschach performance. *Psychological Monographs,* 1950, **60,** Whole No. 316.

Magnussen, M. G. Verbal and nonverbal reinforcers in the Rorschach situation. *Journal of Clinical Psychology,* 1960, **16,** 167–169.

Masling, J. Differential indoctrination of examiners and Rorschach responses. *Journal of Consulting Psychology,* 1965, **29,** 198–201.

Meer, B. The relative difficulty of the Rorschach cards. *Journal of Projective Techniques,* 1955, **19,** 43–53.

Meili-Dworetzki, G. The development of perception in the Rorschach. In Klopfer, B. et al. *Developments in the Rorschach Technique. Volume II· Fields of Application.* Yonker-on-Hudson, N.Y.: World Book Co., 1956.

Peterson, L. C. The effects of instruction variation on Rorschach responses. Unpublished M.A. thesis, Ohio State University, 1957.

Phares, E. J., Stewart, L. M., and Foster, J. M. Instruction variation and Rorschach performance. *Journal of Projection Techniques,* 1960, **24,** 28–31.

Rapaport, D., Gill, M. and Schafer, R. *Diagnostic Psychological Testing. Volume II.* Chicago: The Yearbook Publishers, 1946.

Rorschach, H. *Psychodiagnostics.* (trans. Hans Huber, 1942), Bern: Bircher, 1921.

Schachtel, E. G. Subjective definitions of the Rorschach Test situation and their effect on test performance. *Psychiatry,* 1945, **8,** 419–448.

Schafer, R. *Psychoanalytic Interpretation in Rorschach Testing.* New York: Grune and Stratton, 1954.

Shatin, L. Psychoneurosis and psychosomatic reactions: A Rorschach study. *Journal of Consulting Psychology,* 1952, **16,** 220–223.

Stein, M. I. Personality factors involved in the temporal development of Rorschach responses. *Rorschach Research Exchange,* 1949, **13,** 355–414.

Strauss, M. E. Examiner expectancy: Effects on Rorschach experience balance. *Journal of Consulting Psychology,* 1968, **32,** 125–129.

Strauss, M. E. and Marwit, S. J. Expectancy effects in Rorschach testing. *Journal of Consulting and Clinical Psychology,* 1970, **34,** 448.

Weiner, I. B. *Psychodiagnosis in Schizophrenia.* New York: John Wiley and Sons, 1966.

Wickes, T. A. Examiner influence in a testing situation. *Journal of Consulting Psychology,* 1956, **20,** 23–26.

Williams, M. H. The influence of variations in instructions on Rorschach reaction time. *Dissertations Abstracts,* 1954, **14,** 2131.

Zolliker, A. Schwangerschaftsdepression und Rorsch'scher formdeutversuch. *Schweiz Archeives Neurologie und Psychiatrie,* 1943, **53,** 62–78.

CHAPTER 3

The Issue of Reliability: Temporal Consistency of the Structural Data

The issue of reliability has been prominent in criticisms of the Rorschach. Those who disavow the usefulness of the test frequently point to the problems of establishing evidence of internal consistency on the basis of some form of split-half technique, and to the limited data available concerning the temporal consistency in performance. It is true that the demonstration of split-half reliability for the test poses many problems, none of which have been resolved to the satisfaction of those who critique the test. The "fly" in the split-half "ointment" is the fact that the stimuli of the test are different. They are different for levels of difficulty and complexity, and they are probably different for different kinds of "stimulus pull." Nonetheless, some split-half studies have produced results that are far from unrespectable. Vernon (1933) reported relatively low split-half reliabilities for all the variables in the test except *R*. Conversely, Hertz (1934) published an extensive study of the records of 100 junior high school students in which she used an "odd-even" split of the cards and obtained reliability coefficients ranging from .66 to .97. Ford (1946), following essentially the same approach used by Hertz, but using records of younger children, reported split-half reliabilities comparable to those of Hertz. Orange (1953) reported low positive and significant correlations for the various location scores, reaction times, the inclusion of *S*, and the number of responses for two groups, one nonpatient and one of hospitalized neurotics. He used a unique approach to the split-half method, following both the "odd-even" principle but also attempting to divide the cards into two groups based on degree of ambiguity.

Although the split-half technique does eliminate the disadvantage of prior exposure to the blot, and does control for practice effect, it is probably not a good measure of the "sturdiness" of the Rorschach. The assumption, which must apply in any split-half study, is that the subject will respond to *any* stimulus with essentially the same approach or style; but that is probably not the case. Although it is true that some response styles are more preferred, or have a higher expectancy for occurrence, this does not mean that an individual is totally inflexible and thereby incapable of altering his or her preferred style of response. It has been demonstrated by the data in the preceding chapter that various conditions do alter the structural data, and very markedly in some instances. But if the hypothesis is true that *most or all people do have preferred response styles that will manifest in the majority of their responses;* and *if* the Rorschach is an instrument from which glimpses of those response styles can be derived, *then* those same styles should be evidenced over repeated Rorschach testings. The examination of this premise has encompassed a major portion of the research effort at Rorschach Workshops during the past five years. In other words, does the test reflect a consistency over time; another form of reliability evaluation which may well be the more important in establishing the usefulness of the data collected in any single protocol.

The rationale for, and some of the problems pertaining to, the temporal consistency, or test-retest approach, with the Rorschach is neatly summarized by Holzberg (1960; 1977). He points out that any or all of three conditions that should be met in test-retest situations may not occur in Rorschach testing. The first is the stability of that which is being measured. Holzberg postulates that it may be unfair to assume that personality, as such, will be constant over time. The second condition is the assumption that the set of the subject toward the test will be the same, thereby permitting an "exactness" of data to appear from one testing to another. Since it has been demonstrated that different sets concerning the Rorschach situation do cause alterations in some data, Holzberg suggests that retesting with the Rorschach may in itself create a different set, possibly producing spurious results. The third condition involves memory. Swift (1944) obtained "only fairly satisfactory" retest reliabilities for preschool children when the second testing was completed after 30 days, yet she also found that 47% of the responses given during the first testing were remembered by her subjects. Holzberg assumes that this percentage would be higher for adult subjects, and following Kelley (1942), agrees that the mental operations of the second testing will not be the same as those of the first testing because of the influence of memory.

Although these problems are worth noting, none poses a convincing argument. In fact, two are based on assumptions that are at least partially incorrect. First, while alterations in the subject's set toward the test may vary from one testing to another, the evidence indicates that the impact of this variation is generally seen in content rather than in determinants. Although a subject may be less "defensive" in the second testing, having better understanding of the procedure and knowledge of the stimuli, it seems illogical to assume that the subject will undergo a complete alteration in response styles. On the contrary, it can be postulated that, because the subject is less defensive during a second administration, the response styles will be more exposed or magnified. Thus, while R may be predicted to increase, and the length of articulations may be greater, it is highly unlikely that the response styles of the person are so "fluid" over time as to change the protocol dramatically.

The second semifalse assumption concerns the impact of memory on the retest. If the subject had seen only one or two objects per blot, the possibility of memory influence would be substantial, but, as has been demonstrated in the preceding chapter, most subjects select their responses from a rather significant array of perceived objects. Thus, the memory factor is not based so much on recalling what was seen, *as on what was reported;* and that process requires some fairly sturdy engrams, especially as the time interval between first and second testings become longer. It is true that, during a retest, subjects tend to verbalize a recall of the blot or of an answer. However, in one of the six month retest studies involving 20 phobic subjects who entered a systematic desensitization form of treatment *after* the first testing, six asked, during the retest, if a different set of blots was being used. Eight subjects from that same group prefaced at least one answer with, "Oh yes, this is the . . . " and then proceeded to give an answer quite unlike any that had been given during the first administration. Thus, while memory does play some role in the retest, the nature of the role varies from one subject to another and seems unlikely to change basic personality or response style features.

The issue of the stability of personality itself is a more complex issue. Every approach to the study of personality, ranging from the psychoanalytic to the behavioral models, includes the notion that, at some point in time (usually by early adulthood), a stabilization occurs between response relationships. Whether this postulate is stated in terms of energy forces or response expectancies is less important than the fact that essentially all of psychology has developed from this very premise. It is true that personality changes. This has been well documented in the developmental psychology literature, and the literature from abnormal psychology has illustrated quite well how the disorganization of personality takes place during severe turmoil. Changes have also been noted for people in various forms of treatment oriented toward the reconstitution or reconstruction of the personality; but it is highly unlikely that the "stabilized" personality, not subject to psychopathological disorganization or the influences of treatment, will undergo many changes over relatively short periods, or even over a few years.

Actually, the handful of retest reliability studies that have been reported are reasonably encouraging. Ford (1946) reports reliabilities for the scoring determinants ranging from +.38 to +.86 for a group of young children retested after 30 days. Kerr (1936) had previously reported substantially lower reliabilities for young children retested after one year, results that may logically be attributed in part to the growth factor. Holzberg and Wexsler (1950) deliberately used this technique with a group of schizophrenics, assuming that they would manifest considerable "unreliability." Surprisingly, the schizophrenic sample manifests significantly high and very respectable reliabilities across most scoring variables. Kelley, Margulies, and Barrera (1941) found very little change in the "psychograms" of 12 patients retested two hours after having received ECT, and who demonstrated total amnesia for the first testing, which had been completed just prior to the treatment.

TEMPORAL CONSISTENCY AND INTERPRETATION

One of the fallacies concerning the Rorschach is the notion that temporal consistency should be illustrated for *all* scores. In other words, if the test is "reliable" within the guidelines for this particular kind of reliability, all of its features should be sturdy over time. This is not true. The fallacy rests on the premise that each of the Rorschach scores, ratios, and so on, reflects some unchanging aspect of the person. It is true that many, or even most, of the structural data should remain reasonably constant over time; but any thorough review of research on the many Rorschach variables indicates that some relate specifically to situational phenomena. For instance, the presence of inanimate movement (m) is substantially higher in protocols of persons experiencing stress and feeling somewhat out of control. Part of the validation for that interpretation has been derived from retests of the subjects who give a significantly lower frequency of m at a later time, when the stress elements have been removed. The retest protocols generally show a distinct reduction in the frequency of *m,* often to a zero level. Although this shows a "temporal inconsistency" for that particular variable, it does not make the test unreliable, nor do such findings invalidate the meaningfulness of the variable itself. Spielberger (1966, 1971) has been quite convincing in his demonstration that some anxiety is "state" evoked—that is, situationally related, while other features of anxiety are "trait" related—that is, more durable characteristics of the personality itself. These same concepts of *state* and *trait* apply to Rorschach structural data. Some, like *m,* are state phenomena, while others are related to the more durable response tendencies of the individual. Thus, studies of temporal consistency become important to help differentiate the more enduring traits of the subject from those that may be more transient in nature. Such a differentiation encourages a more sophisticated interpretation and, in cases of psychopathology, adds enormously to the formulation of treatment planning. Problems related to the less permanent features of personality can often be alleviated through brief forms of intervention that do not necessarily focus on, or interfere with, the "trait" features of the person. Conversely, when psychological disarray involves a need to alter some of the more basic features of the personality, brief forms of intervention are typically contraindicated, and longer and possibly more complex forms of intervention will usually be required.

THE RESEARCH PLAN

Any evaluation of the temporal consistency of the test must involve subjects from several different groupings and employ designs that permit retesting at different intervals. The most critical subject group is the adult nonpatient group, representing individuals "stabilized" in personality development who can thus be expected to display consistent behavior over time, assuming relative freedom from psychopathological states. It is assumed that retest data, collected at different intervals from different nonpatient groups, will provide the best illustration of those Rorschach variables that are durable, and those which are variable. Three nonpatient adult groups participated in the "nuclear" studies concerning temporal consistency. The first, with 25 subjects, was retested after seven days; the second, also composed of 25 subjects, was retested after 60 days; and the third, which has been defined as the "focal" group, consists of 100 subjects, who were retested after three years.

Although data from nonpatients are critical to the study of temporal consistency in the Rorschach, so too are data from psychiatric groups. The matrix of studies in this research plan has also included the 30 day retest of outpatients awaiting assignment to therapists or groups (N = 25); newly admitted schizophrenics, untreated over a 10 day evaluation period and retested on the 10th hospital day (N = 20); outpatients retested at a 90 day interval during which brief treatment has occurred (N = 35); and long term outpatients, retested at a 180 day interval (N = 30). Although some sample sizes are smaller than might be desired, especially if only a single study was involved, this matrix of seven projects can still provide meaningful information.

Obviously, these studies were not created simply to study the issue of temporal consistency. In fact, most of the patient-involved studies were designed to review treatment effects as manifest in the Rorschach. Neverthelesss, the data from these groups are amenable to correlational analyses that provide information concerning temporal consistency, and thus, are included here.

THE FOCAL STUDY (Exner, Leura, Armbruster, and Viglione, 1977)

The most significant effort in this complex of studies involved the recruitment of a large sample of nonpatient adults willing to volunteer again, after three years, for a second testing. It was assumed, on the basis of previous research (Exner and Murrilo, 1973; Exner and Murillo, 1976; Exner and Murillo, 1977) that some attrition would occur over this long period of time. Consequently, 170 subjects were recruited in the initial effort. The original sample included 75 males and 95 females, about two thirds of whom were from middle class families, with the remaining one third about equally divided between upper and lower class groups. After volunteering for the project, a "significant other" completed a Form R of the Katz Adjustment Scale (Katz and Lyerly, 1963) concerning the recent behavior of the subject. Volunteers rated by significant others at a level that would imply the possibility of a psychopathological state were eliminated from this project.[1] The 170 subjects who passed this screening were administered the test by one of 26 examiners used in the study, none of whom tested more than 10 subjects. The collected protocols *were not* scored, but instead were stored for the three year interval. A previously devised system was used to maintain some contact with the subjects during this three year period (Exner, Murillo, and Cannavo, 1973). The scheme included telephone contacts at 90 day intervals to reaffirm addresses, and the like, occasional sending of greeting cards, and the completion of a brief behavioral questionnaire at the end of each of the first two years. Beginning with the 34th post-test month, subjects were contacted again to arrange for the retest, which occurred for some subjects in the 35th post-test month, and for others as late as the 38th post-test month. In all, 113 of the original 170 subjects were located and agreed to the retest. Twenty-two examiners were used to complete the retesting, most of whom had not been involved in the first administration. After 100 subjects had been successfully retrieved, the project was terminated. The 200 protocols were then scored by eight skilled technicians, who had previously demonstrated high interscorer reliability across 15 records and had previous scoring experience for no less than 50 records from other projects. Scorers worked "in the blind," with no awareness of the nature of the project *or* of the fact that the sample contained two records for each subject. The final group of 100 subjects contained 58 females and 42 males, aged 24 to 44, with a socioeconomic distribution of 62 subjects from middle class levels, 21 from upper class levels, and 17 from lower class levels.

Nineteen variables were computer coded from the Structural Summary. These

---

[1] Normative data for the R Form of the Katz Adjustment Scale have been published by Hogarty, G. E. and Katz, M. in *Norms of Adjustment and Social Behavior,* available from the Clinical Research Division, NIMH, Rockville, Maryland. On the basis of these normative data as "cutoff" scores, 16 of the original volunteer group were eliminated.

variables were selected because they represent the "core" of structural data from which Rorschach interpretation proceeds. Three of these variables are "collapsed" frequencies of more than one score, since some of the scores occur with such a low frequency that a separate correlational analysis becomes meaningless. These three are: (1) a single sum of shading, which includes all variations of $C' + T + Y + V$; (2) an $FM + m$ score, since m appears with zero frequency in many protocols; and (3) a $CF + C + Cn$ score, since the C and Cn scores appear with zero frequency in most records.

The correlation coefficients and the coefficients of determination for each of these 19 variables are shown in Table 11.[2] It will be noted that substantial correlations occur for almost all variables, with only the sum of shading and $FM + m$ variables correlating at below the .70 level. The fact that the addition of the m scores to the FM scores creates a lower correlation should not be surprising because, as has been mentioned, it is more situational than are other Rorschach features. Similarly, shading scores, particularly Y and V, seem to follow a more transient pattern as the individual is impinged upon by stress that he or she cannot cope with effectively. Probably the most surprising correlation is that for the Affective Ratio, .90. The research concerning the Affective Ratio, or 8–9–10% as calculated in some of the other systems, has been limited and somewhat controversial. The 1974 text stated:

It (the *Afr*) provides some index of the extent to which the subject is affected by the colors and may give a clue to the impact of the external world on his behavior. The *Afr* is probably limited to usefulness in conjunction with the Lambda Index, the $FC:CF + C$ ratio, and the *EB*, all of which convey some information regarding emotionality (p. 322).

The very high retest correlation for the Affective Ratio seems to give much more credence to the notion that it may represent a more basic response style than had been suspected: a style reflecting the extent to which one is willing, or unwilling, to process and respond to stimuli that have emotional features. Overall, the correlation coefficients for this series of variables illustrate considerable sturdiness over time.

A second analysis of these protocols dealt with the extent to which some of the ratios that form a critical basis for interpretation remained directionally constant over this long time period. This is a very important issue, since each of at least four such relationships (*EB, EA:ep, a:p,* and *FC:CF + C*) appear to provide direct evidence of response preferences or styles. Presumably, if the preference or style is among those "stabilized" features of personality, evidence for it should remain reasonably constant over time. It is important to point out that some subjects do not manifest a "distinct" direction for some ratios. The best example of this is Rorschach's ambitent, identified from the *Erlebnistypus (EB)* when the numbers in the ratio are nearly equal, such as 3:3.5, 4:3.0, and so on. Therefore, directionality has been defined, for this analysis, as those ratios in which the number on one side exceeds the number on the other side *by more than* 1.0, so that an *EB* of 3:4.0 *would not* be considered as showing directionality, whereas an *EB* of 3:4.5 *would* be included among those showing directionality.

---

[2] All correlations are positive. Data were processed using the IBM 1130 Statistical System for Linear Regression, Program No. 1130-CA-06X, Code REGR.

Table 11.   Correlation Coefficients and Coefficients of Determination for Two Testings, the Second Taken Between 35 and 38 Months after the First, for 100 Nonpatient Adults

Variable	Description	r	r^2
R	Responses	.79	.63
P	Popular responses	.73	.53
Zf	Z frequency	.83	.70
DETERMINANTS			
F	Pure form	.70	.50
M	Human movement	.87	.76
FM	Animal movement	.72	.52
$Fm + m$	Animal plus inanimate movement	.69	.48
a	Active movement	.86	.74
p	Passive movement	.75	.56
FC	Form dominant color responses	.86	.73
$CF + C + Cn$	Color dominant responses	.79	.63
Sum C	Sum weighted color responses	.86	.74
Sum SH	Sum of all shading responses	.66	.43
PERCENTAGES-RATIOS			
L	Lambda-proportion of F	.82	.68
$X + \%$	Extended good form	.80	.64
Afr	Affective ratio	.90	.82
$3r + (2)/R$	Egocentricity index	.87	.77
EA	Experience actual	.85	.73
ep	Experience potential	.72	.52

The results of this directionality analysis are shown in Table 12, which also provides the Z transformation values for changes in directionality from the first to second testings. Several of the data in Table 12 have striking importance for interpretation. First, of the 77 subjects showing clear directionality in the *EB* at the first testing, 75 showed the same directionality at the second testing. This finding provides strong support for Rorschach's contention that the phenomena of introversion and extratensiveness are basic and stable personality components in the adult. Interestingly, 20 of the 23 subjects who did not show direction in *both* *tests* had *EB*'s in which the two numbers differed 1.0 or less *at the first testing*. In other words, they are ambitents, and 11 of those 20 continued to show the same relationship between *M* and *Sum C* at the second testing. If those 11 subjects are added to the 75 showing the same directionality over both testings, 86 of the 100 subjects manifest a very specific style over the three year interval. A subdivision of these 86 subjects reveals that 35 remained introversive, 40 remained extratensive, and 11 remained ambitents.

The relative stability of the relationship between the *EA* and the *ep* is also very interesting. The *EA* appears to be some index of the extent to which resources are accessible to the person, that is, the extent to which the individual can direct the use of his or her resources. The *ep* appears to provide information about ongoing

Table 12. Test-Retest Frequencies for Five Ratios, with Z Values Concerning Change in Directionality, for 100 Nonpatients

Ratios	Number with Direction in 2 Tests	Number with no Direction in 2 Tests	Number with Direction in 1 Test But Not 2	Number with Direction in 2 Tests Changing Direction	Z Value	p*
EB	77	11	12	2	7.2	< .001
$EA:ep$	71	13	16	2	6.4	< .001
eb	30	29	41	1	1.6	NS
$a:p$	68	9	24	0	5.4	< .001
$FC:CF + C$	50	28	22	0	5.6	< .001

*One tailed.

psychological activity which is not accessible to the person, and which tends to "impinge on him" as a stimulus. In 52 of the 71 cases showing directionality in both testings, EA was higher than ep, and none of these 52 changed direction in the second testing.

The data concerning the $FC:CF+C$ ratio may be slightly misleading. Forty-four of the 50 subjects showing directionality in both tests, and none of whom changed directions in the second test, had more FC than $CF+C$. In fact, 72 of the 100 subjects had more FC than $CF+C$ in the first test. However, in 28 of those cases, the FC score exceeded the $CF+C$ score by only 1.0 and were not considered as "showing directionality." An examination of the scores for those 28 cases shows that 21 continued to have FC greater than CF during the second testing, 14 of these cases exceeding the 1.0 differential. Thus, 65 of the 100 subjects showed more FC than $CF+C$ for both testings. Stated differently, nearly two thirds of the subjects showed a tendency toward modulated affective displays.

The data concerning the active and passive movement responses also tend to confirm substantial stability in that ratio. Only 12 Of the 68 subjects showing directionality in both testings (none of whom changed direction), gave more passive movement answers; and of the 24 subjects showing directionality in one test but not the other, only four gave more passive movement answers in that one instance. As will be elaborated in another chapter, there is evidence that where p exceeds a by more than 1.0, a high correlation exists with behavioral passivity.

The eb shows the most instability of the five ratios, even though there is only one marked changed in directionality among the 30 subjects who showed direction in both tests. Twenty-three of the 41 subjects showing directionality in one test but not the other manifest that directionality during the first test, 12 being higher on the $FM+m$ side, and 11 being higher on the shading side. In the second test, 17 of the 23 went to an absolute zero difference between the two sides of the ratio. Similarly, the 18 subjects who had been at a zero or near zero difference during the first testing split evenly for direction in the second testing, with nine high for $FM+m$ and nine high for shading. These data, plus the relatively low correlations for these two variables, appear to support the notion that the kinds of answers which constitute the *eb are not* reflective of durable styles, but are, rather, more transient psychological experiences.

TEMPORAL CONSISTENCY FOR BRIEF INTERVALS

The Focal Study of temporal consistency offers rich information concerning the degree of sturdiness, or lack thereof, for many of the basic Rorschach variables from which interpretation proceeds. A logical question, however, is whether this sturdiness tends to fluctuate over brief intervals. Four small sample studies were conducted concerning this issue. Two involved nonpatients, and two involved nontreated patient groups.

Nonpatients Retested After Seven Days (Exner and Bryant, 1974)

Twenty-five volunteer nonpatients—16 females and nine males—were retested after a seven day interval. Nine examiners were randomly assigned to subjects, with the restriction that no examiner would test the same subject twice. None of the examiners tested more than four subjects. The 50 protocols were scored by three skilled technicians who were not aware of the purpose of the project or of the type of subjects from whom the records had been taken. The test-retest correlation coefficients and the coefficients of determination are shown in Table 13.

The data in Table 13 show a considerable similarity to the data from the Focal Study, although it is clear that there is much more variance for the elements of the *eb*—that is, $FM + m$ and the sum of the shading responses. Although the study of ratio directionality is less meaningful for such a small group, it is important to note that only six of the 25 subjects showed directionality for the *eb* in both tests. Conversely, 18 of the 25 showed directionality in both tests for the *EB,* and none changed direction at the second testing. Similarly, 21 of the 25 showed directionality in both tests for the *EA : ep* ratio, and none changed directions in the second testing. Twenty of the 25 gave more *FC* than *CF+C* in both tests; and the six subjects giving more passive than active movement in the first test continued to do so in the second testing.

Nonpatients Retested After 60 Days (Exner, Armbruster, and Leura, 1975)

Twenty-five nonpatients (14 females and 11 males) were retested after 60 days by the same nine examiners used in the preceding study. The examiners were randomized across subjects with the proviso that no examiner would test the same subject twice. The 50 protocols were scored by the same three technicians used in the preceding study; they had no awareness of the nature of the study or the characteristics of the subjects. The correlational data from this study are shown in Table 14.

The 60 day retest reveals correlations very similar to those obtained for the three year period, in the Focal Study, and concurrently, these data are very similar to those of the seven day retest group. A study for ratio directionality in this group indicates that 16 of the 25 showed direction in both tests for the *EB,* one of them changing direction in the retest. Eighteen of the 25 showed directionality

Table 13.   Correlation Coefficients and Coefficients of Determination for Two Testings, the Second Taken 7 Days after the First, for 25 Nonpatient Adults

Variable	Description	r	r^2
R	Responses	.86	.74
P	Popular responses	.78	.61
Zf	Z frequency	.88	.78
DETERMINANTS			
F	Pure form	.68	.47
M	Human movement	.81	.66
FM	Animal movement	.63	.40
Fm + m	Animal plus inanimate movement	.56	.32
a	Active movement	.91	.83
p	Passive movement	.84	.71
FC	Form dominant color responses	.93	.87
CF + C + Cn	Color dominant responses	.82	.68
Sum C	Sum weighted color responses	.85	.72
Sum SH	Sum of all shading responses	.51	.26
PERCENTAGES-RATIOS			
L	Lambda-proportion of F	.73	.54
X + %	Extended good form	.88	.78
Afr	Affective ratio	.93	.86
3r + (2)/R	Egocentricity index	.91	.82
EA	Experience actual	.83	.69
ep	Experience potential	.62	.39

for the $EA:ep$ relationship in both tests, with none changing direction in the retest. Four subjects displayed passive movement direction in the first test and remained essentially the same during the second test. Seventeen gave more FC than $CF+C$ in both tests. The eb was, again, the least consistent, with only seven subjects showing direction in both testings and one of the seven changing directions. Fifteen of the remaining 18 showed direction in one test but not in the other, nine being high on the $FM+m$ side.

The most important discovery derived from these two retest studies of nonpatients over relatively brief intervals is that most of the correlations are commensurate with those of the Focal Study. This is even more remarkable in light of the sizes of the samples, both of which are small, and in which minor numerical alterations tend to magnify variance.

Outpatients Retested After 30 Days (Leura, Wylie, and Exner, 1976)

Twenty-five patients (15 female, 10 male), all of whom had been "wait listed" for either individual or group psychotherapy at one of three outpatient clinics, were retested after a 30 day interval. The first testing was completed during the routine screening process at the clinics, and all patients had completed an intake-history

Table 14.   Correlation Coefficients and Coefficients of Determination for Two Testings, the Second Taken 60 Days after the First, for 25 Nonpatient Adults

Variable	Description	r	r^2
R	Responses	.84	.70
P	Popular responses	.84	.71
Zf	Z frequency	.81	.65
DETERMINANTS			
F	Pure form	.74	.55
M	Human movement	.85	.73
FM	Animal movement	.74	.54
$Fm + m$	Animal plus inanimate movement	.67	.45
a	Active movement	.82	.67
p	Passive movement	.78	.61
FC	Form dominant color responses	.83	.69
$CF + C + Cn$	Color dominant responses	.73	.53
Sum C	Sum weighted color responses	.78	.61
Sum SH	Sum of all shading responses	.59	.35
PERCENTAGES-RATIOS			
L	Lambda-proportion of F	.86	.73
$X + \%$	Extended good form	.84	.70
Afr	Affective ratio	.89	.79
$3r + (2)/R$	Egocentricity index	.85	.72
EA	Experience actual	.83	.70
ep	Experience potential	.69	.48

after screening. Eleven of the subjects had been on low dosage medication before applying for clinic service.[3] In each case, the medication had been prescribed by a general practitioner making the referral to the clinic, and in none of these cases was the medication routine altered during the 30 day interval prior to retesting. Five examiners, randomly assigned to subjects, were used in this study, with no examiner testing any subject twice. The protocols were scored by four skilled technicians and one post doctoral fellow, none of whom were familiar with the nature of the subject population. The correlational data from this study are shown in Table 15.

There is considerably more variability among these subjects than among the three nonpatient groups. Correlations for eight of the 19 variables fall below the .70 level, with three of those below the .60 level. Nonetheless, there is considerable similarity between these data and those from the nonpatient groups. The shading variable has the least consistency in all four studies, with the composite variable $FM + m$ running a close second. The Human movement responses, the $X + \%$, Affective Ratio, the Egocentricity Index, the Experience Actual, the Z frequency, and the total R, reflect consistently high correlations throughout

[3] Seven subjects were prescribed valium 5mg.; the other four subjects were prescribed ellavil, 10mg.

Table 15.   Correlation Coefficients and Coefficients of Determination for Two Testings, the Second Taken after 30 Days, for 25 Adult Wait Listed Patients

Variable	Description	r	r^2
R	Responses	.83	.69
P	Popular responses	.69	.47
Zf	Z frequency	.86	.74
DETERMINANTS			
F	Pure form	.57	.33
M	Human movement	.82	.68
FM	Animal movement	.74	.55
Fm + m	Animal plus inanimate movement	.62	.38
a	Active movement	.78	.61
p	Passive movement	.84	.71
FC	Form dominant color responses	.71	.51
CF + C + Cn	Color dominant responses	.57	.32
Sum C	Sum weighted color responses	.68	.47
Sum SH	Sum of all shading responses	.49	.24
PERCENTAGES-RATIOS			
L	Lambda-proportion of F	.65	.42
X + %	Extended good form	.83	.68
Afr	Affective ratio	.86	.74
3r + (2)/R	Egocentricity index	.91	.82
EA	Experience actual	.77	.59
ep	Experience potential	.67	.45

the four studies. It is impossible to determine from the data in Table 15 whether the greater variability for this group is a function of turmoil, chance, or a deliberate effort to dramatize greater disarray so as to hasten the beginning of treatment. Interestingly, the data concerning ratio directionality for this group are not very different from those of the three nonpatient groups. Fifteen of the 25 subjects showed direction in both tests for the *EB*, and none changed direction, while nine of the remaining 10 showed no direction in either test. Fourteen subjects gave more *CF+C* than *FC* in both tests, and the seven subjects who showed a passive direction in the movement answers continued to do so in the second test. The *EA* : *ep* ratio was directional for 19 of the 25 subjects in both tests, and only two changed direction. The *eb* was very inconsistent, with only four subjects showing the same direction in both tests. Nineteen of the remaining 21 showed no direction in the first test, but did in the second; 14 of them loaded high for shading variables. This may reflect greater experience of internal irritation, due either to the basic turmoil of the pathology, or it may be related to the anxiety of the subjects about the prospect of treatment. Although it is not appropriate to compare this group with inpatient schizophrenics, it will be noted in the next study that far less variance appears for such a group retested after a brief period following hospital admission.

Inpatient Schizophrenics Retested After 10 Days (Exner, Schuyler, Schumacher, and Kuhn, 1976)

Although treatment is usually initiated for most patients shortly after admission to a psychiatric hospital, there are instances in which a period of "wait and see" evaluation occurs. Twenty such cases were collected over a period of three years in a small psychiatric facility. The cases included 13 males and seven females. The first testing was completed on the second or third day after admission as part of the routine diagnostic procedure. As these subjects were placed on a wait-and-see routine, arrangements were completed to retest them prior to an initiation of a treatment plan which ordinarily began after a 10 day interval. Thus, all were tested the second time after 10 days. Seven of the subjects had been "stabilized" on antipsychotic medication prior to admission, and that routine was maintained during the 10 day test-retest interval. None of the remaining 13 were on medication during that period. The first testing was accomplished by two psychologists who were responsible for routine assessments at the hospital. The second test was taken by one of three examiners who knew that the subjects had been tested previously but did not know the purpose of the second testing. The protocols were all rescored by two skilled technicians who were not associated with the hospital project or aware of the nature of the subjects. Table 16 provides the correlational data from this project.

Table 16. Correlation Coefficients and Coefficients of Determination for Two Testings, the Second Taken after 10 Days, for 20 Inpatient Schizophrenics

Variable	Description	r	r^2
R	Responses	.89	.79
P	Popular responses	.78	.61
Zf	Z frequency	.80	.64
DETERMINANTS			
F	Pure form	73	.53
M	Human movement	.77	.59
FM	Animal movement	.75	.56
Fm + m	Animal plus inanimate movement	.73	.53
a	Active movement	.86	.74
p	Passive movement	.82	.67
FC	Form dominant color responses	.84	.71
CF + C + Cn	Color dominant responses	.89	.80
Sum C	Sum weighted color responses	.81	.65
Sum SH	Sum of all shading responses	.72	.51
PERCENTAGES-RATIOS			
L	Lambda-proportion of F	.76	.57
X + %	Extended good form	.92	.85
Afr	Affective ratio	.79	.62
3r + (2)/R	Egocentricity index	.75	.56
EA	Experience actual	.82	.67
ep	Experience potential	.71	.50

Tne data for this group are quite remarkable, and *not* because of brief protocols. The average R for the first test was 24.2 ($SD = 3.6$) and for the second 23.7 ($SD = 3.4$). None of the correlations for this group fall below the .70 level, although it is interesting that the correlations for the *AFr* and the Egocentricity Index are somewhat lower than for the five groups previously reported. The highest correlation is for the $X+\%$ (.92), which reflects the consistently *low* frequency of good form quality answers given. Similarly, there is a very high correlation for the $CF+C+Cn$ answers, which do occur with a significantly higher frequency in this group than in any of the other groups. An analysis of ratio directionality reveals a similar consistency. Nine of the subjects loaded high on the $CF+C$ side of the EB in both tests, and eight were high on the M side of the ratio in both tests. Sixteen of the 20 showed a $CF+C$ direction in both protocols, and the four who showed passive directionality in the first record also did so in the second. Only 11 subjects showed direction for the EA : ep ratio in both tests; nine of them were high on the *ep* side. The other nine subjects *showed no directionality* in either test. The *eb* ratios show the greatest variability, with 15 of the 20 subjects manifesting high loadings for the shading side during the first test, but only four remaining directional for the second test. This probably reflects some form of anxiety or internal irritation concerning the process of having been admitted to a hospital and being evaluated. Although only four of these patients remained "directional," continuing to offer a high frequency of shading answers during the second test, it should be noted that 18 of the 20 subjects continued to manifest more shading than $FM+m$ during the second test, although the difference between the two had been reduced significantly.

Inasmuch as nonpatients, over varying intervals, manifest a relative high consistency for most variables and ratios, and newly admitted schizophrenics show similar consistency over a brief period while "wait listed" outpatients show greater variance, the obvious next question to be broached concerns the variability in the Rorschach that may or may not occur under treatment conditions. To this end, two more projects were completed with the goal of studying temporal consistency in addition to other research objectives, such as evaluation of treatment effects.

Studies of Two Outpatient Groups (Exner, Wylie, and Armbruster, 1975; 1976)

In the course of research at Rorschach Workshops, many hospitals, clinics, and private therapists have been solicited in order to obtain the cooperation of patients in studies, most of which would involve two or more testings. During one such recruitment, two groups were "set up" to be retested at a specific interval during or after treatment. One group of 35 subjects was first tested at the onset of "brief" treatment. The treatment modalities varied from supportive psychotherapy to systematic desensitization, but all were oriented to completing intervention within 90 days. Twelve of the 35 subjects in this group were still being treated after the 90 day period had expired but none had altered the treatment modality. The entire group consisted of 21 females and 14 males, the majority of whom were being treated for "reactive depression" conditions. All but two were seen once weekly in their intervention programs. The second group, consisting of 30 subjects, 17 females and 13 males, were entering long term, dynamically oriented psychotherapy, generally for conditions that would be labeled "neurotic," and were seeking extensive personality reorganization. All 65 subjects were tested within a week of the first treatment day, in some cases by psychologists (other than the therapists) at the clinics, or, in 23 of the 65 cases, by one of three examiners from Rorschach Workshops.

The retests of the brief treatment group was taken by six examiners who knew all were outpatients, but not what the project was about. Five different examiners collected the second protocols from the long term treatment group, and assumed that the record was being taken to assess progress. All second protocols were collected between 170 and 195 days after the subjects had entered treatment. The protocols from both groups were scored by the examiner taking the record, and then rechecked by at least two experienced technicians, and any disagreements between the examiner and the technician were resolved by one of the project leaders. The correlational data for each of these groups are shown in Table 17.

The data for the brief treatment group show much consistency except for four

Table 17. Correlation Coefficients and Coefficients of Determination for Two Groups, One of 35 Patients in Brief Treatment, with the Second Record Collected After Approximately 90 Days, and the Second of 30 Long Term Treatment Cases, with the Second Record Taken After Approximately 180 Days

Variable	Description	Brief Treatment Group $N = 35$		Extended Treatment Group $N = 30$	
		r	r^2	r	r^2
R	Responses	.83	.69	.64	.41
P	Popular responses	.81	.66	.76	.57
Zf	Z frequency	.86	.74	.81	.66
DETERMINANTS					
F	Pure form	.77	.58	.51	.26
M	Human movement	.82	.68	.68	.46
FM	Animal movement	.73	.53	.49	.24
$FM + m$	Animal plus inanimate movement	.70	.50	.41	.17
a	Active movement	.87	.76	.81	.65
p	Passive movement	.79	.63	.71	.51
FC	Form dominant color responses	.51	.27	.39	.15
$CF + C + Cn$	Color dominant responses	.44	.19	.47	.22
Sum C	Sum weighted color responses	.49	.24	.38	.14
Sum SH	Sum of all shading responses	.28	.08	.42	.18
PERCENTAGES-RATIOS					
L	Lambda	.64	.41	.48	.23
$X + \%$	Extended good form	.84	.71	.81	.66
Afr	Affective ratio	.89	.80	.73	.54
$3r + (2)/R$	Egocentricity index	.91	.83	.73	.53
EA	Experience actual	.84	.70	.70	.49
ep	Experience potential	.76	.58	.61	.37

variables, all apparently related to the treatment targets. A considerable change occurred for chromatic color responses, and the variation in the shading answers was so extensive that the retest correlation is insignificant. Even though the color variables show much inconsistency, *none of the* 18 *EB's* showing directionality in the first test changed direction. Conversely, 21 of the 35 EA : ep ratios showed directionality in the first test, and eight of those did show a directional change after 90 days. In all eight cases, the shift was from a higher *ep* to a higher *EA*. Changes in the direction of the *FC* : *CF+C* ratio were very prominent. Twenty-four subjects showed directionality for that ratio in the first test, 17 being higher on the *CF+C* side. In the retest, 12 of the 24 had shifted directions, 10 moving from the *CF+C* side to the *FC* side, and two making the opposite shift. Changes in the *eb* were the most marked. Twenty-two subjects showed directionality for the *eb* at the first testing, with 16 higher on the shading side. Fifteen of the 22 subjects continued to show direction in the second test, 10 shifting from high shading to high *FM+m*. Nine of the 35 were directionally high for passive movement in both tests.

The variability among the long term treatment subjects, after six months of treatment, is quite extensive. It will be noted that the correlation for *R* is substantially lower than in any of the preceding studies, including the Focal Study. This is a function of significantly longer second records. The average *R* for the first test is 22.9 (SD = 4.2), whereas the mean *R* for the second test is 27.1 (SD = 5.7). Although this tends to affect all other correlations, there are substantial variations for many variables. The proportional frequency of pure Form answers was substantially lower, while the number of color and shading responses had increased significantly proportionally. There was also considerable variation among three of the five basic ratios. The *FC* : *CF+C* ratio was directional for 18 subjects at the first testing, 15 of whom were higher on the *FC* side. At the retest, only six subjects continued to show directionality, all remaining high for *FC*. In other words, 24 or the 30 subjects showed *FC* : *CF+C* ratios in the second test in which the difference between the two sides of the ratio was 1.0 or less. Thirteen of the subjects were directional for the *eb* in the first test, whereas 19 showed direction in the second test. These 19 included the 13 from the first test, but eight had changed direction. The *EA* : *ep* ratio also was marked by considerable alteration. Twenty of the 30 subjects were directional in the first test, 14 being high on the *EA* side. In the retest, 18 of those subjects continued to show directionality, although 10 of the 14 high *EA*'s had become high *ep*'s, while three of the six who had been high on the *ep* side had changed to the high *EA* side. Only the *EB* and *a* : *p* ratios remained relatively constant. Nineteen subjects had shown direction for *EB* in the first test, and 17 of those 19 continued to do so in the retest. The remaining two altered to "no direction," and five of the 11 who had been nondirectional in the first test became directional in the second. Twenty-six of the 30 showed directionality in the first test for the *a* : *p* ratio, and 24 of those, including seven high for passive movement, remained essentially unchanged six months later.

The results of these two studies indicate that some Rorschach variables, especially those relating to manifestations of emotion, are highly subject to alteration in different forms of intervention. Conversely, at least over periods of up to six months, some Rorschach features remain remarkably stable. *Z* frequencies are highly consistent, as are the *X+%*, the Affective Ratio, the Egocentricity Index, the Experience Actual, and the frequency of Popular responses. Similarly, directionality of the *EB* and *a* :*p* ratios remains stable for most subjects under most conditions, while intervention does have a greater impact on *eb*, the *FC* :*CF+C*, and *EA* : *ep* ratios.

SUMMARY

The matrix of these seven studies offers substantial support for the contention that the majority of Rorschach variables underpinning interpretation are stable over time. The three projects involving nonpatients show that all but two of the 19 variables correlated are very sturdy over different time intervals; and there is even a relatively significant agreement for the two showing the lowest retest correlations, *FM +m* and the sum of shading scores. It is even more important to note that the directionality of four of the five basic ratios is quite sturdy over time for these three groups. The *EB* is clearly the most consistent for direction or nondirection for both patients and nonpatients, while the *EA* :*ep*, *FC* :*CF+C*, and *a* :*p* ratios are very consistent for persons not in treatment. The *eb* has the greatest instability for all groups, and is especially variable for patients in treatment. These seem to be the kinds of responses that reflect "state" characteristics: the *FM* answers represent ideational activity related to need states, the *m* responses being correlated with the experience of stress and the sense of being out of control, and the shading answers are each related to internal emotional experiences that are discomforting for the person. Whereas the *eb* material represents "state" activities, the other four ratios, and the determinant scores that contribute to them, appear to illustrate trait, or response style, activities. These include the human movement answers, the chromatic color responses, and the type of movement answer. Similarly, the high level of consistency found for the *Z* Frequency, the Affective Ratio, and the Egocentricity Index also supports the premise that they reflect response style phenomena.

Finally, it is extremely important to remember the data in the preceding chapter, specifically the fact that each subject selects the response to be given from many possibilities that have been processed. The consistency of the *X I %* in all seven of these investigations suggests that the perceptual accuracy of people is very stable over time, whether it is good or poor. Thus, when people respond with a high consistency to the Rorschach stimuli, they are indeed displaying remarkable stability of personality.

The next two chapters will explore the variety of response styles and "state" features that are represented in the Structural Summary in the light of recent research and the applicability of its findings to interpretation.

REFERENCES

Exner, J. E. *The Rorschach: A Comprehensive System*. New York: John Wiley and Sons, 1974.

Exner, J. E., Armbruster, G. L., and Leura, A. V. Temporal consistency among nonpatients over a 60 day interval. Workshops Study No. 218 (unpublished), Rorschach Workshops, 1975.

Exner, J. E., and Bryant, E. A study of temporal consistency over a seven day period. Workshops study No. 205 (unpublished) Rorschach Workshops, 1974.

Exner, J. E., Leura, A. V., Armbruster, G. L., and Viglione, D. A Focal Study of temporal consistency. Workshops Study No. 253 (unpublished), Rorschach Workshops, 1977.

Exner, J. E., and Murillo, L. G. Effectiveness of regressive ECT with process schizophrenics. *Diseases of the Nervous System,* 1973, **34,** 44–48.

Exner, J. E., and Murillo, L. G. Early prediction of post-hospitalization relapse. *Journal of Psychiatric Research,* 1975, **12,** 231–237.

Exner, J. E., Murillo, L. G., and Cannavo, F. Disagreement between ex-patient and relative behavioral reports as related to relapse in nonschizophrenic patients. Eastern Psychological Association, 1973, Washington, D.C.

Exner, J. E., Zalis, T., Schuyler, W., Schumacher, J., and Kuhn, B. Reevaluation of newly admitted schizophrenic patients after a ten day period. Workshops Study No. 228 (unpublished), Rorschach Workshops, 1976.

Exner, J. E., Wylie, J. R., and Armbruster, G. L. Effects of brief treatment with anxious or depressed patients. Workshops Study No. 216 (unpublished), Rorschach Workshops, 1975.

Exner, J. E., Wylie, J. R., and Armbruster, G. L. A follow-up of patients in long term treatment after the first six months. Workshops Study No. 223 (unpublished), Rorschach Workshops, 1976.

Ford, M. The application of the Rorschach test to young children. *University of Minnesota Child Welfare Monograph,* No. 23, 1946.

Hertz, M. R. The reliability of the Rorschach ink-blot test. *Journal of Applied Psychology,* 1934, **18,** 461–477.

Holzberg, J. D. Reliability re-examined. In Rickers-Ovsiankina, M. A. (ed.) *Rorschach Psychology.* New York: John Wiley and Sons, 1960.

Holzberg, J. D., and Wexler, M. The predictability of schizophrenic performance on the Rorschach test. *Journal of Consulting Psychology,* 1950, **14,** 395–399.

Katz, M., and Lyerly, S. Methods of measuring adjustment and social behavior in the community. *Psychological Reports,* 1963, **13,** 503–535.

Kelley, D. M., Margulies, H., and Barrera, S. E. The stability of the Rorschach method as demonstrated in electric convulsive therapy cases. *Rorschach Research Exchange,* 1941, **5,** 35–43.

Kelley, T. L. The reliability coefficient. *Psychometrika,* 1942, **7,** 75–83.

Kerr, M. Temperamental differences in twins. *British Journal of Psychology,* 1936, **27,** 51–59.

Leura, A. V., Wylie, J. R., and Exner, J. E. Reexamination of prospective patients who have been wait-listed during a 30 day period. Workshops Study No. 231 (unpublished), Rorschach Workshops, 1976.

Orange, A. Perceptual consistency as measured by the Rorschach. *Journal of Projective Techniques,* 1953, **17,** 224–228.

Spielberger, C. D. *Anxiety and Behavior.* New York: Academic Press, 1966.

Spielberger, C. D., Lushene, R. E., and McAdoo, W. G. Theory and measurement of anxiety states. In, Cattell, R. B. (ed.) *Handbook of Modern Personality Theory,* Chicago: Aldine Press, 1971.

Swift, J. W. Reliability of Rorschach scoring categories with preschool children. *Child Development,* 1944, **15,** 207–216.

Vernon, P. E. The Rorschach inkblot test. II. *British Journal of Medical Psychology,* 1933, **13,** 179–205.

CHAPTER 4

Basic Personality Structure: The Four Square

Any competent Rorschach interpretation evolves from a study of the interrelationships among the many variables of the test. Some variables taken alone do provide useful information, but the scope of that information is restricted, and its meaningfulness can be greatly modified by the presence or absence of other variables. Each Rorschach unit, whether structural or verbal, ultimately contributes to interpretation, and none can be casually neglected. Each Rorschach is unique in its total configuration, different from all other Rorschachs, and illustrative of the idiography of the subject from whom it was taken. Thus, the process of interpretation evolves in a step-by-step sequence in which each new datum is reviewed in the context of *all* previously examined data. At almost every step, some proposition occurs that will later be confirmed, modified, or rejected; but few, if any, propositions will be confirmed simply because of the presence or absence of a single variable.

The most logical "starting point" in the interpretation of a Rorschach is with the structural data; and, among the structural data, with a complex of four extremely important variables that have come to be known as *The Four Square*. They include the *EB (Erlebnistypus),* the *EA* (Experience Actual), the *eb* (Experience Base), and the *ep* (Experience Potential). Studied independently, only the *EB* provides very useful information, but taken as a group, with the *EB* as the cornerstone, the informational yield is extended enormously.

The *EB* provides information about one of the basic response styles: namely, whether the person tends toward an ideational or emotional mode of dealing with coping situations. One mode does not necessarily exclude the other, but most people do have a marked preference or tendency toward one or the other in coping situations. Some people are obviously "Ideational." Rorschach (1921) described them as introversive. Others tend toward more marked emotional displays. Rorschach defined them as extratensive. Either activity entails some *deliberate action* by the person, and thus involves the use of available resources. In other words, when these kinds of response are *initiated,* the person responds by drawing on his or her own resources, which have been organized in a way to make them accessible. The kinds of responses included here are those oriented toward effective coping—or, stated differently, oriented toward a reestablishment of greater equilibrium. Not all ideation or emotion is deliberately invoked; in fact, much is not. The *EB,* however, reflects the forms of psychological action, either ideational or emotional, that are provoked by the decision process. Rorschach implied this, but Beck (1960) was the first to recognize its full meaning, and he postulated the *EA* as an index of the extent to which resources were organized in a manner that makes them accessible. Although the actual numerical value of the *EA* has little interpretive significance, it does provide a comparison point.

Klopfer (1954) postulated that some types of Rorschach answers represent response tendencies not fully available to the individual. These included animal and inanimate forms of movement, plus some of the grey-black and shading answers. Exner (1974), working from these two propositions, extended the Klopfer ratio to encompass *all* grey-black and shading determinants to form the Experience Base *(eb),* to reflect ideational and emotional activities that *had not been deliberately* initiated by the individual. Then, following Beck's example, adding the two sides of the *eb* to create the Experience Potential *(ep),* thus forming another comparison point and completing The Four Square.

The Four Square, then, taken as a unit, provides data about the response tendency of the individual when using accessible resources *(EB);* the extent to which accessible resources are greater or less than psychological actions that have not been deliberately initiated by the person *(EA : ep);* and something about the characteristics of actions that are ongoing but not organized in a way that makes them accessible to the person *(eb).* Information like this is very important to the understanding of both pathological and nonpathological states. It is extremely relevant to treatment planning, and it can be crucial to treatment evaluation.

THE *EA : ep* RELATIONSHIP

Although the *EB* is the cornerstone of the Four Square, the *EA : ep* relationship provides substantial clarification about the response style that is illustrated in the *EB,* and especially the extent to which that style is behaviorally pervasive. There are many instances in which a response tendency does not become manifest simply because other elements, or forces, thwart that manifestation. For instance, a person prone to reflectiveness may not exhibit that reflectiveness under conditions of intense anxiety, because anxiety inhibits or fragments the concentrational operations required for reflectiveness. Under other circumstances, a person prone to emotional display may not be able to initiate the display because a stream of ideational activity that is not well organized produces difficulties in the selection of targets for the discharge. Every person experiences these instances, and others like them. Who has not tried deliberately to induce sleep, only to be kept awake by a stream of seemingly disjointed thoughts; or what person has not experienced a sense of irritating uneasiness when attempting to "stay on target" in a problem solving situation? The words "maturity" and "psychological sophistication" are often employed to differentiate those who seem less confounded by such experiences, while those who manifest such disarray are often called "immature" or "primitive."

The *EA : ep* relationship *does not* reflect maturity in the sense of effective adjustment, but it does appear to represent some characteristic of development, or organization of resources, into some form of "stabilized" or semipermanent relationships. Evidence for this conclusion is drawn from three broad areas: studies of children, behavioral studies, and studies of treatment progress or outcome. Among the most important findings is an apparent growth curve that is evident for the *EA : ep* relationship in the reference samples collected for younger clients that are shown in Table 2 of Chapter 1. When only the nonpatient samples are reviewed, a gradual increase is noted in the percentage of records, *at each year level,* where *EA* exceeds *ep*. This increase is consistent from one year to the next, except for 13 and 16 year olds, where a very modest decrease occurs when contrasted with subjects from the preceding year. This increase is presented graphically in Figure 2, which also illustrates increases, or lack thereof, for the two psychiatric group reference samples.

The data represented by Figure 2 indicate that, while the nonpatient sample shows a continuing increase in the frequency with which *EA* exceeds *ep,* one of the psychiatric samples (behavioral problems) increases at a "slower" rate and actually levels at about the 11th year, and the second (withdrawn) shows a greater proportion of higher *EA* through the 10th year, but then reflects a decline in the proportion of higher *EA* subjects after the 13th year. *If the assumption is true that the EA represents an index of accessible resources, and the ep is an index of actions that are not accessible to organization or control,* these data support two additional propositions. The first is that youngsters displaying behavioral problems, that is, acting out forms of behavior, are less able to contend with impulses because they do not have sufficient and/or consistent access to their own resources to initiate behaviors that avoid "impulse ridden" activity. The second proposition is that withdrawn youngsters tend to "overorganize" their resources early in their developmental years, but that this organization falters early in pubescence because the nature of the organization *is not* commensurate with the levels of sophistication required in the more complex world of the adolescent. It is highly probable that the levels of organization noted in the young withdrawn child reflect access to less mature operations that are effective at younger levels, but the development does not continue through the years when social adaptation is required. While theories are interesting, and often provocative, the data remain: Pragmatically, it is obvi-

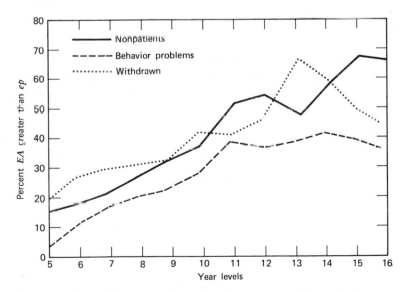

Figure 2.　Percent *EA* greater than *ep* for three groups at 12 year levels.

Table 18.   Means for Three Reference Groups, Ages 5 Through 16, for Four Variables Comprising the EA and ep Ratios

Year	Nonpatients				Behavior Problems				Withdrawn			
	M	Sum C	FM + m	SH	M	Sum C	FM + m	SH	M	Sum C	FM + m	SH
5	0.9	3.1	2.7	1.5	0.5	4.2	2.6	2.7	1.4	2.7	2.2	2.9
6	1.2	3.7	3.0	1.9	0.8	3.7	3.0	1.9	1.5	2.9	2.1	4.0
7	1.5	3.8	3.1	1.7	1.1	4.9	3.4	2.2	2.3	2.8	2.5	3.9
8	1.9	3.1	1.8	1.6	1.3	4.2	3.6	2.4	2.8	2.4	2.3	3.6
9	1.8	2.9	3.2	1.7	1.1	3.9	3.6	1.6	2.8	3.1	2.7	3.4
10	1.9	2.8	3.1	1.8	1.3	4.3	3.0	1.9	2.6	2.7	2.8	3.0
11	2.5	3.3	3.1	1.2	1.9	4.6	3.7	1.2	2.3	3.1	2.4	3.1
12	2.7	3.4	3.3	2.2	1.7	4.9	3.8	0.9	3.1	3.1	2.8	3.2
13	2.7	3.8	3.8	1.7	1.4	4.4	3.6	3.7	3.6	3.1	3.9	3.8
14	2.8	3.6	3.6	1.3	1.6	4.3	3.8	3.2	3.3	3.3	3.5	3.6
15	2.6	3.1	3.3	1.9	2.1	4.7	4.3	3.2	3.6	3.0	3.1	5.0
16	2.8	3.3	3.0	1.9	1.9	4.9	2.2	2.5	3.4	3.3	2.8	4.2

*Standard deviations are shown in Table 2, Chapter 1.

ous that a seemingly natural progression to higher EA occurs among the nonpatient group.

It may be speculated that the more frequent progression to higher EA levels with increasing age in the young nonpatient sample is a function of an increase in the number of M (human movement) responses appearing in the protocols of the adolescent groups. This is *not true.* In both the 11th and 12th year, where the proportion of subjects with higher EA is less than the proportion of high ep subjects, the mean M does increase significantly as contrasted with the 10th year group; however, the mean Sum C also increases, so that throughout all years, the mean Sum C is greater than the mean M. Thus, it is an increase in both the mean M *and* the mean Sum C that contributes to the greater proportion of EA subjects. It is also very important to note that, after the sixth year, the mean FM+m *and* the mean Sum of Shading remain relatively constant through the 16th year, showing only a modest increase. In other words, the shift from a greater percentage of higher ep subjects at the earlier year levels *is not* due to a reduction in the number of FM, m, or grey-black, or shading answers; instead it is a function of an increase in both the number of M and chromatic color answers. The data in Table 18 demonstrate that this is *not* the case for either of the psychiatric groups. Table 18 provides the means, by year level, for each of the three reference groups, for M, Sum C, FM+m, and Sum Shading.[1] In the group of behavior problem subjects, M shows a gradual increase and Sum C remains consistently high throughout the 12 age levels. FM+m increase at about the same rate as does M. A major factor for this group is the significant increase in the mean number of shading and grey-black determinants at the 13th year. Although the data presented in Chapter 3 indicate

[1] The relatively low frequencies of each of the four grey-black, shading variables makes it impractical to list each in this developmental model; however, there are substantial differences across groups, and within groups at different year levels for the kind of grey-black, or shading answers that contribute most to the mean sum of shading.

that these variables are the least stable over time among adult samples, it is compelling to note that the mean frequency for shading and grey-black answers remains relatively high for the behavior problem group through the 16th year.

The withdrawn group shows a remarkably high mean frequency of grey-black and shading answers throughout all 12 year levels, a factor which appears to contribute to the downward slope of the *EA* "growth" curve during the 14th, 15th, and 16th year levels.

The proportion of subjects in the adult reference group (Table 1) who show *EA* greater than *ep* provides another interesting comparison. Slightly more than 70% of the nonpatients have a higher *EA*. Conversely, *EA* is higher for only 47% of the outpatients, 43% of the depressives, 34% of the schizophrenics, and 21% of the inpatient character problems.

The composite data from all the reference groups show that, for older adolescent and adult nonpatients, *EA* exceeds *ep* more often than not. In the older adolescent and adult patient populations, *ep* exceeds *EA* in the majority of cases. A logical conclusion is that the accessibility—or lack—of resources can be a contributing factor to the onset of psychological and/or behavioral difficulties. However, caution must be exercised in the broad application of this hypothesis, for nearly 30% of the adult nonpatients, and more than 35% of the older adolescent nonpatients do show higher *ep, yet evidence no psychopathology.* If the conceptualizations about *EA* and *ep* are correct, then it may be that *EA* reflects something concerning the individual's ability to tolerate frustration or ambiguity. Some support for this premise is derived from the results of two small sample studies. In the first (Exner and Bryant, 1975), two groups of 10 subjects each were selected from a larger sample of college students on the basis of the *EA* : *ep* relationship shown in their Rorschachs, which had been collected by eight examiners during the preceding four months. The 10 subjects in one group showed *EA* greater than *ep* by at least two points. The 10 subjects in the second group had *ep*'s exceeding *EA* by at least two points.

The 20 subjects volunteered for a project concerning a visual motor coordination that used the pursuit rotor. The particular project activity was selected because its performance shows a very low correlation with intelligence while performance can be made more difficult if the speed of rotation or the size of the target disc is varied. The subject is required to keep a metal stylus on the target, which in this instance is about the size of a penny, while the target is rotated on a turntable about the size of a phonograph. The task requires that the subject make a circular motion with his arm while trying to keep the stylus on target, thereby activating a timer which records in fractions of a second. All subjects were given a three minute "warm-up" trial and then permitted to rest for one minute. Subsequently they were instructed to keep the stylus on the target "as long as you can until I stop the disc." The turntable speed was manipulated by the experimenter, so that rotation began at 45 rpm and increased an additional 5 rpm every 60 seconds. The rotation of the turntable was never stopped, so that, in effect, each subject would make a decision to interrupt his or her performance, even though contrary to instructions. Six of the high *ep* subjects interupted their performance during the sixth minute (75 rpm), and two others stopped during the seventh minute (80 rpm). The first of the high *EA* subjects to "drop out" did so during the sixth minute, and two others stopped during the eighth minute (85 rpm). The two remaining high *ep* subjects interupted their performance in the ninth minute, while all of the remaining high *EA* subjects continued to perform into either the eleventh or twelfth minute, with the disc rotating at 100 rpm or higher, making that task very difficult. Interestingly, when the "on-target" times for the two groups were compared for the first five minutes, *the high ep group functioned at a slightly better level.* It is, of course, very possible that other variables, such as self esteem or social desirability, may have contributed to the results; however, the data do suggest a marked difference between the groups for persistence.

The second study (Exner and Bryant, 1976) involved the use of a mirror star tracing apparatus. Thirty adult males, all attending evening continuing education programs, and all of whom had been administered the Rorschach in the standardization project, were selected on the basis of the *EA* : *ep* relationship. Fifteen showed *ep* greater than *EA by more than* 3.0 points, while the remaining 15 showed *EA* higher than *ep* by more than 3.0. The project was identified as a study of visual motor coordination, and each subject was given three trials, using the preferred hand, and instructed to proceed as far as possible in the tracing without crossing either of the boundary lines. After the practice trials, subjects were asked to "take as many trials as necessary," using the *non*preferred hand, to complete a line remaining within the boundaries *that they felt reflected their best performance.* Nine of the 15 high *ep* subjects proceeded to work for an average of seven trials to create a line reaching the second point of the star. Three of the remaining six continued to practice until reaching the third star point. One of the remaining three subjects worked through 15 trials to complete the entire star. The high *EA* subjects performed quite differently. Four, averaging 11 trials, worked to completion of the third star point; while the other 11 subjects used an average of 19 trials to complete the star in its entirety. Again, elements of self esteem or social desirability may have influenced the results. But the fact that a substantially greater number from the high *EA* group did persist in the task suggests that high *EA* people are more willing to contend with a problem solving, or coping, situation for a longer period of time.

Possibly the most definitive data concerning the *EA* : *ep* relationship are derived from studies focusing on treatment effects and relapse. Exner (1974) reported one study in which two groups of 30 subjects each were followed for an 18 month interval during which treatment was ongoing for one group but not for the second. In the treated group, which included 21 patients showing higher *ep* before treatment, 15 of the 21 high *ep* patients reversed the *EA* : *ep* direction after 18 months. Conversely, 22 of the 30 control subjects showed a higher *ep* in the first testing, and 23 of the 30 showed a similar high *ep* after the 18 month interval. These and other kinds of data reported in the 1974 text triggered a series of treatment effects studies focusing on several of the Rorschach variables, including the *EA* : *ep* relation.

THE OUTPATIENT (OP) STUDY (Exner, Wylie, and Kline, 1977)

Many factors make the randomization of subjects across treatments impossible unless a single installation is involved; and even there, both ethical and reality considerations preclude designs that would please the "purist." Nonetheless, it is possible to test a variety of subjects prior to treatment and maintain independence from the treatment decision, thus creating a situation where follow-up data can be collected.

The research plan for the OP study included testing at four intervals: (1) pretreatment, (2) eight to nine months after the onset of treatment, (3) 16 to 18 months after the onset of treatment, and (4) 27 to 29 months after the onset of treatment. Solicitation of clinics, hospitals, and private practitioners yielded 430 volunteer subjects, aged 20 through 36, who entered one of seven different types of treatment between July 1972 and June 1975. Slightly more than one third of these subjects withdrew from treatment or were unavailable for retesting, leaving a sample of 279 subjects who did participate through the fourth testing. The initial testing was completed by psychologists from the various units for 186 cases, while 31 examiners from Rorschach Workshops did the other initial testing and/or the retesting, none testing the same subject twice. The same general procedure described in the preceding chapter for the Focal Study was used with these subjects to maintain contact during and after treatment. The cooperation of the 53 therapists aided greatly in sustaining contact with the patients. The 279 subjects were distributed across the seven treatment modalities with the following frequencies: 56 in a psychoanalytically oriented, uncovering form of psychotherapy *(dynamic);* 32 in a *Gestaltian* form of individual psychotherapy; 43 in a *modeling* form of treatment, often including two therapists and with the major focus on interpersonal habits; 40 in *assertiveness* treatment; 46 in *systematic desensitization;* 34 in transactionally oriented *group* psychotherapy; and 28 in a *biofeedback* form of intervention.

It should be apparent that no effort was made to "match" subjects for pathology or demography. Most were supported by third party payments, although a few of those in all but the modeling treatment paid themselves. Most of the subjects entering the dynamic or Gestalt forms of treatment would probably be described as "neurotic" by most standards. Most of the subjects entering group treatment or assertiveness training complained of interpersonal problems, most often involving marital difficulties. The majority of subjects undergoing systematic desensitization had obsessive or phobic complaints, while the majority of subjects in the biofeed back intervention had somatic complaints. Naturally, intervention programs varied for frequency of contact, both within and across treatments. For example the majority of those in a dynamically oriented form of psychotherapy were seen twice weekly, whereas most in the other treatment modalities were treated once a week. No effort was made to study therapists, except that no patient was included in the study whose therapist had not acquired either the Ph.D. in psychology or an M.D. with at least three years of residency in psychiatry. In some instances, where two therapists were used in a modeling form of treatment, the second was often trained at a subdoctoral level. Ninety-four of the subjects were treated in hospital outpatient units; 121 were treated in clinics not directly a part of a hospital administrative unit, although most did maintain hospital affiliations; and 64 were treated by private practitioners.

The research plan was designed on the assumption that some subjects, especially those in the behavioral forms of intervention, would have terminated treatment by the ninth month, and that others would terminate by the 18th month, thus permitting a posttreatment followup through which subjects could be differentiated in terms of posttreatment effectiveness. This proved to be a less than accurate prediction, although more than half had terminated prior to the second retest, at the 16 to 18 month interval. The "status" of the patient was evaluated concurrently with each testing using the Form R of the Katz Adjustment Scale (Katz and Lyerly, 1963), which was completed at each interval, including the pretreatment point, by a "significant other" designated by the patient (usually a family member). In addition, the therapist completed the same scale at each of the retest intervals.

The OP study also included a "control" group of nonpatients tested at approximately the same intervals. This group consisted of 50 adult subjects, 25 male and 25 female, at the beginning of the project. Attrition, for various reasons reduced the size of the control group to 41 (22 females and 19 males) by the time of the fourth testing.

It is very important to distinguish between this study and those designed to evaluate the effectiveness of different modes of treatment. The OP project would fall far short of such a goal, because neither patients nor therapists were randomized, and there was no attempt to equate patients for psychopathology, or to equate therapists for skills. The object of the OP study was to determine what changes would be manifest in the Rorschach under different modes of treatment in situations where the patient presumably selected the type of therapy. Thus, while some groups will show greater change on some Rorschach variables than other groups, this should not reflect on the utility of any particular mode of intervention. The aims of therapy usually vary greatly with different treatments, and even among therapists using a particular treatment framework. In fact, as will be noted from the data in Table 19, 54 of the 279 subjects were still in treatment at the 28th month; however, 199 of the 279 (71%) were rated as "improved" at the 28th month by their significant others.

Table 19 presents the frequencies for directionality for both the $EA:ep$ and the EB, for each of the eight groups at each of the four testings. Each group is subdivided on the basis of the first testing, to show the frequencies for each of the two directions of $EA:ep$, and each of the three states represented by the EB: introversiveness, extratensiveness, and ambient. Table 19 shows the frequencies for the two ratios; however, some elaboration concerning each of the groups should be made.

Control Group

As might be expected in light of the data from the Focal Study, these 41 nonpatients showed very little change for either of the two ratios. The data remain very consistent at each of the three retestings, confirming once again the apparent sturdiness of these variables over time.

Dynamic Psychotherapy (14 therapists)

This group of 56 subjects (31 female and 25 male) is one of two groups showing considerable variability within their subgroups. The subgroups are divided in terms of their $EA:ep$ ratios, at the beginning of treatment—that is, whether EA was higher than ep and vice versa. Fifteen of the 24 subjects who began treatment

Table 19. **Frequencies for Directionality of the *EA:ep* Relation and the *EB* for Seven Treatment Groups and One Control Group Across Four Testings During 28 Months**

Testings	Dynamic N = 56		Gestalt N = 32		Modeling N = 43		Assertive N = 40	
	EA > ep N = 24	ep > EA* N = 32	EA > ep N = 19	ep > EA* N = 13	EA > ep N = 23	ep > EA* N = 20	EA > ep N = 16	ep > EA* N = 24
PRETREATMENT								
EA > ep	24	0	19	0	23	0	16	0
M > Sum C	10	14	8	5	9	7	10	13
Sum C > M	9	10	7	4	11	12	4	7
M = Sum C**	5	8	4	4	3	1	2	4
9 MONTHS								
EA > ep	9	13	6	6	20	8	14	3
M > Sum C	12	13	8	4	10	7	9	11
Sum C > M	8	10	7	4	11	12	5	8
M = Sum C**	4	9	4	5	2	1	3	5
In treatment	24	32	19	13	23	20	14	16
Rated improved by signif other	6	15	4	5	9	9	8	11
18 MONTHS								
EA > ep	17	22	16	9	21	14	13	2
M > Sum C	11	16	8	4	10	7	8	14
Sum C > M	10	13	9	7	12	10	4	8
M = Sum C**	3	3	2	2	1	3	4	2
In treatment	22	31	19	10	13	8	5	0
Rated improved by signif other	11	19	11	7	17	13	13	16
28 MONTHS								
EA > ep	19	25	15	7	17	11	14	3
M > Sum C	11	15	8	5	10	8	8	13
Sum C > M	9	14	8	7	11	10	4	8
M = Sum C**	4	3	3	1	2	2	4	3
In treatment	21	8	18	4	3	0	0	0
Rated improved by signif other	15	26	14	9	18	15	12	17
PRETREATMENT								
EA > ep	19	0	25	0	16	0	33	0
M > Sum C	7	5	16	9	10	6	14	3
Sum C > M	6	9	5	6	5	4	12	5
M = Sum C**	6	1	4	6	1	2	7	0
9 MONTHS								
EA > ep	16	4	23	9	16	3	31	1
M > Sum C	7	5	15	9	10	5	14	3
Sum C > M	6	8	4	5	4	4	13	4

Table 19   (Continued)

Testings	Group N = 34		Desensitiz N = 46		Biofdbk N = 28		Nonpatient N = 41	
	EA > ep N = 19	ep > EA* N = 15	EA > ep N = 25	ep > EA* N = 21	EA > ep N = 16	ep > EA* N = 12	EA > ep N = 33	ep > EA* N = 8
M = Sum C**	6	2	6	7	2	3	6	1
In treatment	13	10	11	6	7	2	—	—
Rated improved by signif other	5	3	16	12	10	4	—	—
18 MONTHS								
EA > ep	17	7	24	6	16	4	32	1
M > Sum C	7	5	16	8	10	5	15	3
Sum C > M	6	7	6	7	4	4	12	4
M = Sum C**	6	3	3	6	2	3	7	1
In treatment	5	2	0	0	0	0	—	—
Rated improved by signif other	11	8	19	15	11	7	—	—
28 MONTHS								
EA > ep	18	5	24	5	16	5	34	2
M > Sum C	8	6	15	9	9	5	14	4
Sum C > M	8	7	6	7	4	5	13	3
M = Sum C**	3	2	4	5	3	2	6	1
In treatment	2	0	0	0	0	0	—	—
Rated improved by signif other	13	8	19	16	10	7	—	—

*Includes cases where $EA = ep$.
**Includes cases where M is ±1.0 of Sum C.

with EA higher than ep reversed direction during the first nine months. This reversal probably reflects the impact of an intervention plan oriented toward "reconstruction"—a plan that confronts currently organized or *stabilized* psychological features with the objective of reorganization. It is also important to note that 19 of the 24 did show a higher EA at the 28th month, but only three had terminated treatment, although 15 of the 24 were rated improved. Interestingly, six of the nine *who were not* rated improved at the 28th month never reversed the $EA : ep$ direction.

The subgroup that began this form of treatment with ep higher than EA showed a much different progression. Thirteen of these 32 subjects had reversed direction for $EA : ep$ by the ninth month, and 25 had higher EA's at the 28th month. Only eight of these subjects remained in treatment at the 28th month; six of these *were not rated* by their significant others as having shown behavioral improvement. It would appear that "reconstructive" treatment like that represented by this group has a more rapid and successful impact when the patient begins treatment with a higher ep. When EA is higher initially, treatment goals are apparently achieved more slowly, probably because of the time required to "break up" the EA in its pretreatment form of organization.

The frequencies for the *EB* show less variation over the three retest intervals. Thirteen of the 56 subjects showed no marked direction in *EB* at the beginning of Treatment. The same 13 retained their "ambitent" status at the ninth month; beyond that time, however, ten of the 13, eight of whom had been in the high *ep* group, showed a marked direction. At the same time, four other subjects, two from each subgroup, had moved to the ambitent status by the 28th month. Concurrently, three other subjects reversed direction, two from high *M* to high *Sum C*. Overall, 17 of the 56 subjects showed an *EB* at the 28th month that differed from their initial testing.

Gestalt Psychotherapy (6 therapists)

The data trend for these 32 subjects (18 female and 14 male) is very similar to that found for the dynamic psychotherapy group. Thirteen of the 19 subjects in the initial high *EA* group had reversed direction by the ninth month, with nine of the 13 showing a second reversal by the 28th month. Only one of those 19 subjects had terminated treatment by the fourth testing, although 18 of the 19 were rated improved. Seven of the 13 subjects showing a higher initial *ep* had reversed to a higher *EA* by the 28th month. Of the four of the 13 who remained in treatment, *none* had reversed the *EA* : *ep* direction.

Directionality of the *EB* remained very stable during the period of over two years. All who were higher for *M* at the onset of treatment remained high for *M* in the last test. Four subjects who had been ambitent at the initial test moved to an extratensive *EB* by the final testing. Gestalt psychotherapy, like the more traditional dynamically oriented psychotherapy, focuses on reorganization of the personality structure, although it is usually identified as more "developmentally" oriented than reconstructive. If this relatively small sample of subjects is any clue to the process of Gestalt psychotherapy, it seems very similar to the more traditional psychoanalytically oriented therapy, when viewed by only two Rorschach variables. Clearly, subjects beginning treatment with higher *ep* tend to terminate earlier, and undergo less disruption to the more stabilized features of their personality operations.

Modeling Therapy (7 primary therapists)

The data from the 43 subjects in modeling intervention are striking. This form of treatment apparently focuses on interpersonal skills as the primary target, frequently using a second therapist for role playing situations. Seventeen of the 23 modeling subjects with a higher *EA* at the start of treatment continued to display the *EA* : *ep* ratio in the same direction after the 28th month, even though nearly half had terminated treatment at or before, the 18th month, and all but three had ended by the 28th month. Thus it would seem that modeling has little effect on the basic organization of stabilized resources as dynamic and gestalt therapy do. On the other hand, 11 of the 20 high *ep* subjects entering modeling therapy showed higher *EA* at the 28th month, suggesting that this form of intervention does act to "congeal" psychological activities into a more accessible form. At the same time, there is virtually no impact on the *EB*. At the beginning of treatment, nine of the 23 high *EA* subjects reflected an introversive response style. At the 28th month, the same nine persisted in that style, as did one other who had moved from an ambient to an introversive style. Similarly, seven higher *ep* subjects showed introversive traits before treatment, and all seven, plus one ambient, showed introversiveness at the 28th month. Twelve high *ep* subjects were extratensive at the start of treatment, and 10 remained so at the 28th month, with the other two moving to an ambient status. The 11 high *EA* subjects who were extratensive in the initial test continued to display the same *EB* throughout the three retests. Thus, only four subjects changed *EB* through the 28th month. Although modeling is not usually described as a developmental form of intervention, the data here suggest that some form of development has occurred, especially for those who began treatment with higher *ep*'s. It is also very notable that, unlike the dynamic and gestalt forms of psychotherapy, those entering modeling treatment with higher *EA*'s did not appear to undergo the *EA* disorganization observed in the other two groups.

Assertiveness Training (nine therapists)

The 40 subjects in assertiveness training (24 females and 16 males) reflected very little change for either of the two variables. Two of the 16 beginning with a high *EA* reversed by the ninth month and remained that way, as did three high *ep* subjects. All others showed the same *EA* : *ep* relation through the four testings. Two high *EA* subjects, identified as introversive at the first testing, changed to an ambient status by the 18th month, although both had terminated treatment before the ninth month; and one of the 24 high *ep* ambient subjects became extratensive before the 18th month. Thus, it seems that this form of intervention, which yielded an "improved" rating for 29 of the 40 subjects, has relatively little effect on those psychological features manifest in the *EA* : *ep* relation, or in the *EB*.

Group Psychotherapy (four therapists)

This mode of treatment, applied to 34 subjects (18 female and 16 male), produced only modest change for either of the two variables. One of the 19 high *EA* subjects reversed, as did five of the 15 high *ep* subjects. Two of the six high *EA* ambients altered to extratensiveness, and one of the six changed to introversiveness. Two of the high *ep* extratensives also showed a change, one to higher *M* and the second to ambient.

Desensitization (five therapists)

This group consisted of 46 subjects (25 female and 21 male). Twenty-five began treatment with a higher *EA*, and 24 remained that way over the 28 month period, although all 25 had ended treatment before the 11th month. One of the 25 showed an *EB* change from introversive to extratensive. The 21 higher *ep* subjects showed an interesting pattern. Nine had reversed to higher *EA* by the ninth month, and all nine had terminated prior to that time. At the 28th month, however, only five of the nine had sustained the reversal. One of the six ambients in the high *ep* group ultimately changed to extratensive, but the change occurred nearly two years after termination.

Biofeedback (three therapists)

These 28 subjects (16 male and 12 female) were in treatment for the shortest average time period. Nineteen were terminated before the sixth month, the remaining nine terminated between the ninth and 11th months. The 16 higher *EA* subjects remained stable for the *EA : ep* ratio over all testing, and one of the 16 changed from introversive to ambitent. Interestingly, five of the 12 higher *ep* subjects reversed to higher *EA,* with two of those reversals occurring after termination. One of the 12 high *ep* subjects who was introversive at the onset of treatment changed to ambitent at the ninth month, and one ambitent changed to extratensive 18 months after termination.

THE *EA : ep* AS A CONCEPT

The cumulation of data regarding the *EA : ep* relation support some reasonably firm conclusions. First, *EA* is something that develops gradually, so that most nonpatient adults will ultimately manifest more *EA* than *ep.* The *ep* appears to develop earlier and, apparently, much faster than *EA,* so that during childhood and most of adolescence, more *ep* than *EA* will be displayed. *It does not appear* that, as *EA* increases, *ep* decreases, at least in nonpatients; rather, the *ep* tends to reach some asymptotic level for most nonpatients between the 10th and 15th years. This level *is not expressed* as an absolute quantity, but more in terms of a proportion of the functioning psychological operations of the individual. The same is true of *EA;* that is, its meaning should be conceptualized in proportional terms related to the total functioning of the person.

Second, whenever *EA* exceeds *ep,* that relationship is very sturdy over time in both patients and nonpatients. Its sturdiness is not even disrupted by most forms of intervention, whether short or long term, *except* where the intervention aims at broad personality reorganization. The fact that *EA* is higher than *ep does not necessarily indicate good or poor* psychological adjustment or intervention prognosis. About 50% of the OP subjects entered treatment with *EA* higher than *ep,* and 71% of those were rated improved after 28 months (101 of 142). Concurrently, 137 of the 279 OP subjects had higher *ep*'s at the beginning of treatment, and 72% (98) of these subjects were rated improved after 28 months.

Third, when *EA* is high in persons with psychological problems, reconstructive forms of psychotherapy will require a longer period for *effective* intervention than cases where *ep* is higher at the onset of treatment.

Fourth, a smaller proportion of adolescents who manifest psychological problems show *EA* higher than *ep* when contrasted with nonpatients of their own age. Yet, from years five through 11, both nonpatient and patient children show increases *that are about the same* in the proportion of subjects with higher *EA*'s. For example, 4% more nonpatient 10 year olds had higher *EA*'s than did the nonpatient nine year olds, while 7% more behavioral problem 10 year olds showed higher EA's than did their counterpart nine year olds, and 11% more of the 10 year old withdrawn children were higher for EA than the nine year old withdrawn children. This suggests that pathological conditions do not inhibit *EA* growth much, if at all, during earlier years, but that pathological features may, *under some conditions,* cause a sharp decline in *EA or* inhibit its further growth. For instance, the proportion of higher *EA*'s is slightly greater among outpatients than among inpatient depressives—47% and 43% respectively, while only 34% of schizophrenics show a higher *EA,* and only 21% of inpatient character problems have a higher *EA.* There is no way of knowing whether the higher *ep*'s among these subjects existed prior to the pathology, but they do seem related.

Fifth, the data from the two small sample behavioral studies suggest that high *ep* subjects have less tolerance for frustration, or less persistence in nonmeaningful tasks.

These findings suggest that *EA* does, in effect, represent something about the manner in which the person is *able to use* his or her resources in a deliberate way. Thus, *ep,* reflecting the extent to which psychological activity is impinging upon the person, becomes a *critical comparison point* for understanding the effectiveness of *EA* as an asset or liability. When *EA* exceeds *ep,* the person has demonstrated, through the behavioral sampling of the Rorschach, that operations involving accessible resources have "outnumbered" operations that are less controlled. Conversely, when *ep* exceeds *EA,* the record illustrates a person who was more prone to display behavior prompted by psychological actions that are not readily accessible or amenable to direction. Stated differently, the *EA* can be conceptualized as representing the more "sophisticated operations" of the person, while the *ep* reflects the more "primitive operations." Thus, if *ep* is greater than *EA,* the person will be less able to exert direction and/or control in coping situations, whereas the high *EA* individual is more able to do so because more resources are available for use.

It is important again to stress that the concepts "sophisticated" and "primitive" are not used here to differentiate the pathological from the nonpathological. They simply refer to the capability of the person to initiate deliberate action in coping situations. Some who are psychologically sophisticated will initiate pathological actions, while more primitive individuals may follow a less complex but parsimonious coping style. The manner of coping will be determined, essentially, by other responses styles, one of which is represented by the all important *EB.*

THE *ERLEBNISTYPUS (EB)*

The data in the preceding chapter illustrate the remarkable consistency of the *EB* among adults, and the data from the OP study presented in this chapter reaffirm that sturdiness even under a variety of treatment conditions. The Focal Study revealed that 86 of the 100 nonpatients were consistent in *EB* direction, or nondirection, after three years. *Twelve of the 14 subjects* who did show an *EB* change during that period *were ambitents,* or ambiequals. These are people who do not show a distinct response tendency.

A similar pattern of *EB* consistency is revaled in the OP study. A comparison of the initial test data with those of the final retest, taken at about the 28th month, shows that only 38 of the 279 subjects manifest a directional shift for *EB, and 33 of the 38 were at one point or another involved with the ambiequal status.* More precisely, 22 of the directional shifts were *from* the initial ambitent status, 14 moving to an extratensive status and eight moving to an introversive status by the 28th month. Another 11 subjects, five initially testing as extratensive and six as introversive, moved to an ambient status by the 28th month. Of the remaining five subjects who shifted, three tested as introversive in the first test and extratensive in the last test, while the other two reversed in the opposite direction. Seventeen of the 38 *EB* shifts occurred among subjects in the dynamically oriented form of psychotherapy. The remaining 21 *EB* shifts were distributed about equally across the other six therapies, four in gestalt, four in modeling, three in assertiveness training, five in group therapy, two in desensitization, and three in biofeedback.

One of the curiosities of the OP data is the very high proportion of ambients who did shift during or after treatment. Fifty-one of the 279 subjects were ambient in the first test, and 22 of those, or 43%, became either introversive or extratensive by the 28th month. This suggests that the ambient may be much more pliable than either the introversives or the extratensives. This seeming pliability, or flexibility, of the ambient group prompted a reexamination of the Focal Study data on temporal consistency. The protocols of the 100 subjects participating in the Focal Study were separated by *EB* groups on the basis of the initial test, and retest correlation coefficients were calculated for each of the groups (Exner and Viglione, 1977). The resulting data are shown in Table 20.

The Table 20 data reveal that the ambient group, consisting of only 20 subjects, are about as temporally consistent for most variables as are either the introver-

Table 20. Correlation Coefficients for 100 Nonpatients Retested after 35 to 38 Months, for 19 Variables Across Three Groups, Defined by the *Erlebnistypus*

Variable	Introversive $N = 37$	Extratensive $N = 43$	Ambient $N = 20$
R	.85	.79	.71
P	.75	.74	.70
Zf	.89	.75	.83
F	.84	.61	.54
M	.83	.76	.75
FM	.72	.73	.71
FM + m	.69	.72	.71
a	.86	.78	.84
p	.72	.74	.56
FC	.86	.80	.92
CF + C	.64	.67	.68
Sum weighed C	.80	.78	.77
Sum shading	.68	.50	.82
PERCENTAGES-RATIOS			
L	.86	.49	.95
X + %	.77	.80	.85
Afr	.90	.86	.89
3r + (2)/R	.82	.89	.71
EA	.86	.85	.85
ep	.76	.68	.80

sives or the extratensives. It is possible, in light of the small sample size, that they are even more consistent, at least for some variables. The retest correlations for Lambda and for *FC* are remarkably high for a three year interval, and, interestingly, the ambitents show a significantly higher retest correlation for the sum of shading than do either of the other groups. The latter is especially interesting because the retest correlations for all of the groups presented in the last chapter showed the sum of shading to be among the least sturdy features. A review of the raw'' data in the Focal Study, on the assumption that the ambitents may show a high frequency of zero shading scores, yielded very little clarification. Only two of the ambitents showed a zero frequency for shading in the first test, and only one at the retest, and the mean shading scores for the group are about the same at each testing as those for the group of introversive subjects. The very high correlation for *Lambda* among the ambitents is also intriguing. Actually, it is elevated spuriously by a single data point that falls at the extreme of a regression line. If that single case is removed from this small sample, the correlation coefficient for *Lambda* is reduced to .59.

The reasonable consistency of the ambitent group, as illustrated in the Focal Study, and the apparent pliability of these types of individuals, as reflected in the high proportion of *EB* direction shifts in the OP study, raises the issue of whether this sort of response style may be the "most preferred." Is the seeming flexibility of the ambitent an asset in coping situations? Data from two sources suggest *that this is not the case.*

THE RELAPSE STUDY *(RE)* (Exner and Murillo, 1975)

This study, of posthospitalization relapse included 148 patients discharged from hospitalization between June 1971 and September 1972. Seventy-one had been diagnosed as schizophrenic, while the remaining 77 represented a variety of affective and characterological disturbances. The schizophrenic group contained 38 males and 33 females, the nonschizophrenic group had 34 males and 43 females. Approximately 35% of the schizophrenics and 65% of the nonschizophrenics were married. All but six had graduated high school, and 21 had graduated college. One hundred and twenty had been first admissions, while the remaining 28, divided evenly among schizophrenics and nonschizophrenics, had been hospitalized previously. There was a considerable variation in the types of treatment employed, ranging from drug and/or ECT techniques to individual and/or group psychotherapy. One hundred and nineteen of the 148 were discharged with a regular routine of postdischarge medication. The basic purpose of the study was to explore methods of identifying "potential relapse" soon enough after discharge to permit change in the after-care plan to prevent relapse.

The Rorschach was among several sources of data collected at discharge. Seven to nine weeks after his or her discharge, each subject was interviewed by either of two psychologists not associated with the hospital and having no prior contact with the subject or knowledge of the subject's history. Following the interview, the psychologist completed the Inpatient Multidimensional Psychiatric Scale (IMPS), and concurrently the subject completed a Form S of the Katz Adjustment

Scale while a significant other completed the Form R of the same scale.[2] Posthospitalization contact was maintained with the ex-patient *and* the significant other for a 12 month period, or until a relapse (defined by rehospitalization or complete debilitation) occurred. These contacts included telephone calls, the completion of a biographical-medical-occupational questionnaire at the four and six month intervals, and greeting cards sent for special occasions. Thus, it was relatively easy to identify instances of relapse during the 12 month posthospitalization period.

Forty-one subjects—19 schizophrenics and 22 nonschizophrenics—relapsed during the 12 month period, seven during the 3rd month, 25 between the 4th and 6th months, and nine after the 6th month. There was no apparent relationship between the relapse and length of hospitalization or type of treatment; nor was there any relationship between the relapse and seemingly abrupt changes in the aftercare medication routines, whether planned or unplanned. A substantially greater proportion of patients with a history of multiple hospitalizations, 10 of 28, were included in the relapse group.

The *EB* distribution for these subjects at discharge shows that, among the 71 schizophrenics, there were 18 ambitents, 28 extratensives, and 25 introversives. The records of the 77 nonschizophrenics reveal 21 ambitents, 23 extratensives, and 33 introversives. *Eleven of the 18 ambitents were included* among the 19 schizophrenic relapsers, *and 8 of the 21 nonschizophrenic ambitents were among the* 22 relapsing from that group. Overall, 19 of the 39 ambitents (49%) relapsed, as contrasted with nine of the 51 extratensives (18%), and 13 of the 58 introversives (22%). This does not automatically mean that ambitents are "more fragile" after hospitalization, for that is not necessarily the case when the *EA* : *ep* data are included in the analysis. Thirty of the 41 relapsers had higher *ep* in that ratio, as contrasted with only 42 of the 107 nonrelapsers. The *ep* was higher for 13 of the 19 relapsing ambitents. These data indicate that a higher *ep* after hospitalization may represent more limited coping resources, *and when such limits exist in a person who does not manifest firm response styles,* a greater vulnerability to stress may exist. In other words, that person may tend to become more *vacillating* in coping conditions. Naturally, there are many factors that contribute to relapse, and other data from the *RE* study will be discussed later in this chapter and in the next, but before this, the findings of another study concerning the *EB* should be reviewed, since the data are relevant to the issue of the ambitent style as an asset or liability.

A STUDY IN PROBLEM SOLVING (PS) (Exner, Bryant, and Leura, 1975)

Three groups of 15 subjects each, drawn from a 19 and 20 year old college population, were selected on the basis of three criteria: the Rorschach *EB,* the *EA* : *ep* ratio, and the SAT Verbal Score. SAT scores were between 575 and 600. One

[2] Although several Rorschach variables do differentiate the relapsing from non-relapsing groups, the highest level of post-dictive accuracy is derived from a comparison of the Form S and Form R Katz Adjustment Scales, using a *d* score technique for two of the scales related to social and free time behaviors. This technique identifies approximately 75% of the nonschizophrenic relapsers, while misidentifying about 15% of the nonrelapsers as "false positive".

group had *EB*'s that were clearly extratensive, defined by *Sum C* exceeding *M* by 3.0 or more. A second group was clearly introversive, defined by *M* exceeding *Sum C* by at least 3.0. The third group consisted of ambitents, defined in this study as *Sum C* being within 0.5 points of *M*. *EA* exceeded *ep* by 2.0 or more for all subjects.

The problem solving apparatus used was the Logical Analysis Device (Langmuir, 1958). The subject is provided with a display panel containing nine indicator lights arranged in a circle. Each of the nine lights is controlled manually through the use of an adjacent pushbutton. A 10th light is located in the center of the circle and is known as the "target" light. It has no switch. Information about the relationships of the various lights is provided by an arrow diagram placed within the circle of nine indicator lights. Each arrow indicates one relationship, either between the indicator lights on the circle, or between any of these lights and the target light. The only information that the subject does not have is the nature of the relationship between two lights. Figure 3 portrays the display panel at which the subject works. Actually, three kinds of relationships may exist between two lights: an effector relation, which means that one light being activated will cause another light to activate; a preventor, which means that if one light is on, a second is prohibited from lighting; and a combinor, which means that the combination of two lights activated simultaneously, will act either as an effector or preventor for a third light. The object of the task is to light the center light, using only operations created by the switches for the three lower peripheral lights. The subject display panel for the logical analysis device is illustrated in Figure 3.

Before being exposed to the first problem, the subject is taught the rules of problem solution by demonstration, explanation, and practice. The subject may ask questions, take notes, and repeat practice operations, and is encouraged to make a written summary of the procedure. The task of finding the correct combi-

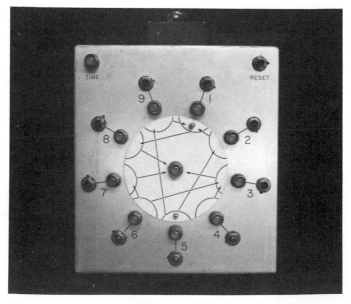

Figure 3. Subject display panel for the logical analysis device.

nation of operations, using only the three lower switches, is one of logical analysis, developed by trial and error, with each trial representing an experimental question posed by the subject concerning various relationships. Ultimately, the subject must synthesize the information developed from each operation he or she has selected, to accomplish the goal—causing the target light to be turned on. Problems vary in complexity; some problems may contain as few as 15 or 20 information yielding operations, while others may have as many as 50 operations that can yield relevant information. Each information producing operation is such that many other possible operations can be eliminated by logical deduction. This procedure is demonstrated and explained during the instruction period; however, each subject must ultimately decide how many operations will be explored, and in what sequence before a final solution is attempted. Each operation is electronically recorded on a continuously moving printout which, when analyzed, provides three data points: (1) total number of operations to solution, (2) total number of extraneous operations, and (3) total number of repeated operations. The latter can be subdivided into repeated relevant and repeated extraneous operations. The time between operations, and total time spent solving the problem, are also recorded.

As Langmuir (1958) points out, subjects vary enormously in their mode of approach to these problems. Some work very systematically, exploring the functions for each of the nine peripheral lights (even though some are often obviously irrelevant), while others tend to repeat, or "verify" information over and over. Still others move almost immediately to the switches controlling the three lower lights that must ultimately be used in the final solution. These individuals, who are not usually successful, have been labeled "organ grinders" by Langmuir. They seldom pause to contemplate the results of their actions, nor do they usually alter their approach in favor of the more elementary analytic procedure provided in the initial instructions. Through the use of data provided on the continuous printout, the problem solving approaches can be reasonably well defined along a continuum of efficiency that ranges from the hyperactively haphazard, crude, and redundant to the deliberately systematic, flexible, and sophisticated.

The 45 subjects used in this study were shown a demonstration problem, then given a simple practice problem, then presented with four "test" problems of gradually increasing difficulty, with time limits of 10, 15, 20, and 30 minutes respectively. Two "experimenters" were assigned randomly across subjects; neither was aware of the basis on which the subjects had been selected. Although a "time limit" was established for each problem, subjects were permitted to continue working on the problem beyond the time limit if they desired; the data analysis, however, was restricted to operations performed within the respective time limits. All subjects completed the first two problems well within the time limit. Six subjects—one introversive, two extratensive, and three ambitent—did not complete the third problem within the time limit, but all completed the problem within an additional seven minute interval. Eight subjects could not complete the fourth problem with the time limit, and six of the eight—two extratensive and four ambitent—elected not to continue. Data were analyzed separately for each problem, using a 3×3 analysis of variance, with total operations, total errors, and average time between operations as the dependent measures. Separate analyses were performed for repeated operations, repeated errors, and total average time to completion for those finishing within the time limits. Means and standard deviations for each of these variables are shown in Table 21.

The data in Table 21 indicate that the introversive group used consistently fewer operations, with longer average times between operations than either of the other two groups. The introversives also had significantly fewer repeated operations for

Table 21. Means and Standard Deviations for Six Variables in Four Logical Analysis Device Problems for Three Groups

Variables	Introversive $N = 15$		Extratensive $N = 15$		Ambitent $N = 15$	
	M	SD	M	SD	M	SD
PROBLEM 1 (10 MIN)						
Total operations	11.4	3.7	16.3	4.2	19.9	4.9
Total errors	3.1	1.6	6.1	2.8	5.4	2.3
Time between operations (sec)	19.3	3.6	13.1	3.3	15.6	3.6
Repeated operations	1.8	1.1	4.6	1.4	3.9	1.6
Repeated errors	0.7	0.4	2.3	1.2	2.8	1.5
Time to solution (sec)						
(passed only)	220.2	43.1	213.6	41.7	310.2*	54.1
PROBLEM 2 (15 MIN)						
Total operations	19.8	4.3	28.4	7.1	23.7	6.7
Total errors	5.7	2.3	11.7	4.8	8.8	3.6
Time between operations (sec)	21.4	3.7	14.7**	4.2	20.9	4.1
Repeated operations	3.6**	1.2	7.2	2.6	6.7	2.8
Repeated errors	2.1**	0.8	4.1	2.0	5.9	2.4
Time to solution (sec)						
(passed only)	423.6	44.2	417.6	49.7	495.6*	57.4
PROBLEM 3 (20 MIN)						
Total operations	41.2**	9.8	61.8	17.1	56.3	15.2
Total errors	11.7**	3.9	26.4	6.7	18.9	5.1
Time between operations (sec)	24.6	6.8	15.9**	4.8	20.4	5.1
Repeated operations	7.3	3.1	9.7	4.7	15.3*	3.8
Repeated errors	3.5**	1.2	6.9	3.3	11.4*	2.7
Time to solution (sec)						
(passed only)	1013.5	67.1	982.6	69.7	1148.6*	61.2
PROBLEM 4 (30 MIN)						
Total operations	51.2	12.1	70.6	11.3	64.9	13.7
Total errors	13.6**	4.2	29.8	8.7	21.7	7.5
Time between operations (sec)	18.2	5.1	13.7	4.4	16.3	4.9
Repeated operations	12.7	3.8	16.2	4.1	24.1*	6.8
Repeated errors	4.3	1.6	6.9	2.7	12.8*	3.3
Time to solution (sec)						
(passed only)	931.8	57.6	967.2	61.8	1057.9*	63.1

*Significantly greater than other two groups at .05.
**Significantly less than other two groups at .05.

each of the last three problems, and tended to repeat errors considerably less. The extratensives used the largest number of operations for each of the last three problems, and had the shortest average time between operations in all four problems, completing the first three in slightly less average total time than the introversive group. While the extratensives repeated more operations while doing the first two problems than did either of the other groups, they repeated slightly fewer errors in those problems than did the ambitents. The ambitents used the longest average time to solution in all four problems, and beginning with the third problem, *repeated significantly more operations and repeated more errors*. In the last two problems, ambitents repeated almost twice as many errors as the extratensives, and nearly three times as many as performed by the introversives. Conversely, it was the extratensive group *that actually made the greatest number of errors in each of the problems*.

An extrapolation from these data suggests that the introversive sample works through problem solving tasks at about the same rate as the extratensives. However, introversives use substantially fewer operations to achieve their goal, whereas the extratensive group explore many more possibilities, often needlessly, and often with much greater replication of operations *and errors,* even though taking about the same amount of time to achieve the "target" as the introversives. The two groups are difficult to discriminate in terms of efficiency if time to solution is used as the criterion. On the other hand, the ambitents are clearly less efficient when compared to either the introversive or extratensive groups. They use more time to solution, but more important, they repeat more operations *and* repeat more errors with a significantly higher frequency than either of the other groups. It would appear that the ambitent needs to verify each manuever or operation, and apparently does not profit as much from mistakes as do either of the other kinds of subjects.

The composite data from the Problem Solving Study, and from the OP and RE investigations, indicate that the ambitents are more pliable, less consistent under stress, more subject to change, and more "unsure" in problem solving situations. The ambitent is probably a vacillator—that is, one who tends to fluctuate between alternatives rather than manifest a firm style, regardless of whether that style is ineffective or effective. They are probably the more suggestible people, versatile in the sense of being able to adopt a variety of styles, but less persistent or secure in the use of a style. Consequently, they are probably more vulnerable to disruption under stress conditions; for it is in those circumstances that the "sturdier" features of response tendencies will persist. This does not mean that ambitents are less well adjusted or effective, for there is no real evidence to suggest this to be the case. But it probably means they are *less consistent* in their behavior; and that lack of consistency can be a liability under various circumstances.

Introversive and extratensive subjects appear remarkably "firm" in their stylistic features, but that firmness can also become a liability in situations requiring flexibility. The introversives, based on the PS Study data, are more ideational in problem solving. They are slower but more systematic in their decisions, and the accuracy of their decisions compensates for the slowness of operation. The extratensive group appears to be more "doer" oriented in problem solving. These individuals are more willing to make mistakes in their operations, but they apparently profit from those mistakes so that their solution times are not greater than for the more reflective introversives. The results of the PS Study parallel the findings of Rosenthal (1954) who used the Katona Matchstick Problems with groups of high *M* and high *Sum C* subjects. Rosenthal found that the high *M* group was "more thoughtful," and took longer finishing the task, while the high *C* subjects manipulated the sticks much more; but he concluded that while the approach to the problem solving was different for the two groups, they were equally proficient in terms of achieving solutions.

The fact that all subjects in the PS study were higher for *EA* sets limitations on the extent to which the results can be generalized. Data from the several studies concerning the effectiveness and characteristics of a style. For instance, Piotrowski (1957) and Exner (1974) have both demonstrated that differences in the requiring greater persistence. In addition, the type and quality of *M* responses, and the chromatic color answers, will, no doubt, create variations within a style concerning the effectiveness and characteristics of a style. For instance, Piotrowski (1957) and Exner (1974) have both demonstrated that differences in the characteristic of *M* responses do relate to behavioral and interpersonal effectiveness. Subjects who give "cooperative *M*'s" are generally more oriented toward socially effective behaviors. Witkin, Dyk, Faterson, Goodenough, and Karp (1962) have found a high positive relation between assertive *M*'s and Field Independence. Wagner and Hoover (1971; 1972) have shown that drama students, drum majorettes, and cheerleaders tend to give significantly more "exhibitionistic" *M* answers. Similarly, a variety of studies demonstrate that the *FC* form of response is much more related to controlled affective displays, while *CF* and *C* answers appear to correlate more with less well modulated forms of emotional expression (Exner, 1974). Thus, any overview of the three forms of response styles illustrated by the *EB* must be couched in a broad conceptual framework. Each form will include some constant elements, but will also be marked by considerable variation.

All introversives tend to be ideational in their coping activities; but if that ideational style exists within the person with a higher *ep* and *M*'s that are predominantly aggressive, the coping manifestations will be notably different than those for the introversive with a higher *EA* and *M*'s that are predominantly cooperative. Both however, will be ideational, and have a greater tendency to exhibit the basic features common to introversives. For example, Blatt and Feirstein (1977) have demonstrated that a significant relationship exists between *variability* of cardiac rate and the number and percentage of *M* responses, during a problem solving situation that used a logical analysis apparatus similar to that used in the PS Study. The Blatt and Feirstein study also reveals that variability of cardiac rate, *during rest periods,* correlates significantly with the percentage of color responses and the tendency to give color answers not dominated by form. In other words, introversive subjects have greater cardiac variability *while solving problems,* while the extratensive subjects tend to have greater variability *during rest intervals.* This is a good illustration of the basic stylistic differences, many more of which have been reviewed in the 1974 text.

The behavioral variability in any group of extratensives is at least as great as, if not greater than, that for introversives. This is because the introversive is defined by a single form of answer, the *M,* whereas the extratensive is defined by any combination of four types of chromatic color answers, *FC, CF, C,* and *Cn.* Thus, the extratensive whose record has *CF* and *C* responses exclusively will manifest a markedly different form of coping action than the extratensive with a record of only *FC* responses. Here again, the presence of a higher *EA* or higher *ep* will contribute substantially to the characteristics of the coping activity, as will many other Rorschach features.

Singer and Brown (1977) have presented an interesting theoretical formulation concerning the *EB*. They speculate on the possibility that the two basic dimensions of the *EB*, the introversive and extratensive variations, may be constitutionally predetermined; however, they also point to many findings in the developmental psychology literature to emphasize how these styles may be reinforced or inhibited in their "natural" development. They suggest that an *EB* that is derived from more precisely defined criteria, versus the more crude and simple *M* to *Sum C* ratio devised by Rorschach, can yield much information concerning the "gross patterns of fantasy, affectivity, motility, and of the spontaneity potential in the ideation and affect of the individual." It is an interesting postulate that, if tested, might render greater understanding of subtle dimensions that are now less than obvious in the ratio itself, such as the types of *M* and *C* responses that have contributed to it.

The accumulated data concerning the *EB* reaffirm the stylistic features it represents; but taken alone, they offer little more information. Any of the three styles can be effective or maladaptive, and it is quite unusual, except in very young children, to find a record *in which one side of the EB has a zero representation.* In the Focal Study, the first administration of the test yielded six who gave zero *M*, and four subjects who gave zero *Sum C*, one of the four being among the six giving no *M*. Thus, only nine of the 100 nonpatients *did not give both M and C* responses. In the second test, three years later, four of the nine persisted with a zero frequency, two continuing to give zero *M*, and two continuing to give zero *C*, *but no subjects were zero on both sides of the ratio, nor were any of the other 96 subjects zero on either side of the ratio.*

A somewhat similar case exists for the 297 subjects in the OP study. At the pretreatment testing, only 28 showed a zero frequency for either *M* or *Sum C*, and only six of those subjects were zero for both sides of the ratio. In the final retest, at 28 months, 11 subjects (4%), all of whom were included in the original 28, were zero for one side of the ratio, and only one subject, from the biofeedback group, remained zero for both sides of the ratio. These are very important data; for while a person may be described as introversive or extratensive, the style *is not necessarily manifest in all behavior.* Instead, the style illustrated by the *EB* is the one with the higher probability of occurrence under most situations, *but it does not exclude* behavior of the opposite style, nor should such an exclusion be expected. In fact, while the ambient appears to be more vulnerable to stress, under certain circumstances the ambient's pliability, taken in lesser extremes, *may be* one of the crucial factors contributing to the effectiveness of adjustment of either the introversive or extratensive person. In general, the style will be only as efficient as it is flexible, and much of that flexibility may well be contingent upon the extent to which resources are available for its support. It is quite likely that none of the three styles represented in the *EB*, will manifest as frequently or as effectively when *ep* is greater than *EA* as in those cases where the reverse is true. This raises the issue of the components of the *ep*—that is, the elements of the Experience Base *(eb)*, which, to this point, have been discussed only in a peripheral manner; yet these are the elements that appear to provoke much behavior, and are directly involved in matters of behavioral effectiveness.

THE EXPERIENCE BASE *(eb)*

Whereas the kinds of responses contributing to the *EB* seem to reflect deliberate and organized actions, the responses that make up the *eb* seem to represent a different form of psychological activity. These answers correlate with "internal stimuli," that is, experiences that *act on* the person in a provocative manner. Quite often, these forms of stimulation precipitate coping behavior, that is, behavior involving *EA* activity; however, in some instances, the frequency and/or intensity of the *eb* activity distorts, directs, or even inhibits *EA* initiated behaviors.

The *FM + m* Component

The *FM* and *m* responses, which constitute the left side of the *eb*, are similar to *M* in some respects. There is no movement in the blot stimuli, and whenever movement is included in the response, it must be "projected" there by the subject. Why is it, then, that *M* responses are considered to reflect "deliberate" forms of ideation, while *FM* and *m* are not? That is clearly one of the still to be solved Rorschach mysteries; but the fact remains that *FM* and *m* are a "different breed" of psychological operation. Data concerning the *m* response offer much more clarity about that operation than is true for *FM* answers. There are at least five studies supporting the hypothesis that *m* answers are related to an experience of stress in which the person has a sense of disruption and feels "out of control." The first of these studies (Shalit, 1965) involved the retesting of Israeli Navy personnel while on board ship during severe storm conditions. He found a significant increase in *m* during the retest.

While it is impossible to replicate the Shalit "design," there are parallel conditions of stress situations that can be used to investigate the phenomenon he described. Exner and Walker (1973) retested 20 depressed inpatients one day before their first ECT treatment. Fourteen of the 20 had produced at least one *m* in their first records, taken shortly after admission, and the mean *m* for the group at that testing was 1.26 (SD = 0.83). The retest protocols showed that 16 of the 20 subjects produced *m,* including all 14 showing *m* in the first record; and the mean *m* for the group increased to 2.57 (SD = 1.1), $p < .05$. A second retest of these subjects occurred at the time of discharge from hospitalization. These third protocols, although generally longer than either of the first two, contained very few *m*'s. Only six of the 20 produced *m,* and only one each.

A second study involved subjects in parachute jump training. Twenty males were tested on one of their first three training days, and all were retested one day before their first actual parachute jump (Armbruster, Miller, and Exner, 1974). Three of the 20 subjects gave *m* answers in their first protocols, whereas 12 of the 20 gave at least one *m* response in the retest.

The third study of this series (Exner, Armbruster, Walker, and Cooper, 1975) focused on elective surgery patients. Twenty-five subjects, 14 males and 11 females, were tested initially during a seven to 10 day interval after arrangements for the surgery had been settled. Ordinarily, such arrangements are made 60 to 120 days in advance of the operation. The types of surgery varied considerably, some being orthopedic, but most being "organ-oriented." All were considered "major" involvements requiring a minimum of seven day's postsurgical care in the hospital, but none were considered to involve a "high-risk" factor. The first of two retests was completed one day before the surgery, after the subject had been admitted to the hospital. The second retest was taken 60 to 70 days after discharge from the hospital. Data from the initial testing reveal that six of the 11 females and four of the 14 males gave a total of 16 m answers, with one record containing three m's, four records containing two m's each, and one m in each of the other five protocols. At the first retest, *a day before surgery and after hospital admission,* 10 of the 11 females produced 24 m responses, and nine of the 14 males gave 17 m answers. There were two records containing 4 m's each, one from each sex, five records including four from females that contained three m's, and six records, three from each sex, that contained two m's. A t test for proportions reveals the difference in m frequencies in the two testings to be highly significant ($p < .01$). The third testing produced the fewest m answers for the group: 14 m responses appeared in the protocols of eight subjects, five female and three male, with 2 m's being the greatest number for any record. All eight subjects had also delivered m answers in the initial testing. Interestingly, these eight subjects showed a higher ep in all three tests, while only two of the other subjects showed a higher ep at any testing, and both were higher ep *only* in the first retest.

The fourth data source, supporting the postulate that m equates with the experience of stress, concerns the 56 subjects in the OP study treated with "dynamically oriented" psychotherapy. Fifteen of the 24 subjects entering treatment with a higher EA produced 27 m responses at the initial testing. Similarly, 23 of the 32 high ep subjects delivered 39 m answers. Thus, both groups averaged slightly more than one m per protocol; or, viewed differently, the high EA subjects *giving m's* averaged about 1.8 each, while the high ep subjects *giving m's* averaged 1.7 each. During the first nine months of treatment, 15 of the high EA subjects, 13 of whom had given m's in the first test, reversed direction for $EA : ep$. It has been postulated that such a reversal represents some form of "breaking up" of the stabilized features of the personality, and if that is true, it should be a stressful experience for the patient. After nine months of treatment, the retest shows that 20 of the original high EA subjects produced 49 m answers, *almost twice as many as in the first test,* and 32 of the 49 m responses were delivered by the 15 subjects who had reversed the $EA : ep$ direction. During the same period, 13 of the 32 subjects who had been higher for ep at the start of treatment reversed the $EA : ep$ direction, they included nine subjects who had given m in their first protocol. The nine month retest shows that 10 of the 13 subjects gave 11 m responses. Conversely, 16 of the 19 high ep subjects *who did not reverse* delivered 28 m answers. In other words, the high EA group, which had produced an average of about one m per subject in the first test, increased to an average of slightly more than two m's per test at the nine month interval, with most of those m's given by subjects who had reversed the $EA : ep$ direction. The high ep subjects who did not reverse direction continued to give about the same average number of m's in the retest, while those who reversed to a higher EA give significantly fewer average m's in their second record.

The third retest, taken at 28 months, shows a much different m pattern for both subgroups. Twenty-seven of the 56 subjects had terminated treatment at that time, and they produced 19 m responses (14 protocols). The 29 subjects remaining in treatment gave 22 m's (17 protocols). At this point there was no discernible difference in m responses between the higher EA versus the higher ep subjects. Most important, 10 of the original high EA subjects who had reversed to high ep and had produced a large number of m's in the first, ninth month, retest, and who *had reversed the EA : ep direction again by the 28th month, showed a zero m frequency in the last testing.*

The frequency of m among nonpatients is not insignificant. Table 1, in the first chapter, reveals an average of 0.73 m answers for the reference sample, while each of the four patient reference groups average about 1.3 m's per protocol. Campo (1977) has reported on 72 patients, each of whom gave at least three m's in their Rorschachs. She concludes that the presence of m does *not coincide* with an increase in the severity of disturbance, but does reflect a severe anxiety experience. She argues that a more precise understanding of the m response can be derived only if the characteristic of the response itself, such as active versus passive m's, is studied in more detail. Campo points out that the m response, which is form dominated, illustrates less disorganization than do those involving little or no form features, and in this context recommends that the symbol F be included for form dominant m answers *(Fm).*

Campo is probably correct in suggesting that the characteristic of the m, and the form domination in the response, are important to interpretation. A review of 170 m answers given by nonpatients shows that 83, or about one half, occur to Card II, usually integrating the DS5 space with the lower red $D3$ area to create the impression of a rocket ship; and 60 of the remaining 87 m's were divided equally between explosions on Cards IX or X, or waterfalling, in the center $DS8$ area of Card IX. Only 27 m's from this group did not fall into one of these four responses, and they represent much more idiographic kinds of material. Nearly 75% of these m's are form dominated, and slightly more are "active" in character.

An examination of 150 m's taken from the reference samples of inpatient depressives show a marked difference from the nonpatient m's. Seventy-eight, or slightly more than half, were passive in character, and almost as many contained very little form use. The Card II rocket ship response, seen most often by nonpatients, was reported only 33 times in this group, while a seed falling response to the $D3$ area of Card X appeared 29 times in this list. The Card IX explosion was reported often, 37 times, but in 28 of those responses, the character of the m was converted from active to passive by making the answer, "a picture of . . . ."

The m answer is probably best viewed as a somewhat broad category of ideational experience, not deliberately evoked by the subject, but occurring in response to threat over which the subject senses little or no control. When form dominates the m answer, the subject probably has less disruption because of this experience than when the form plays a minor role. It is a more transient form of response, and in evaluating treatment effects, it should be expected to disappear over time.

The *FM* response is quite different from *m*. It is more "durable over time," and not subject to extreme fluctuations as a function of stress. *FM* has been shown to increase under diminished states of consciousness, such as those produced by alcohol (Piotrowski and Abrahamsen, 1952) and sodium amytal (Warshaw, Leiser, Izner, and Sterne, 1954). Exner, Zalis, and Schumacher (1976) studied the records of 15 chronic amphetemine users, all of whom were between the ages of 17 and 22. They note a substantially high frequency of *FM* as contrasted with a control group of 15 chronic marijuana users in the same age range. There were, of course, other differences between the two groups. The amphetemine subjects showed many of the features of the acute schizophrenic, while the marijuana users did not illustrate psychotic features. Nonetheless, the *FM* frequency was much higher for the first group. This finding prompted an examination of the protocols of 190 female subjects, half of whom are prostitutes. The prostitute subjects has been classified by intraoccupational socioeconomic level criteria, ranging from the very "high priced" call girl to the addicted part-time streetwalker (Exner, Wylie, Leura, and Parrill, 1977). The streetwalkers, identified in the study as the Class V Group, consisted of only 10 subjects, all of whom were heroin addicted. They were matched, on the basis of marital status, intelligence, birth order, and educational level, with 10 controls who were not prostitutes. There were many features in the protocols of the two groups that differentiated one from another, but one major difference occurred in the frequency of *FM* answers. The 10 addicted prostitutes gave almost twice as many *FM* answers as did the controls. As might be suspected, there was also a statistically significant difference between the groups for *EA : ep*, and *CF + C > FC*, with the addicted prostitutes ranking higher for *ep* and *CF + C*.

The accumulated data concerning *FM*, which are rather sparse by standards of other Rorschach research, suggest that these kinds of answers correlate with ideation created by "need" states. In theory, these are the unprovoked thoughts that occur most often to a person when he or she is not engaged in coping activities. For instance, the kinds of uninitiated thinking that often keeps the intended sleeper awake may be *FM* actions. Two studies have been completed, the results of which bear on this postulate.

Exner, Cooper, and Walker (1975) studied the Rorschach changes of nine *very* overweight males during a 10 day medically supervised dietary program. Each of the subjects began the program with at least 50 pounds of excess weight, and the procedure for the diet involved hospitalization, during which only the intake of fluid was permitted. The "fluid only" phase of the program was the first segment of a more extended weight control regimen. Rorschachs were administered the day before hospitalization, and again on the 10th day of hospitalization. The average weight loss during this period was 18.4 pounds, and at least psychologically, all nine subjects were "very hungry" on the 10th hospital day. The average number of *FM* answers given in the prediet protocols was 3.77, which is very similar to the nonpatient norm. The retest records showed a mean *FM* of 4.96, which is not significantly different from the prediet mean; however, the variation *within* the sample was striking. Two subjects produced considerably fewer *FM* answers at the second testing, one moving from three to zero, and a second from four to one. One additional subject remained essentially at the same point, giving three *FM*'s in the first record and four in the second. The other seven subjects increased substantially for *FM* at the second test, the smallest increase being from two *FM*'s at the first test to four at the second. Thus, while the data are not statistically defensible, the majority of subjects did move upward for *FM,* most showing a considerable change.

The second study in this series involved the testing of 15 juvenile offenders (Exner, Bryant, and Miller, 1975). All were tested at entry to a juvenile detention center and again at the 60th day of detention. All 15 had been sentenced to an "indeterminant period" of detention for offenses ranging from auto theft to assault, an act typically marking a series of antisocial acts in the history of the subject. Most such subjects are released from detention after 75 to 90 days, but others are detained for a considerably longer period. Thus, at the 60 day interval, none of the subjects knew the probable date of release. The average number of *FM* responses at the first testing was 4.27 (SD = 1.3), while at the second testing, the mean *FM* had increased to 6.89 (SD = 1.9). A test for differences between the means yields a t of 4.68 ($p < .05$).

The *FM* response is an interesting phenomenon in that it occurs in almost all records of very young children and tends to increase in frequency to about age 10. According to the reference data in Table 2 (Chapter 1), the average number of *FM* answers is about the same for 10 year olds as for 16 year olds, and only slightly less than the average for adult nonpatients. The highest frequency of *FM* answers occurs among children identified as "behavior disorders." They show a gradual progression in the mean frequency of *FM* to nearly four answers per record in the 14 through 16 year old populations. Similarly, inpatient character disorders show an average of nearly four *FM*'s in their protocols. The reference sample data in Table 2 also reveal that withdrawn children tend to average slightly fewer *FM*'s in their protocols than the nonpatient children to about the 12th year, after which they give slightly more FM responses than the nonpatient group. Interestingly, it is this withdrawn group that gives an average of *more M than FM* at five different year levels, 8, 9, 12, 15, and 16. In the adult samples, only the nonpatients and the schizophrenics give an average of more *M* than *FM*.

Haan (1964) has found that when *FM* exceeds *M,* there is a high correlation with several measures of defensiveness; however, this defensiveness does not seem effective if relapse is used as a criterion. Exner, Murrilo, and Cannavo (1973) followed 105 nonschizophrenic patients for one year after discharge from hospitalization. Twenty-four were rehospitalized during that 12 month interval; 17 of these patients had more *FM* than *M* in their discharge Rorschachs as contrasted with only nine of the 81 nonrelapsers. In the Exner and Murrilo (1975) RE study described earlier in this chapter, 14 of the 22 nonschizophrenic relapsers had more *FM* than *M* as compared with only 10 of the 55 nonrelapsers; and 13 of the 19 relapsing schizophrenics showed a similar *FM* to *M* pattern, while only 12 of the 52 nonrelapsing schizophrenics showed more *FM* than *M*. *These data should not be interpreted to indicate that FM is a negative element,* for that does not appear to be the case. There are several other Rorschach variables that differentiate relapsing from nonrelapsing subjects. For subjects in both these studies, it is likely that relapse was predisposed much more with a lack of coping resources, or a failure to use available coping resources.

The relative consistency of *FM* in the various reliability studies presented in Chapter 3, and the consistency of the means for *FM* in the reference samples of younger clients, makes it quite unlikely that the *FM* component would provoke alteration in coping effectiveness. This is not to suggest that *FM* activity is not involved in situations of debilitation, but the involvement is probably far less direct than in the case of *m* activity. Although more data would be desirable, the composite of information on *FM* provides strong support for the notion that *FM* activity *functions as a stimulus, which, in turn is provoked by need conditions*. It is some correlate of an ideational "signal system" that prompts the person to action and thus serves to complement the coping resources. Obviously, then, when *FM* action is considerable but coping resources are few, a potential for disarray exists; or, if the coping resources are not well organized, the same potential may exist. Thus, while exceedingly high frequencies of *FM* may signal an "overload" of need states that can produce disorganization, very low frequencies of *FM* may signal a different type of malfunction, one in which normal needs have been extinguished or neutralized.

There is another component of the "signal system" of the individual that is manifest in the data in the right side of the *eb*.

The Grey-Black and Shading Component

It has been demonstrated in Chapter 2 that the achromatic colors and the shading features will often be significant to the formulation of responses. This occurs for some kinds of responses far more often than is reflected by the frequency of articulation that refers to these features. There is also considerable variation among the frequencies with which the four elements *T, Y, C',* and *V* appear. The texture determinant appears with the greatest mean frequency for almost all groups. This is true for each year level in the nonpatient reference samples for younger clients *and* adults. It is also true for adult outpatients, inpatients with character problems, and schizophrenics; for all but one age level (12th) of the younger client behavior problem samples; and in eight of the 12 age levels of the younger withdrawn client samples.

The vista *(V)* determinant has the lowest mean frequency for almost all groups, including all nonpatient samples, both adults and younger clients; all adult patient samples except depressives; all younger samples; withdrawn client and in nine of the 12 year levels of the younger client behavior problem samples. The achromatic color *(C')* and diffuse shading *(Y)* determinants vary in their mean frequencies across groups and within the different year levels for the younger clients.

It is interesting to note where the exceptions occur to this highly consistent pattern of mean frequencies. The adult inpatient depressives show the highest average for the *Y* responses, *and the lowest average for T* determinants. The *C'* and *V* determinants occur with about the same frequency for that group. In the four year levels of withdrawn younger clients where *T* is not the greatest mean frequency, the *C'* determinant shows the highest average. The *Y* variable is consistently lower than either *C'* or *T* for that group, but is consistently higher than *V* responses. The *Y* determinant is also at a consistently lower mean frequency than the *C'* determinant in the younger clients with behavior problems.

Although these responses differ in the average frequencies with which they are articulated, all have some common characteristics. Each represents a form of emotional experience for the subject, and *each of those experiences has an irritating effect.* It is this irritation that creates a stimulation or signaling effect. The effect may manifest as tension, anxiety, apprehension, or some other form of internally experienced discomfort. Some of these irritations are probably "chronic" or semichronic; that is, they are trait-like. Others will tend to fluctuate for presence and/or intensity.

The texture *(T)* determinant appears to represent one of the more chronic experiences, although it does fluctuate considerably under various circumstances. The 325 nonpatient protocols used in the Table 1 reference sample show a *zero T* frequency in only 19 cases, even though the mean for *T* in the entire sample is 1.18. In other words, almost everyone delivers one or two texture responses, the overwhelming majority of which occur to Cards IV and VI. Outpatients and schizophrenics tend to give about twice as many *T* responses as nonpatients, and depressives give about a third more *T* responses than the nonpatients. Inpatients with character problems give fewer *T* responses than do nonpatients. A review of the records in the adult patient reference samples provides some interesting food for thought. The character problem group, consisting of 90 subjects, included 23 *T*-less records; the 185 outpatient records included only six *T*-less protocols; the 155 depressives gave 31 *T*-less records; and the 210 schizophrenics included 36 records with no *T* responses. Thus, three of the four patient samples averaged between 18% and 25% *T*-less protocols as compared with about 5% from the nonpatients; *yet two of the three patient groups* (depressives and schizophrenics) *averaged significantly more T responses than the nonpatients, while the third group averaged only slightly fewer T's than nonpatients.* Although the samples are not truly bimodal, there is a bimodal quality about them, since each contains an appreciable percentage of *T*-less protocols yet a considerably larger percentage of protocols in which *T* frequencies are considerably higher than the mean. This is illustrated in Table 22, which provides the means and standard deviations for the *T* determinant for each of the five adult reference groups, plus means and standard deviations for the same groups, but with the *T*-less protocols removed from the calculations.

The data in Table 22 illustrate that when patients do articulate *T* in their records, they tend to do so with a substantially higher frequency than nonpatients. In other words, the form of emotional experience represented by the *T* answer is apparently more intense in the variety of patient groups. This is very interesting when considered in terms of the meaning of the texture response. Exner (1974) sum-

Table 22.   Means and Standard Deviations for Five Adult Reference Samples Concerning the *T* Determinant, Showing the Total Group and Group Sample for Which *T* Occurs

Groups	Total Group			Total Group Minus T-Less Protocols		
	N	*M*	SD	*N*	*M*	SD
Nonpatients	325	1.18	0.9	306	1.23	0.9
Outpatients	185	2.57	1.3	179	2.58	1.3
Character problems	90	1.05	0.8	57	1.68	0.5
Depressives	155	1.78	1.0	124	2.23	0.7
Schizophrenics	210	2.36	1.4	174	2.85	1.1

marized a review of the literature on T by stating, "The texture answer is probably best interpreted as indicating needs for affective interpersonal contact." Most likely, that statement was only *partially* correct. The T appears to illustrate *the emotional impact of the need for affective contact,* rather than the need itself. It is a *correlate* of the need, or at least of the emotional experience generated by the need; and a variety of data indicate that the need itself varies considerably under different circumstances. Two previously mentioned studies reflect this point.

The first (Exner and Bryant, 1974) shows an apparent elevation of T. It is a study involving recently separated or divorced subjects who at the time of testing had no substitute partner. It focused on 30 recently separated or divorced subjects, 18 female and 12 male. All were tested during a period of 30 to 40 days after a formal separation agreement had been reached, or within the first three weeks after a divorce decree had been awarded. The 30 demographically matched controls had been selected from a larger subject sample who had volunteered to participate in the "standardization" project. The controls were paired on the basis of the demographic match plus a marriage judgment rating on which all had rated their marriages as "average," or "above average" for stability and happiness. The divorced-separated subjects gave an average of 3.57 T responses ($SD = 1.21$), and included no T-less records. The control group averaged 1.31 T ($SD = 0.96$) and included two T-less protocols. Inasmuch as there were no baseline data—that is, no preseparation testing—for the divorced-separated group, the Rorschach was readministered to 21 of the 30 subjects after a six month interval.[3] At that time, 14 of the 21 had reestablished "emotional relationships." Those 21 subjects had averaged 3.49 T responses in the first test, as compared with 2.64 T's in the second. Although the means are not statistically significant, the slight reduction in the T frequency suggests a corresponding modest reduction in the affective experience related to the need state.

The second study (Leura and Exner, 1976) involved 32 "foster home" children aged seven to 11 who had had no placement lasting longer than 14 months, and a control group of 32 children of about the same intellectual level who had lived with their true parents since birth. The mean T for the foster-home group was 0.457 ($SD = 0.26$), *and 20 subjects produced "T-less" records.* The mean T for the 32 control subjects was 1.47 ($SD = 0.52$), and only three of those gave "T-less" protocols. A retest after four months of 16 of the 20 "T-less" foster home subjects showed that 15 of the 16 remained T-less. This marked difference cannot be attributed to the "failure of articulation" element. In the first testing, the 20 subjects averaged 1.4 grey-black or shading answers, with 16 of the 20 delivering such responses. Most involved C' or Y. In the retest, the 15 T-less subjects averaged 1.7 grey-black, shading answers with at least one in every record. These data appear to support the premise that, for some subjects, the affective experience of emotional or dependency needs may become "neutralized," and if this experience occurs, it takes on a durable characteristic.

Some other inferences about T may be drawn from a small sample study of 17 promiscuous female adolescents aged 13 to 16. Although small, the sample is truly bimodal for T, with 10 subjects averaging 4.2 T responses, and seven subjects

---

[3] Six of the nine subjects who were not retested after the six month interval refused further participation in the study, while the remaining three could not be located.

giving no T answers. The 10 with T responses also averaged slightly more than one other grey-black, or shading, answers. The seven "T-less" subjects averaged nearly two grey-black, shading responses; such responses appeared in six of the seven protocols.

Overall, the T determinant should be expected to appear in most protocols. The wide variability in its frequency generally occurs only among subjects with psychological difficulties, and when such variability is manifest, it signals some disruption of the experience of affective need or deprivation. This may be most important for the T-less protocol, as it may imply that the subject has abandoned a natural need experience. Thus, intervention planning should first deal with the low level of experienced need before developing treatment modalities oriented to reestablishing interpersonal relations.

The least frequent of the four grey-black or shading answers making up the right side of the eb is the vista (V) answer. The V determinant not only appears with low frequency among almost all groups; it appears also to be more characteristic of a "state" phenomenon in that it does not occur consistently across protocols of retested subjects. The V answer appears with greatest frequency among the protocols of depressive and suicide prone subjects, and, as will be noted in a later chapter, it has a significant positive correlation with the incidence of suicide. It has been pointed out that the V determinant occurs with the lowest mean frequency among all groups in the reference samples, except for the inpatient depressives, and at three year levels among the younger clients defined as behavioral problems. In the 10 year old behavioral problem sample, the V showed the second highest average frequency of the four grey-black, shading determinants; in the 11 year olds for this same sample, the V determinant appeared more often than Y responses; and in the 12 year old sample for this group, the mean frequency for V actually exceeded each of the other three grey-black, shading determinants.

In the OP study, the frequency of V responses nearly doubled at the first retest for those treated by dynamic, gestalt, and group psychotherapy, regardless of whether they entered treatment with a high ep or higher EA, and regardless of which form of EB style was originally manifest. Conversely, most nonpatients do not give V answers, averaging only 0.36 V's per record across the 325 samples in the reference pool. Among the patient samples, the depressive group delivered the higher average frequency of V, 1.89, while the outpatient sample also gave more than one V response per protocol, for an average of 1.13.

Interestingly, the younger clients gave very few V answers in their protocols. Nonpatient children gave no V responses through the seventh year, and again gave none at the ninth and 11th year levels. In the eighth, 10, 12, and 14th years, the mean frequency for V was 0.2, and it was only slightly higher at the 13th, 15th, and 16th year levels. The highest frequency for V occured among the withdrawn samples, being nearly 1.0 at the 14 through 16 year levels.

The accumulation of data on the V response tends to reaffirm the 1974 postulate that it represents a form of internal, and negative, emotional experience associated with self examination or introspection. The fact that it increases among patients in psychotherapy is to be expected, since these subjects are "taught" to introspect, and much of psychotherapy focuses on negative qualities. An important datum concerning V is derived from the RE study. Eighteen of the 22 nonschizophrenic relapsers gave at least one V response at the time of discharge from hospitalization, as contrasted with V answers in only six of the records of nonrelapsing, nonschizophrenic subjects.

The very low frequencies of V across all groups except those in treatment indicates that the presence of even a single V answer should be cause for careful evaluation. It is also very important to distinguish between the apparently "nonemotional introspective process" represented in FD answers, and the more emotionally laden V answers. The FD responses appear to illustrate a "taking of distance" from oneself, seemingly for the purpose of inspection; but the V answer has an affective element associated with it, and that affective element can, and often does, create a distortion of what is seen. In other words, most V responses seem to be associated with introspective efforts in which the conclusion is negative—that is, "I don't like what I see."

The appearance of a V response in the protocol of a child is very unusual. Children are not very introspective, and when they are, the consequence can often be quite painful, for the models against which they tend to judge themselves are typically the much more experienced older siblings and adults. It is quite interesting to note that, at the 10th, 11th, and 12th year levels, the behavior problem reference sample children gave more V than they did at least two of the other three kinds of grey-black, shading responses. These are youngsters who apparently have a greater capacity for complex processes, such as self-examination, than do the younger groups, and the presence of these responses may well illustrate a tendency to self inspection—that is, trying to decide "what went wrong" and how to correct it. Should this be true, the prospects for intervention with younger clients who deliver V answers may be much greater than if V or FD are not present in the protocol.

The Y determinant appears with the highest mean frequencies in two adult reference samples; outpatients and depressive inpatients. Both groups averaged almost twice as many Y responses as nonpatients or either of the two other patient groups. The reference samples of younger clients reveal a consistently higher average Y among withdrawn subjects *at every year level*. These data tend to coincide with those reported in the 1974 text, which indicated that Y occurs more often among subjects characterized as having "constrained" affect. Elstein (1965) reported that high Y subjects tend to be more inhibited and resigned to their situation. Following from that lead, two sets of protocols were extracted from the research pool for closer examination.

The first consisted of 100 records in which ep exceeded EA by more than 1.0, *and that contained at least 2 m responses*. The logic for studying this group is based on the premise that if the accessible coping resources are limited in a person who also senses a loss of control, the internal affective experience of helplessness should be present. A computer drawn control sample of 100 protocols with a zero frequency for m, and with a mixture of $EA : ep$ relationships, was used for comparison. The "test" sample averaged 2.67 Y determinants ($SD = 1.1$), while the control sample averaged 1.36 Y ($SD = 0.7$), $p < .05$. The test sample, which included both patients and nonpatients, showed Y responses in 86 of the 100 records. If the records without Y responses are excluded, the average Y is increased to 3.10. Similarly, the control sample, which also included patients and nonpatients, contained 81 records with one or more Y responses; however, elimination of the 19 "Y-less" protocols increased the average for Y to only 1.68.

The second set of protocols consisted of 55 records in which at least four movement answers, of any of the three varieties of movement *(M, FM, m)*, appeared and in which *all movement answers were scored passive (p)*. The working hypothesis here is that the passive form of movement correlates significantly with behavioral passivity, and that under such conditions a person will be more prone to experience feelings of helplessness in the coping situation posed by the Rorschach. A control sample of 55 records was computer drawn, with the stipulation that no records were acceptable unless they also included at least four movement responses, no more than one of which could be scored passive. All protocols were from adults and included both patients and nonpatients. The "test" sample yielded an average of 2.2 Y $(SD = 0.8)$, while the control sample showed a 1.3 Y average $(SD = 0.6)$; *p is not significant*. A further examination of these records revealed that only 31 of the 55 test records contained Y, while 47 of the 55 control protocols had at least one Y. A second comparison, using only records containing Y shows that the test sample has an average of 3.90 Y, while the controls average only 1.52; $p < .05$. The low frequency of protocols containing Y among those giving all passive movement answers is surprising, since most people (about 86% of all cases) do give at least one Y response in a normal length record. These data suggest that people who are "passive" in ideation, and probably in behavior, do not necessarily feel very helpless, but if they do have that experience, it is intense.

The data from the OP study also yield some understanding of the Y determinant. The 279 patients followed in that study showed an average of 2.35 Y $(SD = 0.9)$ at the initial testing, with no group showing significantly more or less, on the average, than any of the other groups. At the 18 month interval (second retest), 115 remained in treatment, while 164 had terminated treatment. The protocols of the terminated patients show a mean Y of 1.34, while the records of the 115 still being treated at that time show a mean Y of 2.14. When each of the two groups are compared for their respective Y averages at the first testing, the differences are magnified. The 164 subjects who had ended therapy gave an average of 2.53 Y at the initial testing, while the group continuing treatment yielded an average of 2.09 Y in the first test. In other words, the terminated group gave significantly fewer Y answers at the second retest, while the nonterminated subjects gave about the same number as in the first testing.

The C' determinant has also been shown to be related to emotional constraint—more so, in fact, than does Y (Exner, 1974). Among the adult reference samples, the C' response occurs about half as often as Y or T in the records of nonpatients and outpatients. Conversely, the C' response appears slightly more often than T in the records of depressive patients, and with about the same frequency as T and Y in the protocols of patients with character problems. It appears much more often than Y among the protocols of withdrawn younger clients, and is the most frequently delivered grey-black response in four age levels for that group (years 6, 11, 12, and 14). The frequency of C' is considerably greater among psychosomatics and depressives than in any other group in treatment. For instance, in the OP study, the subjects entering biofeedback and systematic desensitization therapies gave nearly twice as many C' responses as any of the other treatment groups, and all treatment groups gave about twice as many C' answers as did the nonpatient controls.

There is apparently an interesting relationship between the C' response and two other ratios in the Structural Summary, the $FC:CF+C$ ratio, and the Affective Ratio. This is illustrated in two studies. In the first (Exner and Leura, 1977), the protocols of 20 male adolescents who had been tested in conjunction with "acting-out" problems were compared with the records of 20 nonpatient adolescents of comparable age. The tests from the acting-out group were taken by one of eight school psychologists as part of a routine diagnostic procedure. The subjects were aware that the psychologists would be making a "recommendation" concerning them, and, as is often the case in these instances, they were not "fully cooperative." The 20 control records were collected from "volunteer" subjects by technicians from Rorschach Workshops, with guarantees that no information about the tests would be shared with the school or with parents. The control subjects had been selected from a larger group identified by teacher ratings as behaviorally active but not destructive.

The acting-out group averaged slightly more than 17 answers, while the controls averaged slightly less than 22 responses. The acting-out group gave 52 chromatic color responses, or an average of 2.6 each. Thirty of the 52 color answers were CF, and six were pure C. This group also gave 159 of its 344 responses to the last three cards, yielding an average Affective Ratio of .815. The control subjects gave 89 chromatic color answers, or an average of 4.45 each. Fifty-one of the color responses were CF, and three were pure C. A total of 204 of the 436 answers from the controls were to the last three cards, with a mean Affective Ratio of .879. Thus, both groups gave about the same proportion of answers to the last three cards, producing much higher Affective Ratios than are usually expected from subjects of this age. This pattern suggests that they respond quite readily to emotionally toned stimuli. The acting-out group, however, gave substantially fewer responses in which the chromatic color features were actually articulated. They also gave 49 C' answers, or an average of 2.4 each. C' responses occurred in 19 of the 20 protocols. The control subjects gave 11 C' answers, or an average of 0.55 each, and these responses appeared in only seven of the 20 records. It is compelling to speculate that the acting-out group would have given many more chromatic color answers had not the pressure of being examined existed, and that the frequency of C' answers might have been lower. Some support for this speculation is derived from a review of 40 protocols collected from inpatient depressives.

Twenty of these protocols showed Affective Ratios between .70 and .90, while the second group of 20 revealed Affective ratios ranging from .30 to .50. The average range for the Affective Ratio among nonpatient adults is .55 to .75, so that one group represented depressives who are prone to respond to emotionally toned stimuli, whereas the second group consisted of those more prone to withdraw from such stimulation. The high *Afr* group delivered 333 answers ($M = 16.65; SD = 3.7$), including 56 chromatic color answers, *and* 51 C' responses. The low *Afr* group gave 319 responses ($M = 15.95; SD = 3.8$), including 44 chromatic color answers, and only 23 C' responses. Thus, both groups averaged slightly more than two chromatic color responses per protocol, but the high *Afr* subjects gave more than twice as many C' answers.

Unlike the sort of internal emotional experience represented by the Y answers, that of helplessness, the C' seems more directly related to constraining features. It is like a psychological "biting of one's tongue," wherein the emotion is internalized rather than externalized and consequently creates irritation. This seems to be one of the reasons for the high frequency of C' responses among psychosomatics and depressives, each of whom are often found to have difficulties with the externalization of affect.

CASE ILLUSTRATIONS

It should be apparent that any of the features of the Four Square yields some information, but that the full measure of interpretive usefulness is derived from an examination of all four elements, mediating conclusions from any one in the context of information yielded from the others. Obviously, any of the three basic styles represented in the EB can be efficient or inefficient. Similarly, a higher EA does not necessarily portend a better adjustment than a higher ep; rather, it signifies a different sort of personality organization, one in which more resources are accessible to cognitive "control and/or direction." The $EA : ep$ relation implies little or nothing about the "kinds" of thinking that go on or about their appropriateness to specific situations. Thus, a higher EA may appear to be more desirable, *but* it can reflect greater accessibility to resources that are organized in a distorted and/or inappropriate manner, as for example in schizophrenia. If the higher EA schizophrenic is contrasted with the higher ep nonschizophrenic, the latter may well be the more desirable, especially if the high ep consists mainly of FM's, some T, and a bit of Y or C'.

But this is all highly speculative, for while the Four Square is a good starting point for interpretation, many other data must be reviewed before the total picture of a person can be developed. This point may best be made by the inclusion of *some* data from six cases that represent a broad diversity of subjects, ranging from apparent "normality" to severe pathological states, such as schizophrenia and suicide. The data presented here will consist of the Four Square, plus the frequencies for chromatic color answers, FM, m, T, Y, C', and V, each of which is important to for clarification of the EB and eb. More structural data will be added to each of these cases in subsequent chapters to illustrate how the structural features are often interrelated, and how the breadth of description expands as the structural data are expanded.

Case 1

Male, age 27, high school graduate, married five years, wife age 24; they have one daughter, age 3. Current employment as mail handler. No psychiatric history.

$EB = 2:4.5$	$EA = 6.5$	$C = 0$	$T = 2$
		$CF = 3$	$Y = 0$
		$FC = 3$	$C' = 1$
$eb = 5:3$	$ep = 8$	$FM = 4$	$V = 0$
		$m = 1$	

This Four Square shows an extratensive subject with a greater probability of emotional discharge, rather than ideation, in coping situations. Although he has access to some important resources, he is also prompted by many psychological features that are not organized in a way to permit their direct use. Instead they serve to stimulate behavior. Many of these features are need states, including the natural feeling of wanting more affection. *If* he experiences anxiety, the latter will be one of the primary causes. However, he also seems a bit uncertain of his emotional controls and tends to internalize emotion on occasion.

The above description is about as much as can be generated from these data. Clearly, some of these data raise additional questions that can be only approached through other features in the record. For instance, is the *m* response cause for concern in this case? To what extent do the *CF* answers illustrate adaptive versus nonadaptive content? To what extent is he actually responsive to emotionally toned stimuli? At this point, little or nothing is really known about the adjustment of this person. He may be quite "healthy," or he may be actively psychotic. All that seems certain at this point is his extratensive style (and a capacity for ideation), plus the seemingly more primitive *EA* : *ep* relation.

Case 2

Female, age 28, single, lives alone, currently teaches 4th grade. Both parents living (ages 53 and 52), plus two siblings, female age 26, male age 24. No psychiatric history.

$EB = 5:2.0$	$EA = 7.0$	$C = 0$	$T = 1$
		$CF = 1$	$Y = 2$
		$FC = 2$	$C' = 0$
$eb = 2:4$	$ep = 6$	$FM = 1$	$V = 1$
		$m = 1$	

In this case, the Four Square indicates an introversive person—that is, one who has a greater tendency to ideation than to emotional display under coping conditions. She has access to an important resource, but at this time is experiencing more "pain and/or irritation" than is common. She seems to feel helpless at times, and *possibly* feels "out of control" during those instances. Apparently, she is also introspective at this time, and that process may be contributing to her sense of irritation or anxiety.

This description places greater emphasis on the presence of a single *m* response than did the last case. This is because of the nature of the *eb*, consisting as it does of only one *FM* plus one *m* on the left side, *and* four shading responses, including one *V* determinant, on the right side. The proportionally higher number of shading answers indicates a reasonably strong sense of discomfort, and the fact that two of the four shading determinants are *Y,* suggests some feeling of helplessness. Other data that would be very important in understanding this situation are the egocentricity index, the frequency of Whole Human answers, the characteristics of the human movement responses, and, of course, the level of reality testing as indicated by the $X+\%$.

Case 3

Female, age 31, one year of junior college completed, recently divorced, retaining custody of two children (male, age 9, female, age 7). No current employment. No psychiatric history.

$EB = 1:6.0$	$EA = 7.0$	$C = 0$	$T = 4$
		$CF = 3$	$Y = 3$
		$FC = 6$	$C' = 0$
$eb = 4:7$	$ep = 11$	$FM = 2$	$V = 0$
		$m = 2$	

Here is another person with a greater tendency to discharge emotion in coping situations. In this instance, the ep is considerably larger than EA, suggesting that she does not have access to, or good command of, many of her resources. The eb is heavily weighted on the right side, consisting of $4T$ and $3Y$. This indicates that she is experiencing an uncommonly intense irritation related to ungratified needs for emotional affiliation; and at times she also seems to sense a "helpless lack of control" over things happening to her and around her. At the same time, the preponderance of FC versus CF responses suggests that when she does act in accord with her extratensive style, most of her emotional displays will be reasonably modulated.

This seems to be a more "primitive" person who may be experiencing the emotional "aftermath" of her recent divorce, or there may be other elements involved. The higher ep, plus the $2\,m$'s, plus the shading answers, suggest that she may not feel "secure" in her thinking and or behavior. Additional data are required here for clarification and elaboration, especially the egocentricity index, the Affective Ratio, the $W:M$ (Aspirational Index), the presence of Whole Human answers, and the like. *This case poses a greater likelihood for problems than either of the first two.* However, *if* there is a problem, it may range from a mild and situationally created experience of apprehension to a more severe psychotic-like state.

Case 4

Male, age 26, high school graduate, single, lives at home with parents (both age 48). Older female sibling (age 28) has been married for five years. He is currently employed as an auto mechanic. No psychiatric history.

$EB = 3:3.5$	$EA = 6.5$	$C = 1$	$T = 0$
		$CF = 2$	$Y = 2$
		$FC = 0$	$C' = 3$
$eb = 6:6$	$ep = 12$	$FM = 4$	$V = 1$
		$m = 2$	

This configuration suggests a real problem potential. The EB reflects the ambitent, who may tend to vacillate in coping situations, although he does have a capacity for either ideation or emotional discharge in those situations. The considerably higher ep indicates the presence of many psychological features that are not accessible yet offer much stimulation to behavior. The more primitive state is compounded by the presence of a pure C response and the absence of FC answers. This suggests that when he does display affect, it probably tends to "get out of control." The presence of the three C' answers may indicate that he has some awareness of this and is attempting to contain emotion more. The absence of T raises an important question about his interpersonal relations. This is also another instance of the composite of two m and two Y answers in the same protocol, which raises the issue of feelings of helplessness or lack of control.

This description is not very positive, and can suggest a person "headed for trouble" if he has not encountered it already. There is no firm style; the emotional controls seem very limited; he is prompted by considerable need provoked ideation ($FM+m$); and he is experiencing much emotional discomfort. Information about his self esteem, his interpersonal relations, his ability to organize, his reality testing, and his susceptibility to emotionally toned stimuli are all necessary before the situation can be understood more thoroughly.

Case 5

Female, age 13, single, living at home with both natural parents, currently in the eighth grade but not doing very well. No work history. No psychiatric history.

$EB = 3:2.5$	$EA = 5.5$	$C = 0$	$T = 1$
		$CF = 1$	$Y = 0$
		$FC = 3$	$C' = 0$
$eb = 6:2$	$ep = 8$	$FM = 5$	$V = 1$
		$m = 1$	

This is another ambitent, but this time a young adolescent. Although the higher ep is less cause for concern at this age level, the ambitent status is a potential problem warranting closer evaluation. An apparently more important issue here is the much larger number of FC responses. This pattern is quite uncommon in youngsters of this age and raises questions about overcontrol. The presence of one V determinant may reflect the natural self examination of the young adolescent, or it may relate to identity problems, which are also not uncommon at this age.

The tendency toward vacillation, plus the apparent overcontrol of emotional discharge makes other data in the Structural Summary quite critical to a distinction between a "normal" growth problem and something more debilitating. The Affective Ratio, the $X+\%$, and the Egocentricity Index will offer much needed information about her emotional responsiveness, her perceptual accuracy, and her self-esteem. Hopefully, her record will contain several H responses, general content that is more positive than negative, a reasonable frequency of Z and $DQ+$ answers, and one or two FD responses.

Case 6

Female, age 24, married no children, one year of junior college plus one year of business school. Husband, age 24, employed in management training position. She is employed as an executive secretary. No psychiatric history.

$EB = 4:7.0$	$EA = 11.0$	$C = 0$	$T = 2$
		$CF = 3$	$Y = 0$
		$FC = 8$	$C' = 1$
$eb = 4:3$	$ep = 7$	$FM = 4$	$V = 0$
		$m = 0$	

Working only from these data, this appears to be a fairly "well put together" person. She is prone to emotional display when coping, but she also demonstrates an obvious capacity for ideation under these circumstances. She has "good" access to many of her resources, and when she is acted upon by features that are not in her "organized" psychological structure, most of that action appears related to "need" states, including a natural desire for emotional affiliation. Although these data seem to be produced by someone who is well adjusted, they can also appear in the same configuration in the record of a severely disabled person.

These six cases provide illustrations of the kind of information that can be "milked" from the Four Square and the data that contribute to it. Any realistic approach to each of the six "bits" of data reviewed thus far *must avoid* any firm judgment concerning pathology or lack of it. In two of these cases, the potential for difficulty seemed rather apparent, while two others seem devoid of such a potential. By the end of the next chapter, sufficient additional data will have been added to each to determine whether these early judgments about potential for pathology were accurate.

REFERENCES

Armbruster, G. L., Miller, A. S., and Exner, J. E. Rorschach responses of parachute trainees at the beginning of training and shortly before their first jump. Workshops Study No. 201 (unpublished), Rorschach Workshops, 1974.

Beck, S. J. *The Rorschach Experiment: Ventures in Blind Diagnosis.* New York: Grune and Stratton, 1960.

Blatt, S. J., and Feirstein, A. Cardiac response and personality organization. *Journal of Consulting and Clinical Psychology,* 1977, **45,** 111–123.

Campo, V. On the meaning of the inanimate movement response. Ninth International Rorschach Congress, Fribourg, Switzerland, 1977.

Elstein, A. S. Behavioral correlates of the Rorschach shading determinant. *Journal of Consulting Psychology,* 1965, **29,** 231–236.

Exner, J. E. *The Rorschach: A Comprehensive System.* New York: Wiley, 1974.

Exner, J. E., Armbruster, G. L., Walker, E. J., and Cooper, W. H. Anticipation of elective surgery as manifest in Rorschach records. Workshops Study No. 213 (unpublished), Rorschach Workshops, 1975.

Exner, J. E., and Bryant, E. L. Pursuit rotor performance and the *EA* : *ep* relation. Workshops Study No. 212 (unpublished), Rorschach Workshops, 1975.

Exner, J. E., and Bryant, E. L. Mirror star tracing as related to different Rorschach variables. Workshops Study No. 222 (unpublished), Rorschach Workshops, 1976.

Exner, J. E., Bryant, E. L., and Leura, A. V. Variations in problem solving by three *EB* types. Workshops Study No. 217 (unpublished), Rorschach Workshops, 1975.

Exner, J. E., Bryant, E. L., and Miller, A. S. Rorschach responses of some juvenile offenders. Workshops Study No. 214 (unpublished), Rorschach Workshops, 1975.

Exner, J. E., Copper, W. H., and Walker, E. J. Retest of overweight males on a strict dietary regimen. Workshops Study No. 210 (unpublished), Rorschach Workshops, 1975.

Exner, J. E., and Leura, A. V. Rorschach performances of volunteer and nonvolunteer adolescents. Workshops Study No. 238 (unpublished), Rorschach Workshops, 1977.

Exner, J. E., and Murillo, L. G. Early prediction of posthospitalization relapse. *Journal of Psychiatric Research,* 1975, **12,** 231–237.

Exner, J. E., Murillo, L. G., and Cannavo, F. Disagreement between patient and relative behavioral reports as related to relapse in nonschizophrenic patients. Eastern Psychological Association, Washington, D.C., 1973.

Exner, J. E., and Viglione, D. Temporal consistency of three *EB* types over three years. Workshops Study No. 242 (unpublished), Rorschach Workshops, 1977.

Exner, J. E., and Walker, E. J. Rorschach responses of depressed patients prior to ECT. Workshops Study No. 197 (unpublished), Rorschach Workshops, 1973.

Exner, J. E., Wylie, J. R., and Kline, J. R. Variations in Rorschach performance during a 28 month interval as related to seven intervention modalities. Workshops Study No. 240 (unpublished), Rorschach Workshops, 1977.

Exner, J. E., Wylie, J. R., Leura, A. V., and Parrill, T. Some psychological characteristics of prostitutes. *Journal of Personality Assessment,* 1977, **41**, 474–485.

Exner, J. E., Zalis, T., and Schumacher, J. Rorschach protocols of chronic amphetemine users. Workshops Study No. 233 (unpublished), Rorschach Workshops, 1976.

Haan, N. An investigation of the relationships of Rorschach scores, patterns, and behaviors to coping and defense mechanisms. *Journal of Projective Techniques and Personality Assessment,* 1964, **28**, 429–441.

Katz, M., and Lyerly, S. Methods of measuring adjustment and social behavior in the community. *Psychological Reports,* 1963, **13**, 503–535.

Klopfer, B., Ainsworth, M. D., Klopfer, W. G., and Holt, R. R. *Developments in the Rorschach Technique. I: Theory and Technique.* Yonkers-on-Hudson, N.Y.: World Book Co., 1954.

Langmuir, C. R. Varieties of decision making behavior: a report of experience with the Logical Analysis Device. Washington, D.C.: American Psychological Association, 1958.

Leura, A. V., and Exner, J. E. Rorschach performances of children with a multiple foster home history. Workshops Study No. 220 (unpublished), Rorschach Workshops, 1976.

Piotrowski, Z. *Perceptanalysis.* New York: Macmillan, 1957.

Piotrowski, Z., and Abramhamsen, D. Sexual crime, alcohol, and the Rorschach test. *Psychiatric Quarterly Supplement,* 1952, **26**, 248–260.

Rorschach, H. *Psychodiagnostics.* Bern: Bircher, 1921 (Transl. Hans Huber Verlag, 1942).

Rosenthal, M. Some behavioral correlates of the Rorschach experience-balance. Unpublished doctoral dissertation, Boston University, 1954.

Shalit, B. Effects of environmental stimulation on the *M, FM,* and *m* responses in the Rorschach. *Journal of Projective Techniques and Personality Assessment,* 1965, **29**, 228–231.

Singer, J. L., and Brown, S. L. The experience type: Some behavioral correlates and theoretical implications. In Rickers-Ovsiankina, M. A. (Ed.) *Rorschach Psychology.* (2nd ed.) Huntington, N.Y.: Robert E. Krieger Publishing Co., 1977.

Wagner, E. E., and Hoover, T. O. Exhibitionistic *M* in drum majors: A validation. *Perceptual Motor Skills,* 1971, **32**, 125–126.

Wagner, E. E., and Hoover, T. O. Behavioral implications of Rorschach's human movement response. Further validation based on exhibitionistic *M*'s. *Perceptual Motor Skills,* 1972, **35**, 27–30.

Warshaw, L., Leiser, R., Izner, S. M., and Sterne, S. B. The clinical significance and theory of sodium amaytal Rorschach testing. *Journal of Projective Techniques,* 1954, **18**, 248–251.

Witkin, H. A., Dyk, R. B., Faterson, H. F., Goodenough, D. R., and Karp, S. A. *Psychological Differentiation: Studies of Development.* New York: John Wiley and Sons, 1962.

CHAPTER 5

Basic Personality Structure: Other Style Indices

The six cases presented at the end of the preceding chapter could have been described more extensively if other Rorschach data concerning styles or response tendencies had also been available. For example, data for the $FC:CF+C$ ratio were evident in the frequencies presented, thus providing some information about control of affective discharge. However, some evidence regarding emotional responsiveness, cognitive flexibility, perceptual scanning and cognitive decisions, and perceptual accuracy would have increased the "descriptive yield" substantially. Since 1973, much new information has accrued concerning the relationship of several Rorschach variables and these response tendencies, the sturdiness of which has been illustrated in the Focal Study (Exner, Leura, Armbruster, and Viglione, 1977). These variables include the $FC:CF+C$ ratio, the Affective Ratio, the Egocentricity Index, the active-passive ratio, and the Zd score. The composite of new information about these variables adds much to their interpretive usefulness and to the validity of the system.

THE FC:CF+C RATIO

This ratio provides an index of the extent to which emotional discharges are modulated. The FC answer reflects the affective discharge, which is more "controlled and/or directed" by cognitive elements than are CF or C responses. Adult nonpatients (see Table 1) give about two and one-half more FC than CF answers, and about seven times more FC than C or Cn responses. If CF and $C+Cn$ are added, the $FC:CF+C$ ratio is about 2:1 for nonpatient adults, whereas the directionality of the ratio is reversed for all of the patient groups. Outpatients give more than one and a half CF answers for each FC. When the pure C responses are added to the CF, the ratio for outpatients is about 1:2.3. Interestingly, the group of inpatient character problems average *slightly more pure C* than FC, and slightly more than two CF for each FC response. Overall, the $FC:CF+C$ ratio for that group is about 1:3.3. This is a larger "right side" average than is found in the schizophrenic sample, for which the ratio is about 1:2.6. The schizophrenics tend to give almost as many pure C as FC responses, and nearly twice as many CF's as FC's. The data for the depressive inpatients are also quite interesting. The depressives tend to give significantly fewer chromatic color responses than any of the other groups, approximately half as many as do the schizophrenics or character problems, and more than one third less than outpatients or nonpatients. Nonetheless, when depressives give a chromatic color answer, the odds are about three times greater that it will be a CF or C rather than an FC answer.

While there is a considerable variance among the $FC:CF+C$ ratios of the patient groups, a substantial majority in each of these four groups display a ratio in which $CF+C$ is greater than FC. This pattern supports the "not surprising" conclusion that patients tend to have greater difficulty modulating their emotional displays than do nonpatients. It is very important, however, to point out that a high "right side" value in this ratio *does not correlate* at a very substantial level with a higher right side value in the EB.[1] In other words, subjects who give more $CF+C$ than FC answers are not "automatically" extensive. The Focal Study of 100 nonpatients retested after three years included 18 subjects who gave more $CF+C$ than FC responses in both tests. Ten of the 18 were extensive, six were introversive, and two were ambient. The reference sample of 325 nonpatients includes 93 cases in which $CF+C$ is greater than FC; these cases include 49 extratensives, 13 ambients, and 31 introversives.

There is a more direct relationship between the higher ep subjects and the higher $CF+C$. Slightly more than 40% (N = 39) of the 96 higher ep subjects in the nonpatient reference sample gave more $CF+C$ than FC, as contrasted with about 24% (N = 54) of the 229 higher EA subjects in that sample. The percentage of higher $CF+C$ subjects in the various patient samples is considerably greater than for nonpatients, and so too is the percentage of higher ep subjects. This suggests that as accessible resources are fewer, the capacity for modulation of emotional displays is also less. This apparent relationship is also illustrated in the reference data from the groups of younger clients. For instance, the seven and eight year old nonpatient samples give slightly more than two times as many $CF+C$ as FC answers' and nearly 80% of those samples show a higher ep. The 15 and 16 year old nonpatients give about as many FC as $CF+C$ answers, and at those levels, nearly two thirds of the samples show a higher EA.

The presence or absence of the pure C response is also quite important in the interpretation of this ratio. The 325 reference sample nonpatients totaled 156 pure C answers among 7,069 responses, or about 2% of all responses. The 156 pure C's were given in 84 of the 325 records, approximately 25% of the group. Conversely, a pure C appeared in slightly more than half the depressive and outpatient protocols: 82 of the 155 depressive records, and 101 of the 185 outpatient records. The schizophrenic group gave 328 pure C answers in 5,082 responses, or slightly more than 6% of all answers. The pure C appeared in 149 of the 210 schizophrenic records. The character problem group gave the highest proportion of pure C answers. Pure C's appeared in 71 of the 90 records from that group, totaling 135 of the 2,012 answers, or nearly 7% of all responses.

The reference samples from the younger clients reveal a somewhat parallel picture. Almost all the five and six year old subjects gave at least one pure C response, *regardless of subgroup*. Similarly, a high frequency of subjects at the eight, nine, and 10 year levels gave pure C, although it appeared more often in the behavior problem groups than among nonpatients, and less often among the withdrawn groups. More than three of every four behavior problem youngsters, at these three age levels, gave at least one pure C, while this occurred in about half of the nonpatient records and in about one third of the records from withdrawn

---

[1] Three samples of 20 subjects each, all of whom show higher $CF+C$ than FC, were drawn from the reference sample pool. Thirty one of the 60 were clearly extratensive, eight were ambient, and 21 were clearly introversive.

children. A more marked change appears for the 12 to 16 year olds. The behavior problem groups continue to give pure C in about three of every four protocols; the nonpatient records show a reduction in the frequency of pure C to about one in every three records at the 12 and 13 year levels, and about one in every four protocols at the 14th through 16th years; and the withdrawn youngsters show a slight increase to about one in each three records.

Some of the data from four of the seven groups who were followed in the OP study (Exner, Wylie, and Kline, 1977) also highlight the importance of the presence or absence of pure C. The 165 subjects who entered dynamically oriented, gestalt, modeling, or group psychotherapy produced 194 pure C answers (98 protocols) at the initial testing. In the third retest, at approximately 28 months, the same group produced 94 pure C responses, 70 of which were *given by 44 of the 56 patients still in treatment*. Interestingly, 39 of the 44 were included among the 98 initial test records that contained a pure C, while only seven of the other 59 subjects who had given pure C in the first test, and had now terminated, gave a pure C response in the last retest.

Another interesting datum from the OP study concerns the $FC:CF+C$ ratio and the ratings of improvement at the 28th month. A total of 199 of the 279 patients were rated improved by significant others in the 28th month. In the initial testing, 116 of the 199 (58%) gave more $CF+C$ than FC, whereas at the third retest only 61 of these subjects (31%) continued to give more $CF+C$ than FC. On the other hand, 54 of the 80 patients *who were not rated improved* at the 28 month retest had also given more $CF+C$ in the initial testing, *and continued to do so in the third retest*.

Stotsky (1952) reported that treatment "success" is achieved more frequently among schizophrenics whose pretreatment records show more FC than $CF+C$. This also appears to hold for posttreatment "survival." In the RE study (Exner and Murillo, 1975), the protocols taken at discharge from hospitalization reveal that $CF+C$ was greater than FC in 17 of the 19 relapsing schizophrenics, as contrasted with only 22 of the 52 nonrelapsing schizophrenics; and $CF+C$ was greater than FC for 18 of the 22 nonschizophrenic relapsers versus only 26 of the 55 nonrelapsers from that group. Obviously, this variable by itself is not a good "postdictor" of relapse because of the high frequency of "false positives." However, it does seem clear that there is some "contributing" relationship between the more limited modulation of emotional discharge and the frequency of psychological disability, *at least for adults*. The nature of this relationship will become somewhat clearer if viewed in the context of two of the variables in the Four Square (*eb* and *ep*), plus the Affective Ratio. These elements appear to interrelate in many cases when the issue of emotional control is critical to the pathology.

THE AFFECTIVE RATIO *(Afr)*

The very high (.90) retest correlation for the Affective Ratio, revealed in the Focal Study, conveys a "stylistic" feature of considerable substance. This high correlation persists even when the subjects are divided on the basis of another style, as illustrated in the Table 20 (Chapter 4) data on the introversives, ambients, and extratensives in the Focal Study. This consistency is more remarkable when the respective *Afr* means are examined for each of the three *EB* groups. The mean *Afr* for the ambitents actually falls between the means for the two other groups, *which are significantly different (p < .05) from each other* (Introversive *M Afr* = 0.6213, *SD* = .13; Ambient *M Afr* = 0.6705, *SD* = .11; Extratensive *M Afr* = 0.7934, *SD* = .14). Thus, each group is relatively consistent within itself, but the two extreme groups, extratensives and introversives, differ considerably in terms of the *proportional* average number of responses to the last three cards of the test. Extratensives give proportionally more responses to those cards than do introversives. This is an intriguing result because it coincides so well with what is known about extratensives as people who tend to "discharge" affect when in coping situations; but caution must be exercised about the broad applicability of these data. *It is not true* that *all* extratensives give a higher *Afr* than *all* introversives. Quite the contrary, there is a considerable overlap in the *Afr* distributions for the two groups. The introversives (N = 37) show a range of .42 to .97, with the median falling at .62. The extratensives show a range of .53 to 1.17, with the median falling at .76. Thus, some introversives will have an *Afr* that exceeds the "normal range" of .55 to .75, while some extratensives will have *Afr*'s that fall below that range.

These findings prompted the question of whether subjects entering treatment, as in the OP study, would have similar mean *Afr*'s *when* subdivided by *EB* styles. The 279 subjects in that study, divided on the basis of the first test, included 51 ambitents, 99 extratensives, and 128 introversives, with *Afr* means of .73, .69, and .67 respectively; *however,* an examination of the *Afr* distributions shows that the distributions for the introversive and extratensive subjects *are almost bimodal.* The introversive sample shows 36 subjects with *Afr*'s of less than .40, and another 31 subjects with *Afr*'s above .80. Similarly, the extratensive distribution has 27 subjects with *Afr*'s below .50 and 33 subjects with the *Afr* above .90. These data suggest that while patients, as a group, or as subgroups, do not differ substantially for the mean *Afr,* they do, when contrasted with nonpatients, show a markedly different distribution of *Afr* scores than is found among nonpatient samples. In other words, patients tend to *fall at the upper and lower extremes considerably more often.*

The next question broached, concerning the subjects in the OP study was whether the *Afr* distributions changed as a function of treatment. In the 28th month (third retest), 199 of the 279 subjects were rated as "improved" by significant others. Of the 199, 172 had remained consistent for *EB* style (10 ambitents, 92 introversives, and 69 extratensives). A review of the *Afr* distributions for the introversives and extratensives reveals means of .63 and .71 respectively, with reasonably "normal" distributions of scores for each group. The bimodality that was evident for these groups at the initial testing was not apparent at the third retest.[2] The mean *Afr* for the subjects *who were not rated improved* was .59, in the third retest, with the distribution showing a majority of subjects falling at either end. This group, consisting of 80 subjects, has 27 with *Afr*'s lower than .55, and 24

---

[2] Examination of the protocols of the first retest, taken at the ninth treatment month, did reveal a bimodal tendency, but it was not as distinct as that in the initial test data. It is also important to note that some of the subjects tested at the 28th month were still in treatment, but were still rated as improved.

with *Afr*'s higher than .75. Among the more fascinating findings here *is the fact that 20 of the 27 subjects with a lower than .55 Afr showed more CF+C than FC, while 18 of the subjects with a higher than .75 Afr gave more CF+C than FC,* but there was no difference between these extreme groups for *EB* style. About as many were introversive as were extratensive; however, when the extreme groups were studied for the *EA : ep* relation, it was noted that a majority in the low *Afr* cluster *had a higher EA,* while the majority in the high *Afr* cluster *had a higher ep.*

Some additional data relevent to understanding of the *Afr* are derived from a study of the grey-black and shading responses. In the preceding chapter, two studies were described that focused on the *C'* response. In the first (Exner and Leura, 1977), two groups of active adolescents, one referred for problems and the second consisting of volunteers, differed for *C'* answers, but both groups had high average *Afr*'s, of .815 and .879 respectively. In the second study, two groups of depressive inpatients were compared, one with *Afr*'s ranging from .70 to .90 and the second with *Afr*'s ranging from .30 to .50. The high *Afr* group gave significantly more *C'* responses than did the low *Afr* group. The results of these two small sample studies prompted a "computer selection" of 200 protocols from the reference sample pool, with no concern for patient versus nonpatient status. One sample of 100 subjects represented protocols (adults) in which at least three *C'* and/or *Y* determinants appeared while the second sample of 100 records showed a zero frequency for *C'* and *Y*. The high *C'+Y* group had a mean *Afr* of .78 ($SD = .16$), while the zero *C'+Y* group had a mean *Afr* of .52 (SD = .12), $p < .05$. When these two groups were reexamined for the presence of *T* and *V* determinants, it was discovered that the *zero C'+Y* group gave significantly more *T+V* than the other group.

Another aspect of the relationship between the Affective Ratio and the *C'+Y* determinants is shown in the protocols used in an earlier study (Exner, 1974) that focused on the *C'+Y* determinants. They study included three groups of 42 adults each, one behaviorally defined as "Unconstrained Affect," a second behaviorally defined as "Constrained Affect," and the third being a randomly selected control group. The Constrained Affect group gave significantly more *C'+Y* than either of the other groups, while the Unconstrained Affect group had *C'+Y* in significantly fewer *Protocols* than the controls. The mean *Afr*'s for the three groups did differ significantly, *but not as might be expected.* The control group had an *Afr* mean of .63 (*SD* = .11), while the two classification groups were both higher (Constrained *Afr* = .69, *SD* = .19; Unconstrained *Afr* = .79, SD = .07). The Unconstrained group differed significantly from the controls but *not* from the Constrained group, the reason being that the Unconstrained and control groups had a relatively modest variance, but the Constrained group showed a broad distribution of *Afr*'s, ranging from .96 downward to .28. The subjects in the Constrained group were mainly psychosomatic and depressed outpatients, who gave a total of 45 *C'* and 57 *Y* responses. The *Afr* distribution reveals that 12 highest *Afr* subjects (.71 to .96) gave 15 of the *C'* and 24 of the *Y* determinants, or nearly 40% of the *C+Y* total. If those 12 subjects are eliminated from the sample, the mean *Afr* for the remainder of the group falls sharply to .51, and the standard deviation is reduced to .10.

The accumulation of data from this series of investigations of the Affective Ratio, may be reflected best in the following statements:

1. The *Afr* seems to represent a very consistent style.
2. Extratensive people tend to have higher *Afr*'s than ambitents or introversives, but there is a considerable overlap across those three *EB* styles.
3. Prior to treatment, patients show a greater frequency of very high or very low *Afr*'s than do nonpatients.
4. Patients who are rated as "improved," during or after treatment, show a more normal distribution of *Afr*'s, while patients who are rated as "unimproved" continue to show a significantly higher frequency of very high, or very low, *Afr*'s.
5. When the *Afr* is high, external *or* internal correlates of affect are more likely to appear than when the *Afr* is low.

The style or operation represented by the Affective Ratio seems to involve a *psychological receptiveness to emotionally toned stimuli*. It reflects the *tendency or expectancy* to process those stimuli in the cognitive operations, *and the processing itself becomes a form of response, which appears then to serve as a stimulus to other responses*. In a broad sense, it is a kind of threshold, probably not so much for specific stimuli as for classes of stimuli.

The relationship between this style and affective control is only indirect, at best. Control involves cognitive modulation of the emotional response, and this is probably best evidenced in the Rorschach by the $FC:CF+C$ ratio; whereas the Affective Ratio simply provides an index of the tendency *for responses to occur* when an emotionally toned stimulus is present.

The development of this style, or response tendency, appears to occur rather early in the formative years if the reference data from the younger client samples are considered. Assuming that the nonpatient samples provide a baseline, it will be noted that, at each year level from five through 16, the behavior problem samples show a higher mean *Afr*, while the withdrawn samples show a lower mean *Afr*. All three groups show a reasonably consistent decline for the average *Afr* as chronological age increases. At the 11th year level, the nonpatient sample gives an average *Afr* of 0.81, as contrasted with a mean of 1.06 for the nonpatient five year olds. Similarly, the behavior problem 11 year olds show an average *Afr* of .96 as contrasted with a mean of 1.36 for the "fives" in this group. Between the 11th and 16th year levels, each of the three groups show a reduction in mean *Afr* of about .10, so that by year 16, the nonpatient mean (0.73) is about the same as for nonpatient adults (0.69), whereas the behavior problem group remains higher (0.85) and the withdrawn sample remains lower (0.58). It is also very interesting to note that, although the withdrawn samples consistently have the lower *Afr* mean at each year level, they also have the greatest variance in the distribution of scores from years 11 through 16. During the same years, the withdrawn group also shows a significantly higher frequency of $C'+Y$ than do either of the other groups.

These findings have particular importance to treatment planning, which often tends to focus more on issues of "emotional control" than on the issue of "emotional responsiveness." Although control is clearly an important treatment target, the phenomena of *overresponsiveness and underresponsiveness* to emotionally "loaded" stimuli can be equally important. For instance, overcontrol may well be linked to overresponsiveness in some cases; that is, the excessive tendency to mediate emotionally toned stimuli may create an "overload" on resources, against which the person defends by overcontrol. The preponderence of *FC* rather than *CF+C* answers in the withdrawn samples of younger clients in just one illustration of this. These are often children who do not manifest the "natural" emotional expressiveness of the child; possibly because they are processing too much of the emotionally provoking stimuli of their world. This seems to be the case in those instances where the *Afr* is noticeably high, signaling a psychological overresponse to stimuli that threaten to overload the cognitive operations. The withdrawal, in these cases, becomes a form of avoiding that overload.

Obviously, any combination of over or under control plus over or under responsiveness can create a potential for disarray, and any personality description or treatment plan that is formulated from Rorschach data should focus on both as *separate* but related psychological features.

THE ROLE OF *LAMBDA*

Lambda probably represents less of a "firm" response style and more of a situational responsiveness to the test condition. The various retest correlations for *Lambda,* including that in the Focal Study, are quite respectable, ranging from a low of .49 for the extratensives in the Focal Study, to .95 for the small group of ambitents in that same study, with most of the other retest studies yielding correlations between .70 and .80. There is, however, a significant fluctuation in *Lambda* during treatment, whether the retest is just a few days after the first, or several weeks later. For instance, in the OP study, the first retest, at the ninth month, showed correlations for *Lambda* that ranged from .37 for the biofeedback group, to .77 for the subjects in group psychotherapy. At the second retest, 18 months after the start of treatment, the correlation between those *Lambda* data and those of the initial testing ranged from .41 for the assertiveness training group to .71 for the dynamic psychotherapy group. When the first and second retests were compared, a similar range was noted, but not for the same groups.

Exner (1974) postulated that *Lambda* would equate with the responsiveness of the subject to ambiguous stimuli, suggesting that subjects whose records show a low *Lambda* would be more "emotionally labile" than would subjects manifesting a high *Lambda* score. This postulate was based on data such as those reported by Henry and Rotter (1956), who found that higher proportions of *F* occurred in records of subjects who understand the purpose of the test; Hafner (1958), who noted a reduction in the proportion of *F* when subjects responded as quickly as they could; Goldman, 1960, and Exner and Murillo (1973), who found that the proportion of *F* increased significantly in "recovering schizophrenics"; and from the early reference samples which showed that all patient groups gave significantly lower average *Lambda* responses than nonpatients.

Beck (1945) and Klopfer (1954) both postulated that the proportion of *F* in the record was related to "affect-delay," suggesting that it is a defense manifestation in which "conscious control" plays some role. This may be true, as is evidenced by the consistently higher mean *Lambda* responses of the behavior problem subjects in the reference samples from age nine to age 16, although the matter of "conscious control" is more questionable. Higher than average *Lambdas* occur for a significant number of the adolescent subjects in the Exner and Leura (1977) study, *but* there is no significant difference between the adolescents being evaluated for "diagnosis" and the volunteer adolescents. In other words, *Lambda* may indicate a more "automatic" tendency to *avoid the complexities of a stimulus situation* when the consequences of the response are not predictable. Some added support for this notion is found in the segment of the Exner, Armbruster, and Mittman (1978) study in which therapists tested their own patients. The *range* of *Lambda* for patients tested by their own therapists was .15 to .57, whereas the range for the patients tested by a therapist other than their own was .46 to .95.

A review of 120 reference sample cases, selected from the Behavior Problem group on the basis of unequivocal behavioral data on "acting out" behavior, shows an interesting distribution of *Lambda*.[3] These subjects ranged in age from 12 to 16, and the average *Lambda* for the entire group was .93 (*SD* = .32). The mean itself is not significantly different from nonpatients in this age range, but the high standard deviation offers a clue to the broad range of scores involved, which extend from .20 to 4.10. Twenty-four cases show *Lambda* falling below the .60 level, while 27 cases have *Lambdas* above 1.35. Thus, the Exner (1974) postulate, that it is the low *Lambda* that reflects "lability," is only partially correct, for a high *Lambda* may also equate with the lack of emotional control.

It may be that *Lambda* is best translated in a context like that of the Affective Ratio, as connoting responsiveness to a stimulus *rather than general emotionality*. In such a framework, the low *Lambda* would probably typify the person willing and/or prone to become "wrapped up" in complex stimuli, whereas the high *Lambda* would reflect the person avoiding the stimulus complexities. Either may be very emotional, or *may not be*, and while a sense of consistency is implied, the consistency is probably much more *situation specific* than generalizable to a broad spectrum of behaviors. Thus, the subject who renders a proportionally high frequency of pure *F* is apparently responding to the stress of the ambiguous test situation by being "ultraconservative" but not necessarily pathological. The *F*, in a sense, is an avoidance response. It occurs in practically all records, and will often be interpreted as a "healthy backing-off" sort of answer. The presence of a pure *F*, following, in the same card, a multidetermined poor form quality answer, is usually taken as a sign of regrouping or resiliency, or an ability to back away from the complexities of the stimulus.

It is only when the frequency of pure *F* is too high or too low that it becomes an important interpretive issue. The low *L* indicates some overinvolvement with the stimulus complexities, while the high *L* suggests a less secure person fearful of the consequences of seemingly excessive stimulus involvement. The most difficult records to interpret are those in which no other determinant but *F* occurs, as they are void of an important bulk of interpretive data. In those situations, interpretation must proceed more cautiously, using only remnants of structural data such as the *W*:*D*, *F*+%, *X*+%, *A*%, *Afr*, the ratios pertaining to content, the location score distributions, and the distribution of contents. Although this approach takes account of many features, style data are lost, for the most part, and information concerning control is limited. The verbal material itself becomes a more critical issue than is desirable, and the entire interpretation may have less depth or breadth. One style oriented variable not eliminated in records that are exclusively

---

[3] These subjects all had histories of assaultive behavior directed against peers or younger children.

pure F is the egocentricity index. It relates not only to issues of security, as may be illustrated in the high L, but to several of the features of the Four Square, and to issues of emotional control.

THE EGOCENTRICITY INDEX $(3r + (2)/R)$

The temporal stability of the egocentricity index is well illustrated by the variety of very high retest correlations presented in Chapter 3, most of which cluster around the .87 correlation yielded in the Focal Study. Analysis of the very large numbers of protocols accumulated in the Rorschach Workshops research pool has reaffirmed many of the earlier findings about this index. The average egocentricity index for nonpatient adults is .37, with a variance that is quite modest, so that the "average range" remains at approximately .30 to .40. Schizophrenics and character problems tend to have significantly higher average indices, while depressives typically have a significantly lower average index.

The many protocols collected from younger clients have also contributed to an understanding of this Rorschach feature. Children are generally quite self centered, especially during the earlier developmental years. This trait is illustrated in the means for the index among the younger client groups, all of which are significantly higher at the five and six year levels than at the 15 and 16 year levels. Each of the three younger client reference groups shows a gradual decline in the mean for the index at almost every year level; however, the three groups also tend to differ significantly from each other at almost every year level, with the behavior problem groups consistently showing the highest average index, and the withdrawn groups consistently having the lowest average index for *any* given year level. This decline phenomenon is illustrated in Figure 4, which also includes data points for the average index for each of the five adult reference samples.

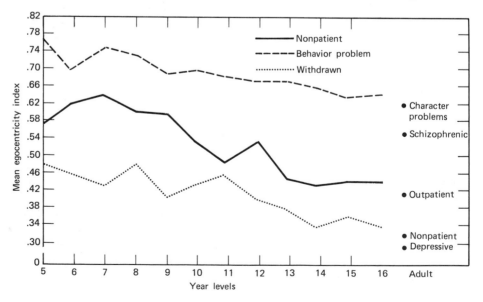

Figure 4.   Mean egocentricity index for three younger client groups and five adult groups.

One element of the egocentricity index that contributes to the significant differences between the three younger client groups is the frequency of the reflection answers *(Fr+rF)*. Nonpatient youngsters before age nine give about two reflection answers for every three protocols. Behavior problems in this age range average slightly *more than* one reflection per protocol, while the withdrawn youngsters average about one reflection for every five records. In fact, the five and six year old withdrawn children have a zero frequency of reflection answers. In the age range from nine to 16, the nonpatients average approximately one reflection for each three protocols, whereas the behavior problem samples average almost *one per record,* while the withdrawn groups average only about one *Fr* or *rF* for every 10 records. Previous findings (Exner, 1969, 1974; Raychaudhuri and Mukerji, 1971) have demonstrated that the reflection response appears very infrequently among adult protocols, *except* for three groups: those with serious sex role confusion, those who are prone to antisocial behavior, and schizophrenics. Each of these groups gives significantly more *Fr+rF* responses than do other pathological groups or nonpatients. The reflection appears to be a more primitive form of self-centeredness, and the fact that it does appear significantly more often among the records of the younger client behavior problem groups may give some clue to the nature of the interpersonal difficulties that they experience. Some evidence for this is noted in a study of adult outpatients in group psychotherapy.

Exner, Wylie, and Bryant (1974) collected peer preference nominations from subjects in four outpatient groups. All subjects had been administered the Rorschach prior to treatment by one of eight examiners who were naive to the purpose of the investigation. Two of the groups consisted of 10 subjects each, each group having two therapists and meeting twice weekly. The remaining two groups had one therapist each and met once a week. One of these groups had nine subjects and the second had eight subjects. The psychopathological manifestations varied across groups, although none of the subjects was schizophrenic or psychotic at the beginning of treatment. All groups were "coeducational," with two having a majority of females and two being equally divided. Although the orientations of the therapists differed considerably, the major focus in each group was primarily "transactional."

The peer nominations were collected after the fourth month of treatment, and consisted of 30 items, with two entries (most and least) for each item. They ranged over a variety of interpersonal preferences and behaviors, such as "most and least trusted," "attending a party with," "seeking advice from," "telling problems to," "borrowing money from," "going on a vacation with," "most humorous," "loaning a car to," "most intelligent," and so on. Subjects responded anonymously and under the condition that the information collected would *not* later be available to the group or to the therapists.

Ten of the 27 subjects had produced reflection answers in their Rorschachs. Seven of the 10 were consistently ranked "least" for 11 of the 30 items, and all 10 were ranked least for the "seeking advice from" and "telling problems to" items. Interestingly, the egocentricity index mean for these 10 subjects (.57) did not differ significantly from the mean index (.46) for 10 other subjects who tended to be rated "most" more than others in the groups. Another interesting finding is that the subjects who were mentioned with the lowest frequencies for all 30 items tended to have substantially lower egocentricity indices than did the other members of the groups. Four of the 27 subjects were not mentioned at all, and they had egocentricity indices of .25, .27, .29, and .33. A review of the 10 cases who did give reflection answers revealed that all would fall into the "hysteroid" or "immature" categories.

At one point, after the egocentricity index had been established, it was postulated that the index might have some direct relationship to either the Field Dependence-Independence phenomenon (Witkin, Dyk, Faterson, Goodenough, and Karp, 1962), or the Locus of Control *(I-E)* variable (Rotter, 1966). Data on this postulate were collected from 70 subjects—38 patients and 32 nonpatients—with the use of a rod and frame apparatus to measure field dependence and the *I-E* Scale to measure locus of control (Exner, Kuhn, Schumacher, and Fishman, 1975). Rorschachs were collected by examiners other than those collecting the rod and frame or *I-E* data. Rank order correlations show low positive, but not significant, relationships, between the egocentricity index and either of these variables *(3r + (2)/R vs.* Field Dependence *Rho = .24; 3r + (2)/R vs. I-E Rho = .21).*

Low egocentricity indices tend to appear with much greater frequency among the records of people with obsessive styles, such as obsessive-compulsives, depressives, phobics, and psychosomatics. The low index is also quite common in the records of effected adult suicides, but taken alone it is not a particularly good "predictor" of suicide proneness.[4]

The data from the OP study tend to confirm earlier findings (Exner, 1974) that a change in the egocentricity index, from too high or too low to the "normal range" of .30 to .40, is noted significantly more often for patients rated as improved than for patients who are not rated improved. This is illustrated by the data in Table 23. These data are shown with the seven treatment modalities divided into two groups, long term and short term, based on the average length of time in treatment. This format groups patients treated by dynamic psychotherapy, gestalt therapy, and modeling in the "long term" classification, and patients in the other four treatment groups in the "short term" classification.[5]

The data in Table 23 suggest that subjects who enter treatment with an egocentricity index in the average range of between .30 and .40 have a higher "success rate," as measured by ratings of significant others, than do subjects who enter treatment with the index higher or lower than that range. However, that datum must be approached very cautiously. There is no effort here to equate for pathology or chronicity of disturbance. It is quite possible that the sorts of difficulties shown by those with "normal" egocentricity scores are not as chronic or debilitating as those of the other two groups. In addition, it is important to note that a substantial number of subjects in the egocentricity "extreme" groups were rated improved, even though *they did not change the class of index.* This point is also

---

[4] The Egocentricity Index correlates with effected suicide at slightly higher than the .30 level, but higher correlations exist between the index and various psychopathological states in which no evidence of suicide is present. Thus, used as a single predictor variable, the index would identify a very high frequency of "false positives."

[5] This differentiation is somewhat arbitrary, since subjects in the treatment modalities classified as "short term" may have remained in treatment longer than some subjects in the "long term" modalities. In general, however, subjects in short term treatment had terminated before 12 months, while the majority of subjects in the long term modalities had remained in treatment beyond the 12th month.

Table 23. Frequencies of High, Low, and Normal Egocentricity Indices in Two Broad Groupings of Outpatients Rated after 28 Months as Improved or Unimproved by Ratings of Significant Others

Category	Treatment Groupings					
	Long Term ($N = 131$)			Short Term ($N = 148$)		
Egocentricity Index Classification	>.40	.30 to .40	<.30	>.40	.30 to .40	<.30
Pretreatment distribution	34	56	41	34	68	46
Rated improved after 28 months	17	49	31	16	52	34
Number improved who changed class of index	12*	4	22*	8*	7	21*
Rated unimproved after 28 months	17	7	10	18	16	12
Number unimproved who changed class of index	2	2	1	0	4	4

*Proportion of subjects showing change is significantly greater than for unimproved group at .05.

emphasized in the results of two "interlocking" studies of *successfully* treated schizophrenics (Exner and Murillo, 1973, 1977).

Two groups of chronic schizophrenic inpatients were followed in these studies. One group of 35 subjects had been treated with a modified form of electroconvulsive therapy plus psychotherapy, while the second group of 30 subjects were treated with either chlorpromazine or haloperidol plus psychotherapy. Thirty-two of the ECT patients, and 21 of the drug treated patients, progressed sufficiently to be discharged from hospitalization. Prior to treatment, the ECT group averaged .53 for the egocentricity index ($SD = .12$), while the drug treated group averaged .51 ($SD = .13$) for the index. The ECT subjects discharged from hospitalization showed a significant reduction in the mean index, to .38, while the discharged drug treated subjects continued to show a relatively high index (.47). During the first 12 postdischarge months, four ECT and five drug treated patients relapsed, but the egocentricity means for the "surviving" subjects remained essentially unchanged one year after discharge (ECT = .37; Drug = .51) *and three years after* discharge (ECT = .35; Drug = .53). It should be noted that ratings of social behavior taken one year after discharge favored the ECT subjects quite significantly, but this difference *did not appear* in the same ratings taken three years after discharge. By almost any standards, these subjects would be considered very successful treatment cases who are not simply "surviving," but rather, functioning very effectively in their respective environments. In this instance, the much higher egocentricity index of the drug treated group does not appear to be a handicap. This appears to be less true when the index is substantially lower than average. In the RE study, 16 of the 22 relapsing nonschizophrenics had egocentricity indices of less than .30 at discharge, while only four of the 55 nonrelapsers from this group fell below the .30 level.

It seems likely that the highly self-centered person is less prone to "malfunction" provided that he or she lives in an environment where self-centeredness is accepted and even encouraged. For instance, Winter and Exner (1973) tested 18 subjects who were successful performing artists with no psychiatric history. The $3r + (2)/R$ for this group averaged .48, with a range from .40 to .62, and *seven* of the records included reflection responses.

Although the egocentricity index is essentially related to "self focusing," the issue of "self-esteem" is probably also manifest, at least when the index is low. This hypothesis is derived from the very large number of depressed subjects who give a low index, and from the relatively high frequency of low indices among suicide prone subjects. On the other hand, when the index is significantly high, it should not be interpreted to indicate a form of self-glorification. Although that may be the case, it is possible that an excessive self-focus *is also related to low self-esteem;* that is, a high frequency of self-focusing behavior can be conceived as a defense or concealment of deeper feelings of little personal worth. There is a "hint" of support for this notion in the fact that about one in every five effected suicide cases, as will be noted in Chapter 7, do have higher than average egocentricity indices. On a more pragmatic level, it seems obvious that when the index is high or low, a potential for problems does exist, and if those problems are manifest, an alteration of the high or low index should be considered as one of the important treatment targets.

THE ACTIVE-PASSIVE RATIOS $(a:p, M^a:M^p)$

The decision to include the active-passive ratios in the Comprehensive System evolved from a series of studies, the results of which led to the conclusion that the basic $a:p$ ratio could provide useful information concerning cognitive constriction or flexibility. A proportional d score technique was devised which revealed that when the larger number in the ratio is three or more times greater than the smaller number in the ratio, an ideational "rigidity" or constriction tends to exist. Conversely, as the numbers in the ratio begin to approximate each other, a greater tendency toward ideational "flexibility" is displayed. It was noted that $a:p$ ratios indicating cognitive or ideational rigidity occur with a significantly higher frequency among patients (Exner, 1974).

The retest correlations in the Focal Study (.86 for active movement; .75 for passive movement) tend to bear out the proposition that there is a stylistic-like consistency to the psychological features reflected by the basic ratio. Correlations from the other retest studies, including those involving treatment for up to six months, cluster at the same level, or slightly higher than the Focal Study correlations.

The issue of cognitive or ideational rigidity is often important in understanding the persistence of seemingly "maladaptive" symptoms, and can be a major element of concern in forms of treatment that aim at cognitive alteration as a function of interpretation, such as in traditional forms of "uncovering" psychotherapy. Practically every therapist has encountered the patient who in one session seems to grasp an important interpretation very profoundly, then in the very next session deals with the same sort of material as if the interpretation had never occurred. Most therapists will interpret this phenomenon as a form of defensiveness or resistance; however, it may also be that cognitive rigidity tends to inhibit a full processing of the interpretation, *or,* if the full processing does occur, the inflexible ideational style is such that the interpretation cannot be "integrated" easily. Some support for this hypothesis is noted in the results of a small study of patients in an uncovering form of psychotherapy.

Exner and Wylie (1974) asked 11 psychoanalytically oriented psychotherapists each to "rate" the responsiveness of two of their patients in three sessions, separated by intervals of two weeks. All 22 patients had been administered the Rorschach previously as part of the OP study. All patient subjects had been in treatment for approximately 10 weeks, usually twice weekly, at the time of the first rating. The rating scale consisted of 20 items, 14 of which focused on the verbal and nonverbal behavior of the patient during the session, such as motor activity, periods of silence, tendency to change topics, aggressiveness, symptom focus, and so on, while the remaining six items concerned the therapist's evaluation of the session in terms of content, motivation, insight, progress, redundancy, *and* an overall evaluation of the session itself. Each item was rated on a scale from one to seven, with the midpoint representing a "not significant" or "average" rating, the higher ratings used for greater than average, and the lower ratings used for less than average. Neither the therapists nor the patients were aware of the purpose of the study.

These specific patients had been selected for evaluation on the basis of several Rorschach variables. Half had higher *ep* than *EA,* all had either high or low *Zd* scores, and the group split evenly for introversiveness or extratensiveness. In addition, 13 of the patients showed active-passive ratios in which one number in the ratio was substantially greater than the second number, while the remaining nine subjects had *a* :*p* ratios in which the values on each side were equal or nearly equal. The rating for the first of the three sessions was considered a "practice" trial and was not included in the data analysis, which focused on the composite of the second and third sessions. The data concerning patient verbal and nonverbal behaviors yielded very little differentiation for any of the selection variables, however, data for four of the six therapist evaluation items did differentiate significantly for the two *a* :*p* ratio groups.

Nine of the 13 patients with *a* :*p* ratios indicating "rigidity" were rated very low (ratings of 1 or 2) in *both* sessions, for insightfulness, progress, and therapist's overall evaluation of the session, and very high (ratings of 6 or 7) for redundancy. Conversely, seven of the nine patients with *a* :*p* ratios suggesting "flexibility" of ideation were rated in the opposite direction *on each of these four items for both sessions.* Although rating scales like this offer clear hazards for research because of the probable interrelationship of items, or the potential for "sets" in which one rating may influence the next, the data are not unimpressive; and it is important to point out that the two ratings used in the data analysis were taken two weeks apart. Certainly, during that interval the therapists conducted many sessions with a number of patients, thereby reducing the likelihood of a set carrying over from one rating to the next. If the results can be presumed reliable, it appears that the therapists did not find the majority of the *a* :*p* "rigid" subjects to be as productive or reinforcing as might have been expected or desired. In other words, they probably "liked" those patients less than they did the more flexible patients.

Some additional support for the *a* :*p* rigidity-flexibility hypothesis is derived from a study of "creative flexibility" (Exner and Bryant, 1974). Thirty high school students, ages 15 or 16, who had been tested as part of the nonpatient reference samples, were used as subjects. Fifteen (9 males and 6 females) were selected because their $a:p$ ratios indicated rigidity (all had zero on one side and a number greater than 4 on the second side), while the other 15 were selected because the $a:p$ ratio indicated flexibility (one side exceeded the other by two or less). All subjects had taken the junior level form of the Scholastic Aptitude Test (PSAT), and the two groups were not significantly different for either the verbal or the quantitative scores. Each subject was presented with a box containing eight items: a paper clip, a book of matches, a metal key, a wooden toothpick, a rubber sink stopper, a bandaid, a golf tee, and one foot of string. They were asked to write, within 20 minutes, as many uses for each of the items as they could formulate, using the item in its natural state or in some modified state (such as reshaping the paper clip into a fish hook). The test also permitted the creative use of two or more items combined—for example, using the paper clip as a fish hook, the key as a sinker, and the string as the fishing line. There was *no* significant difference between the groups for the total number of uses; however, the groups *did differ* significantly for the number of uses listed where the item is not used in its natural state, *and* for the number of uses combining items. In each case, the flexible $a:p$ group gave more responses.

The early work on the $a:p$ ratio did not uncover any important behavioral correlates except a "possible" relationship between a substantially greater number of passive responses and behavioral passivity. This relationship has been explored more extensively using subjects from the OP study. Eighty three of the 279 subjects in that study had $a:p$ ratios in which the passive movements exceeded active movements *by more than one,* such as 3:5, in the first retest after nine months of treatment. A composite index of behavioral passivity was devised. It was based on seven items of the *R1* Scale of the Katz Adjustment Scales (Katz and Lyerly, 1963), dealing with symptoms; nine items from the *R2* Scale, dealing with social behavior; and four items from the *R4* Scale, dealing with leisure activity. All 20 items represent behavioral features that are commonly identified with passiveness, for example, "seems helpless," "has few friends," "entertains very little," "can't make decisions," and so on. The ratings on these items provided by significant others at the ninth month were added to create a "passivity index." A control group of 83 cases was selected at random from the 196 OP subjects whose $a:p$ ratios did not show p exceeding a by more than one. A comparison of the mean passivity index scores yields a highly significant difference between the groups ($p < .01$), with those $a:p$ passive subjects scoring much higher for passive behaviors.

The findings of the OP study data concerning $a:p$ suggested a closer examination of the $M^a:M^p$ ratio (Exner, Armbruster, and Wylie, 1976). Twenty-four nonpatient adults were subjects in this study. All had at least six M responses in their Rorschach's, which had been collected among the reference samples. Twelve subjects gave more M^a than M^p, while the second 12 showed M^p exceeding M^a by more than one. Each subject was asked to write *endings* for each of six TAT stories. The stories, for Cards 1, 3BM, 8GF, 13B, 14, and 17BM, had been written to present the individual in the picture as being in a dilemma situation. The boy in the Card 1 story was presented as having trouble learning a difficult selection; the person in Card 3BM was featured as having lost a job; the woman in 8GF was described as learning that her husband was approaching bankruptcy; the boy in 13B was presented as having wandered away from a picnic and now was lost; the person in Card 14 had been rejected by a girl friend; and the man in 17BM was characterized as trying to escape from a burning apartment house. The story endings, written by the subjects, were given three scores each: one for a positive or negative outcome, the second for an outcome involving the "entry" of new people into the story, and the third for outcomes initiated by the "hero" of the story as against those in which the outcome is contingent on action initiated by someone else. Data regarding the characteristics of the story endings are shown in Table 24.

The data in Table 24 indicate that the high M^p subjects tend to include a new person in the story significantly more often, *and* that the story hero initiates the outcome of the story far less frequently than is the case for the high M^a group. For instance, a very common ending to the story about the lost little boy (13B), given by the high M^p subjects, was that the parent or a search party ultimately located him. Conversely, about half of the higher M^a group subjects ended the story with the boy retracing his way back to the picnic area. Eleven of the 12 high M^p subjects ended the 17BM story by indicating that firemen "came to the rescue," while nine of the 12 higher M^a subjects ended the story with the hero carefully climbing down the rope to safety. The Card 14 "lost girl friend" story showed a total differentiation of the two groups. The high M^p subjects either had the girlfriend changing her mind and returning, or a new girl contacting the hero. All high M^a subjects ended the story with the hero deciding to seek out a new girlfriend.

The combination of the two active-passive ratios will provide considerable information about the ideational, and possibly behavioral, tendencies of some subjects. The $a:p$ offers an input concerning the flexibility or rigidity of the cognitive operations, and when p is higher than a by more than one, there is a strong possibility of a form of behavioral passivity. It also seems that this flexibility-rigidity feature is evidenced in the $M^a:M^p$ ratio, although in many cases, the total number of M's is too small to permit drawing these conclusions about the deliberate ideational activity of the subject. Nonetheless, when the M^p exceeds the M^a by more than one, there is a higher probability that the fantasies of the subject will be marked by a "Snow-White" characteristic—that is, they will be fantasies in which

Table 24.   Characteristics of Six TAT Story Endings Provided by Two Groups of 12 Subjects Each, Differentiated on the Basis of the $M^a:M^p$ Ratio

	Groups	
	$M^p > M^a$	$M^a > M^p$
Characteristic	Endings = 72	Endings = 72
Outcome positive	65	61
Outcome negative	7	11
New person included in story	38*	17
Outcome initiated by hero	23	51*
Outcome initiated by person other than hero	49*	21

*Significantly greater than other group at .05.

the subject responds to events initiated by others, rather than directly initiates behavior.[6] Presumably the person with the high M^p frequency will be more difficult in the traditional therapy situations.

ORGANIZATIONAL ACTIVITY *(Zf; Zd)*

Data concerning the organizational activity of the subject during the test are often crucial for understanding other stylistic features reflected in the Structural Summary. The frequency *(Zf)* of organizational activity offers a clue about the extent to which the subject tries to "grapple" with the stimulus field in a way that is somewhat more psychologically demanding than other mediational approaches. The Z score is assigned to all W answers *that include form,* or to responses in which blot components have been meaningfully integrated. Either of these modes of approach, with the possible exception of a W response to Card V, requires greater mediational activity than the more economical response to a detail area that avoids integration. Every card, including Card V, includes at least one, and usually several, detail areas to which form dominant answers can be generated rather easily; yet most subjects do not follow this more economical route consistently throughout the test. Instead, the typical subject offers a variety of answers differing substantially in complexity, and many involving Z.

It is reasonably well established that Z correlates positively with intelligence (Exner, 1974), but the correlations that have been reported tend to cluster in the low to mid-.40s range, leaving a huge variance unaccounted. In fact, when subjects who are intellectually limited are eliminated from a sample, the correlations between Zf and/or ZSum and various indices of intellect are typically reduced to the mid-.30's. This suggests that while some basic intellectual talent is usually required for Z, the actual frequency and type of organization that occurs will be influenced by many other factors. Data from the reference samples indicate that most adults have Z in about 40% of their answers, and that more than half of those Z answers involve a W response. Younger clients have Z in about half of their responses, and typically, at least three of every four Z are assigned because of a W answer. The tendency of younger clients to give more Z and more W related Z answers probably results from a "devil may care" approach to the blots. Youngsters tend to respond more quickly and are generally less preoccupied with "taking the blot apart." Thus, any interpretation of Zf must always occur in the context of the W frequency. When W is relatively low, and Z is relatively high, there is evidence of a considerably greater attempt to organize than when W and Z are at about the same frequency.

A low Zf can be associated with intellectual limitations, or it can result from an

---

[6] As the fairy tale goes, Snow White's behavior was invariably initiated by others. She was encouraged to flee by a mirror, poisoned by a witch, preserved and protected by the dwarfs, and rescued by a prince. Few, if any, behaviors that she initiated were responsible for anything that happened to her. Passive fantasies like these are usually not oriented toward problem solving as such, but rather involve outcomes in which the actions of others are the crucial elements—for example, being selected to become a movie star while sitting at the counter of a lunchroom, or being informed of the death of a distant but generous relative who has bequeathed millions to the subject, and so on.

unwillingness to tackle the complexity of the stimulus field. A high *Zf* may be a product of intellectual striving, *or* it may indicate a need to deal more carefully and precisely with the stimulus field.

Although the *Zf* yields useful information about the psychological tendency of the subject to organize a stimulus field, it is the *Zd* score that provides data about the efficiency of the overall organizational effort. Approximately 75% of all nonpatient adults show *Zd* falling within the +3.0 to −3.0 range. Similarly, about 65% of all nonpatient children *above the six year level* have *Zd* scores within the ±3.0 range. Conversely, slightly less than 40% of the adult patient groups and about 35% of the younger client patient groups show *Zd* in that range. Patients, both adult and child, who manifest obsessive features tend to have *Zd* scores exceeding +3.0, while patients, both adult and child, who are prone to greater impulsiveness in their actions are prone to have *Zd* scores exceeding −3.0. Leura and Exner (1977) studied the protocols of 15 children, ages 8 to 11, who were behaviorally defined as "hyperactive" and who had abnormal EEG's. No less than 14 had *Zd* scores of −3.5 or more. A series of studies reveals that there are considerable differences between subjects at the two extremes of the *Zd* distribution.

Exner and Leura (1974) videotaped three groups of eight children each playing "Simon Says." All the children had been selected from the nonpatient reference sample pool. Fifteen were age 8 and nine were age 9. Four subjects in each group had *Zd* scores exceeding +3.0, while the other four had *Zd*'s greater than −3.0. Each group was instructed about the game before the test trials, and a teacher and the "game leader" demonstrated the procedure through four steps, such as, "Simon says put your hands on your knees, Simon says put your hands on your head, Simon says put your hands on your stomach, put your hands on your cheeks." The children in each group were told that they were competing, not against each other, but against two other groups, and that the "team" with the least number of errors would win a "special prize."[7] Thus, no child was eliminated from the "contest" if an error was made. Three trials were conducted, with 20 instructional steps in each trial, 11 including "Simon says" and the other nine omitting that critical preface. The videotapes were scored for "errors" by each of three technicians. The errors were divided into two categories: errors that displayed a gesture toward a mistake but did not complete the mistake, and errors that did complete the mistakes. During the first trial, the 12 children with *Zd*'s of −3.5 or greater made 51 mistakes or "near mistakes out of a possible 108, while the 12 children with *Zd*'s of +3.5 or greater made only 20 mistakes or near mistakes. In addition, the group with negative *Zd* scores made 18 incorrect movements to "Simon Says" instructions, for example, putting their hands on their hips when the instruction called for hands on legs. The high plus *Zd* group made only six such incorrect movements. During the second trial, the high negative *Zd* group made only slightly more mistakes than the high positive *Zd* group, and during the third trial the number or errors for the two groups were essentially the same, both being quite low. These findings suggest that the high negative *Zd* subjects are more prone to response before fully mediating the stimuli; that is, they *underincorporate* the stimulus field, while the high positive *Zd* subjects are more careful in their mediation of the stimuli. The results of a second study appear to confirm this postulate.

---

[7] The prize offered, and ultimately awarded to all teams, was an ice cream and cake party.

Exner and Caraway (1974) presented 20 college sophomores, selected on the basis of very high or very low *Zd* scores, with three groups of 10 stimuli each. Ten of the subjects had *Zd* scores exceeding +3.5, and the remaining 10 had *Zd*'s greater than −3.5. The two groups did not differ significantly for mean SAT Verbal scores. The stimuli were presented in an *incomplete* form, with one set consisting of movie titles, a second set of proverbs, and a third set drawn from book titles. The task of the subject, which was presented as a form of new intelligence test, was to try to identify the complete stimulus by working with only parts of the stimulus present. Each subject was tested individually by one of three examiners who were not familiar with the purpose of the investigation. Each item was first presented with only a few of the letters in the title or proverb displayed. At that time the subject would be permitted to "guess" the full stimulus, or "pass" and request an added *stimulus bit*. For example, the movie title *Gone with the Wind* was presented on the first trial as "__o__ _i__ t__ __i_d." The subject knew that the complete stimulus represented a proverb, book title, or movie title, but did not know which. Each subject was allowed to "guess" or "pass" as many times as necessary until the stimulus was correctly identified. There was *no* information imparted in the instructions about a limitation on the number of guesses or passes, nor were either implied to be more desirable than the other. At each pass or incorrect guess, one more letter was added to the stimulus material, with those letters appearing more critical to the solution reserved for later trials. Thus, for example, the sequence of information provided for "Gone With The Wind" was as follows:

Trial 1: "__o__ _i__ t__ __i_d"
Trial 2: "__o__ _i__ t_e __i_d"
Trial 3: "__o__ _i_h t_e __i_d"
Trial 4: "__o_e _i_h t_e __i_d"
Trial 5: "__o_e _i_h the __i_d"
Trial 6: "__one _i_h the __i_d"
Trial 7: "__one _i_h the __ind"
Trial 8: "__one _ith the __ind"
Trial 9: "__one with the __ind"
Trial 10: "__one with the Wind"
Trial 11: "Gone with the Wind"

The stimuli varied in length from a two word book title *(Don Quixote)* to an 11 word proverb ("A bird in the hand is worth two in the bush"). There was considerable variance among the subjects for trials to solution, but overall, the *underincorporators* (high negative *Zd*) used *slightly fewer* trials for the movie and book titles than did the overincorporators (high positive *Zd*), while the two groups took about the same number of trials to achieve correct solutions to the proverbs. The major difference between the two groups appears in the number of "passes" versus the number of "guesses." *The underincorporators guessed* almost three times as frequently as the overincorporators. This probably accounts for their slightly better performance on the movie and book title items. The overincorporators were very conservative with guesses, and often passed when almost all stimuli were present.

Bryant and Exner (1974) compared overincorporators and underincorporators for timed and untimed performance on the Minnesota Paper Form Board Test, which involves the ability to visualize the assembly of two dimensional geometric shapes into a whole design. The subjects for this study were 32 high school students, ages 15 to 17, selected from the nonpatient reference sample on the basis of the Zd score being greater than ± 3.0. Eight of the 16 overincorporators, and eight of the 16 underincorporators, were asked to take the test under a 10 minute time limit, while the remaining 16 subjects were asked to complete the test in as much time as they preferred. A comparison of the two groups operating under a time limit shows that the underincorporators completed almost twice as many problems as the overincorporators, but they also made proportionally more errors, so that the overall performances for correct items were about the same. Given unlimited time, the overincorporators consistently attempted more items and achieved significantly more correct solutions.

Similar results are noted in a serial learning task involving 24 nonpatient adult subjects (Exner and Bryant, 1975). The subjects were selected from an evening division continuing education program on the basis of Zd scores, 12 being above $+3.0$ and 12 exceeding -3.0. The task was to learn a serial of 16 nonsense syllables, with half the subjects in each group limited to 10 training trials, and the other half permitted an unlimited number of training trials. The underincorporator subjects who had been given only 10 training trials were able to identify the next syllable in the serial task correctly more than one-third as often as the overincorporators; *however,* the difference is largely due to the fact that underincorporators tended to "guess" more often, where the overincorporators would "pass" on items quite frequently. Conversely, when given unlimited time to learn the serial, the overincorporators were far superior to the underincorporators in the task.

The data from the reference samples, plus these few studies with nonpatients, indicates that overincorporators are more cautious, almost ruminative, in their approach to a stimulus field. They prefer situations in which they have sufficient time to evaluate stimulus cues carefully and fully, and having done so can formulate their response. Under time pressure, or probably under situations when the stimulus cues are less precise, they are uncertain and less secure than they would prefer and may well make inappropriate responses because of this. On the other hand, the underincorporator also makes many inappropriate or ineffective responses because he or she tends to reach conclusions prematurely. Underincorporators are more willing "risk takers" in the sense of trying to decipher complex stimuli without waiting for the "critical bits" of information to appear. Either of these conditions can contribute to a psychopathological state, and both are issues that can influence the progress of an intervention effort. Underincorporators tend to scan quickly and may often miss critical stimulus bits, while overincorporators are indecisive about what is truly critical and what is not. Both are mediationally inefficient in their respective styles, and this inefficiency can have a grave impact on other response tendencies. Obviously, if the Zd is inordinately high or inordinately low, this element should be considered in any treatment formulation, and it may well become a treatment target itself. For instance, the underincorporative child can probably be trained to delay using a variety of different tactics, such as the Simon Says game. A more careful processing of stimuli can, in turn, lead to a different form of behavioral response less "loaded" with inappropriateness. Similarly, the overincorporative person is potentially handicapped by his or her un-willingness to form responses before a meticulous study of the stimulus field has ensued. This tendency toward "dotting all i's and crossing all t's" is probably an asset in some situations, but it can quickly become a liability in a complex stimulus situation when response time is short.

CASE ILLUSTRATIONS

The material presented in this chapter has focused on six stylistic features; emotional control $(FC:CF+C)$, responsiveness to emotionally toned stimuli (Afr), approach or avoidance of complex stimuli $(Lambda)$, the self-focusing orientation (egocentricity index), ideational flexibility $(a:p, M^a:M^p)$, and organizational activity and efficiency (Zf, Zd). When data about these features are added to data from the Four Square, the descriptive yield is enhanced significantly, and many issues that can be raised using only Four Square data are narrowed or resolved; the yield is increased even more when data on perceptual accuracy $(F+\%, X+\%)$ are included. The latter assist in detecting subjects who have difficulty discriminating the real from the unreal, as well as those who are prone to perceive stimuli in their unique manner as against those who are strongly committed to a more precise stimulus interpretation. Severe perceptual dysfunctions will usually manifest themselves in a high frequency of minus answers, while the perceptually accurate, but more unique, "translator" will be illustrated by the high number of "weak" form quality responses. The more conservative, and less willing to be unique, person will rarely offer a poor form quality response, and will typically show both $F+\%$ and $X+\%$ in excess of 95.

The data relevant to the Four Square were presented for six cases in the preceding chapter, and limited descriptive statements about each of those subjects were generated using those data. The same cases are reviewed again here, beginning with a "recap" of the interpretation developed *only* from the Four Square, followed by an expanded interpretation using the Four Square data plus those derived from the six additional style indices discussed in this chapter. The structural data presented include number of responses (R) to afford a better understanding of the Lambda and the Afr, plus the actual frequencies of pairs (2) and $Fr+rF$ to aid in the translation of the egocentricity index.

Case 1

Male, age 27, high school graduate, married five years, wife age 24. They have one daughter, age 3. Current employment as a mail handler. No psychiatric history.

Interpretation from Four Square Data.   An extratensive subject who has a greater tendency toward emotional discharge in coping situations as contrasted with the tendency toward ideation in those circumstances. Although he has access to some important resources, he is also prompted by many psychological features that are not organized in a way to permit their controlled use. A bulk of these features are need states, including the natural experience of wanting more affection. *If* he experiences anxiety, the latter will probably be one of the primary causes. Al-

Case 1: Partial Structural Summary

R = 22   Zf = 9   ZSum =   P =   (2) = 8

Location Features			Determinants (Blends First)	Contents	Contents (Idiographic)

Location Features

			DQ
W	=		
D	=	+ =	
Dd	=	o =	
S	=	v =	
DW	=	— =	

Form Quality

FQx		FQf	
+	= 0	+ = 0	
o	= 17	o = 6	
w	= 4	w = 2	
—	= 1	— = 1	

M Quality

+	=
o	= 2
w	=
—	=

Determinants (Blends First)

FM.CF = 1
FM.FC = 1
m.FC' = 1

M	= 2
FM	= 2
m	=
C	=
CF	= 2
FC	= 2
C'	=
C'F	=
FC'	=
T	=
TF	=
FT	= 2
V	=
VF	=
FV	=
Y	=
YF	=
FY	=
rF	= 0
Fr	= 0
FD	=
F	= 9

Contents

H	=	
(H)	=	
Hd	=	
(Hd)	=	
A	=	
(A)	=	
Ad	=	
(Ad)	=	
Ab	=	
Al	=	
An	=	
Art	=	
Ay	=	
Bl	=	
Bt	=	
Cg	=	
Cl	=	
Ex	=	
Fi	=	
Fd	=	
Ge	=	
Hh	=	
Ls	=	
Na	=	
Sx	=	
Xy	=	

Contents (Idiographic)

	=
	=
	=
	=
	=
	=
	=
	=

Special Scorings

PSV	=
DV	=
INCOM	=
FABCOM	=
CONTAM	=
ALOG	=
	=

RATIOS, PERCENTAGES, AND DERIVATIONS

ZSum-Zest	=		FC:CF+C = 3:3	Atr	= .83
Za	= +2.0		W:M =	3r+(2)/R	= .36
EB	= 2:4.5	EA = 6.5	W:D —	Com:R	—
eb	= 5:3	ep = 8	L = .69	H+Hd:A+Ad =	
				(H)+(Hd):(A)+(Au) —	
Blends:R	= 3:22		F+% = .67	H+A:Hd+Ad =	
a:p	= 5:2		X+% = .77	XRT Achrom =	
Ma:Mp	= 1:1		A% =	XRT Chrom =	

though prone to emotional discharge, he becomes uncertain of his own controls at times and in those situations does inhibit their expression by internalization.

Expanded Interpretation. The fact that he does inhibit emotions at times is somewhat important, for he is more responsive to emotionally toned stimuli than most adults *(Afr),* and it seems clear that, in some circumstances, his emotional controls falter a bit and his behavior may become directed by the emotion rather than by logic *(FC:CF+C).* His reality testing is quite good *(F+%, X+%),* and he shows evidence of some flexibility in his thinking $(a:p)$. Although he may not be as psychologically sophisticated as many adults $(ep > EA)$, he is not overly self centered $(3r + (2)/R)$, and demonstrates the ability to "back away from" the more complex stimulus situations to avoid becoming too involved in them *(Lambda)*.

Comment.   Although the data thus far do not completely eliminate the presence of psychopathology, most findings are more positive than negative. He has a reasonably well established coping style, good reality testing, and does not appear to be overly troubled by negative emotions. He is more of an externalizing kind of person, and his greatest liability seems to be the fact that he has a bit too much *CF* present and that the *Afr* is somewhat high. These elements can create conditions for some forms of "acting out" behavior. Conversely, he may simply be a person who is more emotional than others, but not necessarily in self-destructive or antisocial ways. The missing data, which now become critical, include the frequency of Popular answers, which would yield some understanding of his awareness of conventionality; the $W:M$ ratio, which focuses on his aspirational level to determine whether he sets goals that are within the boundaries of his functional capabilities; the distribution of *DQ* scores, to reveal more about his cognitive sophistication; the presence or absence of special scores to provide more information on his ideational operations; the presence of human content, and particularly *pure H,* to focus more on his interest in people; and finally, the characteristics of his two *M* responses and of his three *CF* answers. Hopefully, he will not display aggressive or destructive *M*'s, or *M* in *Hd,* any of which could point to more pathology in this case than is now evident. Similarly, *CF* in Botany or Landscape responses would be preferable to *CF* in Explosions, Blood, or Fire.

Case 2

Female, age 28, single, lives alone, currently teaches 4th grade. Both parents living (ages 53 and 52), plus two siblings, female age 26, male age 24. No psychiatric history.

Interpretation of Four Square Data.   A person with a greater tendency to ideation than to emotional display under coping conditions. She has access to many psychological resources, but at this time is experiencing more "pain and/or irritation" than is common. She appears to feel helpless at times, and *possibly* feels "out of control" during those instances. Apparently, she is also introspective at this time, and that process may be contributing to her sense of irritation or anxiety.

Expanded Interpretation.   She is in serious trouble. Although prone to ideation in coping, she often develops fantasies that are oriented more toward escape than to direct problem solving $(M^a:M^p)$. There is also evidence to suggest that she is probably a more passive person than may be desirable for an effective adjustment $(a:p)$. She tends to approach her world in a precise and methodical manner *(Zd),* often devoting more time than may be efficient to the task of sorting out important from unimportant details. Although she tries to be precise in identifying a stimulus field, she often misinterprets cues by translating them in an overly personal manner $(F+\%,\ X+\%,$ *frequency of weak form quality answers)*; thus her reality

Case 2: Partial Structural Summary

R = 16   Zf = 7   ZSum =   P =   (2) = 4

Location Features		Determinants (Blends First)		Contents	Contents (Idiographic)
W =	DQ	M.FY = 1		H =	=
D =	+ =	FC.FY = 1		(H) =	=
Dd =	o =	m.CF = 1		Hd =	
S =	v =			(Hd) =	
DW =	— =	M = 4		A =	=
		FM = 1		(A) =	
		m =		Ad =	=
		C =		(Ad) =	
Form Quality		CF =		Ab =	=
		FC = 1		Al =	
FQx	FQf	C' =		An =	=
		C'F =		Art =	
+ = 0	+ = 0	FC' =		Ay =	=
o = 11	o = 2	T =		Bl =	
		TF = 1		Bt =	=
w = 3	w = 1	FT =		Cg =	
— = 2	— = 0	V =		Cl =	
		VF =		Ex =	**Special Scorings**
M Quality		FV = 1		Fi =	
		Y =		Fd =	
+ = 0		YF =		Ge =	PSV =
o = 3		FY =		Hh =	
		rF =		Ls =	DV =
w = 2		Fr =		Na =	INCOM =
— = 0		FD = 2		Sx =	FABCOM =
		F = 3		Xy =	CONTAM =
					ALOG =
					=

RATIOS, PERCENTAGES, AND DERIVATIONS

ZSum-Zest =		FC:CF+C = 2:1		Afr = .33	
Zd = +5.0		W:M =		3r+(2)/R = .25	
EB = 5:3.0	EA = 7.0	W:D =		Cont:R =	
eb = 2:4	ep = 6	L = .23		H+Hd:A+Ad =	
				(H)+(Hd):(A)+(Ad) =	
Blends:R = 3:16		F+% = .67		H+A:Hd+Ad =	
a:p = 2:5		X+% = .68		XRT Achrom =	
Ma:Mp = 2:3		A% =		XRT Chrom =	

testing will be "off target" at times, and this may cause her difficulties in her world. She tends to avoid emotionally provoking stimuli much more than most adults *(Afr),* and seems to place a lower value on herself than may be healthy *(3r + (2)/R).* She is very introspective *(FV +FD),* a process which, when added to her avoidance of emotionally loaded stimuli and her lower self esteem, suggests a potential for depression, or at least a feeling of being unable to cope effectively. She finds it difficult to extract herself from seemingly complex situations *(Lambda),* and although she appears capable of controlling her emotional displays reasonably well, internal emotions may contribute significantly to some of her problems in identifying stimulus cues more accurately.

Comment.   This introversive and overincorporating woman is experiencing far more internal disruption than would seem healthy. She delivers four shading determinants in this short record, and three of those four ($Y + V$) are of a less desired variety. Even the fourth, a *TF* rather than the more usual *FT,* does not portend well for her. Although the *FD* answer is correlated with a more objective and less emotional form of introspection, in this case it may reflect greater distancing from the self than is adaptive, and the high frequency of the *FD* indicates considerable activity of this sort. One of the blends involves both chromatic color and shading (*FC.FY*). These responses are often an indication of confused or mixed emotions as found in ambivalent experiences. Some of the more critical missing data include the presence or absence of *S,* to gain information about feelings of anger or negativism; the character of her *M* answers, and especially the presence of pure *H* versus the *(H)* or *Hd* contents; the distribution of Special Scores; and the characteristics of her two form quality minus responses. The fact that *EA* exceeds *ep* will require careful consideration in any treatment plan in that this relationship suggests a more "stabilized" psychological operation than if the reverse were true. If her condition is situational—that is, reactive, brief treatment should be reasonably successful; however, if the current condition overlays a long standing character problem or inadequately developed personality structure, the treatment modality and target priority will be crucial to successful intervention that will last over time.

Case 3

Female, age 31, one year of junior college completed, divorced recently, retaining custody of two children (male, age 9, female, age 7). No current employment. No psychiatric history.

Interpretation of Four Square Data.   A person with a greater tendency to discharge emotion in coping situations. In this instance, the *ep* is considerably larger than *EA,* suggesting that she does not have access to, or good command of, many of her resources. The *eb* is heavily weighted on the right side, consisting of four *T* and two *Y* responses. This indicates that she is experiencing an uncommonly intense irritation related to ungratified needs for emotional affiliation; and at times she also seems to sense a "helpless lack of control" over things happening to her and around her. At the same time, the preponderance of *FC* versus *CF* responses suggests that when she does act in accord with her extratensive style, most of her emotional displays will be reasonably well modulated. This seems to be a more "primitive" person who may be experiencing the emotional aftermath of her recent divorce, *or* there may be some other elements involved. The higher *ep,* plus the two *m*'s, plus the shading answers, suggests that she may not feel very "secure" in her thinking and/or behavior.

Expanded Interpretation.   She is much more responsive to emotionally toned stimuli than most adults *(Afr),* and while this does coincide with her basic coping

Case 3:   Partial Structural Summary

R = 25   Zf = 14   ZSum =   P =   (2) = 11

Location Features		Determinants (Blends First)	Contents	Contents (Idiographic)

Location Features

W	=		DQ
D	=	+	=
Dd	=	o	=
S	=	v	=
DW	=	—	=

Determinants (Blends First)

M.Fr = 1
FM.FC' = 1
FM.FY = 1
m.CF = 1
CF.YF.TF = 1

M	=	
FM	=	
m	=	1
C	=	
CF	=	1
FC	=	6
C'	=	
C'F	=	
FC'	=	
T	=	
TF	=	
FT	=	3
V	=	
VF	=	
FV	=	
Y	=	
YF	=	
FY	=	
rF	=	
Fr	=	
FD	=	1
F	=	8

Form Quality

FQx			FQf		
+	= 0		+	= 0
o	= 19		o	= 6
w	= 4		w	= 1
—	= 2		—	= 1

M Quality

+	= 0
o	= 1
w	= 0
—	= 0

Contents

H	=	
(H)	=	
Hd	=	
(Hd)	=	
A	=	
(A)	=	
Ad	=	
(Ad)	=	
Ab	=	
Al	=	
An	=	
Art	=	
Ay	=	
Bl	=	
Bt	=	
Cg	=	
Cl	=	
Ex	—	
Fi	=	
Fd	=	
Ge	=	
Hh	=	
Ls	=	
Na	=	
Sx	=	
Xy	=	

Contents (Idiographic)

=
.... =
.... =
.... =
.... =
.... =
.... =
.... =
.... =
.... =
....
.... =
....

Special Scorings

PSV	=
DV	=
INCOM	=
FABCOM	=
CONTAM	=
ALOG	=
	=

RATIOS, PERCENTAGES, AND DERIVATIONS

ZSum−Zest	=			FC:CF+C	= 6:3	Afr	= .92
Zd	= −4.5			W:M	=	3r+(2)/R	= .56
EB	− 1:6.0	EA = 7.0		W:D	=	Cont:R	=
eb	= 4:7	ep = 11		L	= .47	H+Hd:A+Ad =	
						(H)+(Hd):(A)+(Ad) =	
Blends:R	= 5:25			F+%	= .75	H+A:Hd+Ad	=
a:p	= 5:0			X+%	= .75	XRT Achrom	=
Ma:Mp	= 1:0			A%	=	XRT Chrom	=

style *(EB)*, this responsiveness exacerbates her intense need for emotional affiliation. She is also much more self-centered than most adults *(3r + (2)/R)* and at times may be more juvenile in this self-centeredness than is useful *(1 Fr)*. She is the sort of person who may become overly involved in complex stimuli *(Lambda)*, and will often tend to misinterpret some of those stimuli because she is not careful enough in sorting out the importance of various cues *(Zd)*. She tries to organize her world *(Zf)*, but her tendencies toward underincorporation, plus her excessive responsiveness to emotional stimuli, may greatly reduce the effectiveness of this effort. She often feels helpless when prompted by her more basic needs *(both FM's are blended with FY)*, and probably experiences more feelings of being out of control than is customary for the adult. Her reality testing is adequate $(F+\%, X+\%)$, but her ideation is often characterized by less flexibility than might be desired $(a:p)$, especially in that she will probably need to be flexible to meet her strong emotional needs. It may be that her self-centeredness, plus her tendency to overrespond to emotionally loaded stimuli, interfere with the development and/or maintenance of mature interpersonal relations. She is not as psychologically sophisticated as many adults $(ep > EA)$, and overall problems of maturational failure may be contributing to her current status.

Comment.   This is a challenging record because there is still no clear evidence on the basis of which to distinguish a postdivorce form of reactive helplessness from the more long standing immaturity reaction. In fact, one condition may be superimposed on the other, although the most notable feature at this point remains the very high T frequency. Possibly, the most critical missing data here are the frequencies of human content, especially pure H, and the character of those content. Very immature and dependent people tend to use more (H) and Hd, and will generally report "nonadults" (children, elves, infants, etc.). None of her movement answers are passive, a fact that reduces the likelihood of a long standing dependency phenomenon. However, her cognitive operations do appear somewhat rigid, and her underincorporateness cannot help but cause some problems in her environmental interactions, especially since she is so markedly extratensive and so overly responsive to emotionally toned stimuli. Any treatment plan should include a focus on the underincorporation and probably some reduction in her excessive responsiveness to emotionally loaded and complex stimulus situations. The $W:M$ ratio will also be important here, to determine something about her aspirational level, for it may be that she is targeting on goals which exceed her current level of maturity and/or functioning.

Case 4

Male, age 26, high school graduate, single, lives at home with parents (both age 48). Older female sibling (age 28) has been married for five years. He is currently employed as an auto mechanic. No psychiatric history.

Interpretation of the Four Square Data.   This configuration suggests real problem potential. The EB reflects the ambient, who may tend to vacillate in coping situations, although he does have the capacity for either ideation or emotional discharge in those situations. The considerably higher ep indicates the presence of many psychological features that are not accessible yet account for much stimulation to behavior. This more primitive state is compounded by the presence of a pure C response and the absence of FC answers, suggesting that when he does display affect, it probably tends to "get out of control." The presence of three C' answers may indicate that he has some awareness of this and is attempting to contain emotion more. The absence of T raises an important question about his interpersonal relations. He may be experiencing the irritations of helplessness or loss of control.

Case 4:   Partial Structural Summary

R = 20   Zf = 12   ZSum =   P =   (2) = 10

Location Features		Determinants (Blends First)		Contents		Contents (Idiographic)	
W =	DQ	M.VF	=1	H =			=
D =	+ =	FM.CF	=1	(H) =		....	
		FM.FC'	=1	Hd =			=
Dd =	o =	m.CF	=1	(Hd) =		....	
				A =			=
S =	v =			(A) =		....	
				Ad =			=
DW =	— =	M = 2		(Ad) =		....	
		FM = 2		Ab =			=
		m = 1		Al =		....	
		C = 1		An =			=
Form Quality		CF =		Art =		....	
		FC =		Ay =			=
FQx	FQf	C' =		Bl =		....	
		C'F = 1		Bt =			=
+ = 0	+ = 0	FC' = 1		Cg =		....	
		T =		Cl =			
o = 9	o = 3	TF =		Ex =		Special Scorings	
		FT =		Fi =			
w = 3	w = 1	V =		Fd =		PSV =	
		VF =		Ge =			
— = 6	— = 2	FV =		Hh =		DV =	
		Y = 1		Ls =			
M Quality		YF =		Na =		INCOM =	
		FY = 1		Sx =			
+ =		rF =		Xy =		FABCOM =	
		Fr =					
o = 1		FD =				CONTAM =	
		F =					
w =						ALOG =	
							=
— = 2							

RATIOS, PERCENTAGES, AND DERIVATIONS

ZSum-Zest =		FC:CF+C = 0:3		Afr = .43	
Zd = +5.0		W:M =		3r+(2)/R = .50	
EB = 3:3.5	EA = 6.5	W:D —		Cont·R =	
eb = 6:6	ep = 12	L = .43		H+Hd:A ∣ Ad =	
				(H)+(Hd):(A)+(Ad) —	
Blends:R = 4:20		F+% = .50		H+A:Hd+Ad =	
a:p = 7:2		X+% = .45		XRT Achrom —	
Ma:Mp = 1:2		A% =		XRT Chrom =	

Expanded Interpretation.   This begins to look very much like a schizophrenic case. Reality testing is quite limited and marked by substantial distortion ($F+\%$, $X+\%$, frequency of minus responses). He is more self centered than most adults ($3r + (2)/R$), and appears to be trying to avoid emotionally provoking stimuli (Afr). The latter effort may be due to his very poor emotional controls ($FC:CF+C$, 1 pure C), which will often create a situation in which he is directed by emotion rather than by intellect. Two of the three M answers are minus, indicating some significant ideational distortion, which may be compounded by indications of cognitive or ideational rigidity ($a:p$). Unfortunately, he does not seem to be able to back away from complex stimuli as much as would be useful *(Lambda)*, but instead seems to attempt to organize complex stimulus fields more often than is economical *(Zf)*. In doing so, he will often be overly cautious and at times unable to discriminate easily between important and unimportant stimuli *(Zd)*. He is now experiencing excessive internal emotional disruption *(eb)*, and apparently some of his ideation leads to a negative form of self-inspection (*M.VF*). The composite of poor reality testing, apparent ideational distortion, and poor emotional control sets the stage for major psychological disarray, and his somewhat limited accessible resources (*ep > EA*) do not appear sufficient for effective coping.

Comment. The critical missing data here consist of the distribution of Special Scores and information on Human content. The former are especially important to the identification of a true thought disturbance, while the absence of pure Human content is not uncommon among schizophrenics. The nature of the *M* responses, especially the two minus answers, will also contribute to any final diagnostic decision. The overincorporativeness, *in a case such as this*, may relate to some forms of supersuspicious or paranoid-like ideation. If this is true, the remainder of the structural data will probably include a greater than normal emphasis on human and animal details, a higher than average use of *S*, and a higher frequency of *Dd* answers. The reaction time data may also provide important insights here. If reaction time is long, especially for those cards in which minus responses occur, the condition may be more "severe," since this indicates a struggle to translate the stimulus, a struggle that is ultimately unsuccessful. Very brief reaction times tend to indicate more of a problem in control and delay.

Case 5

Female, age 13, single, living at home with both natural parents, currently in 8th grade but not doing very well. No work history. No psychiatric history.

Interpretation from the Four Square Data. An ambitent who may tend to vacillate in coping situations. Although the higher *ep* is less cause for concern at this age level, the ambitent status may be a potential problem warranting closer evaluation. An apparently more important issue here is the high frequency of *FC* responses. This response pattern is quite uncommon among youngsters of this age and raises questions about overcontrol. The presence of one *V* determinant may reflect the natural self-examination of the young adolescent, or it may relate to some identity problems that are not uncommon at this age.

Expanded Interpretation. A picture of a somewhat isolated and not very secure youngster may be unfolding here. She is an overincorporator, and may have difficulty discriminating important from unimportant stimulus cues *(Zd)*. The previously mentioned preponderance of *FC* answers becomes more important in the light of the relatively low *Afr*, suggesting a tendency to avoid emotionally provocative stimuli. Thus, it appears that she exerts more control over emotional displays than do most adolescents, because she is not comfortable with those displays. Some indirect support for this proposition is noted in her substantially

Case 5:   Partial Structural Summary

R = 21   Zf = 10   ZSum =   P =   (2) = 7

Location Features		DQ	Determinants (Blends First)	Contents		Contents (Idiographic)
W =			FM.FC = 1	H =		=
D =	+ =		m.CF = 1	(H) =		=
Dd =	o =		FT.FV = 1	Hd =		
S =	v =			(Hd) =		=
DW =	— =			A =		
			M = 3	(A) =		=
			FM = 4	Ad =		
			m =	(Ad) =		=
			C =	Ab =		
Form Quality			CF =	Al =		=
			FC = 2	An =		
FQx	FQf		C' =	Art =		=
			C'F =	Ay =		
+ = 0	+ = 0		FC' =	Bl =		=
			T =	Bt =		
o = 20	o = 9		TF =	Cg =		
			FT =	Cl =		
w = 1	w = 0		V =	Ex =		**Special Scorings**
			VF =	Fi =		
— = 0	— = 0		FV =	Fd =		PSV =
			Y =	Ge =		
M Quality			YF =	Hh =		DV =
			FY =	Ls =		
+ = 0			rF =	Na =		INCOM =
			Fr =	Sx —		
o = 3			FD =	Xy =		FABCOM =
			F = 9			CONTAM =
w = 0						ALOG =
— = 0						=

RATIOS, PERCENTAGES, AND DERIVATIONS

ZSum–Zest =			FC:CF+C = 3:1		Afr = .50	
Zd	= +3.5		W:M =		3r+(2)/R = .33	
EB	= 3:2.5	EA = 5.5	W:D =		Cont:R =	
eb	= 6:2	ep = 8	L = .75		H+Hd:A+Ad = (H)+(Hd):(A)+(Ad) =	
Blends:R	= 3:21		F+% = 100		H+A:Hd+Ad =	
a:p	= 5:4		X+% = .95		XRT Achrom. —	
Ma:Mp	= 1:2		A% =		XRT Chrom =	

low self-focus $(3r + (2)/R)$, which may be another signal that she is not very self-confident. Her perceptual accuracy, or reality testing, is better than is usually found in youngsters of this age $(F+\%, X+\%)$, which may reflect an orientation to avoiding mistakes. This orientation, possibly, relates to her tendency toward overincorporativeness. While her ideation appears to be marked by flexibility $(a:p)$, there is also evidence that she may become overly "wrapped up" in passive fantasies $(M^a:M^p)$, a tendency that can contribute to some forms of social isolation.

Comment. Had the *Afr* and egocentricity index been considerably higher, there would be less cause for concern in this case. However, the fact that she appears to be avoiding emotionally toned stimuli, *and* shows less self-focus than most adolescents, *and* is somewhat overcontrolled in her emotional displays, can spell trouble, now and in the future. The missing data that are most crucial to a better understanding of this youngster include the Human content, the frequency of Popular answers, and information on her self-concept. The latter cannot usually be derived from structural data, but instead must be gleaned from the character and content of her verbal material. Her overincorporativeness may be cause for concern; however, that is difficult to judge without more information about her self-concept. If she is becoming more overincorporative in order to avoid being singled out for mistakes, the problem can be more serious than if her overincorporativeness is simply an attempt to identify better the demands of her world. The blend of *FT.FV* is also some cause for concern here. It reflects two uses of shading in the same percept, but, more important, it represents a strong "pain" experience, occurring in a single psychological operation, that involves both a need for greater emotional affiliation and a negative experience produced by some form of self-inspection. This is an unusual composite, and it may signal more irritation than is evident in the available data. Finally, her high $F+\%$ and $X+\%$ suggest that she is less willing to be individualistic than most youngsters or adults. A loss of uniqueness this early in life can be a major liability later on, and this feature should be a major target of any intervention efforts.

Case 6

Female, age 24, married, no children, one year of junior college plus one year of business school. Husband, age 24, employed in management training position. She is employed as an executive secretary. No psychiatric history.

Interpretation from the Four Square Data.   A fairly "well put together" person. She is prone to emotional display when coping, but she also demonstrates an obvious capacity for ideation under those circumstances. She has "good" access to many of her resources, and when acted upon by features that are not in her "organized" psychological structure, most of that action appears related to "need" states, including a natural desire for emotional affiliation.

Expanded Interpretation.   The added data tend to coincide with the earlier speculations developed from the Four Square alone. Her emotional controls appear effective $(FC:CF+C)$, and she is about as responsive to emotionally toned stimuli as most nonpatient adults *(Afr)*. She is appropriately self-focusing $(3r+(2)/R)$ and has very adequate reality testing $(F+\%, X+\%)$. Her ideation shows some flexibility $(a:p)$; she is concerned with organizing her stimulus world, but not overly so *(Zf)*; and when she does organize, the effort is generally marked by efficiency *(Zd)*. She probably becomes overinvolved with complex stimuli a bit more than most people *(Lambda)*, but the nature of her resources, controls, and reality testing all indicate that she is well prepared to handle such situations effectively.

Case 6:   Partial Structural Summary

R = 24   Zf = 10   ZSum =   P =   (2) = 9

Location Features			Determinants (Blends First)		Contents		Contents (Idiographic)	
W	=	DQ			H	=		=
			M.FC	= 2	(H)	=	....	
D	=	+ =	M.FT	= 1	Hd	=		=
			FM.FC	= 2	(Hd)	=	....	
Dd	=	o =	FM.FC'	= 1	A	=		=
					(A)	=	....	
S	=	v =			Ad	=		=
					(Ad)	=	....	
DW	=	— =	M	= 1	Ab	=		=
			FM	= 1	Al	=	....	
			m	=	An	=		=
			C	=	Art	=	....	
Form Quality			CF	= 3	Ay	=		=
			FC	= 4	Bl	=	....	
FQx		FQf	C'	=	Bt	=		=
			C'F	=	Cg	=	....	
+	= 1	+ = 0	FC'	=	Cl	=		
			T	=	Ex	=	Special Scorings	
o	= 18	o = 6	TF	=	Fi	=		
			FT	= 1	Fd	=		
w	= 3	w = 2	V	=	Ge	=	PSV	=
—	= 2	— = 0	VF	=	Hh	=		
			FV	=	Ls	=	DV	=
M Quality			Y	=	Na	=		
			Yr	=	Sx	=	INCOM	=
+	= 1		FY	=	Xy	=		
			rF	=			FABCOM	=
o	= 3		Fr	=			CONTAM	=
w	= 0		FD	=			ALOG	=
—	= 0		F	= 8				=

RATIOS, PERCENTAGES, AND DERIVATIONS

ZSum-Zest	=		FC:CF+C	= 8:3	Afr		= .60
Zd	= +1.0		W:M	=	3r+(2)/R		= .38
ER	= 4:7.0	EA = 11.0	W:D	=	Com:R		=
eb	= 4:3	ep = 7	L	= .50	H+Hd:A+Ad = (H)+(Hd):(A)+(Ad) =		
Blends:R	= 6:24		F+%	= .75	H+A:Hd+Ad		=
a:p	= 5:3		X+%	= .79	XRT Achrom.		—
Ma:Mp	= 2:2		A%	=	XRT Chrom		=

Comment.   This subject continues to reflect a fine level of adjustment when other data are added. The critical data still missing concern her Human content, the distribution of *DQ* scores, and her self-concept as manifest in the verbal material. It seems likely that she will deliver a sufficient number of Popular answers, and probably her range of contents will indicate a healthy interest in a variety of things. At this point, there is no evidence of maladjustment. Quite the contrary, this record appears as "solid" as any of the six presented thus far.

SUMMARY

Each of the six records presented here is far from complete. In two cases (No. 2, the 28 year old single teacher; and No. 4, the 26 year old auto mechanic), the presence of psychopathology is almost certain, and further evaluation will involve issues of more precise diagnosis, intensity of the condition, and treatment formulation. In two other cases (No. 3, the 31 year old divorcee; and No. 5, the 13 year old high school student), there are apparent problems, but in each instance it is not clear whether they are situationally related or more chronic, *or* how debilitating they may be. The remaining two cases (No. 1, the 27 year old mail handler; and No. 6, the 24 year old married executive secretary) appear to reflect reasonably "healthy" protocols, although they differ considerably for maturity, controls, and the like. The remaining features of the Structural Summary, plus the Sequence of Scores, plus an analysis of the verbal material, will confirm, add to, or alter interpretative propositions that have developed thus far; but generally, revisions of those propositions will be very nominal, since all are based on the more sturdy features of the test.

The six records will be presented in their entirety in the subsequent chapters in addition to other protocols with similar, but also different, features that will illustrate how individuals, both adjusted and maladjusted, have some traits in common yet retain their own, very personal, idiographies.

REFERENCES

Beck, S. J. *Rorschach's Test. II: A Variety of Personality Pictures.* New York: Grune and Stratton, 1945.

Bryant, E. L., and Exner, J. E. Performance on the Revised Minnesota Paper Form Board Test by under and overincorporators under timed and nontimed conditions. Workshops Study No. 188 (unpublished), Rorschach Workshops, 1974.

Exner, J. E. Rorschach responses as an index of narcissism. *Journal of Projective Techniques and Personality Assessment,* 1969, **33**, 437–455.

Exner, J. E. *The Rorschach: A Comprehensive System.* New York: John Wiley and Sons, 1974.

Exner, J. E., Armbruster, G. L., and Mittman, B. L. The Rorschach response process. *Journal of Personal Assessment,* 1978, **42**, 27–38.

Exner, J. E., Armbruster, G. L., and Wylie, J. R. TAT stories and the $M^a:M^p$ ratio. Workshops Study No. 225 (unpublished), Rorschach Workshops, 1976.

Exner, J. E., and Bryant, E. L. Flexibility in creative efforts as related to three Rorschach variables. Workshops Study No. 187 (unpublished), Rorschach Workshops, 1974.

Exner, J. E., and Bryant, E. L. Serial learning by over and underincorporators with limited and unlimited numbers of training trials. Workshops Study No. 194 (unpublished), Rorschach Workshops, 1975.

Exner, J. E., and Caraway, E. W. Identification of incomplete stimuli by high positive Zd and high negative Zd subjects. Workshops Study No. 186 (unpublished), Rorschach Workshops, 1974.

Exner, J. E., Kuhn, B., Schumacher, J., and Fishman, R. The relation of Field Dependence and Locus of Control to the Rorschach index of egocentricity. Workshops Study No. 189 (unpublished), Rorschach Workshops, 1975.

Exner, J. E., and Leura, A. V. "Simon says" errors and the *Zd* score in young children. Workshops Study No. 204 (unpublished), Rorschach Workshops, 1974.

Exner, J. E., and Leura, A. V. Rorschach performances of volunteer and nonvolunteer adolescents. Workshops Study No. 238 (unpublished), Rorschach Workshops, 1977.

Exner, J. E., Leura, A. V., Armbruster, G. L., and Viglione, D. A focal study of temporal consistency. Workshops Study No. 253 (unpublished) Rorschach Workshops, 1977.

Exner, J. E., and Murillo, L. G. Effectiveness of regressive ECT with process schizophrenia. *Diseases of the Nervous System,* 1973, **34,** 44–48.

Exner, J. E., and Murillo, L. G. Early prediction of posthospitalization relapse. *Journal of Psychiatric Research,* 1975, **12,** 231–237.

Exner, J. E., and Murillo, L. G. A long term followup of schizophrenics treated with regressive ECT. *Diseases of the Nervous System,* 1977, **38,** 162–168.

Exner, J. E., and Wylie, J. R. Therapist ratings of patient "insight" in an uncovering form of psychotherapy. Workshops Study No. 192 (unpublished), Rorschach Workshops, 1974.

Exner, J. E., Wylie, J. R., and Bryant, E. L. Peer preference nominations among outpatients in four psychotherapy groups. Workshops Study No. 199 (unpublished), Rorschach Workshops, 1974.

Exner, J. E., Wylie, J. R., and Kline, J. R. A long term study of treatment effects as manifest in Rorschach performance. Workshops Study No. 240 (unpublished), Rorschach Workshops, 1977.

Goldman, R. Changes in Rorschach performance and clinical improvement in schizophrenia. *Journal of Consulting Psychology,* 1960, **24,** 403–407.

Hafner, A. J. Response time and Rorschach behavior. *Journal of Consulting Psychology,* 1958, **14,** 154–155.

Henry, E. M., and Rotter, J. B. Situational influences on Rorschach responses. *Journal of Consulting Psychology,* 1956, **20,** 457–462.

Katz, M., and Lyerly, S. Methods of measuring adjustment and social behavior in the community. *Psychological Reports,* 1963, **13,** 503–535.

Klopfer, B., Ainsworth, M. D., Klopfer, W. G., and Holt, R. R. *Developments in the Rorschach Technique. I: Theory and Technique.* Yonkers-on-Hudson, N.Y.: World Book Co., 1954.

Leura, A. V., and Exner, J. E. Some Rorschach characteristics of a group of hyperactive children with abnormal EEG's. Workshops Study No. 239 (unpublished), Rorschach Workshops, 1977.

Raychaudhuri, M., and Mukerji, K. Homosexual-narcissistic "reflections" in the Rorschach: An examination of Exner's diagnostic Rorschach signs. *Rorschachiana Japonica,* 1971, **12,** 119–126.

Rotter, J. B. Generalized expectancies for internal versus external control of reinforcement. *Psychological Monographs,* 1966, **80,** Whole No. 609.

Stotsky, B. A. A comparison of remitting and nonremitting schizophrenics on psychological tests. *Journal of Abnormal and Social Psychology,* 1952, **47,** 489–496.

Winter, L. B., and Exner, J. E. Some psychological characteristics of successful theatrical artists. Workshops Study No. 183 (unpublished), Rorschach Workshops, 1973.

Witkin, H. A., Dyk, R. B., Faterson, H. F., Goodenough, D. R., and Karp, S. A. *Psychological Differentiation.* New York: John Wiley and Sons, 1962.

CHAPTER 6

The Finished Interpretation

The material covered in the preceding chapters has focused on just a few of the many variables in a Rorschach protocol. To be sure, those few variables represent the nuclear data of the test—that is, they are both highly reliable and valid as indicators of some of the more basic features of the personality. Taken separately or analyzed collectively, they reveal much about the Rorschach subject.

Nevertheless, they fall far short of providing the full description of the subject that is possible only when the complete protocol is used. The Structural Summary, taken alone, contains a potential for at least 104 variables in a record *void* of blends or idiographic contents. The absence of many of these variables is often as important to interpretation as their presence. There are an astronomical number of possible scoring combinations that may appear in the Sequence of Scores in even a relatively brief protocol; and the unique combinations of verbal material are almost infinite. It is the use of all of this material, beginning with the structural basics and proceeding carefully through the entire Structural Summary, the scoring sequence, and a review of the verbal material, that will yield the finished Rorschach interpretation. This is not a lengthy task, requiring days of rumination, but it is one that requires thoroughness, logic, and, possibly most important, a knowledge of people.

The concepts of "normality" and "psychopathology" are often very elusive. If normality is defined in terms of a statistical norm, then any uniqueness becomes "abnormal." If normality is defined in terms of the economical conservation of energy when performing a task, then the person who "works harder" must be abnormal. If normality is defined in terms of social values, then any form of nonconformity becomes abnormal. All people have assets and all people have liabilities. All people experience pain, and all people experience pleasure; and, fortunately, all people are unique and different from all other people. The finished Rorschach interpretation should focus on this uniqueness in terms of the assets and liabilities of the subject. It is a *descriptive* interpretation from which the intelligent professional can, within cautious guidelines, draw some logical conclusions and even make some logical predictions. The Rorschach, however, is generally not at its best when used predictively, for the data reflect the present more than either the past or the future, and statements about the past or the future must be of a more speculative nature. For instance, one of the greatest values of the Rorschach is its use for treatment planning. This is not because any particular Rorschach variable can be equated with a particular form of treatment, but rather because the Rorschach will reflect the liabilities of the subject. These can be conceptualized in terms of targets for treatment. In other words, what features of the Rorschach will hopefully be altered as a result of intervention? It is at this point that the interpreter should review his or her knowledge of the variety of intervention modalities as they relate to the relevant targets, asking which of the several available intervention modalities has the greatest expectancy of promoting the desired "change"

Possibly the most important caution to be exercised in Rorschach interpretation concerns the interpreter rather than the test. Most subjects who are administered the Rorschach have problems, and the focus of interpretation is usually oriented to gaining a better understanding of these problems in terms of the cause, character, and correction of the dysfunction. Unfortunately, interpretations often tend to concentrate on the dysfunction and can be very misleading because they neglect to emphasize adequately the positive, and possibly more salient, features of the person. Although these "distorted" interpretations are often a result of "professional sets," or of styles of report writing, some of the distortions may occur because the interpreter is not sufficiently familiar with test data from nonpatients. Normative reference data are useful as guidelines, and are essential to any empirically established test; but deviations from normative reference data do not always signal pathology or undesired characteristics. Therefore, a finished interpretation must be balanced, emphasizing both assets and liabilities. The desired balance is possibly best illustrated by the use of four protocols here. All have been taken from nonpatients, and all will reflect marked liabilities. However, when these liabilities are considered in the context of the assets which are apparent, their importance to the interpretation is considerably reduced.

SOME NONPATIENT PROTOCOLS

The records of three adults and one child are included here. They were drawn from the reference pool of nonpatients at random, with the exception that one protocol would be from a child, and one would reflect an instance in which *ep* exceeded *EA*. Data from two of these records have been included in the preceding chapters as Cases 1 and 6; thus, it seems appropriate to complete those interpretations before presenting the two new records.

Case 1: A 27 Year Old Male

History.   This man was born and raised in a large city. He is the second of four children, having a brother, age 30, and two sisters, ages 23 and 21. His father, age 58, is a telephone repair supervisor, and his mother has been working for the past five years in a bakery. The subject completed high school at age 18 and spent the next two years in the Army; one as a rifleman in Viet Nam. After being honorably discharged, he worked for one year in a laundry as a presser, and since then has been employed by the postal service as a mail sorter. He reportedly enjoys his work and has no plans for an occupational change. Shortly after obtaining his present employment, he married a woman three years younger than himself whom he had met while working at the laundry. She is also a high school graduate and has completed a few courses in liberal arts at a community college. She continued to work at the laundry during their first two years of marriage until she become pregnant. They now have a three year old daughter, and she has no plans to return to work for at least two more years. Two years ago, they purchased a cooperative apartment and feel that they are establishing "roots" in a new neigh-

Case 1

Card	Free Association	Inquiry	Scoring
I	8″		
	1. These are kinda funny aren't they, like I suppose it c.b. a bat if u thk about it That's it. E: If you look at it a bit longer u mite find s.t. else, most people do	E: (Rpts S's resp) S: Well let's c, this part c.b. the body part & ths c.b. the wgs out here. It just kinda gives tht impression if u use u'r mind a little	Wo Fo A P 1.0
	2. Well I guess it c.b. lik a face, not a real face but lik a mask of a face, like an A mask That's really all I can find	E: (Rpts S's resp) S: Yeah, w the big ears out lik a fox or s.t., c the white parts here r kinda slanted lik foxes hav & this is the nose & the mouth down here	WS+ Fo Mask 3.5
II	14″		
	3. Hey, ths is a weird one, like 2 bears really in a big fite w. e.o., man they'r hurt too	E: (Rpts S's resp) S: Yeah, well thy got blood all over themselves, mayb thy aren't hurt but the bld mite be from whatever thyr fiting over lik s.o. animal tht thy killed E: Can u show me some of the features S: Sure, c up here is the heads & the kinda big body & c the red on the heads & down here wld b the bld, its pretty messy	$W+$ $FM^a.CFo$ (2) A (P) 4.5
	4. U kno this red part here c.b. lik one of those hard shell crabs u c on the beach s.t's.	E: (Rpts S's resp) S: Yeah, u kno thy hav these long thg coming out, I d.k. if its tails or what & thyr round lik this is here	Do Fo A

III 5"

5. U know it ll a couple of guys working on s.t.

E: (Rpts S's resp)
S: Well thyr lik trying to pick s.t. up or s.t. I kno, c ths thg down here & here thy r, c the heads & thyv got their arms out down lik here tryg to get this thg

$D+\ M^ao\ (2)\ H\ P\ 3.0$

6. U kn ths thg that thy r after c.b. another crab, but I don't mean for it to b w them I mean if u look at it a littl different u kno what I mean? (E:Yes) Thy r picking at s.t. but not a crab, but u can c it lik a crab too

E: (Rpts S's resp)
S: Well it really c.b. one, not exactly like the other one but a crab tho we go out to the beach alot on the weekends or when I have days off & u c thgs lik ths, the round shells

7. Hey, u kno this thg ll it c.b. crowbar lik u open crates & thgs with

E: (Rpts S's resp)
S: Well yeah, its got tht fork part to it, we use thm all the time where I work, u kno a crowbar

$Do\ Fw\ Crowbar$

IV 7"

8. It ll s.k. of a skin, mayb a bear skin lik a trophy u pu up on a wall I don't c nothin else there

E: (Rpts S's resp)
S: Well its got ths big legs c here & a small head up at the top prt & well, it jus ll a skin, c the lines lik on a bear skin (runs finger over card)

$Wo\ FTo\ Ad\ P\ 2.0$

V 9"

9. Well if its o.k. to tak thes parts off, cause I d.k. what the heck thy r, the rest o' it c.b. a bat lik the other ore, c the wgs - out lik it is mayb flying round

E: (Rpts S's resp)
S: Thes wld b the wings & here r the antennae lik thy use lik radar to find their way & the rest is just the body part

$Ddo\ FM^ao\ A\ (P)$

VI 8"

10. Jeez, I guess it c b another bear skin, just the bo tom prt

E: (Rpts S's resp)
S: This one isn't the same, its more lik a rug mite b instead of a trophy skin, it has more fur (rubs blot), c the lines all over & these extensions r the legs. Ths other part doesn't ll it would go with it tho

$Do\ FTo\ Ad\ P$

Case 1 (Continued)

Card	Free Association	Inquiry	Scoring
VII (6″)	Can u turn thes thgs? E: If u lik		
13″	V11. U kno ths way it re me of thos puppet u c on the TV s.times, I can't thk of who does them but thy sort of ll ths, like 2 puppets with the heads kinda back as if thyr sorta in a position to do s.t. but thyr not moving yet, just in place ready to start movg lik in a dance or s.t.	E: (Rpts S's resp) S: Well the heads r back & here is the leg down here lik u can't c the other one & each one has one arm out, just lik standg there ready to begin doing s.t. but not doing it yet. The kind of puppets I'm thkg of hav heads bigger than the body parts, lik ths	W+ M^{p}o (2) (H) 2.5
	12. Hey, u kno ths way it re me lik a toy my daughter has, her grandfathr got it for her, it has a couple of rabbits on a teeter-totter & u wind it up & thy go up & dwn, her's isnt grey lik ths one tho	E: (Rpts S's resp) S: Yeah, it looks good lik tht lik its going up & down, except it would look more lik one if it had some colors to to, ths grey is dingy, c the rabbits on each end & the cntr w.b. the teeter	W+ m^a.FC'o (2) (H) 2.5
VIII 6″	13. Now tht's a lotta color, it ll a coupl cats going up a tree in the middle	E: (Rpts S's resp) S: Well thy ll 2 cats, c the legs & head & tail & ths cntr is lik a tree, c the green on the top & its kinda colord lik trees in the fall & thyr climbg it	W+ FM^a.FCo (2) A,Bt P 4.5
	14. If u just take the top, it ll a mountain, u kno lik a big volcano or big mt of s.s.	E: (Rpts S's resp) S: It just ll one to me, it has that form to it, lik a big mt.	Do Fo Ls
	15. Ths bttm part kind ll a statue of a coupl of frog heads, lik mayb in a museum	E: (Rpts S's resp) S: Its not the kinda thg I care about for my own house but u c them other places lik a museum, thyr suppos to mean s.t., c a head on each side kinda pointed outward	Do Fo Art

IX 8"

16. This ll a coupl of thos toy clowns lik kids bat around Thes r orange ones with the big pointd hat, we got one s... lik it for our daughter

E: (Rpts S's resp)
S: Yeah, thy hav thes big stomachs so the kinds can punch em & ths are clown ones but thy make em in all diff forms lik seals & cats & thgs

Do FCo (2) Toy

<17. U kno ths green stuff ten me of cheese after it gets all moldy, we went away 4 the wk once & shut off the frig to sav energy but we forgot abt some cottage chees & it ll ths when we got back

E: (Rpts S's resp)
S: Yeah, just sort of a round green mess lik u could almost grow penicillin in there

Dv CFw Mold

X 5"

18. This c.b. another couple of crabs, here in thes prts

E: (Rpts S's resp)
S: Yeah with all the legs & the cntr is the shell part

Do Fo (2) *A P*

19. Thes thgs kinda ll a couple of big collie dogs

E: (Rpts S's resp)
S: Well the head is right here (points) & the legs, frt legs & thy r yellow lik collies are colord yellow lik ths

Do FCo (2) *A*

V20. U kno ι cld mak part of this lik a face of a man

E: (Rpts S's resp)
S: Its not all tht good, but u can c it, here r the eyes & nose & a littl mouth, its kinduva narrow face, weird lookg

DdS– F– Hd 6.0

21. This pink is lik bubble gum

E: (Rpts S's resp)
S: Well its just pink & long lik bubble gum after u chew it, we used to do that all the time when I was a kid

Dv CFw Gum

<22. Ths way I c another dog, lik laying down here, ϲ here (points)

E: (Rpts S's resp)
S: Ths one isn't a collie tho, its just lik some other kind, just layg there, c the head & the body, lik the feet were curled up in under lik dogs lay lik tht

Do FM^{P}o A

161

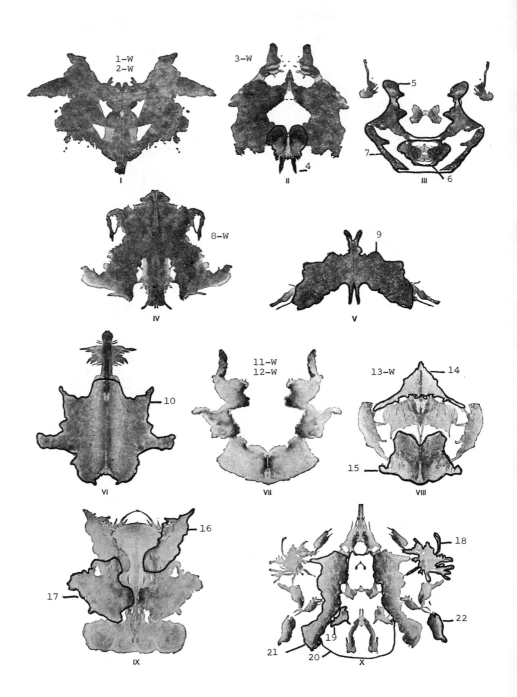

Case 1

CARD	RT	NO.	LOCATION	DETERMINANTS (S)		CONTENT (S)	POP	Z SCORE	SPECIAL
I	8"	1.	Wo	Fo		A	P	1.0	
		2.	WS+	Fo		Mask		3.5	
II	14"	3.	W+	FM^a.CFo	(2)	A,Bl	(P)	4.5	
		4.	Do	Fo		A			
III	5"	5.	D+	M^ao	(2)	H	P	3.0	
		6.	Do	Fw		A			
		7.	Do	Fw		Crowbar			
IV	7"	8.	Wo	FTo		Ad	P	2.0	
V	9"	9.	Ddo	FM^ao		A	(P)		
VI	8"	10.	Do	FTo		Ad	P		
VII	13"	11.	W+	M^po	(2)	(H)		2.5	
		12.	W+	m^a.FC'o	(2)	Toy		2.5	
VIII	6"	13.	W+	FM^a.FCo	(2)	A,Bt	P	4.5	
		14.	Do	Fo		Ls			
		15.	Do	Fo		Art			
IX	8"	16.	Do	FCo	(2)	Toy			
		17.	Dv	CFw		Mold			
X	5"	18.	Do	Fo	(2)	A	P		
		19.	Do	FCo	(2)	A			
		20.	DdS−	F−		Hd		6.0	
		21.	Dv	CFw		Gum			
		22.	Do	FM^po		A			

Case 1:   Structural Summary

R = 22   Zf = 9   ZSum = 29.5   P = 6+2   (2) = 8

Location Features		Determinants (Blends First)	Contents	Contents (Idiographic)

Location Features

W = 7   DQ
D = 13   + = 6
Dd = 2   o = 13
S = 2   v = 2
DW =   — = 1

Determinants (Blends First)

FM.CF = 1
FM.FC = 1
m.FC' = 1

M   = 2
FM = 2
m   =
C   =
CF = 2
FC = 2
C' =

Form Quality

FQx		FQf	
+	=0	+	= 0
o	=17	o	= 6
w	=4	w	= 2
—	=1	—	= 1

M Quality

+ =
o =
w =
— =

C'F =
FC' =
T   =
TF   =
FT   = 2
V   =
VF   =
FV   =
Y   =
YF   =
FY   =
rF   =
Fr   =
FD   =
F   = 9

Contents

H   = 1
(H) = 1
Hd   = 1
(Hd) =
A   = 9
(A) =
Ad   = 2
(Ad) =
Ab   =
Al   =
An   =
Art = 1
Ay   =
Bl   = 0,1
Bt   = 0,1
Cg   =
Cl   =
Ex   =
Fi   =
Fd   =
Ge   =
Hh   =
Ls   = 1
Na   =
Sx   =
Xy   =

Contents (Idiographic)

....Crowbar........   =
....Mask..........   =
....Gum...........   =
....Mold..........   =
....Toy...........   =
....   =
....   =
....   =

Special Scorings

PSV   =
DV   =
INCOM =
FABCOM =
CONTAM =
ALOG   =
       =

RATIOS, PERCENTAGES, AND DERIVATIONS

ZSum-Zest = 29.5-27.5	FC:CF+C = 3:3	Afr = .83
Zd = +2.0	W:M = 7:2	3r+(2)/R = .36
EB = 2:4.5 EA = 6.5	W:D = 7:13	Cont:R = 9:22
eb = 5:3 ep = 8	L = .69	H+Hd:A+Ad = 3:11 (H)+(Hd):(A)+(Ad) = 1:0
Blends:R = 3:22	F+% = .67	H+A:Hd+Ad = 11:3
a:p = 5:2	X+% = .78	XRT Achrom. = 9.0"
Ma:Mp = 1:1	A% = .50	XRT Chrom = 7.6"

borhood. The subject's older brother is a construction worker; he is married and has two children. The older of the subject's two sisters was the first in her family to complete college and currently works as a commercial artist in an advertising firm in another city. The younger sister completed two years at a community college and works in a department store selling cosmetics. There is no psychiatric history in the family except for some form of brief treatment of the sister-in-law following the birth of her second child. The subject is an avid football fan, having "lettered" in football in high school.

Previously Developed Interpretation.   An extratensive subject who has a greater tendency toward emotional discharge, as contrasted with ideation, in coping situations. Although he has access to some important resources, he is also prompted by many psychological features that are not organized in a way to permit their controlled use. Many of these features are need states, including the natural experience of wanting more affection. *If* he feels anxiety, the latter need will probably be one of the primary causes. Although prone toward emotional discharge, he becomes uncertain of his own controls at times and in those situations does inhibit their expression by internalization (preceding analysis developed from Four Square data). The fact that he does inhibit emotions at times is important, for he is more responsive to emotionally toned stimuli than are most adults *(Afr)*, and it seems clear that, under some circumstances, his emotional controls falter a bit and his behavior becomes directed by emotion rather than logic *(FC : CF+C)*. His reality testing is good *(F+%, X+%)* and he shows evidence of some flexibility in his thinking *(a : p)*. Although he may not be as psychologically sophisticated as many adults *(ep > EA)*, he is not overly self-centered *(3r + (2)/R)*, and he demonstrates the ability to "back away from" more complex stimulus situations to avoid becoming too involved in them *(Lambda)*. (This analysis developed from other style indices).

Finished Interpretation.   He does not set goals that exceed his capacities *(W : M)*, and he is able to identify and respond to conventionality with comparative ease *(P = 6 + 2)*. His cognitive operations are relatively well developed *(DQ distribution)*, and he appears to have a broad range of interests *(Cont : R = 9 : 22)*. On the more negative side of the coin, he gives a higher than usual frequency of Animal answers that may reflect less maturity for someone in this age range. Similarly, he displays less Human content than most adults; his protocol has only one pure *H* answer. This suggests that his interpersonal world may be more superficial than is desirable for an adult. His sequence of scores is quite interesting in that all four form quality *weak* and the one minus answer in his protocol are given in response to chromatically colored cards. This pattern seems related to his apparent over-responsiveness to emotionally loaded stimuli and suggests that when he is prompted by emotion, his perceptual accuracy may suffer. It is also notable that his two responses to Card VII include a Human and a Toy content, neither of which appear to reflect the more commonly perceived "female" features of that card. One of his two *Dd* answers occurs on Card V, which is unusual in that this is the lest difficult card and typically provokes a *W* response. He does not really give *Z* responses after his first answer to Card VIII (even though he has a *Z* Score on *X*) another possible illustration of the extent to which emotion tends to restrict his functional capabilities.

His verbal material is quite interesting. Someone has suggested that within every man there still resides a boy, and this case is no exception. Several of his responses illustrate less maturity than might be expected (two Toys, bubble gum, and a mask). The mask answer is probably a response to the examiner's prompting—that is, he is interested in concealment. His first answer to Card II, "bears fighting," is one of the more primitive that he delivers. It is aggressive and loose, although he tends to recover a bit in the inquiry by suggesting that the bears are not hurt, but that the blood comes instead from their prey. In spite of his apparent immaturity, he gives several "barrier" responses, answers whose contents are relatively inpenetrable (three crabs and a crowbar). This indicates that he might be less "reachable" were some form of intervention to take place. In general, his responses to the achromatic cards are much sturdier than those given to the cards with chromatic features. He is probably a bit brighter than his work history and occasional crude language would suggest. Several of his answers are well articulated, and at least two ("puppets" and "teeter" on Card VII) are rather creative. It is also interesting that he seems to become more comfortable as he proceeds through the test, and his verbalizations become considerably longer and often more personalized, "Like a toy my daughter has . . . ," "we got something like it for our daughter. . . . ," "We went away for the week once. . . . ," "We used to do that all the time. . . ." This form of personalization is much more common to the younger client than to the adult, and may again illustrate aspects less mature than might be expected for a person his age.

Case 1 Summary.   This is a fairly emotional fellow who probably "wears his heart on his sleeve." He is somewhat more prone to aggressiveness than may be effective, but he also has some awareness of this and tries to "back away" from such provocative situations. His reality testing is generally good, although it tends to become "colored" under emotional influences. He seems to have some awareness of his semiloose emotional controls, and works toward avoidance and/or control. He is appropriately identified with the masculine role, but also tends to be a bit more "childish" at times than might be preferred. He is brighter than he credits himself to be, but does not appear to be making any concerted effort to extend his intellect. He understands and responds to conventionality about as much as most adults, and is relatively flexible in his thinking. There is no major evidence of pathology, although his apparent immaturity could create difficulties in situations requiring a more sophisticated problem solving approach. He is probably a person who likes to be "cared for," and as long as his immediate environment, especially his home, affords that support, there is no reason to suspect that he will falter in his overall adjustment.

Case 6: A 24 Year Old Female

History.   This woman was born in a small Midwestern community. She is the second of three daughters in a family of four children, the oldest child being a male, age 32, who is currently a high school teacher. Her older sister, age 27, completed college, married shortly thereafter, and is a housewife. Her younger sister, age 22, is an airline stewardess. The father, age 60, operates a grain processing business, and the mother, age 58, assists with the bookkeeping for the business. The subject completed high school at age 19 and entered a junior college shortly afterwards with no specific occupational plans. After one year, she decided to convert to secretarial training and completed a one year program in a business school, after which she accepted the first of three positions as a secretary. Her performance has merited consistently higher paying employment with greater responsibility, so that now she is responsible to an executive vice-president of a textile firm. She was engaged to a high school "beau" for one year after completing high school, but "broke off" the engagement when she entered business school. One year later, she met her husband, whom she married after a 10 month courtship. He is currently a management trainee, having recently completed a B.A. degree in economics. She was essentially responsible for the support of the family during his last two years of college, although his tuition was covered by veterans' benefits to which he was entitled for having served two years in the Army during the Viet Nam war. They have no immediate plans for a "family," although she expresses a desire for "one or two" children "in a few years." She feels strongly committed to her "career" and perceives opportunities for further advancement. She and her husband are outdoor enthusiasts and frequently go hiking or camping during brief vacation periods. There is no psychiatric history in the family, although her older brother was divorced at age 25 after three years of marriage and did seek marriage counseling before the final separation.

Previously Developed Interpretation.   She is prone to emotional displays when coping, but she also demonstrates an obvious capacity for ideation under those circumstances. She has "good" access to many of her resources, and when acted upon by features that are not in her "organized" psychological structure, most of that action seems related to need states, including a natural desire for emotional affiliation. Her emotional controls appear effective $(FC:CF+C)$, and she is about as responsive to emotionally toned stimuli as most nonpatients (Afr). She is appropriately self-focusing $(3r + (2)/R)$ and has very adequate reality testing $(F+\%, X+\%)$. Her ideation shows some flexibility $(a:p)$; she is concerned with organizing her stimulus world, but not overly so (Zf); and when she does organize, her effort is generally efficient (Zd). She probably becomes a bit overly involved with complex stimuli, more so than most people $(Lambda)$, but the nature of her resources, controls, and reality testing all indicate that she is well prepared to handle such situations effectively.

Finished Interpretation   Her aspirational level seems to be compatible with her talents $(W:M)$, and her level of cognitive sophistication seems quite adequate $(DQ$ $Distribution)$, although a slightly larger number of $DQ+$ responses might ordinarily be expected from someone whose occupation probably requires considerable integration of details. The frequency of her Popular response is somewhat higher than is usually found among adult nonpatients and may suggest that she is somewhat more concerned with convention than might be desired; that is, she may sacrifice her own needs and interests at times to insure her social acceptability. She has a broad variety of contents, several of which are quite idiographic, and at least two of these ("antennae" and "umbrella") may relate to her concern for convention. Antennae are a means of "taking in" the signals or cues from the environment, while the umbrella is used as a means of protection from the elements. It is somewhat early in the interpretation to speculate, but the possibility that much of her goal oriented behavior is precise and directed by a need to be socially acceptable is quite intriguing.

The sequence of scores is somewhat unusual, marked by the fact that most of her organizational efforts (Z) occur in responses to the first five cards, and while she delivers an M answer for each of the first four cards, she discontinues this

Case 6

Card	Free Association	Inquiry	Scoring
I	5"		
	1. I thk it c.b. a wm standg in the middle there Should I try to find s.t. else? *E:* Most people c mor thn 1 thg	*E:* (Rpts *S*'s resp) *S:* I has tht outline, the hips & the legs & the upper part & thes mite b her hands raised as if she's just standg there	Do $M^p o$ H P
	2. I suppose the entire thg c.b. a bf I don't c a.t. else tho	*E:* (Rpts *S*'s resp) *S:* Well it has the large wings like bf's have & ths mite b the tail & the feelers in the frnt	Wo Fo A P 1.0
II	11"		
	3. Ths mite b two little dogs playing together, they'r rubbing their noses togthr	*E:* (Rpts *S*'s resp) *S:* Its not really the entire dogs, u can only c them from the waist up just their shoulders & heads & its lik thyr being playful the way dogs rub noses when they play, c here r the noses touching & the rest of the head and so on	$D+$ $FM^a o$ (2) Ad P 3.0
	4. If it doesn't hav to be s.t. really identical, u cld c ths as people at a party	*E:* (Rpts *S*'s resp) *S:* They might be shaking hands or s.t., it c.b. a costume party bec they r wearing big red hats, probably two women who are greeting e.o., c thes r the hats & ths w.b. the rest of them, as if thy hav long dresses on	$W+$ $M^a.FCo$ (2) H 4.5
III	8"		
	5. My, ths c.b. the same party with two people bowing to e.o., the red thgs would be the decorations for the party	*E:* (Rpts *S*'s resp) *S:* Well it if it were the same party thes might b 2 other people, mayb men bec thy r thinner than the other two, as if thy r dressed formally, c the heads & legs & these red parts w.b. the decorations for the party	$W+$ $M^a.FC+$ (2) H P 5.5 *PSV*

168

6. I thk I hav a one track mind bec this cntr red cld also b a mask lik u mite wear at a costume ball

E: (Rpts S's resp)
S: Well it has the shape of one & its red lik thy wore years ago, I don't mean red masks, but very colorful ones. I don't c the holes for the eyes but the form is rite for one

Do FCw Mask

IV 13"

7. Ugh, ths ll some sort of big monster all covered w fur, lik from science fiction, some huge thg just standing there, it ll he has big boots on

E: Can I turn it over?

E: Whatever u prefer

E: (Rpts S's resp)
S: Well its an unusual lcokg thg, s..t from the movies ot s.t., all covered w fur. He has littl arms & these great big boots or s.t. on his feet
E: Covered w fur?
S: It just all looks furry, the shades there

Wo Mp.FTo (2) (H) P 2.0

V8. Its not much more pleasant ths way, it ooks lik a big bat

E: (Rpts S's resp)
S: It has the big wings and the body part here in the middle, I thk thy r shaped lik ths altho I've never seen one up close, & I hope I don't

Wo Fo A 2.0

---

9. Maybe if I just use the head of the monster it ll s.t. e.se, lik a flower, yes thats better

E: (Rpts S's resp)
S: Well it just has tht rounded shape to it lik a flower, I'm not sure what kind, I believe that African violets are formed lik this

Do Fo Bt

V 10"

10. I thot of a bf but thy usually hav bigger wgs, it c.b. a moth tho, its black lik a moth flying around

E: (Rpts S's resp)
S: Well it does hav thes wgs & the small body & its all black or grey, whatevr u want to call it, so it c.b. a moth

Wo FMa.FC' A P 1.0

---

11. If u look just at this top prt it rem u of a TV antennae

E: (Rpts S's resp)
S: It has tht V shape to it, lik the antennae tht r built into the sets, or I thk u can buy them separate, thy just hav this shape

Do Fw TV Antennae

169

Case 6 (Continued)

Card		Free Association		Inquiry	Scoring
VI	15″	12.	The top part ll it c.b. an indian totem pole with the carved feathers coming out from each side	E: (Rpts S's resp) S: It has the form to it, but it should b colored, thy make thm in such beautiful colors, but its does hav the form	Do Fo Ay
		13.	I thk the bigger part c.b. an A skin, lik a blanket or rug	E: (Rpts S's resp) S: Ths one looks furry too, c the shades give that effect & it has the four legs, or what were legs, yes lik a rug I'd say	Do FTo Ad P
VII	16″	14.	This c.b. 2 children, one here & one here, just fr the waist up	E: (Rpts S's resp) S: It ll 2 little girls, w big pony tails, c the nose & chin & ths w.b. the shoulders here	Do Fo (2) Hd P
		15.	These parts here ll cups, lik coffee cups or beer mugs w the handle here	E: (Rpts S's resp) S: They just seemed to rem me of tht the way thy r formed there & the handle out here	Do Fw (2) Cup
VIII	7″	16.	Ths ll s.t. from a biol book, an illustration of internal parts lik the lungs & rib cage & mayb the stomach, I'm not sure of the parts but it does ll those illustrations	E: (Rpts S's resp) S: Well its very colorful, with each color used to portray one part, like the pink mite be lungs or s.t. & so on, just an illustration, not the real thg	W+ FCo An 4.5
		<17.	Ths way it ll a dog standg on some rocks or thigs	E: (Rpts S's resp) S: Well it does ll a dog, c the legs & the head & body & thes wld b lik rocks or s.t., thy was thy r colored it c.b. tht he's in the forest or s.t.	Do FM^p.FCo A P 3.0
		18.	Ths lower part rem me of ex-posed flesh, as if it mite b a burn or s.t. lik that	E: (Rpts S's resp) S: Its lik a brush burn or a fire created burn, pink & orange, lik the skin is not there anymore & just the fleshy part is exposed, ugh	Dv CF- Flesh

				Scoring			
IX	11″	19. I suppose that the upper part c.b. a bf but I can't make anything out of the pink	E: (Rpts S's resp) S: Its very colorful, lik a bf mite be & u cld immagine the orange parts as the out parts of the wigs & the green w.b. the fuller parts of the wgs, I d.k. I just thot of a bf, its so colorful E: Can u run your finger around it? S: (Outlines the bf) c here the wgs & the middle w.b. the body	D–	CF–	A	
IX		V20. If I look ths way the pink part c.b. an umbrella	E: (Rpts S's resp) S: The large area w.b. the umbrella part & this w.b. the handle, its really more lik a beach umbrella that one u carry bec the top is so big in relation to the handle	Do	Fo	Umbrella	
X	6″	21. This all ll a floral design w the different flowers arranged so that one is on each side, its very pretty	E: (Rpts S's resp) S: Well, I can't really identify any of the flowers, thy don't really ll any that I am familar with but thy are very pretty & laid out very, a, neatly, lik a display, with each color selected to offset the others	W+	CFo	(2)	Bt 5.5
		22. Thes brown thgs ll deer lik thy r jumping over s.t., ↓ ɔ horns & thyr brown	E: (Rpts S's resp) S: Thy hav a shape of deer sort of jumpg c the horns & the legs, just deer	Do	$FM^a.FCo$	(2)	A
		V23. Oh, these green parts ll sea horses, thy r really shaped lik that	E: (Rpts S's resp) S: Well they look very much lik them & thyr green, I thk seahorses r usually green lik ths	Do	FCo	(2)	A
		24. Ths c.b. a maple seed, with the little pods on the end	E: (Rpts S's resp) S: Thy r usually brown lik ths & thy are shaped lik an upside down v with the pods on the end lik thes, c here (points)	Do	FCo	Bt	

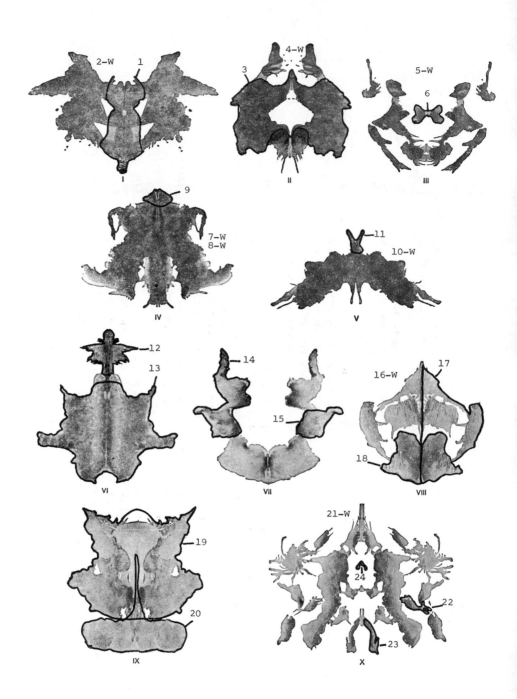

SEQUENCE OF SCORES

Case 6

CARD	RT	NO.	LOCATION	DETERMINANTS (S)		CONTENT (S)	POP	Z SCORE	SPECIAL
I	5"	1.	Do	M^po		H	P		
		2.	Wo	Fo		A	P	1.0	
II	11"	3.	D+	FM^ao	(2)	Ad	P	3.0	
		4.	W+	M^a.FCo	(2)	H		4.5	
III	8"	5.	W+	M^a.FC+	(2)	H	P	5.5	PSV
		6.	Do	FCw		Mask			
IV	13"	7.	Wo	M^p.FTo	(2)	(H),Cg	P	2.0	
		8.	Wo	Fo		A		2.0	
		9.	Do	Fo		Bt			
V	10"	10.	Wo	FM^a.FC'o		A	P	1.0	
		11.	Do	Fw		Antennae			
VI	15"	12.	Do	Fo		Ay			
		13.	Do	FTo		Ad	P		
VII	16"	14.	Do	Fo	(2)	Hd	P		
		15.	Do	Fw	(2)	Cup			
VIII	7"	16.	W+	FCo		An		4.5	
		17.	Do	FM^p.FCo		A	P	3.0	
		18.	Dv	CF-		A			
IX	11"	19.	D-	CF-		A			
		20.	Do	Fo		Umbrella			
X	6"	21.	W+	CF^ao	(2)	Bt		5.5	
		22.	Do	FM^a.FCo	(2)	A			
		23.	Do	FCo	(2)	A			
		24.	Do	FCo		Bt			

Case 6: Structural Summary

$R = 24$ $Zf = 10$ $ZSum = 32.0$ $P = 9$ $(2) = 9$

Location Features		Determinants (Blends First)	Contents		Contents (Idiographic)	
W = 8	DQ	M.FC = 2	H = 3		Antennae = 1	
D = 15	+ = 5	M.FT = 1	(H) = 1			
Dd = 0	o = 17	FM.FC = 2	Hd = 1		Cup = 1	
		FM.FC' = 1	(Hd) =			
S = 0	v = 1		A = 7		Flesh = 1	
DW =	— = 1	M = 1	(A) =			
		FM = 1	Ad = 2		Mask = 1	
		m =	(Ad) =			
		C =	Ab =		Umbrella = 1	
		CF = 3	Al =			
Form Quality		FC = 4	An = 1		=	
		C' =	Art =			
FQx	FQf	C'F =	Ay = 1		=	
+ = 1	+ = 0	FC' =	Bl =			
o = 18	o = 6	T =	Bt = 3		=	
w = 3	w = 2	TF = 1	Cg = 0,1			
— = 2	— = 0	FT =	Cl =			
		V =	Ex =		**Special Scorings**	
M Quality		VF =	Fi =			
		FV =	Fd =		PSV = 1	
+ = 1		Y =	Ge =			
o = 3		YF =	Hh =		DV =	
w = 0		FY =	Ls =		INCOM =	
— = 0		rF =	Na =			
		Fr =	Sx =		FABCOM =	
		FD =	Xy =		CONTAM =	
		F = 8			ALOG =	
					=	

RATIOS, PERCENTAGES, AND DERIVATIONS

ZSum-Zest = 32.0-31.0		FC:CF+C = 8:3		Afr = .60	
Zd = +1.0		W:M = 8:4		3r+(2)/R = .38	
EB = 4:7.0	EA = 11.0	W:D = 8:15		Cont:R = 10:24	
eb = 4:3	ep = 7	L = .50		H+Hd:A+Ad = 5:9	
				(H)+(Hd):(A)+(Ad) = 1:0	
Blends:R = 6:24		F+% = .75		H+A:Hd+Ad = 11:3	
a:p = 5:3		X+% = .79		XRT Achrom. = 11.8"	
Ma:Mp = 2:2		A% = .38		XRT Chrom = 8.6"	

coping approach thereafter. Three of the four *M* answers are in blends, two with *FC* and one with *FT,* suggesting that while she has a good capacity for ideation, that phenomenon alone is generally not sufficient to bring closure to her response operation. This is also apparent in the fact that three of her four *FM* determinants also appear in blends, two with *FC* and one with *FC'*. In other words, although she is a person subject to considerable ideation, the ideation does not ordinarily function as an "end in itself" but instead seems to stimulate some form of emotional response. This is consistent with her basic *EB* style, but it can become a liability, as is suggested by the sequence of scores to the last three cards. In nine responses, she offers only one of her eight pure *F* answers while delivering eight of her chromatic color determinants, including all three of her *CF* responses. Again, this sort of performance is compatible with her natural style, but the rather marked shift from a heavy *M* emphasis during the first four cards to a heavy color emphasis during the last three cards may suggest that *she* is less comfortable with being "extratensive" than might be preferred. She begins the test with an *M*, as if to "sign in" displaying cautious ideational control; but as the stimuli become more emotionally provocative later in the test, her responses are no longer marked by the ideational delay of *M,* but rather by a distinct emotional display, *including both of her minus responses—and both involve CF determinants.* The possibility exists that her preoccupation with conventionality may be *psychologically misleading* for her, bringing her to the point of mistrust or apprehension about her natural extratensive style; and her uncertainty about emotional displays may impinge on her self-confidence.

Her verbal material suggests that her self-concept is not as "firm" as might be expected and may be marked by less maturity than is originally inferred from the structural data. Her first answer is a passive-complaint *M*, involving a woman standing, following by a question to the examiner seeking direction, "Should I try to find something else?" Her first answer to the second card, ". . . two little dogs playing," is not one that might be expected from a bright, dynamic, goal oriented adult, and is followed again by some cautiousness, "If it really doesn't have to be something identical (to the form) . . ." A glimpse of some ideational perseveration is noted in responses 4, 5, and 6, all of which focus on a party or on party things, suggesting that she prefers to cope by stressing "pleasant" things. She appears to have some awareness of this, "I think I have a one track mind . . . ," and she tends to dramatize her need to avoid the unpleasant by her commentary in Card IV, "Ugh . . ."; "It's not much more pleasant this way . . ."; "Maybe if I just use . . . , yes, that's better." Her anatomy and flesh responses on Card VIII, the first of the totally chromatic cards, may indicate something of her inability to set up firmer barriers to the impact of emotional stimuli, and, in general, her contents on the last three cards display less sturdiness of coping or defensive mechanisms than is expected of the truly mature person (anatomy, dog standing, flesh, butterfly, umbrella, floral design, deer, seahorses, and seed pod). Although all but two of these answers (flesh and butterfly) are of good form quality and quite acceptable, they tend to conjoin to imply the avoidance of aggression and a greater orientation to the nonthreatening. Much speculation could be generated from the flesh response to the lower area of Card VIII, *but it would be speculation.* The manner in which she departs or "signs out" from the test is also worth noting. It is the maple seed in Card X, given to a very small but nonetheless common area. It is interesting because she first approaches the card with a fairly good *W* answer. This may reflect her own need to be more precise, and also to reduce the complexity of the stimulus field to a more manageable level. Since all responses represent something of the "projected self," a seed might be taken to illustrate a still to be developed potential for growth, and can also represent some sense of insecurity in the self-image.

Case 6 Summary. She is a fairly emotional person who is probably not completely comfortable with her natural emotional style. She has many assets, including brightness, cognitive sophistication that includes a good ability to organize efficiently, adequate emotional controls, a reasonably good level of reality testing, ideational flexibility, a seemingly healthy breadth of interests, and good access to her resources. Viewed more negatively, her self-concept is more fragile or less "firm" than desired, and she seems to need to avoid looking at the "seamy side" of life. She is overly concerned with doing the "right" thing and may often feel vulnerable when her emotions become intense. She tries to set reasonable goals for herself and in that context may often "sell herself short." It is interesting that her recent adult years have been devoted to "serving others" (supporting the student husband, being a good secretary to her employers) which probably "pays off" by fulfilling her needs for affection and reinforcement of her image. It also seems likely that as she has advanced in her occupation, she has began to feel less confident about her ability to play the conventional role she perceives as required. Obviously, her marital relationship is critical to her stability, and one wonders about the decision to defer a "family" for several years. Who made the decision and how deeply does she feel committed to it? While there is an apparent need for greater maturity, the absence of any current symptoms or psychiatric history suggests that she not only is "holding her own," but, indeed, seems to be flourishing. Quite possibly, her decision to seek continued occupational advancement can pose problems *if* she continues to feel discomfort with her emotional displays. Conversely, she may well detect the fact that her displays can be advantageous to her functioning, intrapersonally, interpersonally, and occupationally, and under such circumstances can be expected to continue a "healthy" life. If she ever does become disabled by the onset of symptoms, the most likely nucleus of the problem would be in two basic areas: her need to reconcile her emotionality with her need to conform, and her tendency to avoid the more "unpleasant" stimulus aspects of her world. Either one, or the two in combination, could provoke a form of hysteroid adjustment that might not be very effective in environments requiring controlled and direct confrontations with reality.

Case 7: A 34 Year Old Male

History. This man is the oldest of six siblings, four males and two females, in a second generation Italian family. He was the first of his family to attend college, completing a B.A. degree in creative writing at 21. After floundering in a minor newspaper reporting assignment for two years after college, he entered the advertising industry and has flourished. He married a fellow newspaper worker (also a college graduate) at the age of 25. She now is also 34. She continues to do "free lance writing" while raising their three children, ages 5, 3, and 1. His father, age 61, is a steamfitter and his mother has never worked outside of the home. His oldest brother (age 30) is employed in manufacturing, the second age 29 in coaching, and the third (age 27) in teaching, while the oldest sister (age 29—a twin) is married with four children, and the youngest sister (age 24) is working in fashion design. Four of the six siblings, including the subject, completed college on scholarship and graduated with honors. The subject is strongly devoted to his family, and "programs" time into his busy schedule to insure that they are not neglected. He is also very religious and attends Mass and a variety of retreats, breakfasts, and the like regularly. He describes himself as one of the "ethical" advertisers, and appears to take considerable pride in that role. He describes himself as a political independent, but qualifies this by indicating that he is somewhat more conservative on many issues than his wife. His two older children are both male and he speaks of "reliving" some of his own childhood through them. The youngest child is female and "she will probably learn to manipulate all of us when she gets older." He feels that a three child family is large enough but is not sure if his wife agrees. There is no psychiatric history in the family. His mother does have a "heart problem" and his youngest sister had open heart surgery at age 12.

Structural Interpretation.   The record is of average length, thus permitting direct application of reference data. The Four Square indicates that he is somewhat introversive, preferring an ideational approach in most coping situations. The $EA:ep$ relationship illustrates an expected adult level of access to his resources, and the eb suggests that most of the psychological features that are not accessible to him, and that have a stimulation character, tend to be of an ideational nature. Interestingly, he offers two m determinants, both in blends, which hint that he is prone at times to feel somewhat out of control. His record is marked by a very large number (9 + 1) of Popular responses, indicating that he is quite concerned with conventional things. This concern may be related to the two m responses in that the Rorschach poses a situation in which guidelines are essentially nil. Consequently, people who "need" to be correct will often feel more apprehensive and less in control when taking the test. This supposition is only *speculative* at this point, and a more precise examination of the two m answers in terms of sequence and content will be required before definitive conclusions about their role in his overall personality can evolve. It is interesting, however, to note also that he is an "overincorporator" ($Zd = +4.0$)—that is, a slow and careful scanner of his perceptual field—who may have difficulty discriminating the important and unimportant stimulus cues at times. The Rorschach situation can produce feelings of apprehension and/or lack of control in such people. His five *blend* answers indicate that he is psychologically complex, but not overly so. The $a:p$ ratio of 7:4 shows ideational flexibility; however, his $M^a:M^p$ ratio of 3:3 reflects more passive M's than might be expected of an introversive person in an active problem solving occupation. On the other hand, his success in advertising may be due, in part, to his ability to generate "Snow White" fantasies, in that some kinds of advertising are directed toward that very phenomenon.

The Afr (.75), while within the "normal" range, indicates that he is quite receptive to emotionally toned stimuli; however, the $FC:CF+C$ (3:2) conveys some evidence that he may become overly emotional in some of his displays. Whether this is an asset or a liability can probably be determined *only* with additional information concerning the receptiveness of his environment to these forms of display. For example, if his *routine* environment requires a sedate and controlled form of behavior, he may experience some conflict between his controls and that world. Conversely, if the routine environment is more accepting of, and/or permissive toward, more intense and less controlled displays, it is unlikely that he will experience much, if any, difficulty with this issue, mainly because his basic style is

Case 7

Card	Free Association	Inquiry	Scoring
I 5″	1. The 1st thg I thk of here is the emblem used by 1 of the motion pic companies in intro their films. It shows a wm standg w her arms out & light radiating around here	E: (Repts S's response) S: Yes, that's rite, its the entire thg. The wm is in the middle, her arms r extended upward, here, & the rest would repr. the light radiating outward. E: (I'm not quite clear about the light) S: Well, its not really here, I mean it doesn't ll light or light rays but the area sort of reminded me of that general image. E: (The general image?) S: Well yes, to think of that emblem or copyrite or whatever it is the radiating lite is an important part. This really doesn't ll that but the overall shape of the thg can b interpreted that way.	W+ $M^p.m^p$+ Art,H P 4.0
	S: Should I see more than one? E: Its up to you, most people see more than one thing.		
	2. U kno, it cld b a mask of s.s. too, sort of a halloween mask	E: (Rpts S's response) S: Yes, all of it again, ths white parts wld b the eyes & mouth I suppose. Its very much lik an A mask of s.s., like a dog or cat	WSo Fo Mask 1.0
II 9″	3. I don't get much from the W thg, but if I just use ths drkr prts it ll 2 dogs rubbing noses	E: (Rpts S's response) S: Rite here (points), its just the upper parts of the dogs, u can't really see the full body, their noses r touchg	D+ FM^ao (2) Ad 3.0
	<4. U kno, if I turn it ths way & leave out the red again it cld b a rabbit sliding across a pond covered w ice	E: (Rpts S's response) S: Yes, it re. me of the rabbit in Bambi, my son has me reading that 2 him all the time. C, here is the rabbit & the white part wld b the ice.	DdS+ $FM^a.FC'$o A,Na 4.5

| III | 6″ | 5. It ll a very formal party, rather colorful with the decorations around | E: (Rpts S's response)
 S: Well, there r apparently 2 men here, dressed in formal attire talking. Ths red prts seem to repres. s.s. of decorations, it cld be A decorations since ths cntr part ll a bf. Mayb its an ecology party or s.t. lik tht. | $W+$ $M^p.FC+$ (2) H,Art P,P 5.5 |

| IV | 10″ | 6. Hum, l. a fellow sitting on a stump, mayb a trapper with a bg fur coat on stretching out for a rest | E: (Rpts S's response)
 S: Well I thot of a trapper bec it ll he's in a fur coat of s.s. which conceals some of his outline, especially his arms.
 E: U mentioned that he was sitting on a stump
 S: Oh yes, rite here is the stump & here r his feet, the perspective of ths thg makes it ll he's leaning backward
 E: I'm not quite clear abbut the fur coat
 S: Well it has a very irreg shape to it & the coloring is very much like furriness | $W+$ $M^p.FT.FDo$ H,Cg P 4.0 |

| | | 7. U kno, if I turn it this way ths part ll a head | E: (Rpts S's response)
 S: Yes, sort of like a dog, here is the snout & the head & ths is a tail | Do Fo Ad |

| V | 8″ | 8. I get the impression of 2 A's lik billy goats or deer butting thr heads, lik thy do in a mating struggle | E: (Rps S's response)
 S: Thrs one on e. sid w. the legs extended, really pushing against e.o. (points) | $W+$ $FM^a o$ (2) A 2.5 |

| | | 9. It cld b a bf too | E: (Rpts S's response)
 S: Well all cf it, ths wld b wgs & here is the tail & the antenae | Wo Fo A P 1.0 PSV |

179

Case 7 (Continued)

Card		Free Association	Inquiry	Scoring
VI	10″	10. The top part ll a totem pole	E: (Rpts S's response) S: Rite up here, it re me of the sort of thg u mite c in the southwest	Do Fo Ay
VII	5″	11. A couple of kids playg indian having a good time	E: (Rpts S's response) S: Rite, a couple of littl boys. Thy hav feathers stickg up in their hair ths why I thot thyd b playg indian, thyr just like laughg at e.o.	D+ M^ao (2) H P 3.0
		V12. Ths way it ll 2 wm dancing, lik dancing the can-can or s.t.	E: (Rpts S's response) S: Thyr heads r thrown bk & thyr spinning around on one leg	W+ M^ao (2) H 3.0
VIII	6″	13. The W thg cld b s.s. of an emblem lik a family crest, its very colorful	E: (Rpts S's response) S: Yes, well its very colorful w the A's on each side & I suppose each of the 3 mid parts repres s.t. of the family hist. The blu mite b flags	W+ FCo (2) Art,A (P) 4.5
		V14. U kno the colors in ths part ll it cld b a rock formation in the painted desert	E: (Rpts S's response) S: Yes, I've always wanted to visit there. The pic's I've seen r usually very colorful like ths, I thk they call them buttes or s.t.	Dv CFo Ls
IX	7″	15. The cntr part ll a vase	E: (Rpts S's response) S: It has tht sort of shape 2 it	Do Fo Hh
		<16. Ths way the grn part ll a fat guy playg a saxaphone	E: (Rpts S's response) S: Oh yea, rite here (points) it ll a big guy & ths prt is the sax	D+ M^ao H 2.5
		<17. Ths a man's head her too	E: (Rpts S's response) S: Rite here (points to pink) it ll he's got a mustache, sort of lik T. Roosevelt	Do Fo Hd P

X   3″

18. Hey, fireworks

E: (Rpts S's response)
S: Yes, it all ll one of thos displays lik u shoot up & it explodes into a pretty design as it falls, it just did that

Wv   m^a.CFw   Ex   5.5

19. Ths cld be a couple of crabs

E: (Rpts S's response)
S: Rite here (points), thy hav a lotta legs lik crabs

Do   Fo   (2)   A   P

20. Ths thgs cld be dogs, one on each side

E: (Rpts S's response)
S: Yes, lik collie dogs, c here is the head & the feet

Do   Fo   (2)   A

√21. If u turn it ths way it ll a floral display, its quite pretty with the different colored flowers organized into a display, like on a head table at a barquet or s.t.

E: (Rpts S's response)
S: Well the pink prts ll a cpl of big flwers w the stems here & the rest is all made up with smaller flowrs & folliage, I'm not very good about what kind of flowers but they are arranged well

W+   FC+   Bt   5.5

181

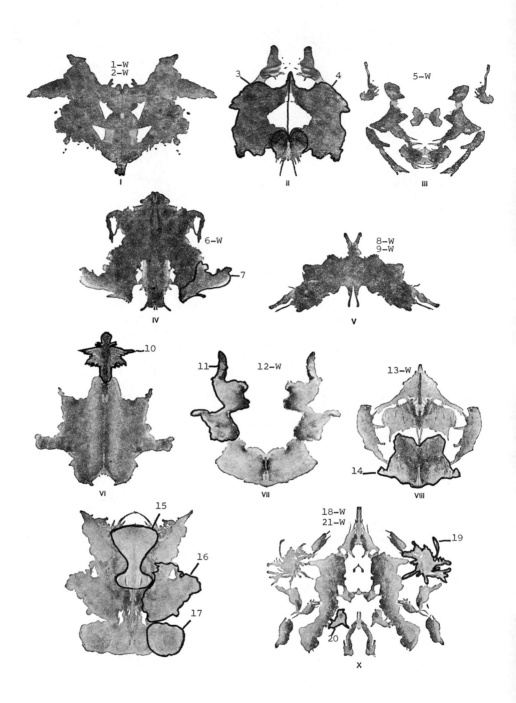

Case 7

CARD	RT	NO.	LOCATION	DETERMINANTS (S)		CONTENT (S)	POP	Z SCORE	SPECIAL
I	5"	1.	W+	$M^p.m^p+$		Art,H	P	4.0	
		2.	WSo	Fo		Mask		1.0	
II	9"	3.	D+	FM^ao	(2)	Ad	P	3.0	
		4.	DdS+	$FM^a.FC'$o		A,Na		4.5	
III	6"	5.	W+	$M^p.FC+$	(2)	H,Art	P;P	5.5	
IV	10"	6.	W+	$M^p.FT.FD$o		H,Cg	P	4.0	
		7.	Do	Fo		Ad			
V	8"	8.	W+	FM^ao	(2)	A		2.5	
		9.	Wo	Fo		A	P	1.0	
VI	10"	10.	Do	Fo		Ay			
VII	5"	11.	D+	M^ao	(2)	H	P	3.0	
		12.	W+	M^ao	(2)	H		3.0	
VIII	6"	13.	W+	FCo	(2)	Art, A	(P)	4.5	
		14.	Dv	CFo		Ls			
IX	7"	15.	Do	Fo		Hh			
		16.	D+	M^ao		H		2.5	
		17.	Do	Fo		Hd	P		
X	3"	18.	Wv	$m^a.CF$w		Ex		5.5	
		19.	Do	Fo	(2)	A	P		
		20.	Do	Fo	(2)	A			
		21.	W+	FC+		Bt		5.5	

Case 7: Structural Summary

R = 21　　Zf = 14　　ZSum = 49.5　　P = 9+1　　(2) = 8

Location Features		Determinants (Blends First)		Contents		Contents (Idiographic)	
W = 10	DQ	M.FT.FD = 1		H = 5,1		Mask = 1	
D = 10	+ = 11	M.FC = 1		(H) =		.... =	
		M.m = 1		Hd = 1			
Dd = 1	o = 8	FM.FC' = 1		(Hd) =		.... =	
S = 2	v = 2	m.CF = 1		A = 5,1			
				(A) =		.... =	
DW =	— = 0			Ad = 2			
		M = 3		(Ad) =		.... =	
		FM = 2		Ab =			
		m =		Al =		.... =	
		C =		An =			
Form Quality		CF = 1		Art = 2,1		.... =	
		FC = 2		Ay = 1			
FQx	FQf	C' =		Bl =		.... =	
		C'F =		Bt = 1			
+ = 3	+ = 0	FC' =		Cg = 0,1		.... =	
		T =		Cl =			
o = 17	o = 8	TF =		Ex = 1		Special Scorings	
		FT =		Fi =			
w = 1	w = 0	V =		Fd =		PSV =	
		VF =		Ge =			
— = 0	— = 0	FV =		Hh = 1		DV =	
		Y =		Ls = 1			
M Quality		YF =		Na = 0,1		INCOM =	
		FY =		Sx =			
+ = 2		rF =		Xy =		FABCOM =	
o = 4		Fr =				CONTAM =	
w = 0		FD =				ALOG =	
— = 0		F = 8				=	

RATIOS, PERCENTAGES, AND DERIVATIONS

ZSum-Zest = 49.5−45.5		FC:CF+C = 3:2		Afr = .75	
Zd = +4.0		W:M = 10:6		3r+(2)/R = .38	
EB = 6:3.5	EA = 9.5	W:D = 10:10		Cont:R = 9:21	
eb = 5:2	ep = 7	L = .62		H+Hd:A+Ad = 6:7 (H)+(Hd):(A)+(Ad) = 0:0	
Blends:R = 5:21		F+% = 1.00		H+A:Hd+Ad = 10:3	
a:p = 7:4		X+% = .95		XRT Achrom. = 7.6"	
Ma:Mp = 3:3		A% = .33		XRT Chrom = 6.2"	

oriented more toward ideation, and emotional displays are not a common feature of his coping routines. It is also important to note that his *Lambda* is well within "normal" limits (.62), suggesting that he does not become overly involved with complex stimulus situations, nor does he seek to avoid them excessively. His *reality testing* is quite good ($F+\% = 100$; $X+\% = 95$). In fact, it is slightly higher than might be anticipated for a subject who is involved in "creative" efforts. Ordinarily, such subjects are prone to offer more unique answers that might be scored *weak*. In this instance, the higher than expected form quality percentages may be the product of a combination of overincorporateness plus excessive concern with convention. In other words, he is probably a person who is concerned with avoiding "mistakes," and prefers not to be challenged by others about his own idiographic needs and perceptions. His *egocentricity index* is appropriate (.38), and there are no reflection determinants in the protocol. The frequency of Animal content is also appropriate for the length of the record. He shows a seemingly healthy interest in people by the presence of six Human contents, five of which are whole humans and none marked by parenthesized features. Two thirds of his responses display some *organizational effort* (Zf = 14), which is slightly more than expected in a protocol of this length, and which probably reflects his substantial intellect plus his motivation to be "certain" of his stimulus field. This characteristic is also illustrated by the somewhat greater frequency (10) of W answers. He also offers two S responses. Although S may indicate tendencies to negativism or oppositionality, and sometimes even anger, it may also illustrate a healthy form of "independence" or defensive resistance. Both of his S answers were responses to the first two cards of the test, a fact that may indicate irritation with the situation and an attempt to avoid a "total" commitment to a stimulus situation that remains ambiguous. The relatively generous breadth of content (9), and the substantial number of $DQ+$ answers (11), indicates both wide range of potential interests and a willingness to extend his intellect to integrate the stimulus features of his world.

Interpretation of Scoring Sequence. An examination of the sequence of scores reveals a fairly consistent high quality performance. His W answers are distributed across seven of the 10 blots, and he "signs in" and "signs out" with $W+$ synthesizing answers. Similarly, his M answers are well distributed across half the blots, although only one occurs during the last three cards. All of his *passive* movement answers occur early in the test, suggesting that this mode of ideation may be more common in situations in which he is unsure and still "feeling his way." He offers multiple answers on all cards *except* Card VI, to which he gives his most "pedestrian" answer (Do Fo Ay), and in which there is no organizational activity; nor does he offer the Popular response. Probably Card VI posed the most complex and/or threatening stimulus for him; although it may be interesting to speculate on this "withdrawal" form of behavior, no firm conclusions can be derived. It is also intriguing to note that while his first answer to Card X, which is truly the most broken and complex blot, is his "poorest" answer ($Wv\ m^a.CFw$), he recovers very well, giving two consecutive pure F responses, and finally giving a synthesized W answer with superior form quality and controlled use of the chromatic color. This indicates a solid resiliency after those situations in which his coping mechanisms have faltered or have not been as sophisticated as is possible for him.

Interpretation of Content. His very first answer is somewhat exhibitionistic and grandiose. It is an emblem that may signify his status needs, and one which also calls attention to the self. He wants to be visible, which is not necessarily surprising in light of the manner in which he describes his occupational success. It is also interesting that after this "self-centered" display, he seeks guidance: "Should I see more than one thing?'' and when left with the ambiguity of the situation, offers a concealment answer (mask), which includes the first of his two uses of white space. He is cautious in approaching the second card, making sure to eliminate the chromatic colors from the areas that he will use. Both answers to this card involve playful animals; the first answer is more cautious than the second, and the second (rabbit sliding) more active and possibly more exploratory (testing the ice). His own cautiousness is conveyed through the next two cards (formal party, trapper sitting, dog's head), but his aspirational competitiveness comes through "loud and strong" in Card V (two animals in a mating struggle). It is even possible that he felt that he was too open with that answer, since the next two, by contrast, are very mild and sedate (butterfly and totem pole). He seems more open and active in Card VII and in subsequent cards, as if he has finally become more sure of himself and feels more in control. The status orientation is implied again by the family crest response on Card VIII, and he gives the first of his two CF answers immediately thereafter; but even though the form is secondary, it is not patently disregarded, and it is important to note that in Card IX, he avoids the use of chromatic color entirely, while reverting more to his basic style (two F and one M answer). This suggests that the concerns about his $FC:CF+C$, raised earlier, are not as important as the ratio itself appeared to convey. In fact, even his second CF answer, in his first response to Card X (fireworks), while illustrating a more childlike entry ("Hey . . .") is not completely uncontrolled, and later, in the inquiry, he tones down the color aspect even more by noting that "it explodes into a pretty *design.*" His ability to inject pure F into the next two answers on card X, and then to sign out with a creative use of the whole blot, including the color features, again supports the notion that his emotions probably do not get out of control very much, and even if they do, he recovers quickly and effectively. All his color answers are positive, and both his CF responses have contents (painted desert, fireworks) that are observed rather than directly experienced. It also seems probable that he presents a "front" of being more grownup than may be the case. The "kids playing Indian," the "fat guy" with the saxaphone, and the "Hey, fireworks" responses present a considerable contrast to the formal party and the floral design ("like on a head table") responses. This is probably healthy, and he may have just enough immaturity to help him avoid becoming overly grandiose or pompous with his success.

Case 7 Summary.   This is a bright and capable person. He seems to be flexible, to a point, showing reasonably rich ideational features and a concurrent ability to use emotion in controlled and effective ways. He is interested in many things, and seems particularly oriented toward people. He has strong achievement needs, but not in excess of his capacities. His reality testing is very good, and he can handle complex stimuli well. He is somewhat too committed to conventionality, and has an overincorporative style of perceptual scanning that may be a sign of excessive caution in approaching his world. While reasonably mature, he may often attempt to display a more emotionally conservative picture than is really the case. In situations with which he is very sure of himself, it is likely that a more ''affective'' person is revealed; however, the difference between the facade and the true person is neither sharp nor distinct. His greatest liability may lie in the fact that he is prone to sacrifice his own uniqueness in order to conform, and this may limit the extent to which his creativeness can be manifest. Nonetheless, he seems "pretty healthy" and if the history is accurate, he is living a very effective life.

Case 8: A 10 Year Old Female

History. This child is the youngest of three children, and the only female in a middle class black family. Her father, age 38, is a policeman in the moderate sized Eastern city in which the subject was born. The father completed two years in a segregated community college in a Southern community at the age of 21, and the next year moved to the Northeast with two of his brothers. Before becoming a policeman, he was a taxi driver for two years and a security guard for two years. The girl's mother was born and raised in a large Northern city and is a registered nurse who currently works part time to supplement the family income. The family lives in an integrated middle class suburban community. The subject's brothers, ages 14 and 12, are in the ninth and seventh grades respectively, and she is currently completing the fifth grade. Her birth was uncomplicated, and her medical history is normal. She is described by her teacher as "diligent" in her efforts, but not outstanding in her performance. She is a good reader but has difficulty with mathematics. She says that she likes "gym and recess" best in school; has several close friends; doesn't like her oldest brother; enjoys visiting her grandmother who still lives in the South; and wants a dog very badly. She is noncommittal about her occupational goals, has a doll collection, likes softball better than basketball, and feels that both of her brothers "get away with murder at home." School records indicate an I.Q. of 109.

Structural Interpretation. The record is of normal length, thus permitting the use of the reference data for 10 year olds. The Four Square data reveal that she is slightly prone toward an extratensive style, but can still "go either way" in terms of style development. As is the case with the majority of nonpatient children of this age, she does not have access to the bulk of her resources ($ep > EA$), and tends to display more stimulation from ideational activity than emotional irritation ($eb - 5:3$). A closer inspection of the features of the eb indicates the presence of two m answers, both in blends, while the grey-black shading side of the ratio consists of one T, one Y, and one C' determinant. The m's may indicate a situational feeling of lack of control, and, interestingly, both are in blends containing a CF answer. This may suggest that when she feels overwhelmed, her seemingly natural tendency toward emotional display is intensified, and she may lose control or direction of her responses for brief periods. In the adult, this might be construed as a marked liability; in the child, however, it is a relatively natural event. Similarly, like that of the typical child, her $FC:CF+C$ ratio is weighed heavily on the $CF+C$ side; but in fact, she actually shows more FC in relation to $CF+C$ than does the typical nonpatient 10 year old. Her $a:p$ ratio does not indicate much flexibility in ideational activity, which could be a problem for her later in life but at this age is not very uncommon. She is very responsive to emotionally toned stimuli ($Afr = 1.00$), which again, is not atypical for the 10 year old and speaks positively to the fact that she is able to deliver as much FC as she does in this record. Her $Lambda$ is somewhat, though not significantly, lower than expected for her age, indicating a very healthy capacity to "back away" from overly com-

Case 8

Card	Free Association	Inquiry	Scoring
I	4″ Oh wow! Are thes really suppos to b s.t.? E: Well they r really inkblots but we want to kno what thy ll, what else thy mite ll		
	19″ 1. A bat or a bf I guess, do I hav to tell which? E: Does it look more like one than the other? S: It cld really be either but I'll say bf, o.k. (Tries to return card) E: I think if you look a littl longer u mite find that it ll s.t. else too	E: (Rpts s's resp) S: Well its got the wgs out here (points) & the body part is smaller & here r the hands and the feet, do u c it now like I c it E: Yes, thank you, you hav the idea	Wo Fo A P 1.0 INCOM
	2. It c.b. lik Tinker Bell on the TV, she flies, she's got magic, she's not flyg yet but she will in a minute	E: (Rpts S's resp) S: Well she's not flying here, but its lik she has her wgs out, lik she is gettin ready to fly, c the wgs & she has littl points on her cap up here & its lik she's standg on her tip toes & c ths top here is her cap, the points r prob magic too	Wo $M^a o$ (H) (P) 4.0
II	3″ Is ths gonna take long? E: Not very long		
	8″ 3. Ths c.b. 2 dogs standg on their frnt legs, no I mean their back legs, pushg w the ft ones S: Can I look the other way too, like ths (inverts card) E: Whichever way u like	E: (Rpts S's resp) S: Well, if u kno a.t. about dogs u kno thy play lik ths s.times, sort of pushg their paws togethr, c thy hav their heads back & here is their ears, lik thy squat down a little when thy do ths, not ths red stuff tho, that doesn't count	D+ $FM^a o$ (2) A P 3.0

4. Ths red part ll s.t. all exploding, lik a bomb. lik it makes a big mess with all the fire

E: (Rpts S's resp)
S: Yeah, bang lik a bomb is goin off rite there & u c the red fire shootin out lik when bombs go off

Dv $m^a.CFo$ Ex

2"

Did u make all of these"
E: No, thy r made by a printer

11"

5. It ll two people cookin s.t. in ths big kettle

E: (Rpts S's resp)
S: Well, it c b. 2 ladies lik at a picnic makin s.t. in ths kettle
E: Can u show me how thy ll ladies to u?
S: Well this here is the head & these w.b. the legs & ths is their front part, ths how u can tell thyr ladies caus thy r bigger in frnt

$D+$ $M^a o$ (2) H P 3.0

6. Ths is lik water wgs tht u use when u learn to swim. can u swim? (E: Yes)

E: (Rpts S's resp)
S: Oh, sure, u fill em w air & thy hold u up, c they come out here, its for littl kids befor thy knc how to swim, I can swim good

Do Fo Waterwings

7. Thes thgs c.b. fishooks too there's no line tho

E: (Rpts S's resp)
S: Well thy come out lik this where the pointy part is & up here is where thy get tied onto the line, my daddy takes me fishin s.times

Do Fw (2) Fishooks

5"

8. Blah, that's an ugly thg lik s.s. of creature, lik a big monster with big feet & a small head, it must be dumb bec the head is so small

E: (Rpts S's resp)
S: C the littl head, lik it doesn't have much brain in there, & here r the great big feet & the littl arms, where the swans are there

Wo Fo (H) 2.0 ALOG

9. These ll the heads of 2 swans, thy r suppos to b white but thes r black

E: (Rpts S's resp)
S: U can't c all of them, just their heads & long necks, mayb thy are special ones cause I think thy aren't suppos to b black, almost all swans are white that I've ever seen

Do $FC'o$ (2) Ad

Case 8 (Continued)

Card	Free Association	Inquiry	Scoring
V	7"		
	10. I d.k., mayb its a flying squirrel, what do most people c in these thgs? E: Many things S: Well I don't c a.t. else in ths one	E: (Rpts S's resp) S: Well he's got his wings out lik he was flying, & his little body & his hands out in the front, we saw them in a movie in school, just like ths I thk	Wo FMªo A 1.0 INCOM
VI	6"		
	11. Thats all furry, its lik a cat, lik on TV, I can't remember his name but he's always gettin run over by s.t. & he gets flat lik ths do u kno which one I mean? (E: Yes, I thk so)	E: (Rpts S's resp) S: Sylvester, thts his name, he's a kinda dumb cat & he's always gettin run over bec he's after a littl bird that always gets away E: What makes it ll that S: The colors there, thy ll fur on his back & here is his nose & head & his legs, lik he got flattened out, ouch!	Wo FTo A P 2.5
VII	3"		
	12. Oh, thts lik 2 girls, lik thy r dancing or s.t. w their hair up, lik pony tail hair up bec thyr dancg, or mayb its not two, just one & she's dancg by the mirror	E: (Rpts S's resp) S: Its lik two Lucy's, from Peanuts, she's always bouncing around & her hair goes up lik this, ths ll she's dancing away in fron of the mirror watching herself, Lucy would do s.t. lik tht, c her nose & her arm is out & its lik she is bent sort of at the waist, lik cartoons do but real people can't do that	W+ Mª.Fr+ (H) P 2.5
VIII	6"		
	13. Finally, a pretty one, its lik a big houseplant, all in bloom, some r beautiful, u should hav given me ths one before	E: (Rpts S's resp) S: It has all the different colors lik it was in full bloom, my mom has some lik it, c the different parts, the petals r pink & some blue & this is the pot	W+ CFo Bt 4.5

190

14. The blue parts c.b. 2 flags too

E: (Rpts S's resp)
S: Just lik two flags, lik thy cross them some-times, c theyr square lik 2 flags

Do Fo (2) Flags

<15. The pink ll an animal if u turn it ths way, lik a cat or s.t., do u have a cat or are u married? (E: I don't have any cats)

E: (Rpts S's resp)
S: Well it has the shape lik a cat & a small head, & the legs, & it just ll a cat to me, one here & one here

Do Fo (2) A P

IX 4"

16. Oh wow, that ll a, ε, one of those poison thgs, a scorpion or s.t., no wait, erase that one

E: (Rpts S's resp)
S: But it doesn't count
E: Its o.k., we'll do all of them, now tell me about the scorpion
S: Well I don't thk it really ll one, but when I first saw it I did, its got these big stingers & its all fat lik thy r & I thk thy mite be orange & green lik ths is, the pink doesn't count

Dd- FC- A

17. I'm using just the orange part now, & it ll 2 witch thgs, thyr not real witches, but lik cartoons of them

E: (Rpts S's resp)
S: O.k., thy hav pointy hats & thy r wearing orange dresses lik witches might on hallo-ween, if thy don't wear black thy wear orange, c one on each side

Do FCo (2) (H)

18. The pink ll some apples, I think four of them but 2 are back behind the frnt two, I'm getting hungry, and these look nice & red lik ready to eat

E: (Rpts S's resp)
S: Well, thyr lik lined up, c the 2 on the outside & 2 more in the middle but u can't c the 2 in the middle too well cause thy r back in there (uses finger to differentiate)

D+ FC.FDo Fd 2.5

X 9"

19. This cne's all mixed up, the blue thgs c.b. spiders but spiders aren't blue

E: (Rpts S's resp)
S: Well thy have all those legs lik spiders but I never saw a blue one

Do Fo (2) A P

20. There's two funny loobg ants too, tteyr trying to carry that stick there

E: (Rpts S's resp)
S: Well, ants are very hard workers & thyr lifting ths stick lik thy are cooperating, lik u c on Seaseme Street, c the littl feelers there & their tiny legs

D+ $FM^{a}o$ (2) A 4.0

191

Case 8 (Continued)

Card	Free Association	Inquiry	Scoring
21.	These yellow things ll s.b. dropped some eggs & thy broke all over, I did that once & was my mom mad, c the yoke is running into the other part like if u break them, the yoke breaks too sometimes & it makes the whole thing yellow lik ths	E: (Rpts S's resp) S: They just look all yellow the way broken eggs look, c them, the darker part in there is whats left of the yoke, like its running into the white part	Dv $m^p.CF.YFo$ (2) Fd
22.	These green thg could be those animals with a horn in their head, lik they use to hav a long time ago	E: (Rpts S's res) S: They aren't real animals, at least not now, but the Greeks used to have them, I don't kno the name but I kno we studied them, u kno what I'm talkg about E: Yes I thk so	Do Fo (2) (A)
23.	This part ll people here, c just the top part of the pink	E: (Rpts S's resp) S: Its just two heads of people, thy look sort of old to me, lik adults E: Adults? S: Well thy don't ll children	Ddo Fo (2) Hd
24.	This cntr blue mite b a bat lik here's one wg & the other and I really don't c a.t. else	E: (Rpts S's resp) S: Well, when I told my mom I was gonna take the inkblot test she said it had some bats, so this must be the one, c it c.b. two wgs here & here & it really just ll that; are we done now? E: Yes S: Boy, I'm beat, this is a hard test, I hope u don't hav to do it every day	Do Fw (2) A

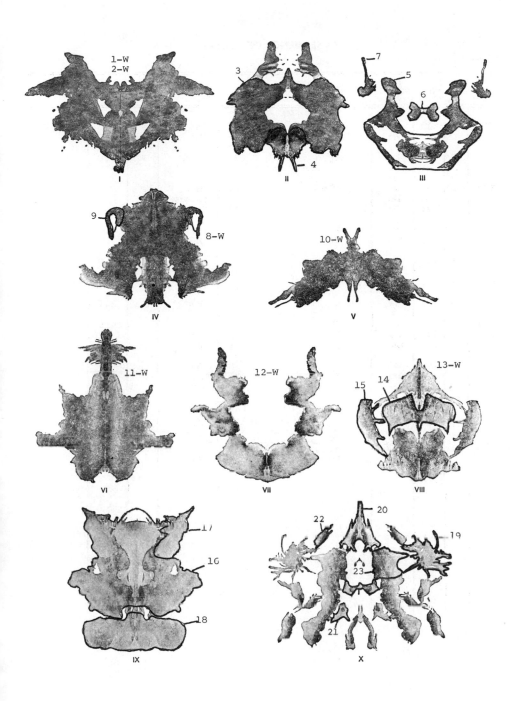

I II III

IV V

VI VII VIII

IX X

Case 8

CARD	RT	NO.	LOCATION	DETERMINANTS (S)		CONTENT (S)	POP	Z SCORE	SPECIAL
I	4"	1.	Wo	Fo		A	P	1.0	INCOM
		2.	Wo	M^ao		(H)	(P)	4.0	
II	8"	3.	D+	FM^ao	(2)	A	P	3.0	
		4.	Dv	m^a.CFo		Ex			
III	11"	5.	D+	M^ao	(2)	H	P	3.0	
		6.	Do	Fo		Waterwgs			
		7.	Do	Fw	(2)	Fishooks			
IV	5"	8.	Wo	Fo		(H)		2.0	ALOG
		9.	Do	FC'o	(2)	Ad			
V	7"	10.	Wo	FM^ao		A		1.0	INCOM
VI	6"	11.	Wo	FTo		A	P	2.5	
VII	3"	12.	W+	M^a.Fr+		(H)	P	2.5	
VIII	6"	13.	W+	CFo		Bt		4.5	
		14.	Do	Fo	(2)	Flags			
		15.	Do	Fo	(2)	A	P		
IX	4"	16.	Dd-	FC-		A			
		17.	Do	FCo	(2)	(H)			
		18.	D+	FC.FDo		Fd		2.5	
X	9"	19.	Do	Fo	(2)	A	P		
		20.	D+	FM^ao	(2)	A		4.0	
		21.	Dv	m^p.CF.YFo	(2)	Fd			
		22.	Do	Fo	(2)	(A)			
		23.	Ddo	Fo	(2)	Hd			
		24.	Do	Fw		A			

Case 8: Structural Summary

R = 24   Zf = 11   ZSum = 30.0   P = 7+1   (2) = 12

Location Features		Determinants (Blends First)	Contents		Contents (Idiographic)
W = 7	**DQ**	m.CF.YF =1	H = 1		Fishooks = 1
D = 15	+ = 6	M.Fr =1	(H) = 4		
Dd = 2	o = 15	FC.FD =1	Hd = 1		Flags = 1
S = 0	v = 2	m.CF =1	(Hd) =		
DW =	— = 1		A = 9		Waterwings 1
		M = 2	(A) = 1		=
		FM = 3	Ad = 1		
		m =	(Ad) =		=
		C =	Ab =		
Form Quality		CF = 1	Al =		=
		FC = 2	An =		
FQx	**FQf**	C' =	Art =		
		C'F =	Ay =		
+ = 1	+ = 0	FC' = 1	Bl =		=
o = 20	o = 8	T =	Bt = 1		
w = 2	w = 2	TF =	Cg =		**Special Scorings**
— = 1	— = 0	FT = 1	Cl =		
		V =	Ex = 1		
M Quality		VF =	Fi =		PSV =
		FV =	Fd = 2		
+ = 1		Y =	Ge =		DV =
o = 2		YF =	Hh =		
w = 0		FY =	Ls =		INCOM = 2
— = 0		rF =	Na =		
		Fr =	Sx =		FABCOM =
		FD =	Xy =		CONTAM =
		F = 10			ALOG = 1
					=

RATIOS, PERCENTAGES, AND DERIVATIONS

ZSum-Zest =	30.0–34.5	FC:CF+C = 3:3	Afr = 1.00		
Zd =	−4.5	W:M = 7:3	3r+(2)/R = .63		
EB =	3:4.5 EA = 7.5	W:D = 7:15	Cont:R = 8:24		
eb =	5:3 ep = 8	L = .71	H+Hd:A+Ad = 6:11		
			(H)+(Hd):(A)+(Ad) = 4:1		
Blends:R =	4:24	F+% = .80	H+A:Hd+Ad = 15:2		
a:p =	7:1	X+% = .88	XRT Achrom. = 5.0"		
Ma:Mp =	3:0	A% = .46	XRT Chrom = 7.6"		

plex stimuli. She is slightly more self-centered than 10 year old nonpatients ($3r + (2)/R = .63$), but not remarkably so, and this also is a rather common feature of children. Her reality testing is quite good ($F+\% = 80$; $X+\% = 88$), and she attempts to organize her stimulus field about as often as do others of her own age ($Zf = 11$). Conversely, she does not organize well, showing a Zd of $-.4.5$. She is an underincorporator, one who tends toward a quick scan of the stimulus field, a proneness toward hasty decision making, and a potential for responding to inappropriate or less relevant stimuli. While this is often common among the very young child, it is found considerably less often among children after the age of eight; and when it does appear in the older child, it may be some cause for concern.

The number of Popular answers that she gives is slightly, but not significantly, higher than normal for her age group, indicating that she can identify and respond to conventionality with comparative ease. Her $W:M$ ratio is more that of an adult than a child; that is, children tend to manifest aspirations that exceed their capacities, while she is much more realistic about hers. This is a bit unusual for the 10 year old and raises the question whether some of her "childish" dreams of accomplishment are being extinguished prematurely by a family system that emphasizes a more conventional adherence to reality. She offers a "healthy" number of Human contents, but most of them are of a parenthesized variety; this pattern raises a question about her capacity to perceive people on a more real plane and her ability to establish more enduring relationships. Again, this is not uncommon among eight and nine year olds, but at 10 there is often a somewhat "sturdier" index of awareness of peer relations, and the self-concept is frequently marked by more interest in the real rather than mythical human. She offers extensive variation in content, with no special emphasis on any category except the predictable high Animal content frequency. Her determinants include one FD answer, which usually represents some tendencies to a healthy introspectiveness. This can be a very worthwhile operation for the preadolescent child.

Interpretation of the Scoring Sequence.   She approaches, or "signs in," with a pure F, Popular answer. This is conservative and "safe," and, when pressed for more answers to the first card, she very appropriately moves to the ideational delay of the human movement response. Both of her m answers occur to chromatically colored blots, which may reflect some potential liability in her overresponsiveness to the color stimuli. Interestingly, both responses also follow FM answers, suggesting that ideational activity created by prompting need states may be partially responsible for her tendency to feel somewhat out of control. She manifests some organizational activity on every card, which is a sign of strength for a child. She will not be overwhelmed by even the most complex stimuli. Her reflection answer occurs to Card VII, which is often perceived as related to "femaleness." This *might* indicate a considerable preoccupation with being feminine, a not uncommon feature of the preadolescent female child; since however, such reflections are more common in the much younger child, she may be tending to overvalue her sex role. Six of her 10 pure F responses occur during the last three cards, a pattern suggesting that the array of chromatic stimuli may be somewhat more intense and/or complex than what she feels comfortable with, and may create a tendency to exert greater control over the natural proneness to respond to emotionally toned stimuli, which is illustrated in the Afr. In fact, her one chromatic color response in Card X is her most complex blend, which includes m, CF, and YF. The presence of both color and shading in a single response hints of mixed, or ambivalent, feelings, and may represent an instance in which "doing what is natural"—that is, responding openly to the color—promotes the pleasurable experience of the emotional discharge but also the painful experience of inability to control that discharge. It is interesting to note that, after this answer, she gives three more responses to Card X, all of which are pure F, as if to revalidate her ability to "back away." She has three Special Scores, two *INCOM* answers and one *ALOG,* all of which illustrate concreteness in her thinking. These sorts of response appear much more frequently in the records of children and are usually not "warning signs" except when the frequency becomes excessive or the character is more pathological, as in some *FABCOM* or most *CONTAM* responses.

Interpretation of Content. Her verbal material includes many commentaries and asides that are very common among the protocols of younger clients. She delays her first answer with a question and uses the same approach on the next two cards. At times, she seeks reassurance, ". . . do I have to tell which . . . ," " ". . . what do most people see in these things?" and ". . . do you know what I mean?" In other instances, she displays a subtle aggressiveness in her chiding of the examiner, ". . . you should have given me this one before," and ". . . do you have a cat, or are you married?" The comment on Card VIII, ". . . you should have given me this one before," may also hint of more defensiveness than is evident on the surface, since it occurs with the first presentation of the card and may relate to her vacillation, noted previously, about becoming too involved in the emotionally toned stimuli. She tends to neutralize most of her aggressive contents; the cat on VI is a TV character, the witches on IX are really cartoons, and the scorpion on IX should be "erased." The latter is additional evidence of the occasional cognitive slippage that marks the psychological operations of the child, as does her clarification on Card II, ". . . two dogs standing on their front legs—no, I mean their back legs . . . ." This process is probably also related to the fact that she is an underincorporator, and prone to more hasty decision making than may be effective at times. Also typical of the child is her tendency to become very personalized in some of her answers and in some of her inquiry comments: ". . . I'm getting hungry and these look nice and red like ready to eat," ". . . I did that once and was my mom mad . . . ," "I can swim good," ". . . my daddy takes me fishing sometimes."

Her movement responses that involve more than one character are all cooperative (ladies cooking, dogs playing, ants carrying), which speaks favorably about her approach to interpersonal relations. Most of her answers reflect the expected child-like immaturity (Tinker Bell, TV characters, cartoon characters), and one in particular offers some "food for thought" concerning her own self-image. This occurs on Card IV in which she describes an ugly creature with big feet and a small head, "It must be dumb because the head is so small." Being the youngest child is often difficult; and very often, the inability to function as effectively as older siblings or adults creates a marked sense of inadequacy.

Case 8 Summary. This is a very interesting, and probably pretty healthy, youngster who fares quite well under the stress of the Rorschach. She is prone to emotional display, but she controls those displays quite well and can generally use them to her advantage. She "banters" with the test and with the examiner to both express and protect herself. Her reality testing is quite good, and although she manifests some of the concreteness of the child, there is no evidence that her thinking is distorted or disturbed. She is very responsive to emotionally provocative situations, and may not be as comfortable with such stimuli as she would prefer; however, she is also able to extract herself from complex stimulus situations very effectively in most instances. Her aggressiveness is more subtle than direct, and she seems to have a sound awareness of the ingredients for healthy interpersonal relations. She is aware of, and responds to, conventionality with ease, although she exhibits many of her own idiographic features with similar ease. She is not fully secure in her cognitive functioning, and may, in fact, harbor more self-doubts about her intellect than is desirable. She formulates responses too hastily at times, and if she persists in this underincorporative style, she may experience difficulties during adolescence and/or adulthood. She focuses extensively on herself, and will ultimately need to give more attention to others in her world. Her thinking is not very flexible, and this too may ultimately create some difficulties for her. Some of her answers are more characteristic of eight and nine year olds, suggesting that her maturational development may be a bit slower than is optimal; however, there is no evidence of any marked retardation in development. Her sex role identification is appropriate, and her cognitive functioning, taken overall, is generally quite sophisticated for some one this age. Her ideation is active and potentially rich, and while she still manifests some of the "magical" thinking of the child, it is not excessive. In general, she is probably a very likable youngster who has many more assets than liabilities.

SUMMARY

The four cases included here illustrate reasonably "healthy" people, free of symptoms, with no psychiatric history, and functioning at effective levels. The first, Case 1, displays more immaturity than might be selected if personality could be ordered, but poses no great cause for concern, especially if his environment continues to offer needed supports. The second, Case 6, illustrates a person who is not fully comfortable with her emotional style and is overly concerned with making appropriate responses while trying to avoid the more unpleasant aspects of her world. The stability of her marriage will be important to her future, but again there is no great cause for concern. Case 7 reflects a very talented businessman with strong achievement needs who may be sacrificing some of his uniqueness in exchange for occupational accomplishments. He is a cautious and precise person who may be overly annoyed by complex ambiguities but is usually able to adapt effectively to them. He is probably the "healthiest" of the three adult cases presented. Case 8 represents a very "sturdy" youngster who probably overreacts at times and is still not completely certain of her emotional controls; but she adapts easily and effectively. She is still quite immature, as would be expected, and possibly even a bit more so than many 10 year olds; but she shows all the characteristics of continued growth, and if she can come to trust her intellect more, her sense of self-trust should improve considerably.

All these subjects have liabilities that are quite evident in the Rorschach data, and any interpretation could focus excessively on them, at the expense of describing and emphasizing assets. The finished or complete interpretation strives to put the assets and the liabilities in a useful perspective, so that the final description does not weigh any features inordinately, but captures the uniqueness of the person. The finished interpretation should represent a beginning from which accurate diagnostic pictures are drawn, and from which appropriate treatment plans are formulated. The following chapters will focus on issues of psychopathology, but in each instance it is equally important that the emphasis on assets not be neglected.

PART TWO

Special Issues of
Diagnosis and Description

CHAPTER 7

The Suicide Potential

The early identification of the potential for suicide has been a persistent challenge for the clinician. The classic works of Shneidman and Farberow (1957) and Farberow and Shneidman (1961) have demonstrated clear relationships between demographic and/or behavioral variables and the ultimate effected suicide; and it is unlikely that any psychological test data, taken alone, will provide greater discrimination of the suicidal risk. Nonetheless, there have been many efforts to glean from various tests, including the Rorschach, significant clues that would add to the early warning system that has gradually evolved.

Any review of the research literature concerning suicide reveals a host of methodological and interpretive problems. The criterion variables often differ considerably. Data from the suicidal subject are often collected too long before, or too long after, the critical event. Possibly even more important is the issue of *intent*, which is extremely difficult, if not impossible, to judge at a very precise level. Some suicides are effected by means that are not ordinarily expected to produce death, such as taking 20 aspirins; yet such deaths are duly recorded as "suicides," while the astonishing survival of a person with a self-inflicted gunshot head wound is recorded as a "suicide attempt." It seems unlikely that the intention to die was greater for the aspirin-taker than for the gunshot victim; yet on a purely demographic basis, the first is an effected suicide while the second is merely an attempt. Although some of these research problems are potentially soluble, they become confounded if research efforts are designed in the context of scientific prediction. Predictive studies on suicide are, in reality, postdictive or retrospective, often based on data collected from subjects identified from other sources as "suicidal" (most commonly by reason of a prior suicide attempt); or, in fewer instances, are based on data collected before the attempted or effected suicide. Thus, even when a potential "predictor" is revealed, typically from small sample research, our moral commitment to suicide prevention takes precedence over the scientific fantasy to test the validity of the predictor by letting events run their full course.

In such a restricted research framework, it is highly unlikely that any single predictor, or group of predictors, will be developed to any "near perfect" level. This point is well stated in an exhaustive review of the literature concerning Rorschach data and the suicidal subject completed by Goldfried, Stricker, and Weiner (1971). They note that past research has included foci on single signs, such as the color-shading response studied by Applebaum and Holzman (1962); multiple sign approaches (Piotrowski, 1950; Martin's Checklist, 1951; Sakheim, 1955; and Fleischer, 1957); content indicators, such as Lindner's "suicide card" (1946); the presence of morbid content (White and Schreiber, 1952; Thomas, Ross, Brown, and Duszynski, 1973); symbolic content (Sapolsky, 1963); and the use of signs and content combined (Hertz, 1948, 1949). Although many of these studies have demonstrated "statistically significant" differences between suicidal and nonsuicidal subjects, the actual number of *true positive* cases identified is often less than two thirds, while the number of *false positive* cases often exceeds one third. The findings from such studies are clearly very important; their clinical utility, however, is often quite limited.

A CONSTELLATION OF CRITICAL VARIABLES

Exner and Wylie (1977) have reported the use of a *constellation* of 11 Rorschach variables, eight or more of which appear in a large percentage of records collected from effected suicide cases within 60 days prior to the event. Initiated in 1974, their research used the entire protocol pool that the various studies leading to the development of the Comprehensive System had generated. The pool contained 41 protocols that had been collected within 60 days before an effected suicide, plus a much larger number of records taken from subjects with a history of suicide attempt, including a small number of these taken within 60 days before an attempt. In an effort to increase the sample sizes, a solicitation letter was sent to 108 clinical installations requesting protocols taken from these types of subjects, plus a completed demography questionnaire about each subject. The end product of this effort was the accumulation of three groups of protocols that formed the basis for their analysis: one group consisting of 59 records of subjects, ages 18 to 57, that were taken within 60 days of an effected suicide; a second group of 31 records from subjects, ages 19 to 50, taken within 60 days before a suicide attempt, and a third group of 33 records from subjects, ages 20 to 62, collected within five days after a suicide attempt. Three control groups were selected by randomization from the protocol pool with the restriction that 60% of each group would be female to match the approximate sex distribution of the three suicide groups. The control groups consist of: (1) 50 depressed inpatients with no history of a suicide attempt; (2) 50 inpatient schizophrenics with no history of a suicide attempt; and (3) 50 nonpatients with no psychiatric history.

The structural data from these records were computer coded, as was the presence or absence of "morbid" content. The first series of analyses focused on the discriminative possibilities of single signs, sign dyads, and sign triads; the group of 59 effected suicide cases was used as the basic "test" group. Some of these analyses did produce significant correlations. For instance, the color-shading blend, cited by Applebaum and Holzman (1962), does correlate at a .34 level ($p < .01$) for the effected suicide group, appearing in 39 of the 59 protocols; however, it also appears in 17 of the 50 records from the control group of depressives, and in 16 of the 50 schizophrenic protocols. Obviously, its discriminatory value is important, but it is also quite limited. Similarly, the dyad of R less than 17 plus more than two vista answers correlates with effected suicide at .33 ($p < .01$), but the same dyad appears in 21 of the 50 control records from depressives, 10 of the 50 schizophrenic control records and six protocols of the 50 nonpatients. Unfortunately, the method of test administration and the rules for scoring the Comprehensive System made it impractical to "test out" the discriminative power of some of the previously reported configurations; however, several of those configurations, or portions of them, were subjected to analyses. None produced useful findings, but in several instances statistically significant results were obtained. For instance, the Sakheim (1955) and Fleischer (1957) indices for "oppressive anxiety" and "neurotic structure" do appear in 31 of the 59 effected suicide records; but they also occur in 14 of the 50 depressives, 10 of the 50 schizophrenics, and seven of the 50 nonpatients. Similarly, the "morbid" content, such as suggested by White and Schreiber (1952) and Thomas et al (1973), did occur with a significantly high frequency among the protocols of the suicide groups; but it also appeared with a high frequency among the records of the control depressives and schizophrenics.

After the first series of 36 analyses had failed to yield any single signs, sign dyads, or sign triads that would effectively discriminate the effected suicide group from the controls, the approach was changed to one seeking constellations of 10 to 15 structural variables that would be common to the effected suicide group. The method used involved a program by which the computer would first screen, on a "yes-no" basis, for the presence or absence of each variable in any suggested constellation. It would then report the frequency for each *variable* within the "test" group, plus the frequency for each arithmetic *combination* of variables in the constellation. For example, if a constellation to be tested included 10 variables, the computer would count the frequency with which each occurred, and also the frequency of protocols in which all 10 occurred, the frequency for nine of the 10, then of eight of the 10, and so on. Whenever a constellation of six or more variables appeared in the "test" group of effected suicides, the computer would seek out the same constellation among each of the three control groups, then would calculate a chi-square, to determine if the frequencies for effected suicides and for controls were significantly different. In the course of these analyses, seven constellations of variables were discovered to appear with a significantly high frequency among the effected suicide group; however, only three of the seven occurred with a significantly greater frequency among effected suicides than in all three control groups, and only one could successfully discriminate effected suicides from all three control groups at a 50% level of accuracy. In other words, the constellation correctly identified at least 50% of the effected suicides while calling no "false positives" from any of the control groups. This finding was not especially exciting, and seemed to confirm the somewhat pessimistic conclusions drawn by Goldfried, Stricker, and Weiner (1971) in their literature review. They had suggested that criterion and methodological problems in suicide research sorely limit the extent to which any Rorschach indices can be validated for the prediction of suicide.

A reexamination of the work of Farberow and Shneidman (1961) prompted speculation that part of the difficulty in discovering an effective discriminator might be related to the issue of intentionality. In accord with their suggestions, each of the three suicide groups was "subgrouped" on a somewhat crude scale devised to estimate intent; the apparent lethality of the method employed was used as the basis for differentiating the groups. The first effort at gauging intentionality followed a schedule described by Tabachnick and Farberow (1961), but this proved too unreliable when completed by multiple raters; thus a broad, three category differentiation was applied, in which the methods used were classified in terms essentially of a *point of no return* element. In this scheme, subjects using techniques that appear to have the greatest probability of producing death, *and* that permit the least amount of time for rescue (firearms, explosives, jumps from great heights, cutting vital organs) are designated as Class I; methods that have a high probability of inducing death but permit a longer rescue time (hanging, drowning, poisoning) are designated as Class II; and Class III includes methods with the lowest probability of inducing death and the greatest available rescue time (cutting nonvital organs, inhaling gases, ingesting analgesics or soporifics).

The data were reanalyzed, with the three suicide groups subcategorized on the basis of the method used, in terms of the constellation of variables that had previously shown the "best" results. It is important to point out that this is a *constellation of variables and not a static configuration;* that is, it is a group of 11 variables, various combinations of which do occur with a significantly higher frequency among the protocols of two of the three suicide groups. The 11 variables included in this constellation are:

$FV+VF+V+FD$ greater than 2
Color-shading blend greater than zero
Zd score greater than ± 3.5
$3r + (2)/R$ less than .30
Experience Potential *(ep)* greater than Experience Actual *(EA)*
$CF+C$ greater than FC
S greater than 3
$X + \%$ less than .70
Pure H (excluding *(H), Hd, (Hd)*) less than 2
P greater than 8 or less than 3
R less than 17

Table 25 presents the frequencies of protocols for two of the three suicide groups, effected suicides and pretested attempters, in which five or more of these critical variables are present. The two groups are shown as subdivided by method employed, and also collectively. Table 25 also shows similar data for each of the three control groups. An examination of the data in Table 25 reveals that when all 11 variables are used as a criterion, only 25% of the effected suicide records, and only 10% of the pretested attempters, are correctly identified, while one depressive control and one schizophrenic control are included as "false positives." The level of accurate identification is increased considerably, however, especially for subjects in the suicide groups who are classified as Class I or II in terms of methods used, when the number of variables present is reduced to 10; concurrently, the number of false positives increases only very slightly. Conversely, if only seven variables are used to identify suicide potential, the accuracy level is increased to 81% for the group of effected suicide cases, and to 45% for the pretested attempters; however, the cost for this level of accuracy is the false positive identification of 58% of the depressive controls, 38% of the schizophrenic controls, and 8% of the nonpatient controls.

The data in Table 25 show that the greatest effective "postdictive" yield for accurate identification occurs when either eight or nine of the critical variables are present. The appearance of eight variables correctly identifies 75% of the effected suicides and 45% of the pretested attempters, while including as false positives

Table 25.   Frequencies of Protocols Identified by Number of Variables, in an 11 Variable Constellation, for Two Suicide Groups Subdivided by Classification of Method Selected, and for Three Control Groups

Group	\#11 N	\#11 %	\#10 N	\#10 %	\#9 N	\#9 %	\#8 N	\#8 %	\#7 N	\#7 %	\#6 N	\#6 %	5 or Less N	5 or Less %
Effected suicides, Class I, $N = 19$	7	.37	11	.58	13	.68	14	.74	17	.89	18	.95	19	100
Effected suicides, Class II, $N = 24$	7	.29	16	.67	19	.79	20	.83	20	.83	23	.96	24	100
Effected suicides, Class III, $N = 16$	1	.06	4	.25	7	.44	10	.63	11	.69	14	.88	16	100
Effected suicides, Combined, $N = 59$	15	.25	31	.52	39	.66	44	.75	48	.81	55	.93	59	100
Pretested attempt, Classes I and II, $N = 7$	3	.43	4	.57	5	.71	6	.86	6	.86	7	100	7	100
Pretested attempt, Class III, $N = 24$	0	0	0	0	2	.08	8	.33	8	.33	9	.38	24	100
Pretested attempt, Combined, $N = 31$	3	.10	4	.13	7	.23	14	.45	14	.45	16	.52	31	100
Inpatient depressed, control, $N = 50$	1	.02	3	.06	7	.14	10	.20	29	.58	41	.82	50	100
Inpatient schizo-phrenics, control, $N = 50$	1	.02	1	.02	2	.04	6	.12	19	.38	34	.68	50	100
Nonpatient control, $N = 50$	0	0	0	0	0	0	0	0	4	.08	7	.14	50	100

Number of Variables Appearing

*From J. E. Exner and J. R. Wylie, Some Rorschach data concerning suicide, *Journal of Personality Assessment*, 1977, 41, 339–348.

20% of the depressive controls, 12% of the schizophrenic controls, *and none of the nonpatients*.

The level of accurate identification of the suicide subjects is clearly reduced by the subjects who fall into the Class III category of suicide method. For example, when nine variables are used as a "cutoff", that criterion identifies only a very small number of controls as false positive, while 32 of the 43 Class I and II effected suicides (75%) and five of the seven Class I and II pretested suicide attempters are identified correctly. Conversely, nine variables identify only seven of the 16 Class III effected suicides (44%) and only two of the 24 Class III pretested suicide attempts (8%). Thus, it appears that there is a distinct relationship between the "lethality of intention" and the number of variables from this constellation that will be present in a protocol. This raises a question about how many of the Class III effected suicides may have been "equivocal"—that is, marked by greater vacillation in the intent, toward self destruction, with the possibility that the method selected may not have been designed to invoke death, but rather to magnify the cry for help that so often characterizes the suicidal person. Unfortunately, the demographic data on these cases are not such as to permit useful approach to that question. It should also be noted that the "cutoff" of eight variables present represents the least number that can be applied while still avoiding false positive identification of any of the nonpatient controls.

A discriminant functions analysis was calculated for the purpose of determining whether any of the 11 variables in the constellation should be weighted more heavily than others. This analysis revealed that three variables (color-shading blend, $FV+VF+V+FD > 2$, and $3r + (2)/R < .30$) each correlate positively and significantly with the effected suicide; however, the correlations are generally low, ranging from .34 to .31. None of the other eight variables, when taken independently, correlate significantly with suicide. Similarly, no dyad or triad of these variables will identify suicide from nonsuicide subjects at a useful level, although some correlations can be raised to the .45 level. In other words, there is no single variable, or combination of two or three variables in the constellation of 11 variables, that is more important than the others in the accurate identification of the potential for suicide.

The data in Table 26 illustrate the problem, or possibly the futility, of using data collected after a suicide attempt has been made to indicate the psychological status of the suicide prone individual. These data show the effected and pretested

Table 26. Frequencies of Protocols, Identified by Number of Variables Appearing in an 11 Variable Constellation, for Combined Effected Suicides and Pretested Suicide Attempt Groups, Post-tested Attempters, Combined Psychiatric Controls, and Nonpatient Controls

| | \multicolumn{14}{c}{Number of Variables Appearing} |
| | 11 | | 10 | | 9 | | 8 | | 7 | | 6 | | 5 or Less | |
Group	N	%	N	%	N	%	N	%	N	%	N	%	N	%
Effected and pretested attempt, Classes I and II, $N = 50$	17	.34	31	.62	37	.74	40	.80	43	.86	48	.96	50	100
Effected and pretested attempt, Class III, $N = 40$	1	.03	4	.10	9	.23	18	.45	19	.48	23	.58	40	100
Postattempt tested, Classes I and II, $N = 6$	0	0	0	0	1	.16	2	.23	3	.50	6	100	6	100
Postattempt tested, Class III, $N = 27$	1	.04	1	.04	2	.08	7	.26	15	.56	21	.78	27	100
Inpatient depressed and schizophrenic controls, combined, $N = 100$	2	.02	4	.04	9	.09	16	.16	48	.48	75	.75	100	100
Nonpatient controls, $N = 50$	0	0	0	0	0	0	0	0	4	.08	7	.14	50	100

*From J. E. Exner and J. R. Wylie, Some Rorschach data concerning suicide. *Journal of Personality Assessment*, 1977, 41, 339–348.

attempter groups, combined by class of method used, as contrasted with 33 subjects from whom Rorschachs were collected within five days *after* an attempt. Table 26 also shows the two psychiatric control groups combined, plus the data for the nonpatient controls. When the criterion of eight or nine critical variables is applied to the posttested attempters, only an insignificant number are correctly identified. In fact, the level of accurate identification for this group is about the same as the number of false positives identified from the control group of inpatient depressives who have no history of suicide attempt. It is also important to note that a subgrouping of the posttested attempters in terms of method used does not enhance the accuracy of identification. These data appear to support the contention that major alterations in the psychological state of the suicidal person do occur subsequent to an actual attempt. Farberow (1950) has postulated that the attempt has a cathartic effect, reducing stresses and altering many of the emotional "impingements" that had previously devastated the individual. In a similar framework, Shneidman (1963) has hypothesized that most people who become suicidal are acutely so only for relatively brief periods during which significant shifts occur among the various psychological features of the person. Whatever the explanation, protocols taken shortly after a suicide attempt has occurred are clearly quite different in structure from those collected prior to an attempted or effected suicide.

The problem of prediction is magnified by these data. It seems that no combination of Rorschach variables can produce the "perfect hit rate" without also identifying a substantial number of false positives; however, some clear implications are present in these data. For instance, the composite of either eight or nine variables does accurately identify a substantial proportion of the effected suicide group, especially those who selected the most "lethal" techniques. Most of the false positives identified through the use of either "cutoff" (eight or nine) are from the control depressives, and it is more than tempting to suggest that some may, in fact, have had suicidal intentions when the Rorschachs were collected. Clearly, these cutoffs do not identify any of the nonpatients falsely. It is also interesting to note that only 38 of the 59 effected suicides were identified as "clearly" depressed from the presuicide history data available. Ten of the 59 had been inpatient schizophrenics, and the remaining 11 subjects had exhibited various forms of psychological and behavioral disarray prior to their deaths, but none could be clearly labeled as psychotic or as "chronically" depressed. In other words, as has been pointed out previously (Shneidman and Farberow, 1957; Farberow and Shneidman, 1961), the potential for suicide erupts in many different types of personalities and under many different conditions. On an operational level, it is clearly in order for the clinician to show intelligent concern about subjects whose protocols contain eight or more of the critical variables in this constellation; but at the same time, he should recognize the fact *that the absence of such a composite* does not necessarily preclude the suicide possibility, as a clear 25% of the effected group, 15 of the 59, had fewer than eight variables present in their records.

It is possible that the greatest significance of these data lies in the kind of information they convey about the psychological activity experienced by persons in whom the intent toward self destruction is strong. Such information may be extrapolated from a review of the 11 variables contributing to the constellation. The vista variable $(FV+VF+V)$ has been described in Chapter 4 as the least frequent of the shading determinants, and, as indicated in the earlier work on the Comprehensive System (Exner, 1974), appears to be related to a negative internal experience evolving from self inspection. The *FD* answer also seems to be related to introspection. Thus, the suicidal person whose record includes this variable is probably doing much self examination, frequently emphasizing his or her negative features. The color-shading blend has been elaborated by Beck (1949) as a form of simultaneous pleasure-pain experience, which Applebaum and Colson (1968) suggest is representative of an aborted form of emotional experience. If a slightly different translation is applied, the color-shading blend may illustrate the experience of ambivalence, an element frequently mentioned in the literature as common to suicidal people. As has been noted in Chapter 5, a low egocentricity index is often found among the records of depressives, and it also appears with relatively high frequency among patients who relapse or do not improve during treatment. It probably represents low self-esteem. Thirty-nine of the 59 effected suicide cases showed a $3r + (2)/R$ of less than .30, while 10 of the remaining 20 subjects in that group had indices higher than .45. This may suggest that whenever the "egocentric balance" (Exner, 1973) shows a greater than usual focus on the self, *or* a greater than usual focus away from the self, self-esteem, as such, tends to be exaggerated in a manner that is potentially damaging to the psychological effectiveness of the person.

It has also been noted in Chapter 5 that subjects with deviant *Zd* scores tend to be less efficient in their perceptual scanning and often inappropriate in their selection of critical stimulus cues. This can often produce maladaptive behavior. In a similar context, many of these subjects display an *ep* that is greater than their *EA*, and, as noted in Chapter 4, they are people who do not have a good command of their own resources, but instead are often "acted on" by psychological activities over which they have little control. Compounding this *ep* > *EA* pattern is the fact that many of these subjects give more pure *C* and *CF* than *FC* in their records, indicating a potential for their emotions to "get out of control" and commanding of their behavior. It is also not uncommon for the suicide prone person to have a low $X+\%$, indicating some limitation in perceptual accuracy, a factor important to decision making, especially in situations involving environmental adjustments. The low frequency of the Whole Human content is generally noted in people who are disinterested in others or who have difficulty in relating easily to them. The *P* response has been well documented (Exner, 1974) as relating to the ability and/or willingness to see conventional things. Low *P* is often found in people who see the world in an unconventional manner, while high *P* occurs among those who sacrifice their own uniqueness for the rigid constraints of convention. Although the presence of some *S* in a protocol can be taken as a sign of independence or a striving for autonomy, an excess of *S* responses seems to offer reasonably clear evidence of oppositional elements (Bandura, 1954; Ray, 1963; Fonda, 1977). These are usually short records in which *R* is less than 17. The presence of more than three *S* answers generally constitutes a remarkably large segment of the protocol and tends to dramatize the "negativism" that many of these people must experience. Finally, the low *R* characterizing many of these records is also common among the protocols of the depressed, some organics, and most very resistive subjects. It may illustrate more of the resistance noted by the high *S*, or it may simply reflect the "slowing down" or retardation of operation that is common to the depressed person.

When the information about all 11 variables is integrated, a picture emerges of a person who is introspective, probably negatively so; who does not, or cannot, express emotions easily or directly and who often aborts them because of that uneasiness or uncertainty; whose emotions tend to "get out of hand" when they are displayed; who does not regard himself or herself very highly in social comparisons; whose resources are not easily or fully available for coping; who may be overly concerned with convention—or may, conversely, have reached a point where convention is disregarded; who does not organize perceptual inputs efficiently, tending to misinterpret stimuli more often than is affordable; who may be quite negative; who has difficulty in creating or maintaining interpersonal relations; and who may be psychologically and/or motorically retarded or inhibited. Although most of the effected suicide and pretested attempted suicide cases do not show all 11 of these variables, most do show "positive" for at least eight or nine of them; and any combination of eight or nine of these characteristics makes for a very disorganized psychology, and a person who must be experiencing considerable pain and frustration. Although this description of the suicide prone person is not particularly new, the fact that it is derived exclusively from structural variables of the Rorschach is important. It serves both to promote better understanding of the test and its usefulness, and to add information to the understanding of the suicide prone person.

SUICIDAL POTENTIAL IN YOUNGER CLIENTS

The constellation of variables that discriminate effected suicide cases and pretested attempted suicide cases from other groups was developed from *adult* records. Subjects in all of the samples ranged in age from 18 to 57 years. The accumulation of a large number of protocols from younger clients has not yielded a substantial number of records taken prior to an effected or attempted suicide; in fact, only 21 cases are available in which the test was administered within 60 days prior to an effected suicide, and only 18 records are available that were collected within 60 days before a suicide attempt. When the two groups are analyzed collectively, there is no obvious constellation of variables that will discriminate those 39 cases from randomly selected control groups of either patients or nonpatients, although several of the variables from the critical constellation for adults do appear in many of these cases. The problems in detecting a critical constellation that will discriminate suicide proneness in the younger client are compounded by the nature of the cases available for study. First, they represent a considerable age range. The 21 effected suicide cases include three 8, 9, and 10 year olds, seven 11 and 12 year olds, and 11 subjects aged 13 to 16. Conversely, 15 of the 18 pretested attempted suicides are 15 or 16 years old. Similarly, 14 of the 18 pretested attempted suicides used Class III methods in their suicide attempts—that is, techniques that have the least probability of actually resulting in death and that allow most rescue time of the methods studied. Conversely, 17 of the 21 effected suicide cases fell into a Class I or Class II modality, most having involved gunshot wounds or hanging.

When the records of the effected suicides are studied separately, there is a constellation of eight variables for which the presence of *seven or more* does discriminate 15 of the 21 cases (71%), while the same cutoff point does not identify *any* false positives from a randomly selected group of 50 nonpatient controls; *however*, seven or more of these eight variables *do appear* in the protocols of 11 of 50 randomly drawn controls from the withdrawn reference samples (22%), and nine of 50 randomly drawn controls from the behavior problem reference samples (18%). When this constellation is applied to the 18 pretested attempter cases, *only* eight (44%) are correctly identified by the presence of seven or more variables. This constellation includes the following variables:

> $FV+VF+V+FD$ greater than 2
> Color-shading blend greater than zero
> $3r+(2)/R$ less than .35
> *Zd* score greater than ±4.0
> Affective Ratio less than .40
> $X+\%$ is less than .70
> *Lambda* less than .35 or greater than 1.20
> Pure *H* (excluding *(H), Hd, (Hd)*) at zero

It will be noted that six of these variables follow from the critical constellation for adults, but that the remaining two (*Afr* and *Lambda*) are related to issues of stimulus complexity: the lower than normal *Afr* indicates an avoidance of emotionally loaded stimuli, and the very low or very high *Lambda* indicates the problem of inability to "back away" from overly complex stimuli.[1] Since this constellation has far less "potency" in differentiating suicidal from nonsuicidal subjects, its utility is far more limited especially in *ruling out* a self-destructive orientation. An examination of the psychiatric and behavioral histories of the 39 effected and pretested attempted suicide cases reveals the same broad range of pathologies and activities that the adult samples did. Only seven of the 21 effected suicide cases and only eight of the 18 pretested attempted suicides exhibit a clear psychiatric history. Four of these 15 were probably schizophrenic, and at least four others had been chronically depressed. Interestingly, six of the effected suicides and four of the pretested attempters showed histories of "acting-out behavior" and manifest little evidence of social isolation. Fifteen of the 21 effected suicides, and 16 of the 18 pretested attempters had no prior suicide gestures or reports of verbal preoccupation with death or suicide. At least 13 of the effected suicides and 14 of the 18 attempts appear to have occurred with some spontaneity, most often after clashes at home or at school. In other words, much like the adult cases, these subjects represent a wide variety of personalities whose suicide oriented activity occurred under very diverse circumstances.

CASE ILLUSTRATIONS

One of the best ways to illustrate the diversity among persons who become overly preoccupied with suicide is through examples. The three cases that follow reflect very different personality styles and histories. Two are effected suicides, and the

---

[1] The other variables from the "adult constallation" also appear with a very high frequency (low R, $ep > EA$, high frequency of S, and $CF+C > FC$). However, the same variables tend to occur very frequently among records of other psychiatric groups and among the nonpatient samples. They are thus nondiscriminatory.

third was prevented, although the act was in progress at the time. The first is a case that was partially evaluated in Chapters 4 and 5.

Case 2: A 28 Year Old Female—Chronic Isolation

History.   This woman is the oldest of three siblings, having a married sister, age 26, and a married brother, age 24. She was born in a moderate sized city in the Western part of the United States where her father, now age 53, has worked for 30 years in the construction industry. The father is a high school graduate. The subject's mother, now age 52, worked full time at a variety of "blue collar," assembly line, type of positions between the ages of 19 and 23, and has done occasional part time clerical work over the past eight years. The subject's younger sister worked as a secretary for two years after completing college, and currently is a full time wife and mother, with two children, ages 2 and 1. The subject's brother completed an engineering degree and currently is a draftsman in the air-craft industry. He has been married for one year. There is no psychiatric history in the family, nor is the medical history especially remarkable although the subject did have surgery at the age of 23 for an ovarian cyst. She completed high school at age 18 and subsequently completed two years at a junior college with no spe-cialization. After working for one year as a library assistant, she decided to reenter college, majoring in elementary education. She completed that degree at age 23, and was hired immediately thereafter to her present position as a fourth grade teacher in an urban elementary school. Her work is highly regarded, and she has been cited twice for particularly creative innovations in her classroom. She is described as slightly overweight, this condition has apparently existed since early adolescence. During high school and college, she would often undertake "crash" diet programs, sometimes losing as much as 15 pounds, but usually regaining the weight within five or six months. She has been an avid reader, and after graduating from college took two creative writing courses at a local university. She has submitted several poems and short stories for publication during the past three years, but none have been accepted. She has taken at least two extended summer vacations with female colleagues in Europe, and during the last year spent two months with a tour group in Asia. She "dated" very infrequently while in high school, but did have a "steady" relationship with a male about 10 years older than she during her first two years of teaching. After that ended with his marriage to someone else, she has dated very infrequently, but does attend various social events (concerts, theatre, lectures, beach parties, etc.) with friends, most female. Her physician reports that prior to her cyst operation, she visited him quite often with complaints about menstruation, but that the frequency of these visits di-minished sharply after surgery. During the past year she has seen him three times, once for infected throat glands, and twice for feelings of "energy loss," for which he prescribed vitamins. Her closest friend, a female of about the same age, reveals that the subject has in recent months often discussed the possibility of adopting a child, while markedly rejecting any notion that she might marry. Approximately one month prior to taking the Rorschach, she made arrangements for a one month tour of Greece for the coming summer and placed a $500 deposit to insure space on the tour, which is sponsored by a teachers' group. At about the same time, she purchased a new automobile, and she is reported to have spent at least three weekends before the Rorschach test driving through mountain areas in her home state. During at least two of those weekends she traveled alone: on the third she was accompanied by two of her female students, ages 9 and 10. The testing was conducted four days after her last visit to her physician, during which she complained again of "lethergy." He referred her to a psychiatrist on the suspicion that she might be depressed, although she denied this explanation. The psychiatrist interviewed her once for approximately 35 minutes, then referred her for psychological evaluation, a routine procedure that he follows. He noted that she was oriented, appropriate, and seemingly cooperative. He did not detect any significant evidence of depression, but did note that she seemed very anxious about the interview. He did not prescribe medication, although her physician had prescribed sleeping medication during one of her earlier visits. The testing was completed by a psychologist in private practice, and a report expressing concern about depression was forwarded to the psychiatrist about six days after the Rorschach was taken. The psychologist suggested that she was a "schizoid personality" and recommended extensive psychotherapy. The psychiatrist notes that she did not appear for a scheduled appointment 10 days after the test, and on the morning of the 15th day after the test she did not appear for work, nor did she contact the school concerning her absence. Her closest friend stopped by her apartment later that day after failing to reach her by phone. The subject had died some time during the preceding 24 hours of an overdose of sleeping medication. There was no suicide note, but a poem dated the day before her death, entitled, "The Peace of the Long Sleep" and containing many references to death, was discovered on a writing desk in her apartment. Her parents, siblings, and friends all deny any possibility that her death was intentional, and her parents report that she was "in good spirits" during her last visit to their home about a week earlier. A coroner's inquest ultimately ruled the death as suicide, largely on the basis of the autopsy, which revealed that the toxicity level in her body could have been reached only by the ingestion of no less than 12 sleeping tablets, when the prescription had called for no more than one in any 24 hour period.

Previously Developed Interpretation.   She is in serious trouble. Although prone to ideation in coping, she often develops fantasies that are oriented more toward escape than toward direct problem solving $(M^a:M^p)$. There is also evidence to suggest that she is probably more passive than may be desirable for an effective adjustment $(a:p)$. She tends to approach her world in a precise and methodical manner (Zd), often devoting more time than may be efficient to the task of sorting out important from unimportant details. Although she tries to be precise in identifying a stimulus field, she often misinterprets cues by translating them in an overly personal manner $(F+\%, X+\%,$ *frequency of form quality weak answers*). Thus, her reality testing will be "off target" at times, and this may cause difficulties in her world. She tends much more than most adults to avoid emotionally provoking stimuli (Afr), and seems to place a lower value on herself than may be healthy $(3r+(2)/R)$. She is very introspective $(FV+FD)$, a process that, when added to her avoidance of emotionally loaded stimuli and her low self-esteem, suggests a potential for depression, or at least a feeling of being unable to cope effectively. She finds it difficult to extract herself from seemingly complex situations $(Lambda)$, and though she seems able to control her emotional displays

Case 2

Card	Free Association	Inquiry	Scoring
I 14″	1. I get the impression of s.t. from Greek mythology, lik a wm standg there, lik a goddess with smoke or fog on each side that's all I c E: Most peopl c mor tha 1 thg S: I'm sorry but tht's all I can c here	E: (Rpst S's resp) S: The goddess is in the cntr & there is the darkness on each side as if it mite b smoke or fog, it sort of illustrates the mysteries about the gods & goddesses E: Show me the wm please S: Here in the cntr, u can c the outline of her, thes r her hands & legs & hips	W+ M^p.FYo (H),Smk P 4.0
II 22″	2. I suppose the cntr c b. a bell	E: (Rpts S's resp) S: I'm not sure exactly why it ll tht, I suppose the shape of it just re me of a bell, lik a church bell	DSo Fw Bell
	3. Ths red top parts c.b 2 gnomes, there is the impression that thy r arguing w e.o.	E: (Rpts S's resp) S: Well these look alive but thyr not lik real people, but thy hav littl heads & sort of shapeless bodies, lik gnomes & thy seem to be yellg at e.o. as if thy don't agree on s.t., c here is the face & the peaked heads & the rest is the body	D+ M^a_w (2) (H) 5.5
III 10″	4. Ths v.b. 2 people, men I thk & thy struggling to if s.t. up	E: (Rpts S's resp) S: Thy seem to be straining over ths in the middl as if thy r trying to lift it but it may b too heavy, c the heads & arms out here & the legs	D+ M^a_o (2) H P 3.0
	V5. It doesn't ll much this way, it c.b. 2 bushes up on a small hill	E: (Rpts S's resp) S: These r the bushes, U u get the impression that thy r back up on a small hill, u c all of this, ths w.b. the hill, mayb thyr small trees & the white & black parts here r the hill, u hav to look in perspective to c it, do u understand? (E: Yes)	DSv FDo (2) Bt 4.5

Case 2 (Continued)

Card		Free Association	Inquiry	Scoring
IV	8″	6. This ll some hideous sc. fict. monster, as if he's sitting on lik a big tail, mayb he's thkg	E: (Rpts S's resp) S: I've heard alot about this test but I didn't realize how gruesome it was, u c it doesn't look very human and yet its not an animal, ths is the big tail & the feet & the little arms, he's sitting lik on his own tail, it must b sc. fict.	Wo M^{P}o (H) 2.0
V	6″	7. If the ends parts are eliminatd it mite b a moth	E: (Rpts S's resp) S: Well thes w.b. the wgs & the small body, it looks very much lik a moth would look	Ddo Fo A
		V8. If I turn it ths way it c.b. a bf, the same part but the tail of the moth would now be the antennae of the bf, it c.b. gliding or floating	E: (Rpts S's resp) S: Its the same part but reversed, but it ll its flying whereas the moth doesn't When bf's glide thy extend the wgs forward lik ths	Ddo FM^{P}o A
VI	16″	9. Ths larger part only, not the top part but just ths bigger section, it re me of a piece of fur	E: (Rpts S's resp) S: It has all of these lines, the shading effect which makes it all look furry to me, it really doesn't have much shape lik anythg, lik a coat or s.t., just a piece of fur	Dv TFo Fur
		10. Ths whole cntr section re me of some sort of organ, lik the tubes in the stomach or some where, as if it is open lik it was dissected	E: (Rpts S's resp) S: Its not a very pleasant thought, but I thk it does ll tht E: I'm not sur I am seeing what u are S: Just ths cntr (points) section, it looks as if the intestine or s.t. had been opened up & u can c in it E: C in it S: Well its much darker in the very cntr as if u r lookg into it	D- FV- An

214

VII	24″	V11.	Ths is a difficult one, but if I look ths way I can c a chair sort of a Victorian chair	E: (Rpts S's resp) S: Well ths is another u hav to c in perspective, the white part here is the seat & ths is the back & thes w.b. the legs, sort of a low back chair, lik a special sort of Victorian chair, do u c it (E: Yes)	W'So FDo Hh 4.0
		V12	It c also ll the lower half of a bow-legged cowbcy, u don't c the upper half but just the trunk & the spread apart legs, its ridiculous	E: (Rpts S's resp) S: I don't kno what made me thk of that, I suppose the arch effect, lik a cartoon character, when the bow-leggedness is overemphasized lik this, u c this is the trunk & these r the skinny legs, thy take this stance s.times	Wo M^p w (Hd) 2.5
VIII	15″	13.	I can't make a.t. out of all of it, but ths lower part ll a very exotic bf	E: (Rpts S's resp) S: It has the big wings & its multi-colored, pink & orange & the colors tend to intermix, that's the way thy do on the prettier bf's, the colors aren't sharply defined but mix together lik ths, its pretty	Do FC.FYo A
IX	18″	14.	The upper part, not the pink, but just the upper prt re me of a picture of an explosion to repres e.t. moving outwrd w all the colors symbolizg the violence of the explos.	E: (Rpts S's resp) S: Yes, as if the artist was trying to capture the intense force with all the colors & the lines emphasizing the moving upward of the explos on	Ddv m^p.CFo Ex
		15.	The cntr c.b. a vase, the white area here	E: (Rpts S's resp) S: It just has that form, lik a vase, c (points)	DSo Fo Vase
X	30″	16.	Oh dear, I can't fnd a.t., except mayb 2 green birds	E: (Rpts S's resp) S: Theyr very small, here & here, with little peaks on their heads, & thyr green, I d.k. what kind thy mite b, just birds	D- FC- (2) A

215

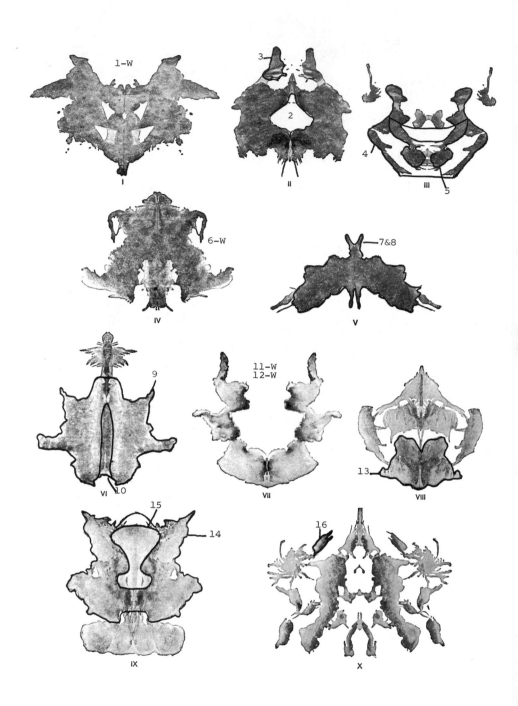

Case 2

CARD	RT	NO.	LOCATION	DETERMINANTS (S)		CONTENT (S)	POP	Z SCORE	SPECIAL
I	14"	1.	W+	M^p.FYo		(H),Smk	P	4.0	
II	22"	2.	DSo	Fw		Bell			
		3.	D+	M^aw	(2)	(H)		5.5	
III	10"	4.	D+	M^ao	(2)	H	P	3.0	
		5.	DSv	FDo	(2)	Bt		4.5	
IV	8"	6.	Wo	M^po		(H)		2.0	
V	6"	7.	Ddo	Fo		A			
		8.	Ddo	FM^po		A			
VI	16"	9.	Dv	TFo		Fur			
		10.	D–	FV–		An			
VII	24"	11.	WSo	FDo		Hh		4.0	
		12.	Wo	M^pw		(Hd)		2.5	
VIII	15"	13.	Do	FC.FYo		A			
IX	18"	14.	Ddv	m^p.CFo		Ex			
		15.	DSo	Fo		Hh			
X	30"	16.	D–	FC–	(2)	A			

Case 2:   Structural Summary

R = 16   Zf = 7   ZSum = 25.5   P = 2   (2) = 4

Location Features		Determinants (Blends First)	Contents		Contents (Idiographic)
W = 4	DQ	M.FY = 1	H = 1		Bell .... = 1
D = 9	+ = 3	FC.FY = 1	(H) = 3		
Dd = 3	o = 8	m.CF = 1	Hd =		.... =
S = 4	v = 3		(Hd) = 1		Fur .... = 1
			A = 4		
DW =	— = 2	M = 4	(A) =		.... =
		FM = 1	Ad =		
		m =	(Ad) =		.... =
		C =	Ab =		
Form Quality		CF =	Al =		.... =
		FC = 1	An = 1		
FQx	FQf	C' =	Art =		.... =
		C' F =	Ay =		
+ = 0	+ = 0	FC' =	Bl =		.... =
		T =	Bt = 1		
o = 11	o = 2	TF = 1	Cg =		....
		FT =	Cl =		
w = 3	w = 1	V =	Ex = 1		**Special Scorings**
		VF =	Fi =		
— = 2	— = 0	FV = 1	Fd =		PSV =
		Y =	Ge =		
M Quality		YF =	Hh = 2		DV =
		FY =	Ls =		
+ = 0		rF =	Na =		INCOM =
		Fr =	Sx =		
o = 3		FD = 2	Xy =		FABCOM =
w = 2		F = 3			CONTAM =
— = 0					ALOG =
					=

RATIOS, PERCENTAGES, AND DERIVATIONS

ZSum-Zest = 25.5 − 20.5	FC:CF+C = 2:1	Afr = .33
Zd = +5.0	W:M = 4:5	3r+(2)/R = .25
EB = 5:2.0 EA = 7.0	W:D = 4:9	Cont:R = 8:16
eb = 2:4 ep = 6	L = .23	H+Hd:A+Ad = 5:4 (H)+(Hd):(A)+(Ad) = 4:0
Blends:R = 3:16	F+% = .67	H+A:Hd+Ad = 8:1
a:p = 2:5	X+% = .68	XRT Achrom. = 13.6"
Ma:Mp = 2:3	A% = .25	XRT Chrom = 19"

---

reasonably well, her internal emotions may contribute significantly to some of her problems in identifying stimulus cues more accurately.

Finished Interpretation. Obviously, the complete Structural Summary raises even more warnings than were developed from the partial summary, beginning with the fact that she displays nine of the 11 critical variables of the suicide constellation (R = 16; P = 2; S = 4; Zd = +5.0; color-shading blend = 1;

$FV+FD = 3$; $X+\% = .68$; $3r + (2)/R = .25$;   and $H = 1$). These collectively
dramatize the pain and confusion she must be experiencing. Not only does she
withdraw from emotionally toned stimuli, as reflected in the very low Afr, but she
also tends to set goals that are considerably beneath her capability ($W:M = 4:5$).
Her cognitive operations, as evidenced by the distribution of DQ scores, are not
very sophisticated; in fact she offers as many "immature" DQv choices as she
does $DQ+$ responses (three each). This is quite unusual for a bright adult and
suggests that there may be some notable decay occurring in these operations. The
fact that she has only two P responses emphasizes her problems in defining conventionality accurately; this problem in definition is related to the earlier observation of her limitations in reality testing because of excessive personalization. She
has more Human than Animal content, another unusual occurrence that may
illustrate a preoccupation with people, *or* that may reflect a "harried" psychological process causing her to "jump around" from one preoccupation to another. The
substantial number of contents (eight) for this brief record suggests that this may
be the case. It is also very important to note that four of her five Human contents
are parenthesized; that is, they are unreal, and probably reflect something about
the way she perceives herself. Her reaction times, on the average, especially to
the chromatically colored cards, are quite long, another possible signal that she is
uncomfortable with emotion and tries hard to avoid it. The four S responses in this
brief record probably convey more than simple oppositionality. She is not a
unique person because she wants to be unique or autonomous; rather, she probably harbors much anger about being unique. If the single TF answer is any
guideline, the anger is probably related, at least in part, to her apparent inability to
gratify her strong need for affection. (It is tempting to note, even at this early point
in the overall interpretation, that during three recent weekends she was driving
through the mountains, twice alone, and the last time with two little girls. She
apparently had no meaningful adults in her life, and that last weekend may have
connoted a desparate reaching out for human contact.)

Her sequence of scores is quite interesting in that she "signs in" with a synthesis answer illustrating her ideational style, but also marked by some experience of
helplessness (FY), and "signs out" with one of her two minus responses
including the use of color, which she had been trying to avoid. It is equally
interesting to note the very long reaction time to Card X, after which she delivers
the very poor form quality answer, *giving only one answer* to the card that often
provokes more responses than any other blot. Quite probably, the disarray of the
stimulus (Card X is the most "broken" blot) overwhelmed her and, in effect, she
gave up. Her S answers are distributed throughout the record, negating the possibility of a situational opposition. Card II was obviously difficult for her, as indicated by the long reaction time plus the fact that she gives two of her three
"unique" weak form quality responses, including her first S. The sequence of
answers on Card VI is also fascinating, with the TF answer followed by her first
minus response and her only vista answer, as if the intense emotional feeling
provoked some negative psychological self-inspection. The color-shading blend is
her only response to Card VIII, raising the possibility that she did, in fact, experience some sense of helpless ambivalence when confronted with the first of the
totally colored blots. Her P *failures* after Card III, and particularly on V, VII, and
VIII, all of which are usually seen with ease, plus the decline in her tendency to

organizational activity after Card IV, and her inability to use pure F more than once in her last nine answers, form a composite suggesting that, as she proceeded through the test, she became more and more helpless and unable to extract herself from the stresses invoked by the blot stimuli. Her apparently "natural" style toward ideational delay, manifest in M answers, almost disappears after Card IV, occurring only once on Card VII, and then in a very unique way that ignores the potential for the Popular. This may illustrate her overall passivity, and it hints that she may be the kind of person who is easily "victimized" by those around her, susceptible to their suggestions and direction and unable to become autonomous.

Much of the verbal material is rich in uniqueness, beginning with her very first answer, which is the unreal goddess, dark and mysterious. The same sense of unreality is evidenced in her third answer, "gnomes," whom she later describes as having "shapeless bodies." They are arguing with each other, as she is with herself; and in her next answer, the figures, "men" are "struggling," again as she is with herself. Something is "too heavy," and when she backs away from this internal conflict, as seems the case in her fifth answer, the result is not very powerful, "two bushes up on a small hill." The *small* hill is interesting here, suggesting that she's not able to take as much distance from herself as she would prefer. More idiography is illustrated in her sixth answer, ". . . some hideous science fiction monster . . . ," revealing more about her very negative and inadequate self-concept. Interestingly, her use of ideation is represented quite well here, ". . . maybe he's thinking." Here she neutralizes the potential aggressiveness of the monster but overdoes it, probably reflecting her own immobility. She really struggles with Card V, manifesting some of her overincorporativeness, but the products, a moth and a gliding butterfly, are not very exciting, both being somewhat fragile and isolated. Response number 10, on Card VI, appears to dramatize her vulnerability, ". . . some sort of organ . . . open like it were dissected." Everything is exposed. There is no defense. Card VII, which usually invokes some conceptualization of femaleness is, for her, ". . . a difficult one," first seen as an antiquated chair, and then as a "ridiculous" lower half of a "bow-legged cowboy." Again, the self-concept is anything but sturdy. The colored blots are obviously very troublesome, and she deals with VIII in her passive way, as a butterfly. On the positive side, she makes the butterfly "exotic," offering a glimpse of some of her ideal self, fragile, delicate, isolated, but exotic. Card IX is apparently an intense stimulus for her, which she neutralizes by making the explosion a "picture" that "symbolizes" the violence. This probably represents her own inability to deal with her aggressiveness and typifies her need to avoid it at all costs. Interestingly, she follows this answer with another S answer and her only pure F response since Card V. She manifests the ultimate in helplessness in her last answer, which occurs in response to a very small area of Card X after a long period of examining the blot, she reveals her feelings, "Oh dear, I can't find anything . . ." The answer is inappropriate in form quality, and the fact that it is marked by the inclusion of color suggests that when she feels overwhelmed, the tight controls that she would prefer to exert over her emotions tend to fail and she does offer the emotionally toned answers. This is the sort of situation in which it would have been intriguing to ask for additional answers to the last card *after* the inquiry had been completed; *or* to Test Limits for the Popular answers on Cards V, VII, and VIII, in order to determine how she might recover under a more directed and structured situation.

Case 2 Summary.   There is an unquestionable fragility to this lonely, passive, and isolated woman. She is clearly bright, but probably never able to function very effectively because of her strongly negative perception of herself and her inability to respond to others with more than a superficial facade of the "attempting to please" follower. She probably became an overincorporator early in her development, finding it important to make the "correct" responses to others; and although this record suggests much uniqueness and disregard for convention, it is likely that her earlier years were marked by a struggle to please, but that she never really achieved the love and acceptance for which she struggled. Teaching elementary school, taking children with her on weekends—these were probably much safer activities than dealing directly with adults. Going on tours, letting others show the way, was safer, but less rewarding than finding her own independence. While much of her behavior might be effective for the true "schizoid" who needs detachment from the world into a more autistically controlled existence, she was apparently never able to become an "effective" schizoid—that is, she longed for others; and probably her suicide was provoked under that unfortunate circumstance in which she sought help but found those around her willing to deal with her only routinely, putting her off, perhaps not listening closely to her *whispers* for help. This is a woman who would "cry in" rather than "cry out," and her cries were too muffled to be readily apparent.

Case 9: A 37 Year Old Male—Rapid Disorganization

History.   This man was born and raised in a rural area in the Midwestern United States. He is the third of four children. His father, who died at age 63 of a heart attack, was a wheat farmer, and his oldest brother, now 44, assumed the responsibilities for that farm at age 27. The older brother is married and has two "grown sons"; both have left the farm and work in distant states. An older sister, now 42, has been married for 20 years and is still raising six children. His mother, 69, lives with that sister and her husband, who is a steelworker in a city about 200 miles away. The younger sister, age 36, is married to a middle management executive and lives on the West Coast. They have very limited contact with her. The subject's wife, age 37, is a high school graduate who married him after working for two years as a cook in a small restaurant. He was 19 at the time of the marriage, which occurred shortly before her 19th birthday. The marriage took place during his second year of service in the Army, and shortly before he was assigned to an overseas post. His wife was pregnant at the time of the marriage, and they now have an 18 year old daughter who will be graduating from high school in approximately two months. After completing his two years of Army service, he purchased, with his father's assistance, a small truck farm noted for its very rich soil, and during the past 18 years he has been extremely successful in raising garden vegetables, especially onions. As his farm flourished, he purchased more and more land and currently employs four full time helpers. During the past 10 years, his income has steadily increased, and he is considered to be very prosperous by local standards. He and his wife have been quite active in a Protestant church, and he has been elected a "deacon" for two three year terms during the last seven years. He often volunteers to teach Sunday School and has contributed significantly to the building fund for the church. He has also been elected president of the PTA twice over a period of nine years, and was elected to the local school board for a four year term when his daughter was entering seventh grade. There is no psychiatric history in the family, and the medical history is essentially unremarkable.

Approximately four months prior to testing, according to his wife, the subject began to display "strange" symptoms. He was much less verbal, subject to insomnia, had a marked loss of appetite, and would often "stay in the fields" considerably longer than usual. Their sexual frequency diminished significantly, and he would often remain home rather than attend church on Sundays. At first, both she and her husband attributed his "symptoms" to the flu or some other "bug." Gradually, however, she became more concerned for his health and "pestered" him to see the family physician. At the first visit, about two months prior to testing, the physician prescribed a vacation and a "better" diet. The vacation was planned but did not occur because of responsibilities on the farm. The diet, however, was followed to no avail. During the second visit, four days before testing, the physician noted a deterioration in affect and suggested immediate psychiatric evaluation on the assumption that the subject, who was nearly "mute" during the visit, might be developing a schizophrenic condition. An interview with a psychiatrist one day prior to the test was conducted at a county community mental health clinic. The psychiatrist noted the apparent depression, and, while tentatively eliminating the possibility of schizophrenia, did raise a question of some organic involvement. The subject, accompanied by his wife, returned to the clinic the following day. The wife had a social history interview while the subject underwent psychological testing; he was scheduled for an EEG and neurological examination late in the day. After completing the psychological testing, and while waiting for the neurological examination to begin, the subject informed the clinic receptionist that he was "going to take a walk." His wife was apparently completing the social history with a social worker at the clinic. The subject proceeded to his automobile and extracted a shotgun from the trunk of the car. He walked, carrying the shotgun, to a small park in the center of town (according to witnesses) and sat on a park bench for a period of at least 30 minutes, during which one passerby asked about his hunting success, and another stopped to ask about the shotgun, which had been made especially for him. He conversed with the second visitor for nearly 10 minutes. Near the end of his 30 minute visit to the park, he took his driver's license from his wallet, wrote a brief note to his daughter on the back, then placed the barrel of the shotgun beneath his chin and, somehow, managed to pull the trigger. The note to his daughter wished her a happy life and asked for forgiveness for the "sin" he felt he was about to commit. Ironically, at about the same time the subject died, the psychologist who did the testing and the psychiatrist who did the interview were discussing the feasibility of hospital admission because of the severity of the subject's depression.

Structural Interpretation. This record contains nine of the 11 critical suicide variables ($R = 15$; $P = 2$; color-shading blend = 1; $FV+VF+V+FD = 4$; ep considerably greater than EA; FC is considerably less than $CF+C$; $H = 1$; $3r+(2)/R = .13$; and Zd is $+4.0$). In light of the history of continued success as a farmer and community participant, the extreme difference between ep and EA suggests that this is a recently developed condition—that is, one of a reactive nature. This conclusion seems particularly defensible in the context of the enor-

Case 9

Card		Free Association		Inquiry		Scoring
I	26″	1 S.t. all torn up, lik a bf I guess	E:	(Rpts S's resp)		WSo FC'o A P 3.5
			S:	Well, its been all torn up, lik by a kid tht caught it & now its decaying, u can c the holes in it & its all blk lik it was decaying		
			E:	Most people c mpre than one thg		
		2. I guess ths cntr prt c.b. a crab or s.t. lik a crab	E:	(Rpts S's resp)		Do Fo A
			S:	Well, its got prongs on it & it just has that shape to it lik one u use fishing		
II	20	3. A hole in the ground, mayb lik a well	E:	(Rpts S's resp)		DS+ VFo Hole 4.5
			S:	Ths cntr part ll a hole in the grnd to me, u can c the folds of the edge around it lik it was just going dwn lik a well		
			E:	I'm not sure I c it as u do		
			S:	Well ths here is the grnd & the hole, if its a well its just been dug cause there ain't no lining yet		
III	67″	4. I guess it c.b. a cpl of African wm pulling an A apart	E:	(Rpts S's resp)		D+ M^a. FC'o (2) H,A P 3.0
			S:	Rite here (points), thy'r all colored lik African wm & thy'r pullin on ths A here, thos people always hav a food shortage so when thy catch s.t. thy pull it apart lik ths		
		V5. If I turn it ths way it ll a cpl of big old maple trees off on a hill	E:	(Rpts S's resp)		Dd+ FDo (2) Bt 3.0
			S:	Rite here (points) c thy hav that big bushiness to them & ths is the hill I guess, thy hav to b way off caus they'r pretty small		

Card	Free Association	Inquiry	Scoring
IV 38″	6. Some old tattered pelt it looks like its still got some fur on it from the marks, but not much & its pretty dirty	*E:* (Rpts *S*'s resp) *S:* Just ths part (points), it c.b. an old jacket or s.t.. its no good anymor tho, its all beat up & dirty *E:* Dirty? *S:* Well ther's not much fur left on it, just here in the cntr & the outer prts r all smudged lik w mud or dirt	*Ddv* *TF.YFo* (2) *Ad*
V 45″	7. I c some roots out here	*E:* (Rpts *S*'s resp) *S:* Here at the end, thy ll bush roots if u pull 'em out of the ground	*Do* *Fo* *Bt*
	8. Tht c.b. a rabbit in the cntr	*E:* (Rpts *S*'s resp) *S:* Well its got big ears & skinny little legs lik it was stndg up lik sniffing s.t.	*Do* *FMªₒ* *A*
VI 85″	9. Ths thg ll a fly	*E:* (Rpts *S*'s resp) *S:* Here at the top, the wgs r here & the body part & there's the ditch. . .	*Do* *Fw* *A*
	10. The cntr c.b. a ditch	*S:* Well, lik an irrigation ditch, its dug down in, u can tell bec its darkr than this other part, its looks muddy arnd it too *E:* Muddy *S:* Yeah, all wet lik mud, c thes colors here (points) they'r lik mud	*Do* *FV.FTo* Ditch
VII 70″	11. Ths don't ll nothin but smoke	*E:* (Rpts *S*'s resp) *S:* Rite, its just a bunch of smoke lik rising upwrd, its all dark lik smoke	*Wv* *mᵖ.Y* Smoke

VIII	15″	12. Some insides or s.t		Wv	CFo	An 4.5

E: (Rpts S's resp)
S: Like if u tear up an A it all looks ths way, kind of bldy on the outside parts & boney insides w all the parts
E: Parts
S: Yeah, just all the inside parts

IX	35″	13. Mayb a waterfall back in a valley or gorge		$D+$	$m^{P}.CF.FDo$	Ls	4.5

E: (Rpts S's resp)
S: Well it ll tht, c here (points) wld b the wtrfall & ths grn stuff wld b trees & bushes lik in the forest, but the wtrfall is way bk in

IX	28″	14. A mapleseed in here		Do	Fo Bt

E: (Rpts S's resp)
S: It just ll one to me, the way its shaped there

		15. Ths pink c.b. a bld stain		Dv	$C.Y$ Bl

E: (Rpts S's resp)
S: Well, it ain't dark enuff to b fresh bld, its liter lik dried bld, just a stain, & u can c the differences in the color lik mayb it was still drying

Note: Testing of limits invoked popular responses on II V, VII, and VIII.

225

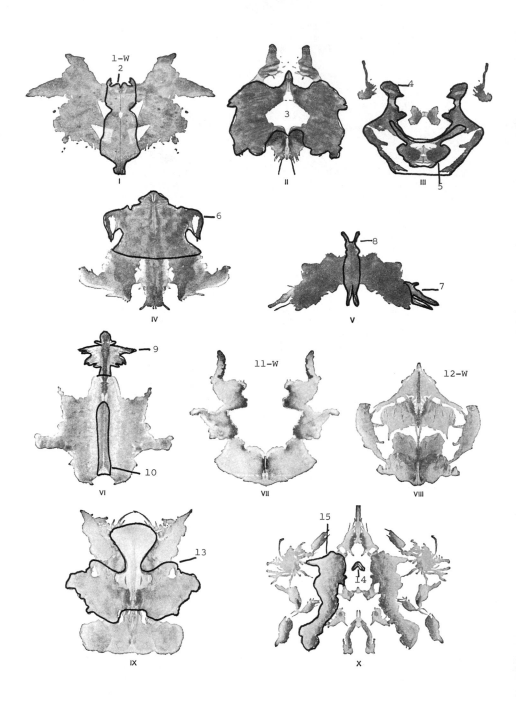

Case 9

CARD	RT	NO.	LOCATION	DETERMINANTS (S)		CONTENT (S)	POP	Z SCORE	SPECIAL
I	26'	1.	WSo	FC'o		A	P	3.5	
		2.	Do	Fo		A			
II	20'	3.	DS+	VFo		Hole		4.5	
III	67"	4.	D+	M^a.FC'o	(2)	H,A	P	3.0	
		5.	Ddo	FDo	(2)	Bt		3.0	
IV	38"	6.	Ddv	TF.YFo		Ad			
V	45'	7.	Do	Fo		Bt			
		8.	Do	FM^ao		A			
VI	85"	9.	Do	Fw		A			
		10.	Do	FV.FTo		Ditch			
VII	70"	11.	Wv	m^p.Y		Smoke			
VIII	15"	12.	Wv	CFo		An		4.5	
IX	35"	13.	D+	m^p.CF.FDo		Ls		2.5	
X	28"	14.	Do	Fo		Bt			
		15.	Dv	C.Y		Bl			

227

Case 9:   Structural Summary

$R = 15$ $Zf = 6$ $ZSum = 21.0$ $P = 2$ $(2) = 2$

Location Features		Determinants (Blends First)		Contents		Contents (Idiographic)	
W = 3	DQ	M.FC' =1		H = 1		Ditch	= 1
D = 10	+ = 4	m.CF.FD =1		(H) =			
Dd = 2	o = 7	m.Y =1		Hd =		Hole	= 1
S = 2	v = 4	C.Y =1		(Hd) =			
DW =	— = 0	TF.YF =1		A = 4,1		Smoke	= 1
		FV.FT =1		(A) =			=
				Ad = 1			
		M =		(Ad) =			=
Form Quality		FM = 1		Ab =			
		m =		Al =			=
FQx	FQf	C =		An = 1			
		CF = 1		Art =			=
+ = 0	+ = 0	FC =		Ay =			
o = 12	o = 3	C' =		Bl = 1			=
w = 1	w = 1	C'F =		Bt = 3			
— = 0	— = 0	FC' = 1		Cg =			
		T =		Cl =		**Special Scorings**	
M Quality		TF =		Ex =			
		FT =		Fi =			
+ = 0		V =		Fd =		PSV =	
o = 1		VF = 1		Ge =			
		FV =		Hh =		DV =	
w = 0		Y =		Ls = 1			
— = 0		YF =		Na =		INCOM =	
		FY =		Sx =			
		rF =		Xy =		FABCOM =	
		Fr =					
		FD = 1				CONTAM =	
		F = 4				ALOG =	
						=	

RATIOS, PERCENTAGES, AND DERIVATIONS

ZSum-Zest = 21.0–17.0		FC:CF+C = 0:3		Afr = .36	
Zd = +4.0		W:M = 3:1		3r+(2)/R = .13	
EB = 1:3.5	EA = 4.5	W:D = 3:10		Cont:R = 9:15	
eb = 3:9	ep = 12	L = .36		H+Hd:A+Ad = 1:5 (H)+(Hd):(A)+(Ad) = 0:0	
Blends:R = 6:15		F+% = .75		H+A:Hd+Ad = 5:1	
a:p = 2:2		X+% = .80		XRT Achrom. = 52.8"	
Ma:Mp = 1:0		A% = .33		XRT Chrom = 33.0"	

mous number of shading responses (9) offered in this very brief record. In other words, it is difficult to conceive of a person becoming financially successful in farming, being elected twice as PTA president, once to the school board, and twice as a church deacon, if so few resources were available over a long period of time. Quite the contrary, the sort of person described in the history was probably a person well in touch with reality and had sufficient resources available to use that "contact" effectively. The nine shading determinants manifest quite an array; two

V's, two *T*'s, two C's, and three Y's, adding up to a great deal of torment. The *Y* answers are especially relevant here, since two of the three are pure *Y* and the third is a *YF* response, suggesting that he must have been experiencing intense feelings of helplessness. The two *V* determinants, in such a short record, are equally devastating in terms of the psychological impact they must have carried, evolving from some very negative self-inspection. The fact that he has two *FD* answers in addition to the two *V* responses, magnifies the tendency toward self-examination that must have existed.

The pure *C* answer, together with the two *CF* determinants, represents something of the intensity of this man's emotions and his inability to control them. The low *Afr* gives some hint of his awareness of this problem of control and his attempts to avoid stimuli that might be overwhelming. The Four Square, especially the *EB,* reveals that he had a natural style of displaying emotions while contending with stresses, and the *a* :*p* ratio illustrates that he probably retained some of his ideational flexibility; however, the dramatically low *egocentricity index* (.13) illustrates the apparently great loss of self-esteem that he must have experienced recently. He was, by style, an overincorporator (*Zd* = +4.0), probably working very hard to sort out important from unimportant details in his life. The six *blend* responses, constituting 40% of the total record, provide a glimpse of the psychological complexity with which he was contending at the time of his death; and the nature of the blends—that is, five of the six including grey-black shading elements—reveals something of the pain that must have been reflected in these psychological operations. For example, one of his blends involves *m, CF,* and *FD.* Assuming this score to illustrate a real psychological experience, it would include an ideational activity related to feelings of loss of control, the uncontrolled delivery of emotion, and the process of introspection; or, stated in a very concrete and somewhat speculative way, "Why do stresses cause me to lose control of what I am doing?"

The presence of only two *Popular* answers suggests that he may have reached the point of disregarding conventionality, a strange turn of events for a PTA president and church deacon. The relatively low *Lambda* affords evidence that he was having difficulty in detaching himself from more complex stimulus situations, yet his reality testing (*F*+%, *X*+%) was quite good. Two more of his blends include the articulation of *two* kinds of shading, texture being involved in both. Shading blends like these are quite uncommon and illustrate an intense disruption. The fact that both did include texture suggests the possibility that he was at a loss concerning his own affectional needs. Another blend, *C.Y,* is also very unusual, and tends to occur when the rampant emotional discharge manifest in the pure *C* response is accompanied by the extreme experience of helplessness or paralysis. It may be linked to an aborted attempt to abort the discharge.

The presence of four *DQv* location selections indicates a level of cognitive maturity or sophistication that, again, is contradictory to his history and suggests some form of disintegration or decay. The very low frequency (1) of *Human* contents illustrates the experience of loneliness that he was probably enduring, and his inability to reach out to someone else for aid in thwarting his disintegration. Interestingly, he could not verbalize his distress to his own physician or directly in the psychiatric interview. This is another case in which the breadth of *content* (9), probably represents the difficulty in focus experienced by those who are psychologically "falling apart." His second largest content category is *Botany*. His *reaction times*, on the average, are very long, issuing notice of his struggle in contending with the complex stimulus figures. His idiographic contents (ditch, hole, smoke) are all of a variety suggesting "no defense," and in light of the very long reaction times, the lack of ability to establish more structure in his responses seems to magnify the feelings of helplessness.

Interpretation of the Scoring Sequence.   He signs in with a W answer, which also includes the feature signifying an inhibition of affect (C'). He signs out with a very poor response $(Dv\ C.Y\ Bl)$, suggesting that he may have been "worn down" in the process of contending with the test and could no longer display the resiliency that he may have shown on Card I, where he followed his C' answer with a pure F response. His shading blends occur on Cards IV and VI, and it is obvious that he had considerable difficulty with Card VII. He has a P failure on several cards, including V, VII, and VIII, all of which are relatively easy Populars. Although he has three W locations, only the first, on Card I, is of substance, with the remaining two, on Cards VII and VIII, involving vague or ill-defined objects, and in both of those instances his focus on form is secondary or nonexistent. Both of his pair (2) responses occur on Card III; none occur afterwards, even though several of the subsequent cards, especially VII, VIII, and X, are particularly conducive to pair answers.

Interpretation of Content.   The self-referential characteristic of *all* Rorschach content is particularly revealing in this record. The subject begins with "Something all torn up . . . ," spelling out rather precisely how he probably feels. On prompting, he offers a "crab," a form of barrier response that may, in retrospect, illustrate something of his inability or unwillingness to share his painful state with those around him. He feels empty, like "A hole in the ground . . . ," and his internal disarray is neatly typified by his response to Card III, ". . . a couple of African women pulling an animal apart." It is tempting to speculate that this may reflect some conflict of emotional allegiance that he may be experiencing between his wife and daughter; *but* that must remain speculation. What is more certain is that he is in conflict with himself and feels torn apart because of it. Probably his best response occurs on Card III, when he inverts the cards and takes distance in something secure, ". . . big old maple trees off on a hill." Unfortunately, he cannot retain that distance, and, beginning with Card IV, it is "downhill all the way." He offers a tattered pelt, exposed roots, a rabbit, a fly, a ditch, smoke, insides, a waterfall, a maple seed, and ends with a blood stain. All are weak, defenseless objects, identified after very long reaction times, and offering the substance of a self-concept equally weak and defenseless. His extremely long reaction times, followed by very mediocre responses on Cards VI and VII, raise the question of concern with potency or the experiencing of aging; however, he is only 37 and not 57 or 67, when such experiences are more common. His inability to identify the Popular female or child figures on VII would ordinarily raise questions about the stability of his marriage, and his relationship to females in general; but again this is of a much more speculative than firm nature. His response of "insides" on VIII dramatizes his own feeling of being exposed, and, interestingly, his next response illustrates another attempt to take distance, but the response is an *m*, a passive *m*, that reflects far less control in the attempt than was manifest in the "old maple trees" on Card III. It is also important to note that he was able to deliver four Popular answers under the structure of Testing Limits (Cards II, V, VII, and VIII). Thus his detachment from convention is probably more a function of cognitive disarray rather than of a true turning away from conventionality; and the fact that these occur under structure is ordinarily a good prognostic sign—that is, the person can respond appropriately when given some direction or support. Quite possibly, had intervention occurred, of a crisis-supportive nature, he could have reacted more openly to the direction provided.

Case 9 Summary.   All suicides are tragic, and some are even more so when the subject slips from the potential grasp of rescue, as in this case. The true causes for his disarray are not obvious in the Rorschach data. It is clear that he felt alone, negative about himself, and unable to contain the impact of intense emotions. The history reveals that he was continually regarded as "very close" to his family, concerned with his daughter's education, strongly committed to his religious values, and equally committed to success in the occupation of his father. His daughter had recently enrolled in a college some distance from home, and it may be that he perceived her "departure" as some "parataxic" loss that he could not surmount. Had he lived, a very careful evaluation of his marriage would have been critically important to any treatment plan. He married at a young age, to a young woman already carrying his child. Was he remorseful? Was his relationship to her more superficial than deep, and was the daughter some form of compensation that he was not psychologically prepared to relinquish? It is important to note that, in this brief record he did give two texture answers, one of which was a *TF* determinant, indicating a relatively strong need for affectional ties, which his marriage apparently did not provide. Unlike the woman in Case 8, who had a basic ideational style, this man appears to have been more extratensive, thus more accustomed to displaying affect; but when the affects became more negative, he appears to have selected a process of internalization rather than display his weaknesses to others; and in doing so he created a process of emotional discharge that ultimately disorganized and destroyed him.

Case 10: A 24 Year Old Female—an Incompatible Hysteroid

History.   This woman has been divorced for two years, and has been an outpatient in a dynamically oriented, uncovering form of psychotherapy during most of that period. She is the second of three daughters; her father, a building contractor, is currently 65. Her mother, age 56, taught elementary school at the age of 22 for one year, but since then has had no employment outside the home. The subject's older sister, age 30, is married with two children. She underwent four years of psychoanalysis after finishing college at age 21. She married at age 24. The younger sister, age 22, is currently a college senior but "on probation" for poor grades. The family resides in a Western city, and would be considered as socioeconomically upper middle class. The subject may best be described as a product of the "drug culture," having begun using marijuana in early adolescence, converted to a variety of "pills" by the age of 16, and used both heroin and hallucinogenics frequently by the age of 18. She did very poorly in high school, but

Case 10

Card	Free Association	Inquiry	Scoring
I	2″		
	1. Oh, a bat I would say	E: (Rpts S's resp)	Wo Fo A P 1.0
		S: Well it has the wgs, look here (points) & thes r the tentacles & ths is the tail	
	V2. Well part of it c.b. a fountain ths way mayb w built in lites, white lites	E: (Rpts S's resp)	DdS+ FC′w Fountain 3.5
		S: I thk if u cut these parts away (points) u cld thk of it as a fountain, c ths top w.b. the peak & the rest is just the sculpted work, except the white, they would be lites	
II	40″		
	V3. Mayb s.k. of donut w a hole in the middle	E: (Rpts S's resp)	DdS− F− Fd 4.5
		S: U ever c the pastries that people mak? They fried them, but thyr not round bec thyr forming them & thy don't come out lik the ones u buy, c lik just ths black part & of course there's the hole	
	4. It c.b. a cell under a microscope, lik when thy r magnified, lik separating lik thy do all the time	E: (Rpts S's resp)	WSv m^a− Cell 4.5
		S: I said that?	
		E: Yes	
		S: Oh yeah, it ll the cells r separating, one on each side, lik it is spreading out, lik when thy separate, the main part is in the middle, the white & the red is like the movement of the cell, its all starting to separate now	
III	10″		
	5. Well, a vase, like u have to look at it lik I am, I've done some drawing & ths has the forms & the shadows lik u mite use if u draw a vase	E: (Rpts S's resp)	DdSo YFo Hh 4.5
		S: The dark parts represents the shadow effect and when u draw u sometimes don't use all the lines, lik u use the shadow effect to create an impression	
		E: I'm not sure I c it	
		S: C rite here (runs finger around area) it c.b. a vase pretty easy if u use u'r imagination	

232

IV	20″	V6.	Well, f u really use u'r imagination u cld make it a mushroom too, the same shadowing effects wld be for the basic shape of it	E:	(Rpts S's resp)		
				S:	Well u use the same part as the vase but u put a tail on it, it wld go dwn here, c this upper part wld b the big round part & the tail wld b down here, if I was going to draw a mushroom, thts how I'd make it, kinda using the shadowy effect to create the outline, making it darker lik this it	DdS– YF–	Mushroom 4.5
		7.	It c.b. be a tree, a pine tree but u hav to discnt these little parts out here	E:	(Rpts S's resp)		
				S:	Ths is the top & it gets wider toward the bttm & here is the trunk, lik a triangle effect, lik pine trees have that u kno?	Ddo Fo Bt	
		V8.	It c.b. a leaf too, a dead leaf, all curled up	E:	(Rpts S's resp)		
				S:	Well ths is the stem, lik for the tree, & the cye markgs on it create sort of a curled effect, lik when leaves dies thy curl up lik ths	Wv FVo Bt	2.00
V	2″	9.	A bf, c the wgs & feet	E:	(Rpts S's resp)		
				S:	Yeah, c the wgs here & the head & the feet	Wo Fo A P 1.0 INCOM	
		10.	I don't get too much more out of ths one unless it cld b a bee too	E:	(Rpts S's resp)		
				S:	Its the same idea as the bf, but u cld c it lik a bee too, with the wgs & head & feet	Wo Fw A 1.0 INCOM	
VI	15″	V11.	Mayb a strange lookg bottl opener	E:	(Rpts S's resp)		
				S:	Well ths prt down here is the part u put in the cork & ths top part is what you turn, the handle so as to get the cork to come cut	Wo Fw Bottl Opnr 2.5	
		V12.	U kno it cld b a sick tree too, lik thy get a disease & turn funny colors & the bark falls off	E:	(Rpts S's resp)		
				S:	Well, it has all the shades there, lik to repres the disease, I don't kno the name but the tree looks sick & the bark falls off, c all the spots are lik that	Wo YFo Bt,	Disease 2.5

233

Case 10 (Continued)

Card	Free Association	Inquiry	Scoring
VII 25"	V13. Mayb a cloud formation lik at nite, its all dark & its lik moving up, all billowy lik when u look up s.times at nite & c the clouds, thy seem to move fast	E: (Rpts S's resp) S: Thts not too good is it, well I was thking lik at nite, its all dark lik tht & the different shadows give it a rounded effect, lik billowy & its all lik moving upward (motions w hands) C its all togthr up here & thes parts r moving up into the full part	Wv YF.m^P.VFo Cl 2.5
	14. If u really use all of it, lik the white part too it is lik a modern design pottery	E: (Rpts S's resp) S: Well u can c the showy part, the drkness all around it & the white part is like the design on it, sort of like an abstract Indian design	DdSo Fo Pottery 4.0
VIII 10"	15. Its lik a glass bowl w a top on it, lik a pretty candy dish or s.t., its very round	E: (Rpts S's resp) S: Well it look full, lik the pinker area makes it look round at the sides, it has the effect of fullness & here is the top & the different colors make it ll it cld b cut glass, u c the drkr colors & the liter colors give it a cut class look, lik a very expensive candy jar or s.t.	Wo FC.FVo Jar 4.5
	V16. It c.b. lik a flower to that is opening up, not really moving but lik a picture tht s.o. took of a flwr when it was opening, lik the time kind of photography	E: (Rpts S's resp) S: Well, its not a real flower, or at least I don't kno what kind, but thes cld b the petals & its lik still not opened up all the way, all the different colord petals r there, lik it may be opening now (gestures with hands) ths wld be the stem & the rest has just started to open	Wo m^P.FCo Bt 4.5

10"

17. Another flower mayb, lik a tulip, lik they plant in the parks

E: (Rpts S's resp)
S: Lik a tulip with orange petals & the green leaves around it & its planted in the kind of soil that they cover w colored stones lik ths pink cld be crushed bricks or s.t.

$W+$ FCo Bt 5.5

18. It c.b. lik a volcano erupting too with all the fire shootg up

E: (Rpts S's resp)
S: Well its all colorful lik an eruption wld be w the orange fire shootg outward & the pink wld be some of the lava

Wv $m^a.CFo$ Ex 5.5

X

5"

19. Colored fireworks, lk thyr look after thy'v exploded

E: (Rpts S's resp)
S: Well its just lik a bunch of colors burstg out all over, lik a design that is created after the explosion

Wv $m^a.CFo$ Ex 5.5

V20. It c.b. stained glass, lik a window that's being put together, a lot of pieces have been selected to give the right color & tone effect

E: (Rpts S's resp)
S: Well right now the pieces are laid out in a design lik all the colors & the white parts still hav to be filled in with other pieces of glass, when u mak a stained glass window you try to use all different shapes for a special abstract effect, & ths is how u mite lay it out when u are beginning
E: U mentioned that the pieces give a color & tone effect
S: Yeah, u don't use solid colors, but ones that have different shades or tones of colors lik some of these here, u can c the different tones in them, deeper in some places and liter in others

WSv $CF.YFw$ Art 6.0

Note: Testing of limits yielded P on cards II and III but not on VII.

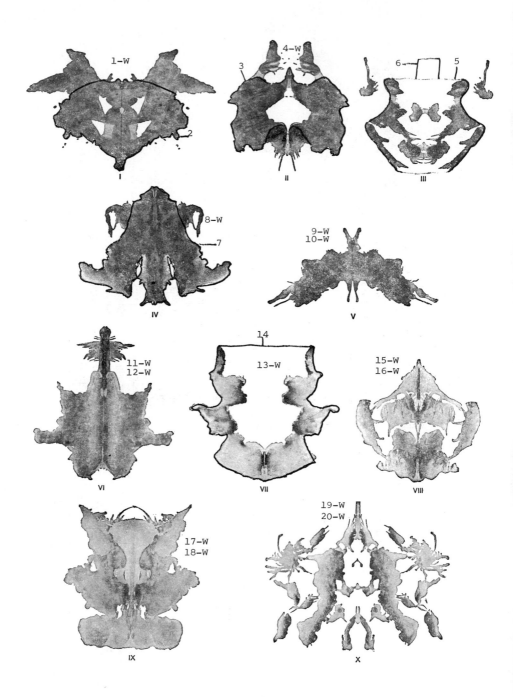

Case 10

CARD	RT	NO.	LOCATION	DETERMINANTS (S)	CONTENT (S)	POP	Z SCORE	SPECIAL
I	2"	1.	Wo	Fo	A	P	1.0	
		2.	DdS+	FC'w	Fountain		3.5	
II	40"	3.	DS−	F−	Fd		4.5	
		4.	WSv	m^a−	Cell		4.5	
III	10"	5.	DdSo	YFo	Hh		4.5	
		6.	DdS−	YF−	Mushroom		4.5	
IV	20"	7.	Ddo	Fo	Bt			
		8.	Wv	FVo	Bt		2.0	
V	2"	9.	Wo	Fo	A	P	1.0	INCOM
		10.	Wo	Fw	A		1.0	INCOM
VI	15"	11.	Wo	Fw	Bttl Opnr		2.5	
		12.	Wo	YFo	Bt, Disease		2.5	
VII	25"	13.	Wv	$YF.m^p.VFo$	Cl		2.5	
		14.	DdSo	Fo	Pottery		4.0	
VIII	10"	15.	Wo	FC.FVo	Jar		4.5	
		16.	Wo	$m^p.FCo$	Bt		4.5	
IX	10"	17.	W+	FCo	Bt		5.5	
		18.	Wv	$m^a.CFo$	Ex		5.5	
X	5"	19.	Wv	$m^a.CFo$	Ex		5.5	
		20.	WSv	CF.YFw	Art		6.0	

Case 10:   Structural Summary

R = 20   Zf = 19   ZSum = 69.5   P = 2   (2) = 0

Location Features			Determinants (Blends First)		Contents		Contents (Idiographic)	
W	= 14	DQ	YF.m.VF	=1	H	=	Bottle Opnr	=1
D	= 1	+ = 2	m.CF	=2	(H)	=		
Dd	= 5	o = 10	m.FC	=1	Hd	=	Cell	=1
S	= 7	v = 6	CF.YF	=1	(Hd)	=		
DW	=	— = 2	FC.FV	=1	A	= 3	Fountain	=1
					(A)	=		
			M	=	Ad	=	Jar	=1
			FM	=	(Ad)	=		
			m	= 1	Ab	=	Mushroom	=1
			C	=	Al	=		
Form Quality			CF	=	An	=	Pottery	=1
			FC	= 1	Art	= 1		
FQx		FQf	C'	=	Ay	=	Disease	=0,1
+	= 0	+ = 0	C'F	=	Bl	=		=
			FC'	= 1	Bt	= 6		
o	= 14	o = 4	T	=	Cg	=		
			TF	=	Cl	= 1	**Special Scorings**	
w	= 3	w = 2	FT	=	Ex	= 2		
			V	=	Fi	=	PSV	=
—	= 3	— = 1	VF	=	Fd	= 1		
M Quality			FV	= 1	Ge	=	DV	=
			Y	=	Hh	= 1		
+	=		YF	= 3	Ls	=	INCOM	= 2
			FY	=	Na	=		
o	=		rF	=	Sx	=	FABCOM	=
			Fr	=	Xy	=		
w	=		FD	=			CONTAM	=
			F	= 7				
—	=						ALOG	=
								=

RATIOS, PERCENTAGES, AND DERIVATIONS

ZSum-Zest	= 69.5-63.0	FC:CF+C = 3:3	Afr	= .43
Zd	= +6.5	W:M = 14:0	3r+(2)/R	= 0
EB	= 0:4.5 EA = 4.5	W:D = 14:1	Cont:R	=13:20
eb	= 5:9 ep = 14	L = .54	H+Hd:A+Ad =0:3 (H)+(Hd):(A)+(Ad) =0:0	
Blends:R	= 6:20	F+% = .57	H+A:Hd+Ad =3:0	
a:p	= 3:2	X+% = .70	XRT Achrom. =12.5"	
Ma:Mp	= 0:0	A% = .15	XRT Chrom =15.0"	

graduated with her class at age 18. Shortly thereafter, she left home in the company of a mixed sex group who were seeking to establish a "commune." Her sexual experiences, beginning at the age of 14, have been frequent and varied, although after high school, she formed a seemingly closer relationship with a young man, a year older than she. He was also heavily committed to drug use, and they cohabited for two years before deciding to marry. She was able to "support" their respective "habits" with funds sent from home, supplemented by various kinds of "day labor" in which he engaged. During their two years of marriage, they also attended classes at two universities as nonmatriculated students interested primarily in design courses. She reports that he would often mistreat her physically when on a "high," and she often required medical attention because of this. During the two years, they "drifted" up and down the West coast of the United States, usually staying in no one place for more than four or five months. Ultimately, his drug involvement became so intense that he was completely disoriented and was committed to a state hospital. She returned home, and at the insistence of her parents filed for a divorce, which was granted in a short time. It was about that time that she entered psychotherapy.

During the last two years she has continued to use drugs, including heroin, "off and on." Also during this period she has had a variety of "affairs" with several men; has been pregnant once and obtained an abortion; and has tried three different jobs, all related to sales work. None of these positions has lasted more than three months. She lived at home during her first postdivorce year, but for the last 10 months has shared an apartment with another young woman who is also a heavy drug user. She drives a car, but has had two serious accidents during the past 15 months, and tries to avoid driving now. Her parents are "at a loss" to understand the deviant behavior of their offspring ("we've done everything for her"). Recently, she has revealed to her therapist that she becomes somewhat violent (breaking objects) when under the influence of LSD, and that she "panics" during sexual intercourse. She has begun using alcohol to apparent excess. Finally, the therapist referred her for evaluation, to "evaluate her present state and to determine if there is an underlying schizophrenia."

Structural Interpretation. This is a record that contains eight of the 11 critical variables of the suicide constellation ($P = 2$; $S = 7$; V's $= 3$; color-shading blend $= 2$; $Zd = +6.5$; $ep > EA$; $3r + (2)/R = 0$; $H = 0$). Although she is an extratensive person, she is not always able to modulate her emotional displays effectively ($FC:CF+C = 3:3$), and, interestingly, she offers no M answers, which is unusual for the bright adult and often signifies that deliberate fantasy may be quite threatening. The eb reveals a great deal of painful internalized emotion, represented by five Y's, three V's, and one C'. The high Y frequency indicates significant feelings of helplessness, magnified even more by the presence of five m's, suggesting that she is overwhelmed and out of control. The absence of T may be very important here, raising the issue of whether she has abandoned expectations for close emotional relationships. The extreme difference between ep and EA indicates that she has little access to her own resources; rather that she is often propelled by activities within her over which she has little or no control. The substantial number of DQv locations is more common to younger clients, and may reflect a serious current disorganization to her cognitive process *or* a failure ever to have developed much cognitive sophistication. Her history suggests that the latter may be more the case. She provides a variety of contents that are far too extensive,[2] and most of these contents are of a more juvenile variety. Her idio-

---

[2] The more precise scorer might argue that the pottery, jar, and vase responses should also be scored as Art, which would reduce the number of contents to 10; however the interpretation would be no different, since the responses would still represent an overly broad number of contents.

graphic contents are diffuse and she has six Bt's. Her $W:M$ is also more like that of the youngster, marked by an excess of W with no M answers, indicating that she probably sets goals that are well beyond her functional level. She seems to struggle to organize her world much more than do most people ($Zf = 19$), and this effort is marked by considerable inefficiency ($Zd = +6.5$). This overincorporative style suggests that she has much difficulty in sorting out important from unimportant details; but it should also be noted that the high Zd score is at least partially created by her continuous use of white space in the formulation of her answers. It is almost as if she cannot, or will not, distinguish figure and ground. This may be a function of a unique perceptual process created by her prolonged drug involvement, *or* it may be a product of intense negativism. In either circumstance, she is a "loser" in her effort to define her world more precisely.

Her reality testing ($F+\%$, $X+\%$) is marginal at best; however, her perceptions are not marked so much by gross distortion as they are by her unique approach to the stimulus field. She is quite individualistic; but when her individualism is taken in light of her *egocentricity index,* which is *zero,* it seems likely that she is not the bright and secure individualist but rather the person who is attempting to avoid any direct comparison between herself and her world. This postulate is supported by the presence of her three V determinants, which indicate an excess of self-inspection and the concurrent experience of pain. Similarly, her two *color-shading blends* signify that she is having trouble with her emotional displays, and may not be very secure with them. The complete absence of *Human* content suggests that her interpersonal world is barren and uncomfortable, and her very low frequency of *Popular* answers indicates that she may be unwilling or unable to perceive and respond to conventionality. A certain naivete is manifest in her failure to use D areas. These are the easiest kinds of response to formulate; yet, when she does not extend herself to W, she persists in her unique approach by selecting Dd areas. Her relatively low Afr suggests that she has some awareness of her inability to modulate her emotional displays effectively, and because of this probably tends to avoid emotionally provoking stimuli whenever possible.

Interpretation of the Scoring Sequence.   The scoring sequence illustrates her emphasis on W responses, with only one non W in her last 13 answers. Similarly, the sequence shows that she gives a "string" of responses that include white space early in the test, with five appearing consecutively in answers 2 through 6. This pattern seems to support the notion that her emphasis on S is probably related to some strong negative feelings that she harbors. Four of her five m determinants occur in her last eight responses, indicating that she experienced less and less control over her feelings as the test progressed. She seems to have had the greatest difficulty with Card II. Her reaction time to that card is nearly twice as long as that for any other card, and she delivers two minus responses to it. Interestingly, both of her answers to Card III have YF determinants, possibly revealing something of her inability to recover from the problems she experienced with the second blot, which may have been intensified by the chromatic color features present on both cards. The sequence also reflects the fact that her answers become more complex beginning with Card VII. Six of her last eight responses are blends. There is also a hint of some rigidity in her thinking at three different points in the sequence. On Card IV, both contents are Botany; on Card V both are Animal and both marked by an Incongruous Combination; and her 18th and 19th responses are both Explosions with the same determinants. This kind of unscored perseverativeness is much more common among children, and may signify the fact that she has difficulty "breaking" her own cognitive set.

Interpretation of Content.   While she signs in to the test in a reasonably conventional manner, many of her subsequent contents are marked by both concreteness and uniqueness, the latter seeming to convey a "not very effective" form of intellectualization. Although many of the contents, such as the doughnut, mushroom, bottle opener, and candy dish, are original, none is characterized by a more sophisticated form of creativeness. Her frequent use of the word "shadows" may indicate something of her own feelings about herself—that is, not very clear. This seems to be illustrated in some of the other contents as well: a doughnut with a hole, a cell under a microscope, a dead leaf, a sick tree, a flower opening but not really moving, and a window being put together. Each of these responses hints at either a vague and not well-differentiated self-concept, or one subjected to the chaos of disintegration and/or decay. There is very little content that could be used to detect something about her sex role identification. The volcano and fireworks probably reflect her volatility. The "not yet" cooked doughnut, the "not yet" opened flower, and the "not yet" completed stained glass window all appear to represent the experience of being truly undeveloped, while the dead leaf and the diseased tree offer a more pessimistic experience of the self. The manner in which she signs out, ". . . a lot of pieces have been selected to give the right color and tone effect," provides another glimpse at the probable fragmentation that currently exists. The fact that the pieces have been "selected" may suggest that she is really a composite of bits and pieces that have accumulated in her personality over time.

Case 10 Summary.   She is a very insecure and probably somewhat hysteroid person who is currently negative about the world and about herself. She is doing a lot of negative introspection; however, this may be a product of the psychotherapy, which has been continuing for a two year period. Nonetheless, her emotions are not well controlled and are often marked by great ambivalence. She feels quite helpless in her world and apparently lives an existence that is emotionally and interpersonally barren. She is like a "burnt" child from whom, occasionally, there are hints of "still to be developed" potentials. If she were 14 rather than 24, these hints might be taken more optimistically; at present, however, her failure to use her ideation constructively, her inability to use her natural extratensiveness with more mature modulation of her emotions, and her intense internal emotional pain combine to portend an ominous future, especially in light of the fact that she has so few resources available to her. Her self-esteem is essentially nil, her self-concept markedly undifferentiated. One of the problems encountered in interpreting a record like this is the fact that no pretreatment data exist; thus it is impossible, or at least difficult, to identify the aspects of the personality that are more chronic from those that may have been created as a result of two years of intervention. As pointed out in Chapter 4, a subject beginning a dynamic form of uncovering psychotherapy with EA higher than ep will often experience considerable disorganization as the process of "rebuilding the personality" takes effect;

and it is not uncommon for such patients to feel that "they are going crazy." Many of the data in this protocol are typical of the extremely immature and undeveloped personality; however, at least some of them may be a treatment effect in which disintegration or "regression" is occurring.

Whether the current undifferentiated state is a chronic feature or a treatment reaction is far less important at this time than the several critical suicide indices that appear. She is helpless, she is angry, she is negative, she is ambivalent, she has trouble with her emotions, she is isolated, she perceives reality in an overly personal way; her self-concept is diffuse and her sex role identity ill defined. Although she is probably bright, her intellect is not functioning at a very useful level, so that she is often concrete and tends to perseverate and/or overgeneralize. She needs to be supported in a manner that will induce integration and development, and any continuation at an "uncovering-interpretive" model of therapy could offer more stress than she is able to contend with at this time.

Case 10 Epilogue.   The assessment report for this case recommended some consideration of a change in therapists, from the male with whom she had been working to a female who might provide a more supportive-developmental approach in which issues like self-esteem, sex role, and emotional control would be the early focal points. The report also recommended the use of a "woman's group" to assist in developing a more mature understanding of the issue of femininity; possibly in a group that also employs "modeling routines" to aid in structuring a more effective interpersonal approach. The report cautioned about her depression and the fact that she might often provide a "good facade" with which to conceal some of her torment; it emphasized her current feelings of being out of control, ". . . she feels like a time bomb, waiting for a time and place to explode . . . ," and stressing the likelihood of a suicidal gesture.

No basic change in the treatment model was implemented, and seven weeks after the evaluation, the subject did ingest a highly lethal variety of pills while alone in her apartment, believing that her roommate had left for a weekend ski trip. Fortunately, bad weather had grounded all airplanes, and the roommate was forced to return to the apartment, where she discovered the subject already in a coma. The subject remained in a coma for three days before regaining consciousness; she was then transferred to a psychiatric facility.

SUMMARY

The three cases presented here fall far short of illustrating the broad variety of personalities who become suicidal. The one thing that all seem to have in common is a deep sense of helplessness and feelings of futility. Their emotions tend to become less well modulated, and their confidence in themselves is rapidly eroded. In some instances, such as Case 8, the ingredients for suicide build over a long period of time, and tend to smolder quietly before building to the ultimate level of disastrous intensity. In other cases, such as Case 9, the ingredients accumulate more rapidly in response to an environment that becomes unmanageable, thus provoking a severe disorganization. Still others, such as Case 10, seem potentially doomed from early life on as they lose the prospect of loving or being loved; they can never establish a firm sense of the self, but instead are relegated to playing a series of roles that are not often compatible with each other. Her attempt at death, like that of many children, was probably much more spontaneous than either of the other two, although the basic ingredients probably existed for a much longer period of time.

A common "lay" misconception is that anyone who is suicidal must be "crazy" or schizophrenic. None of the cases presented here show any evidence of psychosis or schizophrenia, although some schizophrenics, like other human beings, do become suicidal. The differentiation of schizophrenia becomes very important to any treatment plan, including those cases in which suicide potential is present, and the Rorschach technique of detecting schizophrenia is the subject of the next chapter.

REFERENCES

Applebaum, S. A., and Colson, D. B. A reexamination of the color-shading Rorschach test response. *Journal of Projective Techniques and Personality Assessment,* 1968, **32,** 160–164.

Applebaum, S. A., and Holzman, P. S. The color-shading response and suicide. *Journal of Projective Techniques,* 1962, **26,** 155–161.

Beck, S. J. *Rorschach's Test: II. A variety of personality pictures.* New York: Grune and Stratton, 1949.

Exner, J. E. The self-focus sentence completion: a study of egocentricity. *Journal of Personality Assessment,* 1973, **37,** 437–455.

Exner, J. E. *The Rorschach: A Comprehensive System.* New York: John Wiley and Sons, 1974.

Exner, J. E., and Wylie, J. R. Some Rorschach data concerning suicide. *Journal of Personality Assessment,* 1977, **41,** 339–348.

Farberow, N. L. Personality patterns of suicidal mental patients. *Genetic Psychology Monographs,* 1950, **42,** 3–79.

Farberow, N. L., and Shneidman, E. S. (Eds.) *The Cry for Help.* New York: McGraw Hill, 1961.

Fleischer, M. S. Differential Rorschach configurations of suicidal patients: a psychological study of threatened, attempted, and successful suicides. Unpublished doctoral dissertation, Yeshiva University, 1957.

Fonda, C. P. The White-Space response. In Rickers-Ovsiankina, M. (Ed.) *Rorschach Psychology.* (2nd ed.) Huntington, N.Y.: Robert E. Krieger Publishing Co., 1977.

Goldfried, M., Stricker, G., and Weiner, I. B. *Rorschach Handbook of Clinical and Research Applications.* Englewood Cliffs, N.J.: Prentice Hall, 1971.

Hertz, M. R. Suicidal configurations in Rorschach records, *Rorschach Research Exchange and Journal of Projective Techniques,* 1948, **12,** 3 58.

Hertz, M. R. Further study of "suicidal" configurations in Rorschach records. *Rorschach Research Exchange and Journal of Projective Techniques,* 1949, **13,** 44–73.

Lindner, R. M. Content analysis in Rorschach work. *Rorschach Research Exchange,* 1946, **10,** 121–129.

Martin, H. A Rorschach study of suicide. Unpublished doctoral dissertation, University of Kentucky, 1951.

Piotrowski, Z. *A Rorschach Compendium: Revised and enlarged. Psychiatric Quarterly,* 1950, **24,** 543–596.

Ray, J. B. The meaning of Rorschach white space responses. *Journal of Projective Techniques,* 1964, **28,** 315–323.

Sakheim, G. A. Suicidal responses on the Rorschach test. *Journal of Nervous and Mental Disease,* 1955, **122,** 332–344.

Sapolsky, A. An indicator of suicidal ideation of the Rorschach test. *Journal of Projective Techniques and Personality Assessment,* 1963, **27,** 332–335.

Shneidman, E. S. Suicide. In Farberow, N. L. (Ed.) *Taboo Topics.* New York: Atherton Press, 1963.

Shneidman, E. S. and Farberow, N. L. *Clues to Suicide.* New York: McGraw Hill, 1957.

Tabachnick, N. D., and Farberow, N. L. The assessment of self-destructive potentiality. In, Farberow, N. L., and Shneidman, E. A. (Eds.) *The Cry for Help.* New York: McGraw Hill, 1961.

Thomas, C. B., Ross, D. C., Brown, B. S., and Duszynski, K. R. A prospective study of the Rorschachs of suicides: The predictive potential of pathological content. *The Johns Hopkins Medical Journal,* 1973, **132,** 334–360.

White, M. A., and Schreiber, H. Diagnosing "suicidal risks" on the Rorschach. *Psychiatric Quarterly Supplement,* 1952, **26,** 161–189.

CHAPTER 8

Differentiation of Schizophrenia

The issue of identifying schizophrenia accurately has been both complex and controversial for many decades. Although most schemata for the differential diagnosis of schizophrenia begin with the general agreement that a *disturbance in thinking* is the most characteristic feature of the condition, there is much less agreement about the way in which that disturbance is manifest; *and about which* additional features, among the many that characterize schizophrenia, distinguish it from other conditions in which thinking may be impaired. Weiner (1966) has presented a truly classic work that traces abundent research support for the thought process dysfunction in the schizophrenic, neatly demonstrating how the condition pervades cognitive focusing, reasoning, and concept formation. Weiner also notes that the schizophrenic has major problems with perceptual accuracy or reality testing; impairment of "reality sense—"that is, an inability to differentiate the self accurately; problems in object relations; and a system of coping operations that at best are limited in terms of their overall effectiveness. Weiner (1968) has pointed to the necessity of approaching the problem of differential diagnosis of schizophrenia using a "conceptual" approach that is closely aligned to firmly established behavioral characteristics.

In part, the difficulties posed in differentiating the schizophrenic from the nonschizophrenic stem from the basic theoretical conceptions of schizophrenia. Khouri (1977) has pointed to the sharp differences that exist between those who propound a "continuum" concept of schizophrenia and those who identify schizophrenia as a distinct entity discretely different from all other mental dysfunctions. Moreover, theories of schizophrenia are frequently divided into two "camps." One emphasizes the potential genetic element that separates the schizophrenic from the nonschizophrenic, while a second broad grouping of theories focuses on environmental factors as the major cause.

Whatever the cause, the diagnostic manifestations of schizophrenia have also been at issue, except for that common ground, a consensus on the thinking disturbance. Satorius, Shapiro, and Jablensky (1974) have presented a frequency distribution for the presence of 12 behavioral variables that are commonly observed, in a large cross-cultural group, to illustrate the schizophrenic condition. They note that 97% of the schizophrenics studied manifest "lack of insight"; approximately 70% have some form of hallucinations; about two in every three show signs of a delusional operation; and about half have some form of thinking alienation. In a similar context, Carpenter, Strauss, and Bartko (1973) have used a computer analysis of 360 items and 55 combinations of items to differentiate schizophrenics from nonschizophrenics. They have reported that the 12 most discriminating signs of schizophrenia include restricted affect, poor insight, thinking aloud, failure to awaken early, poor interpersonal rapport, lack of depressed facies, lack of elation, widespread delusions, incoherent speech, unreliable information, bizarre delusions, and nihilistic delusions. They find that six or more of these signs will differentiate about two of every three schizophrenics, while falsely identifying only about 4% of nonschizophrenics.

Some of the difficulties in differentiating schizophrenia from nonschizophrenia evolve from attempts to "refine" the diagnosis—that is, to differentiate categories like paranoid, hebephrenic, and the like, or to delineate "degrees" of schizophrenia, like the concepts of "borderline" and "incipient" schizophrenia. For example, Kety, Rosenthal, Wender, and Schulsinger (1968) and Kety, Rosenthal, Wender, Schulsinger, and Jacobsen (1975) have suggested the concept of *spectrum* of schizophrenias. Their conceptualization is based mainly on a series of investigations that have involved elaborate record keeping about adoptive children in Denmark, a design that permits separation of the genetic factor from the environmental influence elements. The spectrum concept, which is not markedly different from the older notion of a "family of schizophrenias" (Bleuler, 1911), is directed at a group of disorders that vary in severity, but all of which appear to be genetically related. In the "hard" or "firm" area of the spectrum lie disorders labeled chronic schizophrenic, "borderline" states, and some acute schizophrenic disturbances. In the less firm or "soft" area of the spectrum appear some of the acute schizophrenic reactions, the schizophrenic personalities, and the schizoid styles. The notion of the "spectrum" is primarily a research classification at this time, but its relation to previously developed conceptualizations of schizophrenia requires attention in any Rorschach oriented research involving differentiation of the condition.

Whatever the approach to classification, it is clear that the diagnostician, regardless of technique employed, confronts a major task in attempting to differentiate the schizophrenic from the nonschizophrenic subject. Although some aspect of this problem is created by the continuing diversity of perspectives on etiology and symptomotology, it is made even more complex by the inclusion of such categories as "reactive" versus "process" (Kantor, Wallner, and Winder, 1953; Phillips, 1953); "acute" versus "chronic" (Meyer, 1907; Kant, 1941; Wittman, 1941); "incipient" versus "remitting" (Miller, 1940; Whitman, 1954; Benjamin, 1944); and "borderline" (Knight, 1953; Grinker, Werble, and Drye, 1968; Kernberg, 1967) or "pseudoneurotic" (Kasanin, 1944; Polatin and Hoch, 1947; Hoch and Polatin, 1949). The bulk of recent research on the treatment of schizophrenia indicates that the response to treatment is generally more positive when the intervention includes a "somatic" core, predominantly some form of drug therapy (May, 1968; Hogarty, Goldberg, Schooler, and Ulrich, 1974; May, Tuma, and Dixon, 1976; Exner and Murillo, 1977). Conversely, there is some evidence to suggest that certain kinds of schizophrenic patients do not respond favorably to drug treatment (Klein, Rosen, and Oaks, 1973; Rappaport, Hopkins, Hall, Belleza, and Silverman, 1976). Although some of these findings are equivocal and require further study, they highlight the importance of a thorough description of the patient before the final treatment plan is formulated, a description focusing especially on the assessment of cognitive functioning and social-interpersonal skills (Keith, Gunderson, Reifman, Buchsbaum, and Mosher, 1976).

RORSCHACH MANIFESTATIONS OF SCHIZOPHRENIA

There have been many attempts to identify the Rorschach variables that will provide a valid differentiation of the schizophrenic from the nonschizophrenic (Rapaport, 1946; Piotrowski and Lewis, 1950; Theisen, 1952; Watkins and Stauffacher, 1952; Beck, 1965; Weiner, 1966). All have achieved some success in differentiating schizophrenia, but with less than consistent uniformity. Diversity in results has typically been created by problems of heterogeneity of samples, and by varying emphases on different subcategories of the overall classification. Weiner (1966, 1971) offers a compelling argument that the most accurate use of the Rorschach for the differentiation of schizophrenia will follow a *conceptual format*—that is, one in which the personality characteristics are defined before an attempt is made to discern any specific Rorschach indicators. In other words, after the features of the condition to be identified are clarified, the Rorschach can be approached in terms of which of its elements best represent those features. It is essentially this approach that has formed the nucleus of two basic studies completed for this work.

THE SCHIZOPHRENIA REFERENCE SAMPLE

The original schizophrenia reference sample (Exner, 1974) included subjects who were inpatients and who had been defined by at least two independent sources as "schizophrenic." These 125 cases had been obtained from four psychiatric hospitals, two public and two private. No special effort had been made to review the cases for specific features that might, as a cluster or constellation, be identified to differentiate those subjects from nonschizophrenics, except that it had been noted that the $F+\%$ and $X+\%$ for the group was significantly lower than for any other reference sample, and the 125 protocols had been screened for the presence of $M-$ answers. The latter screening revealed that 106 of the 125 records contained M responses, and that 92 of those 106 contained at least one $M-$. After the format for the Special Scorings (Exner, Weiner, and Schuyler, 1976) had been developed, it was decided to review that reference sample more carefully in terms of four basic features conceptualized by Weiner (1966) as best characterizing the schizophrenia syndrome. The four are: (1) evidence of a thinking disorder; (2) evidence of impaired perceptual accuracy or reality testing; (3) evidence of poor emotional controls; and (4) evidence of a limited or ineffective interpersonal life.

The rationale used in this review of the sample was that evidence for a thinking disturbance would be noted in the presence of Mw and $M-$ answers, and/or the presence of several of the Special Scorings for Unusual Verbalizations, particularly the neologistic DV's, $FABCOM$'s, and $CONTAM$'s; that evidence of impaired perceptual accuracy would be reflected in low $X+\%$ and $F+\%$, where the majority of poor form quality answers would be *minus* rather than *weak;* that limited emotional control would be illustrated by $CF+C$ being greater than FC, and would usually include at least one *pure C* response; and that the limited interpersonal existence would be illustrated by the relative absence of *pure H* responses, a greater frequency of parenthesized Human contents, M combined with *Hd* contents, and *M* responses that would be characterized by isolation, passivity, aggressiveness, manifestations of self-reference, and/or magical operations (Exner, Armbruster, and Kline, 1976). The evaluation of the 125 cases revealed that 91 were "positive" on all four features, and that an additional 16 were "positive" for three of the four features, with the three including evidence for *both* a thought disorder *and* impairment of reality testing. Only four cases failed to reveal evidence of a thinking disorder, and all gave relatively brief records, while only 18 subjects had *both* $F+\%$ and $X+\%$ in the "normal" range, and 13 of those 18 offered clear evidence for the thinking disturbance.

Beginning in 1974, a broad project was undertaken to increase the sample sizes for all reference groups, including the inpatient schizophrenics. In all, 85 new schizophrenic cases were added to the reference sample for that group, all of whom were first admissions. Two procedures independent of the Rorschach and the hospital diagnosis were used to insure accuracy of classification. First, all subjects were interviewed by one of three psychiatrists or psychologists "in the blind," for approximately 35 to 45 minutes, within one week of the admission, after which the interviewer completed an Inpatient Multidimensional Psychiatric Scale (IMPS) from which a "schizophrenic disorganization" score was obtained (Lorr, McNair, Klett, and Lasky, 1966). Second, a "significant other," knowledgeable about the recent behavior of the subject, completed the Form R of the Katz Adjustment Scale (Katz and Lyerly, 1963) from which a "symptom" score was derived and applied against data obtained in an earlier schizophrenia study (Murillo and Exner, 1973). Thus, all 85 subjects were identified as schizophrenic by hospital diagnosis, by IMPS evaluation, and from the ratings provided by a significant other. These records were then reviewed in terms of the same rationale that had been applied to the initial reference group. The results of this review (Exner, Wylie, and Kline, 1976) show that 64 of the 85 subjects were "positive" for all four features, and that 14 of the remaining 21 were "positive" on at least two of the four features, *including* evidence of thought disturbance. Two control groups of 70 subjects each were drawn from the 245 inpatient cases comprising the depressive and character disorder groups. Thirty-one of the 70 depressive subject cases did show positive for at least two of the four features, but *only four* of those showed evidence of a thinking disorder. Twenty-seven of the 70 character disorder cases were positive on two of the four features, and 11 others were positive for three; however, only six of those 38 subjects were positive for evidence of a thinking disturbance.

When studied collectively, these two studies reveal that 199 of the 210 schizophrenic cases (95%) do manifest evidence of a thinking disorder when the criterion of poor form quality *M*'s, plus the presence of several special scores for unusual verbal material, are used. Conversely, only 10 of the 140 subjects (7%) in the two psychiatric control groups offer such evidence. Similarly, 179 of the 210 schizophrenic cases (85%) show evidence of impaired perceptual accuracy, as contrasted with only 43 of the 140 control subjects (31%). The greatest overlap of features between schizophrenic cases and the controls occurred with respect to evidence of poor emotion control. This is positive in 164 of the 210 schizophrenic cases (78%), and in 112 of the 140 control cases (80%). Obviously, this trait is not something exclusive to schizophrenia, but it does appear very frequently in that condition. A similar finding is noted about some of the evidence concerning interpersonal effectiveness. The 210 schizophrenic cases include 153 (73%) in which pure H is 1 or less; 126 cases with M combined with Hd (60%), and 119 cases in which parenthesized human content exceeds pure H by more than 2 (57%). The 140 control cases reveal 94 in which pure H is 1 or less (67%); 83 cases where M is combined with Hd (59%); and 92 records in which the parenthesized contents exceed pure H by more than two (66%). There is, however, a more marked difference between the groups when the M's are studied for self-referential or magical features. This occurs in 131 of the 210 schizophrenic cases (62%), while appearing in only 26 of the 140 control cases (19%), all 26 among the depressive controls.

These findings suggest that the most critical variables in the Rorschach that are related to the differentiation of schizophrenia are those *related to the issue of the thinking disturbance*. These appear more frequently among the schizophrenic reference sample than do any of the other three features suggested by Weiner, and also with a very low frequency in the protocols of other psychiatric controls. Thus, it seems inappropriate to "call" schizophrenia from a protocol that does not include this feature; however, intelligent caution should be exercised to avoid identifying schizophrenia from this feature alone, especially from the records of younger clients, since as has been mentioned, the incidence of Special Scores for unusual verbal material is not uncommon in children, especially those 12 and under.

The strongest supporting evidence for the presence of schizophrenia concerns the limitations of perceptual accuracy. This phenomenon appears with a very high frequency among schizophrenics and a relatively low frequency among other psychiatric controls. It is particularly interesting to note that, while the $X+\%$ and $F+\%$ may increase in the schizophrenic who is treated "successfully," the elevations may still fall far below what is expected in the nonschizophrenic subject. In the Exner and Murillo (1977) three year follow-up of successfully treated, and *behaviorally effective*, schizophrenics, the mean $X+\%$ and $F+\%$ remained significantly lower than for a control group of nonpatients; *and* those records also included a significantly higher frequency of Special Scores for unusual verbal material than did the controls. In other words, while a much more effective adjustment in the environment can be precipitated by successful treatment, some of the cognitive dysfunction and perceptual inaccuracy does remain, and quite likely, the posttreatment adjustment of the subject will depend, in part, on whether he or she is able to contain those limitations.

Rorschach evidence for poor emotional control and/or limited interpersonal effectiveness does exist in many, but not all, of the schizophrenics studied here. While the presence of either of these features may be considered as useful supporting data in the "diagnosis" of schizophrenic, neither is absolutely crucial to the decision; *and neither, taken alone or as a two-variable composite,* would be sufficient justification for the diagnosis.

These recommendations about the use of Rorschach data for differentiating schizophrenia are by no means a final answer to this complex and important problem. The approach is essentially conservative, based on a format that yields the highest frequency of "true positives" while misidentifying an extraordinarily low frequency of "false positives." If it is flawed, the flaws are in the conservative direction, and could create the misidentification of false negatives, although the data accumulated to this point indicate that this will be unlikely where a "true" schizophrenic condition exists—that is, one falling in the *hard* area of the spectrum defined by Kety (1968, 1975). This approach is also consistent with the Spitzer, Endicott, and Robins (1977) *Research Diagnostic Criteria for Schizophrenia.*

BORDERLINE CONDITIONS

During the last 15 years there has been an ever increasing use of the term "border-line," but unfortunately, the features of the borderline subject have not been defined very precisely, and controversy continues regarding whether the border-line subject should be considered among the "families" of schizophrenia. The concept of borderline schizophrenia has existed for many years. Fenichel (1945) contended that a borderline state reflects a composite of neurotic and psychotic features, while Knight (1953) defined the condition as one in which the "ego" functions are differentially rather than globally impaired. Knight proposed that the borderline person falters in unstructured situations and frequently displays subtle manifestations of the underlying schizophrenic tendencies. More recently, the work of Kernberg (1967) has prompted broader use of the term "borderline" to focus on individuals who are very fearful or rejection or abandonment, avoid pain through discharge of impulses, have concrete values, are very "narcissistic, are fragile under stress, who vacillate between feelings of omnipotence and worth-lessness, who need to control other subjects, and who have inadequate reality testing. Kernberg does not specifically argue that these people are schizophrenic, but rather implies a tendency toward schizophrenic-like episodes under stress conditions.

Grinker, Werble, and Drye (1968) systematically observed 51 patients whom they identified as manifesting the "borderline syndrome." They reported four prevalent characteristics among these patients, including anger as the main or only affect, defective affectional relationships, poor self-identity, and a depressive lone-liness. They divided their subjects into four categories: (1) the psychotic border-line, (2) the core borderline, (3) the adaptive borderline, and (4) the neurotic borderline. They found that, although the social and occupational functioning of these subjects was generally "quite low," only two (both in the psychotic border-line group) manifest true schizophrenic features during a three to five year follow-up. They argued that, because the borderline group was markedly different from the schizophrenic, it constituted a separate diagnostic category. Keith, Gun-derson, Reifman, Buchsbaum, and Mosher (1976) point out that the Grinker *et al* study used a selection criterion for their patients that excluded patients with a psychotic history, a criterion that other investigators have used to establish a "borderline" diagnosis. Willet, Jones, Morgan, and Franco (1973) defined 30 male inpatients as borderline and compared them with 111 psychotic and 168 nonpsychotic patients. They noted that the borderline cases were more often married than the psychotic controls, and used drugs significantly more than the psychotic controls, but significantly less than the nonpsychotic sample. They re-ported that the single variable differentiating the borderline cases from the other two groups was the greater expression of overt anger.

Gunderson, Carpenter, and Strauss (1975) compared 29 schizophrenic patients with 21 subjects identified as borderline, the latter having been selected on the basis of a suspected brief psychotic episode and the absence of the nuclear symptoms of schizophrenia. They found the borderlines to be more angry and anxious, but not more depressed, than the schizophrenics. The borderlines did report more intense "dissociative" experiences, but displayed a somewhat better level of interpersonal functioning. The authors have suggested that, although the borderline patients did not appear to be preschizophrenic, similarities between the groups in premorbid adjustment, some similarities in symptoms, and in prognosis indicate that the two conditions may exist on the same continuum. Kety, Rosenthal, Wender, and Schulsinger (1971) have reported evidence that hints at the possibility that patients called "borderline," who are nonpsychotic, may have genetic backgrounds similar to those of schizophrenics.

In an effort to determine if some discrete features of the borderline subject might be manifest in the Rorschach, 42 patients, each with a history of a brief psychotic-like episode, were selected from four inpatient facilities. Four psychologists and psychiatrists, who identified themselves as using the "Kernbergian" concept of borderline, agree to interview each of the patients, independently, for diagnostic purposes. The interviewers were aware that the study concerned psychotic behavior, but they were not specifically aware that all of the subjects had been diagnosed "borderline" in their respective hospitals. There was complete agreement among the four interviewers that 11 of the 42 patients were schizophrenic, and that 21 cases were borderline. The remaining 10 subjects were "split decisions," with two interviewers calling them borderline and two calling them schizophrenic. Rorschachs from the 21 borderline cases were then compared with those of a group of 25 "remitted" schizophrenics who were in supportive outpatient care and on regular medication routines. Several statistically significant differences were discovered:

1. Although the $F+\%$ and $X+\%$ were generally similar for the two groups, the schizophrenics had significantly more minus answers, while borderlines had significantly more weak responses.

2. $M-$ was present in 18 of the 25 schizophrenic records, but in only two of the 21 borderline protocols.

3. The schizophrenics averaged 3.9 Special Scorings for unusual verbal material, while the borderlines averaged 1.6, usually involving an $INCOM$ or nonneologistic DV rather than the more cognitively impaired $FABCOM$ or $CONTAM$

4. The frequency of P among the schizophrenics averaged 3.6, while among the borderlines it averaged 6.4.

5. The Zd scores of the schizophrenics were quite variable, while among the borderlines, 17 of the 21 showed -3.5 or greater.

6. Borderlines gave about twice as many T determinants as schizophrenics.

7. Borderlines gave about three times as many S responses as schizophrenics.

8. The egocentricity indices for the schizophrenics were quite variable, but averaged .52, while the same indices for the borderlines were consistently greater than .40, with an average of .69.

9. About half the schizophrenics showed EA greater than ep, while 20 of the 21 borderlines showed ep greater than EA.

The two groups were quite similar for several features. Both groups showed a very high frequency of $CF+C$ greater than FC, and approximately two of every three subjects in each group gave at least one pure C response. Both groups also showed a high frequency of Parenthesized Human contents, Blood contents, and Food contents. Both groups also gave a higher than expected frequency of DQv answers.

Taken as a group, the borderlines display a Rorschach structure that can easily be identified as representing the very inadequate or very immature personality. They are quite angry, very self-centered, have poor emotional controls, bend reality to fit their own uniqueness, tend to be underincorporators, and have many features of cognitive concreteness. They perceive conventionality easily but are not always willing or able to respond to it, and they do not have ready access to many of their resources that would be important for coping. They do not manifest the more severe thinking distortion common among schizophrenics, but their thinking is often colored by a unique perceptual approach to the world. Although these data are able to differentiate the 21 subjects from others who are clearly schizophrenic, it is very important to note that 10 other subjects in the original sample were not included in the analysis because the interviewers disagreed sharply on the "diagnosis." Inasmuch as this is a very small sample, involving a small number of "diagnostic experts," it seems very likely that more disagreements would be manifest as the number of patients, and the number of diagnostic experts, was increased. Quite likely, there are institutions where the term "borderline" is reserved for persons with distinct histories and/or behavioral "markings." Conversely, there are probably other places where the term is more broadly applied in traditional terms to include the remitted and incipient schizophrenic. In this confusing context, those working with the Rorschach should be prepared to differentiate, using the basic Rorschach manifestations of schizophrenia as a guideline. In other words, when the characteristics of the schizophrenic appear, the use of the term "schizophrenia" will ordinarily be more beneficial than harmful to the subject, since it will imply the importance of a treatment program with a nuclear somatic component, which can then be added to in the context of specific intervention targets.

CASE ILLUSTRATIONS

The following cases have been selected to illustrate various degrees of impairment that will be evident in the schizophrenic. Two are inpatients, although, as will be noted in the first case, the status of inpatient versus outpatient tells very little about the psychological disarray manifest in this condition.

Case 11: A 24 Year Old Female—the Flighty Butterflower

History.   This 24 year old female is the third of seven children. She has two older brothers, ages 27 and 25, both are married (no children), who work at welding and milk delivery respectively. She has two younger brothers, ages 22 and 18; the 22 year old has been in a state facility since the age of 17 and is diagnosed as schizophrenic. The 18 year old brother is a senior in high school and is apparently doing well. Her sisters are ages 20 and 14. The 20 year old has completed high school and works as a nurse's aide while attending a community college at night. The 14 year old is in the eighth grade and progressing "slowly" in her studies. The father, age 50, is an advertising salesman for several small newspapers, while the mother, age 48, has continued as a housewife since her marriage at the age of 20. Prior to that she worked as a telephone operator for two years after graduating from high school. The father's grandfather was hospitalized as a chronic schizophrenic for 23 years prior to his death; he died before the subject was born. The mother's mother and her older sister, age 57, were both hospitalized for brief periods (not longer than 90 days) for psychotic-like episodes when the subject was in her early elementary school years. The mother currently takes antipsychotic medication.

The subject, who is neat and attractive, tends to mark many of her verbal messages with exaggerated "body language" and an excessive display of affect. She graduated high school with average grades and completed one year at a community college, obtaining all B's, before deciding to seek employment. She worked part time as a waitress for approximately one year; then she and a girl friend decided to "strike out" on their own. After approximately two months of hitchhiking through the country they joined a commune. The subject became pregnant after living in the commune for some five months. She decided to return home and had her child, a female, who is now age two. She has had an extensive drug history; she began at about age 15, using marajuana very frequently, and ultimately using cocaine two or three times a week. There is reason to suspect that she used other drugs before the birth of her child, but this has not been verified. Since the birth of her daughter, she has been essentially drug free.

Shortly after the birth of her daughter she obtained a position as a mail clerk with a large industrial firm. During the past year, her work record has been marked by frequent absence, and her parents complain that she is often missing for two or three day periods without warning. When she was a senior in high school, she voluntarily sought "counseling" from a school psychologist, which continued on a "once a week" basis for about four months and focused mainly on her problems in "keeping" a boy friend. Shortly after her daughter was born, she refused to acknowledge that she had delivered a child, and was seen for three visits by a psychiatrist who labeled her condition as "post-partum" depression. After their third interview she asked for her child and has cared for it, with her mother's assistance, ever since, with the exception of her recent frequent absences from work and home, for which she offers no explanation. Her mother has recently shared her concern for her daughter's welfare with her own psychiatrist, and this prompted an appointment with that psychiatrist for an initial interview. The psychiatrist reported that the subject was generally uncooperative and resistant to questioning concerning her absences from the home. Observing a flatness of affect, some indications of depression, and a form of cognitive concreteness, he requested a psychological and neurological evaluation.

The subject was initially responsive to the "attention" devoted to her during the neurological examination, but during the EEG refused to continue, insisting that the leads be removed. Later, during the same day, she was reasonably cooperative with the psychological evaluation, but, according to the examiner, was occasionally inappropriate in her answers to various questions and often "giggled" during periods when no interchange was occurring. Two days after the examination, the subject made deep cuts into each of her wrists and along the midsection of her abdomen and was hospitalized.

Case 11

Card	Free Association	Inquiry	Scoring
I 10″	1. Oh, mayb a bf but the colorg is wrong is that alright? (*E:* Its up to u) Well, it does ll a bf, I lik bf's so much, ths one has pretty white marks so it must be poisonous (*E:* Most peopl c mor than 1thg)	*E:* (Rpts *S*'s resp) *S:* Yes, I lik it, it has beutiful wgs & a larger than usual body but its very poisonous, u can tell bec of the white marks, look but don't touch u kno	WS+ FC'o A P 3.5 ALOG
	2. I suppose that the cntr c.b. a man who has been run over very gruesome, I don't care for that	*E:* (Rpts *S*'s resp) *S:* He was prob a fat man bec his hips r broad & he's flattened out a bit more there, c his littl hands r up here, his head looks split open, I supp tht happens if ur hit by a car & he looks flattened out to me	Do Fo H (P)
II 15″	3. Oh, I kno, its the littl thgs u c under a microscope, sk of, a, microorganism, I can't rem the name, oh yes, its a preemie	*E:* (Rpts *S*'s resp) *S:* I've seen them & thy do ll ths, w the drk colors & the bright colors, this one happens to hav some reds that join in w the blacks, I thk thy call them preemies, yes preemies *E:* I'm not sur I c it as u do *S:* U must not hav taken biology, thy r just lik ths	W– FY– A 4.5 DV
	4. If I look at it differently I c two peopl but thy hav the bodies of bears	*E:* (Rpts *S*'s resp) *S:* Its unusual to c that. Its really two people, wm I would thk, but thy hav huge bear bodies, thats really unusual	Wo Fo (2) (H) 4.5 INCOM

254

5. It cld also b an airplane flying in a storm, it must be a weather plane, yes of course, thy co that

E: (Rpts S's resp)
S: The white cntr is the plane, quite lik one & all of the darkr part is the storm, lik clds of a storm, dark & stormlike, yes a weather plane, no doubt

$DdS+ \ m^a.YFo$ Plane,Na 4.5 ALOG

III 8"

6. My thats ugly, it ll a man & a wm, as if he's doing s.t. to her, actually he's inside of her with his, u kno

E: (Rpts S's resp)
S: I've nevr watchd sex occur but ths is what it must ll, u can c the penis & she is ex-posed
E: I'm not sur I c it as u do
S: Its very clear, this (points) is the penis & she is open, yes

$Dd- \ M^a- $ Sx 3.0

---

7. Thats a butterflower

E: Rpts S's resp
S: I don't rem that, I thk it must b here a red one, u cn c the large leaves
E: I'm not sur what a buttrflwr ll
S: Oh very much lik ths, & thy r always red

D- FC-A CONTAM

IV 5"

8. My goodness, ths is an owl sitting on a dead tree & staring rite at u

It coudnt possibly b a.t. else

E: (Rpts S's resp)
S: All of ths ll a dead, burnt up stump of an old tree & here at the top is an old owl, the wise old owl, all crouched into a ball so u can only c the head & he's staring rite out at u, c the round body, up here, c it?

$W+ \ FM^Po$ A,Bt 4.0

V 25"

9. Thes r ridiculous cards, dic u make them?
(E: No thy r standard)
Ths ll 2 deer in a death strug-gle, I don't really car for it

E: (Rpts S's resp)
S: Thy r butting heads right now as thy do in thos fierce death struggles that thy hav, c the horns & the legs r extended with the muscles almost bulging thru the skin
E: Bulging thru the skin?
S: It looks pushd out, all of thecolrs there make it look more round, pushed outward as musces do when flexed sternly

$W+ \ FM^a.FVo$ (2) A 2.5

Case 11 (Continued)

Card	Free Association	Inquiry	Scoring
	10. It c.b. an xry of the inner ear, I rem thos fr biology too thy caught ths one as it was vibrating u cn c the tremors of it by the way it is extended on each side	E: (Rpts S's resp) S: Thy r precisely lik ths, I should hav thot of it first, I'm sure the staples r there in the middle E: U said an xry? S: Of course, its all dark as an xry, its clearly the inner ear	W– FY– Xy 1.0 DV
VI 34″	11. There s.t. vulgar about ths, it ll the same thg as before but a diff pict of it	E: (Rpts S's resp) S: Its the screwing, just lik on the other one, here's the penis & its going all the way thru her as if it was almost coming out her rear E: I'm not sur I c it as u do S: I hope not, no one shld c that, its the huge thg here & the rest is her	W+ M^{a}w Sx 2.5 PSV
	V12. Its better ths way, its lik a flag, a Christian flag made from the hide of a cat	E: (Rpts S's resp) S: It must b Christian bec the arms r out, lik the crucifiction & its on this flagpole E: U said it was made from the hide of a cat? S: Its all furry lookg (rubs card)	W– FT– Flag 2.5
VII 7″	13. Ths is how a wm looks if she inspects herself in the mirror for cancer, thes r really awful pictures (giggls)	E: (Rpts S's resp) S: Its as if she's propped up in the stirrups & wld b seeing herself in a mirror or s.t., inspecting her genitals for signs of cancer	W– M^p– Sx 2.5
	V14. It c.b. a negative picture of a wm's face, the black shows her lite colord hair	E: (Rpts S's resp) S: All u can c is her hair which w.b. blonde or white & her face, which is darker is the white part so u can't tell who she is, she has a french style hair do w the puff on top & little wisps coming out at the sides	WS+ FC'w (Hd) 4.0

256

Card	RT	No.	Response	Inquiry	Scoring
VIII	11"	15.	Its the painted desert	E: (Rpts S's resp) S: I didn't mean *the* painted desert but its lik it, all the colors & the bottm is lik the sandstone E: Sandstone? S: It has diff colors mixed lik sandstone	Wv C.Y Ls
		16.	There r tweezers there too, lik eyebrow tweezers	E: (Rpts S's resp) S: The r tiny so they must b eyebrow tweezers, other tweezers r bigger, c this tiny part here, it does ll that	Ddo Fo Tweezers ALOG
IX	37"	17.	I suppose it c.b. a mashed cracked squashed crab	E: (Rpts S's resp) S: Its just all gooey lookg as if thy steppd on it so u can c the claws up here but the shell is all squashed & crashed up E: U said gooey? S: All the stuff, the colors, r running togethr lik it was melting in the sun	W– $CF.YF.m^p$– A 5.5 DV
		V18.	I thk that c.b. a womb in the cntr when u look ths way it has fluid in it, mayb a placenta	E: (Rpts S's resp) S: Wombs r shaped lik ths, lik the hourglass of time & u can c ths one is exactly lik that E: U said it has fluid in it? S: Oh yes, it looks milky, not milk, but milky its lite here & drkr here, milky lik placenta	DS– FY– Sx
X	18"	19.	I thk thats blood running out of ths bug at the top of the poor bug	E: (Rpts S's resp) S: It must be dead or nearly dead bec it has lost so much blood, all ths here & here the poor thg, it was probably a nice bug but s.o. stepped on it	D– $m^p.CF$– A,Bl 4.0 FABCOM
		20.	I lik flowers & I c some tulips here, yellow tulips	E: (Rpts S's resp) S: They r pretty, life should b lik that, c how pretty the yellow is & thy r beautiful	Do CFo (2) Bt

Case 11 (Continued)

Card	Free Association		Inquiry	Scoring
21.	These c.b. spiders, I don't lik spiders, thes r blue spiders tho & thy don't harm thgs	E: S:	(Rpts S's resp) Thy hav so many legs, creepy & crawly thgs but there thy r 2 of them, & thy aren't so bad bec thy r the blue variety or species which makes them friendly	Do FCo (2) A ALOG
22.	A pawnbrokers balls	E: S:	(Rpts S's resp) I don't mean his sex but his sign, the ones that r hung (giggles) on his shop to let peopl kno what he is, he'll lend u money & thgs	Do Fo (2) Pawnshp Symbols
V23.	A tuning fork, it has the big handl & the narrow vibrator part	E: S:	(Rpts S's resp) Rite here, thy look exactly lik that, I don't suppose u ever took music either but thy look just lik tht w the big handle	D– F– Tuning Fork

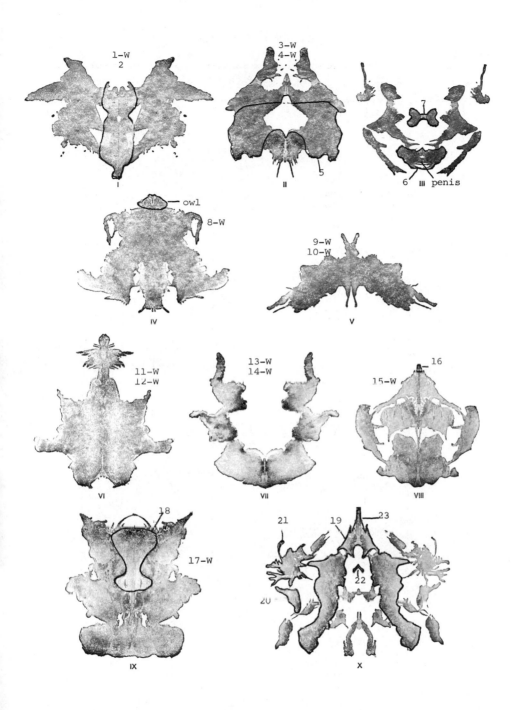

Case 11

CARD	RT	NO.	LOCATION	DETERMINANTS (S)		CONTENT (S)	POP	Z SCORE	SPECIAL
I	10"	1.	WS+	FC'o		A	P	3.5	ALOG
		2.	Do	Fo		H	(P)		
II	15"	3.	W–	FY–		A		4.5	DV
		4.	Wo	Fo	(2)	(H)		4.5	INCOM
		5.	DdS+	m^a.YFo		Plane,Na		4.5	ALOG
III	8"	6.	Dd–	M^a–		Sx		3.0	
		7.	D–	FC–		A			CONTAM
IV	5"	8.	W+	FM^po		A,Bt		4.0	
V	25"	9.	W+	FM^a.FVo	(2)	A		2.5	
		10.	W–	FY–		Xy		1.0	DV
VI	34"	11.	W+	M^aw		Sx		2.5	PSV
		12.	W–	FT–		Flag		2.5	
VII	7"	13.	W–	M^p–		Sx		2.5	
		14.	WS+	FC'w		(Hd)		4.0	
VIII	11"	15.	Wv	C.Y		Ls			
		16.	Ddo	Fo		Tweezers			ALOG
IX	37"	17.	W–	CF.YF.m^p–		A		5.5	DV
		18.	DS–	FY–		Sx			
X	18"	19.	D–	m^p.CF–		A,Bl		4.0	FABCOM
		20.	Do	CFo	(2)	Bt			
		21.	Do	FCo	(2)	A	P		ALOG
		22.	Do	Fo	(2)	Pwnsym			
		23.	D–	F–		Tunfrk			

Testing of Limits was positive for Card VIII
Popular, but negative for Populars on III & VII

Case 11:   Structural Summary

R = 23   Zf = 14   ZSum = 48.5   P = 2+1   (2) = 5

Location Features			
W	= 12	**DQ**	
D	= 8	+	= 6
Dd	= 3	o	= 6
S	= 4	v	= 1
DW	=	—	= 10

Determinants (Blends First)	
CF.YF.m	=1
m.CF	=1
m.YF	=1
FM.FV	=1
C.Y	=1

M	= 3
FM	= 1
m	=
C	=
CF	= 1
FC	= 2
C'	=
C'F	=
FC'	= 2
T	=
TF	=
FT	= 1
V	=
VF	=
FV	=
Y	=
YF	=
FY	= 3
rF	=
Fr	=
FD	=
F	- 5

Form Quality

FQx		FQf		
+	= 0	+	= 0	
o	= 10	o	= 4	
w	= 2	w	= 0	
—	= 10	—	= 1	

M Quality

+	= 0
o	= 0
w	= 1
—	= 2

Contents	
H	= 1
(H)	= 1
Hd	=
(Hd)	= 1
A	= 8
(A)	=
Ad	=
(Ad)	=
Ab	=
Al	=
An	=
Art	=
Ay	=
Bl	= 0,1
Bt	= 1,1
Cg	=
Cl	—
Ex	=
Fi	=
Fd	=
Ge	=
Hh	=
Ls	= 1
Na	= 0,1
Sx	= 4
Xy	= 1

Contents (Idiographic)	
Flag	= 1
Pawnshpsym	= 1
Plane	= 1
Tuning Fork	= 1
Tweezers	= 1
	=
	=
	=

Special Scorings

PSV	= 1
DV	= 3
INCOM	= 1
FABCOM	= 1
CONTAM	= 1
ALOG	= 4
	=

RATIOS, PERCENTAGES, AND DERIVATIONS

ZSum-Zest	= 48.5-45.5		FC:CF+C = 2:4	Afr	= .64
Zd	= +3.0		W:M = 12:3	3r+(2)/R	= .22
EB	- 3:5.5 EA = 8.5		W:D = 12:8	Cont:R	= 11:23
eb	= 5:10 ep = 15		L = .28	H+Hd:A+Ad - 3:8 (H)+(Hd):(A)+(Ad) = 2:0	
Blends:R	= 5:23		F+% = .80	H+A:Hd+Ad = 10:1	
a:p	= 4:4		X+% = .43	XRT Achrom - 16.2"	
Ma:Mp	= 2:1		A% = .35	XRT Chrom = 17.8"	

Structural Interpretation.   Before approaching the issue of schizophrenia, it is important to note that this record contains eight of the critical variables for the adult suicide constellation ($S = 4$; $P = 2 + 1$; color-shading blend = 2; $ep > EA$; $CF+C > FC$; $X+\% = 43$; $3r + (2)/R = .22$, and $H = 1$). Thus, the suicidal gesture, which occurred shortly after the evaluation, should not be surprising, although the gesture would generally fall into a Class III modality.

The evidence for the diagnosis of schizophrenia is very distinct, so much so that it may be surprising to find that she is ambulatory. The thinking disorder is very marked, with all three of her *M* answers being of poor form quality, and two of the three being minus. In addition, she has 11 *Special Scorings,* 10 of which are for unusual verbal material, including four *ALOG*'s, one *FABCOM,* and one *CONTAM.* The latter is especially telling, as the *CONTAM* occurs only about once in every seven schizophrenic records, typically in those in which cognitive distortion has become quite severe. The evidence denoting serious limitations in reality testing is equally strong, with the $X+\%$ very low (.43), and 10 of her 12 poor form quality answers scored minus. Interestingly, her $F+\%$ is .80, hinting at the possibility of a much better level of perceptual accuracy when she is able to extricate herself from complexity. The $FC:CF+C$ is the reverse of what is expected for the adult, and there is one *pure C* in the record, both of which point to her serious limitations in maintaining adequate control over her emotional displays. The fact that her *Afr* falls in the "normal" range highlights the problems of emotional control, for she does not tend to avoid stimuli that might provoke emotional discharge. She has a paucity of *Human contents* (3), and only one pure *H,* suggesting that she probably has some problems in the interpersonal sphere. It is also important to note that she has four *sex* contents, an extraordinarily high frequency for most records regardless of length probably signifying a very intense preoccupation.

The *EB* indicates that she is a person who is more prone to discharge emotion in her coping behavior than to delay through ideation. The substantially larger *ep* denotes that she has many resources that are not organized in a way to make them easily available to her; and the *eb* shows an inordinate number (10) of grey-black, shading answers. A closer look at those responses indicates the presence of *six Y* determinants, one *T,* one *V,* and two *C*'s. The "heavy" emphasis on *Y* discloses some very irritating feelings associated with a sense of helplessness. The record also contains three *m* determinants, conveying a sense of being out of control. In other words, much of her thinking and behavior are produced by impulses acting on her over which she has no control, and she feels somewhat paralyzed because of this. Her *Zf* is slightly elevated, indicating that she does attempt to organize her world, and the *Zd* score, which is within normal limits, indicates that she is reasonably efficient in this effort. The $W:M$ is also elevated; thus, she may be setting goals that are beyond her functional reach at this time, and a failure to achieve those goals may be one factor contributing to her very low self-esteem as is evidenced by the *egocentricity index* (.22). She is not very conventional in the way she interprets her world, as indicated by the low *P* value (2 + 1). This is probably related to her problems with reality testing. The four *S* responses suggest that she is quite negative, and probably angry, at this time. A critical element in the structure is the very low *Lambda* (.28), pointing to the fact that she is unable to detach herself from complex stimulus situations; thus her limited coping resources, plus her problems with emotional control, become even greater liabilities for her. Her long mean reaction times indicate that she does attempt to delay her responses, but delay by itself apparently does not help her "sort out" real from unreal things, nor does it provide her with better overall control. In fact, the reasonably extensive number of contents, especially the several idiographic contents, implies that her cognitive operations may be "flighty" and inconsistent.

Interpretation of the Scoring Sequence. She appears to have some trouble at the very onset of the test. Although she signs in with a *Popular,* she also includes the white space, delivers a C' determinant, and manifests some of her cognitive dysfunctioning with an *ALOG* characterization of the answer. The C' component is possibly a clue, offering a glimpse of her attempt to exert emotional control; and her next answer suggests that she *almost* succeeds, by going to a *pure form* answer that is *nearly* Popular. As it turns out, that pure F is one of only two in the record not marked by some cognitive slippage, the second being in response 22 on Card X. Her remaining pure F answers are either minus or marked by a Special Score. She approaches all but two of the blots with a W response, and this preponderance of W answers often seems to lead to trouble. The approach may relate to her unrealistic aspiration level, or it may simply be a manifestation of an ineffective attempt to protect herself. In either event, this tendency may be a useful treatment target once some of the disordered thinking is contained—useful to orient her to dealing with stimuli in "less large chunks" and to revalidating some of her own conclusions before she formulates responses. She provides a synthesis DQ on several cards, which suggests that there is some cognitive sophistication present that may also offer an asset to a treatment plan. While she has difficulty throughout the test, seven of her minus responses are delivered to the five blots containig chromatic color. This seems to support the notion that when she is provoked to an awareness of emotionally loaded stimuli, her reality testing falters more extensively, and her cognitive dysfunctions become more acute. Eight of her 10 Special Scores for unusual verbal material occur in response to the same blots. Her reaction times show more variation than is represented by the means in the Structural Summary. What may possibly be one of her best answers occurs after her shortest reaction time on Card IV, five seconds, while the answers that occur after her longest reaction times, on Cards VI and IX, are both clearly marked by pathology. This gives rise to the *speculation* that, in her case, when she does delay, her schizophrenic ideation becomes more overwhelming and creates more bizarre responses. It would be interesting, using a different task, to stimulate both fast and slow reaction times to discern if a difference in perceptual accuracy does exist. If such a difference is found, the decision process might be another viable target for the intervention effort.

Interpretation of Content.   She enters the test very precisely, but also seeking support that is not forthcoming, and without it, the cognitive slippage that marks so much of her thinking begins to appear. Although there is no color projection here, there is a hint of the same process as she tries to make the butterfly "pretty" but in doing so reveals the negative mediation, ". . . it must be poisonous," against which she may have been defending herself. The first hint of her depression is seen in her next answer; and the fact that she perceives the Popular female figure as a male stimulates an obvious question about sex role identification. Her next answer may reflect an attempt to make the blot less threatening by making it something "little," and that is probably how she feels about herself, something being examined now. The inappropriate word, "premmie," illustrates her very limited operations, and may tie together with her previously noted sexual preoccupation. A different look at how she perceives herself is evident in her fifth response, ". . . flying through a storm . . . ," which she forces herself to validate by saying, ". . . yes of course, they do that." This answer, occuring after she has perceived two people, but not with people bodies, raises another question about her own sense of self.

Clearer evidence about the nature of her sexual preoccupation is seen in her first answer to Card III, "My that's ugly . . . ," which also gives considerable evidence about her own feelings of vulnerability, ". . . he's doing something to her . . ." and the conflict state that exists within her. This highly idiographic response is followed by her most pathological answer, the *CONTAM,* which probably illustrates her inability to sort out the butterfly percept from the concept of a flower. Instead, they tend to merge, and she is helpless. It is very important that, in the inquiry, she says, "I don't remember that . . . ," but unfortunately she does *not say* something to the effect of "I must have meant butterfly," or, as sometimes will happen with very young children, "You must have written it wrong." Either would demonstrate greater resiliency under structure than is the case here. While providing a creative response on the next card, she also becomes more personal as her ideational disarray continues to be rampant, ". . . and staring right at you." There is some similarity here to answers common among children, to the effect, "It'll get you if you don't watch out." She makes her strongest effort to avoid the test in her approach to Card V: that is, the cards are ridiculous, and probably so too is the examiner. She ultimately gives more evidence of her depressive mood with the death struggle response, after which she offers another "penetration" or vulnerability answer. Card VI again conveys the negative connotation that characterizes her sexual preoccupation, and the Christian flag response may signal some idiosyncratic ideation concerning values. Her answers to Card VII seem to dramatize the very negative self-concept that has been evident throughout the record, the first being an inspection for "cancer," while the second is ". . . a negative picture of a woman's face . . ." She doesn't like herself and probably harbors some rather bizarre delusions about herself and about sexuality. Her *pure C* response is more static than might be expected, but the card appears to be a potent stimulus if her location selection for her next answer is any guideline. She moves from the *W* to a very small detail area, and her first *pure F* response since Card II, but her concreteness reduces the effectiveness of this maneuver. Her answers on Card IX, and her first response on X, illustrate something about the uncontrolled volatility of her emotions, and the fact that two of those three are marked by *m* determinants seems to convey the intense domination that they wield over her. All three contents are morbid and distorted, and while she is ultimately able to detach herself from the emotional discharge in her last two answers, she is only able to do so by using very small blot areas and becoming much more concrete. Much of her word use supports the notion that she is potentially quite intelligent, but obviously her ability to capitalize on that intellect is seriously impaired.

Case 11 Summary.   This woman reflects one of the "hard spectrum" forms of schizophrenia. Her thinking is bizarre, concrete, and probably delusional. Her thoughts often "run together" and handicap her attempt to respond effectively to her world. Her intense, and not well modulated, emotions contribute significantly to her impairment in thinking, and she will often become completely overwhelmed. Interestingly, she appears to have some awareness of her plight, and has been struggling to organize her world and control her affects, but to little or no avail—unless the fact that she has been able to maintain ambulatory status is regarded in an appropriately positive framework. Currently, she seems angry and is experiencing much pain because of her inability to contend with her disarray. Her sexual preoccupation is probably a major element in her confusion, and should be evaluated carefully to discern whether it can be a viable treatment target. Sometimes, magically brutal thoughts with a delusional theme that have arisen very early in life are subject to repair; in other instances, however, it may be better to "compartmentalize the delusion" rather than attempt to rectify it. In this case, the illegitimate child and all the trauma that may have been associated with it may have been a major factor, especially in light of her refusal to acknowledge the child shortly after it was born. In spite of the chronic and severe disorganization that is manifest, this kind of patient is often amenable to intervention if approached cautiously. Containment of the "craziness" and a thwarting of any further disorganization are the primary targets for the immediate future; and subsequently, a structured form of intervention should focus on issues of reentry, the depressive mood, enhancing reality testing, and, most of all, discovering new ways in which she can discharge emotion in a much more modulated fashion. She will need a carefully monitored support system in her environment; it might be built in the context of her relationship with her daughter. It is interesting to speculate that she may perceive the "burden" of her daughter as some bizarre form of punishment. Conversely, the presence of herself, as validated by the presence of the daughter, may have contributed to her ambulatory status. Obviously, much more evaluation of this issue is required.

Case 11 Epilogue. This patient was hospitalized for 10 days, after which she returned home and within one week had returned to work. A more exhaustive evaluation of her sexual preoccupation revealed that she did "hear" the voice of God chiding her for wrongdoings, and God instructed her to become a prostitute to "pay for" her sins. This accounted for her frequent absences from home. A minister volunteered to become involved in her support system "so as to translate God's messages correctly." She was treated with substantial quantities of an antipsychotic drug, added to a group of women who had made suicide attempts, and was seen weekly for individual attention by a psychologist. An evaluation after one year revealed that she was "holding her own," had enrolled in an evening course in a community college, and was, with continued support, reevaluating her occupational goals. She had a very limited social life for the first eight months, but after that time began to accept occasional invitations for dates.

Case 12: An 11 Year Old Male—the Whalechild

History. This youngster is the oldest of two children. Both live with their mother, who has been separated from the father for three years. The mother, age 32, is currently unemployed after having worked for six years in a clerical position. She is a high school graduate. She has been hospitalized twice during the past four years, once for an attempted suicide at age 28 (wrist cutting), and the second time, approximately one year ago, after discussing suicide with a social worker. She has been diagnosed as a "borderline" personality by hospital staff. During the past year there has been some discussion about a foster placement for the children; however, the mother objects to this very strenuously and the father, who lives in another state, indicates no interest in the situation. He is described as an

Case 12

266

Card	Free Association	Inquiry	Scoring
I	2″		
	1. Its a bf w its hands out lik its ready to fite	E: (Rpts S's resp) S: Its got big wings & big hands like he's reachg out to grab s.t. lik mayb he's ready to fite, c the hands r here	Wo FMᵃo A P 1.0 INCOM
	2. Its lik a crab w some wgs too, tell me again what Im supposed to do	E: (Rpts S's resp) S: C the big wgs & the hands & the tail the crab is inside E: Inside S: I didn't say that, I said a crab w wgs thes r the wgs, its a crab thts all	Wo Fw A 1.0 INCOM
	E: (Just tell me what it ll) S: Well it doesn't ll nothing		
II	2″		
	3. Tht's a skeleton & he's got bld on his hands, I don't want to do ths anymore	E: (Rpts S's resp) S: Ths is bld all over here & the skeleton is right inside, lik ths dark part, that's where skeletons always are E: Always are? S: Inside, skeletons are always inside, that's obvious E: I'm not sure what makes it ll bld S: Its red, everybdy know that	W− CF− An,Bl 4.5 FABCOM
III	1″		
	4. Its inside a body, lik bld spurtg out of u'r veins its an accident	E: (Rpts S's resp) S: All the red is the veins with the bld comg out & ths one is the heart, & the rest of it is the body E: U said an accident S: All the bld around so it must be one	W− mᵃ.CF− An,Bl 5.5 INCOM
	5. There's a nose there too tht got hurt, its a bldy nose	E: (Rpts S's resp) S: Sure its here (points) & its got bld on it so it must b a bldy nose lik it got hurt E: Bld on it S: Sure I said tht before didn't u listen	Dd− CF− Hd,Bl ALOG

IV   2"   6.   Its a giant foot, no, wait, erase that, its a giant man with a giant foot, man he's a big one

E: (Rpts S's resp)
S: See the shape of a giant, it really ll one & c the size of his feets thy is giant too, but he ain't got very big hands, c how little thy are no, wait, not hands, I don't c none but he's got little arms

Wo   Fo   (H)   2.0

7.   Its a giant jellyfish too lik he's sittg down on ths post

E: (Rpts S's resp)
S: Yeah, he's a big one too, boy he cld really get u
E: Can u show me some thgs about him
S: Well he's on ths post, just sittg there lik waiting for s.t. to swim by so he can grab it, just trying to look lik he's not there, c he's just there (runs finger around blot) cn ths (points) post

W−   M^p−   A   4.0   FABCOM

V   3"   8.   Thts a big horse, he's runng ths direction

E: (Rpts S's resp)
S: Well he's got his legs out here & here & he's got his head down lik he was coming rite at me, lik when thy race thy put their head down
E: I'm not sure I c the head
S: Its rite in the middle w his ears up here

W−   FM^a.FD−   A   1.0

9.   Say, mayb its tht bf again

E: (Rpts S' resp)
S: Yeah, thts the one in the other pict too, it h as thes wgs on here & here's thos thgs lik bf's have on their heads, whaddaucallem's thyr rite here

Wo   Fo   A   P   1.0   PSV

VI   2"   10.   Oh tht is probably a mosquito & he's eating on ths floor

E: (Rpts S's resp)
S: Well he's probably eating the milk spots
E: Milk spots
S: If u spill milk & leave it, it maks spots lik on ths floor & c the mosquito is there & he's going to eat the milk up, thyr danger-ous cause thy eat holes in things

W+   FM^a.FYo   A   2.5

Case 11 (Continued)

Card	Free Associaton	Inquiry	Scoring
VII 2"	11. Ths r 2 rabbits that r kissing together, lik thyr in love	E: (Rpts S's resp) S: Yep, thyr rite there, & thyr gonna kiss (giggles) so thy must b in love E: Show me the rabbits S: C the ears & the face & thy got thes big lips too, & a funny tail out here	D+ M^ao (2) A 3.0 (ALOG)
VIII 2"	12. Ths 2 A's that got stuck on a tree	E: (Rpts S's resp) S: Well thyr out here (points) & u can c ths is a tree cause its got a top & a middl & a bottm & thy must hav got stuck on it cause thats how thy are	W+ FM^po (2) A P 4.5 FABCOM
	13. There's a dead bird there too, he got smashed & is all blood	E: (Rpts S's resp) S: Well it ll a big bird tht mayb s.b. shot or ran over cause its all blood & its lik dead E: Can u show me some of the bird S: C the wings r here & its all red & pink lik boodly birds get	D– CF– A,Bl
IX 2"	Lets skip ths one, I don't kno what it mite be E: Take u'r time, almost e.-body can c s.t. if thy look longer		
	14. Its a giants face, lookg rite at me & I don't lik it, its mean looking	E: (Rpts S's resp) S: He look mean to me, he's got big ears & he's got his face all scrunched up lik he was mad E: All scrunched up? S: C this all comes out, lik his cheeks & he's got thes funny eyes too lookg rite out, c rite here, lik he is mean	WS– M^a– (Hd) 5.5 DV

X	2"	15. Oh, mayb a whalechild yeah, thats rite a whalechild		D- F- (A) CONTAM

E: (Rpts S's resp)
S: It ll a whale to me, c here, its just lik a whale?
E: U said whalechild?
S: I didn't say that, u wrote it wrong, its a whale & c his face there, here's his nose & his chin & his big long body like a whale

16. Thts a spider tht caught a goat $\quad$ D+ $FM^a w$ (A) 4.0 FABCOM

E: (Rpts S's resp)
S: He's a giant spider, lik he'll get u too if u don't watch where u walk & he's got ths goat, c the goat got a horn so it must be a goat & he's gonna eat him

17. Some chinese blood $\quad$ Dv C Bl ALOG

E: (Rpts S's resp)
S: It's yellow, we learned about tht in school so if its yellow its chinese blood

Note: Testing of limits yielded *P* on Cards II and VII but not on III.

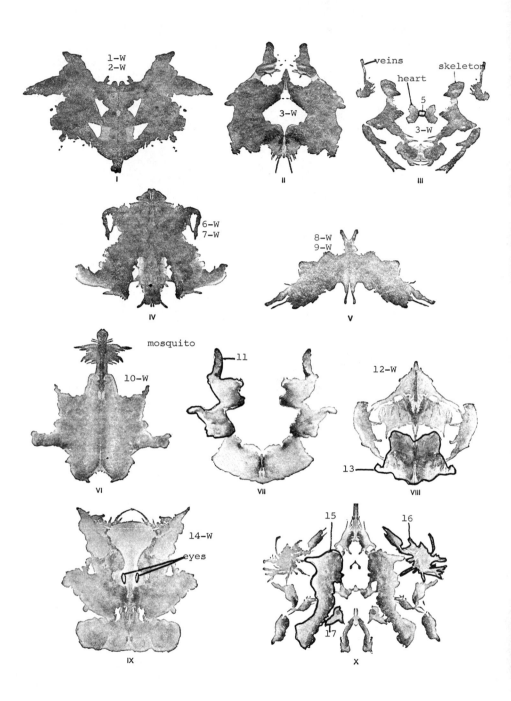

Case 12

CARD	RT	NO.	LOCATION	DETERMINANTS (S)		CONTENT (S)	POP	Z SCORE	SPECIAL
I	2"	1.	Wo	FM^ao		A	P	1.0	INCOM
		2.	Wo	Fw		A		1.0	INCOM
II	2"	3.	W-	CF-		An,Bl		4.5	FABCOM
III	1"	4.	W-	m^a.CF-		An,Bl		5.5	INCOM
		5.	Dd-	CF-		Hd,Bl			ALOG
IV	2"	6.	Wo	Fo		(H)		2.0	
		7.	W-	M^p-		A		4.0	FABCOM
V	3"	8.	W-	FM^a.FD-		A		1.0	
		9.	Wo	Fo		A	P	1.0	
VI	2"	10.	W+	FM^a.FYo		A		2.5	
VII	2"	11.	D+	M^ao	(2)	A		3.0	(ALOG)
VIII	2"	12.	W+	FM^po	(2)	A	P	4.5	FABCOM
		13.	D-	CF-		A,Bl			
IX	18"	14.	WS-	M^a-		(Hd)		5.5	DV
X	2"	15.	D-	F-		(∧)			CONTAM
		16.	D+	FM^aw		(∧)		4.0	FABCOM
		17.	Dv	C		BL			ALOG

Case 12:   Structural Summary

R = 17   Zf = 13   ZSum = 39.5   P = 3   (2) = 2

Location Features		Determinants (Blends First)		Contents		Contents (Idiographic)	
W	= 11	**DQ**		H	=		=
				(H)	= 1		
D	= 5	+ = 4	FM.FY = 1	Hd	= 1		=
			FM.FD = 1	(Hd)	= 1		
Dd	= 1	o = 4	m.CF = 1	A	= 9		=
S	= 1	v = 1		(A)	= 2		
				Ad	=		=
DW =		— = 8	M = 3	(Ad)	=		
			FM = 3	Ab	=		=
			m =	Al	=		
			C = 1	An	= 2		=
Form Quality			CF = 3	Art	=		
			FC =	Ay	=		=
FQx		FQf	C' =	Bl	= 1,4		
			C'F =	Bt	=		=
+	= 0	+ = 0	FC' =	Cg	=		
			T =	Cl	=		
o	= 6	o = 2	TF =	Ex	=	**Special Scorings**	
			FT =	Fi	=		
w	= 2	w = 1	V =	Fd	=	PSV	=
			VF =	Ge	=		
—	= 8	— = 1	FV =	Hh	=	DV	= 1
M Quality			Y =	Ls	=		
			YF =	Na	=	INCOM	= 3
+	= 0		FY =	Sx	=		
			rF =	Xy	=	FABCOM	= 4
o	= 1		Fr =				
			FD =			CONTAM	= 1
w	= 0		F = 4				
						ALOG	= 2,1
—	= 2						=

RATIOS, PERCENTAGES, AND DERIVATIONS

ZSum-Zest	=	39.5—41.5	FC:CF+C	= 0:5	Afr	= .55
Zd	=	−2.0	W:M	= 11:3	3r+(2)/R	= .12
EB	=	3:5.5 EA = 8.5	W:D	= 11:5	Cont:R	= 4:17
eb	=	6:1 ep = 7	L	= .31	H+Hd:A+Ad	= 3:11
					(H)+(Hd):(A)+(Ad)	= 2:2
Blends:R	=	3:17	F+%	= .50	H+A:Hd+Ad	= 12:2
a:p	=	7:2	X+%	= .35	XRT Achrom.	= 2.2"
Ma:Mp	=	2:1	A%	= .65	XRT Chrom	= 5.0"

alcoholic, and was hospitalized twice for alcoholism prior to their separation. The subject is currently in the fifth grade, and is doing very poorly, although the results of two intelligence tests reveal I.Q.'s of 96 and 103. He is described by his teacher as being inattentive and showing inappropriate behavior, frequently "acting out" his aggression toward other children. His brother, age 10, functions at an above average level in the fourth grade. Six months earlier, the subject was evaluated by a school psychologist and identified as a "hyperactive" child, and as such has received special attention in the school. He is of normal height, weight, and build, and has no distinguishing features. He was hospitalized four days before the examination after attempting to stab his mother with a hunting knife. She had apparently argued with him about television, then sent him to the room he shares with his brother. He returned shortly afterwards with the knife, and was restrained by his mother and brother. Since admission he has been cooperative but "detached", often spending much time gazing out the window. He interacts very little with other children in the 10 bed ward where he has been placed, but is reported to have threatened one during a meal. One nurse and one aide report more success in their attempts to interact with him, and during the past two days he has been willing to play checkers with the aide. The physical examination is unremarkable, and an EEG, taken the day of the examination, is within normal limits. A third intelligence testing (WISC-R), administered prior to the Rorschach, yields a Full Scale I.Q. of 99, with no significant scatter in the record. A Bender-Gestalt, administered at the same time, was very well done, although he refused the House-Tree-Person Test. He was resistant to taking the Rorschach, but when given the option of waiting for another day, he chose to complete the examination, most of which was accomplished with the subject and examiner seated on the floor.

Structural Interpretation.   It is very important, when approaching the record of a younger client, to keep that client in proper developmental perspective. This means, for example, that cognitive operations should not be expected to approximate those of the adult, and that some slippage in cognitive activity can be expected. Nonetheless, in this instance, the cognitive disarray is much more extensive than would be typical for the 11 year old, or even a seven year old; and because of the presence of two $M-$ responses, the possibility of a thinking disorder must be considered very carefully. Eleven of his 17 answers are marked by Special Scoring for unusual verbal material, including four *FABCOM*'s, two *ALOG*'s, and one *CONTAM*. This is clearly excessive for a youngster this age, and the presence of the *CONTAM* signals much more trouble than would be expected for most youngsters, regardless of age. Weiner (1977) finds that the average 12 year old will give between two and three responses that are given Special Scores, exclusive of the *CONTAM* types of answer, which are very rare at that age. When this information is added to the fact that there are only three *Popular* answers, and that, although the protocol length is about average, the $X+\%$ and $F+\%$ are both very low and include a high frequency of minus responses (8 of 17), the likelihood of schizophrenia becomes more and more distinct. Although there are five chromatic color determinants, *none are FC*, and a *pure C* is present in the record. The reference data for 11 year olds indicate that they usually give about as much *FC* as *CF + C*, suggesting that he is not able to modulate emotional displays and is often overwhelmed by them. The *Afr* is considerably lower than for any of the 11 year old reference samples. This may signal some awareness of his trouble with control and an attempt to avoid situations that might tend to be overwhelming. However, the *Lambda* is also very low when compared to the data for elevens, indicating that he is not able to back away from situations that include emotionally laden stimuli. It seems likely that he will often find himself "trapped" in those situations, and usually becomes a victim of his own impulses.

The *EB* discloses that he is a person who will discharge affect in his attempts to cope. While this may be a natural style for him, his inability to modulate becomes something of a disaster in many situations. This case is also very interesting because the *EA* is slightly greater than the *ep,* suggesting that he does have access to a considerable resource, and that it is probably organized in a "set" way. The organization, however, is probably primitive and ineffective, and, as he has grown, there has been less flexibility to his coping behaviors. The *eb* reveals very little internal discomfort, but more the evidence of a person strongly prompted by ideation related to need states. He has five *FM* determinants, and while this is not necessarily excessive for his age, his inability to direct those needs in a productive manner is probably a dangerous situation for him. It is also important to note that this is a *T-less* record, suggesting that he may have become "extinguished" concerning his ability to love or be loved. The somewhat extreme differences in the $a:p$ ratio indicate that he does not have much flexibility in his thinking, and although his $W:M$ shows the typical "grandiose" aspirational levels for this age, his *egocentricity index* is inordinately low, suggesting a major loss of the sense of personal worth.

The *Zf* indicates that he attempts to organize his environment more than most youngsters of his age, and the *Zd* score reveals that he is able to do this with relative efficiency. The paucity of *Human content,* including the *absence of pure H,* suggests that he is probably having great difficulty in perceiving and interacting with others. He has a large number of references to *blood,* another "danger sign." Very young children will offer a blood response from time to time, but that has usually disappeared by this age, and the frequency is quite high for even the younger child. The two *anatomy* responses are also interesting, since they would be expected in the younger child but are not typically present at this age. The relatively high frequency of *FM + m,* plus the apparent absence of modulation to emotional displays, can be among the basic ingredients of "acting out," and it will be important to look for some qualitative "feel" concerning his anger as the analysis of content proceeds.

Interpretation of the Scoring Sequence.   He is a very *W* oriented youngster, more like the five or six year old than like others of his own age. This may often "get him into trouble" as he attempts to "bite off more than he can handle." Responses that are truly "good," from a structural view, are few and far between in this record. His first answer to Card IV appears to have those characteristics, as does his second answer to Card V, and possibly his only answer to Card VI; otherwise, his responses are all marked by poor form quality and/or some form of Special Score. While he signs-in with a Popular, it is also an *INCOM,* and his disarray is generally evidenced consistently as he proceeds through the blots, finally signing out with his one *pure C,* which is also marked by an *ALOG.* His *blood* responses occur across four of the five chromatically colored blots, suggesting that this *is not* a manifestation of a simple cognitive slippage, but instead reflects some form of distinct preoccupation. His inability to handle emotionally loaded stimuli is dramatized by the fact that only one of his nine answers to the blots which contain chromatic features is good form, while six of the nine are a minus form quality. The fact that he is able to give four synthesis (*DQ+*) locations across several cards speaks favorably in his behalf, but the huge number of minus answers tends to overshadow this, suggesting that his functional intelligence is severely impaired. His reaction times are all very short, with one exception, and this may illustrate some of the features that others have described as "hyperactive."

Interpretation of Content.   He opens with an aggressive response, ". . . ready to fight," and he probably feels like that much of the time. His remark in Response 2, ". . . tell me again what I'm supposed to do," is probably less of a ploy than a real difficulty in maintaining concentration. Although neither of his answers on Card I is especially "fine," he falls apart on Card II, and with few exceptions, it becomes "downhill all the way." His "blood" preoccupation in the next three cards is obviously important, and when studied in the context of the three contents, a skeleton, body insides, and a nose, may reflect the terrible injury that he has experienced, and probably accounts for some of his own aggressiveness—that is, to "strike out before someone or something strikes at you." The rapidity with which he scans a stimulus field and responds to it often causes him to make cognitive errors, as is illustrated in his approach to Card IV, but he catches himself, which may be an asset to an intervention plan. In other words, he seems to understand when his "scan" has been incomplete and can repair, unlike the underincorporator. The Card IV answers are also loaded with aggressive connotations, a giant and a jellyfish, but he tends to neutralize both later in the inquiry by denying the giant hands, and keeping the jellyfish inactive though alert, like the butterfly on Card I, which is ready to fight. His best "recovery" occurs on Card V, after his *FD* response, and even though the butterfly is a perseverative response it hints that he can grasp conventionality, even when the situation is unstructured, and particularly when it is void of emotionally loaded features.

His response to Card VI may best typify his very weak self-concept; he sees a mosquito eating from the floor. His answer to Card VII is possibly the most positive, although it is much more juvenile than is common for the average 11 year old. His responses to the last three blots are more disaster: he is stuck, he is smashed, he is tormented by his own aggression on Cards VIII and IX, and he enters Card X with what appears to be a *CONTAM*. Interestingly, he attempts recovery from this severe slippage during the inquiry, "I didn't say that, you wrote it wrong . . . ," but then proceeds to talk as if he perceives the composite of the whale and the child in the blot. After the slip, his last two answers manifest an acute concreteness and loss of contact with reality. He is absorbed by the blot and responds quite helplessly to it, offering little more than his strange schizophrenic disarray.

Case 12 Summary.   This schizophrenic youngster is very much out of control. His defenses are fragile, brittle, and ineffective much of the time, and his only effective defense in the past has been some form of acting out of his intense emotions. He feels neglected or abandoned, with few or no prospects, and has been relegated to a pattern of identifications which are developed mainly from his very childish ideation, plus, some modeling based on the conflict he perceived to exist between his parents when the father was in the home. He has also probably "modeled" a bit on his inadequate mother, who often appears to become subject to the commands of her own emotions. He strives to organize, but has not achieved the levels of cognitive sophistication that might permit him to deal with an overly complex world. His self-concept is diffuse and negative, he feels very injured, and he is trying to avoid added injury through his own aggressiveness. His thinking is becoming more and more concrete as his environment becomes more complex, and with chronological but not psychological progress, he is less and less able to handle his world, or even to perceive it very accurately. His ideation is focused so much on his internal turmoil that he is unable to learn more about reality and/or effective patterns of response. He feels lonely, but probably cannot define loneliness. He judges affection through behaviors ("they are kissing, so they must be in love") rather than by feelings. He is the kind of youngster who is very difficult to treat because of the frequent testing out of new found limits, and while he requires a great deal of structure *and* affection, it will be difficult to deliver.

Case 12 Epilogue. This youngster remained in a small unit for seriously disturbed children for approximately 10 months. A thorough neurological examination produced negative findings, and it was concluded that the label of "hyperactive" had been applied inappropriately. During the stay in the hospital, his mother made another attempt at suicide (pill taking) and was hospitalized for three months. In that interval, the younger sibling was placed in a carefully selected foster home and continues to show normal progress in school. The subject experienced several harsh side effects during the time that a medication routine was first explored, but "stabilized" on a phenothiazine during his second hospitalization month. Subsequently, he responded favorably to educational tutoring, and developed a very close relationship with a female nurse's aide, who became his "primary" therapist. At the end of the 10th month, he was placed in a very carefully selected foster home and has continued to progress at a satisfactory rate. He is currently attending public school, and is in his appropriate class.

Case 4: A 26 Year Old Male—a Lonely Island

History. This young man has a long history of medical complaints, dating back to his elementary school years. He has been hospitalized twice, once for pneumonia (two weeks) at age 15, and once for unremitting head pain at age 21 (two weeks). The latter hospitalization included a major neurological examination, including a computerized brain scan. All results of the neurological examination were negative. He has averaged nine visits a year to his family's physician for various complaints, none of which have involved injury or problems with the skeletal structure. Instead, all have focused on "internal" complaints. The Rorschach was administered during a third hospitalization, precipitated by complaints of chronic fatigue, indigestion, and difficulty in breathing. Psychological evaluation was included as a part of a complete examination. The subject lives at home with his parents, who are both age 48. The father is employed as a steamfitter, and has worked with the same firm for 25 years. The mother works part time in a cleaning firm, scheduling rug and house cleaning. She has held her current position for the past 13 years. The subject's older sister, age 28, was married at the age of 23, and continues to be employed as a receptionist in a legal complex, a position she has held since completing two years of business school.

The subject graduated from high school with "average" grades, taking a vocational course of study. Shortly afterwards, he obtained a position as an auto mechanic for an auto sales firm and has retained that position ever since. While in high school, he tried out for several athletic teams but was not accepted until his senior year, when he "made" the track team as a runner for the half mile event. He competed in six track meets, and finished first in three. His heterosexual experiences are limited to a "few" dates while in high school, plus more extended relationships with three women of his own age since his graduation. Each lasted approximately 18 months and usually involved dating once or twice weekly, but according to the subject, all ended as he became more pressured to marry. He indicates an interest in ultimately owning his own business, but is rather vague about what such a business might entail. He perceives his decision to continue to live at home as one benefiting his parents ("I can help out around the place") and also providing him with an opportunity to save money. He was quite cooperative and interested in the psychological testing, but disclaimed any "mental" problems. The assessment question posed from the hospital medical staff concerns the extent to which his chronic medical problems are psychosomatic, plus a request for treatment recommendations.

Previously Developed Interpretation. The partial data from this case, presented in Chapters 4 and 5, prompted questions about the possibility of schizophrenia. Working only from the Four Square in Chapter 4, the interpretation began with: "This configuration suggests a real problem potential. The *EB* reflects the ambitent, who may tend to vacillate in coping situations, although he does have the capacity for either ideational or emotional discharge in those situations. The considerably higher *ep* indicates the presence of many psychological features that are not accessible, yet stimulate much behavior. This more primitive state is compounded by the presence of a *pure C* and by the absence of *FC* answers. This suggests that when he does display affect, it probably tends to get out of control. The presence of three *C'* answers may indicate that he has some awareness of this and is attempting to contain emotion more. The absence of *T* raises an important question about his interpersonal relations. He may be experiencing the irritations of helplessness or loss of control."

When data for other critical ratios and percentages were added to the Four Square data, the interpretation commenced with the comment, "This begins to look very much like a schizophrenic case," and continued with the observation that, "The reality testing is quite limited and marked by substantial distortion *(F+%, X+%, frequency of minus responses)*. He is more self-centered than most adults *(3r + (2)/R)*, and appears to be attempting to avoid emotionally provoking stimuli *(Afr)*. The latter may be because of his very poor emotional controls *(FC:CF+C, 1 pure C)* which will often create the situation directing him by emotion rather than intellect. Two of the three *M* answers are minus, indicating some significant ideational distortion, which may be compounded by indications of a cognitive or ideational rigidity *(a:p)*. Unfortunately, he does not seem to be able to back away from complex stimuli as much as would be useful *(Lambda)*, but instead, appears to attempt to organize complex stimulus fields more often than is economical for him *(Zf)*. In doing so, he will often be overly cautious, and at times, unable to discriminate easily between important and unim-

Card	Free Association		Inquiry	Scoring
I	12″	1. Hum, it kinda ll a weird fly, mayb lik a horsefly thats pretty big	E: (Rpts S's resp)	WSo FC'w A 3.5
			S: Well its big lik a horsefly & its got those white marks on it lik thy do, c the wgs & thes r the marks & the littl feelers	
		S: Thats all		
		E: Most peopl c mor thn 1 thg		
		2. Oh yeah, well I cld say tht thes r hands up here	E: (Rpts S's resp)	Do Fo (2) Hd
			S: Yeah, thy just ll hands, c one here & one here, thats all just hands	
II	27″	3. Well u kno ths is a tough one but I cld mak ths top part into a cockfight, & thyv really been at it cause thyr all bloody	E: (Rpts S's resp)	D+ FMᵃ.CFo (2) A,Bl 5.5
			S: Well thy ll 2 cocks to me, thy have the peaks & the fat bodies & thyr all red, lik thy get after awhile, lik thy all bloody	
		4. That black part ain't nothin, but the white ll a sting ray, lik u mite c at the beach	E: (Rpts S's resp)	DSo Fw A (DV)
			S: Well it sur ll one, thy hav a kinda wg part to them so that when they swim thy really move fast	
III	19″	5. I'd say this is 2 guys who r fiting about s.t.	E: (Rpts S's resp)	D+ Mᵃo (2) H P 3.0
			S: Well, they ll thyr pullg in different directions on ths thg lik thy was each tryg to get it for themselves, I can't c what it is but thy r sure pulling on it	
		V6. U kno, when I look ths way its lik them pict's of the bad black lung disease thes here r the lungs, one here & one here (points)	E: (Rpts S's resp)	D– C'F– (2) An 3.0 ALOG
			S: Oh yeah, it ll them pict's of black lungs, lik u get if u smoke too much, c one is here & one is here & thyr round lik lungs & all black lik thy r if u smoke too much	

IV 9"

7. U kno, tht ll a big gorilla & its funny cause he's got boots on, which thy don't wear, but he's kinda movin along tnere, lik lookg for s.t., kinduva big hulky thg

E: (Rpts S's resp)
S: Well, he's all black, lik a big gorilla with thes big boots here (points) & ths r his arms & his head is kinda pulled in lik he's lookin for s..., or mayb expectin a fite, mean lookin

Wo FM^a.FC'o A P 2.0 FABCOM

V8. U kno ths way its lik them black ungs again but alot bigger here

E: (Rpts S's resp)
S: Well ths is lik a different picture of the same thg, c ths centr wld b lik the back-bone or s... & there's a lung on each side, c thy go upward lik lungs r shaped & thy hav these little ends & thyr all dark lik it was the disease lik thy advertise, its lik the same lungs as in the other pict but taken from close up & tht makes em bigger

W– FY–(2) An 2.0 (PSV)

V 15"

9. Ths ll s.t. that got split apart, lik a rabbit I guess

E: (Rpts S's resp)
S: Well, its lik s.b. took an axe & split ths old rabbit rite dwn the middle & its sorta laid out there, c the leg here & one here

W– F– A 1.0

V10. U kno, ths way it c.b. an eagle or hawk cause it has b g wgs, yeah it must b a hawk cause them wigs is so big

E: (Rpts S's resp)
S: I guess I'd say a hawk, c the big wgs & ths here r the feet that can grab thgs easy when thy are out lookg for prey, thy have these really sharp claws

Wo Fo A 1.0

VI 10"

11. U kno tht ll sort of a lonly island, kinda all alone out there in the water w all the mnts & peaks, and a deep cut in there, just sorta feelg all alone sittg there

E: (Rpts S's resp)
S: Well, I didn't mean that it really felt lonely, but its just that its all alone, the water is all out here, lik the ocean (white around the blot) & the island is lik cut in half by this gorge, its really deep down, almost lik u can't c btm its so dark so its really almost lik 2 but thyr connected in there, & by this peninsula up here

DdSv M^p.VF– (2) Ls 6.5 DV

Case 4 (Continued)

Card	Free Association	Inquiry	Scoring
	12. U kno I c a split brain in there too, yeah, thts wht it is, boy theres some funny thgs in these, it must be a small animals brain cause its so small	E: (Rpts S's resp) S: Yeah, thts what it ll, right down in here, c just ths littl part, lik mayb the brain of a cat or rat or s.t. small, & its almost apart lik thos split brains are s.times c a part is here (points) & the other part is here	D– F– An ALOG
VII 8″	13. I'd say that's just alotta fog	E: (Rpts S's resp) S: Well its just kinda lik fog or smoke, there isn't much shape to it, but its just all dark lik fog or smoke, yeah, probably smog	Wv YFo Fog 2.5
	V14. U kno ths way u can c the head of elephants	E: (Rpts S's resp) S: Well, this is the trunk part & the rest is just the head, c the way its formed there	Do Fo (2) Ad
VIII 9″	15. I'd say thes r a couple of wolves climbing a tree	E: (Rpts S's resp) S: Well thy c.b. wolves I thk, c the legs & thy hav that kind of body & the head kinda crouched in lik a wolf & ths thg in the middle c.b. a tree, c its pointed up here & these c.b. branches & ths wld be the ground I guess except some of the colors r all wrong	W+ FMªo (2) A,BT P 4.5
IX 32″	V16. Ths is weird, it ll the body of a wm, she's got no head but she's lik laying there with her legs apart	E: (Rpts S's resp) S: Oh yeah, the funny one, it just ll a wm to me but u can't c her head, & thes wld b her legs, lik the orange part, she's kinda fat & it ll she's got her legs spread E: I'm not sure I c it lik u do, can u show me a bit more S: Well, thes r her legs & this would b her shoulders & here r her hips & all, thts it	W– Mᵖ– Hd 5.5

V17.	U kno it cld all ll a big implosion too, lik e.t. go ng in all directions & all the fi e shootin up	E:	(Rpts S's resp)		
		S:	Did I say that? I mean explosion, I never heard of a implosion, I mean explosion, c lik its all going up (gestures with hands) & this orange is lik the fire part when tht happens, I didn't say implosion though, explosion, thts what I said	Wv	$m^a.CFo$ Ex 5.5 DV
X	18.	6''	Ths just lik a lotta paint that s.b. threw & it landed tht way	E:	(Rpts S's resp)
				S:	Well it just ll paint lik s.b. got mad & threw it & thats the way it landed, splat, just lik that
				Wv	C Paint
	19.	If I just look at ths brown spot I can make out lik a deer jump-ing there, there's one here too	E:	(Rpts S's resp)	
			S:	Well it could hav horns lik a deer & ths r the legs & it looks stretched out lik it was jumping lik thy do a lot	Do	FM^a (2) A
	20.	U kno ths top part gives a feel-ing of force, lik s.t. growing upwards, lik forcg upward, lik these r two plants & thy come together & thy r pushg up, I don't mean 2 plants, but lik parts of a plant & thy form to-gethr here & this is the stalk going up	E:	(Rpts S's resp)	
			S:	Well, thes side parts c.b. the two parts of the roots or s.t. & thyr coming togethr here & lik pushg on the stalk here, pushg it upward & then it will get buds on it, its not all there rite now, it has to grow a lot before it gets the buds	Dv	$m^a w$ (2) Bt

281

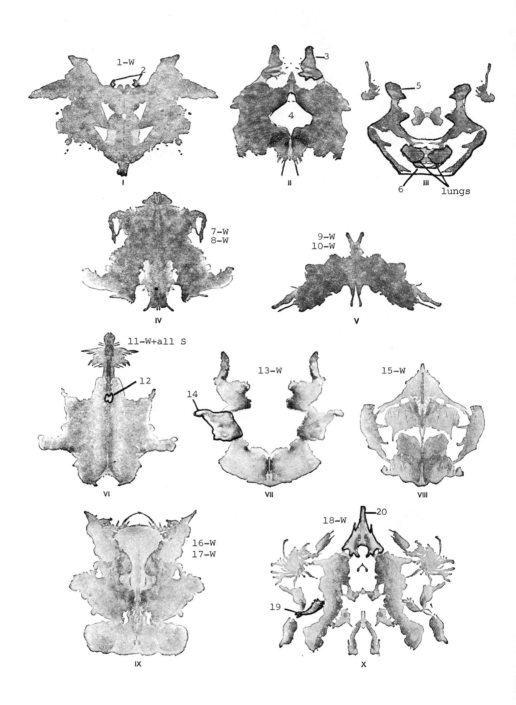

Case 4

CARD	RT	NO.	LOCATION	DETERMINANTS (S)		CONTENT (S)	POP	Z SCORE	SPECIAL
I	12"	1.	WSo	FC'w		A		3.5	
		2.	Do	Fo	(2)	Hd			
II	27"	3.	D+	$FM^a.CFo$	(2)	A,Bl		5.5	
		4.	DSo	Fw		A			(DV)
III	19"	5.	D+	$M^a o$	(2)	H	P	3.0	
		6.	D–	C'F–	(2)	An		3.0	ALOG
IV	9"	7.	Wo	$FM^a.FC'o$		A	P	2.0	FABCOM
		8.	W–	FY–	(2)	An		2.0	(PSV)
V	15"	9.	W–	F–		A		1.0	
		10.	Wo	Fo		A		1.0	
VI	10"	11.	DdS–	$M^p.VF–$	(2)	Ls		6.5	DV
		12.	D–	F–		An			ALOG
VII	8"	13.	Wv	Y		Fog			
		14.	Do	Fo	(2)	Ad			
VIII	9"	15.	W+	$FM^a o$	(2)	A,Bt	P	4.5	
IX	32"	16.	W–	$M^p–$		Hd		5.5	
		17.	Wv	$m^a.CFo$		Ex		5.5	DV
X	6"	18.	Wv	C		Paint			
		19.	Do	$FM^a o$	(2)	A			
		20.	Dv	$m^a w$	(?)	Bt			

Case 4:   Structural Summary

R = 20   Zf = 12   ZSum = 43.0   P = 3   (2) = 10

Location Features				Determinants (Blends First)		Contents			Contents (Idiographic)	
W	= 10		**DQ**	M.VF	= 1	H	= 1		Paint	= 1
D	= 9	+	= 3	FM.CF	= 1	(H)	=			=
Dd	= 1	o	= 7	FM.FC'	= 1	Hd	= 2			
S	= 3	v	= 4	m.CF	= 1	(Hd)	=			=
DW	=	—	= 6			A	= 8			
				M	= 2	(A)	=			=
				FM	= 2	Ad	= 1			=
				m	= 1	(Ad)	=			
				C	= 1	Ab	=			=
Form Quality				CF	=	Al	=			
				FC	=	An	= 3			=
FQx		**FQf**		C'	=	Art	=			
				C'F	= 1	Ay	=			=
+	= 0	+	= 0	FC'	= 1	Bl	= 0,1			
o	= 9	o	= 3	T	=	Bt	= 1,1			=
w	= 3	w	= 1	TF	=	Cg	=			
—	= 6	—	= 2	FT	=	Cl	=		**Special Scorings**	
M Quality				V	=	Ex	= 1			
				VF	=	Fi	=			
+	= 0			FV	=	Fd	=		PSV	= 0,1
o	= 1			Y	= 1	Ge	=			
w	= 0			YF	=	Hh	=		DV	= 2,1
—	= 2			FY	= 1	Ls	= 1			
				rF	=	Na	= 1		INCOM	=
				Fr	=	Sx	=			
				FD	=	Xy	=		FABCOM	= 1
				F	= 6					
									CONTAM	=
									ALOG	= 1
										=

RATIOS, PERCENTAGES, AND DERIVATIONS

ZSum-Zest	= 43.0–38.0	FC:CF+C	= 0:3	Afr	= .43
Zd	= +5.0	W:M	= 10:3	3r+(2)/R	= .50
EB	= 3:3.5 EA = 6.5	W:D	= 10:9	Cont:R	= 8:20
eb	= 6:6 ep = 12	L	= .43	H+Hd:A+Ad = 3:9 (H)+(Hd):(A)+(Ad) = 0:0	
Blends:R	= 4:20	F+%	= .50	H+A:Hd+Ad	= 9:3
a:p	= 7:2	X+%	= .45	XRT Achrom	= 10.8"
Ma:Mp	= 1:2	A%	= .45	XRT Chrom	= 18.6"

portant stimuli *(Zd)*. He is now experiencing excessive internal emotional disruption *(eb)*, and apparently, some of his ideation leads to a negative form of self-inspection *(M.VF)*. The composite of poor reality testing, apparent ideational distortion, and poor emotional control set the stage for major psychological disarray, and his somewhat limited accessible resources *(ep > EA)* do not appear sufficient for effective coping.''

Finished Interpretation.   The remaining data in the Structural Summary offer some added support concerning the probability of a schizophrenic process. Five of his 20 answers include some Special Scores for unusual verbal material, including one *FABCOM* and two *ALOG* answers. He shows only three *Popular* responses, and half his *DQ* scores are either vague or minus, indicating a fairly unsophisticated cognition. It is very important at this point to be able to "rule out" the presence of a significant intellectual deficit, since some of these data may appear in the protocols of those who have "functional" I.Q.'s lower than the average range, but who are not markedly retarded. In particular, a distribution of Special Scores like that noted here (mainly *DV* and *ALOG*), the high frequency of lower level *DQ* scores, the low *P* and slightly elevated *A%*, and the *ep* greater than *EA* may all result from an intellectual handicap; *however*, this record does not appear to be one marked by such a handicap. The *R* is substantial, there are three *M* responses plus four blends, a high *Zf*, and a considerable articulation of shading features, including one *V* determinant. These features are less common among the intellectually deficient, but to be "safe," some other evidence about his intellectual functioning should be obtained (actually a WAIS reveals a Verbal I.Q. of 96, and a Performance I.Q. of 99). The distribution of his content scores indicates a substantial frequency of Anatomy answers that may highlight his somatic preoccupation, *or* may hint at more general issues of body concern. The somewhat lower frequency of Human contents, including only one pure *H*, suggests some interpersonal isolation, and the nature of his *M* answers will be important to a better understanding of this.

Overall, the structural data do include all four indices from which the diagnosis of schizophrenia would be rendered; evidence of some thinking disorder ($2M-$, 5 Special Scores), poor emotional control ($FC:CF+C = 0:3$, pure $C = 1$), very limited reality testing ($F+\% = 50$, $X+\% = 50$), and the low frequency of Human contents, with only one pure *H*.

The scoring sequence indicates a performance that is somewhat "shaky" throughout the test. He has form quality weak or minus answers on all but two cards. His reaction times are quite variable but not particularly meaningful, since in two instances (responses 3 and 5) he is able to deliver ordinary form quality responses, whereas after his longest reaction time, on Card IX, he offers a minus *M* response. His approach is somewhat uneven, although he tends to begin with *W* answers. He signs in with an *FC'* response, which may reflect some of his guardedness about displaying emotion. Both of his *m* determinants occur during the last two cards, which may illustrate the impact that the emotionally loaded stimuli do have on him. One of these is his last answer, which may signify a sense of futility about his capacities.

His verbal material is quite interesting, and, in fact, his first answer may be an *ALOG* (". . . it's big like a horsefly . . ."), although the possibility was not properly pursued by the examiner. It sounds very much like his answer on Card VI, in which he says, ". . . it must be a small animal's brain 'cause it's so small." Several of his contents have an aggressive character (horsefly, cockfight, sting ray, guys fighting, gorilla, hawk, wolves, and explosion), raising a question about how he handles his own aggression. None of his movement answers, except his last response, show any evidence of cooperativeness or effective interaction; instead, all of his movement objects are in conflict, functioning independently, or out of control. This is probably how he sees himself in relation to others, an inference that tends to confirm the earlier postulate that his interpersonal life is quite barren. This isolation may be dramatized by his response to Card VI, ". . . a lonely island, kinda all alone out there in the water with all them mountains and peaks, and a deep cut in there, just feeling all alone sitting there." On the positive side, he seems to recover quite often, sometimes during the Free Association, and in other cases during the inquiry. For instance, when he gives his *FABCOM* on Card IV, a gorilla with boots on, he injects, ". . . which they don't wear . . ."; or in the inquiry to Card VI, he begins by saying, "Well, I didn't mean that it really felt lonely . . ."; or in his last response on Card X, ". . . like these are two plants and they've come together and they are pushing up, I don't mean two plants, but . . ." A different form of resilience is noted in Cards V and VII. In Card V, after opening with a very poor form quality answer, a tendency that many schizophrenics have on this card, he is able to "stay with" the card and produce a near Popular response. Similarly, on Card VII, he opens with a very diffuse, penetration kind of answer, but then, after inverting the card, is able to deliver a good form quality Animal detail response. His response to Card VIII is also an important positive sign in light of his previously noted problems with emotional stimuli and emotional control. Here, he gives a Popular answer and is able to use the entire blot while avoiding the chromatic features. His two "black lung" responses are quite idiographic and probably signify some underlying delusional features. Similarly, two of his responses, the rabbit on V and the brain on VI, include the word "split," which also probably has some very special meaning for him and may represent something of how he feels. It is interesting that his last response has something that is apart now coming together, and the manner in which he ends the inquiry offers some tempting material for speculation, ". . . it has to grow a lot before it gets the buds."

Collectively, his contents offer an indication of an ill-formed self-concept that includes a considerable emphasis on aggressiveness, but that also conveys a sense distortion, inadequacy, and low self-value (big hulky thing, split brain, bad black lung disease, lonely island, weird looking woman). Some of his verbiage is marked by a juvenile quality ("a weird fly . . . boy, there's some funny things in these, . . . just like a lot of paint, . . . I didn't say implosion, though; explosion, that's what I said"), which ties together with the lower level *DQ* scores, and seems to emphasize a clear maturational failure. In other words, he seems *less like* a person who may have progressed and is now deteriorating, and *more like* a person who has never really progressed.

Case 4 Summary.   While marked by the characteristics of the schizophrenic, this man is not necessarily "falling apart." In fact, he is probably "holding his own" pretty well in spite of his disordered thought. It is very likely that his frequent physical complaints and symptoms are ways in which he defends himself against further disorganization, and it may be very dangerous to confront that system of defense at this time, since it seems to be effective in its own peculiar way. In that his history is free of any major psychiatric disruptions (although the incident of unremitting head pain may be a very negative sign), there is no reason to assume that he cannot continue to function with some reasonable effectiveness, marked by interludes of excessive physical preoccupation. Diagnostically, he would fall more into the Kety "hard spectrum" form of schizophrenia, but he has many "soft spectrum" characteristics; that is, he is free of *obvious* psychosis, hallucinations, marked delusional operations, and the like, and his disabilities are intermittent, or "reactive." He could probably profit from chemotherapy and a psychotherapy support system, consisting of little more than periodic visits to review his state of health, especially if he denies any psychiatric difficulties. A more direct confrontation with his illness might trigger massive denial, anger, and withdrawal, thus making him less available to support over time. A positive response to the support might lend itself to a broadening of the support system with the inclusion of some group or activity therapy, and/or an increase in individual visits. Major targets for a case like this consist of aid in the development of better emotional controls, improvement of perceptual accuracy, and development of more effective interpersonal skills. None, however, can proceed extensively before there is some containment of the thought disorder and a "shoring up" of the self-concept.

Case 4 Epilogue.   This man was treated with 75 mg of chloropromazine daily and placed on a routine of biweekly visits to a psychiatrist, during which the focus was generally on problems of everyday living. After approximately four months, the subject agreed to participate in a "support" group on a trial basis, but withdrew after three sessions. During the 11th treatment month, the frequency of visits was altered to once monthly. During this period, the frequency of physical complaints diminished slightly but not significantly. However, the amount of time he lost from work because of these complaints was reduced substantially. He continued living at home, and during the sixth treatment month began dating a woman with whom he had "kept company" previously.

Case 13: A 20 Year Old Male—An Incipient Snowman

The preceding cases have all illustrated a major segment of the so-called "hard spectrum" of schizophrenia. In each, the evidence for the thinking disturbance is quite clear and meshes easily with other data concerning the psychological disarray. In other cases, however, the evidence of the thinking disorder is "less firm" and the diagnosis of schizophrenia may be more equivocal. Ordinarily, such cases represent instances of early or incipient deterioration, the borderline *schizophrenia* described by Knight (1953). They present a more stringent challenge to the diagnostician, and in some instances, data from the Rorschach are better used to render a thorough description than to form a diagnostic conclusion. The following case reflects this issue reasonably well.

History.   This young man agreed to psychiatric treatment after a court hearing regarding his apprehension by police while exposing himself to three female third grade students who were walking home from school. He had no prior history of such behavior or any previous court record. He is a high school graduate who works as a stock boy and lives at home with his parents. His father, age 66, has worked in business machine repair for nearly 40 years. His mother does not work outside the home. He has four older sisters, ages 38, 36, 33, and 30, all married and living in the same community. The second and third sisters have both been in psychiatric treatment, the older having been hospitalized at age 25 for about four months. The subject was referred for psychiatric care by a school psychologist at age 16 because of acute anxiety attacks during examinations. At the time, the

Case 13

Card	Free Association	Inquiry	Scoring
I	1" 1. A bf, I kno how to mak thes too	E: (Rpts S's resp) S: Yeah, bf, well ths is the wgs & the body, c the wgs r out lik E: Outlik? S: Thats the way thy shld b on a bf	Wo Fo A P 1.0
	(Most peopl c mor thn 1 thg) 2. Well it c.b. a lobster. Do u want me to say a.t. else? (E: Its up to u) (S: Well I've done pretty well on ths)	E: (Rpts S's resp) S: Well ths littl thgs r the claws & ths cntr ll the shell fishes body, and ths is the tail but lobsters don't hav a tail	D– F– A
II.	9" 3. U kno, wht ths is? A gunshot wound, w bld dripping out of it	E: (Rpts S's resp) S: Well, the red stuff is bld here & ths ll a piece of wounded flesh rite here w the hole in it & the bld is comg out the front	DdSv m^P.CF.FDo Wound,Bl 4.5
	4. And its a raven	E: (Rpts S's resp) S: Well ths r wgs & the head w.b. here & ths black part w.b. the tail E: Black part? S: Yeah, the black under the red, not the red but black, lik the black tail of a raven	D– FC'– A
III	14" 5. 2 wm pullg apart a purse Thats it	E: (Rpts S's resp) S: Yeah, ths r the wm & ths is the purse E: I'm not sur I c it as u do S: Well ths ll a bag, u kno, purse & ths ll faces & breasts & limbs of women c rite here	D+ M^a o (2) H P 3.0 FABCOM

288

			Response	Inquiry	Scoring
IV	1"	V6.	Its a moth, a grey moth	E: (Rpts S's resp) S: Yeah, ths is the thorax, ths is the head & thes r the wgs & its grayish lik moths I've seen	Wo FC'o A 2.0
		7.	And the abominable snowman ha, ha, ha, he's lik weird lik thy built him funny or mayb he's built so his feet r out forward more lik ths & his littl head 's back more	E: (Rpts S's resp) S: I said that? (laughs) I d.k. (pause) Yeah, its big, massive, a grey hulk, ll dirty snow all piled up lik a snowman E: I'm not sur I c it as u do S: Ths w.b. the feet & thats the arm & ths w.b. the enormous body, I discounted ths piece when I lookd at it	Ddo FC'.FDo (H) (DV)
V	2"	V8.	Its a sting ray	E: (Rpts S's resp) S: Yeah, it looks exactly lik a sting ray Any pict's I've seen of em hav thes 2 littl tails & head & thes wgs, so evenly apart lik ths	Wo Fw A 1.0
		9.	And its a raincld, all the diff dark colors mak it lik a raincld	E: (Rpts S's resp) S: Yeah it just ll a raincld E: I'm not sure what maks it ll tht S: The diff colors, the shades it has, I gotta headache	Wv Y Cl
		10.	And a pair of shears, clip clip	E: (Rpts S's resp) S: On ths one? I thot it was a diff one E: No, it was ths one S: Oh, ths ll the scissors & thes w.b. handles here, r u writing dwn e t I say? (E: no resp)	D- F- Shears (DV)
		11.	And a bf, I got alot outta ths one	E: (Rpts S's resp) S: Ths, yeah, its lik a bf, ths rem me of a whole body & ths r the wgs & the wgs r out ths way lik a bf has wgs out ths way	Wo Fo A P 1.0

Case 13 (Continued)

Card		Free Association		Inquiry		Scoring
VI	1″	12. Its a butterchurn, yeah a churn	E: S: E: S: E: S:	(Rpts S's resp) Oh yeah, ths is the penis too Yes but 1st lets do the butterchurn Ths wb. the handl & the churn part & its kina colord tht way too Colord tht way? The diff coloring maks it ll tht, lik the handl is darkr than the churn	*Do FYw* Butterchurn
		13. And a penis being circumcised, that's it	E: S: E: S:	(Rpts S's resp) Yes, ths is the penis & ths is the foreskin being cut off, it has the color of the fore-skin The color? Ths color ll skin to me, the part being cut is liter colors & ths object is the penis	*Do M^p.FYw Sx*
VII	5″	14. Its a collision of rainclds, thun-der, its prob the same one I saw before but now in a colli-sion	E: S:	(Rpts S's resp) Yeah ths is the same colors as rainclds its dark grey, & its the exact shape of rainclds & ths is the collision point dwn here	*Wv m^a.C'Fo* (2) *Cl* 2.5 *PSV,DV*
VIII	12″	15. Two beavers climbg a tree, I dk if thy climb trees or not but it doesn't matter does it? (ITS UP TO U)	E: S:	(Rpts S's resp) Yeah, ths r the legs & tht ll the heads of beavers & thes r their tails & ths grn ll a trunk & thyr climbg a tree, can I chng it to a possum? (Its up to u) O.K. then I'll say thy ll possums better than beavers, 2 possums	*D+ FM^a o* (2) *A,Bt P* 3.0

IX	1"	16. A nuclear reactor exploding, now ths is a hard one, just a nuclr reactor exploding, I've seen pics of one, but no ones ever seen it lik ths

E: (Rpts S's resp)

S: Yeah lik in pics ths cntr is the reactor & all the colors outside ll an explo, a fisson explo or s.t lik that, all colors

Wv $m^a.CFw$ Ex 5.5 DV

X	16"	17. Let me study it, ah, 2 crabs ftg to get at a wishbone, c ths is the wishbone here its split in 2 ends

E: (Rpts S's resp)

S: Ths r the crabs & the wishbones, ths w.b. antennae & claws & the round body, so thy - lik crabs

$D+$ $FM^a{}_o$ (2) A 4.5 FABCOM

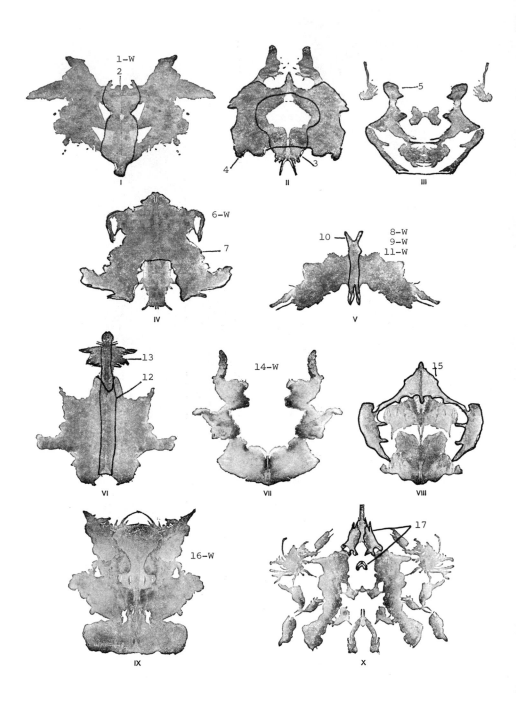

Case 13

CARD	RT	NO.	LOCATION	DETERMINANTS (S)		CONTENT (S)	POP	Z SCORE	SPECIAL
I	1"	1.	Wo	Fo		A	P	1.0	
		2.	D–	F–		A			
II	9"	3.	DdSv	m^p.CF.FDo		Wound,Bl		4.5	
		4.	D–	FC'–		A			
III	14"	5.	D+	M^ao	(2)	H	P	3.0	FABCOM
IV	1"	6.	Wo	FC'o		A		2.0	
		7.	Ddo	FC'.FDo		(H)			(DV)
V	2"	8.	Wo	Fw		A		1.0	
		9.	Wv	Y		Cl			
		10.	D–	F–		Shears			(DV)
		11.	Wo	Fo		A	P	1.0	
VI	1"	12.	Do	FYw		Buttrchrn			
		13.	Do	M^p.FYw		Sx			
VII	5"	14.	Wv	m^a.C'Fo	(2)	Cl		2.5	PSV,DV
VIII	12"	15.	D+	FM^ao	(2)	A,Bt	P	3.0	
IX	1"	16.	Wv	m^a.CFw		Ex		5.5	DV
X	16"	17.	D+	FM^aw	(2)	A		4.5	FABCOM

Case 13: Structural Summary

R = 17   Zf = 10   ZSum = 28.0   P = 4   (2) = 4

Location Features		
W = 7	DQ	
D = 8	+ = 3	
Dd = 2	o = 7	
S = 1	v = 4	
DW =	— = 3	

Determinants (Blends First)

M.FY	=1
m.CF.FD	=1
m.CF	=1
m.C'F	=1
FC'.FD	=1

M	= 1
FM	= 2
m	=
C	=
CF	=
FC	=
C'	=
C'F	=
FC'	= 2
T	=
TF	=
FT	=
V	=
VF	=
FV	=
Y	= 1
YF	=
FY	= 1
rF	=
Fr	=
FD	=
F	= 5

Contents

H	= 1
(H)	= 1
Hd	=
(Hd)	=
A	= 8
(A)	=
Ad	=
(Ad)	=
Ab	=
Al	=
An	=
Art	=
Ay	=
Bl	= 0,1
Bt	= 0,1
Cg	=
Cl	= 2
Ex	= 1
Fi	=
Fd	=
Ge	=
Hh	=
Ls	=
Na	=
Sx	= 1
Xy	=

Contents (Idiographic)

Butterchurn	= 1
Shears	= 1
Wound	= 1
	=
	=
	=
	=
	=

Form Quality

FQx		FQf	
+	=0	+	= 0
o	=8	o	= 2
w	=5	w	= 1
—	=3	—	= 2

M Quality

+	= 0
o	= 1
w	= 1
—	= 0

Special Scorings

PSV	= 1
DV	= 2,2
INCOM	=
FABCOM	= 2
CONTAM	=
ALOG	=
	=

RATIOS, PERCENTAGES, AND DERIVATIONS

ZSum-Zest	= 28.0-31.0			FC:CF+C	= 0:2	Afr	= .21
Zd	= -3.0			W:M	= 7:2	3r+(2)/R	= .23
EB	= 2:2.0	EA	= 4.0	W:D	= 7:8	Cont:R	= 8:17
eb	= 5:7	ep	= 12	L	= .42	H+Hd:A+Ad	= 2:8
						(H)+(Hd):(A)+(Ad)	= 1:0
Blends:R	= 5:17			F+%	= .40	H+A:Hd+Ad	= 10:0
a:p	= 5:2			X+%	= .47	XRT Achrom.	= 4.4"
Ma:Mp	= 1:1			A%	= .47	XRT Chrom	= 10.4"

subject visited the psychiatrist for about six months and was prescribed valium (10mg daily). The subject continued on medication for approximately one year, but has had no psychiatric contact since that time.

He obtained his present position as a stock boy for a department store shortly after completing high school with the help of one of his brothers-in-law. His work record is good, with a very low absentee rate. His father is surprised at the charges, indicating that he saw no evidence that there was anything wrong. He reports taking the subject fishing quite often for the past several years. The father admits that he has often "yelled" at the subject because of his preference for very loud music. The mother notes that the subject remains at home more than might be expected for someone his age. They play checkers a great deal. The subject maintains a model train set in the basement of his home and devotes considerable time to it. He reports that he had a "few" dates while in high school, but has had none since. He denies any drug history, but reports that some of his high school classmates, with whom he plays volley ball occasionally, do use various drugs quite often. He offers no explanation for his exhibitionism other than "something just came over me." He is somewhat reluctant about psychiatric treatment but feels that "maybe it will help me in the long run." A WAIS yields a full scale I.Q. of 108 (verbal I.Q. = 110; performance I.Q. = 104), with his best performance on Information and Similarities (scale scores of 13), and his weakest performance on Arithmetic and Picture Completion (scale scores of 8). The assessment question raised by the referring psychiatrist asks for a differentiation of a schizoid style from a schizophrenic process.

Structural Interpretation.   The structural data reveal the presence of three of the four most common features among schizophrenics; poor reality testing ($F+\% = 40$; $X+\% = 47$), limited emotional control ($FC:FC+C = 0:2$), and limited interpersonal interest and/or relations (*two Human contents, 1 pure H*). However, there are *no pure C* responses, and, more important, the data regarding ideational distortion are equivocal. There are no $M-$ answers, although there are only two M's in the record and one is of weak form quality. There are five, and possibly seven, Special Scorings, six for unusual verbal material plus one perseveration, and including two *FABCOM* answers. This is excessive for the adult, and offers reasonably firm evidence of some kind of ideational or cognitive slippage. However, the absence of $M-$, *CONTAM, ALOG,* and *pure C* responses requires caution and a more careful review of the entire protocol before any firm conclusions can be reached about the basic assessment question, at least regarding the issue of schizophrenia.

It is clear from the structural data that the subject does not have many easily accessible resources ($ep > EA$); that he has an acute sense of being out of control (3 m's); that he is experiencing much internal irritation about the inhibition of emotional display (4 C's) and feelings of paralysis or helplessness (3 Y's); that he cannot back away easily from complex stimuli ($Lambda = .42$); that he tends to avoid emotionally provoking stimuli ($Afr = .21$); that his self-esteem is significantly low ($3r + (2)/R = .23$); and that his distortions of reality are marked by some very unique perceptual interpretations (*FQx distribution has 5 weak and 3 minus answers*). The DQ distribution includes seven scores reflecting a lower developmental level (4v, 3 minus), offering a hint that his cognitive development may have been markedly impaired. He gives four *Popular* answers, which is slightly lower than expected, but still provides evidence that he can perceive and respond to conventionality. The $a:p$ ratio indicates some ideational flexibility, while the Zf suggests a reasonable organizing approach which falls within the range of "efficiency." This is a *T-less* record, which may indicate that he is not prone to expect close emotional relationships, a factor that may relate to the low frequency of Human contents. Two of his three m determinants appear in blends that also involve *CF* features, while the third involves a blend with a *C'F* determinant. This suggests that his emotions intensify, and tend to "get out of control," when he loses his sense of control over situations. The two *FD*'s in the record may indicate a healthy form of self-examination, or they may be related more to his recent confrontation with the law and his present commitment to treatment.

Interpretation of the Scoring Sequence.   He enters the record with two pure *F* responses, the second of which is a minus, a fact suggesting that he is not sure when his task of coping has been successfully completed. All his *m* determinants occur to chromatically colored cards, which is not surprising in light of his problems with emotional control and his attempts to avoid emotionally provoking stimuli. Both of his answers to Card IV involve the *C'* determinant, which may indicate that he feels a strong need to inhibit emotional displays when confronted with stimuli that suggest authority or aggressiveness. He has a great deal of trouble with Card V, giving four answers to the blot, three of which are not very effective; however, he is able to recover from the difficulties he experiences there and sign out from the blot with a Popular response. Similarly, both of his answers to Card VI are characterized by unique qualities, but in that instance he does not display the recovery phenomenon, and this is the only blot to which he is unable to demonstrate some form of organizational action. Other than his minus responses, his most pathological answers appear to occur on Cards VII, IX, and X, all of which are marked by unusual verbal material, while the *DQ* for two is vague, and the form quality for two is weak. His best answers appear to be his Populars, all of which involve good form quality, and only one of which (Card III) is marked by a Special Score. He seems to have a *W* orientation, but it is not very distinct, and, taken as a whole, the sequence does not offer much evidence of strength.

Interpretation of Content.   Although his opening response is adequate, his comment, ". . . I know how to make these too" is rather inappropriate for an adult. Similarly, after asking the examiner for directions on giving more answers, he offers a second comment that is somewhat juvenile, "Well, I've done pretty well on this." This occurs after having given a minus response, which indicates something of his limitations in testing reality very effectively. His first answer to Card II is quite "labile" and "out of control." If this represents a self-percept, it is clearly negative and pathological. His first answer on Card III probably conveys something of what is going on inside of him (pulling himself apart), and marks the first clear evidence of cognitive slippage. His second answer may be the most revealing of his self-concept. He is the abominable snowman, ". . . like they built him funny . . . ," and although he attempts to make light of the percept, it would seem to be quite important to him. It is three times longer than any previous answer, and will remain the longest in the protocol. It is after that answer that he has so much difficulty with the next blot, beginning with an aggressive answer, then giving a very dysphoric and diffuse answer, then moving to a substantial form distortion, before recouping with the Popular response, to which he appends another juvenile sort of unrealistic comment, ". . . I got a lot out of this one." He seems to recognize that he was "carried away" in his responsiveness, and is trying to counteract the negative impact. His first answer to Card VI may be quite revealing about him, ". . . yeah, a churn," conveying the notion that he has a lot going on within him. The following response is an *idiographic classic,* "and a penis being circumcised . . . ," and few theories would ignore the symbolism that seems inherent there. Certainly, if there are questions about the features underlying his exhibitionistic behavior, a rich clue is provided here. His answer to Card VII is quite interesting, partly because most people associate this blot with "femaleness," but even more so because he describes a ". . . collision of rainclouds, thunder . . ." This gives rise to more questions about his feelings of masculinity, and more important, his conception of females. This seems especially relevant in light of the fact that he is the only male, and the youngest of five siblings. His sisters would have been approximately 18, 16, 13, and 10 when he was born, while his mother, now age 57, would have been 37, with 10 years spacing her fourth and fifth children. It would be interesting to know whether he was planned, which seems unlikely, and what roles the older siblings, two of whom have had psychiatric problems, had in his rearing. Whatever the answers to those questions, the Card VII response suggests that he does not perceive females in a positive light, and, in fact, may perceive them as very threatening. His continuing need for support, as manifest again on Card VIII, ". . . but it doesn't matter does it?" tends to magnify his own need to validate his environment and his role in it. He is saying, in effect, "I don't know if this is all right or not," a characteristic that probably marks much of his behavior. His last two answers are very marginal, the first because of the *DV* quality, ". . . but no one's ever seen it like this," while the second is marked by a semibizarre *FABCOM* that involves an area of the blot rarely integrated with the part that he identifies as crabs.

Case 13 Summary.   Much of his performance is schizophrenic-like, and, certainly, there would be little reluctance to identify him as a schizoid. On the other hand, the loose controls, the interpersonal detachment, the very limited reality testing, and some very marked cognitive slippage, could easily be used to support a diagnosis of incipient or borderline schizophrenia. His thinking is concrete and juvenile, and although he seems to have some awareness of his plight, his overall approach to the task is often very childish, but at the same time he becomes very "wrapped up" in some of his unique and/or distorted responses. Much of his word usage, such as thorax, circumcised, reactor, and the like indicates a very bright and knowledgeable person, but his juvenile comments and his inability to cope effectively in this situation suggest that he is functioning considerably below his potential. He seems very confused about his sex role, confused by the identities of others, especially females, and lacks the mechanics or the experience from which he can experience further growth. He feels impotent, incompetent, and insecure, and will often lose control of his behavior when emotionally provoked. His reality testing appears to be gradually deteriorating, and he approaches the world more and more frequently through his own "idiographic" glasses. There is evidence that he feels tormented by his own helplessness, and is struggling to maintain an effective "lid" on his emotions. His self-esteem is very negative, and his self-concept terribly diffuse and negative.

It is very important to note that, with so little in the way of assets, he is not more disorganized or delusional; and that may be to his credit in any treatment plan.

While intervention should probably begin from a somatically oriented base, it would be very naive not to include some long term treatment objectives, such as building a better capacity to respond to emotionally loaded stimuli, dealing directly with the issue of sex role confusion, developing a technique for validating his perceptions, and "sorting out" his tendency to merge sexuality and aggressiveness. His awareness of his helplessness may provide a starting point for such an intervention program, and if a therapist can "break through" his tendencies to remain distant from his environment, a "frightened little boy" may emerge who will stretch out his hand if the opportunity is presented.

Case 13 Epilogue.   It was ultimately decided to treat this patient as a schizophrenic, and in that context, he was prescribed 40mg Haldol daily, and entered in a "modeling" form of psychotherapy involving two therapists, one male and one female. He would meet with the male therapist once weekly, and with the two therapists on alternate weeks. They established treatment objectives to include the development of better perceptual accuracy and the development of useful interpersonal skills. In addition, the entire family (except one sister) was involved in family therapy for approximately seven months on a once per week basis. The subject responded very favorably to this approach, did develop several useful interpersonal skills, and was able to deal more directly with emotionally provoking situations. He changed jobs after some five months of treatment to a maintenance position involving interaction with people, and began a night school course in electronics. After approximately one year, he decided to move into his own apartment and by that time had established some friendships with coworkers. He has remained in treatment to this time but continues to show progress. Is he schizophrenic? He remains on the antipsychotic medication, and according to those who see him, he occasionally "slips" into a form of concreteness that may reflect schizophrenia. Nonetheless, his progress is reinforcing to those working with him as well as to him. He could be called schizophrenic on the basis of the data here; or he could be called schizoid on the basis of the same data. In either event, he would fall into the "soft spectrum" when the overall issue of schizophrenia is reviewed.

SUMMARY

Some issues concerning schizophrenia have not been included here and remain "open." The problem of differentiating the schizophrenic from the manic-depressive condition is far from full resolution. A more careful look at the borderline phenomenon, the problems posed by "reactive" psychosis, and the issue of *early* identification of schizophrenia in the child are all "grist" for further research, without which the diagnostician using the Rorschach must rely more heavily on his or her ability to integrate the description generated from the total record with information about appropriate "diagnostic" criteria for these conditions.

REFERENCES

Beck, S. J. *Psychological Process in the Schizophrenic Adaptation.* New York: Grune and Stratton, 1965.

Benjamin, J. D. A method for distinguishing and evaluating formal thinking disorders in schizophrenia. In Kasanin, J. S. (Ed.), *Language and Thought in Schizophrenia.* Berkeley: University of California Press, 1944.

Bleuler, E. *Dementia Praecox or the Group of Schizophrenias* (1911). New York: International Universities Press, 1950.

Carpenter, W. T., Strauss, J. S., and Bartko, J. J. Flexible system for the diagnosis of schizophrenia: Report from the WHO International pilot study of schizophrenia. *Science,* 1973, **182,** 1275–1278.

Exner, J. E. *The Rorschach: A Comprehensive System.* New York: John Wiley and Sons, 1974.

Exner, J. E., Armbruster, G. L., and Kline, J. R. A review of the schizophrenia reference sample. Workshops Study No. 234 (unpublished), Rorschach Workshops, 1976.

Exner, J. E. and Murillo, L. G. A long term follow-up of schizophrenic treated with regressive ECT. *Diseases of the Nervous System,* 1977, **38,** 162–168.

Exner, J. E., Weiner, I. B., and Schuyler, W. *A Rorschach Workbook for the Comprehensive System.* Bayville, N.Y.: Rorschach Workshops, 1976.

Exner, J. E., Wylie, J. R., and Kline, J. R. Construction of a new schizophrenia reference sample. Workshops Study No. 235 (unpublished), Rorschach Workshops, 1976.

Fenichel, O. *The Psychoanalytic Theory of Neurosis.* New York: Norton, 1945.

Grinker, R., Werble, B., and Drye, R. *The Borderline Syndrome.* New York: Basic Books, 1968.

Gunderson, J. G., Carpenter, W. T., and Strauss, J. S. Borderline and schizophrenic patients. *American Journal of Psychiatry,* 1975, **132,** 1257–1264.

Hoch, P. H., and Polatin, P. Pseudoneurotic forms of schizophrenia. *Psychiatric Quarterly,* 1949, **23,** 248–276.

Hogarty, G. E., Goldberg, S. C., Schooler, N. R., and Ulrich, R. F. The collaborative study group: Drug and sociotherapy in the aftercare of schizophrenic patients II. Two year relapse rates. *Archives of General Psychiatry,* 1974, **31,** 603–608.

Kant, O. A comparative study of recovered and deteriorated schizophrenic patients. *Journal of Nervous and Mental Disorders,* 1941, **93,** 616–624.

Kantor, R. E., Wallner, J. M., and Winder, C. L. Process and reactive schizophrenia. *Journal of Consulting Psychology,* 1953, **17,** 157–162.

Kasanin, J. S. The disturbance of conceptual thinking in schizophrenia. In, Kasanin, J. S. (Ed.) *Language and Thought in Schizophrenia.* Berkeley: University of California Press, 1944.

Katz, M., and Lyerly, S. Methods of measuring adjustment and social behavior in the community. *Psychological Reports,* 1963, **13,** 503–535.

Keith, S. J., Gunderson, J. G., Reifman, A., Buchsbaum, S., and Mosher, L. R. Special report: Schizophrenia, 1976. *Schizophrenia Bulletin,* 1976, **2,** 510–565.

Kernberg, O. F. Borderline personality organization. *Journal of the American Psychoanalytic Association,* 1967, **15,** 641–685.

Kety, S. S., Rosenthal, D., Wender, P. H., and Schulsinger, F. The types and prevalence of mental illness in the biological and adoptive families of adoptive schizophrenics. In

Rosenthal, D., and Kety, S. S. (Eds.), *The Transmission of Schizophrenia*. Oxford: Pergammon Press Ltd., 1968.

Kety, S. S., Rosenthal, D., Wender, P. H., and Schulsinger, F. Mental illness in the biological and adoptive families of adopted schizophrenics. *American Journal of Psychiatry*, 1971, **128**, 302–306.

Kety, S. S., Rosenthal, D., Wender, P. H., Schulsinger, F., and Jacobsen, B. Mental illness in the biological and adoptive families of adopted individuals who have become schizophrenic: A preliminary report based on psychiatric interviews. In Fieve, R. R., Rosenthal, D., and Brill, H. (Eds.), *Genetic Research in Psychiatry*. Baltimore: Johns Hopkins University Press, 1975.

Khouri, P. Continuum versus dichotomy in theories of schizophrenia. *Schizophrenia Bulletin,* 1977, **3**, 262–267.

Klein, D. F., Rosen, B., and Oaks, G. Premorbid asocial adjustment and response to phenothiazine treatment among schizophrenic patients. *Archives of General Psychiatry*, 1973, **29**, 480–484.

Knight, R. P. Borderline states. *Bulletin of the Menninger Clinic,* 1953, **17**, 1–12.

Lorr, M., McNair, D., Klett, C. J., and Lasky, J. *Inpatient Multidimensional Psychiatric Scale*. Palo Alto, Calif.: Consulting Psychologists Press, 1966.

May, P. R. A. *Treatment of Schizophrenia*. New York: Science House, 1968.

May, P. R. A., Tuma, A. H., and Dixon, W. J. Schizophrenia—A follow-up study of results of treatment: I. Design and other problems. *Archives of General Psychiatry*, 1976, **33**, 474–478.

Meyer, A. Fundamental concepts of dementia praecox (1907). In Lief, A. (Ed.), *The Commonsense Psychiatry of Dr. Adolph Meyer*. New York: McGraw Hill, 1948.

Miller, W. R. The relationship between early schizophrenia and the neuroses. *American Journal of Psychiatry*, 1940, **96**, 889–896.

Murillo, L. G., and Exner, J. E. The effects of regressive ECT with process schizophrenics. *American Journal of Psychiatry*, 1973, **130**, 269–273.

Phillips, L. Case history data and prognosis in schizophrenia. *Journal of Nervous and Mental Disorders*, 1953, **117**, 515–525.

Piotrowski, Z., and Lewis, N. D. C. An experimental Rorschach diagnostic aid for some forms of schizophrenia. *American Journal of Psychiatry*, 1950, **107**, 360–366.

Polatin, P., and Hoch, P. H. Diagnostic evaluation of early schizophrenia. *Journal of Nervous and Mental Disorders*, 1947, **105**, 221–230.

Rapaport, D., Gill, M., and Schafer, R. *Psychological Diagnostic Testing. Volume II*. Chicago: Yearbook Publishers, 1946.

Rappaport, M., Hopkins, H. K., Hall, K., Belleza, T., and Silverman, J. Acute schizophrenia and phenothiazine utilization. I. Clinical outcome. Final Report, National Institute of Mental Health, NIMH Grant 16445, 1976.

Satorious, N., Shapiro, R., and Jablensky, A. The international pilot study of schizophrenia. *Schizophrenia Bulletin,* 1974, **1**, 21–34.

Spitzer, R.L., Endicott, J., and Robins, E. *Research Diagnostic Criteria* (RDC) for a selected group of functional disorders. New York State Psychiatric Institute, 1977.

Thiesen, J. W. A pattern analysis of structural characteristics of the Rorschach test in schizophrenia. *Journal of Consulting Psychology*, 1952, **16**, 365–370.

Watkins, J. G., and Stauffacher, J. C. An index of pathological thinking in the Rorschach. *Journal of Projective Techniques*, 1952, **16**, 276–286.

Weiner, I. B. *Psychodiagnosis in Schizophrenia*. New York: John Wiley and Sons, 1966.

Weiner, I. B. Rorschach diagnosis of schizophrenia: Empirical validation. VII International Congress of Rorschach and other Projective Techniques, London, 1968.

Weiner, I. B. Rorschach diagnosis of schizophrenia: Empirical validation. *Rorschachiana,* 1971, **9,** 913–920.

Weiner, I. B. Rorschach indices of disordered thinking in patient and nonpatient adolescents. IX International Rorschach Congress, Fribourg, Switzerland, 1977.

Whitman, R. M. The use of the Rorschach test in schizophrenia. *Psychiatric Quarterly Supplement,* 1954, **28,** 26–37.

Willet, A., Jones, A., Morgan, D., and Franco, S. The borderline syndrome: An operational definition. American Psychiatric Association, Honolulu, 1973.

Wittman, P. A scale for measuring prognosis in schizophrenic patients. *Elgin State Hospital Papers,* 1941, **4,** 20–23.

CHAPTER 9

Some Forensic Issues

The application of psychological assessment techniques to cases where legal issues are involved is difficult, at best; and this includes the Rorschach. This is not so much because the techniques are limited, but more because the kinds of questions that are posed to the "expert" witness or consultant often exceed the theoretical, philosophical, and ethical boundaries on which psychology and psychological assessment are based. Unfortunately, most laws that pertain to issues of mental health have been formulated within the guidelines of the adversary system, which, though designed to protect any defendant and to guarantee a "right" to a fair trial, is not always conducive to descriptive material, especially that which may involve conjecture.

A great many cases that include testimony or consultation from the assessment expert focus on issues of mental competency or legal sanity. Courts are rightfully concerned with the capacity of a defendant to participate in his or her own defense, or to understand charges that have been leveled; and quite often a defense may be based on such issues as whether a defendant knew the difference between "right and wrong" at the time of an offense, or whether an act was committed under "diminished" capacity or "irrestible impulse." Interpretations of behavior are usually *not* the rule in such cases; rather, issues tend to focus more narrowly on diagnostic labels and on inferences drawn from those labels.

Although many such cases involve acts of violence or property damage, there are many other kinds of legal issues in which "psychodiagnostic experts" have become involved. These typically involve hearings rather than trials, but are no less comfortable for the psychologist in that the context of procedure remains within a legalistic framework, as do most kinds of questions posed. Potential for rehabilitation, fitness for child custody, potential for recidivism, and causes of intellectual and/or psychological dysfunction are among the more commonly broached issues facing the expert.

If trial procedures are involved, the expert will often encounter a situation in which much rich material is ignored or prohibited. Quite often, questions focus on narrow issues, sometimes selected from a broader context, and thus are difficult, if not impossible, to answer from most data. Even when a question is answerable, the expert will sometimes find himself in the position of being interrupted by a jurist, or more commonly by one or the other of the legal adversaries who suspect that the answer may be damaging to their case. In other instances, obvious "next" questions are left unasked by lawyers who have clearly "not done their own homework."

The majority of psychologists who have been called upon to serve in an "expert" witness capacity learn very quickly that they must be able to defend their statements and/or opinions using scientific evidence. Conclusions derived from "clinical impression" can be "torn apart" very easily by an alert barrister. Most psychologists involved in forensic issues will admit to a preference for the role of *amicus curiae,* or advisor to the court, in which the adversary system plays far less of a role, and in which the descriptive material, derived from psychological assessment, can be more fully elaborated. Those situations generally provide a broader range for questioning and elaboration of responses.

The material presented here is designed to illustrate how Rorschach data may be used as contributions when forensic issues are involved. In other words, disregarding the legal procedures that may be present, how can data from the Rorschach be used to approach various questions that may be posed?

MALINGERING AND SIMULATION

One of the chronic problems facing any assessment expert who is examining an unwilling subject, or one who may be motivated to conceal information, is that of *malingering* or *simulation.* Simulation is the attempt by the subject to appear more well adjusted, or less pathological, than is truly the case; while malingering is the attempt to appear more disturbed than is real.

As noted in Chapter 2, the Exner and Sherman (1977) study, using a small sample of schizophrenics, indicates that it is very difficult, if not impossible, for most schizophrenics to simulate a performance. Schizophrenics give schizophrenic-like records. However, nonschizophrenic subjects can often conceal pathology by reducing the length of their record, usually to less than 15 responses, and delivering a very high frequency of pure F responses. For example, Exner and Miller (1974) reviewed the protocols of 30 convicted males who were newly admitted to a detention unit while awaiting sentencing. All had been convicted of crimes involving violence, and all had histories that included at least one conviction for a similar crime. The protocols were collected by six second year graduate students who had no familiarity with the nature of the crime, but were aware that all had been convicted. Each of the examiners had administered no less than 10 Rorschachs prior to this study, and all had been judged competent in the procedures of administration and scoring, through observation and monitoring, prior to this study. Twenty-one of the 30 protocols included less than 14 answers, and 16 of the 21 were records containing *only* pure F answers. Although interpretation of those protocols was generally possible, the kind of information available from the interpretation was substantially less broad and/or rich than that in the more common protocol of average length. A retest of seven of the 16 subjects who delivered only pure F answers was completed after 10 days. A representative of the Legal Aid Society assisted in recruiting the subjects for the retest and guaranteed confidentiality of the data. All seven retest records are substantially longer, averaging 19 answers, and all have more indices of limited emotional control; in fact, three contained at least one pure C response. A similar increase in "pathological indicators" was noted in the Exner, Bryant, and Miller (1975) study, mentioned in Chapter 4, which involved a retesting, after 60 days, of 15 juvenile offenders. In other words, *some* concealment of pathology is apparently possible for nonschizophrenic subjects, when they reduce the length of the record sharply and restrict their articulations.

The malingering of pathology is a much different sort of task, and one which is probably impossible *if* the protocol is collected in accordance with standard procedures. The Exner and Wylie (1975) study, mentioned in Chapter 2, revealed that only one of 12 reasonably well trained graduate students could produce a schizophrenic-like protocol within a two hour time limit, even though all had familiarity with schizophrenic protocols; however, Albert (1978) has produced some results from an interesting study on malingering, suggesting that malingering is possible under certain circumstances. He used 46 judges, each rating four protocols drawn from a pool of 24 selected records. Six of the records were taken from inpatient paranoid schizophrenics, six were collected from "normals," and 12 were records in which normal college students were asked to fake a paranoid schizophrenic record. Six of the 12 "fakers" were provided some information about paranoid schizophrenia by audiotape prior to the testing. Albert permitted the judges, all Fellows of the Society for Personality Assessment, to approach the Rorschachs using whatever mode of interpretation they preferred. They had no information about the purpose of the study. Slightly less than half the judges identified the true records from patients as reflecting psychosis. However, 33 of the 46 judges identified the records of the informed fakers as psychotic, 21 of the 46 called records of the uninformed fakers as psychotic, and 11 of the 46 identified the records of normals as psychotic. Unfortunately, there is no information about the modes of interpretation used by various judges, or any information on whether the judges took the time to score the protocols. The latter is quite important, since malingerers will often use very dramatic verbiage in attempting to approximate pathology, and the Albert records were seemingly "overloaded" with verbiage, produced mainly because of an inordinate number of inquiry questions to each response, many, of which appeared to have precipitated more dramatic verbiage. Since very wide differences remain among scoring systems (Exner, 1969, 1974), plus the fact that many interpreters do not score at all (Exner and Exner, 1972), it is possible that the inaccuracies among judges reflect more about their use of the Rorschach than about the test itself.

The protocol pool used for the development and study of the Comprehensive System includes 23 records of cases in which attempts at malingering have been validated. All are marked by longer than usual Free Associations; all contain at least several responses that are highly personal ("This makes me think of my dead aunt . . ."; This is too frightening, I can't look anymore"); and all contain a majority of answers that are very "dramatic." For instance, one subject responded to Card III as, "Oh my God, this is vulgar, it's two naked men who are pissing in a basket of laundry, I used to do that to make my mother angry." The response is ultimately scored as $D + M^a o$ (2) $H, P, 3.0$, which reveals the cognitive and perceptual accuracy that has been involved and falls far short of being a psychotic response. The following protocol is very typical of attempts at malingering.

Case 14: A 42 Year Old Male—a Frightened Fake

History. The fellow is apparently a professional malingerer who, before the administration of the Rorschach, had been found disabled by three competent professionals. The subject claimed the disability as a result of an industrial accident, and when administered the WAIS, obtained a full scale I.Q. of 56 (verbal I.Q. 61;

Card		Free Association		Inquiry	Scoring

| I | (7″) | I d.l. the black it makes me feel more depressed, it makes me nerv. | | | |

	32″	1. It's a terrible black Bf, I don't c thm very often, its very very ugly, it makes me nervous, the way its flyg around there	E:	(Rpts S's resp)	Wo FC'.FM^{a}o A P 1.0
			S:	It has wings, big wings (yawns), its terrible, all black, its making me depressed again, lik I'll loose my mind looking at it, it even shows the little feelers up here on the body	
		E: Most people c mor thn 1 thg			
		S: I can't look anymore, its too frightening, it maks me feel crazy			

II	12″	2. I don't lik ths either, there's anothr BF down here, lk gettg ready to land on this black part ths so ugly, why woud a bf which is so beautiful land on ths ugly part, mayb bf's r blind	E:	(Rpts S's resp)	D+ FM^a.FC.FC'.FDo A,Ls 3.0
			S:	Dwn here's the bf, pretty, c a pretty red one. I lik pretty red one's but it's gonna land on ths black dirt, its ugly dirt, it scares me about what will happen to the bf	
			E:	I'm not sur how u c it abov the dirt	
			S:	It just is & the dirt is down below, if its flyg the dirt must b below	

		3. Thes - bloodstains, ugly, do I hav to look at it. I don't lik it	E:	(Rpts S's resp)	Dv C (2) Bl
			S:	Ooh there awful, I don't lik them	
			E:	What is there tht makes thm ll bldstns?	
			S:	Just the red, oo its awful	

III	38″	4. Ha, that's terrible, its a very funny picture, I don't thk I can tell u about them, its too awful	E:	(Rpts S's resp)	D+ M^{a}o (2) H P 4.0
			S:	I just can't say, its too awful	
			E:	Take ur time, we'r in no hurry	
			S:	Its, its vulgar, its 2 men peeing	
			E:	Two men peeing?	
			S:	I told u it was awful, vulgar, it maks me sick to look, c them (outlines) I can't look anymore	

Case 14 (Continued)

Card		Free Association		Inquiry	Scoring
		5. Only the cntr is a clear picture, its a bf, that same red one, he got away	E: S:	(Rpts S's resp) I'm happy for him, c he's flyg again, rite there, don't look at the other part tho	Do $FM^a.FCo$ A P PSV
IV	35″	6. Oh, I d.l. ths one, its terrible lik my nitemares, Oh God, its that monstr chasing me, big black w thos huge feet trying to crush me, I can't look or I'll go crazy again	E: S:	(Rpts S's resp) Do I hav to look, its so scary, oh I can't, its just big & scary lik my nitemares only I'm not asleep I just c it all the time trying to crush me, I cnt look at it (hides head in arms)	Wo $M^a.FC'o$ (H) 2.0
V	75″	7. Oh God, what is it, all the pic's r so scary, just a black ugly bird flyg there, so depressing, its makg me sick to c it, take it away	E: S:	(Rpts S's resp) Not again, I can't look again at that bat, its too terrible and scary, its an ugly creature	Wo $FC'.FM^ao$ A P 1.0
VI	27″	8. Oh God, I can't look, I dk what is is, its so ugly E: Take u'r time, we hav all day			
		8. Its s.t. tht crawls, lik an ant, it cld get on u & bite u, the big ones r so scary, one bit me once, thy can fly	E: S: E: S:	(Rpts S's resp) Its so ugly I can't look Show me the ant Oh no, up here, c the ant lik w wgs lik he'll fly up & bite, I can't look its too awful (sobs)	Do Fo A
VII	5″	9. Ha, ha, a funny cloud	E: S: E: S:	(Rpts S's resp) Its dark lik clouds but its funny too cause it goes around in a half circle, lik part is missing Half circle There's so tog to it	Wv YFo Cl 2.5

10. Oh its magic too, lik 2 genies rising fr a magic lamp go to cast a spell on the world

E: (Rpts S's resp)
S: Thy 'l smok, lik the clouds but thy hav faces & body parts & here is the magic lamp, its spocky but I lik it cause I understand magic

$W+$ $M^p.YFo$ (2) (H) (P) 2.5

VIII 2"

11. Aha, better, I lik colors, mayb its a tree up here, a magic tree

E: (Rpts S's resp)
S: It has a mgic point on the top, lik to mak thgs happen when u don't kno thy will, & a littl trunk, magic trees always hav a littl trunk

Do Fo B_1 ALOG

>12. An A jumping, I don't kno why mayb he's scared lik me, & he is seeig himself down here in the water

E: (Rpts S's resp)
S: Its really strange but bettr than the others, its a scared A, scared out of his wits, he's jumpg across all of ths thgs & seeing himself do it down here in the water
E: Water?
S: The blue is water, anybody knows that

$W+$ $FM^a.Fr.CFo$ A,Ls P 4.5

IX 18"

13. Oh God, I dk, I can't take much more, its lik a plant that can eat u up, its terrible, don't mak me look at it or I'll b crazy more

E: (Rpts S's resp)
S: Oh no, its got those big branches up here that grab u, I've seen them, thy eat peopl in the parks, c the green leaves thy r deceiving but the orange leaves can reach out & grab u
E: I'm not sure I c it lik u do
S: Well u'r not crazy mayb but thy r real, I kno, I don't want to look

Wo FCo B_1 5.5

Case 14 (Continued)

Card		Free Association		Inquiry	Scoring
X	6″	14. I lik ths color, there's a map there, lik islands	E:	(Rpts S's resp)	*Dv Fo* (2) *Ge*
			S:	Its a map of two big islands, I can't rem the name but I used to kno	
		15. Oh God there's 2 creatures too thy terrible, thy scare me	E:	(Rpts S's resp)	*Do FCo* (2) *a* INCOM
			S:	Lik big blue lobsters that can eat u up thy hav them some places & thy can get u with all the big legs & claws, thyr terrible, I can't look, its too scary, it maks me depressed	

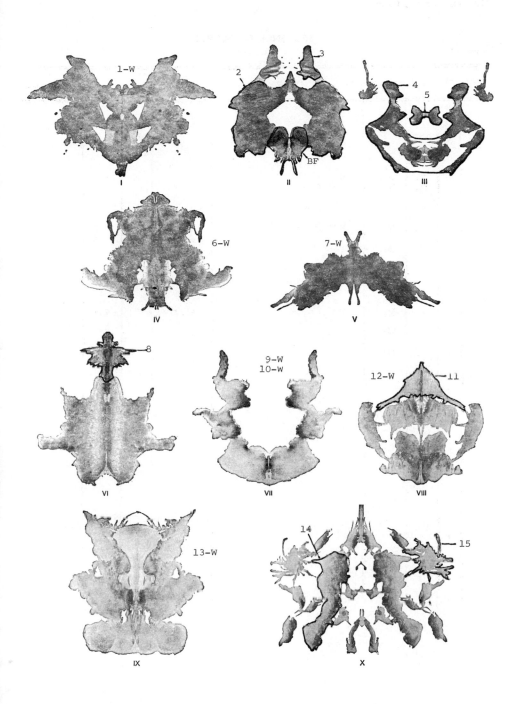

SEQUENCE OF SCORES

Case 14

CARD	RT	NO.	LOCATION	DETERMINANTS (S)		CONTENT (S)	POP	Z SCORE	SPECIAL
I	32"	1.	Wo	$FC'.FM^a o$		A	P	1.0	
II	12"	2.	D+	$FM^a.FC.FC'.FDo$		A,Ls		3.0	
		3.	Dv	C	(2)	Bl			
III	38"	4.	D+	$M^a o$	(2)	H	P	4.0	
		5.	Do	$FM^a.FCo$		A	P		PSV
IV	35"	6.	Wo	$M^a.FC'o$		(H)		2.0	
V	75"	7.	Wo	$FC'.FM^a o$		A	P	1.0	
VI	52"	8.	Do	Fo		A			
VII	5"	9.	Wv	YFo		Cl		2.5	
		10.	W+	$M^p.YFo$	(2)	(H)	(P)	2.5	
VIII	2"	11.	Do	Fo		Bt			ALOG
		12.	W+	$FM^a.Fr.CFo$		A,Ls	P	4.5	
IX	18"	13.	Wo	FCo		Bt		5.5	
X	6"	14.	Dv	Fo	(2)	Ge			
		15.	Do	FCo	(2)	A			INCOM

performance I.Q. 54), with scale scores ranging from zero on Picture Arrangement to five on Vocabulary and Digit Symbol. His MMPI profile is somewhat elevated on the right side ($8627*31''5'94F'LK$?) and could equate with severe pathology.

There is little "credible history" available concerning the subject. It is known

Case 14: Structural Summary

R = 15   Zf = 9   ZSum = 26.0   P = 5+1   (2) = 5

Location Features			Determinants (Blends First)	Contents		Contents (Idiographic)
W = 7		DQ	FM.FC.FC'.FD = 1	H = 1		=
D = 8	+ = 4		FM.Fr.CF = 1	(H) = 2		.... =
			FM.FC = 1	Hd =		
Dd = 0	o = 8		FC'.FM = 1	(Hd) =		.... =
S = 0	v = 3		M.FC' = 1	A = 7		
			M.YF = 1	(A) =		.... =
DW =	— = 0			Ad =		.... =
			M = 1	(Ad) =		
			FM =	Ab =		.... =
			m =	Al =		
			C = 1	An =		.... =
Form Quality			CF =	Art =		
			FC = 1	Ay =		.... =
FQx	FQf		C' =	Bl = 1		
			C'F =	Bt = 2		....
+ = 0	+ = 0		FC' =	Cg =		
			T =	Cl — 1		....
o = 14	o = 3		TF =	Ex =		**Special Scorings**
			FT =	Fi =		
w = 0	w = 0		V =	Fd =		PSV = 1
			VF =	Ge = 1		
— = 0	— = 0		FV =	Hh =		DV =
M Quality			Y =	Ls = 0,2		
			YF = 1	Na =		INCOM = 1
+ = 0			FY =	Sx =		
			rF =	Xy =		FABCOM =
o = 3			Fr =			
			FD =			CONTAM =
w = 0			F = 3			
						ALOG = 1
— = 0						=

RATIOS, PERCENTAGES, AND DERIVATIONS

ZSum-Zest =	26.0-27.5		FC:CF+C = 4:2		Afr = .50
Zd =	-1.5		W:M = 7:3		3r+(2)/R = .53
EB =	3:4.5	EA = 7.5	W:D = 7:8		Com:R = 0:15
eb =	5:6	ep = 11	L = .25		H+Hd:A+Ad = 3:7
					(H)+(Hd):(A)+(Ad) = 2:0
Blends:R =	7:15		F+% = 100		H+A:Hd+Ad = 10:0
a:p =	7:1		X+% = .93		XRT Achrom — 30.0"
Ma:Mp —	2:1		A% — .47		XRT Chrom = 15.2"

that he is foreign born and has completed a university education. He gives several different dates and places of birth. He has worked as a licensed X-ray technician. It was ultimately established that he was malingering in this case, and had done so successfully in at least one other compensation case.

Structural Interpretation. A glance at the Structural Summary soon eliminates the possibility of schizophrenia and/or intellectual deficit. There are no significant data reflecting a thinking disorder; all three M answers are good form quality and, while there are three *Special Scorings,* the unusual verbal material is modest in frequency and character. The $FC:CF+C$ ratio is weighted on the FC side in spite of the presence of a *pure C* response, and the *Afr* is slightly lower than might be expected from one who becomes overwhelmed by emotions. The $F+\%$ and $X+\%$ are both within the normal range, suggesting that there is no perceptual distortion present. The number of Human contents is also modest, including only one *pure H,* suggesting problems in the interpersonal sphere; but this does not equal schizophrenia when "standing alone." The presence of four $DQ+$ answers, three M's, and the high form level accuracy are simply inconsistent with the possibility of severe intellectual deficit as manifest on the WAIS.

A closer inspection of the structural data does reveal a fairly primitive person who does not have good access to resources ($ep > EA$); one who is very self-centered ($3r + (2)/R$ = .53, plus one reflection response); one who has difficulty avoiding stimulus complexity (*Lambda* = .25), and one who is making a significant effort to control and/or inhibit emotional displays (four of the six grey-black, shading answers are of the C' variety). He organizes relatively well (Zf = 9; Zd = -1.5), and offers relatively few lower developmental DQ responses (3). His ideation appears somewhat inflexible ($a:p$ = 7:1), and he offers more blends than would be customary for such a short record as this. His long mean *reaction times* may evidence the fact that he approaches the blots cautiously, but in spite of that caution, he still reveals himself rather openly. He offers five clear *Populars,* and one other that is nearly *Popular,* indicating that he responds somewhat conventionally in most situations. Possibly, in this case, his most interesting answers include those containing the two YF determinants, signifying a feeling of helplessness, which in this instance may be situationally related.

Interpretation of the Scoring Sequence. His longest reaction time is to Card V, after which he yields a Popular answer. This may reflect his trouble in "breaking the blot apart" to offer some more pathological response. His blend on Card II is very complex, indicating both control and some self-examination. Both of his YF answers occur to Card VII, which may represent something of the kind of difficulty he has discriminating females, and offers a hint that his own identity may be in question. He is very cautious on the last two cards, delivering two FC and one pure F response. This may suggest some problems with emotionally toned stimuli. Three of his four pure F responses appear in the last three cards, which may tend to validate the speculation that he does, in fact, try to avoid emotionally provocative situations for fear of loss of control. He organizes on most of the cards, and has no significant P failures.

Interpretation of Content. Most of his contents illustrate the frequent dramatization that is common in the records of malingerers, ("I don't like this one . . . . , ". . . do I have to look . . . ," ". . . it's terrible like my nightmares . . . ," ". . . all the pictures are so scary . . . ," "Oh God, . . . I can't take much more . . . ," and so on). After the excessive verbiage is sorted out, some of his responses are rather revealing. Several of his responses include animals that are generally more "fragile," two butterflies, an ant, and a scared animal. He also gives at least two "penetration" answers, bloodstains and cloud, suggesting a less than adequate system of defending himself; while the remainder of his responses usually involve isolation or aggression—a monster, magic genies, a magic tree, a plant, islands, and lobsters. Most are juvenile, and none are common among more mature persons. He seems to rely on the childlike fantasies to convey his notion of disturbance, and he signs out with a reaffirmation of his fears, this time of creatures that turn out to be lobsters.

Case 14 Summary.   This fellow is disturbed, but not in the way that he would prefer to convey. He is immature and probably impulsive at times. Although bright, he is very self-centered and has only limited interpersonal skills to create and maintain smooth or deep interpersonal contacts. His thinking is concrete at times, probably reflecting something of his immaturity, and he does have trouble guarding himself from excessive emotional displays with which he is not comfortable. His self-concept is fragile and isolated, and he probably becomes overly aggressive sometimes in order to defend himself from the perceived aggressive potential of others. Obviously, his history indicates that he has been relatively successful at his "con" games, which have probably evolved as a result of his inability to adapt himself to a more adult world.

Case 14 Epilogue.   As a result of the detection of malingering, a legal survey was completed on the earlier history of the subject, and a previous case was discovered in which the subject had successfully feigned disability as a result of an "accident" and was compensated with a sizable "pension." That discovery led to the filing of charges of attempted fraud. Those charges were dropped, however, when the subject withdrew his disability claim.

COMPETENCY ISSUES

The question of competency appears among the more common forensic cases. Competency may be variously defined, in terms of "mental retardation (either genetic or organic), "legal insanity" (usually defined as an inability to distinguish between right and wrong), or "diminished capacity" (usually defined as currently psychotic and thus unable to understand charges or participate in a defense). Thus, the issue of competency, depending on the specific statute, may involve questions of schizophrenia, or questions of intellectual or functional retardation. The following protocol illustrates a case in which the attorney for the defense informed the prosecution and the court of the intent to file a "not guilty" plea concerning a homocide, using *all three* premises for the basis of the plea—that is, arguing that the subject was intellectually deficient, neurologically impaired, and psychologically incompetent. In this instance, the two attorneys and the presiding jurist agreed to a "consulting" examination, the results of which would be presented at a pretrial hearing.

Case 15: A 27 Year Old Male—a Growling Mugger

History.   This is a tall, neat, reasonably attractive black man who is the oldest of two children. He has a sister, age 26, but does not know her whereabouts. His father, age 47, is an iron worker in a distant city. He lived with the father after the parents separated when he was 14, but decided to "strike out" on his own upon completing high school. He has had no contact with the mother, age 45, since she and the father separated. He worked as a truck loader for approximately one year, on highway maintenance for nearly two years, and for the past six years has divided his work time. During the "on season" he does various jobs at a race track (walking and caring for horses, cleaning stables, landscaping, etc.), and when the race track is closed, he works in a meat packing plant. Shortly after obtaining the position at the race track, he also enrolled in evening courses at a community college and completed one year, receiving one C and four D's in basic liberal arts courses.

He has had several confrontations with the law, the first at age 20, when he was charged with grand theft (auto). That charge was reduced on an agreement for a guilty plea, and he was sentenced to one year's probation. A year later, he was arrested and convicted of assaulting an elderly woman and robbing her of $19. He was sentenced to "one to five years" in prison and paroled during his 11th month. Six months after parole, he was arrested for the sale of narcotics; the charges were dismissed, however, because of technicalities concerning the arrest procedure. Approximately one year later, he was arrested again on charges of grand theft (auto) and attempted assault on a middle aged woman. The assault charge was dropped after a guilty plea to the auto theft, and he was sentenced to "one to five years" in prison. He was paroled during the 14th month of the sentence, and has worked steadily during the past 16 months. His most recent arrest involves a charge of homicide during an assault. He was "mugging" an elderly woman in the elevator of her apartment. Apparently she suffered a heart attack and expired during the act; thus the subject could be formally charged with homicide. In part, the decision of the defense attorney to consider action based on the issue of competency stems from the results of an intelligence test administered to the subject during his first prison term. Those data indicate a Full Scale I.Q. of 69 (Verbal I.Q. = 70; Performance I.Q. = 67), and an accompanying report describes the subject as "mentally retarded." The subject rejected the possibility of testing at the first suggestion, but later agreed to participate, although somewhat reluctantly. A WAIS was administered prior to the Rorschach and yielded a Full Scale I.Q. of 96 (Verbal I.Q. = 94; Performance I.Q. = 97) with scale scores ranging from eight on Comprehension and Picture Arrangement to 11 on Picture Completion.

Structural Interpretation.   This is another record in which a "quick glance" tends to eliminate the possibility of schizophrenia. The single M response is of good form quality, and there is only one possible Special Score. Thus a thinking disturbance is unlikely. Nonetheless, the emotional controls appear quite limited ($FC:CF+C = 2:3$, *plus one pure C*). There is an absence of pure H, although there are three Human contents, and the $F+\%$ and $X+\%$ are both low, suggesting some limitations in reality testing. A closer look at the form quality distribu-

Case 15

Card	Free Association	Inquiry	Scoring
I	17"		
	1. It don't ll much, mayb a wm there in the middl but she doesn't hav a head	E: (Rpts S's resp) S: Well u can c the legs here & I guess ths wld b hands or s.t. & I don't kno what thos bumps r, mayb knockers but thts kinda funry	Do Fo Hd P
	Most people c mor than 1 thg		
	2. I guess it c.b. a wolf kinda growling	E: (Rpts S's resp) S: Its the head, c the eyes & the mouth here & the way the white goes up its lik he was growling & his ears r stickg out too, lik when an A gets mad his ears go out lik that	WS+ FM^{a}o Ad 3.5
II	34"		
	3. Man thes r weird, I guess it c.b. sk of insect there in the middl	E: (Rpts S's resp) S: I dk much about them, ths one is weird cause its got ths pointy thg coming out the top, lik a stinger, c up here & the rest of it is whte lik sk of weird insect E: Weird? S: I nevr saw any white insects lik ths one but I guess thy must b somewhere	DS- FC'- A 4.5
	V4. U kno, ths way it ll a stone crab, thy got'em in Florida thyr really good to eat	E: (Rpts S's resp) S: It just has tht shape to it, c thes r the longr thgs lik thy hav on thm, it really looks alot lik thy do	Do Fo A
	V5. U kno ths stuff ll ketchup dwn here	E: (Rpts S's resp) S: I don't kno wht made me thk of that, mayb I'm hungry, its just all red lik ketchup but u sur don't put it on stone crab	Dv C Fd

315

Case 15 (Continued)

Card		Free Association	Inquiry	Scoring
III	25"	6. Ths is anothr weird one, tht ll a red bf there but I don't thk I evr saw a red bf, mayb its an African one, thy got alot of weird thgs there	*E:* (Rpts *S*'s resp) *S:* Well its just ll one, c the wgs & the littl body, its kinda pretty I'd lik to c a real one lik tht	*Do FCo A P* (ALOG)
		V7. It mite b an xry of s.t. I guess	*E:* (Rpts *S*'s resp) *S:* Well just ths part here, its colord lik an x-ry, black, u kno, its probably s.b. head or s.t. *E:* Head? *S:* Yeah, I guess so	*D− FC'− Xy*
IV	8"	8. Thts lik a monster tht u mite c in a comic book	*E:* (Rpts *S*'s resp) *S:* Well he's sur got a long tail draggin there, & littl arms & big monster feet lik he's just lumbering along nice & easy	*Wo M^{a}o (H)* 2.0
		9. Hey, u kno ths part c.b. a rock	*E:* (Rpts *S*'s resp) *S:* I saw it lik his head, the monster tht is, but if u look just separate it ll a rock *E:* I'm not sur why it ll a rock *S:* Its just round lik one	*Dv Fw* Rock
V	5"	10. Man thts a bat, a black bat	*E:* (Rpts *S*'s resp) *S:* It has the wgs & the claws out front lik it was attacking, u kno charging s.t., thy swoop dwn & grab thgs w their claws	*Wo FC'.FM^{a}o A P* 1.0
VI	9"	11. Thts lik a voodoo doll up there on the top	*E:* (Rpts *S*'s resp) *S:* Well thy mak them lik ths, usually thy put littl wgs on em lik this, u can c a littl figur of the body there & the wgs lik a voodoo, yeah really lik tht	*Do Fo (H)*

		Response	Inquiry				
		12. U kno, tht top c.b. a bullet too, lik it just went thru ths stuff & its comg out the othr side	E: (Rpts S's resp) S: I don't kno what its going thru, just stuff but its coming out ths side, u can c the path it took, it ll tht to me	W+	m^aw	Bullet	2.5
VII	15"	V13. I guess its an island & ths prt is lik a harbor, u kno	E: (Rpts S's resp) S: It just ll it c.b. an island & ths part c.b. the harbor, u kno lik where ships go to keep away fr a storm or bad weather	WSv	Fo	Ls	4.0
		V14. U kno its lik those muscl build-ers too	E: (Rpts S's resp) S: Thes r the handl & u pull em apart & ths thg in the cntr contains a spring lik thg & it pulls against u & u do that a lot evry day to build up u'r muscles	Wo	Fw	Muscl Bldr	2.5
VIII	30"	15. I dk, just a lot of garbage I guess, it doesn't mak much sense to me	E: (Rpts S's resp) S: Just a bunch of junk, lik trash & garbage piled up there, all diff kinds of things, all ths down here (pink) looks rotted E: Rotted? S: Yeah, lik its all red lik rotted stuff gets red lik ths	Wv	CFw	Garbage	4.5
IX	22"	16. Thts ik one of thos badges tht a forest ranger wears	E: (Rpts S's resp) S: Well it has ht look to it, c thes thgs go up here & its green in here lik for the trees & such, each of thos colors is for some kind of forest thg	Wo	FCo	Art	5.5
X	27"	17. Well there's sea coral there its the kind u can get bad cuts on	E: (Rpts S's resp) S: Ths pink, red, u kno, its lik sea coral tht u c skin divig, its kinda long lik this & its red, tht means is can be poison if u get cut on it	Dv	CFo	Bt	

Case 15 (Continued)

Card	Free Association	Inquiry	Scoring
18.	Thes thgs here ll crabs & thyr fitig over ths weed thg in betwn them, each is pullg on it	*E:* (Rpts *S*'s resp) *S:* Well thy ll crabs w the long feelers, claws & thy got ths weed or whtevr betwn them & thyr lik fiting ovr it	D+ FM^{a}w (2) A,Bt 4.0
19.	U kno thers anothr white bf in ther, mayb a moth not a bf caus bfs aren't white, thats moths	*E:* (Rpts *S*'s resp) *S:* C the wgs r here & the body, hey it really looks alot lik a moth, c (traces) it really does, yeah	DdSo FC'w A

Note: Testing of limits yielded P on III but no on VII.

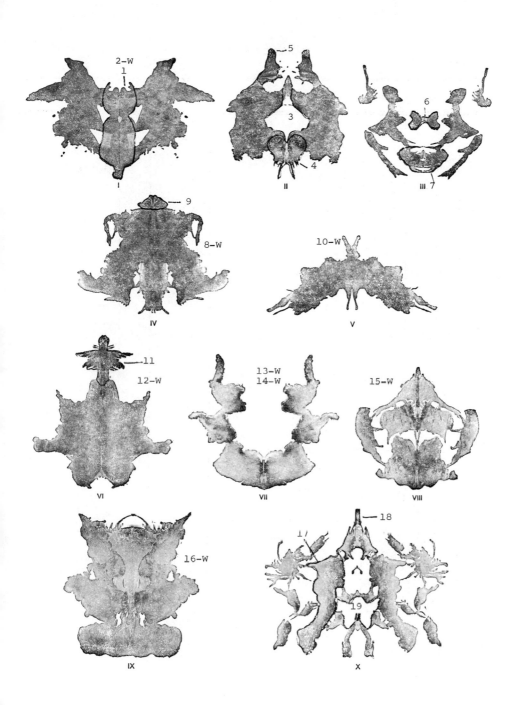

SEQUENCE OF SCORES

Case 15

CARD	RT	NO.	LOCATION	DETERMINANTS (S)		CONTENT (S)	POP	Z SCORE	SPECIAL
I	17"	1.	Do	Fo		Hd	P		
		2.	WS+	$FM^{a}o$		Ad		3.5	
II	34"	3.	DS–	$FC'-$		A		4.5	
		4.	Do	Fo		A			
		5.	Dv	C		Fd			
III	25"	6.	Do	FCo		A	P		(ALOG)
		7.	D–	$FC'-$		Xy			
IV	8"	8.	Wo	$M^{a}o$		(H)		2.0	
		9.	Dv	Fw		Rock			
V	5"	10.	Wo	$FC'.FM^{a}o$		A	P	1.0	
VI	9"	11.	Do	Fo		(H)			
		12.	W+	$m^{a}w$		Bullet		2.5	
VII	15"	13.	WSv	Fo		Ls		4.0	
		14.	Wo	Fw		Muscbldr		2.5	
VIII	30"	15.	Wv	CFw		Garbage		4.5	
IX	22"	16.	Wo	FCo		Art		5.5	
X	27"	17.	Dv	CFo		Bt			
		18.	D+	$FM^{a}w$	(2)	A,Bt		4.0	
		19.	DdSo	$FC'w$		A			

Testing of Limits yielded P on III but not on VII

320

Case 15:   Structural Summary

R = 19   Zf = 10   ZSum = 34.0   P = 3   (2) =1

Location Features		Determinants (Blends First)	Contents	Contents (Idiographic)

Location Features

W = 8   **DQ**

D = 10   + = 3

Dd = 1   o = 9

S = 4   v = 5

DW =   — = 2

Form Quality

FQx		FQf	
+	= 0	+	= 0
o	= 10	o	= 4
w	= 6	w	= 2
—	= 2	—	= 0

M Quality

+	= 0
o	= 1
w	= 0
—	= 0

Determinants (Blends First)

FC'.FM =1

M	=	1
FM	=	2
m	=	1
C	=	1
CF	=	2
FC	=	2
C'	=	
C'F	=	
FC'	=	3
T	=	
TF	=	
FT	=	
V	=	
VF	=	
FV	=	
Y	=	
YF	=	
FY	=	
rF	=	
Fr	=	
FD	=	
F	=	6

Contents

H	=	
(H)	=	2
Hd	=	1
(Hd)	=	
A	=	6
(A)	=	
Ad	=	1
(Ad)	=	
Ab	=	
Al	=	
An	=	
Art	=	1
Ay	=	
Bl	=	
Bt	=	1,1
Cg	=	
Cl	=	
Ex	=	
Fi	=	
Fd	=	1
Ge	=	
Hh	=	
Ls	=	1
Na	=	
Sx	=	
Xy	=	1

Contents (Idiographic)

Bullet	=	1
Garbage	=	1
Musclebuilder	=	1
Rock	=	1

Special Scorings

PSV	=	
DV	=	
INCOM	=	
FABCOM	=	
CONTAM	=	
ALOG	=	0,1
	=	

RATIOS, PERCENTAGES, AND DERIVATIONS

ZSum-Zest	= 34.0–31.0			FC:CF+C	= 2:3	Atr	= .36
Zd	= +3.0			W:M	= 8:1	3r+(2)/R	= .05
EB	= 1:4.5	EA	= 5.5	W:D	= 8:10	Com:R	= 11:19
eb	= 4:4	ep	= 8	L	= .40	H+Hd:A+Ad = 3:7 (H)+(Hd):(A)+(Ad) = 2:0
Blends:R	= 1:19			F+%	= .67	H+A:Hd+Ad	= 8:2
a:p	= 5:0			X+%	= .53	XRT Achrom	= 10.8"
Ma:Mp	= 1:0			A%	= .37	XRT Chrom	= 27.6"

tion, however, reveals the presence of only two minus answers, suggesting that the lowered form quality percentages are a function of unique interpretation of stimuli rather than of true perceptual distortion. The relatively high *Zf* and adequate *Zd* score would ordinarily not be expected in the record of a person who is intellectually limited. However, based solely on the structural data, that possibility *could not be ruled out*. This illustrates the importance of the intelligence test data. For instance, there is only one *M*, one blend, three Populars, and seven lower level

DQ scores, including five that are vague. There is no real articulation of shading features, but rather an emphasis on the grey-black colors. Such a composite could appear in the record of a subject of "subnormal" or "borderline" intelligence.

The *EB* indicates that he usually displays or discharges emotion in coping situations; however, the *ep* is greater than the *EA*, showing that he does not have ready access to many of his resources. The high frequency of *C'* determinants tends to offer some information about the issue of emotional control; that is, he is currently experiencing much internal irritation because of inhibited emotions. This suggests that under ordinary circumstances, he might be more prone to emotional discharge in accord with his basic coping style. Yet it is also evident that when he does discharge affect, it often will overwhelm him and direct his behavior, as is manifest, for example, in the pure *C* type of response. The very low *Afr* indicates that he tries to avoid the kinds of situations that might provoke emotion; however, the low *Lambda* indicates that he has some difficulty in extracting himself from stimulus complexity. The very low *egocentricity index* illustrates very low self-esteem, yet the *W* : *M* ratio suggests that he will often set goals that may exceed his functional capacities. The high frequency of *S* answers reveals a considerable negativism or anger, and, when combined with the low *P* and high frequency of form quality *weak* answers, tends to mark a person who is going to approach his environment in terms of his own needs rather than with concern for convention. In other words, he seems to be a person with an impulsive style who may easily disregard convention in striving for his own aspirations.

Interpretation of the Scoring Sequence.   Both of his minus answers, and half of his weak form quality responses, occur to the chromatically colored cards, even though he takes considerably longer reaction times on those cards than on any of the achromatic cards. This tends to offer support for the notions that he does have trouble with emotional control *and* that emotionally toned stimuli can overwhelm him. His *S* responses occur across four cards, including the first and last, tending to rule out the possibility of a situationally created negativism.

Interpretation of Content.   Several of his answers convey an aggressive tone (the woman on Card I is headless, the wolf in response 2 is growling, the weird insect on Card II has stingers, there is a monster on IV, an attacking bat on V, a voodoo doll and a bullet on VI, some dangerous coral, and crabs fighting on X). This feature, which appears in nearly half of his answers, probably is an accurate reflection of both his feelings and his own self-image. He is an angry man who tends to feel out of place (weird) and quite vulnerable at times (butterflies, ketchup, x-ray, and garbage). His island and harbor response on Card VII convey both his feeling of isolation and needs to "feel safe." In the inquiry to that response he mentions, ". . . you know, like where ships go to keep away from a storm or bad weather." Interestingly, it is white space that forms the harbor, hinting at the probability that he uses his negativism as a shield to protect himself. Undoubtedly, his situation contributes to his anger and his feeling of helplessness, and both may be somewhat exaggerated here. However, when these data are merged with the structural data and with his history, it is not difficult to understand a person who might easily feel that if you do not take advantage of others, they may take advantage of you.

Case 15 Summary.   The composite of the Rorschach and intelligence test data provide a base from which the issues of schizophrenia and intellectual retardation can be ruled out; however, while neither contain data that would be commensurate with a neurological condition, it would be unwise to draw conclusions about that possibility without a more thorough assessment, including a complete neurological examination (which was accomplished in this case, yielding uniformly negative results). Overall, he appears to be a primitive and immature person, who perceives the world in a very unique and somewhat unconventional way. He is probably frustrated quite often when his aspirations exceed his functional capacities, and the resulting anger tends to set off emotions that will often direct or command his responses. Much of his antisocial behavior may be part of an elaborate defensive system designed to conceal his very low self-value. This is another *T-less* record, raising the possibility that he may have developed in a psychological framework that excludes the expectation of close emotional relationships; consequently, he has failed to develop the interpersonal skills that might promote a healthier congruence with his world. His perception of people in general, and of himself in particular, is quite negative and often distorted. He would be difficult to treat because the condition has evolved and become strongly "stabilized" over many years. While a long term, "developmental" form of therapy would be optimal, he is a person who is probably more responsive to immediate gain; thus, behavioral intervention might have a greater likelihood of sustaining some treatment motivation, especially if the focus was on interpersonal skills plus new techniques for the delay of emotional discharge.

Case 15: Epilogue.   After a review of the psychological and neurological testimony, the subject's attorney decided against using the competency issue and instead, entered into an agreement with the prosecution on a guilty plea to a lesser charge. Ultimately, the subject was sentenced to five to 20 years in prison.

CUSTODY AND PLACEMENT

Among the more complex forensic issues are those involving children. Some of these cases, usually the more simple, focus on pending decisions of the court about whether a "delinquent" child should be placed in a residential treatment center or in a "reformatory." In some states, the "street wise" youngster will opt for the reformatory, where the length of stay is fairly specific, while assignment to a residential treatment facility may be for an indeterminate length. In such instances, the subject will usually attempt to simulate a relatively healthy record, or more commonly, will be extremely resistant to testing and give few responses. In other states, the reverse is true; that is, assignment to a residential treatment center will often mean an earlier release than commitment to a reformatory; and here, subjects will often attempt to appear more "retarded" on intelligence tests and more bizarre on the Rorschach. Although both these situations are a challenge for the professional, both are also resolved with comparative ease by descriptions that avoid psychiatric labels and focus, instead, on the assets and liabilities of the subject.

Cases in this category, which are often more difficult for the professional, involve issues of custody and/or placement. Custody issues often include some form of evaluation of both parent and child, neither of whom may be cooperative, and some jurists will often pose questions of "compatibility;" that is, can the child develop normally in the custody of one or both parents? These are questions of a predictive nature, and almost impossible to answer from most assessment data, and especially from Rorschach data. There are, however, instances in which the personality structure of the child "speaks for itself" in terms of maturity, adaptability, controls, reality testing, and so on. For instance, if a youngster is schizophrenic, it is very doubtful that he or she will fare well in any environment that is not oriented toward treatment, especially in an environment in which the parents claim, "But we love him so much." Similarly, the child who manifests evidence of a reasonably "sturdy" personality will probably not flourish as much as possible in an environment controlled by parents who are primitive or periodically psychotic. The following case involves such a youngster, and also includes the even more complex issue of possible child abuse.

Case 16: A 12 Year Old Female—the Unopened Flower

History.   This youngster is thin and small for her age, but very cute. She has a rather hectic history, both at home and in school. Her father, age 33, is a construction worker, and her mother, age 29, works part time as a waitress. Her sister, age 11, is mentally retarded, and has been in a residential treatment center since the age of seven. The parents have separated twice, each time for approximately two months, once when the subject was age three, and a second time shortly after the sister was committed. The subject has a rather marked history of acting out in school, beginning at least as early as the second grade. She is currently in the sixth grade, but is not doing very well; in fact her teachers during the past three years have all regarded her work as substandard, even though she has been "passed" at each year level. Her current teacher reports that she antagonizes the male students and has been in physical combat with at least three during various recess periods. This sort of behavior has been frequent since the third grade, when her fighting behavior prompted examination by the school psychologist. At that time she was labeled a "hyperactive" child and placed in a special training class for part of the day. At that time, her mother concurred with the diagnosis, reporting her to be difficult to manage at home. During part of her third and fourth academic years, she was prescribed various medications to reduce the hyperactivity, including ritalin. During her fourth academic year, she injured an older boy by hitting him with a discarded metal pipe and consequently, experienced her first contact with the court. At that time, her parents complained that they could not control her, and she was made a "ward of the court" and placed in a foster home. Subsequently, the parents regretted their decision to relinquish custody and appealed to the court for her return, which was granted. Approximately two months before the present examination, she came to school with several obvious bruises on her face and legs. When queried by the teacher, she refused to provide details of her injuries. The teacher asked the school nurse to examine her, and the nurse requested a more thorough examination by a consulting physician. The physician discovered three broken ribs and numerous contusions and abrasions. When questioned by the physician, the subject reported that she had been beaten by her father while her mother held her. In addition, the subject accused the father of having broken her arm approximately four years earlier (an injury that is medically documented), and that approximately seven months earlier, her mother had burned her by immersing her hands in boiling water. The teacher has confirmed that the subject attended school with her hands bandaged for nearly two weeks, but reports that the subject said she had burned them by placing them on a barbecue grill. The physician reported the youngster's story to police, who in turn confronted the parents. The parents claim that her injuries were caused when the subject, in a "fit of temper," threw herself downstairs. Her mother reports that she has become more difficult to control during the past year, and that "she often goes crazy like that and there's nothing we can do." (It should be noted here that the parents had a conference with the teacher about the child's poor academic performance three days before the "accident."). The jurist for the juvenile court requested a psychiatric evaluation, and the youngster was interviewed by a psychiatrist, who reported that the child was uncooperative and mute during most of the interview. He raised the possibility that the child might be schizophrenic. Thus, the psychological assessment ordered by the court poses several questions. First, is she schizophrenic? Second, is her hyperactivity due to brain damage? Third, and in light of the first two questions, should she be placed in a residential treatment center, or would it be possible to place her in a closely supervised foster home? At this point, the parents are willing to relinquish custody, and the school is very ambivalent about her continuation. During a period of 10 days prior to the examination, the subject has been housed at a children's shelter, and when first approached by the examiner, was extremely reluctant to participate. The examiner decided to delay the examination until sufficient "rapport" had been established, and devoted most of one half day in the company of the child, talking casually, playing a "scrabble" game, and walking in a nearby park. On the second day, the "scrabble" game was repeated, and in the afternoon, the examination was completed, with the subject and examiner seated on a sofa most of the time. The results of the WISC-R reveal a full scale I.Q. of 117 (verbal I.Q. = 121; performance I.Q. = 115), with no significant scatter among the subtests, scale scores of which ranged from 10 on Picture Completion to 14 on Coding and Arithmetic.

Structural Interpretation. The structural data are very inconsistent with the history and with the assessment questions posed. There is no evidence whatsoever of schizophrenia. Her three M's are all good form quality, the two *Special Scores* are not unusual for a 12 year old, and neither reflects the more distinct "slippage" that would be indicated by *FABCOM* or *CONTAM* answers. The $FC:CF+C$ (3:0) indicates greater emotional control than would be expected for a 12 year old, and this may hint at a problem to be explored more fully. Her reality testing, as indicated by the $F+\%$ (100) and $X+\%$ (89), is quite good, and she offers four *Human contents*, including two pure H responses. The absence of any schizophrenic indices is, of course, no justification for ruling out the possibility of an organically provoked hyperactivity; however, this record does not manifest any of the characteristics that will often appear in the protocols of hyperactive children. The term "hyperactive" has, unfortunately, been used to identify a multitude of conditions, ranging from mild negativism to gross organic involvement, but when

Case 16

Card	Free Association	Inquiry	Scoring
I	1. I don't lik ths one, it looks lik a dead cat (*E*: Most peopl c more than 1 thg)	*E*: (Rpts *S*'s resp) *S*: Yep, it ll one to me, c the face of it, here r the ears & its got its tongue out lik it was dead & there aren't no eyes, just holes lik after u die	*WS+* *Fo* *Ad* 3.5 ALOG
	∨2. Ths way it ll a spooky house	*E*: (Rpts *S*'s resp) *S*: Well the lites r on but its not lik a real hous, more lik a spook house *E*: The lites r on? *S*: Thyr white lik lites on, if thy weren't on it wld all b black, ths is the littl chimney	*WS+* *FC'o* House 3.5
II	3. Thats lik 2 teddy bears kissg	*E*: (Rpts *S*'s resp) *S*: Its just their tops & thyv got their noses together, thts how thy kiss *E*: I'm not sur I c them as u do *S*: Thes r the noses & the heads & thes r their necks	*D+* *FM^ao* (2) *Ad* *P* 3.0
	4. Mayb that c.b. a top or not a top but a thg u pull w a string & it goes fast & balncs for a long time, my sister had one once	*E*: (Rpts *S*'s resp) *S*: I don't rem what u call them, gyplane or s.t., u wrap a string on them & pull & they balance lik ths for a long time	*DSo* *m^ao* Top *DV*
III	5. Oh thats funny, its lik 2 peopl doing their washing or s.t. but ty don't ll real people	*E*: (Rpts *S*'s resp) *S*: One here & one here & thyr r washing clothes in this tub *E*: U said it lookd funny *S*: Thy look all funny, scrawny lik thy didn't eat much, mayb thyr clowns caus u c clowns doing s.t. lik tht to be funny *E*: Clowns *S*: I dk. just somebody funny	*D+* *M^ao* (2) (*H*) *P* 3.0

IV	2"	6. Yuck, ths a black widow spider	E: (Rpts S's resp) S: I thk thts what thy ll, I've nevr seen one but thyr all black & fuzzy lik ths one E: Fuzzy S: Lik thy hav little bits of fur on them lik in here (points) & thy r black & hav thes big kinda legs	W– FC'.FT– A 2.0
		V7. I lik it better lik ths, now that's a bird, lik an eagle zooring up	E: (Rpts S's resp) S: Its got the wgs way out & its lik going up cause the head is out to c where its going E: The head is out? S: Well usually thy don't stick their heads out this far	Wo FMªw A 2.0
V	3"	8. There's 2 alligators there, & thyr peekg out from behind a big bush or s.t. waiting to catch s.t., wow I wldn't want to b around there	E: (Rpts S's resp) S: Well c here, theres 1 here & 1 here & thyr behnd ths big bush & thyr waitg to eat s.t. up E: Behnd ths bush? S: Sur u can only c their noses lik thyr ready to chomp on u	W+ FMª.FD+ (2) A,Bt 2.5
VI	4"	9. Yuck, a snake up there in the bush, crawlg along there, I don't lik snakes do u E: Not very much	E: (Rpts S's resp) S: Well its in there, c the darkr part is the snake & all ths is a bush & its lik crawlg thru it, under it E: Under it? S: It ll its inside the bush, c its a diff color here so its higher up, the bush c it?	D+ FMª.FVo A 2.5
VII	2"	10. Oh, thats littl girls, ik thyr playg or fiting	E: (Rpts S's resp) S: Well thy r here & here, c the long hair so thy must be girls, littl ones & it ll thyr fiting mayb, cause thy r pointg in diff ways, mayb thy don't knc which way to go & thyr fiting about it w e.o.	W+ Mªo (2) H P 2.5

Case 16 (Continued)

Card	Free Association	Inquiry	Scoring
VIII 2"	11. Yuck, what's this, mayb a Xmas tree, it has all the diff colord lites on	E: (Rpts S's resp) S: Well its all diff colord lites lik on a Xmas tree & here is the top where u put the star, and here are the two dogs too.	Wo FCo Bt 4.5
	<12. Theres 2 dogs too, one here & one here	E: Well one is up here & one down here but thy r alike, just dogs, c the legs & the tail, I wish I had a dog	Do Fo (2) (H)
IX 3"	13. Yuck, thats funny, its got 2 witches up here but thyr not real ones	E: (Rpts S's resp) S: C thy hav the big hats on lik witches wear & big noses but thyr not really witches E: Not really? S: Nope, witches aren't fat lik ths, ths is lik toy witches that u punch in school & thy fall ovr & bounce back up at u	D+ FC.FV+ (2) A,Bt 2.5
	V14. Ths way thy ll birds, thyr hiding	E: (Rpts S's resp) S: Well here & here, lik littl birds & thyr under ths bush, c the green is the bush & thy r lik oriole birds caus thyr orange lik oriole birds & thy r under c where the bush covrs part of them rite here lik thy r hiding	D+ Fo (2) A P
X 2"	15. Ugh, more spiders, up here there's 2, c the blue ones	E: (Rpts S's resp) S: Thy hav all thos legs, here the blue c thy r ugly lik spiders, yuck	D+ FMᵃo (2) A,Bt 4.0
	16. And up here theres 2 more eating this stick	E: (Rpts S's resp) S: Thy r a diff kind of spider cause thy can even stand up on their legs lik ths & thyr eating ths thg, mayb a stick	D+ Mᵃo (2) H 4.0
	V17. There 2 men here & thy r fiting	E: (Rpts S's resp) S: Thyr lik boxing at e.o., c each one has his arms out lik thy are hitting e.o.	Do FCo (2) Bt
	18. Thts lik a flowr before it opens up	E: (Rpts S's resp) S: 2 of em, c the yellow its lik, whatdaucallem	

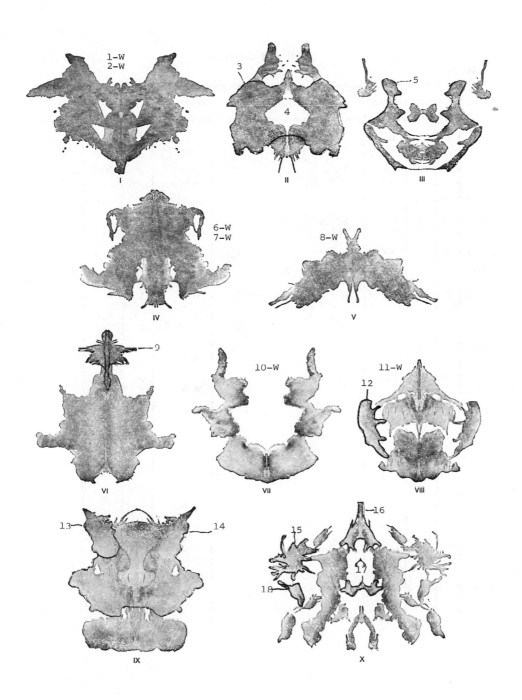

Case 16

CARD	RT	NO.	LOCATION	DETERMINANTS (S)		CONTENT (S)	POP	Z SCORE	SPECIAL
I	5"	1.	WS+	Fo		Ad		3.5	ALOG
		2.	WS+	FC'o		House		3.5	
II	3"	3.	D+	FM^ao	(2)	Ad	P	3.0	
		4.	DSo	m^ao		Top			DV
III	2"	5.	D+	M^ao	(2)	(H)	P	3.0	
IV	2"	6.	W−	FC'.FT−		A		2.0	
		7.	Wo	FM^aw		A		2.0	
V	3"	8.	W+	FM^a.FD+	(2)	A,Bt		2.5	
VI	4"	9.	D+	FM^a.FVo		A		2.5	
VII	2"	10.	W+	M^ao	(2)	H	P	2.5	
VIII	2"	11.	Wo	FCo		Bt		4.5	
		12.	Do	Fo	(2)	A	P		
IX	3"	13.	Do	Fo	(2)	(H)			
		14.	D+	FC.FV+	(2)	A,Bt		2.5	
X	2"	15.	Do	Fo	(2)	A	P		
		16.	D+	FM^ao	(2)	A,Bt		4.0	
		17.	D+	M^ao	(2)	H		4.0	
		18.	Do	FCo	(2)	Bt			

Case 16: Structural Summary

R = 18   Zf = 13   ZSum = 39.5   P = 5   (2) = 10

Location Features		Determinants (Blends First)	Contents	Contents (Idiographic)
W = 7	**DQ**			
D = 11	+ = 10	FM.FD =1	H = 2	House .... = 1
Dd = 0	o = 7	FM.FV =1	(H) = 2	
		FC.FV =1	Hd =	Top .... = 1
S = 3	v = 0	FC'.FT =1	(Hd) =	
			A = 8	.... =
DW =	— = 1		(A) =	
		M = 3	Ad = 2	.... =
		FM = 3	(Ad) =	
		m = 1	Ab =	.... =
		C =	Al =	
Form Quality		CF =	An =	.... =
		FC = 2	Art =	
FQx	**FQf**	C' =	Ay =	.... =
		C'F =	Bl =	
+ = 2	+ = 0	FC' = 1	Bt = 2,3	.... =
		T =	Cg =	
o = 14	o = 4	TF =	Cl =	**Special Scorings**
		FT =	Ex =	
w = 1	w = 0	V =	Fi =	
		VF =	Fd =	PSV =
— = 1	— = 0	FV =	Ge =	
		Y =	Hh =	DV = 1
M Quality		YF =	Ls =	
		FY =	Na =	INCOM =
+ = 0		T =	Sx =	
		Fr =	Xy =	FABCOM =
o — 3		FD =		
		F = 4		CONTAM =
w = 0				
				ALOG = 1
— = 0				=

RATIOS, PERCENTAGES, AND DERIVATIONS

ZSum-Zest = 39.5–41.5		FC:CF+C – 3:0	Afr = .80	
Zd = –2.0		W:M = 7:3	3r+(2)/R = .56	
FB = 3:1.5	EA = 4.5	W:D – 7:11	Cont·R = 5:18	
eb = 6:5	ep = 11	L = .29	H+Hd:A+Ad = 4:10 (H)+(Hd)·(A)+(Ad) = 2:0	
Blends:R = 4:18		F+% = 100	H+A:Hd+Ad = 12:2	
a:p = 9:0		X+% = .00	XRT Achrom = 3.2"	
Ma:Mp = 3:0		A% = .56	XRT Chrom = 2.4"	

it includes some form of perceptual dysfunctioning, Rorschachs tend to show evidence of "underincorporation," loose controls, low self-esteem, a higher than usual frequency of *m* responses, an emphasis on *W* or *Dd,* substantial *S,* and difficulties with Human content. In addition, the *DQ* scores will usually indicate some cognitive "retardation" as manifest in a notable frequency of *vague and minus* answers. In contrast, this record is more compatible for the fairly intelligent child who has experienced at least adequate cognitive growth. She gives three *M* responses, and has 10 *DQ* synthesis answers, with no vague selections. Her four *blends* are about average for her age, as are the five *Popular* responses. The *S* is slightly elevated, but by no means substantial. If the record were examined "in the blind"—that is, without any history, it is very doubtful that the issue of hyperactivity would be considered as a potential. Thus, at this point, it is "back to the drawing board" to generate a full description that will be useful in attempting to understand this youngster.

The *Four Square* indicates that she is prone to introversiveness; that is, she will show a tendency toward the use of ideation when coping (*EB* = 3 : 1.5). There is a marked difference between *ep* and *EA* (11 : 4.5), indicating that she has only limited access to many of her resources, and that there is much psychological activity that she experiences but over which she has little control. Five of the six elements on the left side of the *eb* are *FM*, suggesting that she experiences much ideation created by need states. The right side of the *eb* contains one *T*, which is predictable; two *V*'s, which are not predictable, and which indicate that she is more introspective than most children, and in a way that yields negative emotional experiences; and two *C*'s, also significantly more than most children display of this age, suggesting that she is often uncomfortable because of emotions that have been blocked from expression.

The *a* : *p* ratio (9 : 0) indicates that she is not very flexible in her ideation and probably will have trouble "breaking sets." Her *Afr* (.80), while slightly high for an adult, is average for a 12 year old, indicating that she is naturally responsive to emotionally loaded stimuli. Her *egocentricity index* (.56), conveying a considerable self centeredness, is also about average for a 12 year old. Most 12 year olds will give about as many *CF* and *C* as *FC*, and the complete absence of *CF* or *C* connotes an overcontrol that is very uncommon. It probably also accounts for the two *C*' responses; that is, she does not want her emotions to get out of hand. While her *W* : *M* (7 : 3) would be normal for an adult, it reflects a slightly lower level of aspiration than is common among children. Most children set very high goals for themselves that are often well beyond their capacities. She does not. The very low *Lambda* offers another clue to some of her difficulties (.29). She has real trouble in extracting herself from complex stimulus situations, and when viewed in the context of her ideational inflexibility and her limited accessibility to internal resources, this difficulty suggests that she may not be a very effective "problem solver"; that is, she probably tends to perseverate solutions that may not be effective, and, unfortunately, she cannot "back away" easily to review her errors.

She has both a color-shading blend (*FC.FV*), and a shading blend (*FC'.FT*), each of which are unusual in most records, especially those of younger clients. The former probably indicates a sense of ambivalence or confusion concerning her emotional displays; that is, she is not sure of the "right" way to express her emotions. The latter indicates an inordinate experience of pain, and, interestingly, it contains her one texture determinant. Although it is risky to speculate from a single score, the uniqueness of the score, plus the other data in the record previously mentioned, lend themselves to the question of whether she is confused about how to express her own need for affection, and in fact, whether she may feel that it is necessary to inhibit those feelings. She has a rather restricted range of contents, and interestingly, *five* of her 18 responses contain some form of Botany, which may offer added clues about her and her behavior. The *Zf* (13) shows that she organizes quite a bit, while her *Zd* score suggests that her organizational actions are generally efficient. Her mean reaction times are brief, which is common for children, and important in this instance, since she apparently did not attempt to conceal herself.

Interpretation of the Scoring Sequence.   All three of her *S* answers occur early in the test, suggesting some situational negativism or anger. Her approach is reasonably consistent, and she manifests organizational activity on every card. It seems clear that she has the greatest difficulty with Card IV, to which she gives both of her poor form quality responses and her shading blend. Her *M*'s are well distributed, as are her Popular answers. Although she signs in with a pure *F* answer, it is clear that she is not able to avoid other features of the blots in most cases, and pure *F,* as a style of coping, is not her "strong suit," although she does enter both Cards IX and X using a pure *F* answer, after having given a third pure *F* to Card VIII. This tends to reaffirm an earlier speculation about her overcontrol of affect; that is, she seems to be very reluctant to "let herself go" in a more typical childlike manner.

Interpretation of Content.   Her contents are much more morbid and phobic than is conveyed in the structural data. She "opens" with a dead cat, and after prompting, inverts the card to find a "spooky house." During the test, she sees spiders, witches, alligators, and a snake, none of which are very positive in the context of self-concept, and all are marked by the potential threat that they possess. In most instances, she attempts to counteract the threat component, sometimes through an openness, ". . . wow I wouldn't want to be around there"; ". . . I don't like snakes, do you?"; while in other instances she uses a form of denial to neutralize the threat, ". . . but they are not real ones." Her *M* contents are especially interesting and probably indicate much of how she sees herself in the interpersonal sphere. In the first, "people washing," she seems to have trouble with the cooperative aspects of the percept, ". . . but they don't look like real people." In the second *M* answer, given to Card VII, she is unable to distinguish whether the little girls are "playing or fighting," and in the third, on Card X, she sees, ". . . two men . . . and they are fighting." In other words, her perceptions of people and their interactions seem to presuppose the probability of aggressive exchanges rather than cooperation and harmony. Her most positive answers include the "teddy bears kissing" (bears kiss but humans fight?), "birds, they're hiding," and the "flower before it opens up." All three of those answers are not only void of aggressive content, but they also suggest a very timid and gentle person. Her response to Card IV, "Yuck, that's a black widow spider" tends to suggest her awareness of the damage that evolves from aggressiveness. Some Rorschachers would find it very tempting to speculate that this reflects her father; *however,* there is no empirical justification for such a speculation. In fact, many people in her life, including herself, can be reflected in that percept. Similarly, it is tempting to speculate that her response to Card V, alligators, ". . . peeking out . . . waiting to catch something" may represent her attitude toward the world. This may be true, but it may not be true. All that we know for certain is that she selected the percept; in that context, it illustrates something of her own psychological operations—namely, that things exist within her that can "grab her." The

Card VI "snake in the bush" response seems terribly symbolic and again may raise speculation about a "primal scene" or sexual thoughts, but on a more conservative level, it is simply a perseveration of the alligator response; that is, something "lurks" within that can be very damaging to her.

Her answer to Card IX, the hiding birds, is her color-shading blend, and seems to dramatize her fears and her struggle to conceal. But at the same time, she selects an attractive bird; this is another hint of her gentleness. In her earlier use of color, on Card VIII, she is also positive, "a Christmas tree," while her very last answer, on Card X, ". . . a flower before it opens up," of a gentle and potentially warm youngster who is almost waiting for the moment to spring forth.

Case 16 Summary.   The hostile, vicious, uncooperative and crazy child described in the history is nowhere to be seen in this record. Certainly, she perceives herself negatively, appears to have many phobic thoughts and expectations, and is acutely committed to the notion that to be emotional is "bad." Much of her word use is less sophisticated than might be expected from her intelligence test performance or from the structural data, and this limitation may relate to some of the more immature kinds of comments that she offers. But she seeks support and direction from the examiner, is willing to be quite personal with the examiner, *and does not* deliver any of the wildly aggressive or labile sorts of responses that might have been predicted from the pretesting description. She is in need of considerably more development than has been the case thus far, but she seems very amenable to such development. It seems very likely that her acting out behavior in school has been a function of her confusion about interpersonal relations in general, and also a mode of protecting herself from some sense of impending damage from others. The same phenomenon would account for her inattentiveness, and probably for considerable anxiety, which others have labeled as "hyperactive."

In the context of the assessment questions, the data raise clear questions about the credibility of the parents regarding the various injuries the child has experienced. Unless the child is epileptic, it is very difficult to conceive of her behaving in the extremely uncontrolled ways that they describe. Thus, the first recommendation to the court is for a complete neurological examination, including an EEG, to investigate the possibility of epilepsy or some other organic condition. Second, and concurrent with the neurological, would be a second form of psychological assessment, focusing on the issue of perceptual dysfunction. Third is that there is no apparent need for residential treatment; however, foster home placement may be in order pending a more thorough investigation of the parents. Fourth, the child should be in a form of developmental treatment. In this instance, a one-to-one relationship, preferrably with a female therapist, focusing on the development of interpersonal skills, but more importantly, "talking through" some of the phobic ideation that is present, and working on a better use of resources for problem solving.

Case 16 Epilogue.   All neurological data were within normal limits, and the assessment was for perceptual dysfunction also proved essentially negative, although some of her visual motor functioning revealed a "tilting" tendency, which later proved to be a function of partial sight impairment in the left eye. A more thorough history derived from teachers revealed that several of the "fighting" incidents may have been provoked by others who tended to "tease" the subject because of her isolation from peers, and because she had been identified frequently by the teachers as "troublesome." A more thorough investigation of the parents reveals that the father is noted for excessive use of alcohol, and that the mother has been arrested twice in the past three years on charges related to prostitution. Apparently her husband was aware of her occasional "part time business" ventures and endorsed them.

When confronted by the court with the accumulation of data, the father admitted that they had beaten the child because of her refusal to "go to bed" when instructed, although, contrary to the child's story that father did the beating while mother held her, the father stated that the reverse was true, and also accused the mother of beating the child quite frequently in the past. Conversely, the mother accused the father of the frequent beatings. Subsequently, both were charged with child abuse and child neglect; however, those charges were dropped later. The child was placed in a foster home in another school district, and entered individual psychotherapy with a female therapist. After one year she has been reported to be progressing satisfactorily in her new school, but is reported by the foster parents to continue to have frequent "nightmares." The therapist's reports are generally optimistic about the child's progress.

SUMMARY

The issues broached here focus on only a few of the varied and complex problems confronting the professional who is frequently involved in forensic cases. Nonetheless, the Rorschach approach to these many issues remains essentially the same. That is, the interpreter relies on the descriptive data available from the test as a basis for all conclusions, and concurrently, recognizes the limitations of the test to answer *all* questions. In most forensic cases, the Rorschach cannot stand independently, but can often provide the focal point from which a more thorough understanding of the person originates.

REFERENCES

Albert, S. The susceptibility of the Rorschach to faking psychosis by normal individuals. Unpublished doctoral dissertation, Arizona State University, 1978.

Exner, J. E. *The Rorschach Systems*. New York: Grune and Stratton, 1969.

Exner, J. E. *The Rorschach: A Comprehensive System*. New York: John Wiley and Sons, 1974.

Exner, J. E., Bryant, E. L., and Miller, A. S. Rorschach responses of juvenile offenders. Workshops Study No. 214 (unpublished), Rorschach Workshops, 1975.

Exner, J. E., and Exner, D. E. How clinicians use the Rorschach. *Journal of Personality Assessment*, 1972, **26**, 403–408.

Exner, J. E., and Miller, A. S. Protocols of newly admitted prison inmates. Workshops Study No. 200 (unpublished), Rorschach Workshops, 1974.

Exner, J. E., and Sherman, J. Rorschach performance of schizophrenics asked to improve their protocols. Workshops Study No. 243 (unpublished), Rorschach Workshops, 1977.

Exner, J. E., and Wylie, J. R. Attempts at simulation of schizophrenic-like protocols by psychology graduate students. Workshops Study No. 211 (unpublished), Rorschach Workshops, 1975.

PART THREE

Treatment Planning
and Evaluation

CHAPTER 10

Treatment Planning

There is no magic in the Rorschach from which intervention decisions can be made easily. In fact, taken alone—that is, without some knowledge about the presenting complaints and/or the recent behavior of the subject—Rorschach data could easily become misleading to the formulation of a treatment plan. This is because all humans are fragile, and all have liabilities, or flaws, in their personalities. Thus, as noted in Chapter 6, any person can be psychologically dissected and, if judged against "optimal" standards, be made to appear much more pathological than is the case. For instance, a striking feature of the subject in Case 1, in Chapter 6, is an *ep* somewhat greater than *EA*. He simply does not have his own resources organized in a way that makes them easily accessible in coping situations. Yet he has no apparent problems. He was described as a person who "probably wears his heart on his sleeve," which is not always a disadvantage in an interpersonal world; but supposing that he expressed some concern about being "overly emotional."

Would the best approach to treatment be one that focused on his gaining greater accessibility to his own resources? Although this may appear to be the most optimal target for intervention, it is not necessarily the most optimal in the context of the goals of the subject, especially when viewed in terms of a *cost-benefit analysis*. The subject wants "better" emotional control. It may be that the most parsimonious treatment plan would be one that stresses simple behavioral tactics of delay, without focusing extensively on the reorganization of resources, as would be required if a reversal of the *ep-EA* relationship were a primary target of intervention. On the other hand, if the subject complains of a more extensive "inability to control," then the treatment plan would probably involve a longer term, developmentally oriented, form of intervention, in which better resource accessibility would become a major target or objective; however, other factors must also be considered before any final decision about the plan itself is made. For example, the subject in this particular case is married, has a youngster, and is gainfully employed in a "blue collar" position. Any treatment approach must develop in the context of those environmental relationships—that is, in a context that permits the subject to maintain whatever harmony he has already created in the world, one that hopefully would mesh greater psychological sophistication with the life situation he has "carved out" for himself. Otherwise, the *cost factor* to the client may go well beyond what he is willing to pay in terms of the disruption of his life.

In recent decades, psychology and psychiatry have been marked by many gains in achieving greater diversification among the modes of intervention. Some treatment modalities are highly effective for certain objectives but not necessarily for others. The literature on the many intervention methods has grown rapidly, especially since the milestone publication of Bergin and Garfield (1971), through a variety of annual publications that seek to consolidate the stream of empirical data concerning treatment effects. Any intelligent treatment plan should be formulated in concert with this growing knowledge. For example, a person complaining of chronic headaches usually wants quick relief from the headaches. It may be that such a person will be revealed as having difficulty expressing emotion, especially anger. Under some circumstances, it may appear *optimal* to promote some reconstruction of the personality in which the expression of emotion occurs more freely and spontaneously. This may involve a long term intervention plan. Conversely, a reconstructive approach might jeopardize some other personality features that are precariously interdependent, and under such circumstances, the treatment of choice will probably be one that does not attack that organization, but does focus on the major objective of headache elimination. There are several brief treatment modalities that may be useful in such a situation, such as biofeedback, desensitization, assertiveness training, and so on.

THE RORSCHACH AS A STARTING POINT

The use of the Rorschach for the selection of treatment targets and treatment modalities does begin with the so-called "optimal state," that is, with the speculative question: what features of the test would be altered if a magic wand were available? If the Rorschach is a valid index of response styles, then a "road map" is presented in the composite data from which the effectiveness of those styles can be ascertained, some notion of their interrelationship gleaned, and, most important, liabilities detected. These liabilities become the focal points for treatment consideration, beginning with the question of how serious they seem to be in the total context of the personality, extending through speculation on how easily they can be altered, and ending in the context of the immediate and long range goals of the subject. Overall, the treatment formulation must include a cost-benefit analysis, which requires that the goals be identified in relation to the immediate needs and the environmental circumstances of the subject, as well as the attainability of certain goals within specific time frames. Thus, Rorschach data will aid in detecting the features that should be altered under ideal conditions; but the data *do not* identify the *reality factors* that may be involved if those features are selected as treatment targets. The reality factors are identified only by sound clinical logic that inductively joins information on potential treatment targets with other information about the subject and the effectiveness of various treatment modalities, and that deductively arrives at treatment options, including a cost-benefit analysis for each.

There are Rorschach data that may be quite important to the cost-benefit speculation, and that can often provide important information for therapists once a treatment plan has been selected. They do not necessarily identify specific forms of treatment as being more likely to succeed, but they do offer some information about the expected responses of subjects in different forms of treatment.

The *EA* : *ep* Relation

The results of the OP Study (Exner, Wylie and Kline, 1977) indicate that when a reconstructive treatment approach is applied to a subject beginning therapy with *EA* greater than *ep,* the treatment time can be expected to be longer than when the reverse is true. In the same context, patients entering a reconstructive therapy with *EA* higher than *ep* will often experience considerable disorganization during the first nine months of intervention. Such disorganization is frequently very marked for these subjects, and reports of "feelings of going crazy" are not uncommon. This does not appear to be the case when a "modeling" approach is used with these subjects. However, the long term modeling approach is not always oriented toward a focus on reconstruction of the overall personality, and seems less effective in "mobilizing resource accessibility" than do the more traditional reconstructive techniques. In fact, when a subject begins modeling treatment with *ep* exceeding *EA,* only about half can be expected to reverse that relationship after 24 months. Although this is a significantly greater proportion than would occur under the various brief treatments, it is a significantly smaller proportion than that found when subjects participated in a more reconstructively oriented form of treatment.

The *FC* : *CF* +*C* Ratio and *Afr*

Almost half of the subjects in the OP Study entered treatment with their Rorschachs showing more *CF*+*C* than *FC*. Less than 25% of these subjects continued to display more *CF*+*C* after termination *if* they were rated as improved. Conversely, nearly 75% of those rated as unimproved continued to display more *CF*+*C* than *FC*. This seems to indicate that when issues of affect modulation appear in the responses of subjects presenting complaints, they should be seriously considered an important treatment objective if success is to be expected. Similarly, it was discovered that, after 28 months, the overwhelming majority of patients rated as unimproved continued to display *Afr*'s considerably higher or lower than the average. In other words, these patients seemed to be people who could not deal very effectively with complex emotional stimuli. Again, if an unusual *Afr* appears at the beginning of treatment, the modification of responsiveness to emotional stimuli should be considered important among the variety of treatment targets. This is not to imply that these Rorschach variables must change, but when considered in the light of simple expectancies, they may be very important to treatment decisions.

The Egocentricity Index

The results of the OP study also reveal that a subject entering treatment with an excessively high or excessively low egocentricity index has a significantly lower probability of being rated improved after two years than if that index is altered to a more "normal" range. These findings coincide with those in the RE Study (Exner, Murillo, and Cannavo, 1973) and in the long term study of schizophrenia (Exner and Murillo, 1977). Although it is clear that subjects with higher than average egocentricity indices have a higher posttreatment "survival" rate than do those with significantly lower indices, the same subjects display a greater frequency of interpersonal difficulties after treatment and tend more toward social isolation.

The Active-Passive Dimension

There are two elements in the active-passive ratios that may be of concern in treatment planning. First, when the basic $a:p$ ratio contains numbers in which one is three times greater than the other, the subject seems to have difficulty in making "ideational shifts." The thinking is not very flexible; and to the therapist who is oriented to producing new insights, this can create a significant obstacle. Insight oriented therapists tend to rate these types of patients less kindly than they do patients who show flexibility. Consequently, the therapist working with the less flexible patient is best forewarned about the importance of revalidating translations and interpretations by simply reviewing over and over the point to be made. In the same context, subjects who offer a greater number of passive than active M's are marked by tendencies to manifest "Snow White" fantasies. In treatment, these subjects often appear to be helpless—that is, unable to initiate topics or pursue important conclusions. In fact, of the 151 subjects who did withdraw either from treatment or from participation in the OP Study, 89 showed more M^p than M^a, and when therapists reviewed the causes for their withdrawal from treatment, their most common descriptive phrase was, "could not, or would not discuss or focus on relevant topics in treatment."

Variations in Zd

The work with the Zd "variant" is far from complete; however, it does seem that the underincorporative subject, especially the child, can be trained to delay much easier than the overincorporative subject can be trained to make quicker decisions. Therapists tend to rate the overincorporator as "resistive" and "ruminative," whereas therapists working with underincorporators often rate them as "drawing conclusions too hastily." Nonetheless, most therapists seem to prefer the underincorporating patient to the overincorporating patient, possibly because external controls become more effective with the former but not so much with the latter.

Although these structural issues should be important to any treatment formulation, they are not, by any stretch of the imagination, the keys to intervention success, mainly because of the many extraneous variables that will ultimately coagulate the treatment plan. Every diagnostician and/or therapist will be confronted with the struggle between the optimal and the necessary, a conflict illustrated quite effectively by the treatment planning quandaries posed by Case 3, first described in Chapter 4, and elaborated with additional data in Chapter 5.

Case 3: A 31 Year Old Female—the Reflective Hysteroid

History.   This 31 year old mother of two children, a boy of 9 and a girl of 7, was married at 19 to a man 23 years old. He had completed college, majoring in business, a year earlier, and had already obtained a position in industrial sales, one in which he now continues. She is the second of three sisters, whose father has been a successful self employed plumber, and is now aged 60. Her mother, 59 years old, has no significant work history. Her older sister, age 34, is a high school science teacher who has been married for nine years and has a child of six. Her younger sister, age 28, completed two years of college and currently works as a legal secretary. She is engaged. There is no psychiatric history in the family, and the medical history of the subject is unremarkable.

The subject was acquainted with her husband for approximately three years before her marriage. During their first year of marriage, she worked as a "pool" secretary for a large manufacturing firm but left after becoming pregnant. During her nearly 10 years of marriage, she has occasionally become involved in "volunteer" work in elementary schools (crossing guard) and hospitals (candy striper), but not usually for long periods of time or with extensive commitments. During her fifth marital year, shortly after the birth of her second child, she discovered that her husband was "involved with other women" during his frequent trips away from home. They agreed to seek "marital counseling" at that time, which was arranged through the services of a mutual friend of the family. They participated in nine marital counseling sessions, after which a full reconciliation appeared to have occurred. About four years later, she was confronted by her husband, who stated his intention to seek a divorce in order to marry someone else. The subject claims no awareness that her husband had been seeing "another woman" (apparently for about two years), and underwent a deep depression at the time of the separation. She was prescribed valium by her physician during the early trauma of the separation, but discontinued the medication after two months. She feels that she has been given considerable support during the process of divorce by her family, especially her older sister, and by several friends. The divorce became final about four months prior to the psychological examination, which was precipitated by recurring visits to her physician with various complaints, most focusing on her inability to "reestablish" an independent lifestyle. She is fully supported by generous alimony, but has sought work unsuccessfully. She has no developed occupational skills, and has placed limitations on the amount of time she is willing to commit to work because of "responsibilities to my children." Her current complaints include periodic feelings of nervousness, frequent insomnia, and sometimes inappropriate crying (during lunch with friends, while viewing TV, driving her car, standing in line at the bank). She is described as attractive, although slightly overweight (about 10 pounds), of average height and weight, and in good physical health. Her children are both doing average or better work in school. Her ex-husband has periodic visiting privileges, but does not exercise them often.

The attending physician has referred the subject for a psychological evaluation, asking whether psychiatric intervention is required, or whether some form of continued supportive "medical" treatment is appropriate. The physician, a woman, also asks for some direction if she is to continue supporting the subject, or a statement of treatment objectives if the subject is to be referred for some form of psychiatric intervention.

Previously Developed Interpretation.   The partial data from this case, presented in Chapters 4 and 5, identified her as a clearly extratensive person ($EB = 1:6.0$)—

Case 3

Card	Free Association	Inquiry	Scoring
I 19″	1. I supp I cld c a design lik a sculpture that mite b on a bldg w the gargoyls on the sides	E: (Rpts S's resp) S: Well, its the same on both sides & u sort of get the pict of 2 A's on the sides, lik gargoyles, I think thyr sort of lik lions but not really, c the legs & body but thy hav wgs or s.t., lik A's from mythology, its all like a crest or emblem	Wo Fo (2) Art 1.0
	E: I think if you take ur time and look you'll probably find other things too		
	2. I suppose it c.b. a moth too, w its wgs out lik it was flyg, but not with ths side parts out here	E: (Rpts S's resp) S: Yes, thts rite, thes wld b the wgs (points) but not w the extensions, c ths is the body & the antennae E: U said a moth? S: Yes, well moths are dark lik this, it prob cldn't b a bf cause thyr not dark, thy hav lots of different colors	Ddo FMᵃ.FYo A (P)
II 6″	3. Oh, ths seems to b two dogs, just ths part here (points)	E: (Rpts S's resp) S: It does ll tht, u c the head here & the body, I don't kno what kind but thy hav littl ears & noses	Do Fo (2) A
	4. U kno, ths way it ll a top lik we used to hav for my son when he was littl	E: (Rpts S's resp) S: It was when he was really small, before he was old enough to work it himself, & it had a stand lik ths one & so u'd mak it go & set it in the stand, c the white is the top & the stand w.b. down in here (traces an outline of the stand in the lower D3 area using only part of the area)	DdS+ mᵃo Top 4.5

344

			Free Association	Inquiry					
III	16"	5.	I don't get much of ths one except, u kno, ths midcl red part c.b. lik a clown's mouth, the lips, I'm not sur if u kno what I mean, but it c.b. lik u mite paint human lips to exaggerate them, that's all though	E: (Rpts S's resp) S: Well it does sort of ll tht, if u've ever made up a kid for a school play, lik to b a clown, or for halloween, thts how u might paint the lips, brite red & sort of in ths shape, u just exaggerate the features, it c d ll ths (Adds, Oh, u kno, It mite b lik two puppets too, I didn't c it before, here in the dark part, it ll puppets (Popular area)	Do	FCw	Hd		
IV	18"	6.	Oh, I kno, its lik a frog, I was tryg to figure out the bumpiness of it	E: (Rpts S's resp) S: Well here is the head (points) & the legs are out here on the side, it just ll a frog E: U mentioned bumpiness? S: Oh yes, c the dark spots, it ll if u touch it it would feel bumpy, u know?, lik a frog	Wo	FTw	A	2.0	
V	9"	7.	That re me of that moth again, the one I saw befor flying along w its wgs out	E: (Rpts S's resp) S: Well, it has wgs & its dark too, this how moths are, not very pretty, just dull & dark, c thes r the antennae, its not exactly lik the other one, but it mite be	Wo	$FM^a.FYo$	A (P)	1.0	PSV
		V8.	U kno, if I turn it ths way it ll a boney structure, mayb lik a pelvic bone	E: (Rpts S's resp) S: Well, it just ll one, a pelvis to me, thats all, it has tht form to it, thats all	W-	F-	An	1.0	
VI	7"	9.	That re me of a squashed cat	E: (Rpts S's resp) S: It has the head & the whiskers, & it does look furry & its all flat like it had been squashed, c the legs are way out to the side E: U said it looks furry? S: C this coloring in here, it gives that impression to me, & it wldn't b a cat if it wasn't furry	Wo	FTo	A P	2.5	

345

Case 3 (Continued)

Card	Free Association	Inquiry	Scoring
	10. It mite be a bush too, lik a littl plant, in a planter	E: (Rpts S's resp) S: Well ths top part w.b. the plant, c the branches here & ths w.b. the pot down here, c thes would be the handles on it, its almost lik a small tree, ot s.k. of bush	$W+$ Fo Bt 2.5
VII 14″	11. U kno, tht re me of fried shrimp, thts probably a funny thg to see	E: (Rpts S's resp) S: The top ones hav littl tails, lik shrimp, & all the pieces ll thyv been breaded, probably with cracker meal, or s.t. lik shake & bake, to mak them crispy when thyr fried, c the way thy look grainy lik (rubs blot to convey), there are about six of them I guess	Wv FTo Fd 2.5
	V12. Oh, ths re me of a wm, sort of lookg herself over in a mirror, she's lookg over her shoulder, lik to c if e.t. is alright	E: (Rpts S's resp) S: Ths wld b her head & her arm & legs, lookg over her shoulder in the mirror & here's her reflection, mayb she's checkg to c if her skirt is straight or s.t., women do tht a lot I suppose	$W+$ M^a.Fro H 3.0
	13. U kno ths littl part here ll a town or littl village way off in the distance, one on each side	E: (Rpts S's resp) S: The bldgs r so smll, thy must be way off in the distance, & thy ll on ths mt, c ths part here w.b. the mt, c the peaks of the bldgs r here (points & outlines with her fingernail)	$Dd+$ FDo (2) Towns 1.0
VIII 5″	V14. Ths re me of s.t. from a bio book, illustrating the insides, e.t. is in pairs, almost everythg	E: (Rpts S's resp) S: Well its all in different colors, lik thy use to illustrate the diff organs, lik the liver & the stomach & the lungs, and mayb the chest bones here (points), I mean ribs, & all of tht, c some of it is in pairs, lik the thgs that we hav two of, lik the lungs & thgs.	Wo FCo (2) An 4.5

15. Ths c.b. tree roots I guess, the way thy come out on the sides, there's cne on each side just roots

E: (Rpts S's resp)

S: Thy just come out here, one on each side, the tree isn't there, but just ths prt (points), its lik roots, c the littl finger lik ends, lik roots

Ddv Fo (2) Bt

16. Ths lower prt c.b. ice cream or mayb sherbet, yes, like orange & raspberry sherbet

E: (Rpts S's resp)

S: It does look lik tht but a littl melted lik the flavors ran togethr, mixed togthr u cld thk of sherbet more than ice cream

E: More than ice cream?

S: Well its grainy lookg, the littl markgs in the color makes it look more grainy, not as pure as ice cream, more crystals

Dv CF.TFo Fd

17. U kno, ths way it ll a badge too, mayb lik a campfire girl wears, cr someone w s.t. to do w the outdoors

E: (Rpts S's resp)

S: Well it has 2 A's on it, one on each side & a lot of different colors, it re me of s.t. tht mght b on an environmental poster or button, ths mite be a tree on top I suppose if u use the middle too, its just an emblem sort of thg

W+ FCo (2) Art P 4.5

IX 8"

18. The centr white part makes me thk of a keyhole

E: (Rpts S's resp)

S: Well it has tht shape to it, sort of an hourglass shape like a keyhole, thts how thy are

DSo Fw Keyhole

19. Thes cutr red parts ll two candy apples

E: (Rpts S's resp)

S: Thyr lik u mak in the fall, at least I do for the kids, thy ll thyv been dipped in the red candy syrup, when u do ths thy take on ths color. c just thes round parts here (points)

Do CFo (2) Fd

20. U kno, all of it c.b. a plant, it w.b. a very exotic one I thk bec the orange petals, thts a very unusual color for a plant

E: (Rpts S's resp)

S: Well, its pretty w the orange blooms or petals & the green is the leaves & this pink is the base, the root system

Wv FCo Bt 5.5

347

Case 3 (Continued)

Card	Free Association	Inquiry	Scoring
X			
4″	21. It c.b. the 4th of July, like fireworks exploding	E: (Rpts S's resp) S: Its all different colors lik when thy explod outward to form a pattern lik ths, lik a rocket going off, its makes a pretty pattern	Wv $m^a.CFo$ Ex 5.5
	22. Ths top ll a grey lizzard, ugh! Its sort of a greyish blue, not lik the other grey lik for the moths	E: (Rpts S's resp) S: Well, thy hav thes small legs, there's one on each side, c (points) & thy have thes littl antennae lik points on their heads I really don't kno if it ll one the more I look at it	$D-$ $FC-$ (2) A
	23. Ths cntr blue ll part of a bone structure, not the whole bone, what do u call it, the sternum I thk, ths is lik half of it	E: (Rpts S's resp) S: Well I thk its wider than ths, but both halves r there, one on each side, its the chestbone, I really am not sure if its called the sternum but I thk so, anyhow its a major bone part, it just looks formed lik a bone	Do Fo (2) An
	24. Ths other blue thgs ll crabs	E: (Rpts S's resp) S: Thy hav a lot of legs, just lik crabs, I suppose ths what thy ll, thyr not blue tho not real crabs	Do Fo (2) A P
	25. Ths littl green parts c.b. grass-hoppers	E: (Rpts S's resp) S: Well thy r small, lik grasshoppers & thy hav he littl antennae on them, & thyr green too like a grasshopper, c one here & here (points)	Do FCw (2) A

348

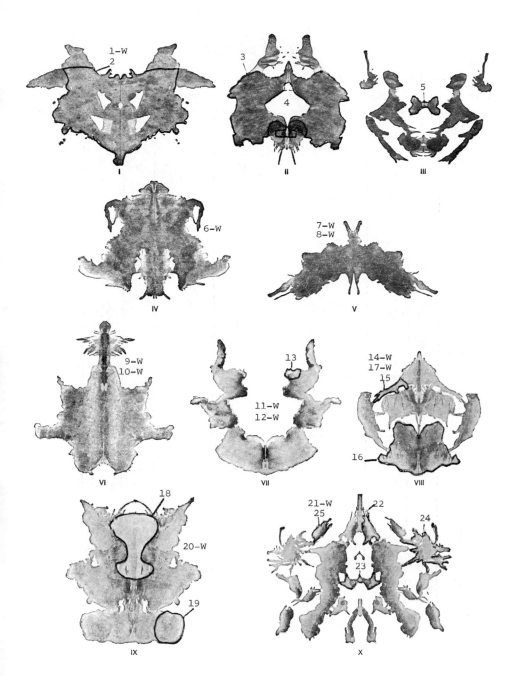

Case 3

CARD	RT	NO.	LOCATION	DETERMINANTS (S)		CONTENT (S)	POP	Z SCORE	SPECIAL
I	19"	1.	Wo	Fo	(2)	Art		1.0	
		2.	Ddo	FM^a.FC'o		A	(P)		
II	6"	3.	Do	Fo	(2)	A	P		
		4.	DdS+	m^ao		Top		4.5	
III	16"	5.	Do	FCw		Hd			
IV	18"	6.	Wo	FTw		A		2.0	
V	9"	7.	Wo	FM^a.FYo		A	(P)	1.0	PSV
		8.	W−	F−		An		1.0	
VI	7"	9.	Wo	FTo		A	P	2.5	
		10.	W+	Fo		Bt		2.5	
VII	14"	11.	Wv	FTo		Fd		2.5	
		12.	W+	M^a.Fro		H		3.0	
		13.	Dd+	FDo	(2)	Towns		1.0	
VIII	5"	14.	Wo	FCo	(2)	An		4.5	
		15.	Ddv	Fo	(2)	Bt			
		16.	Dv	CF.YF.TFo		Fd			
		17.	W+	FCo	(2)	Art	P	4.5	
IX	8"	18.	DSo	Fw		Keyhole			
		19.	Do	CFo	(2)	Fd			
		20.	Wv	FCo		Bt		5.5	
X	4"	21.	Wv	m^a.CFo		Ex		5.5	
		22.	D−	FC−	(2)	A			
		23.	Do	Fo	(2)	An			
		24.	Do	Fo	(2)	A	P		
		25.	Do	FCw	(2)	A			

Case 3:   Structural Summary

$R = 25$ $Zf = 14$ $ZSum = 41.0$ $P = 4+2$ $(2) = 11$

Location Features		Determinants (Blends First)		Contents		Contents (Idiographic)	
W = 12	**DQ**	M.Fr = 1		H = 1		Keyhole	= 1
D = 9	+ = 5	FM.FC' = 1		(H) =		Top	= 1
Dd = 4	o = 13	FM.FY = 1		Hd = 1		Towns	= 1
S = 2	v = 5	m.CF = 1		(Hd) =			
		CF.YF.TF = 1		A = 8			
DW =	— = 2			(A) =			
		M =		Ad =			
		FM =		(Ad) =			
		m = 1		Ab =			
		C =		Al =			
Form Quality		CF = 1		An = 3			
		FC = 6		Art = 2			
FQx	FQf	C' =		Ay =			
		C'F -		Bl =			
+ = 0	+ = 0	FC' =		Bt = 3			
		T =		Cg =			
o = 19	o = 6	TF =		Cl =		**Special Scorings**	
		FT = 3		Ex = 1			
w = 4	w = 1	V -		Fi =		PSV	= 1
		VF -		Fd = 3			
— = 2	— = 1	FV =		Ge =		DV	=
		Y =		Hh =			
M Quality		YF -		Ls =		INCOM	=
		FY =		Na =			
+ = 0		rF -		Sx =		FABCOM	=
o — 1		Fr =		Xy =			
w = 0		FD = 1				CONTAM	=
		F = 8				ALOG	=
— = 0							=

RATIOS, PERCENTAGES, AND DERIVATIONS

ZSum-Zest = 41.0-45.5		FC:CF+C — 6:3		Afr — .93	
Zd = -4.5		W:M = 12:1		3r+(2)/R = .56	
EB = 1:6.0 EA = 7.0		W:D = 12.9		Cont.R = 10.25	
eb = 4:7 ep = 11		L = .47		H+Hd:A+Ad = 2:8	
				(H)+(Hd):(A)+(Ad) — 0:0	
Blends:R = 5:25		F+% = .75		H+A:Hd+Ad — 9:1	
a:p = 5:0		X+% — .76		XRT Achrom — 13.4"	
Ma:Mp = 1:0		A% = .32		XRT Chrom — 7.8"	

that is, one prone to discharge emotion in times of coping. Her *ep* is substantially greater than her *EA* (10:7), suggesting that she does not have ready access to many of her resources. Her *eb* contains two *m* determinants, suggesting feelings of being out of control, and that ratio is also heavily weighted on the right side, which consists of four *T* and two *Y* determinants. This indicates that she is experiencing uncommonly intense irritation related to ungratified needs for emotional affiliation, and that she probably feels helpless in dealing with her own needs. The preponderence of FC versus $CF+C$ responses indicates that her emotions are fairly well modulated when discharged, but the higher ep and the nature of the eb signal that she is not very secure in her thinking and/or behavior. She is much more responsive to emotionally toned stimuli than are most adults ($Afr = .92$), and although this responsiveness does coincide with her basic coping style, it may also exacerbate her intense need for emotional gratification. She is also much more self-centered than most adults ($3r + (2)/R = .56$), and this may be more juvenile than is useful at times ($Fr = 1$). She is also the sort of person who may tend to become overly involved with complex stimuli ($Lambda = .47$), and she seems prone to misinterpret some of those stimuli because she is not careful enough in sorting out the more important stimulus cues ($Zd = -4.5$). She works hard to organize her world ($Zf = 14$), but her tendencies to underincorporate, plus her excessive responsiveness to emotionally provoking stimuli, may reduce the effectiveness of that effort considerably. She probably feels helpless when prompted by her more basic needs *(both FM's are blended with FY)*, and this probably contributes much to her occasional feelings of being out of control. Her reality testing is quite good ($F+\% = .75$; $X+\% = .76$), but her ideation is typically characterized by less flexibility than might be desired ($a:p = 5:0$). This is particularly important since she needs to be flexible in attempting to meet her strong needs for affiliation. It may be that her tendency to overrespond to emotionally loaded stimuli, plus her excessive self-centeredness, may interfere with the development and maintenance of mature interpersonal relations. Overall problems of maturational failure may be contributing significantly to her current status.

Finished Interpretation.   The full Structural Summary does tend to support the postulate that some of her marked disarray may be directly attributable to the trauma of her recent divorce. However, there is also considerable evidence that this reaction overlays a more fundamental immature personality structure. The basic "clues" to the reactive phenomenon appear in the very high T frequency, which would be quite unusual for a chronic state, especially among those who have married; the presence of three Anatomy answers, which are somewhat unlikely in a person with no prior psychiatric history; plus the many contents that convey a sense of being "uprooted" (roots, root system, squashed cat, fried shrimp), or that convey emotions which do not exist (clown's lips, an exotic plant, a "greyish-blue" lizard). All these answers suggest a sense of vulnerability and/or exposure to the environment.

Nonetheless, there are other data, including some mentioned above, that may easily indicate a more long standing immature and/or dependent sort of personality structure. She offers seven lower level DQ scores (five v and two minus), suggesting a less mature cognitive development. The presence of a color-shading blend signifies some ambivalence about emotional displays, yet she is clearly an extratensive person. She offers only two Human contents, hinting that her conceptions of, and interactions with, people are not developed at a fully nature level. Her aspirational ratio $W:M = 12:1$) indicates that she probably strives for goals that are well beyond her functional capacity. At the same time, she delivers three Anatomy and three Food responses, the former possibly being related to some egocentric body concerns, while the latter is often found among the protocols of children or dependency oriented adults. Several of her answers denote a sense of the more immature (bumpy frog, squashed cat, ice cream, candy apples), yet her two emblem responses signal a fairly clear status orientation. This is a very unusual composite for most adults. There is little question that her self-concept is fragile (moths, squashed cat, fried shrimp, a keyhole, grasshopper, and so on) and her inquiry comment to her second "moth" response, ". . . that's how moths are, not very pretty, just dull and dark . . ." reflects something of how she views herself. Even her reflection answer conveys a sense of concern about the self; that is, she is inspecting to "see if everything is alright." This seems to link with the *FD* response, in which she is apparently trying to take some distance from herself. Thus, while she is very self-centered, there is reason to believe that she does not feel secure in her egocentricity but, rather, has a brittle and somewhat negative self-image.

Her sequence of scores indicates some attempt at control early on in the test. She "enters" the first two cards with pure *F* responses and generally restricts the number of answers that she delivers; however, she seems very "caught up" in the last three cards, providing a glimpse of the difficulty that she has in extracting herself from emotionally dominant stimuli. During the sequence to those three blots, she delivers four of her five vague *DQ* location selections, three of her six poor form quality responses, and all three of her *CF* responses. Although she manifests organizational activity in 10 of her 13 answers to Cards I through VII, she organizes in only three of her 10 responses to the last three blots. Some hint of an awareness of her excessive vulnerability to emotionally loaded stimuli is seen in the fact that she delivers four of her eight pure *F* answers during the last three cards, and she also becomes very preoccupied with the symmetrical characteristics of the blots during the same sequence, giving eight of her 11 pair answers. The colors appear to "turn her on," and while she tries to combat this impact, she remains prompted to an excessive level of responsiveness. Her response to Card III is especially interesting by reason of its content, and the fact that she ignores the Popular human figures until the inquiry. The response, ". . . a clown's mouth . . . you might paint human lips to exaggerate them . . . ," suggests rather superficial efforts at denial—that is, trying to convey emotions that are not there (laughing on the outside, but not on the inside).

Case 3 Summary.   This is a somewhat naive and immature woman who *is not* without many resources, but who currently feels quite helpless, ambivalent, and negative about herself. She is truly vulnerable, and while some of that vulnerability may be attributed to her sense of abandonment, it has been long predisposed by a failure to achieve full maturity. Emotions and emotional stimuli play a very important part in her life. It is her style, and she is very responsive to the features of her world that promote feelings; *and,* in spite of her helplessness, she generally modulates her affect quite well. There are no pure *C* answers here, and only one of her *CF* responses (fireworks) gives any hint of volatility. Although her *ep* is higher than her *EA,* the difference might best be judged as a function of the elevation in *T;* that is, she has become more "impacted" by her strong needs for affiliation. If those needs were gratified, or even reduced somewhat, her resources would probably sustain her coping requirements with relative effectiveness, as apparently was the case before her separation. Thus, while she has probably never achieved a full level of "maturation," a factor that may ultimately have contributed to her marital disarray, neither is she a totally inadequate person continually destined to failures of adjustment. Overall, her style is not unlike the hysteroid, who will often ignore or deny unpleasantness in the world, but who, under most circumstances, can also deliver affect in appealing and useful ways that often create and/or sustain interpersonal contacts, provided that the demands of those contacts are not too great.

Case 3: A Treatment Plan.   Using the Rorschach data as a starting point, it appears as though either or both of two approaches might be used in this case. Structurally, her most significant liabilities are her underincoporativeness, the higher *ep*, the overresponsiveness to emotional stimuli as represented in the *Afr*, the seemingly unrealistic aspirational level manifest in the $W:M$, her ideational inflexibility indicated by the $a:p$ ratio, her excessive egocentricity, and most of all, her strong need for affiliation illustrated by the high *T*, and her feelings of helplessness suggested by the composite of two *m* and two *FY* answers. A review of the content shows her to be quite immature and currently feeling very vulnerable.

In the context of a cost-benefit analysis, her most immediate problems, those of emotional affiliation and feelings of helplessness, can possibly be reduced or resolved through relatively brief treatment of a supportive nature, oriented toward a focus on emotional and social issues. She is already seeking support through her female physician; however, it is too indirect, since she must offer a physical complaint to achieve the contact. Although the physician could become a supportive therapist, the content of their interaction must be more directly oriented toward her psychological rather than her physical ills. Regardless of whether it is the physician or another supporting therapist, the contact should probably be supplemented by some form of group participation, possibly in a "women's" group, or, preferably, a heterosexual group of participants who have recently experienced the loss of a spouse. The goals of this approach, viewed from the context of the Rorschach, would be a reduction of the *T* related needs, the development of a sense of greater control (*m* and *Y*), and, hopefully, a reduction of the magnitude of *ep*, thereby creating a better balance between available resources and inner promptings. Such an approach might also reduce the body concern and some of the feelings of vulnerability reflected in the contents; *however*, in terms of the "optimal state," this treatment approach would leave several psychological stones unturned.

This approach for example, would probably do little about her underincorporativeness (although some delay tactics could be built into the individual support framework); it would probably not reduce the high level of egocentricity significantly; there would probably be little reduction in her overresponsiveness to emotional stimuli, or in her ideational inflexibility; it would be unlikely to substantially develop her maturity; and while her aspirational level might alter somewhat, it is doubtful that there would be a sudden shift to a more realistic form of aspiration. The approach would be "reconstitutive" rather than "reconstructive," and that may be sufficient. Again, viewed from a cost-benefit perspective, it would probably be worth trying with a view to reevaluation after some specific time interval.

In a more optimal framework, there is need for much more personality growth, which can be achieved only by a longer term form of intervention. Such treatment would focus on issues of "supportive development" rather than an uncovering focus on the past. The treatment would be insight oriented, and the therapist would have to learn to contend with her ideational inflexibility and her tendency to couch translations or interpretations into the more concrete cognitive approach that she currently manifests. It seems logical to assume that the success of such an approach would depend, in part, on an early development of trust in herself and, consequently, an alteration in the now negative self-image. Ultimately, the treatment focus would have to include the elements of her overresponsiveness to emotional stimuli, and, more particularly, the entire issue of self-concept and sex role identification. Although this approach may be the more "optimal" in terms of goals, it is also fraught with potential problems. She is dependency oriented, and this dependency may be reinforced by a long term relationship, which could be difficult to sever. Her underincorporativeness and her lack of ideational flexibility are almost certain to create many difficulties, especially early in the treatment; and her current tendencies to avoid ideation (there is only one M in the record) may pose many problems for her when she is required to produce "ideational" material. This is not to suggest that a long term approach might fail, for there is no evidence to that effect in the record; but when viewed in the spectrum of cost-benefit, the cost may be too great for her at this time. Naturally, the options should be hers to whatever degree is possible. She might opt for a "growth oriented" form of treatment rather than one that is primarily supportive; or, even if she selects the short term supportive approach, some of the obvious features, such as the immaturity and low self esteem, may be stronger than is recognized here, and may ultimately generate a longer term "contract."

Case 3: Epilogue.   This patient did opt for weekly "supportive" sessions with her physician, during which they began to discuss openly the pain and agony resulting from the marital trauma and her fears of being isolated and not being able to "raise" her children properly. During the sixth session, the issue of occupational independence was broached, and she ultimately decided to enroll in a technical school for skill training. During the second treatment month, she also joined a heterosexual group that focused on interpersonal transactions. During the fifth treatment month she began dating, and the frequency of support sessions was reduced by half. All treatment was terminated during the eighth month, except for occasional visits thereafter, and she was ultimately successful in gaining employment at the end of her first school year. A second Rorschach completed at that time revealed that she continued to be more egocentric than most, and less mature than might be desired; however, the T frequency had reduced, and the m and Y variables had disappeared. Although the Anatomy responses did not appear, she continued to give three Food answers, and the Zd score was -4.0. Nonetheless, she reported herself to be in excellent health, responsive to her children, and no longer confronted with her earlier feelings of loneliness. Although she reported dating often, she had no immediate plans for marriage but suggested the possibility for the future.

Cases 17 and 18: Two 25 Year Olds—Marital Disarray

Although treatment planning for one subject involves many decisions, the alternatives often increase in geometric proportions when a couple is involved. Most couples who seek therapy anticipate being treated as a couple; however, there are many instances in which such an approach can be potentially disastrous to one of the pair, if not both. Unfortunately, all marriages are not made in heaven, nor are they necessarily sustained through faith alone. While the presenting problems of a couple may often appear to be "marriage based," the treatment plan may require that each of the pair be considered separately as well as a couple. The following is a useful example.

History.   The male (Case 17) offers the presenting complaint. He is impotent. He is unable to achieve an erection under most circumstances, and when that rarity does occur, he becomes flacid at the moment of penetration. They have been married for three years, with no children. He reports a satisfactory adjustment during their first marital year; however, the achievement of an erection has become more and more difficult during the past seven months. Their first contact was with a general practitioner, who, after examining both, offered them a "manual" on sexual adjustment that both had read previously. He then referred the male to a neurologist who, after a complete examination, found no positive signs and referred both to an internist. After another thorough physical examination, the internist suggested the possibility of "sex therapy." The sex therapist suggested that before they became involved in sex therapy, a psychological evaluation would be in order, and directed the referral that resulted in the testing.

The male, age 25, is the third of four children, having an older brother, age 35, an older sister, age 33, and a younger sister, age 23. All of his siblings are married. The brother is a college graduate and owns a small business. The older sister is also a college graduate and teaches science in a junior high school. She has two children. The younger sister completed two years of college before marrying and moving to a distant state. She also has two children. His father, age 62, is a printer, while the mother, age 63, has worked as a receptionist for a dentist during the past 10 years, but has no prior work experience outside of the home. The subject completed college as a secondary education major, specializing in history, at age 21, and obtained a position teaching history in high school shortly thereafter. One year later he was appointed an Instructor in a social sciences department of a community college, and has held that position for the past three years. He describes himself as a "quiet, hard working" person who dated only occasionally during his high school years. His first heterosexual experience occurred at age 16 with a prostitute. He continued to visit prostitutes during his first two college years, but then established a "sexual" relationship with a young woman in one of his classes. That relationship continued until shortly after his graduation, when she accepted a position teaching in another state. He claims that there was no discussion of marriage, although neither dated others during the last two college years. He met his wife during his year of teaching high school, at which time she was working as a secretary for the school. They dated very frequently during the remainder of that year, and began having intercourse frequently, which each describes as "mutually" satisfying. They ultimately became engaged, and married approximately two months before he accepted his college teaching position. He is described as being of average height but slightly overweight. His medical history is unremarkable.

The female, age 25, is equal in height to her husband, but considerably thinner than expected for her height and body frame. Her medical history includes an appendectomy at age 14, and treatment for a spastic colon between the ages of 16 and 18. She reports no recurrence of that condition after age 18, at which time she graduated from high school. She is the fourth of five children, having three older sisters, ages 34, 32, and 27, and a younger brother, age 18. Her oldest sister is a high school graduate, was married at age 19, and has three children. Her 32 year old sister also married at age 19, and continued for one more year in secretarial school. She worked four years as a pool stenographer before having the first of her two children. Her 27 year old sister is a college graduate, and currently teaches elementary school. She was married at age 25 and is now pregnant. Her brother is a senior in high school. Her father, age 60, is a foreman in a lumber yard. Her mother, age 57, has not been employed outside the home. When the subject was age 15, the mother entered psychiatric treatment for "nerves" and has been a periodic patient. Her 27 year old sister has also received psychiatric treatment during the past three years for an undescribed problem, and has participated in group psychotherapy in the past year on a regular basis. After graduating high school, the subject entered formal secretarial training, and after one year obtained the position she was holding when she met her husband. Shortly after her marriage, she obtained a better paying position as an assistant manager in the office of a social service agency. She is currently in her third year in that position, which she now describes as putting excessive pressure on her. She has been considering leaving the job for about two months. She complains of being given too much responsibility and too many confusing directives from her supervisors. She reports that she has become increasingly tense and nervous during the last two months, and has recently become fearful of driving a car. She freely admits that her marriage has been "unfulfilling" during the past 18 months, but attributes part of this to the pressures of her job, and denies any consideration of divorce or separation. She feels that her husband's sexual difficulties contribute in only a minor way to her overall view of her marriage. On the other hand, her spouse identifies "their" sex problem as the major cause of their difficulties since their first marital year. He regards the possibility of sex therapy with some optimism, but she is much more cautious about it.

The basic approach in formulating a treatment plan for this couple is to evaluate each as individuals, identifying assets and liabilities, and establishing a priority of possible treatment targets. Subsequently, the information from each record should be integrated, in a comparative way, to evaluate similarities and differences in styles, and especially in terms of targets for intervention. The mixture of data should provide significant clues to the characteristics of the problems of each of the pair and provide a base from which meaningful treatment recommendations can be formulated. The record of the male will be approached first here, since he offers the presenting problem.

Case 17: Structural Interpretation

The data of the Four Square reveal several important features. First, the EB (2 : 2.5) indicates that he is an ambitent, having no marked coping style, and is possibly prone to some vacillation in situations that require coping. Second, the ep is substantially greater than EA, reflecting a person who is impinged upon by many

Case 17

Card		Free Association		Inquiry	Scoring
I	16″	1. I suppose it c.b. a bf, its rather torn tho, lik it was decaying	E: S:	(Rpts S's resp) It seems lik it w.b. dead to be lik this, its all dark & its ragged @ the edges, lik some of the wings had already fallen off thru the decaying process	WSo m^p.FYo Ad (P) 3.5
			E:	Can u show me a bit more of why it ll that?	
			S:	Well there r the holes in it too, but I thk bec its all dark is mainly why I thot of decay	
		E: Most people c more than 1 thg			
		2. The cntr part c.b. a crab	E: S:	(Rpts S's resp) Its got the prongs up here & it has that general body shape to it, lik a crab (points) c here	Do Fo A
II	38″	V3. If I turn it this way it ll an explosion up here, lik flames coming out	E: S:	(Rpts S's resp) Well it re me of a gas well expl or s.t. lik that with the flames shooting out, c here	Do m^a.CFo Ex
			E:	What is it there that makes it ll flames?	
			S:	Well its all red & c the pointed shapes, lik an explo	
		4. U kno the cntr part c.b. a top, lik it was balanced lik when they r spinning	E: S:	(Rpts S's resp) I wasn't really thkg of a top, but a gyroscope, u kno u pull the string & thy stay balanced lik this bec they spin a long time, its a pretty good shape of one, just the white area	DSo m^ao Top
III	55″	5. Well ths ll 2 people pullg s.t. apart, thy sort of ll cannibals	E: S:	(Rpts S's resp) I'm not sure if thyr men or wm but thyr black lik African peopl & I guess thats what re me of cannibals & thyr pullg on ths thg I dk what it is	D+ M^a.FC'o (2) H P 3.0

			E/S	Response / Inquiry	Scoring
IV		V6.		U kno ths way the darker area ll an x-ray of the pelvic area, u can c the pelvis & some of the borey structure of the upper leg	
			E:	(Rpts S's resp)	Do FYo Xy
			S:	Well it has that shape to it & its dark lik an x-ray is, c ths r the upper leg parts & ths is the pelvis (points)	
	21″	7.		Ths ll a pelt to me, lik the skin off of some furry A	
			E:	(Rpts S's resp)	Wo TFo Ad P 2.0
			S:	Well its all furry looking the way the colors r there & its sort of jagged around the edges lik a pelt w.b.	
		<8.		If u turn it ths way ths part ll a seal, it ll he's honking for food or s.t.	
			E:	(Rpts S's resp)	Do $FM^{a}o$ A
			S:	Well ths is the head & here is the body, c the nose is up like he was honking for food the way they do in the circus	
V	13″	9.		That ll a bat if u don't use the outer parts	
			E:	(Rpts S's resp)	Ddo Fo A (P)
			S:	Here r the big wgs & the body, it just ll a bat to me	
		10.		Those outer parts sort of ll tree roots	
			E:	(Rpts S's resp)	Do Fo (2) Bt
			S:	Thy just rem me of that, thy have that shape to them, c on either side, just tree roots	
VI	27″	11.		Ths top part ll an insect, maybe lik a fly	
			E:	(Rpts S's resp)	Do $FM^{a}o$ A
			S:	It has the wgs out lik it was flying along & the narrow body, I guess lik a draginfly rather than a house fly bec of the narrow body, house flies have a fatter body than this	
		12.		Ths cntr part c.b. a canal to, lik down in a ditch	
			E:	(Rpts S's resp)	Do FVo Canal
			S:	Just the part (points) the line here is darker so it w.b. the canal & then it comes up, c it gets lighter (shows w hands)	

Case 17 (Continued)

Card		Free Association		Inquiry	Scoring
VII	70″	13. Gee all I can thk of here is a bunch of clouds moving along	E:	(Rpts S's resp)	Wv $m^p.YFo$ Cl 2.5
			S:	Well thyr all dark lik storm clds or s.t., just a bunch of them	
			E:	A bunch?	
			S:	Well lik a group of them the way thy r laid out there, its really one cloud but its sort of broken apart, like thy were moving to take different positions	
VIII	18″	14. Ths ll a cpl of A's climbg a tree or s.t.	E:	(Rpts S's resp)	$W+$ FM^ao (2) A,Bt P 4.5
			S:	C one on each side & the middle w.b. the tree, c its kind of pointed at the top & has a fuller lower part, thy ll cats or s.t. c the legs & bodies & heads	
IX	45″	<15. Ths part re me of a man playg a saxophone	E:	(Rpts S's resp)	$D+$ M^a+ H 2.5
			S:	He's a chubby guy, c here's his head & big body & ths w.b. the sax here (points) its narrower at the upper part & then comes to the horn below it	
X	15″	16. Ths c.b. a maple seed lik its falling off a tree & spinning down	E:	(Rpts S's resp)	Do m^po Bt
			S:	It has that shape to it w the littl seed pods on the ends, lik an inverted V, u kno what I mean?	
		17. I guess that pink c.b. a bld stain, dried up	E:	(Rpts S's resp)	Dv $C.Y$ Bl
			S:	Well its its pink rather than the deep red of fresh blood & u can c the way the different colors r there that its more lik a dried stain, thyr not uniform, so it looks dried up, o.k.?	

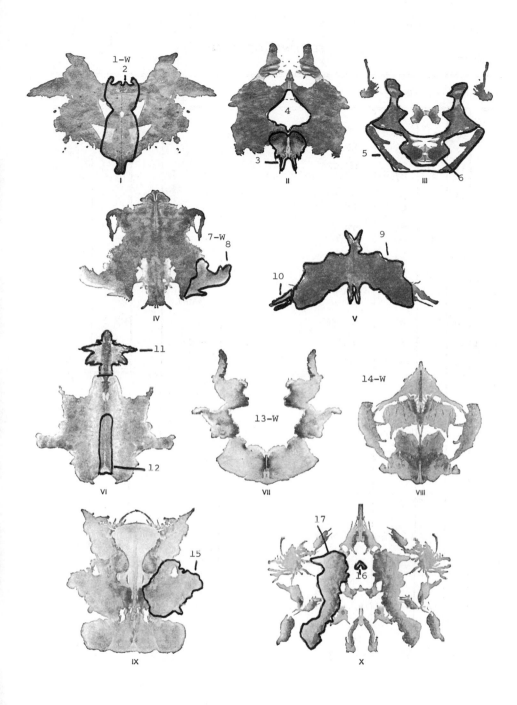

Case 17

CARD	RT	NO.	LOCATION	DETERMINANTS (S)		CONTENT (S)	POP	Z SCORE	SPECIAL
I	16"	1.	WSo	m^p.FYo		Ad	(P)	3.5	
		2.	Do	Fo		A			
II	38"	3.	Do	m^a.CFo		Ex			
		4.	DSo	m^ao		Top			
III	55"	5.	D+	M^a.FC'o	(2)	H	P	3.0	
		6.	Do	FYo		Xy			
IV	21"	7.	Wo	TFo		Ad	P	2.0	
		8.	Do	FM^ao		A			
V	13"	9.	Ddo	Fo		A	(P)		
		10.	Do	Fo	(2)	Bt			
VI	27"	11.	Do	FM^ao		A			
		12.	Do	FVo		Canal			
VII	70"	13.	Wv	m^p.YFo		Cl		2.5	
VIII	18"	14.	W+	FM^ao	(2)	A,Bt	P	4.5	
IX	45"	15.	D+	M^a+		H		2.5	
X	15"	16.	Do	m^po		Bt			
		17.	Dv	C.Y		Bl			

Case 17: Structural Summary

R = 17   Zf = 6   ZSum = 18.0   P = 3+2   (2) = 3

Location Features			Determinants (Blends First)		Contents		Contents (Idiographic)	
W	= 4	DQ	M.FC'	=1	H	= 2	Canal	=1
D	= 12	+ = 3	m.CF	=1	(H)	=		
			m.YF	=1	Hd	=	Top	=1
Dd	= 1	o = 12	m.FY	=1	(Hd)	=		
			C.Y	=1	A	= 5		=
S	= 2	v = 2			(A)	=		
					Ad	= 2		=
DW =		— = 0	M	= 1	(Ad)	=		
			FM	= 3	Ab	=		=
			m	= 2	Al	=		
			C	=	An	=		=
Form Quality			CF	=	Art	=		
			FC	–	Ay	=		=
FQx		FQf	C'	=	Bl	= 1		
			C'F	=	Bt	= 2,1		=
+	= 1	+ = 0	FC'	=	Cg	=		
o	= 15	o = 3	T	=	Cl	= 1	Special Scorings	
w	= 0	w = 0	TF	= 1	Ex	= 1		
—	= 0	— = 0	FT	=	Fi	=	PSV	=
			V	=	Fd	=		
M Quality			VF	=	Ge	=	DV	=
			FV	= 1	Hh	=		
+	= 1		Y	=	Ls	=	INCOM	=
o	– 1		YF	=	Na	=		
w	= 0		FY	= 1	Sx	=	FABCOM	=
			rF	=	Xy	= 1	CONTAM	=
—	= 0		Fr	=			ALOG	=
			FD	=				=
			F	– 3				

RATIOS, PERCENTAGES, AND DERIVATIONS

ZSum-Zest	= 18.0–17.0		FC:CF+C	= 1:2	Afr	= .31	
Zd	= +1.0		W:M	= 4:2	3r+(2)/R	= .18	
EB	= 2:2.5	EA = 4.5	W:D	= 4:12	Cont:R	= 9:17	
eb	= 8:7	ep = 15	L	= .21	H+Hd:A+Ad	= 2:7	
					(H)+(Hd):(A)+(Ad)	= 0:0	
Blends:R	= 5:17		F+%	= 100	H+A:Hd+Ad	= 7:2	
a:p	– 7:3		X+%	= .94	XRT Achrom	= 29.4"	
Ma:Mp	– 2:0		A%	= .41	XRT Chrom	= 34.2"	

spontaneous psychological activities that far exceed his immediately available resources. The *eb* includes five *m* responses on the left side, representing a very frequent experience of feeling out of control, while the right side of that ratio includes four *Y* determinants, plus one each *V*, *C'*, and *T*. The four *Y* answers signal strong feelings of helplessness, while the single *V* response probably hints at an introspective process that is having a negative yield. Although he gives only three chromatic color responses in this record, one is a *CF*, while a second is a pure C, indicating that when he does engage in affective discharge, he has much trouble modulating the discharge and may often become overwhelmed and directed by it. The *Afr* (.31) offers a clue that he may have some awareness of his dilemma and tries very hard to avoid situations that are emotionally provocative. Nevertheless, his *Lambda* (.21) is very low, indicating that he finds it difficult to extract himself from complex stimulus situations. His *egocentricity index* (.18) is also inordinately low, revealing very low self-esteem. This probably relates to the lower than expected $W:M$ (4:2), signaling that he does not set very high aspirations, and his relatively low frequency of organizational activity ($Zf = 6$). His reality testing appears quite adequate ($F+\% = 100$; $X+\% = 94$), although he offers a lower number of *true* Populars than would be expected. The color-shading blend ($C.Y$) appearing in the record indicates considerable ambivalence about emotional displays. This is especially interesting in the light of the very long average reaction times, which suggest that his attempts at delay are often quite unsuccessful. Overall, the structural data suggest a fairly primitive and/or very immature person, with only limited resources effectively organized in an accessible form, who has no marked style of coping and feels out of control very often and helpless in contending with that feeling. He seems somewhat withdrawn, but vulnerable, and with markedly low self-esteem.

Interpretation of the Scoring Sequence. Both of his S answers appear early in the record, and can probably be attributed to some irritation at being scrutinized. All his reaction times are very long, suggesting that when he does offer a particularly revealing answer, he may have been overwhelmed by the need state itself in the "final selection" process. His Z efforts appear somewhat erratically, and, interestingly, the only color response that appears during the last three cards is his "sign out" response, which is both a color-shading blend and a pure C answer. It follows his fifth m answer, as if to signal that the complexity of the last blot finally overwhelmed him, as contrasted with his more "effective" productions on Cards VIII and IX.

Interpretation of the Content. His first answer speaks of his troubled state; he is fragile, torn, and decaying. It is a morbid, helpless, and pessimistic sort of answer; however, when prompted for an additional response, he is able to withdraw a bit by presenting a "barrier" form of response, even though the content, a crab, is not very positive. His reaction time more than doubles when presented with Card II, and, interestingly, he never responds to the grey-black area of the card. Instead, after the very long period of examination, he seems to yield to his internal disarray, giving both the m and CF determinants in the explosion content, from which he withdraws to the white space and implies feelings of precariousness in the spinning top. His first Card III answer, ". . . two people pulling something apart . . . ," illustrates his own internal conflict, and on a more speculative level, may represent his own marital conflict. It is interesting that, following that answer, a third penetration form of answer is delivered, a pelvis, which he identifies as congruent with his own "problem area," ". . . you can see the pelvis and some of the boney structure of the upper leg." There are several other answers in the record which also signify his helplessness and vulnerability; a seal "honking" for food on IV, exposed tree roots on V, an insect and a ditch on VI, a falling maple seed on X, and the interesting 70 second ". . . bunch of clouds . . ." response on VII. The latter is important here, since most people identify the Popular response, Humans, either as women or children, rather easily. His best response seems to be the Card IX, ". . . man playing a saxophone," another form of honking. There are very few "sturdy" contents among his responses, the crab on I, a bat on V (but with the extremities of the blot omitted), and the animals climbing a tree on VIII; and these are the only contents, other than the man playing a saxophone, that seem to reflect a more adult kind of answer, that is, aspects of maturity.

Case 17 Summary.   The Rorschach composite defines a man in acute pain because of his helplessness and inability to gain control over his own emotions. He tries to withdraw from, but will often become trapped by, emotionally loaded situations, and he lacks the mature access to resources that would aid him in warding off current stresses. He seems to vacillate between aggressive barriers that he "puts up" to defend against stress, and almost total feelings of a fragile vulnerability to those stresses. He does not modulate emotion well, and probably has trouble establishing and/or maintaining effective interpersonal contacts. He is an intense person with deep and often frightening feelings, and seems not to have learned to differentiate between anger and assertiveness, volatility and modulated delivery of affect, and adequate coping techniques to use in everyday stress situations. He is completely "open" or aggressively "closed," and at least some of his current problems seem to be a direct product of this overall maturational lag. Ordinarily, he might be considered a good prospect for an insight oriented form of developmental psychotherapy; however, such a recommendation should be deferred until this material can be viewed in the context of data collected from his wife.

Case 18: Structural Interpretation

This is a very unusual Four Square for an adult, primarily because the EB contains *no* chromatic color component. She is clearly a very introversive person, but more than that, during the entire test situation she never acknowledges the chromatic features of the five blots in which they exist. Many people will deliver only one or two color answers while favoring an M approach; however, the complete absence of color in a record that is otherwise rich tends to signal an unusual constriction. Although her cp is slightly higher than her EA, it is not completely clear whether she has sufficient coping resources available in light of the color constriction. The logic here is that everyone, unless massively paralyzed psychologically, delivers some affect at times; and this woman is not paralyzed, as is evidenced by the huge number of M responses that she gives. Interestingly, her Afr (.62) shows no withdrawal from emotionally toned stimuli. The data in the eb may offer some clue to this. The left side is predominantly FM (4), while the right side of that ratio consists of one T, one Y, and *two* C' responses. The latter may represent emotions that are currently being inhibited, but that may be more available under other circumstances. While giving a normal length record, she also delivers slightly fewer blends than might be expected, suggesting a reduction in natural complexity. Her *egocentricity index* (.52) indicates that she is much more self-centered than

Case 18

Card		Free Association		Inquiry	Scoring
I	3"	1. I suppose it ll different kinds of moths or insects, I'll say a Bf	E:	(Rpts S's resp)	Wo Fo A P 1.0
			S:	What made me thk of it first was the BF wings there I guess & the body part in the middl	
		E: Most peopl c more than 1 thg			
		2. It c.b. a bat too, its all black it c.b. one I suppose, that's all tho	E:	(Rpts S's resp)	Wo FC'o A P 1.0
			S:	Cuse its blk, c the wgs & body, just lik the bf only u c it black here	
II	7"	3. I wonder who drew these pictures, thyr really hard to make out, I suppose it c.b. 2 peopl having their hands together	E:	(Rpts S's resp)	W+ M^{p}o (2) H 4.5 DV
			S:	Well thy dont really ll peopl, but u cld guess that if u let this top b the heads & here wld b the hands & there r the bodies, the dark part	
				It just ll 2 people w their hands togethr, I really don't kno what made me thk of that	
		4. It cld ever: ll a cats face, at least this part here, there's 2 of them & they hav their paws together	E:	(Rpts S's resp)	D+ FM^{p}o (2) A (P) 3.0
			S:	Well its s.k. of A w its paws togethr one on each side, it has a small ear & the nose & the paw, c thy r touching, one on each side, U can hardly make it out ths r so weird its hard to make anythg of them	
III	9"	5. Thy don't ll much, I can't b sure but mayb its 2 people facing e.o. lik thyr standg up there & thy hav their hands down at their sides	E:	(Rpts S's resp)	D+ M^{p}o (2) H P 4.0
			S:	I really don't kno what it is, but I said 2 peopl cuz u cld stretch u'r mind to thk that lik here is the head & the bodies & the arms, just down at their sides, lik they r just facing e.o., u kno, lik lookg at e.o., but not really doing a.t.	

366

IV	15"	6. Ths ll sk of monster or s.t. there's really big ft & a face up here, lik the face of a bird or s.t.	E: (Rpts S's resp) S: Well it has this whole body here & the face is lik a bird & the big feet, just lik s.k. of monster, i:s big lookg	*Wo Fo (A)* 2.0
		7. If I just look at the face part & these littl parts here it remind me of a big hairy bird, its separate from the monster & if u look at these lines it ll a lot of hair	E: (Rpts S's resp) S: Its a weird bird, lik it, has ths beak & a really hairy face & small wings lik hunched up just in a big hairy ball E: I'm not sure I c it as hairy S: C these lines, thy look hairy to me	*Do FTw A*
V	12"	8. I'd say it ll to me s.k. of flying insect	E: (Rpts S's resp) S: U really can't tell what kind, just an insect w the wgs out lik its flying & the head is here (points), weird looking	*Wo FM^{a}o A (P)* 1.0
		9. These ll legs out here one on each side	E: (Rpts S's resp) S: I d.k., it ll some kind of leg lik of a person w the toes curled up E: Curled up? S: Well u can't c the foot well so it must be kind of curled up	*Do Fo (2) Hd*
VI	52"	10. To me it ll a person on a post w his arms out & legs dwn & down here is a lot of blood lik they shot him	E: (Rpts S's resp) S: Oh yes, I rem the blood, well its up here, the person c the head, a face is there vaguely. & the arms r down at the sides & the way he's on the post it ll s.b. shot him & this is the pool of blood out in front of him, lik coming out toward u E: Out toward u? S: Well its bigger lik closer, its all runny c the lines in it make it look all runny lik a pool of blood	*W– M^P.Y.FD– H,Bl* 2.5 (ALOG)

367

Case 18 (Continued)

Card	Free Association	Inquiry	Scoring
	11. If u just take the top part it cld b an Indian chief w his arms spread out & he's got feathers on his arms, lik an Indian costume	E: (Rpts S's resp) S: I'm looking at it different now, just the top & these wld b the feathers on his costume like a ceremonial robe & he has his arms stretched out lik calling or signaling	Do M^Po (H)
VII	12. It ll the faces of two pigs in here	E: (Rpts S's resp) S: Thy hav big ears & the short snout its just the faces, u can c the eye in the one, c here (points)	Do Fo (2) Ad
25″	13. Up here it ll 2 girls lookg at e.o., thy each have a pony tail	E: (Rpts S's resp) S: It just rem me of that, c the pony tail & the forehead & nose & chin, lik thyr just lookg at eo.	D+ M^Po (2) Hd P 3.0
VIII	14. Ths part re me of ribs or s.t. lik some insides	E: (Rpts S's resp) S: This is the spine & the ribs, c rite here, u can c its shaped like that is shaped	Do Fo An
28″	15. On the sides r 2 A's crawling up, lik up a tree, lik thy r tryg to reach a branch	E: (Rpts S's resp) S: C the animals r on the side, lik small a's, legs here (points) & ths is the head & this down here c.b. a rock & the rest is a tree mayb & thy r reaching up for this branch, I suppose it c.b. a.thg mayb a bush rather than a tree, but thy r reaching up for this part	W+ FM^ao (2) A,Bt P 4.5
IX	16. 2 peopl w a funny hat on & thy hav guns just lik thyr shootg at e.o.	E: (Rpts S's resp) S: Up here, the orange part, c the pointy hats & these wld b the guns & the faces & fat bodies & the way its here u can c the bullets going back & forth, c these lines here, these w/b the bullets from the guns, shooting at e.o.	D+ $M^a.m^ao$ (2) H 4.5 ALOG
62″			

X	67"			

17. It ll 2 spiders up here

    E: (Rpts S's resp)

    S: C the way thy r drawn here w a the legs makes them ll that, lik spiders

    Do Fo (2) A P

18. Ths ll s.k. of animal w big horns, c 2 of them, lik thy were leang forward

    E: (Rpts S's resp)

    S: C here, big horns on them, & its lik the legs were up in under, u can't c them well, lik thy r leapg but I dk what kind of A it is

    Do FM^{a}o (2) A

19. Ths part is lik 2 weird peopl tryg to hurt e.o. w this big stick lik thg

    E: (Rpts S's resp)

    S: U can't really make out their faces very well, thy hav liitl legs & weird shaped heads & t 1yr trying to hurt e.o. w this big thg in the cntr, ths stick lik thg

    D+ M^{a}o (2) (H) 2.5

20. There is another face dwn here, w horns too

    E: (Rpts S's -esp)

    S: C its here (points), it has horns on it, lik some weird animal I guess, just the face part

    Do Fo Ad

21. Ths prt ll a weird lookg persn kind of lik staring at u, ugh that's all

    E: (Rpts S's resp)

    S: He has a funny peak to his head & these white eyes, lik mayb he's glaring, just staring straight ahead, & he has big bushy sideburns that harg down below his face too c here r his nostrils (points) & his chin is here so thy go down below his face, really weird looking, mean looking, just staring out lik that

    DdS- M^p.FC'- Hd 6.0

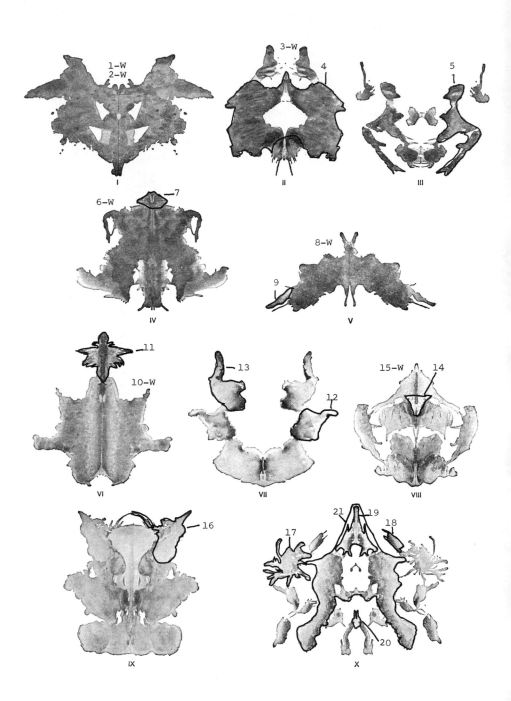

Case 18

CARD	RT	NO.	LOCATION	DETERMINANTS (S)		CONTENT (S)	POP	Z SCORE	SPECIAL
I	3"	1.	Wo	Fo		A	P	1.0	
		2.	Wo	FC'o		A	P	1.0	
II	7"	3.	W+	M^po	(2)	H		4.5	DV
		4.	D+	FM^po	(2)	Ad	(P)	3.0	
III	9"	5.	D+	M^po	(2)	H	P	4.0	
IV	15"	6.	Wo	Fo		(A)		2.0	
		7.	Do	FTw		A			
V	12"	8.	Wo	FM^ao		A	(P)	1.0	
		9.	Do	Fo	(2)	Hd			
VI	52"	10.	W−	M^p.Y.FD−		H,Bl		2.5	(ALOG)
		11.	Do	M^po		(H)			
VII	25"	12.	Do	Fo	(2)	Ad			
		13.	D+	M^po	(2)	Hd	P	3.0	
VIII	28"	14.	Do	Fo		An			
		15.	W+	FM^do	(2)	A,Bt	P	4.5	
IX	62"	16.	D+	M^a.m^ao	(2)	H		4.5	ALOG
X	67"	17.	Do	Fo	(2)	A	P		
		18.	Du	FM^ao	(2)	A			
		19.	D+	M^ao	(2)	(H)		2.5	
		20.	Do	Fo		Ad			
		21.	DdS−	M^p.FC'−		Hd		6.0	

Case 18

R = 21   Zf = 13   ZSum = 39.5   P = 6+2   (2) = 11

Location Features		Determinants (Blends First)	Contents	Contents (Idiographic)

Location Features

W = 7

D = 13   **DQ**

Dd = 1   + = 7

S = 1   o = 12

DW =   v = 0

            — = 2

Form Quality

FQx   **FQf**

+ = 0   + = 0

o = 18   o = 7

w = 1   w = 0

— = 2   — = 0

M Quality

+ = 0

o = 6

w = 0

— = 2

Determinants (Blends First)

M.m   = 1
M.Y.FD   = 1
M.FC'   = 1

M   = 5
FM = 4
m   =
C   =
CF =
FC =
C' =
C'F =
FC' = 1
T   =
TF =
FT = 1
V   =
VF =
FV =
Y   =
YF =
FY =
rF =
Fr =
FD =
F   = 7

Contents

H   = 4
(H) = 2
Hd   = 3
(Hd) =
A   = 7
(A) = 1
Ad   = 3
(Ad) =
Ab   =
Al   =
An   = 1
Art =
Ay   =
Bl   = 0,1
Bt   = 0,1
Cg   =
Cl   =
Ex   =
Fi   =
Fd   =
Ge   =
Hh   =
Ls   =
Na   =
Sx   =
Xy   =

Special Scorings

PSV   =

DV   = 1

INCOM   =

FABCOM   =

CONTAM   =

ALOG   = 1,1

         =

RATIOS, PERCENTAGES, AND DERIVATIONS

ZSum-Zest =	39.5-41.5		FC:CF+C = 0:0	Afr	= .62
Zd	= -2.0		W:M = 7:8	3r+(2)/R	= .52
EB	= 8:0	EA = 8.0	W:D = 7:13	Cont:R	= 3:21
eb	= 5:4	ep = 9	L = .50	H+Hd:A+Ad = 9:11 (H)+(Hd):(A)+(Ad) = 2:1	
Blends:R	= 3:21		F+% = 100	H+A:Hd+Ad = 14:6	
a:p	= 6:7		X+% = .86	XRT Achrom = 21.4"	
Ma:Mp	= 2:6		A% = .52	XRT Chrom = 26.6"	

most adults, and the slightly lowered *Lambda* (.50) signifies that she may not be able to back away from complexity as much as is usual. One of the most striking features of the structural data is the nature of her movement answers. While the *a* : *p* ratio (6 : 7) might ordinarily suggest ideational flexibility, the preponderance of passive movement answers is somewhat unique, as most people will give a few more active movement responses; however, the $M^a : M^p$ ratio (2 : 6) provides some clarification. Most of her deliberate ideations are passive—that is, marked by a "Snow White" sort of fantasy. In other words, although she uses ideation as her major coping technique, she is not usually oriented toward problem solving, but rather to some form of "passive escapism." In addition, two of her M responses are *minus,* and thus raise a question about a thinking distortion or disturbance. The record contains only two *Special Scores;* nonetheless, the two $M-$ answers issue an alert for close examination of their characteristics, and especially for evidence of severe distortion. In a possibly related context, there are several features in the structure that may indicate a kind of super-suspiciousness or guardedness. These include the slightly elevated Zf (13), the constricted number of contents (3), the substantial emphasis on Human contents (9), and the disproportionate number of Hd and Ad contents in relation to H and A. Such a configuration, while not necessarily definitive, is relatively common to those who try to narrow their world to more precise levels, and who are generally very guarded against the potential "intrusions" of others. When studied in relation to the M minus responses, these elements could signal what might be described as a "paranoid style" (Shapiro, 1965)—that is, the style of a person who remains distanciated in the world, has considerable difficulty in the interpersonal sphere, and often seeks shelter in a fantasy world that may easily violate reality. Her disproportionate $W:M$ (7:8) reveals that she is not very willing to extend the utilization of her functional resources. She has two unusual blends, one including both Human and inanimate movement, suggesting that some of her ideation provokes a sense of loss of control. The second involves M, Y and FD, and may relate to the first; that is, it may indicate an initiated ideation with a concurrent feeling of helplessness and an introspective operation. Her reality testing is quite good, as is evidenced by the high $F+\%$ and $X+\%$, and while she has a higher than usual Z frequency, her Zd score is within normal limits. Overall, the structural data reveal a person unwilling or unable to discharge affect deliberately; who appears to cope quite often by using a very passive fantasy existence; who is much more self-centered than is common; who shows some evidence of an ideational distortion; and who manifests some of the features common to those who are often quite distant and guarded in their world.

Interpretation of the Scoring Sequence.   Although she begins with a W oriented approach, she tends toward a greater D emphasis as the test progresses. Her pure F answers are well distributed, and she "enters" five of the 10 cards using only that determinant. Both these features suggest some cautiousness, as do her progressively longer reaction times. Her only S location in the record occurs in her last answer to Card X, and is joined with one of her two M minus responses. She manifests organizational activity on every card and has no significant P failures, although she does neglect the *true* Populars on III and V.

Interpretation of the Content.   She begins with a considerable qualification of her response, "I suppose it looks like different kinds . . .", but then proceeds to offer a Popular. This is probably part of her very cautious style. She leaves her options open, needing to defend her judgment. Her second response, another Popular, has a similar qualification, "It could be . . . it could be one I suppose . . .", and the same format appears in her first response to the second blot, ". . . they are really hard to make out, I suppose it could be . . ." Her description of the interaction between the humans on Card II is both guarded and peculiar, ". . . having their hands together," and similarly, the humans perceived on Card III, ". . . have their hands down at their sides." None of the humans in those responses are identified by sex, which is also true in her answers on Card IX (two people with funny hats shooting at each other) and X (two people trying to hurt each other with this big stick). In fact, other than the butterfly response on Card I, and the two girls looking at each other on Card VII, none of her contents would be particularly identified as "feminine," raising a question about her self-concept and her sex role identity. Several of her responses are quite aggressive in character (a person shot, people shooting, a face with horns, people trying to hurt each other, and a weird person staring at you). The last answer is her M minus response on Card X, and has a very marked "paranoid" flavor. The other M minus, on Card VI, is much more gruesome. She identifies a man on a post who has been shot, and a large pool of blood in front of the post. Neither of these minus answers has the gross distortion of form common to the schizophrenic, but both do convey a sense of very unique ideational activity. In fact, several other answers are also marked by a strangeness, although they are generally of good form quality (cats rather than the more common dogs on Card II, a monster with the head of a bird on IV, a hairy bird on IV, and animals with big horns on X). She tends to interpret most of these stimuli very uniquely, probably in a way that reflects her own very unique ideational process and illustrates her own superguarded idiography. Her only active M's involve aggression, and four of her eight M answers are linked with Hd or (H) content, all of which are less mature, and potentially more pathological.

Case 18 Summary. Although there is no clear evidence of schizophrenia present, this woman manifests many of the characteristics that could be associated with the Kety *et al* (1968, 1971) "soft spectrum," which includes those who are often identified as "schizoid." She seems very isolated, in an autistic world often marked by considerable distortion and aggressiveness. She is supersuspicious and extremely guarded against interpersonal intrusions. She is unwilling, or unable, to display affect in a realistic manner, possibly because such displays might be overwhelming to her. Although she is very self-centered, her self-concept is negative and diffuse, and there is no significant evidence of an appropriate sex role identity. Her control is "excessive," that is, unlikely to be sustained over a long period of time without creating internal havoc, which would be much more pathological than is now the case. If considered separately from her marriage, she should probably be approached as a "crisis" patient, for she is very fragile and brittle, and could easily disintegrate under further stress. Medication should be considered in light of her complaints of nervousness and tension, and an immediate supportive program should be undertaken to instill a sense of reassurance, with a longer term objective of easing the internal strife and initiating an intervention program that will ultimately restore the capacity to deliver emotion in a useful and modulated way, and that will focus on the reorganization of the self-concept.

A Treatment Plan for the Pair

First, and in light of her pathology, it would be very inappropriate to consider treating them as a couple, and especially not in sexual therapy, at this time. She is much too fragile, and beneath her excessive guardedness there may be a "boiling cauldron" that might be tipped easily if she is "forced" into a physical or psychological confrontation for which she is not fully prepared. This does not preclude some form of supportive relationship therapy; however, before such a decision is reached, it is best to review the specific therapeutic targets that might be formulated for each of the pair, using the "optimal" status as a starting point, and subsequently considering the achievement of those objectives in a cost-benefit framework that considers a variety of treatment modalities. Second, it is important that each of the potential treatment objectives be considered in the context of the marital situation. Unfortunately, it is not uncommon for effective treatment of one partner to exacerbate symptoms of the other partner, with ultimate negative consequences for the relationship. Thus, it is also important to work in the context of the original referral. The male has the precipitating complaint, and while the female admits to distress, she issues no direct signal that could be interpreted as "strong" motivation for intervention.

The *optimal* treatment objectives for the female, listed in a logically developed priority, include: (1) some immediate relief from the pressure she is now feeling for greater emotional closeness than she is prepared to deliver. This will require reassurance, and probably some medication to contend with her nervousness; (2) the gradual reestablishment of techniques for the controlled discharge of affect. This may involve some modeling form of therapy, but can also be developed through a more straightforward individual supportive approach; (3) a concurrent review of her perceptions of people and her role in interacting with them. The longer term objective here is to reduce her superguardedness and make her more available to the development of interpersonal skills; (4) an improvement in her level of self-esteem and the gradual development of aspirations more compatible with her functional capabilities; (5) the ultimate development of a better defined sex role identity and concurrent improvement in self-concept.

The *optimal* treatment objectives for the male, also listed in a logical order of priority, include: (1) reduction in the feelings of loss of control and feelings of helplessness. Direct support should aid considerably; (2) the development of more effective techniques for the modulation of affective displays. As with his wife, a modeling approach may be appropriate to this objective, and, quite possibly, their mutual need to learn to display emotion differently could form the basis of some "relational" therapy; (3) an improvement in self-esteem, which will probably occur under a supportive structure; (4) an overall increase in maturational level, which may require a long term, "insight" oriented effort; (5) the establishment of more effective interpersonal skills, which in turn will relate to his own self-concept.

Any plan designed to achieve these optimal objectives would probably require contact with at least three different therapists. It would include for her a relationship to a female therapist who would initiate a supportive relationship, and would ultimately expand into the areas of sex role identity and self-concept. Similarly, he would probably profit more from contact with a male therapist, who would also commence treatment in a supportive framework and would gradually work toward a more insight based, developmental approach. Concurrent with each of the individual therapies, a third intervention, focusing primarily on the "affective interaction," should be initiated. This would be a form of marital therapy, but the major area of concentration would involve the issues of emotional "delivery," with a subsidiary target of reorganizing or strengthening the pattern of communication between them. It is feasible, assuming that each of the individual therapies proceeds effectively, that the marital therapy could ultimately focus on the original presenting complaint, that of sexual dysfunction; *however,* that should not be stressed as an issue early in any of the therapies, mainly because she is too fragile to handle such a direct confrontation. Instead, it should be "put aside" in early recommendations, with the suggestion that it is more a by-product of other problems, and a symptom that *might* be eliminated by some alteration in other areas. This assumption is based on the possibility that better communication and more effective emotional interaction may alleviate some of her guardedness and reduce some of his aggressiveness. Obviously, if there is improvement in the individual treatments, but no remission of the sexual symptom in him, a more direct form of sexual therapy would be in order, *but only* when she is clearly amenable to such an approach. It is also quite important that regular interaction occur between the therapists, so that gains or problems in one of the treatments can be studied in the context of the other two modalities, with very special attention to any signs that would suggest that she is becoming more fragmented. In effect, the total treatment "package" must evolve in light of her progress or lack thereof.

Cases 17 and 18: Epilogue

This couple manifested a stormy treatment history during the first four months of intervention. At the beginning, she was extremely amenable to individual supportive treatment with a female therapist, but he became somewhat resistant to a similar effort, although he agreed to "try it out." Conversely, she was quite resistant to the mutual treatment, so much so that it was deferred during the first eight weeks. She was prescribed medication (valium, 10mg twice daily), but with the proviso that it was to continue only for two or three months. She responded very well to the supportive treatment, but became very resistant as the therapy began to broach issues of goals and sex role identity at about the third treatment month. The mutual therapy began at the end of the second treatment month, and she was remarkably capable of discussing her problems in displaying emotion. Conversely, her husband had great difficulty in defining "emotional blunders," and even though some modeling demonstrations between wife and therapist were used to convey some of his loss of temper, his changes in anger display were short lived. By the end of the third month, they decided mutually to enter sex therapy, since the primary dysfunction had not abated completely, although they had been able to have intercourse several times during the preceding three weeks. After eight sessions of sex therapy, which were not very productive, she opted to terminate sex therapy on the grounds that too many demands were being made on her. During a reevaluation of progress, involving all the therapists and the two clients, several new decisions were made. She decided to continue individual "supportive" treatment for an additional three month trial period. He opted to enter a more intense form of individual treatment, involving twice a week contact. They decided to discontinue the mutual therapy for at least three months. At the sixth month, she had improved considerably in her ability to express emotion, and was far less defensive. In fact, at that point she opted to enter a women's group while reducing the frequency of individual treatment to twice monthly. He did not show any substantial improvement until the eighth treatment month, when many of the developed "insights" began to congeal more meaningfully for him. The sex activity increased in frequency shortly after she joined the women's group, and by the end of a year there was no evidence of dysfunction, and both reported much gratification. She terminated individual treatment at the 11th month, but continued in the women's group for an additional three months. He was reevaluated after 17 months of treatment, showed considerable overall gains, and decided at that time to continue in the intensive form of individual treatment. She was also reevaluated at the same time, and showed some improvement; many of the guarded characteristics were still present, but were not nearly as marked as before treatment. Interestingly, her reevaluation protocol contained three Special Scores (two *INCOM* and one *ALOG*), but no *M* minus answers. She did give one *Mw* response. In other words, some of the ideational fragility noted earlier had dissipated, but there were some signs of the "soft spectrum" possibility.

SUMMARY

The three cases presented here illustrate the technique of using Rorschach data to identify appropriate treatment targets. Obviously, the skilled clinician must synthesize these findings with other material concerning the subject, then integrate that composite with the reality factors confronting the treatment situation. In many instances, extraneous elements, such as financial resources, immediate issues, environmental demands, and treatment availability, will play a major role in determining the ultimate treatment decision. However, there are many ways to approach the achievement of a single objective, and it may border on the unethical when objectives are not appropriately identified and the variety of alternatives to achieve those objects remain unexplored. Vorhaus (1977) has offered an interesting demonstration, using a single case, of how the professional obligations of assessment can be sorely neglected when the "diagnostician" fails to seek out the potential for change that is inherent in the test data. It is not a more difficult process than generating a description, and its inclusion in the regular assessment routine can often have substantial benefits for the client and for those who work with the client. This is expecially true for the younger client whose life is involved with a variety of "controlling" authorities, such as parents, siblings, other family members, teachers, and so on. The next chapter focuses on the nature of some of those complexities as they relate to the identification of treatment objectives and the formulation of a treatment plan for the younger subject.

REFERENCES

Bergin, A. E., and Garfield, S. L. (Eds.), *Handbook of Psychotherapy and Behavior Change.* New York: John Wiley and Sons, 1971.

Exner, J. E., Murillo, L. G., and Cannavo, F. Disagreement between patient and relative behavioral reports as related to relapse in nonschizophrenic patients. Eastern Psychological Association, Washington, D.C., 1973.

Exner, J. E., and Murillo, L. G. A long term follow-up of schizophrenics treated with regressive ECT. *Diseases of the Nervous System,* 1977, **38,** 162–168.

Exner, J. E., Wylie, J. R., and Kline, J. R. Variations in Rorschach performance during a 28 month interval as related to seven intervention modalities. Workshops Study No. 240 (unpublished), Rorschach Workshops, 1977.

Vorhaus, P. Watchman, what of the future? *Journal of Personality Assessment,* 1977, **41,** 427–433.

CHAPTER 11

Younger Clients

While adults usually take an active role in treatment decisions for themselves, this is less often the case for younger clients. Parental judgments and decisions become critical, and in many instances, successful intervention with a youngster may require the cooperation and/or participation of the "significant others" who are major focal points in the immediate environment. Quite often, referrals for evaluation of youngsters come from some formal agencies, such as schools, social service units, courts, and the like, and usually treatment decisions must also involve close contact with those agencies. Unfortunately, there are far too many cases in which treatment decisions are rendered more in the context of the needs of the family, or the requirements of the "concerned" agencies, than in light of the needs and potentials of the youngster. Management is often perceived as more important than remediation or growth. However, it seems likely that in many of these cases, management issues become a focal point simply because there is no precise identification of potential treatment objectives other than those which stem directly from the behavior of the child. The mother of the enuretic child will typically seek out "quick success" methods of ending the enuresis without much concern for other related variables. Similarly, teachers confronted with disruptive children are more concerned with ending the disruptiveness than changing the factors that may, in fact, be creating the disruption. And so it goes; and it is no small percentage of youngsters who find themselves in forms of treatment that may subjugate their own personalities so that other objectives, deemed important to those around them, can be achieved. In reality, many basic treatment objectives important to the child can be achieved in treatment programs that also focus on the needs and demands of the environment, provided those objectives have been identified and the treatment program is formulated in such a manner as to include them. In this context, the Rorschach data can be used with a younger client in the same way that they are used with an adult; but, even more important than with most adult cases, a thorough knowledge of the youngster's *significant environment* is critical to the logical development of a treatment plan once the optimal objectives have been identified.

As has been noted in several of the cases involving younger clients that were presented in earlier chapters (Case 8, Chapter 6; Case 12, Chapter 8; Case 16, Chapter 9), the fundamentals of Rorschach interpretation remain the same, regardless of the age of the client. That is, the Rorschach features have the same interpretive significance. *However,* it is very important that the interpreter be fully aware of the developmental expectancies for children of different ages. For example, a pure *C* response reflects an almost totally unmodulated form of emotional discharge, regardless of the age of the subject; nevertheless, if given by a six year old, it is much more "expectable" than if given by a 16 year old. Six year olds do not modulate well, whereas most 16 year olds have learned that modulation is important and are better able to invoke it. Similarly, a very high egocentricity index in the record of a seven year old is not unexpected, because children of that age are still very egocentered, while the same high index in the record of an 18 year old would be cause for concern because 18 year olds are expected to have developed a much greater concern for the demands of the environment. Treatment objectives must be defined in this same context; that is, focusing on those issues that are unique and deterimental for the child of a given age. If $CF+C$ is greater than FC in an 11 year old, it would not necessarily be considered as a target for intervention, for most 11 year olds will have ratios in that very direction, as contrasted with most adults where the reverse will be true. The first case to be reviewed here, which has been partially described in Chapters 4 and 5, is a good example of the importance of working within the developmental framework.

Case 5: A 13 Year Old Female—the Funny Statue

History.   This young girl was referred to a school psychologist because of failing grades in two of five eighth grade courses (English and social studies) and marginal work in the remaining three (math, science, and home economics). Her seventh grade performance had also been marginal, although she passed in all subjects. This lowered performance is considered a contrast to her evaluations in grades one through six, in which all of her marks were average or above. In fact, during the fifth grade year, all of her marks were "B" or better. A group intelligence test, administered during her third grade year, yielded an I.Q. of 114, and an individually administered WISC-R, completed one week before the administration of the Rorschach, reveals a full scale I.Q. of 111 (Performance I.Q. = 108; Verbal I.Q. = 113) with no significant scatter among the subtests except Picture Completion, on which the scale score of 7 was three points lower than that in any of the other subtests. She claims that she studies diligently, and her mother confirms the fact that she devotes at least one hour each night to study. Her teachers tend to disagree in evaluating her effort, with two reporting that she seems to make a sincere effort, while two others suggest that she does not "seem to try" very hard.

Her father, age 40, is a Protestant minister and, when interviewed about his daughter's school problem, expressed both concern and dismay. The mother, age 37, also expressed dismay about her daughter's performance. Both parents are college graduates. Various routines have been attempted in the home, in which one or both parents have monitored homework assignments, but to no avail in terms of improving performance.

The subject is described as being of average height and weight for her age. She has no outstanding features except braces on her teeth that do mark her appearance. She dresses neatly, albeit conservatively for her peer group. She openly reports a dislike for school, but does not offer specifics. She has two "close" friends with whom she usually shares lunch, but has only occasional interaction with them after school hours. She speaks very negatively about most of her peers, implying that they cheat on examinations and probably do not commit themselves to as much study time as she does. She reports no hobbies, although she has developed a sizable collection of science fiction books and seems very knowledgeable about astronomy. She has several favorite TV programs, but also suggests that none is of overwhelming importance to her. Her medical history is unremark-

Case 5

Card	Free Association	Inquiry	Scoring
I	21″		
	1. I thk it ll a cat but I'm not sure	E: (Rpts S's resp)	WSo Fo Ad 3.5
		S: Well, its lik the face of a cat, its has the ears out here & the puffy cheeks, c here (points) and thes r the eyes, kinda slanty lik a cat & the mouth is here	
	E: I thk if u take u'r time & look a bit longer u'll probably c more thgs too		
	>2. Well, if I look at it ths way, ths part (points) c.b. a donkey I thk, is that enuff? He's just stndg there	E: (Rpts S's resp)	Do FMᵖo A
		S: Well it has a big ear lik a donkey, & its lik he's just stndg there, c (points) thes r his legs & the head & this mite b a tail it really c.b. one I thk	
	E: (Its up to u)		
	S: I thk tht's all		
II	11″		
	3. Oh, ths ll 2 dogs, not all of them but just from the middl up & thy'r playing togthr, lik sniffing at e.o. the way dogs do that	E: (Rpts S's resp)	D+ FMᵃo (2) Ad P 3.0
		S: U can't c the whole dog, just from the middl, c mostly their heads, this (points) is the nose & the littl ear, I never had a dog but we could't hav one at the parish	
	<4. If I turn it again, lk ths the uppr part c.b. mts suppose, is that o.k.?	E: (Rpts S's resp)	Ddv Fo Ls
		S: Well it just re me of mts I thk, the line is all jagged, u kno? Its just lik a mt range mite look	
	E: Whatever u c is fine		
III	14″		
	5. Well I thk ths mite b 2 wm doing s..., mayb lik carryg ths basket they'r funny lookg wm tho	E: (Rpts S's resp)	D+ Mᵃo (2) H P 3.0
		S: Well u kno thy look all out of shape, lik thy are thin & thy don't hav much hair showg, well anyhow, thy r lik wm, & thy r probably carrying this basket here	

Case 5 (Continued)

Card	Free Association	Inquiry	Scoring
	6. The middle red part re me of a brite red bow I used to wear in my hair when I went to Sunday School	E: (Rpts S's resp) S: Well its shaped really well lik a hair ribbon My mom got it for me & at first I liked it but then I thot it was too big, I don't remember what ever happened to it but I thk I lost it, c it bows out here & here (points)	Do FCo Cg
IV 26″	7. Oh, tht ll some kind of big thg, lik out of sc. fict. just sort of standg there	E: (Rpts S's resp) S: Well, I'm not exactly sur what it is, but it re me of the kinds of creatures fr outer space, just great big thgs, c this one has big feet & little arms & it just ll its standg there	Wo Mᵖo (H) 2.0
	8. U kno, ths little part rite here (points) cld b a golf tee, I've caddied for my dad a couple of times	E: (Rpts S's resp) S: It just has that shape to it, like a golf tee, it really ll tht, c the point here & here its bigger where u put the ball	Ddo Fo Golf Tee
V 18″	9. Ths is a hard one but I guess it c.b. a bf if u don't hav to include thes thgs out here	E: (Rpts S's resp) S: Well it has the big wgs, bf's hav those, & it has a littl body lik a bf, it just ll one but not these parts out here	Ddo FMᵃo A (P)
	10. It c.b. a man's head too, its lik a side view u kno, just lik an old man mayb with a beard too, one here too	E: (Rpts S's resp) S: Well u can c the forehead & the beard wld b down here (points) & ths wld b the nose & chin, it just ll tht to me	Do Fo (2) Hd
VI 25″	V11. Well, ths way it ll a piece of marble, we saw one once on a film about fossils & it sort of lookd lik ths with the rough top part & some bigger cuts in it, like ths middle part here (points)	E: (Rpts S's resp) S: Well I don't rem what it was a fossil of, but it was a fossil, & it ll ths, sortof like a prehistoric animal w a big tail lik ths & bec it was in stone it lookd all rough lik ths but when it hardened & bec a fossil it sorta cracked in the middle & the middle part was	Wo FT.FVw Fossil 2.5

382

	Response	Inquiry	Scoring
		lost or s.t., c here it ll its a V there, lik it goes down in, it is all dark there & up here (points) whre its darker is kinda lik a roughness that fossils have	
	12. Ths way u can c ano:her persons' side view agair. lik on the last one	E: (Rpts S's resp) S: Well, it just ll the head of a person to me u can c the nose (points) & the forehead, just lik a sideview but I don't kno anythg else about it	Ddo Fo Hd
VII 16"	13. Ths ll two statues, lik of people who are lookg at e.o. ts kinda funny, u kno?	E: (Rpts S's resp) S: Well it doesn't really ll real people but statues tht r supposed to ll people, not ths part but ths (points) mayb lik two wm, I'm not sure, just lik s.body made them to ll two people lookg at e.o., c the pony tails (points) & the nose & the chin, just lik a side view	D+ M^po (2) (Hd) P 3.0
	<14. If I turn it ths way it re me of a dog's head, lik a dcg with the flat nose I can't remember, oh, yeah a scotty	E: (Rpts S's resp) S: Yes, right here (points) its like a scotty dog, just the head, lik from the side, I kno a girl tht has one & it really ll ths, mostly bec of the nose, its flat lik ths	Do Fo Ad
VIII 20"	15. Well, part of it ll 2 A s who r tryg to get up ths tree but I don't kno what ths bttm part is	E: (Rpts S's resp) S: Well u really hav to use ur immagin to c the tree, its just ths top & middl I guess out not the bottom, mayb its lik a couple of cats or s.t. but theyr not really pink, out the tree c.b. o.k. for the color, lik a pine tree, thyr s.times grey & bluish & here's a cat on each side lik they'r climbg up, c the legs & the body lik a cat (points)	Dd+ FM^a.FCo (2) A,Bt P 3.0
	16. Ths white part ll a bird, c the wgs wya out lik (points)	E: (Rpts S's resp) S: Well it just has that form to it, lik a big bird, lik a condor mayb or an eagle or some bird that has great big wgs lik ths	DdSo Fo A

383

Case 5 (Continued)

Card	Free Association	Inquiry	Scoring
IX 15"	17. Ths white part in here ll s.t., lik a waterfall mayb with the kind of blue around it lik a waterfall has, c its ths white part (points) & it has some blue & then out here its lik green lik around a waterfall	E: (Rpts S's resp) S: Well ths part (points) w.b. the waterfall part & its kinda blue around it, lik mayb the lite was hitting it to give that blue color, its lite blue, but its blue I'm sure	DdSv m^p.CFo Ls 5.0
	18. Ths slits here c.b. eyes too, lik fr a science fict monster or s.t.	E: (Rpts S's resp) S: Well theyr not lik real eyes, I mean lik round, but thyr lik funny eyes lik s.t. from science fict wld hav mayb even two thgs, two eyes, one here & one here	DdSo Fo (2) (Hd)
X 10"	V19. Well, if I turn it over lik ths it c.b. b s.k. of design lik thy hav on graves, lik when thy lay out the flowers	E: (Rpts S's resp) S: Well when thy bury s.o. thy usually lay out the flowers lik in a design on the grave, u kno e.body sends flowers & thy hav to do s.t. w them, & thy try to get the colors to match, sort of lik ths c the colors r the same on each side, lik a design, its lik tht	Wv FCo Bt 5.5
	20. Up here, if I turn it ths way it ll two little ants r tryg to lift a big stick or s.t., lik here c it (points) here thy r	E: (Rpts S's resp) S: C there's one on each side of the stick, thy hav littl antennae lik ths & it ll thyr really wrkg to lift it up	D+ FM^ao (2) A 4.0
	V21. The top of ths pink kind re me of a caterpillar's head, I used to hav a collection of thm when I was a kid	E: (Rpts S's resp) S: Well if u've ever seen a caterpillar u kno thy ll ths, its just a side view of one in the profile u kno, it really looks a lot lik one, c the little nose & the sort of scrunched up face, tht's the way thy look, just here (points)	Ddo Fo Ad

384

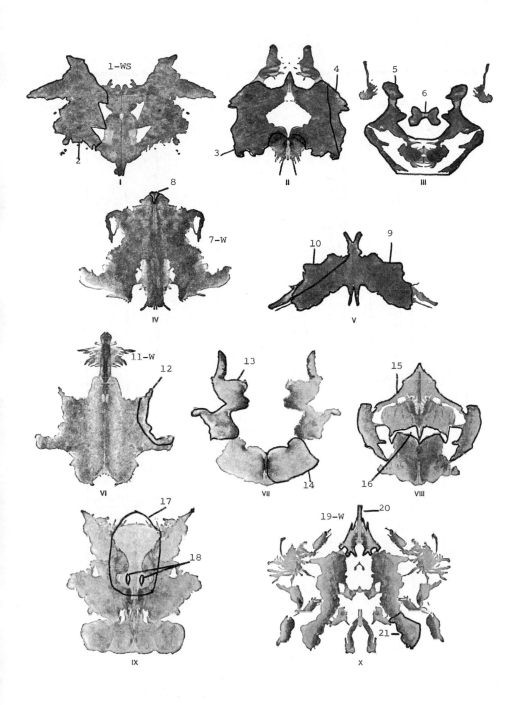

385

SEQUENCE OF SCORES

Case 5

CARD	RT	NO.	LOCATION	DETERMINANTS (S)	(S)	CONTENT (S)	POP	Z SCORE	SPECIAL
I	21"	1.	WSo	Fo		Ad		3.5	
		2.	Do	FM^po		A			
II	11"	3.	D+	FM^ao	(2)	Ad	P	3.0	
		4.	Ddv	Fo		Ls			
III	14"	5.	D+	M^ao	(2)	H	P	3.0	
		6.	Do	FCo		Cg			
IV	26"	7.	Wo	M^po		(H)		2.0	
		8.	Ddo	Fo		Golf Tee			
V	18"	9.	Ddo	FM^ao		A	(P)		
		10.	Do	Fo	(2)	Hd			
VI	25"	11.	Wo	FT.FVw		Fossil		2.5	
		12.	Ddo	Fo		Hd			
VII	16"	13.	D+	M^po	(2)	(Hd)	P	3.0	
		14.	Do	Fo		Ad			
VIII	20"	15.	Dd+	FM^a.FCo	(2)	A,Bt	P	3.0	
		16.	DdSo	Fo		A			
IX	15"	17.	DdSv	m^p.CFo		Ls		5.0	
		18.	DdSo	Fo	(2)	(Hd)			
X	10"	19.	Wv	FCo		Bt		5.5	
		20.	D+	FM^ao	(2)	A		4.0	
		21.	Ddo	Fo		Ad			

able, and there is no psychiatric history in the immediate family. She describes her parents as "O.K." but privately admits that she sometimes becomes bored with their demands for her regular attendence at Sunday school. She also reports that she had a "transitional" object, a teddy bear, which she cherished until about the age of eight. She denies any "wish" for siblings, although she does admit to an imaginery playmate in the year or two before she entered kindergarten. She has no

Case 5:   Structural Summary

R = 21   Zf = 10   ZSum = 34.5   P = 4+1   (2) = 7

Location Features				Determinants (Blends First)			Contents			Contents (Idiographic)	
W	=	4	DQ	FM.FC	=1		H	=1	Fossil	=1
D	=	8	+ = 5	m.CF	=1		(H)	=1	....
Dd	=	9	o = 13	FT.FV	=1		Hd	=2	Golf Tee	=1
S	=	4	v = 3				(Hd)	=2	....
DW	=		— = 0				A	=5		=
				M	= 3		(A)	=	....
				FM	= 4		Ad	=4		=
				m	=		(Ad)	=	....
				C	=		Ab	=		=
Form Quality				CF	=		Al	=	....
				FC	= 2		An	=		=
FQx		FQf		C'	=		Art	=	....
				C'F	=		Ay	=		=
+	= 0	+	= 0	FC'	=		Bl	=	....
				T	=		Bt	=1,1		=
o	= 20	o	= 9	TF	=		Cg	=	....
				FT	=		Cl	=	
w	= 1	w	= 0	V	=		Ex	=	**Special Scorings**
				VF	=		Fi	=	
—	= 0	—	= 0	FV	=		Fd	=	PSV	=
M Quality				Y	=		Ge	=	
				YF	=		Hh	=	DV	=
+	= 0			FY	=		Ls	= 2	
				rF	=		Na	=	INCOM	=
o	= 3			Fr	=		Sx	=	
				FD	=		Xy	=	FABCOM	=
w	= 0			F	= 9					CONTAM	=
—	= 0									ALOG	=
											=

RATIOS, PERCENTAGES, AND DERIVATIONS

ZSum-Zest	= 34.5-31.0		FC:CF+C	= 3:1	Afr	=	.50
Zd	= +3.5		W:M	= 4:3	3r+(2)/R	=	.33
EB	= 3:2.5	EA = 5.5	W:D	= 4:8	Cont:R	=	7:21
eb	= 6:2	ep = 8	L	= .75	H+Hd:A+Ad =		6:9
					(H)+(Hd):(A)+(Ad) =		3:0
Blends:R	= 3:21		F+%	= 100	H+A:Hd+Ad =		7:8
a:p	= 5:4		X+%	= .95	XRT Achrom.	=	21.2"
Ma:Mp	= 1:2		A%	= .43	XRT Chrom	=	14.0"

firm occupational objectives, but does talk openly about the possibility of becoming a nurse.

Previously Developed Interpretation.   She is an ambient who may have a tendency to vacillate in coping situations. Although the higher *ep* is less cause for concern at this age level, the ambient status may be a potential problem warranting closer evaluation. She offers a significantly greater number of *FC* responses than is common for youngsters of this age, and this raises questions about over-control. The presence of one *V* determinant may reflect the natural self-inspection of an adolescent, or it may relate to identity problems, which are also not uncommon at this age. She is an overincorporator, and may have some difficulty discriminating important from unimportant cues. The preponderence of *FC* responses takes on additional importance in the context of her relatively low *Afr*, suggesting a tendency to avoid emotionally provocative stimuli. She seems to try to exert more control over emotional displays than is normal for the adolescent, probably because she is quite uncomfortable with these displays. Some indirect support for this proposition is gleaned from the substantially low egocentricity index, which may be another signal that she is not very self-confident. Her perceptual accuracy is better than that usually found in youngsters of this age and may represent an orientation to avoid making mistakes. This may also relate to her overincorporativeness. While her *a* :*p* ratio indicates some ideational flexibility, there is also some evidence to suggest that she may become "wrapped up" in a passive fantasy existence, which can contribute significantly to some forms of social isolation.

Finished Interpretation.   The complete Structural Summary raises many more "warning flags" than the partial data suggested. She has a clear *Dd* emphasis in her location choices, suggesting that she is either trying to narrow her world, *or* is perceiving her world in a very unique way. The sizable number of *S* responses (4) indicates a substantial negativism, and an examination of the scoring sequence reveals that they are generally distributed through the record, and therefore cannot be attributed to some situationally provoked negativism. She gives a greater number of Human contents than might be anticipated; however, all but one are parenthized, or *Hd*, indicating some difficulties with her sense of people, and possibly with her perception of herself. In addition, she shows a strong emphasis on *Hd* and *Ad* contents as contrasted with Whole Human or Animal percepts. This often equates with the very guarded or overly suspicious person, and is particularly uncommon for most adolescents. When combined with her *Dd* emphasis, overincorporativeness, and elevated *S*, an important question is raised about the possibility of an early "paranoid style." Her mean reaction times are also much longer than is common for the younger client, or even for the adult, signifying that she is trying to be very cautious in her approach to the blots. There is little question about her brightness, as evidenced by her five *DQ+* answers, the 10 *Z*'s, and the three *M* answers. However, the structural data appear commensurate with the picture of an extremely cautious and not very secure person, and, when viewed in the context of the typical 13 year old, of a very insecure, overly controlled, and semi-isolated youngster. The Sequence of Scores indicates that she organizes on every card except the easiest (V), and generally reports the most commonly perceived Popular answers. The only hint of a loss of control occurs on Card IX, where she combines a white space location with unusual details of the blot and uses an *m.CF* determinant. On the other hand, her very strong and unusual control is manifest in the fact that her last answer to eight of the 10 cards is a pure *F*. She does not permit herself to become involved with complexity, nor is there sign cognitive slippage, as is commonly seen in a Special Score at this age.

The verbal material also reveals a very cautious approach in many of her answers, ". . . it could be . . . I'm not sure . . . I think . . . is that O.K.?" A large number of her answers (6) involve profiles, which is not necessarily unusual for the very cautious person, but is unusual for the average 13 year old. It is also important to note that she is not as openly resistant as are most young adolescents. Generally, the group from 12 to 15 who are examined in conjunction with some problem will make light of the test, identifying it as "stupid, dumb," and so on, or backing away from the task with reports of, "It could be anything. . . . It's just an old inkblot." She does neither of these "numbers" on the examiner, and though she seems to be very cooperative, her contents lack the liveliness of the young cooperative adolescent who will often become very involved in the "Blotto" game.

Her first response, a cat's face, is very typical for the adolescent. However, the following answer, after prompting, a donkey, is far less common and may signify her "stubbornness." Her cautious approach to the world is also evidenced in her Card II response, ". . . playing together, like sniffing at each other . . ." On at least three occasions, she does become more like the child who will often personalize an answer, ". . . like I used to wear in my hair . . . I've caddied for my dad a couple of times . . ." The third instance, which occurs in her last answer to the test, may offer a very important clue to the role she is trying to play, ". . . I used to have a collection of them when I was a kid." She tries very hard to be precise, but in doing so, she abrogates many of her natural childish qualities, and in one response she provides a glimpse of the "morbid" cost that her overcontrol may be exacting, ". . . like they have on graves, like when they lay out the flowers." The only hint of aggressiveness appears in the science fiction monster perceived on Card IV, but it is quickly neutralized, ". . . just sort of standing there." She is the monster, ill defined and immobilized. Another clue to her apparently destitute self-image is seen in the variety of lifeless objects she reports, mountains, a fossil, statues, and a design on a grave. Her only pure H response, on Card III, probably illustrates something of her perception of herself, ". . . two women . . . they are funny looking women though," a postulate that seems supported by her approach to Card VII, ". . . two statues, like people who are looking at each other, it's kinda funny . . ." to which she adds in the inquiry, ". . . doesn't look like real people, but statues that are supposed to look like people . . ." While she does not manifest sex role confusion, she also does not manifest any sense of adolescent vibrance, or even ambivalence about femininity, which is the more common feature of the young female in the throes of pubescence. Instead, most of her contents have a vague aura of morbidity and depression, and like the structural data, portend no good for this youngster.

Case 5 Summary. Overall, this appears to be a youngster who is much more depressed than may be readily apparent in her behavior. And she is gradually withdrawing from a world that she has not been able to sort out; or, if she has sorted it out, she is not able to respond to what she sees. She has been trying to play a role that denies the existence of her childhood. Both her structure and her contents are almost like a "little old woman" who will peek through a crack in the door to see who is knocking, but will not "come out to play." She is a very unreal 13 year old, who has not experienced the world as do most youngsters her age, and she has become very "bound up" in a pattern of thinking and behavior that stresses overcautiousness. Her poor schoolwork is due, at least in part, to her depression. It may well be her only way of struggling out of the psychological coffin into which she has been placed, of rebelling against the demands of her significant others to grow quickly. She has apparently been reinforced for patterning herself upon some fictional adult role model rather than adopting the more natural, and sometimes loose, behavior of the child.

A Treatment Plan.   There are many objectives for intervention in this case, and many are interrelated. Her depression is not acute, but it should not be neglected. In that context, she needs close positive emotional contact quickly. Her extreme guardedness will make this difficult, and ideally the mother should be the basic source of contact. If the mother is not available for this part, then a surrogate becomes necessary, since a key goal of her therapy will be to elevate her egocentricity index and to eliminate the form of self-inspection that is producing the vista kinds of responses. It also seems important to try to reestablish more extensive peer relationships, which can be very useful in reorienting her self-image, and to help "loosen" her rigidly controlled emotions. Success in this area would probably increase the *Afr,* and would possibly eliminate some of her tendencies toward passivity in both ideation and behavior. The whole issue of being an adolescent female requires some approach; again, although the mother may be the optimal source, she may also be constricted, so that a therapist-surrogate would have to be involved in this area. It was noted, for instance, that her one outstanding feature, at the time of the examination, was braces. While orthodontial repair may be important to her teeth, it can have a very negative impact on the youngster seeking an identity. An increase in self-esteem, and a more positive self-concept, should combine to raise her levels of aspiration, which, in turn, can help her develop a more distinct coping style. However, the current ambient status, and the higher *ep* than *EA,* are not important targets at this time, since, hopefully, she will still experience considerable growth before reaching her early adult years. Once she is able to overcome her current guardedness and establish more extensive peer group contact, that growth pattern should be facilitated considerably. One of the complications requiring attention is her poor schoolwork, which was the reason for referral. Ideally, that issue should not be very relevant to the treatment plan, but it is a reality factor. Some peer tutoring might be useful in raising her performance and at the same time could provide an avenue for peer contact. However, the emphasis on grades at this time should be minimized, and appropriate school authorities should be cautioned to reduce their manifestations of concern. If poor performance is primarily a function of her depression, improvement should appear quite soon after "affective contact" is established. Conversely, if the poor performance is a function of angry rebelliousness, then any improvement in performance can be expected to occur at a much more gradual pace, and only after she begins to experience a new sense of herself.

Case 5 Epilogue.   The subject responded cautiously, but positively, to the feedback, which focused mainly on issues of "adolescent bewilderment" and her feelings of inadequacy in peer interaction. She was not identified as chronically depressed but as "occasionally sad," to which she readily agreed. She admitted to great distress about her braces, and also revealed much of her naiveté about menstruation, which had begun about 15 months earlier. She was willing to enter "counseling" with a female therapist on a weekly basis, and also agreed to seek out peer group tutoring. Her parents were considerably less responsive, especially her father, who found it very difficult to accept that something "psychological" might be wrong. He insisted on a thorough medical examination, which revealed nothing except that the youngster was in good physical health. The mother was much more responsive after the physical examination, and, during the child's third treatment month, sought out a brief treatment program for herself designed mainly to focus on her relationship to her daughter, who was beginning to bewilder her with some newly unfolding behavior.

The girl's treatment was begun in late February with no real optimism about the prospect for improvement in school performance; however, she did "pass" all courses, with two D's, two C's and one B. Treatment was interrupted during the summer vacation months, but began again in the fall. The subject's grades were considerably better during the first half of her ninth grade year; she was much more active among peers, and a reevaluation after one year showed a substantial increase in the egocentricity index and the *Afr*.

Case 19: A 15 Year Old Female—the Hidden Angel

History.   This youngster, also a school referral, presents a case illustrating how depression in younger clients may often lead to behavioral problems other than the guarded withdrawal behavior noted in the previous case. The subject was referred for a multitude of problems. She is now in the ninth grade, but is failing or near failing in all of her courses. She has a very high absentee rate, which has been persistent during the past two years. When in school, she is boisterous, inattentive, and argumentative with her teachers. Various administrative disciplinary measures have failed to curb her disruptiveness, and her parents have been informed that she may be suspended unless some change in her behavior occurs. She has a notable reputation among her classmates for being promiscuous, and also for being involved with drugs. Her performance in grades one through six was unremarkable, and she achieved average grades. The behavioral disruptiveness began in seventh grade, and, according to reports, has increased steadily since then. Her father, a 42 year old construction worker, reports that he has punished her with various methods, including physical, but that she has simply become "more stubborn." The mother, age 40, who works part time as a waitress, reports that the subject has "always been independent" but was never a "real" problem at home. Both parents are mystified by the high absentee rate, but the subject has refused to reveal where she goes when she is not in school. She is the youngest of three siblings. Her older sister, age 19, married after graduating from high school, and currently works in a blue collar assembly line job. Her older brother, age 17, is now a senior in high school, and plans to join the Navy after graduating. Both older siblings maintained average grades in school, and neither has had any unusual behavioral problems. The medical history of the subject is unremarkable,

Case 19

Card	Free Association	Inquiry	Scoring
I	5"		
	1. It ll there's an angel there if u cld c her better u cld c the gold & silver on her dress, she has her arms out lik this (demo's) sort of lik she's gettg ready to fly but she's not yet	E: (Rpts S's resp) S: Here, c the wgs r coming across & ths is her body part in the middl E: U mentioned that if u cld c her better u cld c gold & silver on her dress S: Well u can almost c it now, c the different colors, lite here, that's the silver & darker here, that's the gold, lik angel r	Ddo $M^p.FYo$ (H) (P)
	2. Ths cntr ll s.t. too, a beetle I thk, or s.k. of bug, its all black, ugly, I lik the angel better, ths has a hard shell, u cn tell	E: (Rpts S's resp) S: Well I thk a beetle, thyr black lik ths, lik w a hard shell lik ths one has, & the littl claws E: U said a hard shell? S: Sure c the shinyness of the color maks it look hard lik beetles	Ddo $FC'.FTo$ A
II	16"		
	3. I c a rabbit, 2 rabbits, one on each side, thyr looking at e.o.	E: (Rpts S's resp) S: Ths red part is the ears, altho thyr not supp to b red & here is the head & the body part & littl feet	$W+$ $FM^p w$ (2) A 4.5
	4. Ths part here c.b. a shell fish of s.s. we study them in science thy hav the funny shell w the crease in it	E: (Rpts S's resp) S: I'm not sure of the name, but thy hav a shell that goes in in the cntr lik ths one does & they hav these spikes coming out here E: U mentioned the shell goes in S: Yeah, it lik folds inward, c here at the cntr, it looks lik it goes inward lik thy do	Do FVo A

III	19"	5. Well, its like a cats face if u ask me, w a pink nose, not the nose, thats white, but the holes, u kno, the nostrils	WS- FC.FC'- Ad 5.5
		E: (Rpts S's resp)	
		S: Well he has black eyes, here & ths is the nostrils, c thy r red or pink & these r the ears c the other red things & out here r the cheeks, thyr fat looking lik a cat's face	
		E: I'm not sure I c it as u do	
		S: Repeats essentially same descript.	
		>6. Ths part c.b. a fish oo	Do Fo A
		E: (Rpts S's resp)	
		S: It has the fin on it, lik a tuna or s.kind, c the head & the tail	
IV	9"	7. That l an old blanket, some of the fur has worn off	Wv TFo Blanket P 2.0
		E: (Rpts S's resp)	
		S: Well its not a new one, its lik one of my grandmothers had I thk a fur blanket, she said thy used them in the car, c the fur is all there but part of it is gone, c the liter places	
		8. It c.b. an old tree too, I dk what kind, big tho	Wo Fo Bt 2.0
		E: (Rpts S's resp)	
		S: This is the trunk & the rest is all the branches & leaves, just all spread out lik a big tree	
V	3"	9. That's lik a bf, a pretty one	Wo FYo A P 1.0 (Cp)
		E: (Rpts S's resp)	
		S: These r the wgs & the littl body & u can c the streak of colors in it, lik there wld b on a real bf, lik if the colors that r supp to be were really there	
		10. Armadillos, one on each side w just the leg stickg out the rest is all in the shell	Do Fw (2)
		E: (Rpts S's resp)	
		S: Well u can't c the head, except mayb just a littl in the cntr & this is the leg & the rest is the big shell that thy hav	

Case 19 (Continued)

Card		Free Association		Inquiry	Scoring
VI	4″	11. Up here it ll a sunrise, w the rays of the sun just showing fr behind ths thg, mayb a tree	E: S:	(Rpts S's resp) Well thy r shaped lik sun rays & thy r behind ths tree or post lik the sun was just coming up	D+ m^a.FDo Na 2.5
		12. This other part ll a bear skin of s.k.	E: S:	(Rpts S's resp) Well its all furry, lik the other one, u kno? the blanket but this one ll it has feet or legs, cut out here & here so I thot of a bearskin	Do FTo Ad P
VII	16″	13. It cld all b a cats face too its white & grey	E: S:	(Rpts S's resp) It has a white forehead & a grey chin & whiskers & the eyes r not so clear but thyr rite here, its a pretty good cats face	WS– FC′– Ad 4.0
		V14. If u turn it upside dwn lik ths the cntr ll a mushroom	E: S:	(Rpts S's resp) All of ths white part, it just has the same shape as a mushroom	DSo Fw Bt
VIII	24″	15. Ths bottom is lik when the sun hits the water, it ll that	E: S:	(Rpts S's resp) Well it has the pinkish orange color just lik when the sun hits water that's very still	Dv C Na
		<16. This way it ll a bear crossing a pond & he's seeing himself in the water	E: S:	(Rpts S's resp) Well, ths is the bear & here he's reflected dwn below & the blue is the water, water is blue like that & the rest is stones & thgs, all showing again in the water dwn here	W+ FM^a.FC.Fr+ A P 4.5

394

IX	36"	V17. Ths pink is lik a cloud that is all fluffy & colored bec the sun is hittg it	E: (Rpts S's resp) S: Well e.body knos clds r white but s.t. when the suns hits lik ths they get colored, ths one is pink lik mayb the sun w.b. behind it or s.t. just pink & c the lines in there, thy make it look fluffy, lik some clds r	Dv CF.VFo CL
X	46"	V18. When u look ths way it ll a mad horse	E: (Rpts S's resp) S: Well, here r the eyes & the nostrils & the shaggy chin & he has a white forehead, his eyes r slanted sort of & so he must b mad	DdS− M^p.FC′− Ad 6.0 ALOG
		19. These brown thgs ll 2 buffaloes, brown & shaggy	E: (Rpts S's resp) S: Thy just hav that shape to them & buffaloes r trown lik this & thy look shaggy E: Shaggy? S: C the different colors of brown there makes it ll some places the fur on him is thick & some is thinner, thyr r lik that if u ever go to the zoo u c them lik this	Do FC.FTo (2) A
		20. I guess the blue thg c.b. spiders too	E: (Rpts S's resp) S: Thy hav lots of legs lik ths, thy c.b. spiders but spiders aren't blue I'm sure of that	Do Fo (2) A P

Note: Testing of limits produced *P* on III but not on VII.

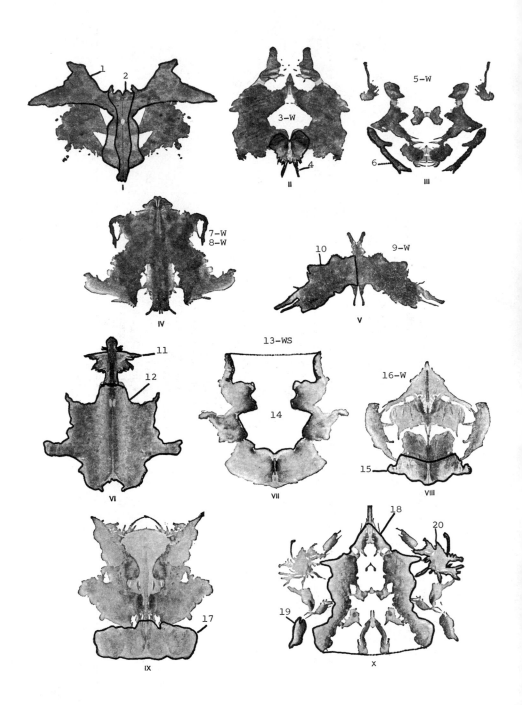

Case 19

CARD	RT	NO.	LOCATION	DETERMINANTS (S)		CONTENT (S)	POP	Z SCORE	SPECIAL
I	5"	1.	Ddo	M^p.FYo		(H)	(P)		
		2.	Ddo	FC'.FTo		A			
II	16"	3.	W+	FM^pw	(2)	A		4.5	
		4.	Do	FVo		A			
III	19"	5.	WS−	FC.FC'−		Ad		5.5	
		6.	Do	Fo		A			
IV	9"	7.	Wv	TFo		Blanket		2.0	
		8.	Wo	Fo		Bt		2.0	
V	3"	9.	Wo	FYo		A	P	1.0	
		10.	Do	Fw	(2)	A			
VI	4"	11.	D+	m^a.FDo		Na		2.5	
		12.	Do	FTo		Ad	P		
VII	16"	13.	WS−	FC'−		Ad		4.0	
		14.	DSo	Fw		Bt			
VIII	24"	15.	Dv	C		Na			
		16.	W+	FM^a.FC.Fr+		A	P	4.5	
IX	36"	17.	Dv	CF.VFo		Cl			
X	46"	18.	DdS−	M^p.FC'−		Ad		6.0	ALOG
		19.	Do	FC.FTo	(2)	A			
		20.	Do	Fo	(2)	A	P		

397

Case 19:   Structural Summary

R =20   Zf = 9   ZSum =32.0   P = 4+1   (2) = 4

Location Features			Determinants (Blends First)		Contents		Contents (Idiographic)	
W	= 7	DQ	M.FC'	=1			Blanket	= 1
			M.FY	=1	H	=	....	
D	= 10	+ = 3	FM.FC.Fr	=1	(H)	= 1		=
			m.FD	=1	Hd	=	....	
Dd	= 3	o = 11	CF.VF	=1	(Hd)	=		=
			FC.FT	=1	A	= 9	....	
S	= 4	v = 3	FC.FC'	=1	(A)	=		=
			FC'.FT	=1	Ad	= 4		
DW	=	— = 3	M	=	(Ad)	=	....	
			FM	= 1	Ab	=		=
			m	=	Al	=	....	
			C	= 1	An	=		=
Form Quality			CF	=	Art	=	....	
			FC	=	Ay	=		=
FQx		FQf	C'	=	Bl	=	....	
			C'F	=	Bt	= 2		=
+	= 1	+ = 0	FC'	= 1	Cg	=	....	
			T	=	Cl	= 1		
o	= 12	o = 3	TF	= 1	Ex	=	Special Scorings	
			FT	= 1	Fi	=		
w	= 3	w = 2	V	=	Fd	=	PSV	=
			VF	=	Ge	=		
—	= 3	— = 0	FV	= 1	Hh	=	DV	=
M Quality			Y	=	Ls	=		
			YF	=	Na	= 2	INCOM	=
+	=		FY	= 1	Sx	=		
			rF	=	Xy	=	FABCOM	=
o	= 1		Fr	=				
			FD	=			CONTAM	=
w	=		F	= 5				
							ALOG	= 1
—	= 1							=

RATIOS, PERCENTAGES, AND DERIVATIONS

ZSum-Zest =	32.0−27.5	FC:CF+C	= 3:2	Afr	= .43
Zd	= +4.5	W:M	= 7:2	3r+(2)/R	= .35
EB	= 2:4.0 EA = 6.0	W:D	= 7:10	Cont:R	= 6:20
eb	= 3:12 ep = 15	L	= .33	H+Hd:A+Ad = 1:13 (H)+(Hd):(A)+(Ad) = 1:0	
Blends:R	= 8:20	F+%	= .60	H+A:Hd+Ad	= 10:4
a:p	= 2:3	X+%	= .65	XRT Achrom.	= 7.4"
Ma:Mp	= 0:2	A%	= .65	XRT Chrom	= 28.2"

and there is no psychiatric history among the members of the immediate family, although the older sister did seek counseling while in her senior year about her intentions to marry against the wishes of her parents.

The subject is described as being an attractive, long haired youngster of average height and weight who looks slightly older than her age. The examiner, a female school psychologist, reports that the subject approached the testing situation with apparent anxiety at the onset but relaxed after a short period. The subject reports a regular menstrual cycle, with occasional "first day cramps." She freely admits to smoking marijuana frequently, and also to sexual relationships with numerous "boys." She indicates that she will usually resist intercourse "unless I'm stoned," and that she really does not "get that much out of it." She has no special boyfriend, but "dates a lot." She feels that she has many friends, but points out that she likes animals much better than people. She is quite aware that her current status in school may be in jeopardy, but has resigned herself to the probable suspension. She feels that school "is pretty dumb," and although she aspires to be a nurse, she expresses an unwillingness to "put up with all this" to be one. She describes her family as a "constant hassle," identifying her father as a cruel dictator and her mother as simply "stupid." She claims that her sister would not have married so quickly had the home been a "happier" place, and she also expresses doubt that her brother would have made such a hasty commitment to the Navy had he been able to "get along better" at home. She says that if she is suspended from school, she will seek work.

Prior to the Rorschach, she was administered a Benton Visual Retention Test, on which her performance was satisfactory, and a WISC. The Full Scale I.Q. is 117, with no significant scatter among the subtests.

Structural Interpretation.   The structure signifies much chaos, and includes six of the eight variables that occur with high frequency among suicidal youngsters ($FV + VF + V + FD > 2$;   color-shading blend > 0; $Zd > \pm 4.0$; $X + \% < .70$; $Lambda < .35$; pure H is 0), and a seventh ($3r + (2)/R < .35$) is exactly on the "margin." Although the constellation is not as "firm" as the one developed for adults, in that it will identify as "false positive" between 10% and 20% of young patients, the presence of these six features remains striking and should be cause for concern. Even if a suicidal potential does not exist, that constellation in itself marks some of the disarray she is experiencing.

Approaching the structural data more methodically, it is noted that she tends toward extratensiveness ($EB = 2 : 4.0$), but that the ep is significantly greater than the EA. Normative data indicate that, by the age of 15, slightly more than two of every three nonpatients will show a higher EA, and when the difference is as substantial as in this case (6.0 : 15), it is probably a matter for concern. It indicates that she has many psychological activities occurring within her, like alarms going off, but that she does not have access to many resources to contend with that psychic bombardment. The eb reveals that many of these psychological activities have an emotional rather than ideational character. She has 12 grey-black shading features in the record, including four T, four C', two Y, and two V determinants. This composite is six times greater than that expected for the 15 year old nonpatient, and *four* times greater than expected for the 15 year old behavior problem. It is even more than twice as much shading as would be expected from the 15 year old withdrawn youngster. The high T frequency signals an intense need for emotional affiliation, while the high C' frequency indicates that she is inhibiting a great deal of emotion that might otherwise be discharged. This is quite interesting in terms of the $FC : CF + C$ *ratio* and the *Afr*. The former (3 : 2) reflects considerably more modulation of her affective deliveries than would be expected for most 15 year olds, while the latter hints that she may have some awareness of the potential "danger" inherent in emotional displays, and that she tries to avoid situations that are emotionally provocative. It is interesting to consider these data in the light of her report that she engages in sexual intercourse *only* "when stoned"—that is, when controls are diminished and needs that may otherwise be controlled are more difficult to modulate and direct. It is also important to note that the "high T" component is probably important in its relation to her promiscuous behavior. In other words, sexual activity, which she says she does not "get much out of," affords a way of being close to someone. The two V determinants and the single FD answer suggest that she does much more introspection than might be suspected from her "devil may care" history.

Both of her M responses, one of which is a minus, have a passive character, suggesting that she is not very prone to deliberate ideation for problem solving; *yet,* the $+4.5 Zd$ score indicates that she is an overincorporator. This has probably evolved from an awareness that people can and do manipulate her. She has essentially no *Human* contents, except for one parenthesized Human, and thus is probably confused about people as well as about herself. Her low *Lambda* (.33) indicates that she has considerable difficulty in extracting herself from complexity, and the low $F+\%$ and $X+\%$ signify that she will often distort reality, a problem that adds to the vulnerability created by her inability to avoid complex stimulus features. Although her $W:M$ (7 : 2) is within a reasonable range, the high $A\%$ (.65) suggests that she is far less mature than is desirable to achieve some of her aspirations. She gives slightly fewer *Popular* answers than might be predicted, but is still clearly able to define and respond to conventional stimuli. Her very long reaction times to chromatically colored cards hint at some of her trouble; that is, she simply cannot handle emotional stimuli, and the four S locations that she includes equate with negative or even angry feelings about this.

Interpretation of the Scoring Sequence. The sequence confirms that she has much difficulty with the chromatic series, showing reaction times that are much longer than to the achromatic cards. In addition, her S locations are well distributed through the test, indicating that the oppositionality cannot be attributed to situational factors. She manifests an interesting P failure on Cards III and VII, which may signify something about her interpersonal problems as well as problems with her own identity. The fact that she uses S in both of her answers to Card VII seems congruent with that proposition; that is, she becomes more upset when confronted with a stimulus that may denote something about "femaleness." In the same context, both of her answers to Card VII are of poor form quality. Some sense of her limited emotional control may be found in her first response to Card VIII. When confronted with a totally chromatic stimulus, she can only offer a pure C response, although it is a healthy sign to note that, after being confronted with three such stimulus figures in consecutive order, she "signs out" with a pure F, Popular answer.

Interpretation of the Content. Her entry, or sign in, response provides the only glimpse of Human content, an angel, somewhat grandiosely elaborated, ". . . if you could see her better you could see the gold and silver on her dress . . ." This answer is also quite revealing in that she says, ". . . sort of like she's getting ready to fly, but she's not yet." After being so revealing, she moves to a classic "barrier" answer, a beetle, but ultimately admits that she prefers the angel. There are at least three other instances in which she "enters" a card by giving a "vulnerable'' answer but then reverts to a ''barrier'' form of response. In Card II, she begins with ''rabbits,'' but then moves to a ''shellfish,'' and in Card IV, she opens with a ''blanket'' but moves to a tree, and in Card V, she enters with a ''butterfly'' but moves to an ''armadillo.'' There is a sense of ambivalence in this process, almost as if she wants to expose herself, but then backs away to a more concealing answer. Two of her answers seem quite pathological and raise questions about her drug involvement. But involve ''nostrils'' (Card III and Card X). This is an unusual response, but it is not uncommon among people who have become involved with ''hard'' drugs. She also gives three sun responses, and all have a somewhat positive quality although two involve a dimensional determinant and a third is pure C. The first, to Card VI, is nearly concealed, ''behind this thing, maybe a tree,'' while the third, on Card IX, is more juvenile and vibrant; it is fluffy and colorful. Her two responses to Card VII, previously mentioned for their unique scoring features, are a bit mystifying: a cat's face and a mushroom. These answers clearly reflect something of herself, as do all of her responses, but it is difficult to sort out what the meaning is in this instance. She is a bit more transparent on Card X, beginning with a mad horse, but then moving to the shaggy buffalo, and ultimately departing from the card with the Popular, but nonetheless, negative spider response. Her pure C response, the second of her three ''sun involved'' answers, is encouraging in some ways. It is not a violent pure C, nor does it imply a real loss of control, as is frequently the case in the pure C answer. Instead, it conveys an intense emotional feeling, but not one that may be ''out of reach.'' Overall, the contents do not seem to reflect an obnoxious or disruptive person, and although the structural data convey a sense of emotional disruption, the answers imply more of a defensive, vacillating, very emotional person. There is very little aggressive content, and that is restricted mainly to the angry horse identified on Card X. It is true that she tends to place ''barriers'' around her, but they seem to be ''short lived'' and not very sturdy over a ''long haul.''

Case 19 Summary.   This youngster is essentially a fragile, gentle person who wants very much to be loved, but who also has great difficulty in containing her own emotions. In fact, she is extremely ambivalent about her emotions, and seems to vacillate between open exposure of her feelings and a strict barrier that tries to conceal them. Her strong need for emotional affiliation seems to collide with her apprehensions about becoming overly emotional. As a consequence, her self-esteem has diminished significantly, her self-concept is in some disarray, she has not progressed developmentally at a normal pace, she resorts too much to a passive fantasy life, and she has become more and more prone to interpret reality in a personalized and sometimes distorted framework. Although she tries very hard to sort through her complex stimulus world, she often has difficulty in distinguishing important from unimportant stimuli. As she has become more and more frustrated in her semi-helpless and ungratified status, she has lost contact with people and with herself, and is building a negativism that can become very self-destructive, if such a consequence has not already taken place.

A Treatment Plan.   This young girl, very much like the one presented in Case 5, is depressed; *but* she is much more volatile and in jeopardy of losing control. Her ''acting out'' behaviors have apparently served to create some form of defense in the past, but her environment is "catching up" with her, and, consequently, she should be treated as a "crisis" problem. The most immediate objective would be to relieve some of the environmental pressure she is feeling. Under optimal conditions, any decision about suspension from school should be deferred, for at least a trial period during which a more thorough evaluation of the family constellation can be completed. On a more direct level, she needs close human contact that can offer reassurance and direction. This should be oriented to provide some reduction of the high T need, and permit a reduction in the feelings of helplessness manifest in the Y responses. Treatment should not necessarily focus, at the onset, on her acting out behavior, and inevitably, she will be prone to test the limits of any interaction until she feels a sense of security in the theraputic relationship. Then, and only then, can a longer term intervention program be initiated to focus on the basic issues of self-concept, peer interaction, social skills, and greater perceptual accuracy. She needs a different perception of people—that is, one less defensive and suspicious of being manipulated—and she needs to learn that she can give and receive affection on a more mature level. Any intervention effort with this youngster will not be easy or quick, since she has a "rugged track record." She will find it difficult to change this pattern, which, no doubt, has reinforced counterproductive behavior that will continue to persist for some time.

An optimal treatment program would not only include evaluation of the family constellation, but also, probably, some form of family therapy in which the elements of inadequate communication can be reduced or eliminated and closer emotional ties created. Concurrently, her academic difficulties might be minimized for the moment, until some realistic remedial program can be instituted; *but* that probably cannot occur until she feels comfortable and "in control" of her situation. This is a long and complex treatment case, which must be planned with loose parameters, to be reevaluated as each step in the process is achieved. She is fragile and chaotic, and somewhat like an accident looking for a place to happen, if that accident has not already taken place. The therapist will require frequent and flexible contact; flexible in terms of adaptability to both brief or extended sessions. Ultimately, the therapist may want to include the assistance of a second therapist, possibly male, for some sorts of role playing to develop social skills and achieve better modulation of emotional discharge. This youngster has a rich psychological endowment, but it has grown in bits and pieces, and it lacks consistency and/or continuity.

Case 19 Epilogue.   The subject was cautiously receptive to most of the feedback, although she vigorously denied any experience of depression or sadness, and was very angered at the suggestion. Later in the feedback session, she did cry openly and for a long period when the issues of her peer group and family relations were broached. She agreed to daily brief contact therapy (in school), and, for the first few days, appeared at the therapist's office well before the appointed time. Subsequent teacher reports also indicate that she did not miss any classes during this period, and that her disruptiveness had subsided considerably; *however,* her parents were very resistant to any involvement (although her brother did volunteer a useful social history and agreed to make himself available). Unfortunately, the bureaucratic wheels of the educational system could not be halted, and she was suspended from school "for the remainder of the year." Shortly thereafter, she left home, and was reported as a "runaway" by her parents. Approximately eight months later, she was placed in a children's shelter, after having been arrested for "soliciting." She reported in a subsequent interview that she had considered suicide shortly after her first venture as a "prostitute," but took no direct action. After four weeks in the children's shelter, she was placed in a residential treatment center, from which she walked away after two months in residence. There is no further information available, although it is impossible to believe that she is not in some sort of disarray wherever she is now.

Case 20: A 9 Year Old Male—the Mixed Up Guitar

History.   This boy is a referral from a physician, at the request of the parents. He has been labeled as "hyperactive," a diagnosis initially offered by an examining school psychologist. He is currently in the fourth grade, and is described as having a very erratic performance that ranges from slightly better than average to completely inadequate. His performance in the second and third grades ranged from low average to average, with the greatest difficulty manifest in reading and math comprehension. During the third grade, the teacher noted an "out of seat tendency" but did not regard it as more serious than that of several others in the class; however, the current teacher reports a significantly higher out of seat frequency, and identified him as a major problem. In addition, he has been observed fighting frequently with peers during lunch and play periods. His parents confirm that he is a seemingly overactive youngster, are seeking ways to reduce the excessive activity, and have requested their family physician to examine the child with the possible objective of medication. Ritalin has been suggested by a consulting school physician, but the parents want a more thorough examination before any final decision is rendered.

The boy was adopted at the age of six months, and no information is available on the genetic parents, except for the indication from the social agency processing the adoption that there is no remarkable medical history for either of the genetic parents. The adoptive father, age 40, is a machinist, while the adoptive mother, age 38, does not work outside the home. Both appear conscientiously concerned with obtaining the best mode of intervention for their son. The father reportedly devotes much time to the boy, and has been active as an adviser to the Cub Scout Pack to which the boy belongs; he plays baseball with his son, and they often go fishing or camping. The father reports that he started to teach the boy some of the "fundamentals" of carpentry, but stopped after becoming concerned that the boy might injure himself using some of the tools.

Prior to the psychological examination, the youngster was subjected to a complete physical and neurological examination. His eye scan and acuity are normal, his hearing is within normal limits. All laboratory studies were negative, as were the "bulk" of the neurological data. However, a computerized EEG reveals a slightly greater frequency of slow wave activity than would be expected. The consulting neurologist describes the EEG as "questionable." The youngster was somewhat resistant to the psychological examination, and ultimately, three separate testing sessions were required. His performance on a WISC revealed a Full Scale I.Q. of 108 (Verbal Scale = 108; Performance Scale = 109) with a consistent performance throughout. He reads at a level slightly lower than third grade,

Case 20

Card	Free Association	Inquiry	Scoring
I	53″		
	1. It ll a crocodile's face lik its gonna bite (stands up)	E: (Rpts S's resp) S: C the nostils & the big mouth is open lik to bite u & u can c back in to his tonsils c here (points) he has a little tonsil down in there E: Can u run u'r finger around the face S: Sure c all this & this, all of it c these r the ears	WS– $FM^a.FD$– Ad 3.5
	2. Mayb its a bat too, ugh all black like a bat, lik its gonna get something (sits down)	E: (Rpts S's resp) S: These r the wgs & the body & the big claws sticking out lik it was grabbing for s.body	Wo $FM^a.FC'$o A P 1.0
	<3. Hey, ths way its lik a witch w a funny hat lik a witch (stands up)	E: (Rpts S's resp) S: C this is one of those mixed up hats lik thy wear	Do Fw (Hd)
II	68″		
	√4. I don't lik these, I d.k. I guess an explosion (still standing, leaning on table)	E: (Rpts S's resp) S: C the red here, the fire lik an explos, lik its starting to explode c the way its going out, lik a big bomb going off mayb	Dv $m^a.CF$o Ex
	<5. U kno there's almost 2 of everything (sits) ths part c.b. a mountain, 2 mountains if u turn it, one on each side, lik 2 countries	E: (Rpts S's resp) S: C its piled up lik a mountain & ths one is the same, just a big mountain	Dv Fo (2) Ls
	6. It c.b. 2 hunters too, thy r holding their guns out & thy hav red hats on so other people will c them o.k. and not mistake them for a bear or s.t.	E: (Rpts S's resp) S: C this way, thy'r big & they have their guns here (cntr) c the guns r pointg away, back toward there & they have red hats on E: U said the guns r pointed away S: C they get smaller lik thy were going that way	W+ $M^a.FC.FD$o (2) H (P) 4.5

III 65″

7. I can mak a combination here those r 2 A's fiting (sits on floor)
E: (Rpts S's resp)
S: Oh I just thot of that, thy c.b. u kno
E: I'd lik to c them as u did
S: I'm tired, thy r rite here c on their back legs lik thy r getg ready to fite e.o., c the heads & legs, lik kangaroos

D+ FM^{a}w (2) A 3.0

3. (layng down) That wld mak a good necktie I guess, its a pretty one, all red, yeah lik a necktie for a clown
E: (Rpts S's resp)
S: Yeah, thy go in lik this when thy hav a knot & out lik ths each end its lik a big necktie that clowns wear

Do FCo Cg

9. Those thgs c.b. hockey sticks
E: (Rpts S's resp)
S: Yeah, thy go dwn lik that, thy r straight till u get to here & then thy bend lik ths, ths one over here is the same

Do Fw (2) Hockey Stick

IV 37″

10. Its a monkey w a hard tail, lik he's sittg on it (starde up), let's do s t. else
E: Let's finish this fi'st (S's sits down agan)
E: (Rpts S's resp)
S: Ths is his tail & he's got big feet, its lik he's leaning bkwrds (demo's) c lik ths & he's got his arms back too (demo's)
E: I'm not sur how u c him leang back
S: C his feet r so big lik out front

Wo FM^p.FDo A 2.0 INCOM

V 51″

11. A bat, exactly lik a bat c his wgs r spread out lik he's zooming along
E: (Rpts S's resp)
S: Its really kind of lik one, c the big wgs out, he's flyg, & he has claws out too, c here

Wo FM^{a}o A P 1.0

12. It c.b. a monster too yeah lik a big monster
E: (Rpts S's resp)
S: He's got a big black coat on & his arms r out (demo's) lik ths & he's got a funny hat on c up here

Wo M^a.FC'o (H) 1.0

405

Case 20 (Continued)

Card	Free Association		Inquiry	Scoring
VI	62″	13.	Tht's like a mixed up guitar (stands up) a one string guitar but its mixed up bec its got bumps on it	E: (Rpts S's resp) S: Yeah, a one stringer, c ths is where the string goes, c the line rite down the middl, there's supposed to be more, at least most have more but ths has only one E: U said it has bumps on it S: Yeah, c all the bumps on it & arnd the edges (feels card) c here in the cntr it ll bumps, c it, lik littl bumps	*Wo FTo* Guitar 2.5
		V14.	Ths way it ll a skate, lik in the ocean, lik a sting ray skate w the big tail	E: (Rpts S's resp) S: Sting ray skates have got long tails lik ths, or is it the neck, I don't remember, it doesn't matter but it does ll ths here looks, c all big here & the tail here	*W– F– A* 2.5
VII	32″	15.	That w.b. a U drawn by a sloppy writer	E: (Rpts S's resp) S: Sure, that does ll a U, also its not very straight so it must be sloppy writing	*Wo Fw Al* 2.5
		V16.	Hey, this c.b. a couple of ele-phants, c the long trunk thyr up on one leg lik in the circus (stands up & demo's)	E: (Rpts S's resp) S: Yeah, its 2 elephants & thyr balancg lik thy do in the circus, c just one leg is down & the others r up, thy can b pretty good at that	*Do FM^{a}o* (2) *A*
VIII	45″	17.	C.b. 2 lions & thy r walkg up this jungle mountain (sits on floor)	E: (Rpts S's resp) S: Its a very colorful mountain, thats how u kno its a jungle mountain & these r the lions, c the legs & the head, thy look exactly lik lions & thy r tryg to get to the top of this mountain	*W+ FM^a.FCo* (2) *A,Ls P* 4.5

IX   31″

18. Tht's a very colorful fire up there, lik u c in a freplc

> *E:* (Rpts *S*'s resp)
> *S:* Well, it c.b. that, c up here its very color-ful lik a fire, thats how I thot of it, just fire, c its orange lik fire

Dv   C   Fi

>19. It c.b. a jungle mt too lik covered w all the green lik in a jungle
(gets off floor into chair)

> *E:* (Rpts *S*'s resp)
> *S:* I'm not sure why, its just green, is this stuff really important?
> *E:* Well, I'd lik to c what u c
> *S:* Well its all green & that's how jungle mts r, really!

Dv   CFo   Ls

X   60″

20. Ths s just a bunch of colors, c the red & yellow & green & brown

> *E:* (Rpts *S*'s resp)
> *S:* Yeah, tht's what I thot of first, just a bunch of colors c all of 'em

Wv   Cn   Colors

21. I've got something else, c dwn here is lik a weird monster & 2 more in here c these r really weird w bumpy bellies am I done now?

> *E:* (Rpts *S*'s resp)
> *S:* Yeah, weird monsters, c down here this one is all brown, lik he was burnt up or s.t. lik out of a fire & these r closer, c thy r bigger & thy r red & thy hav bumpy bellies, thy look lik thy got no legs, lik thy just crawl along & scare people, there's 2 of each of them

Do   FCo   (2)   (Hd)   (DV)

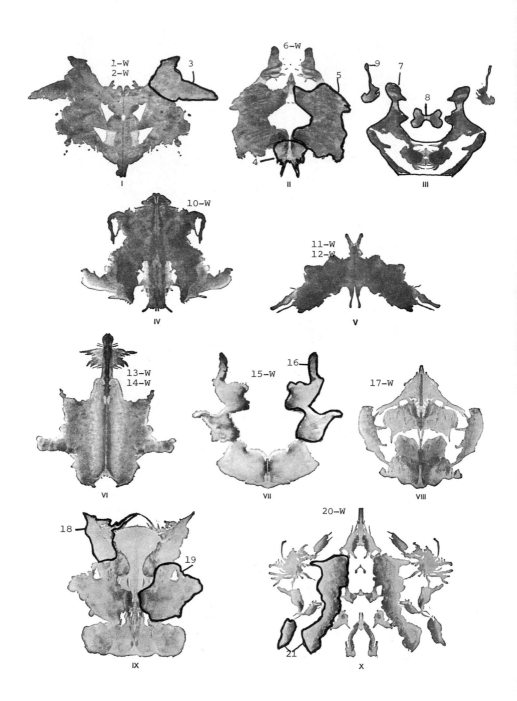

Case 20

CARD	RT	NO.	LOCATION	DETERMINANTS (S)		CONTENT (S)	POP	Z SCORE	SPECIAL
I	53"	1.	WS–	$FM^a.FD-$		Ad		3.5	
		2.	Wo	$FM^a.FC'o$		A	P	1.0	
		<3.	Do	Fw		(Hd)			
II	68"	v4.	Dv	$m^a.CFo$		Ex			
		<5.	Dv	Fo	(2)	Ls			
		6.	W+	$M^a.FC.FDo$	(2)	H	(P)	4.5	
III	65"	7.	D+	FM^aw	(2)	A		3.0	
		8.	Do	FCo		Cg			
		9.	Do	Fw		HockeyStk			
IV	37"	10.	Wo	$FM^p.FDo$		A		2.0	INCOM
V	51"	11.	Wo	FM^ao		A	P	1.0	
		12.	Wo	$M^a.FC'o$		(H)		1.0	
VI	62"	13.	Wo	FTo		Guitar		2.5	
		v14.	W–	F–		A		2.5	
VII	32"	15.	Wo	Fw		Al		2.5	
		v16.	Do	FM^ao	(2)	A			
VIII	45"	17.	W+	$FM^a.FCo$	(2)	A,Ls	P	4.5	
IX	31"	18.	Dv	C		Fi			
		>19.	Dv	CFo		Ls			
X	60"	20.	Wv	Cn		Colors			
		21.	Do	FCo	(2)	(Hd)			(DV)

Case 20:   Structural Summary

R = 21   Zf = 11   ZSum = 28.0   P = 3+1   (2) = 7

Location Features		Determinants (Blends First)	Contents		Contents (Idiographic)

Location Features

			DQ
W	= 11		
D	= 10	+	= 3
Dd	= 0	o	= 11
S	= 1	v	= 5
DW	=	—	= 2

Determinants (Blends First)

M.FC.FD	=1
M.FC'	=1
FM.FC	=1
FM.FC'	=1
FM.FD	=2
m.CF	=1
M	=
FM	= 3
m	=
C	= 2
CF	= 1
FC	= 2
C'	=
C'F	=
FC'	=
T	=
TF	=
FT	= 1
V	=
VF	=
FV	=
Y	=
YF	=
FY	=
rF	=
Fr	=
FD	=
F	= 5

Form Quality

FQx		FQf	
+	= 0	+	= 0
o	= 13	o	= 1
w	= 4	w	= 3
—	= 2	—	= 1

M Quality

+	= 0
o	= 2
w	= 0
—	= 0

Contents

H	= 1
(H)	= 1
Hd	=
(Hd)	= 2
A	= 7
(A)	=
Ad	= 1
(Ad)	=
Ab	=
Al	= 1
An	=
Art	=
Ay	=
Bl	=
Bt	=
Cg	= 1
Cl	=
Ex	= 1
Fi	= 1
Fd	=
Ge	=
Hh	=
Ls	= 2,1
Na	=
Sx	=
Xy	=

Contents (Idiographic)

Colors	= 1
....	
Guitar	= 1
....	
Hockey Stk	= 1
....	=
....	=
....	=
....	=
....	=
....	=
....	

Special Scorings

PSV	=
DV	= 0,1
INCOM	= 1
FABCOM	=
CONTAM	=
ALOG	=
	=

RATIOS, PERCENTAGES, AND DERIVATIONS

ZSum-Zest = 28.0-34.5		FC:CF+C = 4:4		Afr = .31	
Zd = -6.5		W:M = 11:2		3r+(2)/R = .33	
EB = 2:7.0 EA = 9.0		W:D = 11:10		Cont:R = 10:21	
eb = 8:3 ep = 11		L = .31		H+Hd:A+Ad = 4:8 (H)+(Hd):(A)+(Ad) = 3:0	
Blends:R = 7:21		F+% = .20		H+A:Hd+Ad = 9:3	
a:p = 9:1		X+% = .62		XRT Achrom. = 47.0"	
Ma:Mp = 2:0		A% = .38		XRT Chrom = 53.8"	

but shows an adequate memory for designs, and was able to copy the Bender Gestalt figures in a "sloppy" but accurate way, with no rotations, collisions, or reversals. Nonetheless, he was very active throughout all of the testing, a pattern that persisted through the collection of the Rorschach data.

The assessment question being studied here is essentially one dealing with the possibility of psychological factors provoking the hyperactive behavior pattern. The term "hyperactive" has erupted in an almost "faddish" manner in recent years, and quite often is used to describe many conditions. There are, of course, several well developed theoretical positions on hyperactivity, hyperkinesis, or minimal brain dysfunction; however, research in this area has been modest in terms of refining understanding of the syndrome. Stewart (1970) has proposed that it is a condition of genetic origin. Much earlier, Pasamanick and Knobloch (1959) had suggested a physical trauma hypothesis as the originating element. Silver (1971) and Wender (1971) have posited the view that it occurs from a neurochemical imbalance, while Weithorn (1973) has discussed it more broadly as a dysfunction of the central nervous system. Feingold (1974) has argued that many hyperactive children are products of dietary deficiencies or dietary toxics. A basic problem remains the definition of the syndrome and the ability to differentiate it conclusively from an overactive pattern of behavior promoted by psychological factors. Unfortunately, the Rorschach is quite limited in the extent to which it can contribute to such a differentiation, and, ordinarily, inputs from other sources and other tests are required before true "hyperkinesis" can be diagnosed. The Rorschach data can provide a description of the subject and his or her response styles, personality assets, and liabilities, but it can neither confirm nor negate an "MBD" diagnosis. It has been included in this case because all other data are negative or equivocal, and with the anticipation that it may offer some direction concerning intervention.

Structural Interpretation.   The structural data reflect a very complicated youngster. He is quite clearly an extratensive ($EB = 2 : 7.0$), which is neither surprising, nor a liability, but it is obvious that he has a marked tendency toward emotional discharge as a mode of coping. While the ep exceeds the EA, the difference between the two is modest and, again, not surprising for one this age. His eb is heavily weighed on the left side, consisting primarily of FM responses; he is prompted by many needs, but this too is not necessarily surprising for a youngster of this age, except for the high FM frequency, which is twice as great as that for most nine year olds. In other words, he experiences a great deal of ideational activity related to need states, and this may create a sense of confusion. He also delivers about twice as many *blend* answers as most children of this age, signifying a much more complex psychological existence. The extreme $a : p$ ratio indicates that he is not very flexible in his ideation, and this also may create some problems for him. There is proportionally more FC in the $FC : CF + C$ ratio, but in this instance that is probably an asset, because he also delivers pure C responses. Interestingly, his Afr is substantially lower than that for most nine year olds, hinting that he is aware of possible problems in the modulation of affect, and that he tries to avoid situations that might exacerbate such problems. Unfortunately, the *egocentricity index* is also considerably lower than normal for this age, revealing a considerably lower self-esteem than may be "healthy"; in this context, it is very possible that some of his "hyperactivity" especially fighting behavior, is a reaction against feelings of lowered self-value. He is a severe *underincorporator,* a phenomenon not uncommon among very young children, but also relatively common among children with clear evidence of minimal brain dysfunction (as evidenced by neurological features). This may also be contributing to some of his overactiveness, in that underincorporators seem to arrive at decision making very hastily and often prematurely. The low *Lambda* (.31) may be related to the underincorporativeness; that is, he has great difficulty avoiding or backing away from complexity. The lower than expected $F+\%$ and $X+\%$ can be a major problem in a case such as this. He does not tend to "distort" reality severely, since there are only two minus responses in the entire record; however, he does tend to personalize his interpretations in unique ways. When combined with the fact that he offers only three true *Popular* answers, the question arises whether he is too individualistic, and not sufficiently concerned with social demands. He has many contents, at least two or possibly three more than is expected for the average nine year old. It is not clear whether this derives from a broad range of interests and/or information, or whether he may be avoiding specific content areas. He gives only one pure H, suggesting that he does not have a very firm "handle" on people; probably this applies to himself, too. Three of his four Human contents are parenthesized, indicating a less than typical approach to people, even for this age. He has three FD determinants in the record, which may represent an attempt at introspectiveness but may be related to the situation of being examined by many people. His reaction times are very long, but, as the record indicates, he was continually changing positions.

Interpretation of the Scoring Sequence.   His basic approach is to the W, which is not uncommon for nine year olds, but which may be a problem for him in that he is underincorporative and may not devote enough time to a scan of the entire stimulus. He has a P failure on both Cards III and VII, and it would have been desirable for the examiner to "test limits" for these two Populars in order to obtain a bit more evidence about his view of people. Six of his seven blends appear during the first five cards, and three of the six include an FD determinant. This may support the notion that the "attempting to take distance" is more a function of being examined than a continually ongoing form of introspection. However, in either instance, it would signal that he is looking at himself, which could be an asset to any intervention plan. Although he has considerable difficulty with IX and X, he is able to depart from the test with a modulated color response, indicating a capacity for recovery even when confronted by the kinds of stimuli that create discomfort for him.

Interpretation of the Content.   He enters the test with a very angry response, and after a very long reaction time. In fact, many of his answers include aggressive objects or activities (a bat going to get something, an explosion, two hunters, animals fighting, a bat zooming, a big monster, lions, and two weird monsters). Although aggressive contents are not uncommon among children, especially latency age males, they do raise questions about identification patterns and styles of defense. His "sign-in" crocodile's face sounds a warning to the examiner, but also provides a glimpse of the way he sees himself and tends to protect himself. Quite likely, some of his fighting behavior is a defense against attacks on his facade, which may be quite fragile. His third response on Card II provides some support for this notion, ". . . two hunters . . . and they have red hats on so other people will see them O.K. and not mistake them for a bear or something." The fear implicit here is that if others misidentify the hunters, they may be injured. Possibly he operates on the premise that a good offense is the best defense. His first response to Card II, during which time he is standing and holding the card inverted, also suggests this possibility, "I don't like these, I guess an explosion."

Many of his responses are marked by the bantering commentary very typical for most children (Hey, this is funny, I don't like these, let's do something else, I've got something else, I can make a combination here). He also presents the pseudopreciseness that children often convey to avoid being challenged, (You know there's almost two of everything; yeah, a one stringer; I don't remember, it doesn't matter, but it does look like this here; exactly like a bat).

His response to Card IV, "It's a monkey with a hard tail . . ." suggests some tempting "food for thought" about sexuality, but it is possibly his response to Card VI that is the most unique, ". . . like a mixed up guitar, a one string guitar but it's mixed up because it's got bumps on it." It is the tactile features that make the guitar "mixed up," suggesting that he is probably in great conflict about how to make his needs known, or, possibly, is questioning himself about whether he should have needs. It is a very concrete, yet very revealing, answer. He has "only one string"—that is, he is very limited in his response repertoire. His first answer to Card VII is also quite interesting, ". . . a U drawn by a sloppy writer." In the inquiry, he points out that ". . . it's not very straight so it must be sloppy . . ." It is an "either-or" proposition, and raises a question about his own value system and that in his immediate environment. For instance, have his parents been overly precise in the things that they expect of him, or imply that they expect? He obviously becomes very "wrapped up" in the chromatic color, and all answers except his last one to Card X seem heavily influenced by the color features; the lions on VIII are on a jungle mountain identified as such because it's very colorful; the fire is fire because it is orange on Card IX; the jungle mountain on IX is such because it's all green; and X is ". . . just a bunch of colors . . . ." The latter is a color naming response (Cn) that is not uncommon among the records of organic subjects, *but* is also not uncommon among very young children, especially four, five, and six year olds. Thus, its presence here may be related to an MBD feature, *or* it may simply be a manifestation of less cognitive maturity than might be expected for a nine year old. His last answer provokes a recall of the "bumpy" guitar answer on Card VI. He signs out with ". . . weird monsters . . . with bumpy bellies," elaborated in the inquiry as ". . . just crawl along and scare people . . ." Much can be speculated about bumpy bellies, but it would be speculation. Probably it is more important to focus on the bumpiness itself, as a perseverated concept, and one that is very unique. He perceives himself as weird and mixed up, and is clearly aware of his own "monster" characteristics.

Case 20 Summary. Any approach to the basic assessment question raised in this case—can the hyperactivity be of psychological origin?—must be equivocal in light of the EEG finding. However, there are considerable data in the Rorschach that suggest a potential relationship between the psychological and behavioral elements. He is very complicated and not very flexible. He underincorporates, but concurrently strives to "master" his entire stimulus field. His thinking is sometimes very concrete, and he becomes even more so when confronted with emotionally loaded stimuli. He modulates his emotional displays reasonably well, but only when he has some alternative stimuli available on which to base a response. His self-esteem is very limited, and his self-concept seems to be more diffuse than might be expected. He is very aggressive, but much of that aggressiveness is a defense against his own feelings of vulnerability. He has frequent and strong needs, which provoke much ideational activity, but he is not certain about how to control the ideation or reduce the need states. His natural style is to discharge emotion when coping, but his concreteness, underincorporateness, and inability to avoid complexity will often provoke a stronger emotional discharge than he prefers, or apparently than is acceptable to others. He does not have a very good perception of people, and is also quite vague about himself. There may be some "lag" in cognitive development, and this contributes to his tendency to perceive things in terms of "black versus white," or "right versus wrong." Although this is not unusual for a child, it probably complicates his life, since he attempts to integrate his extratensive style with the demands of his environment; and with each behavioral "failure," his self-esteem is reduced and his self-concept inhibited in its natural development. Although he attempts to be introspective, his concreteness will tend to reduce the likelihood that this effort will be effective, and, in fact, he may be prone to "sort himself out" in concrete ways that simply add to his miseries. In other words, he may try to oversimplify his self-inspection to a "pass-fail" level, which can lead to disastrous interpretations about personal worth and create grave distortions in his overall pattern of identification.

A Treatment Plan. Although none of the descriptive elements in the summary would negate the possibility of a *true* MBD condition, there is reason to believe that some of these psychological features do contribute significantly to his less desired behavior patterns. Thus, while a treatment program *might* include some focus on "perceptual retraining," that process could be placed lower on a priority scale and possibly deferred, until attempts to achieve other objectives could be evaluated. The same criterion would be applied to the use of medication at this time. However, it is obvious that the treatment "package" will require multiple intervention modalities, and must be carefully monitored to insure that one is not counterproductive to the others.

First, it is very important that the father-son relationship be more carefully evaluated. The boy appears to equate "masculinity" with aggressiveness; yet, according to the history, the father is presented as a concerned and conscientious parent. Has the father, in his conscientiousness, dominated the boy? The father consults to the boy's Cub Scout pack. Ordinarily, though not always, it is mothers who are most involved at the Cub Scout level. Even if the father's participation is not unusual, however, does his presence have a negative impact on the boy? It is also important to note that the father began to teach carpentry skills to the boy, but then stopped for fear that the boy might injure himself. Did the father overreact in that situation? Very few nine year olds will become skilled carpenters, and almost every parent will feel some apprehension watching a child with a hammer and nail, no less a saw. Does the boy know that he is adopted? It is customary to be open with children about this, but sometimes an overemphasis on the issue can be frightening or confusing. Adoptive parents will often tell children that "they are special," but the child may reject that notion and live in psychological terror that the adoptive parents will decide that is not really true. What then?

There are many useful methods for evaluating the interaction between parent and child, the best involving several behavioral samples taken under "natural" conditions. When this is not possible, behavioral paradigms can be created. For instance, a parent can be taught the principles of a labrynth maze game in which either of two knobs will cause a platform to be tilted in one direction or another. The platform has many holes, and the object of the game is to roll a metal ball as far as possible through the maze on the platform without having the ball fall through the many holes along the way. After the parent is instructed about the operation of the game, he or she is then asked to explain it to the child, and in the course of 10 minutes, see how far they can roll the ball, *working together,* with the parent operating one knob and the child working the second knob. A behavioral scoring of the interaction of the parent and child can be quite revealing. Similarly, a parent may be asked to have the child draw a house, a tree, and a person, supplying the parent with much paper and a box of crayons, then behaviorally assessing the interaction as the parent directs the child's performance. In this case, the evaluation of the child-parent interaction would be designed to study the "conscientious overprotectiveness" hypothesis. If this proves positive, then the intervention program must include some focus on a reorganizing of the interaction patterns between the parent, or parents, and the child to increase the child's sense of security and, hopefully, his self-esteem.

On a different level, the child should probably be involved in a form of directed play therapy designed to uncover more information about his aggressiveness. The use of a Make-A-Picture Story (Shneidman, 1952) or some other form of apperceptive instrument can be very useful to this end, the objective being to induce the child to discuss openly his feelings about aggressiveness, including his own aggressive behavior. This technique can also include some features oriented toward the structuring of a "delay" system, so as to reduce the impact of the underincorporativeness. There are many techniques that could be useful, including the "Simon Says" routine, although that may be too "childish" for a nine year old. Thus, incomplete figures, problem solving tasks, similarities games, and the like might be employed.

A third mode of intervention must occur in the school. A behavioral baseline concerning any disruptive behavior, such as out of seat frequency, would be an important starting point, and in collaboration with the teacher, a list can be developed of the reinforcements she can use to reward desired behavior when it occurs. If the child is as insecure in his identity as seems the case from the Rorschach data, her ability to reassure him through reinforcements for acceptable behavior will aid him in distinguishing productive from nonproductive behaviors.

An ultimate, but not necessarily immediate, goal will be to enhance his use of a natural style to display emotions when coping, but in ways that retain a realistic level of modulation without stifling some of the natural looseness common to children of this age.

Case 20 Epilogue.   The behavioral evaluations of the father-son and mother-son interactions did, indeed, reveal that each was considerably more overprotective, in negative ways, than would be desired. For instance, the father, while interacting with the son in the labrynth maze game, offered three times as many "corrective" statements as positive reinforcements. Similarly, when the mother directed the child to draw the house-tree-person, she made almost continuous suggestions about color choices, location of parts, and the like, and even suggested that the tree be repeated because the original drawn was "not very good." None of these comments was "bitter" or openly aggressive, but all had a destructive impact.

Subsequently, both parents agreed to a TV monitoring of their respective interactions with the child, and seemed to profit considerably from the focused feedback technique. The child was less responsive to the play therapy than had been hoped, but, by the third treatment month, he began interacting more openly with the female therapist and was able to deal, in a limited way, with issues of aggressiveness when they occurred. The greatest immediate gains were made in the classroom. The teacher was very cooperative, and seemed relieved at the presence of a "collaborator," who at the onset was responsible for establishing the baseline data and assisting in developing a list of reinforcers the teacher should use. The boy's classroom performance improved markedly during the first five weeks, and there was a corresponding improvement in his schoolwork, most of which returned to an "average" level, with greater improvement in math. His EEG, persisted as "borderline," according to the consulting neurologist, on the basis of the higher than usual frequency of slow waves. However, no medication was employed, since by that time, the boy's level of activity now fell within acceptable limits, although he was still regarded as among the most active in his class.

REFERENCES

Feingold, B. F. *Why Your Child is Hyperactive*. New York: Random House, 1974.

Pasamanick, B., and Knobloch, H. Syndrome of minimal cerebral damage in infancy. *Journal of the American Medical Association,* 1959, **170**, 1384–1387.

Shneidman, E. A. *The Make-A-Picture-Story Test*. New York: The Psychological Corporation, 1952.

Silver, L. B. A proposed view on the etiology of the neurological learning disability syndrome. *Journal of Learning Disabilities,* 1971, **4**, 123–133.

Stewart, M. A. Hyperactive children. *Scientific American,* 1970, **222**, 94–98.

Weithorn, C. J. Hyperactivity and the CNS: An etiological and diagnostic dilemma. *Journal of Learning Disabilities,* 1973, **1**, 46–50.

Wender, P. *Minimal Brain Dysfunction in Children*. New York: John Wiley and Sons, 1971.

CHAPTER 12

Treatment Evaluation

Another increasingly important use of Rorschach data is for treatment evaluation. Quite frequently, issues of treatment progress or treatment termination are raised by patients or by therapists. Just as the Rorschach data include no magic formulae for making intervention decisions, neither are there magic cues to signal that treatment should be continued, or terminated; however, assuming that a pretreatment protocol is available, a second, or even third, record, taken during treatment or at a tentative termination point, can be used to identify areas of change, and to provide a new review of assets and liabilities. If evaluated logically and in the proper context, the new evaluation can offer significant insights for the patient and/or therapist experiencing difficulty in the progress, of treatment, and can highlight areas of strength and/or concern to which the terminating patient may be alerted.

The history of assessment has focused largely on issues of diagnosis, and more recently on the use of assessment in the formulation of treatment plans; but the "helping" professions have also been plagued with relatively high relapse rates, allegations of ineffective treatment, and a seemingly large number of "revolving door" patients. Viewed from the cost-benefit perspective alone, it is much more realistic to have reevaluation procedures embedded into the routine intervention process to provide information on gains and alerting signals to potential pitfalls. This seems especially logical where intervention has focused specifically on a crisis situation, such as a suicide gesture, loss of significant others, or environmental disruption; or in instances in which hospitalization has occurred and problems of reentry have yet to be directly experienced. Reevaluation can also be very important in the long term treatment case, probably less to study the issue of termination and more to study gains, or to identify obstacles that appear to be inhibiting progress.

The procedure of reevaluation is essentially no different than that involved in treatment planning; that is, the instrument is used to define the subject as he or she is currently. The major difference is that a second, or "baseline," protocol is used to judge some changes that have occurred. It is very difficult to accomplish effective treatment evaluation without a second record—one taken before, or at the start of treatment. Attempting to evaluate treatment without a baseline protocol offers a multitude of problems, mainly because liabilities will be noted in all subjects, and the absence of a valid baseline makes it extremely difficult to view those liabilities in a realistic perspective. There are instances in which other forms of assessment can be used as a substitute baseline. Usually, these are well developed forms of behavioral assessment. For instance, if it is clear that a patient was very lethargic, was motorically retarded, had a very poor appetite and frequent insomnia, and openly complained of sadness or depression before treatment, a Rorschach taken later could target on the potential for future depressions.

However, it could not reveal with any precision what changes have occurred in the personality structure, particularly in the cognitive-affective sphere, as a result of the intervention process. Sometimes changes are modest but sufficient, whereas in other instances, changes may have been significant, but still insufficient in terms of the overall treatment objectives. The ultimate judgments about sufficiency or insufficiency will be revealed by the behavior of the patient, but before that time, the intelligent clinician can integrate new Rorschach findings with accumulated knowledge about the patient and can make some logical deductions, *provided that some reasonable baseline data are available.* Ideally, that baseline will derive from a previously administered Rorschach. The following case illustrates the basic process.

Cases 21 and 21A: A 24 Year Old Male—The Little Bird

History.   This man was originally referred by his family physician. He had undergone an extensive medical examination as a result of chronic back pain and occasional blurring of vision. That examination proved negative, and the next logical step was a psychiatric evaluation. The subject graduated from college at age 21, with a B.A. degree in economics. Shortly thereafter, he obtained a position as a teller in a bank, and after 18 months was promoted to a position of "credit manager" in one of the smaller branches of the bank. He has held that position for nearly three years. He also married in the first month after graduation from college. His wife, who is 10 months older than he, was a first year law student at that time, and has since completed her law degree and has been admitted to practice. She is now a member of a firm specializing in corporate law.

His parents are both living in a distant city. His father, age 46, is an accountant, and his mother does not work outside of the home, although she is involved in many volunteer projects in the community. He is a twin, having a fraternal sister who was born approximately 20 minutes before he was. She also has a college degree, in education, and currently teaches elementary school. She is engaged and expects to marry shortly.

He is described as a "pleasant looking" individual of average height and weight, with no distinguishing features. He expressed some skepticism about the possibility of a psychological factor contributing to his symptoms, but was quite responsive during the examination.

PreTreatment Evaluation.   The pretreatment Rorschach suggests a very slight tendency to extraversion, but he could be as easily "called" an ambitent. While he does appear to have considerable access to his resources ($EA > ep$), his $FC:CF+C$ indicates that he does not modulate affect well, and, in fact, displays a pure C response, indicating that the affect can become very volatile. His $a:p$ ratio suggests marked behavioral passivity, and he offers a substantial number of passive human movement features, revealing a tendency toward the more passive, Snow White kinds of deliberate ideations. While his reality testing is quite good, he is overly self-centered ($3r + (2)/R = .45$), but does not appear to set goals that are very high ($W:M$). His six human contents, including three pure H, indicate a natural interest in people; however, he has a V and FD determinant, hinting that he may be comparing himself unfavorably to whatever standard he expects of

Case 21

Card	Free Association	Inquiry	Scoring
I	14″		
	1. It ll a bat to me, w its wgs spread out, glidg alng	E: (Rpts S's resp) S: Well, the W thg ll tht, the wgs r sprd out lik it was glidg along, here is the tail (points)	Wo FM^{po} A P 1.0
	2. It c b. also a person, its seems lik he's—well I d.k. if its a man or wm, anyway, whatever, he's tied to a stake in the middle & other people r dancing around it, the darkness makes it ll there's smoke there too	E: (Rpts S's resp) S: I suppose it is a wm, altho I really didn't c it as clear before. Anyhow, she's tied to ths stake in the cntr w her hands up in the air, like she was cryg for help, its lik she was being burnt at the stake bec of all the smoke around her & these other people seem to b in costumes of s.s. E: Costumes? S: Well, u can't c them clearly so thy must b in costume	W+ M^{p-a}.YF+ (2) H,Smk P 4.0
II	39″		
	3. It ll a delta wgd plane or rocket takg off w the fire comg out	E: (Rpts S's resp) S: Well, it ll tht to me it has the shpe of a delta wgd plane lik for the future & there is fire bursting out of the rear, c the red here	DS+ m^a.CFo Plane,Fi 4.5
III	11″		
	4. It ll two people pulling s.t. aprt, lik thy r fiting over it	E: (Rpts S's resp) S: Thy c.b. either men or wm, I guess wm bec of the breasts & hi heels & thy'r pull-ing on ths thg, lik a basket of food	D+ M^{a}o (2) H,Fd P 3.0
	5. The entr c.b. lungs or s.t.	E: (Rpts S's resp) S: Its got the shape & the color to it, at least I always thot of lungs as red lik ths	Do FCo An

Case 21 (Continued)

Card		Free Association		Inquiry		Scoring
IV	41″	6. It ll some big monster out of sc. fict. sittg on a stump		E: (Rpts S's resp) S: It looks furry all over, lik I was sittg at his feet bec the feet look so big, & the rest is so grotesque, just lik a monster fr sc fict., c here is the head & the arms (points)		W+ M^p.FT.FDo (H) P 2.0
		7. These c.b. the heads of dead geese, just sort of hangg fr a basket or s.t.		E: (Rpts S's resp) S: Its lik thy were being taken home fr the butcher shop or s.t., just the shape of goose necks & heads		Do Fo (2) Ad
V	9″	8. It ll 2 people who r mad at e.o., sitting back to back		E: (Rpts S's resp) S: Well, each has a foot out & not doing a.t., just sittg, w their heads sort of dwn E: U said thy were mad at e.o. S: Well, u don't sit tht way unless u'd b mad, it may be a man & wm who just had a fite & thy'r too tired to go on		W+ M^p+ (2) H 2.5
		9. The W thg c.b. a bf too		E: (Rpts S's resp) S: The wgs r spread out, lik it was glidg along, c here is the little body part (points) & these r the wgs		Wo FM^po A P 1.0
VI	86″	10. I d.k. what ths top part c.b., maybe s.s. of insect		E: (Rpts S's resp) S: It c.b. a fly, if u stretch u'r immag, it mite be a dragonfly come to thk of it w the wgs here (points) & the body		Do Fo A
		V11. If u don't mind my lookg at it ths way it ll 2 littl birds in a nest waitg for their mother to feed them		E: (Rpts S's resp) S: It ll their mouths r open waitg for food from the mothr, & ths part is the nest, its pretty clear		Dd+ FM^po (2) A 2.5
VII	17″	12. It ll 2 littl girls who r talkg to		E: (Rpts S's resp)		D+ M^ao (2) Hd P 3.0

tails stug up, mayb my just whittd around . . . lik arguing

Card	No.	Response	Inquiry	Scoring
			E: (Rpts S's resp) S: I'm not sure about it now, I guess ths white all ll s.s. of anchor, I didn't kno tht I'd hav to find them again E: Can u show me? S: Just the white, it has that shape	DS- F- Anchor
VIII	13.	Ths ll an anchor to me		
	14."	It ll insides, lik s.b.'s insides, all bloody	E: (Rpts S's resp) S: Well its lik u c in medical books, lik the insides of a person, there is lungs & the stomach & the ribs	W+ CFo An,Bl 4.5
	V15.	A milk bottle in here	E: (Rpts S's resp) S: These r hard, I saw it rite here in the cntr white part (Points), it has to b a milk bottle cause it is white lik it has milk in it	DdSo FC'o Fd ALOG
IX	16.	A couple of baby heads down here	E: (Rpts S's resp) S: Thy r pink lik littl kids, babies that is, & u can c the forehead & the facial features, there's one on each side	Do FCo (2) Hd P
	8"			
	17.	The orange & green ll a sunset in a storm	E: (Rpts S's resp) S: It ll clds, the green & the orange is the sun, shining thru the clouds before the storm, the color is back in the distance, lik the clouds are closer bec of the coloring	Dv m^p.CF.VFo Na,Cl 2.5
X	18.	It c.b. insides again, lik an A that got splttrd all over	E: (Rpts S's resp) S: Just internal parts, all gory, the way thy r colord, lik bld & guts, just all over	Wv C An
	12"			
	19.	The pink c.b. coral reefs	E: (Rpts S's resp) S: One on each side, lik 2 coral reefs, thy r colord pink lik ths in the Bahamas	Dv CFo (2) Bt
	20.	These mite b eggs, fried eggs u can c the yolk	E: (Rpts S's resp) S: Thy r yellow lik fried eggs, & the yolk is a darker yellow, c one on each side, no toast tho	Do FCo (2) Fd

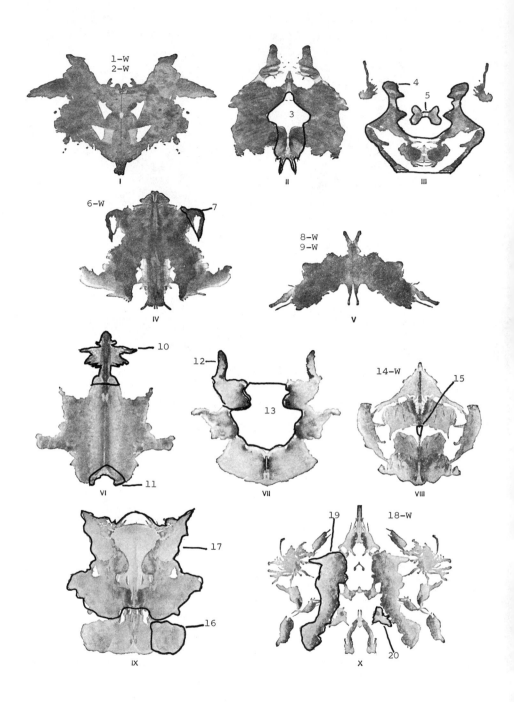

Case 21

CARD	RT	NO.	LOCATION	DETERMINANTS (S)		CONTENT (S)	POP	Z SCORE	SPECIAL
I	14"	1.	Wo	FM^po		A	P	1.0	
		2.	W+	M^{p-a}.YF+	(2)	H,Smk	P	4.0	
II	39"	3.	DS+	m^a.CFo		Plane,Fi		4.5	
III	11"	4.	D+	M^ao	(2)	H,Fd	P	3.0	
		5.	Do	FCo		An			
IV	41"	6.	W+	M^p.FT.FDo		(H)	P	4.0	
		7.	Do	Fo	(2)	Ad			
V	9"	8.	W+	M^p+	(2)	H		2.5	
		9.	Wo	FM^po		A	P	1.0	
VI	86"	10.	Do	Fo		A			
		11.	Dd+	FM^po	(2)	A		2.5	
VII	17"	12.	D+	M^ao	(2)	Hd	P	3.0	
		13.	DS-	F-		Anchor			
VIII	14"	14.	W+	CFo		An		4.5	
		15.	DdSo	FC'o		Fd			ALOG
IX	8"	16.	Do	FCo	(2)	Hd	P		
		17.	Dv	m^p.CF.VFo		Na,Cl		2.5	
X	12"	18.	Wv	C		An			
		19.	Dv	CFo	(2)	Bt			
		20.	Do	FCo	(2)	Fd			

Case 21

R = 20   Zf = 11   ZSum = 32.5   P = 7   (2) = 9

Location Features			Determinants (Blends First)		Contents		Contents (Idiographic)	
W	= 7	DQ	m^p.CF.VF	=1	H	= 3	Anchor	=1
D	= 11	+ = 8	m^a.CF	=1	(H)	= 1		
Dd	= 2	o = 8	M^{p-a}.YF	=1	Hd	= 2	Plane	=1
S	= 3	v = 3	M^p.FT.FD	=1	(Hd)	=		
DW	=	— = 1			A	= 4	Smoke	=0,1
					(A)	=		
			M	= 3	Ad	= 1		
			FM	= 3	(Ad)	=		
Form Quality			m	=	Ab	=		
			C	= 1	Al	=		
FQx		FQf	CF	= 2	An	= 3		
+	= 2	+ = 0	FC	= 3	Art	=		
o	= 16	o = 2	C'	=	Ay	=		
w	= 0	w = 0	C'F	=	Bl	= 0,1		
—	= 1	— = 1	FC'	= 1	Bt	= 1		
			T	=	Cg	=		
M Quality			TF	=	Cl	= 0,1	Special Scorings	
			FT	=	Ex	=		
+	= 2		V	=	Fi	= 0,1		
o	= 3		VF	=	Fd	= 2,1	PSV	=
w	= 0		FV	=	Ge	=	DV	=
—	= 0		Y	=	Hh	=		
			YF	=	Ls	=	INCOM	=
			FY	=	Na	= 1	FABCOM	=
			rF	=	Sx	=		
			Fr	=	Xy	=	CONTAM	=
			FD	=			ALOG	= 1
			F	= 3				=

RATIOS, PERCENTAGES, AND DERIVATIONS

ZSum-Zest	=	32.5-34.5	FC:CF+C	= 3:5	Afr	= .54
Zd	=	-2.0	W:M	= 7:5	3r+(2)/R	= .45
EB	= 5:7.0	EA = 12.0	W:D	= 7:11	Cont:R	= 8:20
eb	= 5:4	ep = 9	L	= .18	H+Hd:A+Ad	= 6:5
					(H)+(Hd):(A)+(Ad)	= 1:0
Blends:R	=	4:20	F+%	= .67	H+A:Hd+Ad	= 8:3
a:p	=	4:7	X+%	= .90	XRT Achrom	= 33.4"
Ma:Mp	=	3:3	A%	= .25	XRT Chrom	= 16.8"

people, and, more particularly, of himself. He gives slightly more *S* than most adults, which may indicate some oppositional features, but far more important is his emphasis on food contents (2 + 1), which is unusual for an adult and usually points to sharp dependency needs. His three anatomy answers are not really surprising in terms of his complaints, but they also may reveal a different sort of body concern—that is, one that deals more directly with the self-concept. His mean reaction times are very long, making the idiographic answers even more revealing, since they have been selected from a much broader range of possible answers. This may relate to his very low *Lambda,* which signals problems in avoiding complex stimulus situations. He also offers a very unusual *M* response containing both active and passive movement features. These kinds of answers probably signify elements of vacillation or ambivalence.

His scoring sequence indicates the *S* answers to be broadly distributed, suggesting that the negativism is more trait related. While he is a *W* oriented person, he has more difficulty with the last three cards, and delivers all three of his *DQv* locations to the last two. In fact, all of his answers to the last three cards involve some form of color response, suggesting that he becomes more involved in emotionally loaded stimuli than the *Afr* of .54 suggests. Similarly, both of his *m* answers occur in responses which also contain a *CF* determinant, indicating that the impact of the emotional discharge often causes him to feel out of control.

Much of his content is very idiographic. He enters the test with a unique form of passive movement, a bat, but "gliding along." He follows this with a much more dramatic answer, a person, described as a man tied to a stake. This seems to reflect his current helplessness and feeling the inner turmoil. His people on Card III are aggressive, "pulling something apart," again reflecting the internal conflict and raising speculation about his perception of the interpersonal world. Some possibly symbolic "heads of dead geese" are identified on Card IV, and, after an enormously long reaction time on Card VI, he focuses on the upper D area, "I don't know what this top part could be, maybe an insect." Immediately thereafter, he seems to dramatize his own dependent helplessness with, ". . . two little birds in a nest, waiting for their mother to feed them." Other responses, such as little girls, milk bottle, and baby heads, tend to reinforce the postulate that he is far less mature than would be expected and has some strong dependency needs. In addition to the aggressive response on Card III, his first answer to Card V seems to strengthen the proposition that he anticipates a stormy rather than harmonious interpersonal existence. Some of that feeling appears to be reflected in his second response to IX, a sunset in a storm, and the same sense of pessimistic vulnerability is noted in two of his three anatomy answers, one on Card VIII and the other on Card X, both of which signal penetration and destruction. There is little evidence of a sturdy masculine identity in the record, and his "sign out" response, fried eggs, probably typifies much of how he perceives himself. The contents are immature, incongruous, and clearly unexpected for an intelligent and successful young banker. If the record were to be viewed "in the blind" with no data about the subject, it would be unlikely that marriage or a responsible occupation would be associated with this seemingly very immature, fragile, dependent, self-centered person who has great difficulty in modulating his emotional displays. When considered in the context of his presenting physical problems, it seems likely that the symptoms are rather primitive and not very effective ways of avoiding whatever stresses may be presented in his occupation; but more importantly, they are probably related to some form of marital disarray, which may include areas of sexual dysfunction. He is a passive-dependent style, and whenever he is forced into situations of greater independence and/or responsibility than those for which he is prepared, some form of psychological "malfunction" has a high probability of occurring. He has clear problems about his own sex role identity, which would make for difficulty in any close heterosexual situation, especially marriage, and which would generalize negatively across a broad spectrum of interpersonal relationships.

The Treatment Plan.   Although this subject is obviously immature and more dependent than might be desired, the original cost-benefit evaluation, structured in the context of the realities of his marriage and occupation, seemed to encourage a supportive rather than insight oriented treatment plan. More specifically, the recommended intervention program included two basic components. First, was supportive individual therapy, designed to permit some ventilation, but also to explore avenues of emotional discharge that would be more effectively modulated than those he was using. It appeared that he experienced considerable difficulty defining interpersonal relationships, and might often be inhibiting the expression of his own thoughts and needs in order to preserve a more passive-dependent role. Thus, the supportive treatment would ultimately focus on some form of assertiveness training, differentiating assertiveness from aggression, and hopefully providing a basis from which the pattern of identification could be strengthened. Second, because there appeared to be the possibility of a sexual problem, a family therapy approach would also be employed, focusing mainly on the verbal and nonverbal techniques used by the marital partners to communicate ideas and emotions. It was postulated that this mode of intervention would also help strengthen his weak self-concept, and if a greater sense of security could be produced in the marriage, some symptom relief might be forthcoming.

The Final Treatment Decision.   His wife, an attractive woman of about his own height, declined to become involved in any form of therapy. She perceived the basic problem to be "his," and although she would give "moral support" to his treatment, she felt that her own involvement would be counterproductive. He was also reluctant about marital therapy and probably reinforced her position. Among the alternatives offered was long term treatment, designed toward a developmentally based goal of "reconstruction." He was cautioned that such a program might not bring the immediate relief that he sought, but that over a longer intervention period, he would have an opportunity to focus on more objectives. He opted for the longer term, insight oriented approach, with his wife's blessing. In retrospect, he probably made this decision because it did appear to offer a more sustained support system than might be expected in either the supportive or marital forms of treatment.

Treatment began on a twice weekly basis, with a male therapist who described his own approach as "eclectic" but whose training was predominantly in the traditional "dynamic" framework. Major symptom relief was reported by the end of the fourth treatment month; however, the therapist reported that once the subject began focusing on his conceptions of masculinity, in about the fifth treatment month, a series of secondary symptoms, such as forgetfulness, insomnia, headache, bouts of fatigue, and the like would appear for brief periods, usually lasting no more than two or three weeks.

After 13 months and 93 treatment sessions, both the therapist and the patient feel that considerable gains have occurred; however, the therapist notes more signs of resistance, ordinarily manifest in periods of silence, during the past 10 treatment sessions. He has suggested a reevaluation through testing, to identify

Case 21A

Card	Free Association	Inquiry	Scoring
I	7"		
	1. Oh yes, this is the bat	E: (Rpts S's resp) S: It has the wings & the tail & here r the ft paws or feelrs or whatever thy are	Wo Fo A P 1.0
	2. U kno, it c.b. a mask too possibly w hair on it	E: (Rpts S's resp) S: An animal mask, lik a cat, c here r the eyes & mouth & ths w.b. the ears E: U mentioned tht it possibly had hair on it S: Yes, c the puffy cheeks, ll hair, u see some of those on fancy masks in New Orleans at Mardi Grais, its fuzzy lookg to me	WSo FTo (Ad) 1.0
II	12"		
	3. Ths seems lik 2 pecple at a costume party, lik thy r dancing, no mayb toastg s.o., clinkg glasses togthr	E: (Rpts S's resp) S: Thy would hav to b in costume w big red hats on, lik clowns or s.t. lik that, c here is where thy r touchg their glasses	W+ $M^a.FC+$ (2) H (P) 4.5
	<4. Ths way it ll a rabbit, lik he's crouchg down	E: (Rpts S's resp) S: It has a good shape of one, lik he was crouchg down, c here is the head & the body & tail	Do FM^Po A
III	10"		
	5. Ths 2 men liftg s.t. thy ll thy r negro	E: (Rpts S's resp) S: Well, it ll thy r liftg ths thg up, its hard to tell what it is, mayb a basket or s.t. E: U mentioned that thy ll negros S: Well thy are black & thy hav negroid features, around the head	D+ $M^a.FC'o$ (2) H P 3.0
	6. Ths cntr rem me of s.t. last time, but I'm not sure what, I thk mayb a bow, lik a hair-ribbon	E: (Rpts S's resp) S: Well it has that form to it, & of course its red, colorful lik a hair-ribbon w.b.	Do FCo Cg

Case 21A

Card	Free Association	Inquiry	Scoring
IV 18″	7. I thk I saw ths as a big gorilla, laying down	E: (Rpts S's resp) S: Well, he's layg down bec the ft r so much bigger than the rest, lik closer to you, as he was layg dwn & the whl thg ll a lot of fur, u don't c his head much	Wo $FM^p.FD.FTo$ A P 2.0
	V8. U kno, ths way it c.b. a horse just his head, lookg thru a bush or s.t.	E: (Rpts S's resp) S: It looks rather lik a horses head here & he's back behind ths bush, lookg thru E: I'm not sure I c the bush as u do S: Rite here (points), I'm assumg its a bush bec of the irreg shape, it c.b. something else, lik rocks too	W+ $FM^p.FDo$ Ad,Bt 4.0
V 7″	9. Ths ll anothr bat to me	E: (Rpts S's resp) S: Well it has the wgs again & the body & here r the feelers, its all black too lik a bat w.b.	Wo $FC'o$ A P 1.0
	10. I cld also b bookends, I thk I saw that before too, metal bookends	E: (Rpts S's resp) S: It ll metal bookends of 2 animals each w its head towrd the cntr & the legs outstretched to convey the impression of pushing, mayb 2 rams E: U said it ll metal? S: Yes, the way it is color'd givs that impression, lik it w.b. hard to the touch, lik metal, u kno it c.b. bronze or steel or s.o. metal, it looks hard tho	W+ $FM^p.FT+$ (2) Bkends,(A) 2.5

VI 5"

11. Ths lowr prt c.b. a bear rug I d.k. what the top is tho
   E: (Rpts S's resp)
   S: Well, its all furry lookg & it has that form to it of a bear rig spread out, c the legs r here, there doesn't seem to b a head

   Do FTo Ad P

12. The side c.b. a statue of a face, lik the bust of a king, u can z the crown
   E: (Rpts S's resp)
   S: Its quite good really, the crown it here (points) & the jaw part has been empha-sized to signal determination, as if it is carved in stone
   E: Carved in stone
   S: Yes, bec of the jaw emphasis, it isn't real so it has to be a statue that is carved that way

   Ddo Fo (Hd)

VII 6"

13. I rem ths one, its the two wm lookg at e.o., thy r standg behind s.t.
   E: (Rpts S's resp)
   S: Young wm, w pony tails, just their heads, at least u can't c much of the body, lik mayb thy r behind s.t., lik a rock or fence, u get some of the upper body but not much, mostly just the heads
   E: I'm not sure I c them as u do, that is standg behind s.t.
   S: Well thy r here (points) so thy must be be-hind ths thg, ths fence bec u can't c the lower parts of them

   W+ M^P.FDo (2) Hd P 2.5

V14. Ths c.b. the head of an eleph
   E: (Rpts S's resp)
   S: It has the trunk & the general form lik the head of an elephant & then the village

   Do Fo Ad

15. U kno ths litl prt c.b. a village off in the distance
   S: Well, u can c the bldgs, lik the church spire & town hall & that sort of thg, its far off lik cn a hill or s.t.

   D+ FD+ Village 1.0

Case 21A (Continued)

Card		Free Association		Inquiry	Scoring
VIII	16″	16. It c.b. a coat of arms I don't rem seeing that before	E:	(Rpts S's resp)	W+ FC̲o̲ (2) Art P 4.5
			S:	Its all in symmetry, the animals on the sides & the shields in the cntr & the peaked part, each part repr some form of family history, the great events of the family & its put together in a very colorful fashion so that the colors set off each part	
IX	22″	17. Oh yes, I didn't care for ths one before, I thk I rem seeing it as a forest w the waterfall in the middle canyon	E:	(Rpts S's resp)	D+ m^p.CF.FD+ Ls 2.5
			S:	Its lik a canyon in the center leadg back to ths waterfall, it has a hazy effect to it bec of the mist of the waterfall & the green is all of the trees, I d.k. what the orange prt c.b., may another part of the forest being lit up by sunlight, ths pink isn't included tho	
	<18.	U kno, if I turn it ths way it ll a fellow playg a saxaphone	E:	(Rpts S's resp)	D+ M^a+ H 2.5
			S:	C, (points) rite here, he's a fat man & ths is the saxaphone, its quite clear	
X	14″	19. I suppose these c.b. crabs	E:	(Rpts S's resp)	Do Fo (2) A P
			S:	Ths blue thgs, all the legs & the middle is the body	
		20. Ths pink thgs c.b. worms just hatched	E:	(Rpts S's resp)	Do FC.FTo (2) A
			S:	Newly developing worms, thy r still pink as if thy just hatched & thy r rather wrinkly lik a worm	
			E:	Wrinkly?	
			S:	Thy just ll tht, I suppose the way the picture is there makes them look wrinkled to me	

430

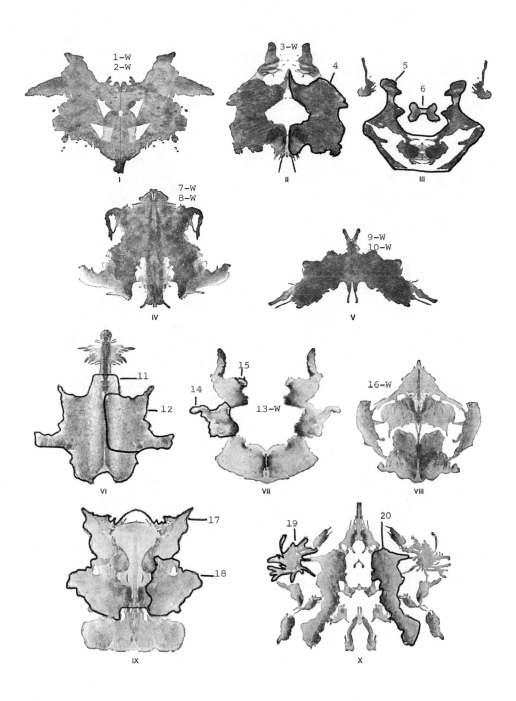

SEQUENCE OF SCORES

CARD	RT	NO.	LOCATION	DETERMINANTS (S)		CONTENT (S)	POP	Z SCORE	SPECIAL
I	7"	1.	Wo	Fo		A	P	1.0	
		2.	WSo	FTo		(Ad)		1.0	
II	12"	3.	W+	M^a.FC+	(2)	H	(P)	4.5	
		4.	Do	FM^po		A			
III	10"	5.	D+	M^a.FC'o	(2)	H	P	3.0	
		6.	Do	FCo		Cg			
IV	18"	7.	Wo	FM^p.FD.FTo		A	P	2.0	
		8.	W+	FM^p.FDo		Ad,Bt		4.0	
V	7"	9.	Wo	FC'o		A	P	1.0	
		10.	W+	FM^p.FT+	(2)	Bkends(A)		2.5	
VI	5"	11.	Do	FTo		Ad	P		
		12.	Ddo	Fo		(Hd)			
VII	6"	13.	W+	M^p.FDo	(2)	Hd	P	2.5	
		14.	Do	Fo		Ad			
		15.	D+	FD+		Village		1.0	
VIII	16"	16.	W+	FCo	(2)	Art	P	4.5	
IX	22"	17.	D+	m^p.CF.FD+		Ls		2.5	
		18.	D+	M^a+		H		2.5	
X	14"	19.	Do	Fo	(2)	A	P		
		20.	Do	FC.FTo	(2)	A			

R = 20   Zf = 13   ZSum = 32.0   P = 8   (2) = 7

Determinants

Location Features				Contents		Contents (Idiographic)	
		M^a.FC	=1				
		M^a.FC'	=1	H	= 3	Bookends	=1
W = 9	**DQ**	M^p.FD	=1	(H)	=		
D = 10	+ = 9	FM^p.FD.FT	=1	Hd	= 1	Village	=1
Dd = 1	o = 11	FM^p.FT	=1	(Hd)	= 1		
S = 1	v = 0	FM^p.FD	=1	A	= 6		
		m^p.CF.FD	=1	(A)	= 0,1		
DW =	— = 0	FC.FT	=1	Ad	= 3		
		M = 1		(Ad)	= 1		
		FM = 1		Ab	=		
		m =		Al	=		
		C =		An	=		
Form Quality		CF =		Art	= 1		
		FC = 2		Ay	=		
FQx	FQf	C' =		Bl	=		
		C'F =		Bt	= 0,1		
+ = 5	+ = 0	FC' = 1		Cg	= 1		
o = 15	o = 4	T =		Cl	=		
w = 0	w = 0	TF =		Ex	=	**Special Scorings**	
— = 0	— = 0	FT = 2		Fi	=		
		V =		Fd	=		
M Quality		VF =		Ge	=	PSV =	
		FV =		Hh	=		
+ = 2		Y =		Ls	= 1	DV =	
o = 2		YF =		Na	=		
w = 0		FY =		Sx	=	INCOM =	
— = 0		rF =		Xy	=		
		Fr =				FABCOM =	
		FD - 1					
		F = 4				CONTAM =	
						ALOG =	
						=	

RATIOS, PERCENTAGES, AND DERIVATIONS

ZSum-Zest = 32.0-41.5		FC:CF+C = 4:1		Afr = .33	
Zd = -9.5		W:M = 9:4		3r+(2)/R = .35	
EB = 4:3	FA = 7.0	W:D = 9:10		Cont:R = 7:20	
eb = 5:7	ep = 12	L = .25		H+Hd:A+Ad = 5:10 (H)+(Hd):(A)+(Ad) = 1:1	
Blends:R = 8:20		F+% = 100		H+A:Hd+Ad = 10:5	
a:p = 3:6		X+% = 100		XRT Achrom = 8.6"	
Ma:Mp = 3:1		A% = .50		XRT Chrom = 14.8"	

gains more precisely, and to reidentify relevant treatment goals. The patient has agreed quite enthusiastically to the second examination.

Case 21A: Reevaluation of a 25 Year Old Male

A reevaluation, using two protocols, is ordinarily best accomplished by setting the records "side by side" and making item by item comparisons, beginning with the structural data. Naturally, both records are reviewed in their entirety; however, for purposes of convenience here, the retest protocol is shown first, and is then followed by an integrated Structural Summary sheet containing the scores, ratios, and so on, from both records, followed by side-by-side comparisons of the Free Associations of both records. It is from this comparative data that the reevaluation builds.

A Comparison of the Structural Data.   Several striking changes have occurred in the basic structure, among the more important of which is the sharp reversal in the $EA : ep$ relationship, moving from a higher EA (12:9) to a higher ep (7:12). As noted in Chapter 4, this is not uncommon among subjects who enter an "uncovering" form of psychotherapy with a higher EA, but it is important to alert the therapist to this finding, since the subject is currently experiencing considerable psychological activity and may not have adequate readily accessible resources to contend with his internal stress. It is also interesting to note that a possible reversal has occurred in the EB itself. This is very unusual, and since both ratios contain figures that closely approximate each other, it is likely that he was an ambitent at the first testing and continues to display that style. One of the major factors contributing to the shift in the $EA : ep$ relation is a marked evaluation in the T variable. The new record contains five of these determinants, and signifies that he is experiencing much irritation because of ungratified needs for emotional affiliation. Again, it is very important to alert the therapist to this, and to recommend an evaluation of the marital situation. It may be that changes in the subject are beginning to have a negative impact on his relationship with his wife, and if this is the case, it should be broached directly.

One of the major objectives in the original treatment plan concerned a better modulation of affective displays. This change has clearly occurred, with a distinct reversal in the $FC : CF + C$ ratio and the elimination of the pure C response. The markedly reduced Afr, from .54 to .33, indicates that the subject is now prone to avoid emotionally provoking stimuli. While this may be acceptable in terms of reality factors, a question must be raised as to whether the withdrawal is too marked, especially in light of the now slightly excessive number of FC responses. In other words, while the new found modulating is desired, it should not exist under conditions in which withdrawal is a critical element. Another positive gain appears in the reduced *egocentricity index,* which is now in the "normal" range; and, concurrently, the aspirational level, as indicated by the $W : M$, has improved slightly.

The *Lambda* is still considerably lower than may be adaptive, and the subject may still be vulnerable to complexity. This is especially important in light of the drastic alteration in the Zd score, moving from -2.0 to -9.5. This severe form of underincorporativeness is likely to be a major handicap for him, especially in his

R = 20-20   Zf = 11-13   ZSum = 32-32.5   P = 7-8   (2) = 9-7

Determinants

Location Features				(21)	(21A)	Contents Primary Only		Contents (Idiographic)	

Location Features

						Contents Primary Only		**Contents (Idiographic)**	
W	=7-9	DQ		M^p.FT.FD	M^a.FC	H	= 3-3	Anchor	=1-0
				M^p.a.YF	M^a.FC'	(H)	= 1-0		
D	=11-10	+	= 8-9	m^a.CF.VF	M^p.FD	Hd	= 2-1	Bookends	=0-1
				m^a.CF	FM^p.FD.FT	(Hd)	= 0-1		
Dd	=2-1	o	= 8-11		FM^p.FT	A	= 4-6	Plane	=1-0
					FM^p.FD	(A)	=		
S	=3-1	v	= 3-0		m^p.CF.FD	Ad	= 1-3	Village	=0-1
					FC.FT	(Ad)	= 0-1		
DW	=	—	= 1-0	M	= 3-1	Ab	=		=
				FM	= 3-1	Al	=		
				m	=	An	= 3-0		=
				C	= 1-0	Art	= 0-1		
Form Quality				CF	= 2-0	Ay	=		=
				FC	= 3-2	Bl	=		
FQx		FQf		C'	=	Bt	= 0-1		=
				C'F	=	Cg	= 0-1		
+	= 2-5	+	=0-0	FC'	= 1-1	Cl	=		
				T	=	Ex	=	**Special Scorings**	
o	= 16-15	o	=2-4	TF	=	Fi	=		
				FT	= 0-2	Fd	= 2-0	PSV	=
w	= 0-0	w	=0-0	V	=	Ge	=		
				VF	=	Hh	=	DV	=
—	= 1-0	—	=1-0	FV	=	Ls	= 0-1		
				Y	=	Na	= 1-0	INCOM	=
M Quality				YF	=	Sx	=		
				FY	=	Xy	=	FABCOM	=
+	= 2-2			rF	=				
				Fr	=			CONTAM	=
o	= 3-2			FD	= 0-1				
				F	= 3-4			ALOG	= 1-0
w	= 0-0								
									=
—	= 0-0								

RATIOS, PERCENTAGES, AND DERIVATIONS

ZSum-Zest	= 32.5-34.5 (32.0-41.5)	FC:CF+C	= 3:5 (4:1)	Afr	= .54 (.33)
Zd	= -2.0 (-9.5)	W:M	= 7:5 (9:4)	3r+(2)/R	= .45 (.35)
EB	= 5:7 (4:3) EA = 12 (7)	W:D	= 7:11 (9:10)	Cont:R	= 8:20 (7:20)
eb	= 5:4 (5:7) ep = 9 (12)	L	= .18 (.25)	H+Hd:A+Ad	= 6:5 (5:10)
				(H)+(Hd):(A)+(Ad)	= 3:0 (1:1)
Blends:R	= 4:20 (8:20)	F+%	= .67 (100)	H+A:Hd+Ad	= 8:3 (10:5)
a:p	= 4:7 (3:6)	X+%	= .90 (100)	XRT Achrom.	= 33.4 (8.6)
Ma:Mp	= 3:3 (3:1)	A%	= .25 (.50)	XRT Chrom	= 16.8 (14.8)

435

	Case 21			Case 21A	
I	14″	1. It ll a bat to me, w its wgs spread out, glidg alng 2. It c.b. also a person, its seems lik he's—well I d.k. if its a man or wm, anyway, whatever, he's tied to a stake in the middle & other people r dancing around it, the darkness makes it ll there's smoke there too	I	7″	1. Oh yes, this is the bat 2. U kno, it c.b. a mask too possibly w hair on it
II	39″	3. It ll a delta wgd plane or rocket takg off w the fire comg out	II	12″	3. Ths seems lik 2 people at a costume party, lik thy r dancing, no mayb toastg e.o., clinkg glasses togthr <4. Ths way it ll a rabbit, lik he's crouchg down
III	11″	4. It ll two people pulling s.t. aprt, lik thy r fiting over it 5. The cntr c.b. lungs or s.t.	III	10″	5. Ths ll 2 men liftg s.t. thy ll thy r negro 6. Ths cntr rem me of s.t. last time, but I'm not sure what, I thk mayb a bow, lik a hair-ribbon
IV	41″	6. It ll some big monster out of sc. fict. sittg on a stump 7. These c.b. the heads of dead geese, just sort of hangg fr a basket or s.t.	IV	18″	7. I thk I saw ths as a big gorilla, laying down V8. U kno, ths way it c.b. a horse just his head, lookg thru a bush or s.t.
V	9″	8. It ll 2 people who r mad at e.o., sitting back to back 9. The W thg c.b. a bf too	V	7″	9. Ths ll another bat to me
VI	86″	10. I d.k. what ths top part c.b., mayb s.s. of insect V11. If u don't mind my lookg at it ths way it ll 2 littl birds in a nest waitg for their mother to feed them	VI	5″	10. I cld also b bookends, I thk I saw that before too, metal bookends 11. Ths lowr prt c.b. a bear rug I d.k. what the top is tho 12. The side c.b. a statue of a face, lik the bust of a king, u can c the crown

VII   6"

13. I rem ths one, its the two wm lookg at e.o., thy r standg behind s.t.
V14. Ths c.b. the head of an eleph
15. U kno ths litl prt c.b. a village off in the distance

VIII   16"

16. It c.b. a coat of arms I don't rem seeing that before

IX   22"

17. Oh yes, I did't care for ths one before, I thk I rem seeing it as a forest w the waterfall in the middle canyon
<18. U kno, if I turn it ths way it ll a fellow playg a saxaphone

X   14"

19. I suppose these c.b. crabs
20. Ths pink thgs c.b. worms just hatched

VII   17"

12. It ll 2 littl girls who r talkg to e.o.
13. Ths ll an anchor to me

VIII   14"

14. It ll ir sides, lik s.b.'s insides, all b.oody
V15. A milk bottle in here

IX   8"

16. A couple of baby heads down here
17. The orange & green ll a sunset in a storm

X   12"

18. It c.b. insides again, lik an A that got splttrd all over
19. The pink c.b. coral reefs
20. These mite b eggs, fried eggs u can c the yolk

occupation, where precise decision making is usually expected. It can also be a distinct handicap in his interpersonal world, which is probably still developing, and in which hasty decisions about the cues given off by others can lead to some disastrous exchanges. The therapist should be encouraged to use an approach that will restore the delay factor.

Another potential liability at this point is the very high $F+\%$ and $X+\%$. There are no weak or minus answers in the record, and usually, when this occurs, the individual is sacrificing some personal uniqueness in an attempt to avoid behavioral mistakes. This commitment to perceptual accuracy may be positive in the context of the severe underincorporation; however, neither will be useful to long term effective adaptation.

Although there are a large number of blends in the record, suggesting an excess of psychological complexity, three of the blends include FD determinants, which are expected to increase during individual psychotherapy, since the focus is on introspection. In fact, there are five FD's in the record, which convey a great deal of self-inspection, but most will probably disappear shortly after effective intervention, and need not be a cause for concern at this time. The $a:p$ ratio remains in the passive direction and probably has a marked behavioral correlate; however, the $M^a:M^p$ ratio has altered to a favorable direction, suggesting that he is now probably using his deliberate and controlled ideation in a more problem solving oriented manner.

Comparison of the Free Association.   The second record does not "reek" of the helplessness of the verbal material in the first protocol. However, there is still a marked sense of cautiousness and uncertainty. The sign-in response is still a bat, but no longer "gliding," and instead of a person tied to a stake, the second answer is one of concealment, a mask, which includes the first of the five texture determinants. Similarly, there is an improvement on Cards II and III, but the people on Card II are not dancing, but toasting, and the rabbit is "crouching down," another concealment answer. The people on III are no longer violent, and now they are men, and the lungs have been replaced with a hair ribbon. The entry response to Card IV is still an aggressive creature, and still neutralized, but the "dead geese" have vanished, and have been replaced by a horse's head, ". . . looking through a bush . . . ." The latter is a very interesting response, and it probably indicates his current approach to the world—that is, looking at it, but from a safe and somewhat concealed position. The angry people, and the butterfly, are no longer perceived on Card V, being replaced by a bat and some bookends. In the inquiry, the bookends are described as the figures of ". . . two animals each with its head toward the center and the legs outstretched to convey the impression of pushing . . . ." It may well be that he has developed a facade of more sturdiness than is truly the case; in fact, some of his reluctance in therapy could relate to false impressions that he may have reported earlier about his overall progress. Again, it would be important to alert the therapist to this possibility.

The weak and dependent responses previously given on VI have also disappeared, to be replaced by more conventional answers, including the bust of a king, suggesting an orientation to status that was not evident previously. He also handles Card VII much more effectively in the second testing, although he conceals the Popular woman figures. Similarly, there is considerable improvement on VIII, moving from penetration and dependency answers to a second status response. More improvement is noted in the way he handles Card IX, with his second answer, ". . . a fellow playing a saxaphone," having a marked positive quality, especially in terms of the several concealment answers reported earlier in the record. He is less creative on X, but not as volatile or vulnerable as in the first testing. His sign-out response is particularly interesting in light of his situation, ". . . worms just hatched," an answer that may well reflect much of what he is now.

Cases 21 and 21A Summary.   There is no question that this man has made substantial gains in therapy. He is markedly less dependent and much more mature than before. His content indicates that he is still testing his newly discovered self and will continue to do so for some time, as his growth continues. His emotional controls have improved enormously, and he may now be prone to overcontrol. He seems to have lost access to some of his resources, but signs are favorable that another reversal will occur with continued treatment. The two major problem areas are a distinct tendency toward underincorporativeness, and, currently, a very strong need for emotional affiliation. New delay techniques will be important for him, and his marriage should be examined more closely. His current resistance may relate to his attempts at concealment, or it may be related to his quandary about his strong affective needs. He should become more individualistic; however, that need not be a concern at this time, while he is still in the developmental process.

Most, or all, of these findings should be shared with the subject, with particular emphasis on the obvious gains that have been made. This feedback can be delivered by the therapist, but may have greater favorable impact if it comes directly from the consulting clinician, probably in the presence of the therapist (with the patient's permission).

SUMMARY

The reevaluation process identified here is not very time consuming and can often thwart or circumvent significant problems that arise during, or at the end of, treatment. It represents the completion of the "full circle" assessment process, which should become more and more a part of the total intervention effort. It is designed to maximize the utilization of assessment technology, and the specific technique employed is far less important than is the commitment to the reevaluation. Where the Rorschach is involved, it will have some obvious advantages but also some limitations. For instance, in the preceding case, there is no factual information on the marriage, which seems to be a very important variable. Other assessment methods might have included more definitive data about the marital situation. Conversely, other assessment techniques might not have defined some of the other liabilities that should be current cause for concern, such as underincorporateness, or the tendency to overcontrol. The final decision concerning technology will be that of the therapist and the assessment consultant, but whatever the decision, the technology is available.

CHAPTER 13

An Overview

Some of the storm that surrounded the Rorschach for so many years during the late 1950s and throughout most of the 1960s appears to have subsided. Those who were "anti-Rorschach" presumed to have witnessed its demise, while some Rorschach advocates often "went into the closet," experiencing a sense of futility in trying to defend the test under the scrutiny of those who cried for "reliability" and "validity" data. Some reports were issued suggesting that the Rorschach had been abandoned, and was floundering (Shemberg and Keeley, 1970; Bierderman and Cerbus, 1971). But in reality, the test was being taught and used with about the same frequency as had been the case previously. In fact, as the literature of the 1970s has unfolded, there appears to be a renewed interest in all assessment, and a gradual increase in the use of assessment techniques, including the Rorschach (Gough, 1971; Lubin, Wallis, and Paine, 1971; Weiner, 1972; Garfield and Kurtz, 1973; Garfield and Kurtz, 1974; Levy and Fox, 1975; Brown and McGuire, 1976; Ritzler and Del Gaudia, 1976; and Weiner, 1977). A recent survey of practicing clinicians (Wade and Baker, 1977) indicates that the Rorschach continues to be regarded as the most important test to be mastered by the psychology graduate student.

The Rorschach has not survived and flourished because of some "mystique," but rather because it is truly valid for certain things that are important. All the Rorschach systematizers, Beck, Klopfer, Hertz, Piotrowski, and Rapaport, have known this, and most have conveyed aspects of that validity in their own works. Had they worked closely, in collaboration, it is very likely that the sturdiness of the instrument would have been demonstrated more markedly long before this time; but many factors caused them to work separately—different theories, different approaches, different interests, and possibly even different geographies. And they worked in a different time, when research methods were less sophisticated and data analysis was much more difficult. In spite of those handicaps, each made some remarkable contributions to our understanding of the Rorschach (Exner, 1969). Their work, added to Rorschach's original conceptions about perception and perceptual styles, formed the nucleus from which the Comprehensive System has developed.

One of the "core" objectives of the system has been to test out Rorschach's postulates in the context of contemporary psychology and the methodology it reflects. Considerable gains have been achieved to this end, but the work is far from finished. In fact, it may be that the surface has hardly been dented. There are a multitude of questions that remain unanswered, beginning with the characteristics of the stimulus figures themselves. It is fascinating to review the voluminous Rorschach literature and yet find fewer than 50 studies dealing directly with the stimulus elements. Similarly, much more work is required concerning the very intriguing response process, which is apparently so complex and so delicate. Much more ambitious and extensive work is required to expand the clinical utility of the test, in both the areas of treatment planning and treatment evaluation. Each of these areas remains relatively unexplored, although it is becoming clearer that they are the future pathways for all assessment.

The complexity of the test, and of the process that occurs when a subject is responding to it, are such that it can relate to almost any area of psychology, such as perception, cognition, motivation, interaction, decision making, information processing, to mention only a few. Although its clinical utility is often remarkable, its research potential is often awesome. It is valid for some things but not for other things; and it may be valid for things we have yet to explore. This is part of the intrigue of the Rorschach; that is, it seems to tap into a very complex human operation with a multitude of component parts that are often difficult to identify, difficult to understand, and even more difficult to research. For instance, what is there about the pair response that makes it related to self-focusing or self-centered behavior? Or, even more intriguing, what is there in the Zd score, partially developed from a set of weighted scores established over 40 years ago, that identifies so-called over- and underincorporators? From a strictly pragmatic view, these things exist, but from a conceptual view they are often difficult to understand. Why is it that the EA has considerably greater temporal stability than the ep? One contains no more stimulus elements than the other, and both contain a stimulus element that does not, in reality, exist in the blots, *movement*.

These are just a few of the unanswered Rorschach questions, and there are probably many that have not even been asked. The coding or scoring for the Comprehensive System seems complete, but there may be a need to differentiate responses in still other ways, so as to strengthen the structural data that the test yields. Following from the Beck quotation cited on the first page of this work, "Those . . . who will be using the test will confirm what is sound. They will discard what they cannot confirm . . ."; it may be more appropriate to suggest that those who will be using the test will discover new potentials for its study and for its use. And in some future decade, it may be possible to think of the Rorschach as truly complete.

On a more concrete level, those who use it now should recognize its limitations. When the test data are taken appropriately, scored accurately, and interpreted conservatively, they will afford a uniquely rich insight into the psychology of a person, *as a person*. This is the Rorschach legacy, and it is unlike any other assessment approach available to psychologists. Its full use requires a very intelligent understanding of people and a special appreciation for frailty, for the Rorschach seems to detect that in almost everyone. It is an easily abused technique, but in the "hands" of the skilled clinician its yield can be enormously important to any of its subjects, and that, of course, is what assessment is all about.

REFERENCES

Biederman, L., and Cerbus, G. Changes in Rorschach teaching. *Journal of Personality Assessment*, 1971, **35**, 524–526.

Brown, W. R., and McGuire, J. M. Current psychological assessment practices. *Professional Psychology,* 1976, **4,** 475–484.

Exner, J. E. *The Rorschach Systems.* New York: Grune and Stratton, 1969.

Garfield, S. L., and Kurtz, R. M. Attitudes toward training in diagnostic testing: A survey of directors of internship training. *Journal of Consulting and Clinical Psychology,* 1973, **40,** 350–355.

Garfield, S. L., and Kurtz, R. M. A survey of clinical psychologists: Characteristics, activities, and orientations. *Clinical Psychologist,* 1974, **28,** 7–10.

Gough, H. G. Some reflections on the meaning of psychodiagnosis. *American Psychologist,* 1971, **26,** 160–167.

Levy, M. R., and Fox, H. M. Psychological testing is alive and well. *Professional Psychology,* 1975, **6,** 420–424.

Lubin, B., Wallis, R. R., and Paine, C. Patterns of psychological test usage in the United States, 1935–1969. *Professional Psychology,* 1971, **2,** 70–74.

Ritzler, B. A., and Del Gaudia, A. C. A survey of Rorschach teaching in APA approved clinical graduate programs. *Journal of Personality Assessment,* 1976, **40,** 451–453.

Shemberg, K. and Keeley, S. Psychodiagnostic training in the academic setting: Past and present. *Journal of Consulting and Clinical Psychology,* 1970, **34,** 205–211.

Wade, T. C., and Baker, T. B. Opinions and use of psychological tests: A survey of clinical psychologists. *American Psychologist,* 1977, **32,** 874–882.

Weiner, I. B. Does psychodiagnosis have a future? *Journal of Personality Assessment,* 1972, **36,** 534–546.

Weiner, I. B. Approaches to Rorschach validation. In, Rickers-Ovsiankina, M. A. (Ed.), *Rorschach Psychology* (rev. ed.), New York: Krieger, 1977.

Author Index

Abrahamsen, D., 107, 121
Abramson, L.S., 39, 59
Ainsworth, M.D., 121, 155
Albert, S., 304, 335
Ames, L.B., 13, 35
Applebaum, S.A., 201, 202, 208, 243
Armbruster, G.L., 41, 46, 51, 52, 60, 67, 71, 76, 79, 80, 104, 120, 122, 129, 136, 154, 155, 248, 299

Baker, T.B., 440, 442
Bandura, A., 208
Barrera, S. E., 65, 80
Bartko, J.J., 245, 299
Baughman, E.E., 40, 53, 54, 58, 60
Beck, S.J., 3, 35, 120, 128, 154, 208, 243, 247, 299
Belleza, T., 246, 300
Benjamin, J.D., 246, 299
Bergin, A.E., 340, 377
Biederman, L., 440, 441
Blatt, S.J., 27, 35, 102, 120
Bleuler, E., 246, 299
Bohm, E., 27, 35
Brown, B.S., 201, 244
Brown, S.L., 103, 121
Brown, W.R., 440, 442
Bryant, E.L., 57, 60, 71, 80, 85, 86, 97, 108, 111, 120, 131, 135, 141, 154, 155, 303, 335
Buchsbaum, S., 246, 250, 299

Campo, V., 106, 120
Cannavo, F., 67, 80, 108, 120, 341, 377
Caraway, E.W., 140, 154
Carp, H.L., 40, 60
Carpenter, W.T., 245, 250, 299
Cerbus, G., 440, 441
Claparede, E., 38, 60
Cleveland, S.E., 21, 35
Coffin, T.E., 39, 60
Colson, D.B., 208, 243
Cooper, W.H., 104, 107, 120
Cox, F.N., 40, 60

Dahlstrom, L.E., 42, 60
Dahlstrom, W.G., 42, 60
Del Gaudia, A.C., 440, 442
Dinoff, M., 39, 60
Dixon, W.J., 246, 300

Draguns, J.G., 52, 61
Drye, R., 246, 250, 299
Duszynski, K.R., 201, 244
Dyk, R.B., 102, 121, 132, 155

Elstein, A.S., 113, 120
Endicott, 250
Exner, D., 304, 335
Exner, J.E., 3, 17, 21, 29, 30, 35, 36, 37, 39, 41, 46, 48, 51, 52, 53, 54, 55, 57, 58, 60, 61, 67, 71, 72, 75, 76, 79, 80, 82, 85, 86, 95, 96, 97, 102, 104, 107, 108, 110, 111, 114, 115, 120, 121, 122, 124, 126, 128, 129, 131, 132, 134, 135, 136, 138, 139, 140, 141, 154, 155, 202, 208, 243, 246, 247, 248, 249, 299, 300, 303, 304, 335, 336, 341, 377, 378, 440, 442

Farberow, N.L., 201, 203, 207, 243, 244
Faterson, H.F., 102, 121, 132, 155
Feingold, B.F., 404, 416
Feirstein, A., 102, 120
Fenichel, O., 250, 299
Fisher, S., 21, 35
Fishman, R., 132, 154
Fleischer, M.S., 201, 203, 243
Fonda, C.P., 208, 243
Ford, M., 63, 65, 80
Fossberg, I.A., 40, 61
Foster, J.M., 40, 61
Fox, H.M., 440, 442
Franco, S., 250, 301
Frank, L.K., 37, 61
Friedman, H., 27, 35, 38, 61

Garfield, S.L., 340, 440, 442
Gibby, R.G., 39, 40, 61
Gill, M., 36, 61, 300
Goetcheus, G., 39, 61
Goldberg, S.C., 246, 299
Goldfried, M., 201, 203, 243
Goldman, R., 128, 155
Goodenough, D.R., 102, 121, 132, 155
Gough, H.G., 440, 442
Greaves, S.T., 39, 61
Grinker, R., 246, 250, 299
Gross, L., 39, 61
Gunderson, J.G., 246, 250, 299

Haan, N., 108, 121
Hafner, A.J., 128, 155

Haley, E.M., 52, 60
Hall, K., 246, 300
Hamlin, R.M., 27, 35
Harrow, M., 27, 36
Henry, E.M., 128, 155
Hersen, M., 39, 61
Hertz, M.R., 63, 80, 202, 243
Hoch, P.H., 246, 299, 300
Hogarty, G.E., 67, 246, 299
Holt, R.R., 121, 155
Holzberg, J.D., 64, 65, 80
Holzman, P.S., 201, 202, 243
Hoover, T.O., 102, 121
Hopkins, H.K., 246, 300
Horiuchi, H., 38, 61
Hutt, M., 39, 61

Izner, S.M., 107, 121

Jablensky, A., 245, 300
Jacobsen, B., 246, 300
Jensen, A.R., 27, 35
Jones, A., 250, 301

Kant, O., 246, 299
Kantor, R.E., 246, 299
Karp, S.A., 102, 121, 132, 155
Kasanin, J.S., 246, 299
Katz, M., 67, 80, 88, 121, 136, 155, 248, 299
Keeley, S., 440, 442
Keith, S.J., 246, 250, 299
Kelley, D.M., 65, 80
Kelley, T.L., 64, 80
Kernberg, O.F., 246, 250, 299
Kerr, M., 65, 80
Kety, S.S., 246, 250, 251, 299, 300, 374
Khouri, P., 245, 300
Klein, D.F., 246, 300
Klett, C.J., 248, 300
Kline, J.R., 86, 121, 124, 155, 248, 299, 341, 378
Klopfer, B., 82, 121, 128, 155
Klopfer, W.G., 121, 155
Knight, R.P., 246, 250, 287, 300
Knobloch, H., 404, 416
Kuhn, B., 75, 80, 132, 154
Kurtz, R.M., 440, 442

Langmuir, C.R., 98, 99, 121
Lasky, J., 248, 300
Leiser, R., 107, 121
Leura, A.V., 48, 57, 60, 61, 67, 71, 72, 79, 80, 97,
    107, 111, 115, 120, 121, 122, 126, 128, 139,
    155
Levy, M.R., 440, 442
Lewis, N.D.C., 247, 300
Lindner, R.M., 201, 243
Lord, E., 39, 61
Lorr, M., 248, 300
Lubin, B., 440, 442

Lushene, R.E., 80
Lyerly, S., 67, 80, 88, 121, 136, 248, 299

McAdoo, W.G., 80
McGuire, J.M., 440, 442
McNair, D., 248, 300
Magnussen, M.G., 39, 61
Margulies, H., 65, 80
Martin, H., 201, 243
Marwit, S.J., 40, 62
Masling, J., 40, 61
May, P.R.A., 246, 300
Meer, B., 44, 61
Meili-Dworetzki, G., 38, 61
Metraux, R.W., 35
Meyer, A., 246, 300
Meyer, M., 6, 35
Miller, A.S., 104, 108, 120, 303, 335
Miller, D.R., 40, 61
Miller, W.R., 246, 300
Milton, E.O., 39, 61
Mittman, B.L., 41, 46, 51, 52, 60, 129, 154
Molish, H.B., 35
Morgan, D., 250, 301
Mosher, L.R., 246, 250, 299
Mukerji, K., 131, 155
Murillo, L.G., 29, 35, 67, 80, 96, 108, 120, 124,
    128, 155, 246, 248 249, 299, 300, 341, 342,
    377, 378

Neiger, S., 27, 36

Oaks, G., 246, 300
Orange, A., 63, 80

Paine, C., 440, 442
Parrill, T., 107, 121
Pasamanick, B., 404, 416
Peterson, L.C., 40, 61
Phares, E.J., 40, 61
Phillips, L., 21, 35, 52, 60, 246, 300
Piotrowski, Z., 17, 35, 102, 107, 121, 201, 244,
    247, 300
Polatin, P., 246, 299, 300
Pope, B., 27, 35
Pottharst, K., 39, 61
Powers, W.T., 27, 35

Quarrington, M., 27, 36
Quinlan, D.M., 27, 36
Quirk, D.A., 27, 36

Rapaport, D., 21, 36, 52, 61, 247, 300
Rappaport, M., 246, 300
Ray, J.B., 208, 244
Raychaudhuri, M., 131, 155
Reifman, A., 246, 250, 299
Ritzler, B.A., 27, 35, 440, 442
Robins, 250
Rodell, J.L., 35

Rorschach, H., 37, 61, 81, 121
Rosen, B., 246, 300
Rosenthal, D., 246, 251, 299, 300
Rosenthal, M., 102, 121
Ross, D.C., 201, 244
Rotter, J.B., 128, 132, 155

Sakheim, G.A., 201, 203, 244
Sapolsky, A., 201, 244
Sarason, S.B., 40, 60
Satorius, N., 245, 300
Schachtel, E.G., 46, 61
Schafer, R., 21, 36, 46, 61, 300
Schooler, N.R., 246, 299
Schreiber, H., 201, 203, 244
Schulsinger, F., 246, 251, 299, 300
Schumacher, J., 75, 80, 107, 121, 132, 154
Schuyler, W., 21, 30, 35, 41, 53, 61, 75, 80, 247,
    299
Shalit, B., 104, 121
Shapiro, R., 245, 300, 373
Shatin, L., 52, 62
Shavzin, A.R., 40, 60
Shemberg, K., 440, 442
Sherman, J., 52, 60, 303, 336
Shneidman, E.S., 201, 203, 207, 243, 244, 415, 416
Silver, L.B., 404, 416
Silverman, J., 246, 300
Singer, J.L., 103, 121
Sleman, A.G., 27, 36
Smith, J.G., 21, 35
Spielberger, C.D., 66, 80
Spitzer, 250
Stauffacher, J.C., 27, 36, 247, 300
Stein, M.I., 37, 62
Sterne, S.B., 107, 121
Stewart, L.M., 40, 61
Stewart, M.A., 404, 416
Stotsky, B.A., 124, 155
Strauss, J.S., 245, 250, 299
Strauss, M.E., 40, 62
Stricker, G., 201, 203, 243
Swift, J.W., 64, 80

Tabachnick, N.D., 203, 244
Thiesen, J.W., 247, 300
Thomas, C.B., 201, 203, 244
Tuma, A.H., 246, 300

Ulrich, R.F., 246, 299

Vernon, P.E., 63, 80
Viglione, D., 17, 35, 67, 80, 95, 121, 122, 155
Vorhaus, P., 377, 378

Wade, T.C., 440, 442
Wagner, E.E., 102, 121
Walker, E.J., 104
Walker, E.L., 40, 61, 107, 120, 121
Walker, R.N., 35
Wallner, J.M., 246, 299
Wallis, R.R., 440, 442
Warshaw, L., 107, 121
Watkins, J.G., 27, 36, 247, 300
Weiner, I.B., 21, 27, 30, 35, 36, 39, 41, 53, 61, 62,
    201, 203, 243, 245, 247, 273, 299, 300, 301,
    440, 442
Welthorn, C.J., 404, 416
Welsh, G.S., 42, 60
Wender, P., 404, 416
Wender, P.H., 246, 251, 299, 300
Werble, B., 246, 250, 299
Wexler, M., 65, 80
White, M.A., 201, 203, 244
Whitman, R.M., 246, 301
Wickes, T.A., 39, 62
Willet, A., 250, 301
Williams, M.H., 40, 62
Winder, C.L., 246, 299
Winter, L.B., 134, 155
Witkin, H.A., 102, 121, 132, 155
Wittman, P., 246, 301
Wylie, J.R., 17, 36, 52, 55, 60, 72, 76, 80, 86,
    107, 121, 124, 131, 135, 136, 154, 155, 202,
    243, 248, 299, 304, 336, 341, 378

Zalis, T., 80, 107, 121
Zolliker, A., 52, 62

Subject Index

Achromatic color responses (C'), 114-116
Active-passive movement scores, 16-20
  temporal consistency, 70-79
Active-passive ratios (a:p,M^a:M^p), 134-138
  cognitive flexibility, 135
  Snow-White fantasies, 137-138
Affective ratio, 124-128
  treatment effects, 125-127
Ambitent, *see* Erlebnistypus
Articulation, 53-58
Autistic logic (ALOG):
  criterion, 22
  interpretation, 25-29

Borderline conditions, 250-252

Children:
  normative data, 7-12
  suicide potential, 209-210
  treatment planning, 379-416
Chromatic color responses (FC,CF,C):
  FC:CF+C ratio, 122-124
  temporal consistency, 69-79
  treatment effects, 124
Color projection, 17
Color shading blend, 202, 208
Competency issues, 313-323
Contamination (CONTAM):
  criterion, 23
  interpretation, 26-29

Developmental quality scoring, 14-15
Deviant verbalizations (DV):
  criterion, 21-22
  interpretation, 25-29
Diffuse shading responses, 113-114

EA:ep relationship, 82-94
  treatment planning, 341
Egocentricity index (3r+(2)/R), 130-134
  field dependence-independence, 132
  locus of control, 132
  relapse, 133
  suicide potential, 204, 208
  treatment effects, 130-134
Erlebnistypus (EB), 94-104
  problem solving, 97-104
  relapse, 96-97
  temporal consistency, 70-79, 95

treatment effects, 86-93
Experience Actual (EA):
  temporal consistency, 70-79
  treatment effects, 86-93
Experience base (eb), 81-121
  FM+m Component, 104-109
  Grey-Black shading component, 109-116
  treatment effects, 105-106
Experience Potential (ep):
  temporal consistency, 65-79
  treatment effects, 86-93
Extratensive, *see* Erlebnistypus

Fabulized combination (FABCOM):
  criterion, 23
  interpretation, 26-29
Forensic issues, 302-336
  competency, 313-323
  custody, 323-335
  malingering, 303-313
Form dimension responses (FD), 113
Form quality scores:
  consistency within records, 41, 44-45
  scoring criteria, 15-16
  temporal consistency, 69-79
Form Responses, *see* Lambda
Four square, 81-121
  treatment effects, 86-93

Good form quality, 41-45
  schizophrenia, 247-249
  temporal consistency, 69-79

Human content:
  in movement responses, 247-249
  in treatment planning, 352, 373, 381

Inappropriate combination, 22-29
Incongruous combinations:
  criterion, 23
  interpretation, 26-29

Lambda, 128-130
Logical analysis device, 98-99

Malingering, 303-313
Movement responses, animal, 106-109
  situational stress, 107
  treatment effects, 108-109

Movement responses, human, 102-103
  field dependence-independence, 102
  schizophrenia, 247-248
  social behavior, 102
Movement responses, inanimate, 104-106
  stress effects, 104-105
  treatment effects, 105-106

Nonpatients:
  normative data, 4-5
  sample protocols, 157-198
  temporal consistency of response patterns, 67-72
Normative data, 3-12
  adults, 4-5
  children, 7-12

Organizational Activity (Zf,Zd), 138-142
  problem solving, 140-141
Overincorporator, 139-142
Overview, 440-442

Pair Responses, *see* Egocentricity index
Perceptual accuracy in response process, 51-53
Perseveration (PSV):
  criteria, 24-25
  interpretation, 29-30
Popular responses :
  alteration of stimuli, 54-58
  social desirability, 45-47
Procedures, 6, 13-14

Queer Responses, *see* Deviant verbalizations

Reflection Responses, *see* Egocentricity index
Reliability, 63-80
  temporal consistency, 65-79
  test-retest, 63-65
  treatment conditions, 72-79

S responses, 204-208
Schizophrenia, 245-301
  borderline conditions, 250-252
  diagnostic concepts, 245-246
  normative data, 4-5

perceptual accuracy problems, 52
  sample protocols, 252-298
  special scores, 5, 247-249
  temporal consistency of diagnosis, 75-76
  X+%, 247-249
Scoring :
  active-passive movement, 16-20
  color projection, 17
  developmental quality scores, 14-15
  form quality scores, 15-16
  special scores, 21-30
Shading responses, 109-116
  temporal consistency, 69-79
Social desirability influences, 46-51
Special scores, 21-30
Structural summary blank, 31-34
Suicide potential, 201-244
  critical constellation, 202-210
  sample protocols, 210-242

Texture responses (T), 57-58, 110-112
Treatment effects, 86-96
  assertiveness training, 89, 92
  biofeedback, 89, 93
  desensitization, 89, 92
  dynamic psychotherapy, 88-91
  gestalt psychotherapy, 89, 91
  group psychotherapy, 89, 92
  modeling, 89, 91-92
Treatment evaluation, 417-439
  sample protocols, 418-439

Underincorporator, 139-142

Vista Responses (V), 112-113

White space responses, 204-208

X+% :
  consistency, 41, 44-45
  schizophrenia, 247-249
  temporal consistency, 69-79

Zd, 138-142
Zf, 138-142